TEXAS

To Magdalena Hernández de la Teja, Paula Eyrich Tyler, and Mark E. Young for their love and support.

TEXAS

2e

Crossroads of North America

Jesús F. de la Teja
Texas State University

Ron Tyler
Amon Carter Museum of American Art, retired

Nancy Beck Young
University of Houston

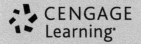
CENGAGE
Learning·

Australia • Brazil • Japan • Korea • Mexico • Singapore • Spain • United Kingdom • United States

Texas: Crossroads of North America, Second Edition
Jesús F. de la Teja, Ron Tyler, and Nancy Beck Young

Product Director: Suzanne Jeans

Product Manager: Clint Attebery

Senior Managing Content Developer: Joanne Dauksewicz

Content Developer: Naomi Friedman

Media Developer: Kate MacLean

Marketing Brand Manager: Kyle Zimmerman

IP Analyst: Alexandra Ricciardi

IP Project Manager: Amber Hosea

Manufacturing Planner: Sandee Milewski

Art and Design Direction, Production Management, and Composition: Lumina Datamatics, Inc.

Cover Image: ©iStockphoto.com/THEPALMER/Roberto A Sanchez

For product information and technology assistance, contact us at **Cengage Learning Customer & Sales Support, 1-800-354-9706**

For permission to use material from this text or product, submit all requests online at **cengage.com/permissions**
Further permissions questions can be e-mailed to **permissionrequest@cengage.com**

Library of Congress Control Number: 2014956304

ISBN-13: 978-1-133-94738-7

Cengage Learning
20 Channel Center Street
Boston, MA 02210
USA

Cengage Learning is a leading provider of customized learning solutions with office locations around the globe, including Singapore, the United Kingdom, Australia, Mexico, Brazil, and Japan. Locate your local office at: **www.cengage.com/global**

Cengage Learning products are represented in Canada by Nelson Education, Ltd.

To learn more about Cengage Learning Solutions, visit **www.cengage.com**

Purchase any of our products at your local college store or at our preferred online store **www.cengagebrain.com**

Printed at CLDPC, USA, 08-18

Brief Contents

Contents

3 | New Opportunities, New Rivalries, 1767–1800

68

PART II   DEFINING TEXAS 169

6 | Revolution, 1835–1836 172

7 | Texas Independent, 1836–1845 204

10 | Creating an Infrastructure, 1876–1898   301

PART III TEXAS DEFINED   333

11 | A Contradictory Movement: Texas Progressivism, 1900–1929   336

12 | Depression and War, 1929–1945   370

13 | A "Confluence of Anxieties": Texas from 1946 to 1960   401

14 | The Conundrum of Lyndon Johnson's Texas, 1960–1978   435

15 | Recognizing Old and New Realities   467

Preface

The idea for this textbook arose out of the experience of the first edition authors as consultants for the Bob Bullock Texas State History Museum in Austin. In struggling to present the entire scope of the Texas experience within the limited confines of three floors of approximately 30,000 square feet of exhibit space, we were forced to hone the messages we wanted visitors to gain during their visit. The more we thought about the contexts that could only be hinted at in the museum, the more attractive the idea of a Texas history survey became to us. We wanted to tell a balanced story that would appeal to an increasingly diverse twenty-first century Texas audience.

For this second edition, that process of reflecting and honing, now taking into account reaction to what we did and did not do well in the first edition, has taken on new twists. Concern for the need to cover the republic era separately from the first statehood period and the need to treat recent events in more detail required a major reorganization. Part 1 now covers the history of Texas up to the revolution, requiring the regrouping of material for the Spanish colonial period. Part 2 still covers the Texas frontier experience with five chapters detailing the story from the struggle for independence from Mexico to the end of the nineteenth century. And, the material in Part 3 has been regrouped and a chapter has been added to bring the story well into the twenty-first century.

Reassignment of writing responsibilities also took place because of the departure for personal reasons of first edition coauthor Paul Marks. As a replacement, we are fortunate to have Nancy Beck Young, a scholar of twentieth-century political history. Consequently, the book's 15 chapters have been equally divided among the three of us, with Jesús de la Teja responsible for Part 1, Ron Tyler responsible for Part 2, and Dr. Young responsible for Part 3.

Themes

In *Texas: Crossroads of North America*, second edition, we tell the story of this region as a dynamic process, beginning with the ways in which people—natives, adventurers, government representatives, immigrants, and residents—perceived the opportunities offered on this Indian, Spanish, Mexican, and Anglo frontier, in this republic and state. That suggests our first major theme—that Texas was a crossroads of intersecting geographies and cultures. People pursued these opportunities both as individuals and groups, first in the land itself, then through more complex ways of achieving social, economic, and political independence and power, which reflects our second major theme of opportunity. They found often formidable challenges, in part by coming into contact with representatives of other cultural and ethnic groups with different perspectives and agendas. As certain groups gained power—including the power to define "Texas" and "Texans" in their way—their definitions were repeatedly challenged by the vastness and energetic diversity of the state and its population, which suggests our third major theme of Texas as a "cultural centrifuge." In this geographic and cultural mix, myth and reality have combined to make and keep Texas a distinctive place.

Approach

This is a distinctly modern history of Texas. We tell the story that constitutes one of the most dramatic and colorful histories of any state in the nation, but we try to make sense of that legacy and show how it relates to present-day Texans and those to come. We haven't lost the focus on our Hispanic, African American, or German heritage, or on the courageous soldiers who participated in the Texas Revolution, the war with Mexico, the Civil War, World Wars I and II, and more recent conflicts, but we also show the many roles of Mexican Americans, African Americans, and women, and the struggle for civil rights that continues as society becomes ever more mindful of inequities in opportunity. While not forgetting the accomplishments of Cabeza de Vaca, Stephen F. Austin, Sam Houston, James Stephen Hogg, Lyndon B. Johnson, or the presidents Bush, we have also told the stories of Rosa María Hinojosa de Ballí, Ignacio Pérez, Oveta Culp Hobby, Barbara Jordan, and Michael Dell. We recognize the enduring contributions of the Texas Rangers, one of the most storied law enforcement organizations in the country, but we also tell the story of the brave citizens who helped reform the Rangers and restore them as a useful state agency when others would have disbanded them.

Texas: Crossroads of North America, second edition, tells the story of the people who lived within the state's borders before there was any idea of Texas or when Texas was defined in very different terms than it is today. Our text recognizes that the building blocks of today's Lone Star State have been in the making for not hundreds, but for thousands of years. This book offers a dynamic introduction to Texas as a place by emphasizing the interrelationship between people and nature as soon as people arrived. It stresses the cultural diversity of the native peoples of Texas, relying on recent archeological findings and newer interpretations of the ethnographic evidence. Throughout Part 1 there is a concern for reminding the student that the indigenous peoples of the region were autonomous actors in their own right.

Just as *Texas: Crossroads of North America* pays greater attention to the indigenous background it also gives greater emphasis to the story of Spain and Mexico in what is now Texas. Among the strengths of our textbook is a concern with keeping in mind the stories of those parts of today's state that were part of other jurisdictions in the past. Consequently, considerable attention is given to settlement in the El Paso and lower Rio Grande, areas that have greatly contributed to the state's unique cultural legacy. Whether talking about Nacogdoches, San Antonio, or Paso del Norte, a conscious effort has been made to balance the lives of missionaries and soldiers with those of ranchers and merchants. Integrated into these stories is extensive coverage of women's roles in the development of the Spanish frontier.

In moving the chapter on Mexican Texas to Part 1, the authors feel strongly that they are laying out a more coherent foundation for students to understand and appreciate the advent and process of Anglo-American colonization. We strive to show more fully how this colonization occurred within the context of the new Mexican nation and of local Mexican frontier governing structures, and what opportunities and challenges it posed for the existing Mexican population of Texas. This foundation helps us make more sense of the cultural context in which our Mexican American population is more fully appreciated as part of the Texas experience. In other words, we show how the Mexican period was one of transition, a period marked by Mexico's search for nationhood out of its colonial past, and how that search created a space for settlers from the United States who grew increasingly frustrated by Mexico's inability to achieve political stability.

We devote a full chapter to the Texas Revolution. In part because of its strength as a "creation myth" for Texas, it remains the most dramatically engaging point of entry into the state's modern history and a cornerstone of a distinctly Texan identity for many readers. We think it important to illuminate the confusion and complexity of the struggle, to get beyond simplistic and ethnocentric understandings, to see the revolution as an event within Mexico itself, with a varied and sometimes conflicted cast of characters.

In the republic era, we point up the political and economic fragility of the fledgling nation, and the uncertainty of opportunity, particularly for increasingly marginalized groups. In the early statehood era, we trace Texas's increasing identification as a southern state, and therefore one willing to throw away its hard-won annexation to join the confederacy.

We try to provide a broad and varied picture of Texas and Texans during the Civil War, including those Texans who resisted identification with the southern cause. Our emphasis in Reconstruction is on laying out clearly the various policies and requirements of the federal government, how Texans responded, and how and why the state reverted to conservative Democratic policies as soon as possible, undercutting any hoped-for gains by African Americans.

While Texas was still largely an agricultural state in 1900, we point out that in addition to being among the most productive agriculturally, these years also witnessed the beginnings of industrialization. The huge growth in population, the spread of railroads throughout the state, the fluctuations of the cotton market, and the discovery of oil at Spindletop in 1901 all characterized the state's modernization in the early twentieth century. A parallel development was the emergence of one-party rule and its impact on economic and cultural problems. The economic structure, based on one-crop agriculture began to falter in the aftermath of World War I and would have collapsed under the weight of the Great Depression of the 1930s, had not politicians in Washington, D.C., come to the rescue. This story reveals the state's increased reliance on and contributions to the federal government, a major theme in twentieth-century Texas history. During and after World War II the cultural superstructure did collapse in the face of civil rights challenges by women, Mexican Americans, and African Americans, and we have not yet finished its reconstruction.

The increasingly significant role that the federal government played in the state's development proved contentious even as it boosted the region's economy. World War II, in particular, spurred development in Texas, with the completion of the "Big Inch" and "Little Inch" pipelines and the construction of the world's largest petrochemical complex along the Gulf coast. Federal government expenditures in Texas, which today dwarf the state's own budget, suggest its huge role in the state, and the state's significant role in the federal government. The impact of all these factors combined with increasing challenges of taxation, civil rights, education, water, and continued growth helps explain why the Democratic Party, for decades the only relevant forum for discussion of the state's problems and goals, began splitting between its liberal and conservative branches in the postwar years. Just as important in the making of two party Texas was the highly successful Republican challenge.

Recent history can easily descend into a general recitation of diverse events and developments. In dealing with the end of the twentieth century and the early twenty-first century, we have identified three significant themes—the ways in which Texas exhibits old and new identities in both politics and economics; the challenges of governing a state experiencing uneven growth and opportunity; and awareness of environmental issues, particularly in regard to water needs and availability—and we have examined them from the perspective of the ongoing conflicts regarding modernization and interaction with the federal government.

Throughout this work, we have tried to engage where possible with individual stories, with the ways in which people have responded to the opportunities and challenges they found in Texas, and how these responses have led to the geographic, cultural, political, and economic landscape we have today. As a result, *Texas: Crossroads of North America* is as much a history of Texans as it is of Texas.

In writing this book the authors benefited from discussing subject matter or having chapters read by a number of knowledgeable individuals. Among those with whom we consulted were William H. Goetzmann, Creekmore Fath, and Will Wilson, Sr., all now deceased. Along with those readers for the first edition, we also wish to thank Timothy Perttula, Juliana Barr, Joaquín Rivaya-Martínez, Robert Utley, Randolph B. Campbell, Stephen L. Hardin, and Patrick Cox for reading portions of the new text, and Naomi Friedman, our new editor, who has been sympathetic to our vision for the work while challenging us to be clearer in how we present it to our audience.

Jesús F. de la Teja
Ron Tyler
Nancy Beck Young

1

UNDEFINED TEXAS

t was not a destination for the European adventurers who traipsed across the southern half of North America in the early sixteenth century. It was not a final destination for hunter-gatherer bands that followed the buffalo, the seasons, and the spirits throughout central North America in the same era. It was not a recognizable political unit, even for the widely dispersed and varied native peoples who made it their home then. It would be hundreds of years before Texas resembled the place we recognize today as the second largest state in the Union. For three centuries, conflict, competition, and cooperation among Euro-Americans and indigenous peoples continually reshaped and redefined Texas.

The history of Texas—that is, the story found in records—begins during the age of the conquistadors, but the story of what is now Texas stretches back thousands of years before the Spaniards' arrival. From the very earliest Paleoindian hunters to cross what are now the state's borders and begin the occupation of every environmental zone of Texas, to the advanced but very distinctive agricultural societies of East and far West Texas on the eve of European contact, people made Texas their home even though they did not think of their home as Texas.

The same motives that led them to explore the rest of the New World brought the first Spaniards to Texas from the 1520s to the 1540s: the search for fabulous treasures to plunder, natural resources to exploit, and civilizations to subjugate and put to work. A century later, other Spaniards, such as military men and religious missionaries, began to explore the region with a much different purpose: the defense of Spanish claims against rivals and the search for souls to save. Accompanying them were soldiers, their wives and families and, eventually, artisans and merchants. These early settlers faced many obstacles: great distances between settlements, a difficult climate, and Indian resistance to encroachment into their territories.

Relatively few thought of themselves as *Tejanos* (Hispanic residents of Texas) and for them Texas began just south of San Antonio and stretched beyond the Sabine River into what is today western Louisiana. The ranching communities that occupied the lower Rio Grande valley were part of Nuevo Santander. The people who lived in these settlements traded with Texas settlements, but identified themselves in terms of what is today the state of Tamaulipas. Neither were the residents of the Paso del Norte area, what is today El Paso-Juárez, Tejanos. Living on both sides of the river, these people descended from the sixteenth-century settlers of New Mexico, from some of the Pueblo groups that had allied themselves with the Spanish, and from other Spanish colonials who found the area perfect for cultivating the vine and raising livestock. Also, the various native peoples who predated the arrival of the Spaniards and the eighteenth- and early-nineteenth-century migrant tribes that moved south of the Red River and onto the Texas plains certainly did not see themselves as Texans.

It took events far beyond the control of the people living north of the Rio Grande at the start of the nineteenth century to alter and expand the definition of Texas. The Louisiana Purchase, the Mexican War of Independence, and the consequent political upheavals and new migration patterns brought new and very different people into the region: Euro-Americans, African Americans, and eastern Indians. Texas became contested ground as the newcomers saw opportunities west of the Sabine—rich cotton bottomlands, vast and fecund hunting grounds. That Texas had no large and prosperous cities, no grand cathedrals or imposing public monuments, and no well-developed roads or ports helped foster the impression that it was a wilderness ready to be tamed. Neither the millennia of Indian habitation nor a century of Spanish settlement could be easily wiped away, however. And, without understanding that history we cannot understand who Texans are today.

First Texans, First Encounters: Prehistory to 1554

Looking out from behind the dune vegetation of what is now Follets Island on a crisp November morning in 1528, the area's inhabitants beheld a strange sight. In the wreckage of a large makeshift boat, a group of strangely dressed men sat close together, shivering and muttering in an incomprehensible language. In the days that followed, the scene was repeated three more times on other Texas barrier islands. In all, over 200 members of Pánfilo de Narváez's Florida expedition had by happenstance become the first Europeans to arrive in Texas. This first recorded meeting between Texas Indians and Europeans took place on peaceful terms. The Indians offered fish, roots, and nuts, while the Spaniards reciprocated with hawkbells and beads. The chronicler of this meeting, Álvar Núñez Cabeza de Vaca, records that when he and his men were unable to relaunch their boat and lost all their possessions in the heavy surf, "the Indians, at sight of what had befallen us, and our state of suffering and melancholy destitution, sat down among us, and from the sorrow and pity they felt, they all began to lament so earnestly that they might have been heard at a distance, and continued so doing more than half an hour." In the months to come, the shrinking number of survivors, undernourished, suffering from exposure, and increasingly at odds with the local inhabitants, would transfer some of their negative feelings to the island, naming it Mal Hado ("Misfortune.") Eventually, only four men, Cabeza de Vaca and two other Spaniards along with the North African slave belonging to one of them, returned to Christendom. Their adventures inspired other Spaniards to venture into the interior of North America and participate in other encounters with the land's original inhabitants during the opening chapters of Texas's modern history.

Chapter 1 First Texans, First Encounters: Prehistory to 1554	
2.4 MILLION–10,000 YEARS AGO	Palo Duro canyon cut, Padre Island and other barrier islands begin to form, modern Texas ecosystems emerge
13,000 YEARS AGO	Arrival and spread of Paleoindian hunter-gatherers
10,000 TO 2,000 YEARS AGO	Archaic period cultures—increased cultural specialization by region
2,000 TO 800 YEARS AGO	Emergence of Jornada Mogollón culture in far West Texas, Antelope Creek Phase culture in the Panhandle, Caddo culture in East Texas, and Karankawa culture in coastal Texas
1,300 YEARS AGO	Arrival of Proto-Apaches on southern plains
1492	Christopher Columbus's voyage opens Western Hemisphere to European exploitation
1519	Álvarez de Pineda becomes first European to explore Texas coast
1521	Hernán Cortés completes Spain's conquest of the Aztec Empire
1528	Narváez's expedition to Florida marooned on Texas coast; survivors Álvar Núñez Cabeza de Vaca and companions provide earliest information on Texas Indians
1541	Francisco Vázquez de Coronado visits the Texas Panhandle during his 1540–42 expedition to Arizona, New Mexico, and the Plains
1542	Luis de Moscoso leads the remains of the Soto expedition (1539–43) into East Texas before returning to the Mississippi River
1554	Hurricane wrecks Spanish treasure fleet off Padre Island, confirming accounts of hostile Indians

When humans first set foot on what is now Texas soil, the natural history of the region was already hundreds of millions of years in the making. Understanding the processes that shaped the landscapes and environments of Texas seems the best place to begin the story of the Lone Star State. Texas contains all of the major land forms and most climatic environments to be found in the Western Hemisphere, making it a natural crossroads of North America.

Humans adapted to life in these varied ecological zones, from the semitropical riverine environment of South Texas to the humid pine forests of East Texas to the short grass plains of the Panhandle. For well over 10,000 years the first Texans hunted, fished, farmed, and made war in what became a crossroads of native cultures. When Europeans finally arrived on the scene, what they perceived as a wilderness was in reality the home of well-adapted and diverse cultures. They brought with them, however, the seeds of radical change, physical and cultural, that eventually would make Texas a crossroads of empires.

As you read this chapter, consider the following questions:

1. How did changing environmental conditions affect the development of human cultures in Texas from Paleoindian to Late Prehistoric times?
2. What evidence exists supporting the assertion that the Texas region's Indian peoples during the Late Prehistoric period were not isolated, backward natives as we commonly think?
3. The earliest European exploration of Texas took place during the initial phase of Spain's conquest of Mexico, yet Spaniards did not immediately colonize Texas. Why?

Texas Takes Shape

A little over a billion years ago, give or take a hundred million years, in the last quarter of the Precambrian era, what is now North America collided with another continental plate. As in an automobile accident, some parts went flying, others crumpled, and still others were completely consumed by the collision. Mother Nature cleared the wreckage over the next few hundred million years— mountains flattened out through erosion, sediment covered depressions—but today we can still see the effects of that earth-shattering event. In Llano County, at Enchanted Rock State Park, for example, a granite dome sticks up out of the countryside, a beautiful reminder of the intense heat and pressures created by that long-ago collision that also brought granite near the surface as far east as Marble Falls. Texas underwent numerous cycles of uplifting and submergence, cooling and heating, wetness and drying out, and countless species of animals and plants arose and vanished before humans arrived to claim the land for themselves about 15,000 years ago.

The last Ice Age, which lasted from about 2.4 million to about 10,000 years ago, brought about the final major changes to the North American landscape, both topographical and biological, that created present-day Texas. Erosion did its job on West Texas, producing the magnificent Palo Duro Canyon and the impressive Caprock Escarpment. The state's major streams moved the eroded sediments eastward to the gulf coast, where they continued to add to the Texas landmass—that is, until the Ice Age glaciers began to melt about 15,000 years ago. Then, sea levels began to rise rapidly, flooding the lower courses of most Texas streams to create the distinctive shallow bays and estuaries of the Texas coast. The silt and sand that continued to flow southeastward now formed barrier islands such as Galveston and Padre Island, which have proven so valuable to students seeking a respite from the arduousness of college coursework each spring.

Life in Texas was also seriously affected by the Ice Age. Megafauna such as mastodons and mammoths, giant sloths, longhorn bison, camels, and horses all died out completely. The long-horned bison (ancestor of the American buffalo), which had crossed the land bridge also died out. Most species of cat predators also disappeared, the mountain lion and jaguar remaining as the dominant representatives of the group in the Lone Star State. Modern bears also survived.

By the time the first Texans arrived, approximately 13,000 to 15,000 years ago, the land looked much as it does today, as nature had rearranged the flora. The warming climate sent the conifer and juniper (Texas cedar) forests of West Texas back up the mountain slopes from where they had descended during the Ice Age, and grasslands returned with a vengeance to the West Texas plains. Piñon pines and junipers disappeared from the canyons of the Rio Grande and Pecos River and tributaries as this part of the state became increasingly arid. They were replaced with desert plants such as cacti and sotol. In the central Texas Hill Country, scrub oaks took the place of piñon pines next to junipers, while east of the Balcones Escarpment the older deciduous species of the Ice Age were replaced with warmer weather varieties, such as walnuts and pecans, oaks and elms. Also on the scene were loblolly pines, which although not yet dominant, made up an increasing proportion of the East Texas woods. The drying of the climate also played a major hand in the retreat of South Texas scrub oaks to protected and moist areas, allowing for the spread of cacti and mesquite throughout the flat and underwatered region.

Although no Garden of Eden, the land that we call Texas today had much to offer: abundant woods and water, fertile soils and mineral wealth, and ample herds and flocks. Not surprisingly, the first Texans quickly moved to occupy just about every ecological niche the land had to offer. The human story of Texas was about to begin.

Early Prehistoric Texas, 13,000-1 BC

It is hard to know exactly when the first human residents of Texas arrived within the modern state's boundaries. New archaeological discoveries and increasingly sophisticated scientific techniques continue to readjust the timeframe for the movement into Texas of the first hunter-gatherer family groups that made up North America's Paleoindian population. Assertions about a human presence in Texas earlier than 12,000 years ago and perhaps as early as 40,000 years ago remain controversial. Also controversial is where the earliest Texans came from. The traditional North Asian Beringia land bridge between Siberia and Alaska view remains prevalent, but some researchers argue for seaborne South Asian and even European migrations, as well as seaborne migrations along the western coast of North America.

Whenever they arrived and wherever they came from, the earliest Texans soon spread throughout the state. They became the base population for some (but not all) of the cultures found in Texas when Europeans first arrived in the early sixteenth century. The story of the first Texans is shrouded in the mysteries of stone tools, scarred animal bones, geometrically decorated rocks, the remains of cooking pits, and several human burial grounds. Yet archaeologists, with the assistance of other scientists, have begun putting more and more clues together, allowing us to understand the dawn of Texas history in ever greater detail.

Radiocarbon dating, site and artifact interpretation, and differences in methodological approaches all conspire to prevent the development of a single narrative framework for the story. In general, the Paleoindians were the first humans to make a home in North America, and a particular stone tools technology known as Clovis (from a site in New Mexico) has been given the distinction of representing this earliest culture in North America. As these first people adjusted to environmental changes and developed adaptations to deal with new conditions their cultures diversified, and scientists have grouped these changes into a long period they call the Archaic, from a Greek word for old. Finally, the Late Prehistoric refers to the few thousand years, when the arrival of new technologies and domesticated crops created the cultural patterns present when Europeans arrived.

Where the divisions between the Paleoindian, Archaic, and Late Prehistoric periods should come remains unsettled, mostly because it is clear that the cultural attributes associated with the different periods are present—or in some cases not present—at different times in different parts of Texas. When did the first humans arrive in Texas? Did early cultures succeed each other or overlap? How much and exactly what plants did Paleoindians gather compared to their Archaic successors? We do know enough to tell the basic story of the original settlement of Texas, a story as full of danger, adventure, and adaptation as any from the days of Spanish explorers or Anglo-American frontiersmen.

Big-Game Hunters Populate the Land

Although there is some controversial evidence for a pre-Clovis human presence in Texas, for instance at Cueva Quebrada in Val Verde County or the Debra Friedkin site in Bell County, a solid archaeological record dates to about 13,000 years ago and is associated with Clovis technology. The Clovis toolkit, which includes not only the famous fluted projectile points but also blades, scrapers, and hammerstones, has been found from the Trans-Pecos to East Texas, most importantly at a central Texas site known as Gault. The same site provides clear evidence for the presence of the successor technologies to Clovis during the Paleoindian period such as Folsom (also from a site in eastern New Mexico), which in some parts of Texas lasted until about 11,500 years ago. These excavations make clear that Paleo-Texans were not just mobile, but adaptive. They were not just big-game hunters but versatile foragers. Where mammoths were scarce, they turned to the last remaining populations of elephant, camel, horse, and giant bison for meat, and even to frogs, birds, and small mammals, along with a large variety of plant foods.

In general, hunting provided the principal subsistence for Paleoindians, and they were efficient and resourceful killers. They took special care to select the finest flints from which to make their lethal projectile points, which changed over time to reflect changing prey species. Around cooking pits and campfires in the days and weeks preceding a communal hunt, a group's hunters sat exchanging stories and ideas and meticulously working flint cobbles collected at sites such as what is now Alibates Flint Quarries National Monument in the Texas Panhandle. When all was ready, the group would venture near the herd. Their strategies included going after the matriarch, the weakened or wounded peripheral animals, or cornering groups of animals in blind canyons as well as driving them off cliffs.

Just how long the good life lasted for Paleo-Texans is not clear. As the climate dried and the megafauna died out, the first Texans were challenged to adopt new subsistence practices. About 11,500 years ago a new, smaller and more versatile projectile point specifically associated with South Texas known as Golondrina appeared. It indicates a switch in quarry for hunters who attached the un-fluted points to both spears and knives. These and related Paleoindian descendants of the early Paleo-Texans also increasingly relied on foraging practices that made ever greater use of plants.

For centuries Texas provided well for Paleoindians. Hunting was good, water was plentiful, and a bounty of useful plants provided whatever they might need, even as the climate became drier and warmer and the biggest of the megafauna died out. Around the campfires there was leisure time, evidenced by the production of stones with geometric designs and the presence of shells, ochre, and decorative stones, canine tooth necklaces, and bone needles. The careful burials of a young female at Leander, near Austin, and two males near Lake Whitney, along the banks of the Brazos River, suggest that Paleo-Texans also gave thought to the vastness of the universe and the possibility of a hereafter.

Diversifying Ways of Life

The transition from Paleoindian to Early Archaic ways of life happened between about 10,000 and 9,000 years ago depending on the region. Greater experimentation with tool forms, particularly projectile points, and increasing reliance on more varied foodstuffs denote the arrival of a new age in Texas, one marked by greater cultural diversity in response to environmental changes. For the next 7,000 to 8,000 years, Texas was home to an increasing number of more regionalized hunting and foraging cultures; this period is known as the Archaic. Population growth fostered both trade and territoriality, evidence for both of which can be found in Archaic-period cemeteries such as the Ernest Witte site near the Brazos River in Austin County.

The Early Archaic period was marked by a greater reliance on locally available resources. Early Archaic Texans launched their darts, generally tipped with small points made from locally available stone, from atlatls, but now they aimed them at smaller mammals. Around their hearths they probably worked on developing new methods of catching animals such as traps and nets. Early Texas women also probably spent an increasing amount of time experimenting with new ways of preparing and cooking the plant foods that they gathered and that now made up a greater share of their diet.

Rock shelters such as Fate Bell at Seminole Canyon State Historical Park, near the confluence of the Rio Grande and Pecos River, served as housing for early Texans. Paintings on the shelter's walls have survived thousands of years of weathering to remind us of our kinship with the Paleoindians, who dreamed of great hunts and spiritual journeys.

Successful adaptation to Texas environments created a population boom beginning about 4,500 to 5,000 years ago. Over the next 2,500 years Texas hunter-gatherers became so adept at exploiting the regional ecosystems that territoriality emerged as a cultural characteristic. Some groups occupied coastal bays and estuaries; other groups claimed more arid, but still fertile, environmental niches in western and southwestern Texas. From the Panhandle to central Texas some cultures maintained an ancestral connection to the bison. Farther south, along the middle stretches of the Rio Grande, resourceful desert dwellers relied on smaller game and a wide variety of plants. Growing archaeological evidence suggests that at least some far West Texas Archaic communities began cultivating corn as early as 4,000 to 3,500 years ago. Fish and shellfish furnished a plentiful food supply to coastal groups for a large part of the year. For the remainder of the year, these groups also lived off the small game and various plants available on the coastal prairies.

Emerging Sense of Place

These hunter-gatherer groups adapted so successfully to their local environments that the temporary rock shelters and stream-side camps they had established in the past became more permanent homes. In far West Texas archaeologists have uncovered the remains of circular structures dating to between 5,000 and 3,500 years ago. A sense of home is also evident among Archaic peoples in their treatment of the dead, their evolving aesthetic, and the diversity of their material goods. Well-defined burial grounds in which men, women, and children found a final resting place are further marks of increasing attachment to place. Settlement sites cannot be considered villages in the modern sense, for the hunter-gatherer bands needed to move, at least seasonally, to ensure adequate food supplies. However, within their well-established ranges, which would also have included mineral and flint deposits, they used the same campsites over numerous generations, providing groups with a sense of identity.

Seasonally occupied sites at rock shelters became canvases for the early Texans' imagination. Archaic artists decorated their dwellings with inspired representations of the natural and supernatural world around them. Archaic rock artists transformed anonymous caves and megaliths into recognizable places where a band communed with the spirit worlds. Each succeeding generation reinforced the group's association with a place and continuity in religious beliefs by adding to the earlier artwork—the inclusion of men on horses and images of buildings with crosses on them implying continuity well into the modern era.

Elaborate burials also attest to the increasing value placed on status and material possessions and the development of trade networks. The presence of stones from as far away as the Ouachita Mountains of Arkansas and Oklahoma is evidence that territoriality had fostered the development of long-distance trade, another sign of increased materialism. Shell ornaments, chert knives, and even deer skulls in some graves may have been intended to introduce the departed to the afterlife as an important individual. Dart points embedded in the bones of some corpses bespeak the darker side of increased contact between groups—violent competition for land and resources.

The last centuries of the Archaic period also mark the end of a purely hunter-gatherer Texas. Far to the south, in today's central and southern Mexico, human cultural evolution had followed a similar track until about 6,000 years ago, when people started planting the seeds of various plants whose wild relatives they had been gathering for generations. By about 5,500 years ago, early gardeners had transformed the wild teosinte into domesticated corn. Farming eventually produced sedentary populations of considerable size, with increasingly sophisticated cultures. At the same time, technological and agricultural developments in what is now the U.S. Midwest and Southeast, where sunflowers were domesticated 4,000 to 5,000 years ago, also influenced the development of complex sedentary societies. In time their technologies spread into the American Southwest, where they had an impact on the cultural development of Texas.

Late Prehistoric Texas, 1–1528 AD

About two millennia ago the increasing diversification of cultures moved Texas into the last period of prehistory. For some groups from central Texas to the Panhandle, the buffalo and other large mammals remained basic to human

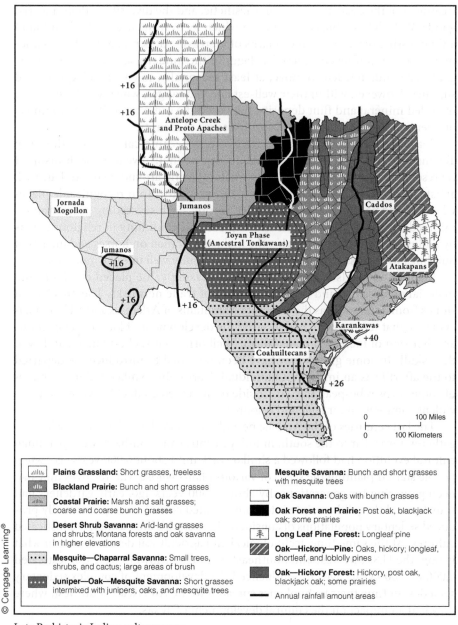

Late Prehistoric Indian cultures map

subsistence, while others along the Texas coast and the southernmost prairies continued to rely on seasonal migration to exploit locally available resources, even as they refined their toolkits and adopted the bow and arrow around 1,300 years ago. But, at the eastern and western ends of what one day became Texas, sedentary agricultural societies representing two very different cultural traditions tied the region to cultural developments in adjoining parts of North America and Mesoamerica. All of these native groups were active in an expanding east–west and north–south trade system that made Texas a crossroads of cultural and technological exchange that Europeans little understood when they began to intrude themselves into the lives of the region's peoples in the sixteenth and seventeenth centuries.

Buffalo Hunters of Western Texas

In the case of central and Panhandle Texas, the paucity of archaeological evidence makes it difficult to tie Archaic and Late Prehistoric populations to those groups encountered by Spaniards in the sixteenth, seventeenth, and eighteenth centuries. The history of the Panhandle–Llano Estacado region is easier to piece together than that of central Texas. Late Archaic hunter-gatherers in the Panhandle either were absorbed by eastward-moving Puebloans and Mogollón peoples, or were pushed farther east to the Hill Country of central Texas. The result was that between 800 and 500 years ago, during a period called the Antelope Creek phase, the broad expanse of northwestern Texas was home to a culture that combined bison hunting with horticulture and the construction of permanent stone dwellings.

Antelope Creek people settled near playa (rainwater) lakes and permanent springs fed by the Ogallala Aquifer and adapted to local conditions by adding buffalo hunting to their agricultural subsistence strategy. Antelope Creek people became important intermediaries in a trade network that linked agricultural societies to the east and west. With buffalo hides and, perhaps, dried meat as trade items, they acquired ceramics from both the Pueblos of present-day New Mexico and the Caddo peoples to the east. They also traded luxury items such as turquoise, Alibates lithic raw material, obsidian, and seashells.

Successful as they were in adapting to conditions on the southern Plains, the Antelope Creek people were incapable of meeting the long-term challenge of a new intruder group that arrived in the Panhandle region about 700 years ago as the climate cooled and became wetter. For over 1,000 years, Athabaskan-speaking bands of hunter-gatherers had been moving down the eastern slopes of the Rocky Mountains, adapting to conditions on the fringes of the Great Plains on the way to becoming the most formidable pre-horse buffalo people of Texas. Between 700 and 600 years ago, as buffalo herds moved into the increasingly verdant southern plains, they were followed by bands of these Athabaskan-speaking hunters, who in historic times came to be known as Apaches. Some groups of proto-Apaches settled east and others west of the Rockies. Highly adaptive, the eastern proto-Apaches not only became the most proficient bison hunters of West Texas, but they also took up gardening, mimicking to a small degree the subsistence strategy of the Antelope Creek people they eventually replaced, sometimes violently as the archaeological record makes clear. Dominant in northwestern Texas on the eve of the arrival of the Spaniards to the interior of North America, the ancestral Plains Apaches were among the earliest people to be described by Spanish explorers.

The prehistory of the people inhabiting central Texas is not as well established because European penetration of this region came rather late—in the last decades of the seventeenth century. For a long time, informed opinion maintained that the Tonkawas were the descendants of the region's Archaic Indians. The current consensus is that the Tonkawas represent the merger of late-arriving southern Plains hunters and surviving central Texas hunter-gatherer bands that were no longer independently viable.

Regardless, for 1,000 years before the arrival of Europeans, central Texas was home to a succession of hunter-gatherer cultures that relied extensively on the buffalo for subsistence. Highly mobile, and continuing to make use of rock shelters, by 1,300 years ago these Indians had adopted the bow and arrow and made use of pottery. Within the next few centuries, the central Texas Indians joined in the interregional trade system that had developed across the expanse of Texas. Ceramics imported from the east as wells as seashells and stone from hundreds of miles away survive to point out the extent of this trade. But the life of these Toyah-phase people (the name given to the central Texas culture dated to 1300–1700 AD) was not an entirely idyllic life of following the buffalo and gathering berries and nuts. They were, it seems, basically territorial, and some of their burials, with arrowheads found among the skeletal remains, indicate that the deceased suffered violent death.

Foragers and Fishermen of South Texas and the Gulf Coast

The violence experienced by the Toyah-phase people may have been the result of conflict with some of their southeastern hunter-gatherer neighbors. The assemblage of culturally similar hunter-gatherer groups inhabiting most of southern Texas and neighboring northern Coahuila and Tamaulipas is commonly referred to as Coahuiltecan. Up the coast from the Coahuiltecans lived another culture group with distinct characteristics and a long history of interaction with Euro-Americans in historic times. Collectively known as the Karankawas, these people of the bays and barrier islands from Corpus Christi to the lower Brazos River can be traced through the archaeological evidence to about 800 years ago. And, from Galveston Bay eastward and inland into the coastal prairie lived hunter-gatherers with many of the same characteristics as the Karankawas.

These cultural groups shared common traits that permitted such successful adaptation to local environmental conditions that agriculture did not take hold among them. The absence of manos and metates (hand stones and grinding slabs) at their sites indicates that they did not experiment with corn or other seeds requiring heavy grinding, although they most certainly had contacts with neighboring corn-farming Jornada Mogollón and Caddo peoples.

Generally, Coahuiltecan, Karankawa, and Galveston Bay peoples were mobile band communities that occupied open campsites and relied on temporary brush or hide shelters to protect them from the elements. All were ceramic-making cultures among which about 1,300 years ago the bow and arrow made an appearance. As hunter-gatherers, the ancestral Coahuiltecans relied mostly on small mammals such as rabbits and rodents, snakes, and freshwater fish and shellfish for the meat portion of their diet. As the bison moved south in the centuries immediately preceding the arrival of Europeans, the Coahuiltecans increasingly hunted buffalo, an adaptation that may well have brought them into conflict with bison hunters to the north as their hunting ranges overlapped.

Coastal Coahuiltecans, Karankawas, and Galveston Bay peoples made extensive use of marine resources. They employed seashells for a wide variety of purposes: whelks became hammers, sunray clams became scrapers, and some turned conch and clamshells into projectile points. They also used shells to create jewelry and other ornamentation for exchange purposes. Coastal Coahuiltecans, for instance, traded their shell creations with other hunter-gatherer cultures of the interior and with the Mesoamerican cultures of central Mexico, from whom they received ceramics, obsidian, and jadeite.

Arriving at their winter campsites in the fall after hunting season in the interior, Coastal Coahuiltecans, Karankawas, and Galveston Bay bands repaired or constructed dugout canoes, prepared fishing nets and traps, and chipped away at flint cobbles or shells to fashion the arrowheads and other stone tools necessary to process the catch of fish and shellfish on which the group would feed until early spring. Some group members, mostly women and children, did not go fishing or hunting but went out to gather roots, nuts, and leaves for food, basketry, and dyes. Some returned to camp at the end of the day with supplies of clay for pottery and asphaltum (naturally occurring marine tar) with which to coat or decorate pottery and to waterproof baskets.

Surviving funerary evidence suggests a wide range of beliefs regarding territoriality and the afterlife. Their individual and scattered burials indicate that interior Coahuiltecans seem to have had little attachment to specific sites, while well-established Karankawa cemeteries in which individuals were buried with personal belongings indicate both a strong sense of place and of a hereafter. Group movement for most bands, therefore, took place in the context of seasonal needs in combination with territorial boundaries. Evident in the remains of the camps of both Rockport area Karankawas and interior Coahuiltecans is shared use of their boundary area, for the sites of the former indicate spring-summer use while the camps of the latter indicate fall-winter use.

The archaeological record clearly demonstrates that the successful subsistence strategies of Coahuiltecans, Karankawas, and Galveston Bay peoples provided a level of material prosperity that allowed them to reject a sedentary way of life. Contrary to Spanish judgment, Coahuiltecans were not backward people. Although violence is part of the archaeological record, there is nothing in it to suggest excessive belligerence. Contrary to common opinion, the Karankawas were not cannibals. However, because their success depended on strict management of population size to avoid outstripping the environment of its capacity to support them, South and coastal Texas peoples came under severe pressure when caught between the advance of Spaniards from the south and powerful Indian adversaries from the north. Violence was a natural response.

Desert Farmers of West Texas

The people of far West Texas began combining some gardening with their hunting and gathering ways at the latest by about 3,500 years ago, during the Late Archaic era. For hundreds of years various hunter-gatherer groups experimented with gardens of corn, squash, beans, and local plants, while still relying on foraging and hunting for their basic subsistence needs. By about 2,000 years ago, some of the communities in the region had adopted a more sedentary way of life that included technological and cultural characteristics known as Mogollón, a culture area extending west to southern Arizona and New Mexico and south into Chihuahua. These farmers built pit houses next to their fields of corn and beans. As soon as the harvest was in, however, it was off to hunt and gather in order to meet the rest of the year's subsistence needs. Seasonally occupied villages thus became a common settlement pattern for hundreds of years.

Even in the best of times, farming was a challenge in this perennially arid region. There is no evidence that the Jornada Mogollón people ever attempted irrigation agriculture on a sizable scale, as the Hohokam did in Arizona, but they did divert runoff. By placing their fields at the foot of a mountain, the Jornada Mogollón could tap spring rain runoff to give their crops a chance. In time, some communities developed on the margins of the area's playas and settlement construction followed more complex Puebloan "apartment" style dwellings. Nevertheless, these settlements were hit-and-miss propositions, and many farming and village sites had to be abandoned after a year or two, when they were unable to support group needs.

At a select few sites, conditions were right for long-term settlement. As the pit-house dwellers succeeded in raising surpluses of corn and beans, they began to construct simple adobe pueblos, usually consisting of a number of apartments arranged in a row and containing a large room thought to be a ceremonial or communal space. Builders often plastered the floors of their pueblos and built a variety of outbuildings and cooking pits. Even in pueblo times the Jornada Mogollón did not entirely abandon their traveling ways. In some villages, including Firecracker Pueblo (so named for an abandoned fireworks stand across the road from the site north of El Paso), they scooped out storage pits in which to keep corn and other food supplies during their absences.

Increasing dependence on corn made the Jornada Mogollón people focus increasingly on developing agricultural tools and instruments. They had to make manos and metates and transport them to the village from wherever the stone deposits were located, sometimes a considerable distance away. Given its fragility, they had to make pottery on a regular basis for storage, cooking, and eating purposes. Utilitarian as the pots, bowls, pitchers, and ladles they made were, the human need for artistic expression found its way into animal motifs and geometric designs that have acquired the designation "El Paso polychrome style."

The Jornada Mogollón people remained foragers and hunters, and archaeological sites have turned up dozens of nondomesticated plant species, including cacti and mesquite, that were in common use. Animal protein, leather, bone,

Firecracker pueblo was a small settlement of the Jornada Mogollón culture just north of El Paso. Used during the part of the year when its residents were tending to their neighboring fields, the village was left vacant during long stretches when the inhabitants dispersed to hunt and forage for the rest of their subsistence needs.

and sinew were essential products that could only be obtained through the hunt. Whereas rabbits, rodents, birds, and snakes provided everyday meals, deer, antelope, and bison supplied not only the village table, but its workshops as well. Killed, skinned, and butchered in the field, the animals' hide, meat, and useful bones were brought back to the village for processing. Because the Jornada Mogollón people used stone tools, they were forced to spend a considerable amount of time preparing arrow tips, dart points, scrapers, knives, and hammers from stones that sometimes came from hundreds of miles away.

And travel, whether to hunt, gather, or procure stone for tools, brought the Jornada Mogollón into contact with neighboring groups and cultures. Sometimes they brought back a pot or bowl from one of the western Mogollón or Hohokam villages, or from an Anasazi pueblo. From exchanges with other hunting parties, they obtained obsidian, turquoise, and even seashell beads. Although more important symbolically than economically, these interactions provided the Jornada Mogollón with vital links to the technological and cultural trends of the region.

By the early fourteenth century, the Jornada Mogollón peoples of the Trans-Pecos were entering a period of crisis. So successful during earlier (and wetter) times in establishing a corn-farming subsistence base for themselves, they had outstripped their capacity to survive prolonged drought and underproduction. This was not unique to the Jornada Mogollón, for the Hohokam, Anasazi, and western Mogollón were suffering from the same combination of environmental and demographic factors. Drought conditions emptied reservoirs and meant that not enough runoff came down mountain slopes to allow the large pueblos to survive. Dispersing in their efforts to survive, some of the Jornada Mogollón moved north into the Rio Grande valley of central New Mexico to join Anasazi migrants from the northwest. Other Jornada Mogollón groups entirely abandoned agriculture and returned to a hunter-gatherer way of life, especially the easternmost groups, which had easy access to migratory buffalo herds on the southern Plains.

By the time they arrived in the region, sixteenth-century Spaniards identified various Indian groups inhabiting the lower parts of the southern Plains and parts of the Trans-Pecos as Jumanos. Although they described some of these groups as purely bison-hunting societies, they described others as floodplain agriculturalists. At least some of these groups were undoubtedly the descendants of the Jornada Mogollón culture, some of which had clung to their agricultural ways and others of which had become important traders across Texas. Slowly over the next two centuries, the Jumanos disappeared from the scene, some incorporated into other regional culture groups and others absorbed into northern Mexican colonial society.

Mound-Building Farmers of East Texas

As late as the last decades of the seventeenth century, Jumano traders were crossing the great expanse of Texas to trade with agricultural peoples, the Caddos, who inhabited the eastern fringes of the Great Plains and the western river valleys of the Mississippi basin. Some of these Caddos lived as far west as the Trinity River and represented an even more successful Texas agricultural tradition than the Jornada Mogollón. By the time the Spanish arrived, their culture extended back about a thousand years, and they would continue to be an important factor in Spanish colonial Texas history up to the eve of Mexican independence.

About 2,000 years ago the peoples of the Sabine River and nearby drainages had begun to practice some gardening, making or acquiring utilitarian ceramics, and practicing a more sedentary life way, creating a tradition that had much in common with other Indian cultures of the eastern United States known as Woodland. Mound-building, ceremonial centers, and dispersed villages eventually became a part of the settlement pattern after about 800 AD in northeastern Texas. Some ceramics shared features with those of other Trans-Mississippi groups, and trade goods found in burials indicate long-range trade connections with other peoples.

Out of these Woodland-period developments, about 1,200 years ago, there emerged a distinctive culture that has come to be known as Caddo. The Caddo culture area centered on the Red, Sabine, Angelina, and Neches rivers of Texas and adjacent portions of Louisiana, Arkansas, and Oklahoma. The Caddo spoke one of a number of related languages called Caddoan today, of which Wichita, Pawnee, and Arikara are other examples, and eventually the Caddo language developed dialects associated with the major political divisions of the Caddos that Europeans encountered in the four-state region.

In time, the Caddos became the dominant culture of the region, a process that took place over hundreds of years during which Caddo society developed into a sophisticated system of interrelated kinship-based political entities that late seventeenth-century Europeans described as confederacies. In fact, the three confederacies of historic times—the Kadohadacho, Hasinai, and Natchitoches—were the product of successful adaptations to environmental conditions in East Texas, western Louisiana, southwestern Arkansas, and southeastern Oklahoma. In this well-watered and heavily forested region, early Caddo farmers took advantage of abundant natural resources that enabled them to establish dispersed sedentary communities. By about 800 years ago corn became the principal staple, while squash, beans, sunflowers, and a variety of other annuals and nuts rounded out the plant base of Caddo subsistence. Caddos also hunted deer and turkey, as well as small game, to meet the balance of their dietary requirements. The occasional bear and bison provided leather and furs for other needs.

Like Mississippian cultures to the east, the Caddos were prolific mound builders. As their culture became more sophisticated, they developed a settlement pattern based on scattered agricultural villages of widely dispersed conical-shaped thatch dwellings and specialized ceremonial centers. Mounds near villages continued to serve the basic purpose of containing the remains of high-status individuals, and mounds were also built at a number of these ceremonial centers that served to elevate temples in which Caddo priests and leaders could commune with the spirit world.

The prosperity indicated by widespread mound building is also evidenced by extensive interregional trade and sophisticated crafts activities. Through Plains intermediaries, Caddos exchanged their bois d'arc bows, ceramics, tanned goods, and perhaps even corn, for turquoise from New Mexico, copper from the Great Lakes region, seashells from the Gulf of Mexico, and buffalo hides from the Plains. They produced sophisticated agricultural and woodworking toolkits of stone and shell that included digging tools, hoes, and axes for clearing timber. In the stone-scarce environment in which they lived, the Caddo even relied on wood to make the large

Courtesy of Friends of Northeast Texas Archaeology and Timothy K. Perttula

The Caddo were prolific pottery makers who took advantage of East Texas's abundant clay resources. Vessels such as this one, from a site in Camp County and dating from ca. 1600 CE, were part of the trade goods that Caddos exchanged with neighboring groups.

mortars and long wooden pestles they used to grind corn into meal. Caddo pottery and basketry from the centuries immediately preceding the arrival of Europeans was among the finest in North America. French and Spanish descriptions of their tanned and decorated animal-skin apparel indicate a long tradition of craftsmanship.

Due to extensive observation by Europeans in the late seventeenth and early eighteenth centuries, a great deal can be inferred about Caddo society on the eve of the arrival of Europeans. Overall, the Caddos were largely peaceful tribes before the eighteenth century, although defensive warfare was part of life. At the most basic level of society—the family—organization was matrilineal, meaning that descent was traced on the mother's side. Marriage took place between members of different clans, and families were grouped in clans, usually named for animals, which were hierarchically ranked. Commoner families typically lived in individual homesteads surrounded by the agricultural field assigned to them.

Political organization outside the home combined egalitarian and hierarchical practices and was partly theocratic in nature. Chiefdoms composed of groups of scattered homesteads, one or more villages, and a ceremonial center, operated under the leadership of a hereditary caddi, or community chief. He governed with the support of elders called canahas, but in times of war villages would select war chiefs from among proven warriors. Religious leadership in each Caddo tribal group was in the hands of the Xinesi, also a hereditary position in the male line, who conducted ceremonies to communicate with the spirit world. His mediation with the supreme being, and his leadership during important annual feasts to celebrate planting, harvesting, and the hunt, were indispensable to the continuation of Caddo society.

The decline of Caddo fortunes coincides with sustained European contact, which brought new diseases and economic disruptions that were intensified by a number of factors. Warfare with neighboring Indian groups such as the Choctaws, Osages, Wichitas, and Tonkawas became more violent as the region's animal resources became a source of contention in trade relations with the French. Epidemic diseases, which may have struck even before the first European set foot in East Texas in the 1540s, but certainly had a documented effect after the 1680s, decimated whole villages, forcing survivors to consolidate into fewer and fewer groups. Attempting to adapt to the changing conditions of the eighteenth century, the Texas Caddos became involved in the French fur trade and began to hunt bison on horseback, an adaptation that brought them into the realm of people for whom the buffalo had always been at the core of life and culture.

European Arrival, 1528–1554

The first Spaniards to explore Texas lived during that restless period of frenzied searching for precious metals and great civilizations that we refer to as the Age of Conquest. From their experiences in the Caribbean and Mesoamerica (Mexico and Central America), Spaniards looked upon the conquest of Indian peoples and the plunder of their wealth as legitimate goals of exploration. In fact, it was Hernán

Cortés's triumph over the Aztec Empire that created high expectations for what might be found in the rest of North America. From the 1520s through the 1540s, numerous expeditions made their way north from Cuba and the land of the Aztecs seeking other Mexicos. Eventually, members of three of these expeditions came into contact with most of Texas's geographic regions and many of its culture groups.

Spain and Europe in the Age of Conquest

The Spaniards who followed Christopher Columbus to the New World in the early sixteenth century were part of a highly militarized culture that combined martial virtues with militant Christianity. For seven centuries Spaniards had participated in their own crusade against Iberian Muslim kingdoms that came to be known as the Reconquista. This Christian recovery of the Iberian Peninsula from the descendants of North African invaders who had overrun Visigothic Spain and Portugal in the early eighth century gave Spain its strong Catholic identity. It was an identity that its rulers at the end of the fifteenth century, Fernando of Aragón and Isabel of Castile, took advantage of in advancing their aims to make their respective kingdoms strong and wealthy. Strength and wealth could best be accomplished by securing cultural cohesion and expanding dynastic and economic opportunities beyond the borders of Spain. Not surprisingly, then, 1492 was the year of the first published European vernacular language grammar— Castilian; it was also the year that Jews were forced to convert to Christianity or leave the kingdoms of Castile and Aragón; and, it was the year in which Christopher Columbus undertook his royally sanctioned voyage of exploration, really an economic reconnaissance mission with unexpected consequences.

That voyage itself was the product of cultural and technological changes in Europe that had been in process for centuries. Unlike the Americas, which by about 7,000 years ago had become isolated from the other continents, Europe was part of the "Old World," interacting with Asia and Africa and benefiting from those interactions in ways that would make the continent home to the world's modern empires. As the heirs to ancient Mediterranean civilizations, Europeans shared a number of characteristics, including written languages, agricultural technologies such as numerous cultigens (domesticated plants) and livestock (domesticated fowl and mammals), advanced metallurgy, and similar architectural and cultural forms. From Portugal to Austria and Norway to Italy, Europeans operated under similar political principles, economic rules, social conventions, and cultural practices. Most importantly, they felt themselves superior to non-European peoples.

Trade and warfare, including the Crusades of the eleventh through thirteenth centuries, contributed to the emergence of a powerful Europe by the sixteenth century. From their Asian visits, European merchants brought home new technologies like gunpowder and paper along with the silk and spices that constituted the bulk of intercontinental trade. Europeans adapted Middle Eastern maritime technologies for oceanic travel and continuously improved instruments and charts that gave them greater ability to navigate farther and farther from home.

And, most importantly, the homegrown invention of the printing press allowed Europeans to quickly and efficiently share all of that new information, producing a snowball effect.

With the 1492 conquest of Granada, the last Muslim kingdom on the Iberian Peninsula, all of Western Europe was uniformly Christian and ready to take on the world. Much of that Europe was already engaged in a struggle with the Ottoman Empire, a Muslim polity that controlled significant portions of southeastern Europe and most of the Middle East. And, even as they fought Muslims in the east, Christian Europeans fought among themselves for dynastic and economic reasons; as the sixteenth century progressed they would also fight over competing versions of Christianity. The quest for a competitive advantage, particularly with regard to what is referred to as the "spice trade," provided an opening to men such as Christopher Columbus.

A merchant explorer who advanced the theory that Asia could be reached by sailing west across the Atlantic, Columbus shopped his ideas among European monarchs until he found a receptive hearing in Castile. Columbus did not propose to discover a "New World" but a new way to get to the other end of the Old World. Norsemen and fishermen had pushed northwest beyond Greenland and Iceland, so educated Europeans also had some idea of the presence of western lands. Columbus hoped to prove it was possible to reach Asia by sailing across the Atlantic Ocean before water and provisions ran out onboard the tiny ships. As it turned out, if the American continents had not stood in the way, Columbus would have been literally dead wrong, for by the time his three-ship fleet reached the Bahamas in October 1492, there were not enough supplies remaining for a return voyage.

The Conquest Begins

Columbus's gamble did not pay off personally in the long run. He remained convinced that he had reached Asia (all the evidence to the contrary, and with the result of the indigenous population mistakenly being referred to as Indians), he mismanaged the settlements that he established, and he failed to make good on his promise of Spanish access to the riches of the Orient. Instead, he enslaved the island populations to produce a source labor in the new settlements and to generate revenue back in Spain, where slavery was still common as a result of the interethnic warfare between Iberians and North Africans. Ironically, following his third voyage, Columbus returned to Spain in chains to face criminal charges of maladministration and cruelty.

From the beginning, then, Spanish settlement in the New World relied on an indigenous population that was often subjected to brutal forced labor practices. Pope Alexander IV's bull (decree) of 1493, *Inter Caetera*, issued shortly after Columbus's return to Spain, granted the Catholic Kings of Spain dominion over most of the newly discovered lands. Spain, in return, was responsible for assuring the conversion of the Indians to Christianity. It was an obligation that Fray Bartolomé de Las Casas and other clergymen would not let the Crown forget. In 1511, Spanish jurists had drawn up a document called the *Requerimiento* to be read to Indian communities that Spaniards were about to subjugate; it traced the history of the world from a biblical perspective, explained the Pope's decree, and required those hearing it to submit willingly or be subjugated by force. Catholic missionaries, especially Franciscans and Jesuits, soon became part of the machinery of empire, accompanying expeditions or sometimes leading them. Almost from the beginning a spiritual conquest of the New World accompanied its physical conquest.

Just as important to the Crown as the harvest of souls, if not more so, was the acquisition of wealth. Working from medieval precedents established during the Reconquista, Castilian monarchs issued *capitulaciones* (royal charters) to *adelantados* (leaders) for *entradas* (conquest, colonization, or settlement expeditions) that granted specific privileges in return for the *quinto real*, the Crown's one-fifth share of the proceeds of the endeavor. In this arrangement the members of the expedition outfitted themselves, bore all the expenses and, therefore, the risk, while the Crown gambled little. In the event an entrada met success, some of its members would certainly receive *encomiendas* (grants of Indian tribute, either as labor or goods), which would divert tax income from the royal treasury to the encomenderos' pockets, but that was a small price to pay for bringing new lands under Spanish control. And, after all, as in the case of Columbus, there were ways of terminating agreements that were not favorable to the Crown.

In the years after Columbus's voyages, Spaniards expanded their area of control to the major islands of the Caribbean and soon came into contact with the more sophisticated societies of Mesoamerica. By 1519, the governor of Cuba had set his sights on the nearby Yucatán Peninsula, from which accounts had been received of advanced societies that offered better business opportunities than had so far been discovered. To lead this initial commercial venture he appointed Hernán Cortés, an ambitious conquistador who had participated in the conquest of Cuba. After initial stops along the Yucatán Peninsula, Cortés landed on the Mexican coast, founded the town of Vera Cruz, had the new settlement's officials (whom he had chosen) vote him their governor, and broke away from the authority of Cuba's governor. In two years' time, through a combination of brute force, masterful diplomacy, and artful betrayals Cortés brought down the Aztec Empire, launching the Spanish conquest of Mexico, a process still not completed 300 years later when Spain's presence in North America came to an end.

The First Conquistadors in Texas

When Pánfilo de Narváez presented his petition to King Charles I of Spain (better known as Charles V, Holy Roman Emperor) to conquer Florida in 1526, he was hoping to surpass the accomplishments of his rival and personal enemy, Cortés. From various slaving expeditions and explorations in the 1510s, including one by Álvarez de Pineda in 1519 that mapped the entire gulf coast from Florida to Tampico, Spaniards became curious about the vast land north of Mexico that came to be known as Florida. Narváez, who had sided with the governor of Cuba against Cortés during the conquest of Mexico, had lost an eye in

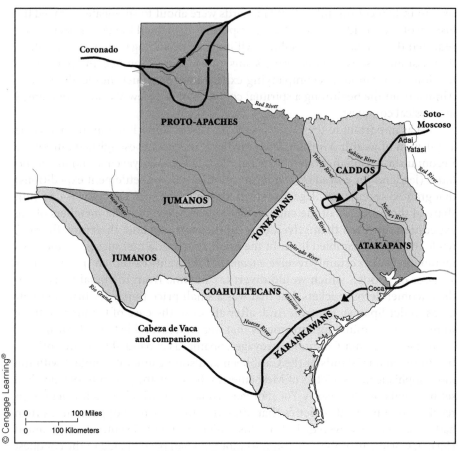

Sixteenth-century Texas conquistadors and native peoples.

battle attempting to arrest the conqueror of the Aztecs. Captured, humiliated, and then abandoned, he had returned to Spain intent on getting his due; this, he believed, could be accomplished in Florida.

There would be no quinto real from this venture, however, and no spoils for Narváez and his men, either. Misfortune dogged the expedition from the time its five small ships reached the Caribbean. One hundred forty men deserted at Santo Domingo, and then a hurricane off the Cuban coast sank two ships and killed the sixty men on board. After wintering in Cuba, the expedition again set sail in February, encountering other storms that threatened disaster. Finally, in April 1528, the Spaniards reached the gulf coast of Florida, where they entered what was probably Tampa Bay. Their luck did not improve, however. Despite the warnings of his treasurer Álvar Núñez Cabeza de Vaca that the land forces should not separate from the fleet, Narváez marched his men inland in a futile attempt to reach the supposedly gold-rich Kingdom of Apalachee. After four months of hostilities with Indians and forced marches through swamps and jungles, the men had found no gold or other tangible wealth and there was no sight of the expedition's fleet. The entrada's morale was broken. In September the men constructed five crude boats at St. Mark's Bay, Florida. Overcrowded with almost 250 survivors, they set sail for Mexico.

Soon after passing the mouth of the Mississippi a storm battered the boats toward the Texas coast. In the days that followed Narváez's boat was lost, and in early November, one after another of the remaining craft beached just south of Galveston Island. Suffering from exposure, starvation, and dehydration, the would-be conquistadors were at the mercy of the Indians who inhabited the area. The initially friendly meeting between Indians and Spaniards soon took a turn for the worse as misunderstandings between the two cultures developed. Some Spaniards died of exposure and others disappeared in attempts to reach civilization; a fortunate few found "employment" among the Indian groups that took them in. Of the dwindling number of expeditionaries, only four would live to tell the tale. One of these four was Cabeza de Vaca.

For six years, the survivors dwelt among the Galveston Bay, Karankawa, and Coahuiltecan Indians of coastal and South Texas, sometimes as "slaves," sometimes as merchants, but also as healers. In 1532, Cabeza de Vaca finally abandoned his single remaining companion, Lope de Oviedo, and made his way inland. Captured by another group of Indians, he soon discovered the presence in the region of three fellow Spaniards, Captains Alonzo del Castillo and Andrés Dorantes and the latter's North African slave, Estebanico. Two years of planning resulted in a successful escape from their captors, and the beginning of an odyssey that took the four Christians across parts of present-day Texas, New Mexico, and northern Mexico, from the Gulf of Mexico to the Gulf of California between 1534 and 1536. Everything he could remember having seen and heard during his odyssey Cabeza de Vaca wrote down in his *Relación*, the first Texas literature and the first ethnographic work on North America.

Coronado and the Seven Cities of Gold

Antonio de Mendoza, first viceroy of New Spain, as greater Mexico was known during the 300 years of Spanish rule, had only recently arrived in the New World when Cabeza de Vaca came out of the northern "wilderness." For Mendoza, who was the Spanish king's chief administrator in New Spain, underwriting an expedition to discover and conquer the "Seven Cities of Gold" that the wanderers reported hearing about would be financially rewarding, would reduce the slave raiding that contributed to social and economic instability in the country, and would be a way to rid central Mexico of the large number of idle Spanish "gentlemen" who were a constant source of trouble. A prudent and sensible administrator, however, Mendoza was not about to invest his limited financial resources and reputation on unsubstantiated rumor. To establish the veracity of Cabeza de Vaca's reports, he sent out a scout: a Franciscan friar with considerable New World experience, Marcos de Niza. He was to be guided by none other than Estebanico, Cabeza de Vaca's companion, whom the viceroy purchased from Dorantes because none of the three Spaniards was willing to retrace their steps into the interior.

Although the 1539 Niza–Estebanico expedition turned out to be an utter disaster, with Estebanico being killed by the Zuni inhabitants of Hawikuh in present-day Arizona, Niza's assertion that the town was "bigger than Mexico City," gave Viceroy Mendoza the answer he wanted. To carry out the conquest, Mendoza turned to Francisco Vázquez de Coronado. Already the governor of Nueva Galicia, at age thirty, Coronado now had the honor of leading an expedition that would bring new glory and subjects to the Crown, new souls to Christ, and great wealth to himself, the viceroy, and those sturdy enough to see the enterprise to its conclusion. A thousand Spanish men-at-arms, thousands more Indian servants and camp followers, immense herds of horses, mules, and cattle, and flocks of sheep and goats, marched out of Culiacán, Sinaloa, in April 1540.

What the villagers of Hawikuh thought of armored Spaniards riding horses making unintelligible demands for shiny yellow and white metals they had never seen can only be imagined. Coronado, not to be denied, took the town by storm on July 7, 1540. Having found no gold or silver in the first city of Cíbola, as the region was called initially by Spaniards, the expedition moved on to the other cities, then eastward to the Rio Grande and Pecos River pueblos (towns), where bloodshed and disappointment mixed. Niza's enthusiasm had proved a lie. At the Pecos River pueblo of Cicuye, however, the Indians gave reason for hope. Far to the east, beyond the great flat lands, they promised, was the Kingdom of Quivira, where gold and silver awaited the Spaniards in plenty.

Quivira turned out to be another disappointment for Coronado and his men. To get there they had to cross a portion of today's northwestern and Panhandle Texas. In the spring of 1541 they visited the Blanco and Tule canyons region, where they recorded their impressions of the unprecedented flatness of the land, the region's immense bison herds, and the tipi-dwelling, buffalo-hunting proto-Apaches who had recently made the southern Plains their home. And, when they got to Quivira, actually Wichita Indian villages in central Kansas, they found no gold or silver, or anything else that they valued for that matter. Although some of his men desired to stay in the country, Coronado, broken both psychologically and physically (a fall from his horse had caused permanent injuries), brought his humbled expeditionaries back to Culiacán in the spring of 1542 with nothing to show for their efforts.

Their reports on the Rio Grande country, although optimistic about future prospects for the region, did not encourage Spanish settlement. The High Plains of Texas, remote and almost totally devoid of human residents, offered even fewer attractions. One lasting legacy of Coronado's bold venture seems to have been a lingering resentment on the part of the town-dwelling Indians, who henceforth would be called Pueblos by the Spaniards, and who within fifty years would confront more determined Spanish conquerors.

Conquistadors in East Texas

Cabeza de Vaca had his own ideas about how Spanish settlement of Florida might best be carried out, and he hoped to gain permission from Emperor Charles V to attempt a new colonization effort. He returned to Spain in the summer of 1537 to find that he had been preempted by one of the heroes of the conquest of the Inca Empire, Hernando de Soto. This ruthless conquistador had come away from the Peruvian adventure a rich and powerful man. For him, as for most of his contemporaries, adventure and conquest had become an addiction. God, gold, and glory, although usually not in that order, were his driving motives. In the spring of 1536 Soto arrived in Spain laden down with his share of the spoils taken from the Incas and by the end of April 1537, he had obtained the governorship of Cuba, a knighthood in the Order of Santiago, and a charter to colonize Florida. Wisely, Cabeza de Vaca turned down Soto's offer of a place in his expedition when the conquistadors met.

In the spring of 1539, after almost a year of final preparations in Cuba, Soto landed his 600-man expedition somewhere in the Tampa Bay area of Florida. He was much better equipped than Narváez had been a decade earlier on his Florida misadventure, but Soto's quest for the wealth that had eluded that earlier expedition turned out no better. Wherever he and his men traveled throughout southeastern North America between May 1539 and May 1542, the least resistance from the indigenous peoples they encountered was met with steel, lead, and war dogs. Finally, racked with fever and discouraged by his failure to find

Shortly after Cabeza de Vaca's 1555 edition appeared, the Gentleman of Elvas published his account of the Soto-Moscoso expedition at Evora, Portugal, in 1557. His account is the first European report on the Caddo country of East Texas.

the precious metals that lured him to North America, Soto died on the banks of the Mississippi River, leaving behind only a legacy of slaughter and destruction that imperiled the expedition's survival.

Succeeding Soto in command was Luis Moscoso de Alvarado, who held a council at which the Spaniards decided to abandon the enterprise. Having decided to try for an overland march to New Spain, as the region conquered by Cortés and his successors was called, Moscoso led his men across the Red River in the summer of 1542. Only slightly less brutal now that Soto was no longer in command, expedition members fought and tortured their way through the Caddo country of northeast Texas. The Caddos encountered by the Spaniards in Texas, members of the Kadohadacho and Hasinai confederacies, must have had word of the Spaniards ahead of time. For, according to a Portuguese chronicler, as soon as Moscoso and his men approached,

> The people were called out, who, as fast they could get together, came by fifties and hundreds on the road, to give battle. While some encountered us, others fell upon our rear; and when we followed up those, these pursued us. The attack continued during the greater part of the day, until we arrived at their town. Some men were injured, and some horses, but nothing so as to hinder travel, there being not one dangerous wound among all. The Indians suffered great slaughter.

Despite the rumors of Christians far to the south or west, and certain knowledge that New Spain lay to the southwest, Moscoso and the other expedition leaders based their decision to abandon the overland march on Cabeza de Vaca's experience. They recognized the country they were entering to be the one in which, according to Cabeza de Vaca, "the Indians wandered like Arabs, having no settled place of residence, living on prickly pears, and the roots of plants, and game; and that if this should be so, and they, entering upon that tract, found no provision for sustenance during winter, they must inevitably perish." At that point, the conquistadors retraced their steps to the Mississippi, where they wintered and built boats to carry them to New Spain. In September 1543, the surviving 311 members of Soto's great expedition arrived at Pánuco. They left behind a trail of destruction from the Atlantic coast to eastern Texas. Most disruptive were epidemic diseases that wreaked havoc on the native populations of the southeastern United States.

The disheartening results of the Coronado and Soto–Moscoso expeditions convinced the Spanish to direct their attention to other parts of the New World. The absence of precious metals, the unsuitability of the native peoples for assimilation, and the difficulty of access to the region deterred a permanent Spanish presence. The absence of any foreign threat in the Gulf of Mexico further disinclined the Crown from expending more resources there. Consequently, for the next four decades, the little contact Spaniards did have with what is now Texas was restricted to the gulf coast, where hurricanes and other storms sometimes drove Spanish ships sailing between Veracruz and Havana.

The most famous of these incidents, the 1554 wreck off Padre Island of the Santa María de Yciar, San Esteban, and Espíritu Santo, three of four ships in a treasure fleet containing over two million pesos in gold and silver, did nothing to improve the reputation of Texas. The 250 castaways who attempted to march back to Spanish-held territory overland were attacked by Indians all along the whole way. The lone survivor, Fray Marcos de Mena, told stories of cannibal Indians and a waterless desert by the sea. The salvage expedition sent to recover the 1.5 million pesos on board the three ships found the shallow waters off Padre Island treacherous and lacking in adequate anchorages. If the interior of Texas offered few attractions for the fortune-seeking conquistadors, the coast of the Gulf of Mexico represented only danger for the sailing men bearing treasures from the New World to the old.

Conclusion

At the beginning of the sixteenth century the land we now call Texas had already been a cultural crossroads for thousands of years. It was the meeting place of eastern Woodlands, Plains, and southwestern cultures. It was home to both simple hunter-gatherers and sophisticated agriculturalists. Its people spoke a number of unrelated languages and maintained widely varying traditions, although their cultures made pottery and used stone tools and bows and arrows. Almost all Texas Indians had something else in common: to one degree or another they all made use of the buffalo, a grazing animal that due to changing environmental conditions in the Late Prehistoric period was extending its range southward and eastward across almost the entire breadth of Texas.

Not a single Indian living within the state's present boundaries would have understood the concept of Texas, however. With the exception of the complex, hierarchical, socially stratified Caddos, no prehistoric Texas Indian group appears to have had much use for any kind of political organization beyond the local chief or head man and his group of trusted advisors. And, although most cultures had become territorial by Late Prehistoric times, that territoriality was at most a simple defense of hunting grounds or a finely tuned subsistence strategy based, as in the case of the Karankawas, on seasonal exploitation of locally available resources.

In other words, the land that the Spaniards encountered in the first half of the sixteenth century was not a wilderness or a land of savages. Crisscrossed by trade networks that tied the Rockies to the Mississippi and the Great Lakes to the Gulf of Mexico, its people were exposed to, contributed to, and were influenced by the major cultural, sociopolitical, and technological changes of pre-Columbian North America. Occupying every possible ecological niche the state had to offer, its people had adapted to conditions with dexterity.

Most of these adaptations, which relied on extensive rather than intensive exploitation of the land, seemed odd and primitive to the technologically advanced and socially complex Europeans who encountered them. Certainly, the early indigenous cultures of Texas paled in comparison to the technological and social complexity of some Mesoamerican, South American, and Old World civilizations; and, so, they were ill prepared to meet the challenge of the New World coming into existence. In the course of the next 500 years, this New World would leave little room for the descendants of the first Texans to call the state home.

Happenstance brought the first Europeans to the northwest corner of the Gulf of Mexico, to a land that had no name, no boundaries, and in no way approximated modern Texas. The accidental exploration of present-day coastal Texas and parts of northern Mexico by Cabeza de Vaca and his fellow survivors of the Narváez conquest was followed by the more purposeful exploits of the Soto–Moscoso and Coronado expeditions: Dreams and tales of treasure had brought these conquistadors into the forests of East Texas and the plains and canyons of West Texas. The great disappointment at finding no gold or silver and no new Aztec empires to conquer dampened their enthusiasm. This vast and sparsely settled land turned out to be nothing more than the least inviting corner of Spain's North American ambitions.

Suggested Readings

The study of early Texas requires a little ingenuity, given the existing nature of the literature. Entries in the *New Handbook of Texas* (NHOT) covering most of the subjects treated in this chapter will prove extremely useful as a basic introduction.

Texas Takes Shape

The essay "Geology" in the NHOT gives a clear overview that complements the information in *Roadside Geology of Texas* by Darwin Spearing (1991). Dividing the state into sections, focusing on the geological features encountered on or near the state's byways, and profusely illustrated, *Roadside Geology of Texas* is a great companion for weekend excursions. Terry G. Jordan et al., *Texas: A Geography* (1984) remains the best survey on the subject.

Early Prehistoric Texas, 13,000–1 BC

In the last few years the archaeological literature on Texas, which used to consist largely of highly technical reports of fieldwork and efforts to reconcile findings in different parts of the state from approximately the same timeframe, has blossomed. Nevertheless, the reader is forewarned that archaeologists do not all agree on the boundaries between prehistoric periods, or on the precise taxonomy to apply to their findings, although they do tend to agree broadly on Paleoindian, Archaic, and Late Prehistoric as the major periods. These issues, along with many others, are presented by Linda Cordell in *Archaeology of the Southwest* (2nd ed., 1997). Although concerned only with western Texas as part of her definition of "Southwest," the text is very useful in understanding the general currents of development during Paleoindian times in Texas. For those wishing to begin with a more general introduction to North American prehistory, look to Brian M. Fagan's *The Great Journey: The Peopling of Ancient America* (rev. ed., 2004).

The best synthesis of Texas during prehistoric times is Timothy K. Perttula's edited volume *The Prehistory of Texas* (rev. ed., 2013), which brings together some of the state's leading archaeologists to provide surveys of each of the state's culture regions from Paleoindian to Late Prehistoric times. A very readable survey by an ethnohistorian is David La Vere's *The Texas Indians* (2004), which tells the story of the state's indigenous peoples through the twentieth century. W. W. Newcomb, Jr., provides the text to a marvelously illustrated volume on *The Rock Art of Texas Indians* (1967), the paintings for which were done by Forrest Kirkland from original sketches and photographs.

Late Prehistoric Texas, 1–1528 AD

Texas Indians during Late Prehistoric to early historic times have received unequal attention from scholars. Articles in the NHOT on individual tribes are uneven in how up-to-date they are, but generally serve as a good introduction to the background of each group. The evidence for the mysterious Jumanos, their possible origins, and what might have happened to them is presented by Nancy Parrott Hickerson in *The Jumanos: Hunters and Traders of the South Plains* (1994). Toyah Phase peoples and their relationships to other Texas Indians are explored in the controversial and inappropriately named *Land of the Tejas: Native American Identity and Interaction in Texas, A.D. 1300 to 1700* by John Wesley Arnn III (2012). The story of the Apaches' arrival in Texas is told in the opening part of Thomas A. Britten, *The Lipan Apaches: People of Wind and Lightning* (2009), as well as in William B. Carter, *Indian Alliances and the Spanish in the Southwest, 750–1750* (2009). The work of Robert A. Ricklis—in particular The *Karankawa Indians of Texas: An Ecological Study of Cultural Traditions and Change* (1996)—has revolutionized our understanding of these long-maligned people. The Atakapans and other East Texas Indians are the subjects of Lawrence E. Aten, *Indians of the Upper Texas Coast* (1983).

Of the indigenous peoples of Texas at the time of the European encounter, none has received more attention than the Caddos. The opening parts of four works provide a useful introduction: *Caddo Indians: Where We Come From*, by Cecile Elkins Carter (1995); *"The Caddo Nation": Archaeological and Ethnohistoric Perspectives*, by Timothy K. Perttula (1992); *The Caddo Chiefdoms: Caddo Economics and Politics, 700–1835* (1998) by David La Vere; and *The Caddo Indians: Tribes at the Convergence of Empires, 1542-1854*, by F. Todd Smith. A very different approach to Caddo origins is taken by Vynola Beaver Newkumet and Howard L. Meredith, *Hasinai: A Traditional History of the Caddo Confederacy* (1988).

Finally, for those readers who wish to dig into Texas Indian prehistory themselves, there are a number of out-of-print works that can serve as invaluable guides: Parker Nunley, *A Field Guide to Archeological Sites in Texas* (1989); Ellen Sue Turner and Thomas R. Hester, *A Field Guide to Stone Artifacts of Texas Indians* (1985); and, of course, Hester's *Digging into South Texas Prehistory* (1980).

European Arrival, 1528–1554

Several works provide overviews of Spanish North America, including the area that is now Texas, in the Age of Conquest. Anyone with a deeper interest in the conquest of Mexico and the establishment of Spanish institutions in

North America can begin to explore the subject in Michael C. Meyer, William L. Sherman, and Susan M. Deeds, *The Course of Mexican History* (9th ed., 2010). The first three chapters of David J. Weber's *The Spanish Frontier in North America* (1992) provide a comprehensive survey of what is now the southern half of the United States through the end of the sixteenth century. The same chronological period is covered, in a very different, but highly entertaining way, in the opening chapters of John L. Kessell, *Spain in the Southwest: A Narrative History of Colonial New Mexico, Arizona, Texas, and California* (2002). For those interested specifically in Texas, the most complete survey of this era can be found in Chapter 2 of Donald E. Chipman, *Spanish Texas, 1519–1821* (rev. ed., 2010). Emphasizing the Indian side of the story are two very different works: Elizabeth A. H. John, *Storms Brewed in Other Men's Worlds: The Confrontation of Indians, Spanish, and French in the Southwest, 1540–1795* (reprint; 1996), and Gary Clayton Anderson, *The Indian Southwest, 1580–1830: Ethnogenesis and Reinvention* (1999). For an understanding of conquest-era Spain, see J. H. Elliot, *Imperial Spain, 1469–1716* (2nd ed., 2002). A primer on Spanish history from prehistoric times is William D. Phillips, Jr., and Carla Rahn Phillips, *A Concise History of Spain* (2010.)

Of the conquistadors who traveled across Texas, none has received more scholarly attention than Álvar Núñez Cabeza de Vaca, who set down the story of his adventures in North America in a work titled *Relación*. It has been translated numerous times, including the very readable and well-illustrated *Castaways: The Narrative of Alvar Núñez Cabeza de Vaca*, ed. Enrique Pupo-Walker, trans. Frances M. López-Morillas (1993). Cabeza de Vaca's experiences have also produced a cottage industry of anthropological, ethnohistorical, and historical work and literary criticism on Indian-Spanish contact. The best of these studies is Andrés Reséndez, *A Land So Strange: The Epic Journey of Cabeza de Vaca* (2007).

Interpretation of the Coronado and Soto-Moscoso expeditions has changed significantly over the last century. The first historian to put together the story of Soto-Moscoso was the mestizo historian Garcilaso de la Vega, whose *The Florida of the Inca*, which first appeared in 1605, has been translated and edited by John Grier Varner and Jeannette Johnson Varner (1980). Bringing up to date the state of research on Moscoso's route in Texas is James E. Bruseth and Nancy A. Kenmotsu, "From Naguatex to the River Daycao: The Route of the Hernando De Soto Expedition Through Texas," *North American Archaeologist* (1993). A very good brief summary of the expedition can be found in Robert S. Weddle, *Spanish Sea: The Gulf of Mexico in North American Discovery, 1500–1685* (1985), Chapter 12. In Chapter 13 of the same book, Weddle tells the story of the 1554 treasure fleet shipwreck. The current trend in research on the Coronado expedition can be found in the works of Richard Flint and Shirley Cushing Flint, in particular Richard Flint's *No Settlement, No Conquest: A History of the Coronado Entrada* (2008). The best short summary of Spanish exploration in West Texas during this period is John Miller Morris, *El Llano Estacado: Exploration and Imagination on the High Plains of Texas and New Mexico, 1536–1860* (1997), part 1.

New Spain's Northeastern Frontier to 1767

Tired, sick, but full of hope and enthusiasm for their work, the nine Franciscan priests who participated in the reoccupation of Texas finally sat down together on July 22, 1716, to pen a joint petition to the viceroy seeking further aid for their work. "We have conceived great expectations that this province will become a New Philippine, having, firstly, Your Excellency's protection and, on the Indians' part, the great friendliness with which they have received us. We believe that their docility and good demeanor merit that our generous and Catholic King and Lord (whom God protect) attend to them as his beloved children, and extend his powerful hand to put in ours the wherewithal for them to cover their nakedness, cultivate their lands, and raise livestock for their subsistence." With a bit of hyperbole, they hoped to flatter King Phillip V by comparing their work among the Hasinais with the efforts of earlier missionaries in the Philippine Islands under Phillip II 150 years earlier. These friars and their successors represented one of the principal tools of Spanish colonial expansion, although royal support was never as generous as they hoped it would be. Along with presidios and ranches, missions were an indispensable institution of the Spanish North American frontier until the last third of the eighteenth century. Missionaries firmly believed that their work served both majesties—glorifying God and expanding the dominions of the king. In Texas both these assumptions would be tested and the reality of Spanish imperial might put to the test by indigenous peoples with very different world views and the means to successfully ward off the Spanish challenge.

For a century and a half before the missionaries tasked with the permanent occupation of Texas sat down to write about their hopes and dreams, Spaniards (generally, all subjects of the Spanish Crown, whether European or American of

33

Chapter 2 New Spain's Northeastern Frontier to 1767	
1598	Juan de Oñate's expedition crosses the Rio Grande at Paso del Norte
1659	Fray García de San Francisco establishes Mission Nuestra Señora de Guadalupe, first Spanish settlement at Paso del Norte
1680	Pueblo Revolt leads to founding of Ysleta for friendly Tigua Indians, and other settlements at Paso del Norte
1685	La Salle expedition lands at Matagorda Bay, builds Fort St. Louis
1690	San Francisco de los Tejas becomes first Spanish settlement in the province of Texas
1693	Spaniards abandon Texas
1714	St. Denis founds Natchitoches and makes contact with Spaniards at Rio Grande
1716	Ramón expedition reoccupies East Texas for Spain
1718	Governor Alarcón founds mission-presidio complex of San Antonio de Béxar
1720	Mission San José y San Miguel de Aguayo, "Queen of the Missions," founded by Fray Antonio Margil de Jesús
1721	Marqués de Aguayo establishes Presidio de los Adaes, future capital of Texas; founds mission-presidio complex of La Bahía
1731	Querétaro missions from East Texas transferred to San Antonio; Canary Island immigrants establish first civil settlement at Béxar
1746	Mission-presidio complex of San Xavier begins to form
1749	Escandón orders transfer of La Bahía to present location; settlement of lower Rio Grande valley begins
1755	Laredo founded
1758	Mission San Sabá, established for Apaches, destroyed by Indians hostile to Apaches
1767	Distribution of land grants in lower Rio Grande valley begins

any ethnicity) had on occasion traveled north of the Rio Grande and east of the Pecos. Measuring the Indian societies they encountered by European standards, they failed to see the thriving and dynamic world that the diverse Indian peoples of the region had created for themselves. The various culture groups of what is now Texas had developed a vast and sophisticated trade network based on regular exchange gatherings in the Colorado–Brazos area of central Texas. Indian trade fairs included a wide variety of products, including buffalo robes and dried meat, tools, pottery, mass-produced stone projectile points, corn, some jewelry, and, most prized of all, horses.

This Indian world was only vaguely understood by the Spaniards, who could not accept that an Indian political economy might complement rather than threaten the Spanish imperial system. It would take much of the eighteenth century to bring Spanish policymakers around to accepting that Indians could be allies or trade partners rather than merely enemies or heathens awaiting salvation. By mid-century Spanish Bourbon policymakers were exploring new ways of colonizing without overly relying on missions. Texas, however, proved a largely insurmountable challenge to Spanish religious, political, and economic principles. Despite the success of settlement areas around today's San Antonio, Goliad, Laredo, and El Paso, the vastness north of the Rio Grande was very much an Indian world and would remain so for a century to come.

As you read this chapter, consider the following questions:

1. How did the various Indian peoples of Texas and the surrounding region respond to the arrival of Europeans in their territories?
2. How was the Spanish settlement of Texas the result of far off imperial political and economic rivalries?
3. Aside from the effective resistance of the most powerful of the region's native peoples, what other challenges did Spaniards face in colonizing Texas?

 ## The Paso del Norte Corridor, 1598–1690

In the years after Coronado returned from the land of the Pueblos, tensions between Spanish colonials and the Indians of northern New Spain again erupted into an armed conflict. The native peoples involved, referred to collectively as Chichimecas by the Aztecs and then the Spaniards, actively resisted encroachment of their hunting grounds by Spanish ranchers intent on expanding the developing livestock industry of the colony. A series of silver strikes, beginning in 1546 at Zacatecas, brought about a new type of colonial expansion, however—the silver rush. Silver lodes were rarely located at the site of good agricultural land along easily accessible travel corridors. Consequently, the initial occupation of the north was a spotty affair, in which Spaniards occupied strategic locations while the Chichimecas retained control of much of the countryside. Eventually, this frontier process once again brought Europeans into contact with the indigenous peoples north of the Rio Grande and, ultimately, Texas, this time by way of a natural route of travel that acquired the name Paso del Norte in the area of far West Texas.

New Spain's Northern Frontier Society

The Chichimecas of the mining frontier area were very different from the sedentary Aztecs and Mayas. Throughout what is today northern Mexico lived numerous band peoples that followed a hunter-gatherer way of life and a few semi- or fully sedentary groups that practiced subsistence agriculture. They spoke a variety of languages, contested each other for territory and resources, and proved highly resistant to Spanish efforts to subjugate them. As disease and warfare reduced the viability of some groups, surviving members fled beyond the reach of the Euroamericans, and through a process of ethnogenesis (cultural reinvention) or absorption combined with members of other groups to forge new band or tribal identities.

Militarized and mobile, Chichimecas resisted Spanish encroachment in a series of conflicts that lasted most of the latter half of the sixteenth century. To exploit mines, open farms, and fight and enslave the indigenous peoples, Spaniards, Afro-Hispanics, Hispanicized Indians, and a growing mixed-blood population made its way north. A lucky few Spaniards, both *peninsulares* (European-born) and *criollos* (American-born) made fortunes as miners, merchants, and *hacendados* (owners of large landed estates—haciendas—that produced both livestock and crops for market). Some organized their own militias, which in time became the seeds of the presidio frontier military garrison system. The vast majority of frontiersmen, however, simply sowed the seeds of modern North Mexican society.

Eventually, an important new element was added to this mixed lot of Spaniards, Africans, and Indians—the mestizo. *Mestizaje*, as the process of race mixing in the Spanish world has come to be known, created an ever-increasing population of mixed-bloods known collectively as *castas*. The ordering of society according to a racial-ethnic hierarchy was called the *sistema de castas*. Often the product of extralegal unions or of rape, the mestizo population found the expanding northern frontier more welcoming to them. Military service, ranching, farming, and other economic activities were more accessible on the frontier, as was the possibility to "pass" into the ranks of the criollos.

At the same time that Spaniards, Africans, mestizos, and acculturated Indians flocked to each new *bonanza* (rich mineral deposit), Spanish missionaries established new centers for the conversion of the small local Indian populations. The Catholic religious order primarily responsible for undertaking the conversion of Chichimecas was the Franciscans. Having arrived in New Spain in the mid-1520s at the behest of Cortés, their job had at first seemed a strictly religious one—to turn the "civilized" Indian societies of central Mexico away from their native gods and toward Christ. The farther north they expanded their efforts, however, the more complicated the problem became. Preparing hunter-gatherers and semisedentary people for life in the Spanish Empire was not merely a matter of religious reeducation but of completely transforming their ways of life. Indians gathered together in communities that came to be known as missions were subjected to the regimentation of European civilization: strict and complex divisions of labor and gender roles, routinized work modes, and monogamy. Although the friars were the ultimate authorities in the missions, the Indians were trained in the ways of Spanish local government and responsibilities to the greater colonial society. The goal of these efforts was the re-creation of Spanish social, political, and economic institutions, with peninsulares and criollos as the lords of the land.

New Mexico and Far West Texas Explored Again

As the silver frontier expanded northward, it was only a matter of time before New Mexico again drew the attention of Spaniards. By the early 1580s missionaries and fortune seekers, including the Rodríguez–Chamuscado and Espejo expeditions, had made their way into the land of the Pueblos, the survivors returning with fanciful tales of wealthy native kingdoms. King Philip II was quite interested in this "new" Mexico, as the Pueblo country was being referred to, not only for the reports of silver and other riches and the possibility of claiming new souls for God, but for its supposed strategic importance. Spain's European rivals had been probing the peripheries of Spanish dominions for over a decade and there continued to be talk of a northern water passage between the Atlantic and Pacific Oceans. With little sense of the true geography of North America, Spaniards believed the occupation of New Mexico would keep their rivals at bay and bring untold new souls to God.

In 1595, twelve years after Philip II's initial authorization for the "pacification" of New Mexico, the viceroy settled on an acceptable *adelantado* (expedition leader) for the campaign. Juan de Oñate, the son of one of the discoverers of the Zacatecas silver mines, was rich, well connected, and had substantial administrative experience. Oñate's expedition, which finally set out in 1598, included about 130 Spanish soldier-settlers and their families, over 200 other soldiers, and hundreds of Indian servants. The religious goals of the entrada (colonization campaign) were represented by ten Franciscans. Herds and flocks accompanied the colonists, who hoped to establish a successful mining colony among the sedentary Pueblo Indians.

After a three-month crossing of the Chihuahuan desert, Oñate's caravan crossed the Rio Grande at the site of present-day Juárez-El Paso. Today's El

Courtesy of Jesús F. de la Teja

Now called "The Equestrian" and residing at the entrance to El Paso's international airport, this monumental bronze of Juan de Oñate sparked controversy with the area's native peoples. Hero to some, villain to others, Oñate brought a permanent Spanish presence to what is now far West Texas.

Pasoans claim that by virtue of the date of their arrival, on April 30, 1598, Texas can claim to be the site of the first Thanksgiving. According to one of the colonists, "there was a sermon, a great ecclesiastical and secular celebration, a great salute and rejoicing, and in the afternoon, a comedy."

As Oñate took control of the upper Rio Grande valley, he sent out expeditions to explore the region. In 1601 he repeated Coronado's trek across the Texas Panhandle in search of the mythical Kingdom of Quivira. As disappointed as Coronado had been before him, Oñate settled for establishing a modest colony among the Pueblos. A few hundred Spanish colonists lived among thousands of agricultural Indians who came under the tutelage of Franciscan missionaries. In the absence of precious metals, New Mexico became a land of sheep ranches and subsistence farms, hardly the prosperous and populous colony envisioned.

Despite the lack of development, Spanish New Mexico needed to be able to communicate with rest of New Spain; the only route by which this could occur lay along the Rio Grande and Paso del Norte. Spanish convoys headed to and from Santa Fe stopped there to rest and take on water, but for many years no one thought to establish a mission, presidio (garrison), or town at the crossing. Not until 1659 did Friar García de San Francisco gather a group of local Mansos Indians in Mission Nuestra Señora de Guadalupe de los Mansos. Within a short time a number of Spanish colonists established farms in the area and in 1665 the Franciscans started a second mission, San Francisco de los Sumas. During this time Paso del Norte was officially incorporated into the province of New Mexico with the appointment of an *alcalde mayor* (lieutenant governor) under the authority of the governor in Santa Fe hundreds of miles to the north.

The Pueblo Revolt and the Growth of Paso del Norte

Life at Paso del Norte was uneventful until the Pueblo Revolt of 1680 brought a mass of Spanish refugees to its doorstep. The rebellion resulted from Spanish abuses of the native population: missionaries suppressed local beliefs and humiliated traditional leaders; Spanish colonists exploited Indian labor; and, missionaries and secular officials fought over control of the province and of the Indians. In 1680, these abuses sparked the Pueblo Revolt. Although their numbers had declined significantly due to epidemic diseases and dropping fertility rates, the Pueblos still numbered in the tens of thousands in 1680, whereas the Spanish population included only about 3,000 men, women, and children. In a coordinated assault throughout the province, the Pueblos killed 21 missionaries and almost 400 settlers. The survivors fled to Paso del Norte, arriving with little more than the clothes on their backs.

When Governor Antonio de Otermín took stock of the refugees in October 1680, he found that fewer than 2,000 had made it out safely; among them were over 300 Piro and Tiwa Pueblos whose close association with the Spaniards put them at odds with other Pueblos. With no prospects of reoccupying the upper Rio Grande valley in the immediate future, Otermín set about establishing settlements for the Spanish and Indian populations. By 1684 a string of five communities lined the south bank of the river: Guadalupe, San Lorenzo, Senecú, Ysleta, and Socorro. Although the last three of these settlements were intended to serve the friendly Pueblo refugees, Spanish settlers soon moved in among the Indians. For the next 150 years these settlements, along with a small number of haciendas and smaller *ranchos* (the root of the English term ranch), flourished in New Mexico's southernmost district. The area became an important wine-producing and Indian trade center and the key way station on the Santa Fe-Chihuahua *Camino Real* (royal road).

With the Spaniards' expulsion from New Mexico, a group of Franciscan missionaries turned their attention to Indians who had been visited in the 1580s and who periodically came to trade at Spanish outposts. East of the Mansos and Sumas, in what is today western Texas, southeastern New Mexico, and northern Chihuahua, lived various indigenous groups known collectively as Jumanos by the Spaniards, descendants of the Jornada Mogollón culture of prehistoric times. Among these groups there were both sedentary agriculturalists, some of whom had been visited by Cabeza de Vaca, and nonsedentary buffalo hunters and traders. Over the course of the seventeenth century, various groups of Apaches had moved southward into the region and had begun engaging in cycles of warfare and trade with the Pueblos and other Indian groups in the interior. Also finding their way into this area were groups of Indians from Spanish frontier settlements fleeing harsh working conditions and loss of their traditional ranges. Thus, by the late seventeenth century there were thousands of Indians in the area with enough knowledge of Spaniards and enough interest in European trade goods and livestock to foster trade and missionary contacts.

In 1681 the Jumano chief Juan de Sabeata arrived in Paso del Norte asking for missionaries to visit his country. Sabeata spoke Spanish, claimed to have been baptized at the mining town of Parral, and had conducted many trade expeditions to the Hasinai country of eastern Texas, where he exchanged Spanish wares and horses for dressed hides and other native trade goods. In response, the governor, responding to the opportunity to gain additional Indian allies, sent his lieutenant, Juan Domínguez de Mendoza, and Friar Nicolás López to investigate the possibility of establishing a Spanish presence among the Jumanos in the vicinity of the Conchos–Rio Grande junction, an area that came to be called La Junta de los Ríos. Between December 1683 and June 1684, the Mendoza–López expedition ventured as far northeast as the Edwards Plateau, somewhere along the Colorado River. There the escort hunted for buffalo hides while López and his companions baptized a number of Plains Indians and made plans for establishing a permanent mission field.

When Mendoza and López returned to Paso del Norte they left behind two missions, La Navidad and Apóstol Santiago, near what is today Presidio, Texas. Fathers Juan de Zavaleta and Antonio de Acevedo, who were left in charge, were soon forced to withdraw to Parral, however, when the Julime and other tribes in the area joined a general insurrection against the Spaniards. Word of the successful rebellion of the Pueblos had spread among other tribes under Spanish

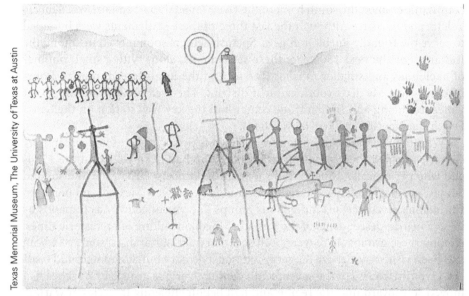

The expansion of Spanish colonization in the direction of the Rio Grande in far West Texas altered Indian life ways even in areas where the Spaniards never gained a foothold. At Meyers Springs, just east of the Big Bend, a rock shelter contains Indian artists' rendering of these contacts in the form of church towers with crosses.

control, and the whole northern frontier was aflame in an insurrection that has come to be called the Great Northern Revolt. Missions and haciendas burned, missionaries became martyrs, and herds were scattered, stolen, and slaughtered.

Despite various efforts to reestablish the La Junta missions in the years that followed, neither La Navidad nor Apóstol Santiago proved sustainable in the long run. The Spaniards turned their attention to recovering New Mexico, where their honor and their strategic interests had been wounded by the first major successful Indian revolt against Spanish rule in New Spain. As the Franciscans returned to their burned-out churches and their torn-down friaries and abandoned fields, they poured what resources they could muster into New Mexico. Little could be spared for the marginal stations at La Junta. Nevertheless, it was at these missions that Spanish authorities in Mexico first received word of the first successful intrusion by other Europeans into the colony's territory.

La Salle and the Spanish Rediscovery of Texas, 1684–1694

Fathers Joaquín Hinojosa and Agustín de Colina were working at La Junta late in 1687, reestablishing the missions abandoned three years earlier during the Great Northern Revolt, when Chief Juan Sabeata of the Jumanos arrived with disturbing news. He had returned from the annual Indian trade fair in Hasinai country with word that other Spaniards were actively trading with the Indians of the region. Asked to bring back proof, Sabeata returned from the next fair at the beginning of 1689 with pages torn from French books, a picture of a ship with French writing on the back, and the reassuring news that other Indians had attacked and destroyed the French settlement and all its occupants. In this way the Spaniards first learned of the fate of René Robert Cavelier, Sieur de La Salle's ill-fated colony on the Gulf Coast.

The French Threat, 1684–1689

From the time of his arrival in the vicinity of Montreal in 1666, La Salle, a French-born Canadian, took an interest in the fur trade and in creating a personal commercial empire in the interior of North America. During a search for new trade opportunities in 1682, he reached the mouth of the Mississippi River, claiming the entire basin, which he named Louisiana, for France. La Salle intended the name to flatter Louis XIV, before whom in late 1683 he laid out a plan to establish a fortified colony at the mouth of the river. From a warm water port there, the French could both control the fur trade of much of the continent and pursue the conquest of the silver mining districts of nearby New Spain.

Misfortune dogged the fleet. Breakdowns, a hurricane, pirates, and desertions left the expedition with considerably fewer than the 400 men, women, and children with which it had started. In January 1685 the ill-fated fleet sailed past the mouth of the Mississippi, finally making landfall at Matagorda Bay, where the expedition's supply ship soon foundered. When the naval commander decided to take the fleet's lone warship home, a significant number of colonists chose to abandon the venture. Finally, the following winter La Salle lost his remaining ship, *Belle*, which sank in Matagorda Bay during a storm.

La Salle soon established his settlement on Garcitas Creek, where a small compound, now referred to as Fort St. Louis, began to take shape. A number of the weaker members of the party died during the first months, and the "artisans" recruited for the colony turned out to be a rather useless lot overall. The company proved ill equipped to farm under the prevailing conditions, and the first crops were lost. In addition, the local Karankawas, whom La Salle had initially decided to treat as hostile, kept the settlement under siege.

Men abandoned the post, and some deserted La Salle during his explorations of the country. Henri Joutel remarked that two sailors had gone native: "They had . . . so perfectly inured themselves to the customs of the natives, that they became mere savages. They were naked, their faces and bodies with figures tattooed on them like the rest. They had taken several wives . . . and they had been forced to learn to shoot with bows and arrows." Another member of the expedition had done so well among a group of Coahuiltecans that by the time the Spanish found him he was the chief of a sizable village. With each desertion or death by snakebite, alligator mauling, or disease, the colony became weaker.

The last chapter of the La Salle colony began in January 1687. The settlement was down to about forty people, including some women and children, and under constant attack by the Karankawas. On January 12, La Salle and his strongest seventeen men again set out for the Mississippi to seek help. Arrogant and abusive toward his men, by March 19 members of the party had had enough and mutinied, killing La Salle, his brother, and two servants. As six survivors made their way to Canada, including Henri Joutel, who wrote the best existing account of the expedition and its tragic end, conditions at the post worsened as food ran out and disease felled the survivors. Likewise, the Karankawas had had enough of the French encroachment and during Christmas 1688 a large war party attacked the compound, making off with some children and killing the remaining colonists.

The Spanish Search for La Salle and the First Occupation of Texas, 1689–1694

Spaniards had no way of knowing that the Texas coast and its native peoples had taken care of their problem. With only a rough idea of which direction La Salle's ships had sailed, colonial authorities organized a number of maritime and land expeditions to search for the French. Ultimately successful in locating the site of the French colony was Alonso de León, governor of Coahuila and seasoned frontiersman. Born in Nuevo León in 1639, he had studied in Spain and served in the Spanish navy before returning to the frontier and becoming an accomplished Indian fighter. In 1689, accompanied by Friar Damián de Massanet, he undertook a fourth land expedition during which he came upon the ruins of the French post. The sight of human remains, of loose pages torn from books, of everyday household belongings scattered within the compound moved one of León's men to compose a poem commemorating the event. The first verse, as translated by La Salle historian Robert Weddle, reads in part:

> Sad and fateful site
> where prevails the dark of night
> because misfortune's whim
> brought thy people death so grim,
> . . .
> the cruel enemy pressed
> his heartless hand upon thy breast,
> upon thy innocence so mild,
> sparing not the smallest child.

Although the smallest child had not been spared, five children had survived the final Indian attack. Karankawa women protected four of the Talón family children and one other boy, all of whom were adopted into the tribe but later ransomed by the Spaniards.

In spring 1690, León and Massanet returned to Texas one last time to make sure the French were gone and to establish relations with area Indians. After carrying out the viceroy's orders to burn the French post and recovering some of the surviving French children from various Indian groups, León proceeded to the land of the Tejas, where, assured of the Hasinais's continued interest in conversion, he placed Massanet in charge of Mission San Francisco de los Tejas. He also invested the headman of the neighboring village with the symbol of Spanish authority—a staff with a cross. This ritual, in León's perspective, initiated Caddo vassalage to the Spanish Crown. What the Hasinai leader thought of León's instructions that he and his people should respect the missionaries, learn the Catholic faith, and become Christians we will never know. According to León, the headman willingly accepted the staff and promised to do as asked.

The Hasinai caddí most certainly did not see this and other early exchanges the way the Spaniard did. Caddos had long been in indirect communications with Spaniards from New Mexico and northern New Spain through their Jumano trading partners. The horses and trade goods that they acquired through middlemen might now be available directly from the new arrivals, who seemed to be offering gifts and a willingness to remain among the Caddos to make relations permanent. Hasinai leaders were probably very wary of the Spaniards because there were no women and children among León's company (for the Caddos and neighboring peoples all-male groups tended to indicate hostile intentions, while mixed groups signaled peaceful intent) but the presence of images of the Virgin Mary seems to have served as an adequate substitute. The willingness of Spaniards and Frenchmen to participate in a variety of Caddo rituals that helped establish trust and alliance, also acted in the Europeans' favor at the beginning. What Spaniards took as Indian deference was, from the Hasinai perspective, merely the establishment of diplomatic and commercial ties with new partners. Nevertheless, the absence of women among Spaniards and the celibacy of the missionaries did not sit well with the Hasinai and would shortly prove disastrous to Spanish interests.

Thus, Spaniards thought they had incorporated the Kingdom of the Tejas, the portion of modern Texas that extends from the Trinity River eastward into present-day western Louisiana, as a Spanish province with the appointment of Domingo Terán de los Ríos as its governor in January 1691. The Terán de los Ríos-Massanet expedition, which lasted from May 1691 to April 1692, proved that Spain was not ready to occupy Texas. Throughout the entrada, which was meant to secure a permanent Spanish presence and remove any lingering Frenchmen in the area, the governor and missionaries quarreled. The winter of 1691–92, which caught Terán de los Ríos in what is now the Red River country of Texas, Louisiana, and Arkansas, proved harsh and sapped what was left of the expedition's morale. In the end Terán de los Ríos had nothing to show for his year-long wanderings through East Texas and the expedition withdrew in failure.

These first Spanish efforts to occupy Texas did not go well. Mission Santísimo Nombre de María, which had been founded a few months after the establishment of Mission San Francisco de los Tejas, was swept away in a flood. When the missionaries at San Francisco ran out of gifts and it became obvious that the

Spaniards had little interest in establishing reciprocal trade relations on their terms, the Tejas saw little incentive in supporting, or even accepting, a Spanish presence among them. Not only had the Spaniards failed economically, becoming dependent on the Tejas for food, they had also failed morally. Ironically, both the absence of women among the friars and the licentious behavior among the handful of soldiers toward Indian women created hostility among area Hasinais. Even the religious ministrations of the friars contributed to the tension, as the Tejas began associating the waters of baptism with death. Finally, in October 1693, Chief Bernardino, now sporting a French suit of clothes, warned the Spaniards to leave. By the end of the month Friars Massanet and Francisco Hidalgo and a handful of soldiers were on their way to Coahuila. Ironically, waiting for them in Monclova, the capital of Coahuila, when they arrived in February 1694 was an order from the viceroy to abandon the province of Texas.

 ## The French Challenge, 1714–1722

Overextended and underpopulated, by the end of the seventeenth century, the Spanish Empire was a feeble power—just like its king, the sickly and often irrational Charles II. Hoping to forestall French penetration of the Gulf, in 1698 Spaniards established a fort at Pensacola, but the garrison there could do little but watch as French Louisiana came into being, first at Biloxi, then at Mobile and along the lower Mississippi River. Further complicating the situation was the death of the childless Charles II. When Philip of Anjou, grandson of Louis XIV, ascended the Spanish throne in 1700, the War of the Spanish Succession (known as Queen Anne's War in English North America) followed. France and Spain were allied against the English, Austrians, Dutch, and various German states. By the end of the war in 1714, Frenchmen occupied a series of Indian trading posts and a handful of strategic ports. Despite their erstwhile alliance with France in Europe, the Spaniards regarded France as their most serious rival in North America.

A French Trader Helps Spain Settle Texas

The new French threat did not take long to materialize. Governor Antoine de la Mothe, Sieur de Cadillac, charged with making Louisiana profitable, ordered traders westward to establish commercial relations with the Caddo confederacies. He entrusted a most sensitive assignment to one of the oldest and most experienced residents of Louisiana, Louis Juchereau de St. Denis, whose mission was to establish contact with frontier Spaniards as a prelude to opening direct trade with the silver mining region of Nueva Vizcaya. A vigorous, Canadian-born Indian trader and royal official, the thirty-seven-year-old commander at Biloxy already had a dozen years of experience among the lower Mississippi tribes.

In September 1713, St. Denis ventured up the Mississippi to the mouth of the Red River, then westward to the site of a Caddo village, where he established the trading post of Natchitoches. In the course of the next few months, St. Denis slowly made his way southwestward in search of a Spanish outpost. With him were Pierre and Robert Talón, who as children had survived the La Salle expedition. Finally, in July 1714 he crossed the Rio Grande near present-day Guerrero, Coahuila (about thirty-five miles southeast of Piedras Negras-Eagle Pass), and approached Presidio San Juan Bautista del Río Grande. On arrival, St. Denis told the commander of the small post, Diego Ramón, that Governor Cadillac had sent him on a mission to find the Franciscan missionary who had written the French governor of Louisiana two years previously requesting assistance in the conversion of the Hasinais.

With the arrival of St. Denis at the Rio Grande outpost, Friar Francisco Hidalgo must have believed his prayers were answered. It was he who had written to the French in Louisiana for support in Christianizing the Caddos. The friar knew that the appearance of a Frenchman on the Coahuila frontier would require a Spanish response in Texas. St. Denis's testimony at the viceroy's court proved conclusively that the French had designs, not only on Texas but on the interior mining provinces. The viceroy issued orders for the reoccupation of Texas on terms favorable to the Franciscans but unwittingly to the French as well: four missions to be protected by a garrison of twenty-five men, to be established as close as possible to the westernmost French post. While Hidalgo and his fellow Spaniards would return to the country of the Tejas, Governor Cadillac would have his point of contact with New Spain, and St. Denis would have an expanded market for the goods and services his Natchitoches post could supply.

In command of this important expedition to establish a Spanish presence in Texas was Captain Domingo Ramón (son of presidio commander Diego), an experienced frontiersman. Setting out from Saltillo in February 1716, he continued to collect materiel and people along the way. By the time the caravan arrived in the land of the Tejas in June, it consisted of twenty-six men, seven of them with their families, twelve missionaries, and a number of civilians. In accepting that Massanet's model of a purely religious occupation could not produce the desired results, Spanish officials also came to terms with the Caddos' expectation that peace missions include women and children.

Ramón's expedition also included missionaries representing both the Querétaro and Zacatecas colleges, including the now aged Hidalgo, who in his thirty years of service had helped establish numerous missions in northern New Spain and was now given the honor of serving as the first resident priest at Nuestro Padre San Francisco de los Tejas, the first mission established by the Ramón entrada. Querétaro friars established two other missions between the Angelina and the Neches, while Zacatecas missionaries established Mission Nuestra Señora de Guadalupe at the principal Nacogdoche settlement, future site of the town of Nacogdoches. Clustered between the Neches and Angelina rivers, the four missions came under the protection of Presidio Nuestra Señora de los Dolores.

Officially the leader of the Zacatecas friars was Friar Antonio Margil de Jesús, the most renowned Franciscan in early eighteenth-century New Spain and cofounder of the Queretaro and Zacatecas colleges, who had been too ill to make the initial entrada with Ramón. Early in 1717 he directed the founding of two new missions to the east, closer to the French post of Natchitoches, including Nuestra Señora de los Dolores at an Ais Indian village outside today's San Augustine and San Miguel de los Adaes near present-day Robeline, Louisiana. The considerable distance between these two missions and the presidio-mission complex on the Neches could only mean that Margil had accepted St. Denis's assurance of protection and assistance. It was a decision he and his fellow friars would later regret.

Although they had made a good start, Ramón and the missionaries were uncomfortable with the precariousness of their outpost. The Hasinais, happy to receive the gifts brought by the Spaniards to establish friendly relations, proved indifferent to the friars' preaching once all the goods had been distributed. Growing trade with the French helped keep the Hasinais in the driver's seat in what the Spaniards liked to think of as their new province. The two-dozen-man garrison was certainly not big enough to provide protection to the new settlement, carry out construction and escort duties, and keep an eye on the French. Also, the immense distance between the Neches presidio-mission complex and the Rio Grande settlement, more than 400 miles, made it exceptionally hard to communicate with the interior and obtain supplies. Perhaps more importantly, the Crown's resources were by the early eighteenth century stretched too far to provide adequately for settlement based on government funding. The presidio-mission settlement model, which had worked to help secure for the Crown considerable portions of the frontier hundreds of miles to the south for over a century, had reached its limits.

Spanish Occupation Expanded

The missionaries' letters and memorials and reports by the Ramóns reached Mexico City about the same time as new warnings that St. Denis and the French in Louisiana were intent on the commercial penetration of northern New Spain. The viceroy was determined not to duplicate the bungled 1690–93 experience. When his war council recommended occupying strategic locations on the coast and on the San Antonio River, he moved quickly. The viceroy named Martín de Alarcón governor of Coahuila and Texas and ordered him to establish a presidio-mission complex on the upper San Antonio River and resupply the East Texas establishments.

Alarcón proved to be the wrong man for the job, however. His recruitment efforts were half-hearted; he had barely enough men to carry out the first part of his mission—establishing a settlement on the San Antonio River. Friar Antonio de San Buenaventura y Olivares, who was responsible for founding a mission at the site of the new outpost on the San Antonio, was so upset with the governor, especially over the quality of the recruits, that he refused to travel in his company. Trailing along with all the property and a few Indian servants from the now-closed Mission San Francisco Solano, the friar met Alarcón at the San Antonio River on May 1, 1718. There Olivares immediately took possession of land and water in the name of the local Indians for the founding of Mission San Antonio de Valero, today's Alamo. Four days later Alarcón founded a settlement that he called the Villa de Béxar, in honor of the viceroy's brother and military hero, the Duke of Béjar, which would soon be known as Presidio de San Antonio de Béxar. Presidio de Béxar and Mission Valero would thus become the core of modern San Antonio.

Although he visited all of the East Texas missions later in the fall, Alarcón failed to reinforce Presidio de los Tejas. He also failed to establish a Spanish presence on the coast. He antagonized the missionaries and other Spanish residents, further alienated the Hasinais, and provoked the nearby French by confiscating their trade goods. Well past his prime, the navy and army veteran was ill prepared to deal with the challenges of a province that existed more on paper than in reality. The viceroy sought a more vigorous man to take charge of the situation when war broke out between Spain and France in 1719.

In the aftermath of the War of the Spanish Succession, Spain had been an unwilling party to the Treaty of Utrecht, which parceled out various Hapsburg possessions, including the islands of Sardinia and Sicily. When Spain attempted to retake these former possessions, France joined in a general European war against Spain. Word of this conflict reached Spanish Texas in a curious way. One morning in June 1719 a small troop of French soldiers from Natchitoches surprised the missionary and guard at Mission San Miguel, and took prisoner all the occupants of the mission henhouse. While Lieutenant Philippe Blondel and his men returned to their post with their feathered captives, Captain Ramón ordered the abandonment of East Texas. The episode, known in Texas history as the "Chicken War," set off a chain of events that expanded and solidified Spain's presence in Texas.

Spanish Texas Reinforced

By the time word of the French action reached Mexico City, officials were already preparing to secure their border with Louisiana. A royal decree arrived in May ordering construction of fortifications at Matagorda Bay, the strengthening of missionary activity at San Antonio, and military protection for all missions. Fortunately for the viceroy, the selection of a leader for this expedition proved simple. The Marqués de San Miguel de Aguayo had had his eye on Texas for some time; the prospect of serving the king by going to the Texas missionaries' rescue might further his ambitions to expand his wealth and property.

While he prepared his campaign, Aguayo authorized Margil to establish a mission for the Zacatecas College at San Antonio. Dedicated on February 23, 1720, Mission San José y San Miguel de Aguayo was destined to become the "Queen of the Missions." Even before setting foot in Texas, the Marqués de Aguayo had already carried out one part of his instructions—to strengthen the missionary effort at San Antonio.

Whereas previous expeditions to Texas had been makeshift, underprepared, and largely unsuccessful, the Aguayo entrada proved an unqualified success. By the time it set out from Monclova in mid-November, it consisted of almost 600 men, about 4,000 horses, thousands of head of cattle, sheep, and goats, and hundreds of pack-mules. It was the largest and best equipped Spanish force so far to enter Texas. Sending one detachment to San Antonio to prevent a French occupation, Aguayo dispatched another to occupy Matagorda Bay at the site of La Salle's post. By the time Aguayo and St. Denis (who was in command of Natchitoches) met on August 1, 1721, hostilities between France and Spain had ended and conditions in East Texas had improved. Various Caddo headmen pledged their allegiance to the Spanish king, and St. Denis was pleased at the opportunity again to do business with the restored missions and the new presidio that Aguayo had ordered built near Mission San Miguel de los Adaes.

For the next few months Aguayo executed his plan for strengthening and reinforcing Texas. Where there had been two presidios before his arrival now there were four, including Presidio Los Adaes in East Texas, and Presidio La Bahía at the site of La Salle's failed colony. He also increased the military personnel in the province from approximately 50 to over 250 men. Aguayo reopened all of the East Texas missions that had been abandoned in 1719 and authorized the construction of new ones, including one at La Bahía called Nuestra Señora del Espíritu Santo de Zúñiga. More important, Aguayo seems to have done a good job at Indian relations and left the Spaniards in Texas at peace with all of the Indians except the Apaches, who inhabited the Edwards Plateau and seemed unwilling to enter into friendly relations.

Spanish Texas Takes Shape, 1721–1731

Friar Hidalgo did not return to the East Texas missions following Aguayo's restoration of Spanish settlements there in 1721. He remained in San Antonio, where he labored at Mission Valero. It was an exciting and dangerous time at the presidio-mission complex on the edge of the Edwards Plateau. The south-central Texas native peoples who entered the missions spoke a variety of Coahuiltecan dialects and were sometimes antagonistic toward each other. Their hunter-gatherer ways were so at odds with Spanish notions of civilized life that misunderstanding, resistance, and, sometimes, violence colored their relations with

Spanish colonials. A mission, Hidalgo well understood, was a risky undertaking, and failure could come from the most unexpected source.

Early Spanish–Indian Relations

Mission San Francisco Xavier de Nájera was a case in point. Chief Juan Rodríguez of the Sanas, one of several central Texas Indian groups collectively known as the Ranchería Grande, had quickly befriended the Spaniards and offered his services in return for a mission for his people. Early in 1722 he and fifty families of Sanas arrived in San Antonio eager to enter the mission. Their eagerness was in part due to depredations from Apaches, whose increasing raids against them made the Sanas all the more interested in an alliance with the Spaniards. When resources for a mission failed to materialize after more than a year, Chief Rodríguez and about a dozen warriors and their families, fearing annihilation at the hands of the Apaches if they stayed at the unprotected Nájera site, befriended the Xarames at Mission Valero and took up residence there. As for the Sanas who decided to return to the Ranchería Grande, they made their sentiments clear: "The Spaniards want us to work for them; we want to be their friends and to fight no more; but to live near them, or be placed in a mission, we do not want even to speak of it."

The Sanas' concern with Apache attacks was well founded. Lipan Apache raids made life dangerous in San Antonio, both at the presidio and at the missions. Retaliatory campaigns by Spaniards, some of which were little more than thinly disguised slave raids, only increased the level of enmity. Soon the friars of the Querétaro College came to see the Apaches not as aggressors, but as the victims of corrupt military commanders and their debauched troops. A chronic state of warfare between Apaches and Spaniards ensued for the next twenty years, as the San Antonio presidio-mission complex made an inviting target for these plains hunters who were slowly migrating to the south in the early eighteenth century.

As another southward moving hunter-gatherer people, the Comanches, cut off their access to the Pueblos and Spanish New Mexico, the Apaches raided Spanish-Texas horse herds to replace mounts lost to their enemies. The Apaches attacked supply convoys for manufactured items they did not have access to. Human beings also became the object of raiding, as both Apaches and Spaniards took women and children as hostages and slaves. The Apaches perceived that the Spaniards of Texas had allied themselves with their enemies: the Hasinais, Ranchería Grande, and other eastern Indians. The assimilation of other Indian groups and Spanish captives would give rise to a distinctive Lipan Apache identity. And, the Lipans' presence in the Edwards Plateau west of San Antonio would influence Indian–Spanish relations throughout the eighteenth century.

Conflict was not confined to the Apaches, however, as the Karankawa tribes along the Texas coast also proved to be antagonistic to a Spanish presence at

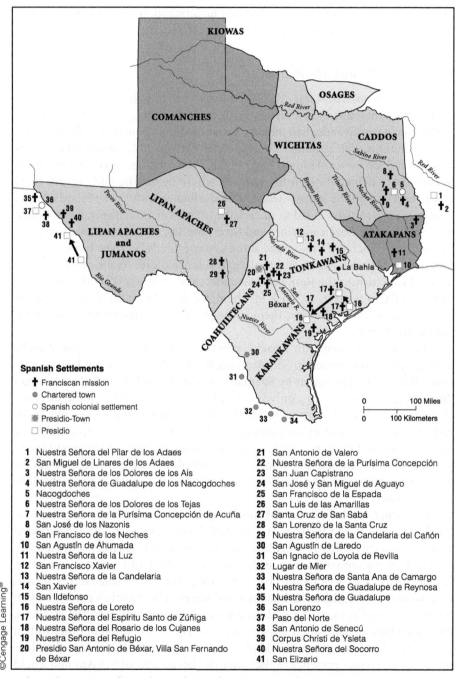

Spanish Settlements

✝ Franciscan mission
● Chartered town
○ Spanish colonial settlement
◉ Presidio-Town
☐ Presidio

1 Nuestra Señora del Pilar de los Adaes	**21** San Antonio de Valero
2 San Miguel de Linares de los Adaes	**22** Nuestra Señora de la Purísima Concepción
3 Nuestra Señora de los Dolores de los Ais	**23** San Juan Capistrano
4 Nuestra Señora de Guadalupe de los Nacogdoches	**24** San José y San Miguel de Aguayo
5 Nacogdoches	**25** San Francisco de la Espada
6 Nuestra Señora de los Dolores de los Tejas	**26** San Luis de las Amarillas
7 Nuestra Señora de la Purísima Concepción de Acuña	**27** Santa Cruz de San Sabá
8 San José de los Nazonis	**28** San Lorenzo de la Santa Cruz
9 San Francisco de los Neches	**29** Nuestra Señora de la Candelaria del Cañón
10 San Agustín de Ahumada	**30** San Agustín de Laredo
11 Nuestra Señora de la Luz	**31** San Ignacio de Loyola de Revilla
12 San Francisco Xavier	**32** Lugar de Mier
13 Nuestra Señora de la Candelaria	**33** Nuestra Señora de Santa Ana de Camargo
14 San Xavier	**34** Nuestra Señora de Guadalupe de Reynosa
15 San Ildefonso	**35** Nuestra Señora de Guadalupe
16 Nuestra Señora de Loreto	**36** San Lorenzo
17 Nuestra Señora del Espíritu Santo de Zúñiga	**37** Paso del Norte
18 Nuestra Señora del Rosario de los Cujanes	**38** San Antonio de Senecú
19 Nuestra Señora del Refugio	**39** Corpus Christi de Ysleta
20 Presidio San Antonio de Béxar, Villa San Fernando de Béxar	**40** Nuestra Señora del Socorro
	41 San Elizario

©Cengage Learning®

Eighteenth-century Indian tribes and Spanish settlements.

Matagorda Bay. Shortly after its founding, Mission Espíritu Santo attracted members of various Karankawa bands, but relations between the military and the Indians in the missions soon deteriorated. By 1726 the new commander at Presidio La Bahía had arranged for the presidio-mission complex to relocate at what is today called Mission Valley in Victoria County. The new location was more healthful (higher ground, better water supply) and secure, and the missionaries were able to attract bands of Aranamas and Tamiques, Coahuiltecan-speaking residents of the coastal prairies. Unfortunately, even at its new location, the community was an extremely isolated and was unable to attract civilian settlement. For the next twenty years Presidio La Bahía, understaffed and undersupplied, struggled to survive, until one final move in 1749 brought it to the present location of Goliad. In the meantime, the area's independent Indians dictated the terms of their relationship with the presidio-mission complex there, visiting the Spanish establishment only when it suited them.

Perhaps the greatest disappointment to friars and colonial officials alike was the lack of progress they had made with the Hasinai villagers in eastern Texas. As in the 1690s and just before the Chicken War, the Hasinais and other Caddo groups had no real interest in the Christian conversion program. In addition, the Tejas blamed the Spaniards for the epidemics and crop failures they experienced. Within a few years of their reestablishment, the missions were almost completely devoid of Indians, who only tolerated an occasional visit from the friars. Consequently, neither the missionaries nor the East Texas presidios could feed their residents, and they were forced to rely increasingly on the Tejas, French Natchitoches, or far-off San Antonio. These conditions did not bode well for a Spanish long-term presence. An infusion of new blood was needed.

A New Plan to Colonize Texas

From the perspective of Mexico City, the northern frontier, Texas in particular, seemed to be little more than a money pit, where missionaries, governors, presidio commanders, and colonists exchanged charges of corruption, incompetence, and cruelty toward the natives. The viceroy, determined to get the situation under control, appointed Colonel Pedro de Rivera to carry out a thorough inspection of the frontier defense system with the goal of saving money and instilling discipline. When Rivera arrived in Texas in August 1727, what he found was shocking. In East Texas there were no Indians at the missions and, given the peaceful relations with both the Hasinais and the French, the presidios were overstaffed and undisciplined. At San Antonio and La Bahía the missionaries were more gainfully employed, but the presidio companies were similarly overstaffed as they appeared to have successfully handled the Apaches. Rivera's draconian reforms called for abandonment of Presidio de los Tejas, the closing of East Texas missions, reductions in the complements of the remaining three presidios, and the recruitment of civilian colonists.

The viceroy was extremely pleased with Rivera's efforts. Instead of four presidios and 269 men, Texas was left with only three garrisons with a total of 144 billets. The Franciscans were displeased, however, not only because the Querétaro missionaries were forced to abandon East Texas, but because they would get less assistance from the remaining smaller garrisons. Rivera had failed to consider the symbiotic relationship between presidios and missions. Presidios not only protected nearby missions, they also provided the overseers and instructors that helped train the neophytes, new Indian converts, and served as markets for the food crops and animals that the neophytes produced.

Because the development of Texas could not rest solely on a few soldiers and neophytes, Rivera agreed with Spanish officials who had recognized the need for civilian settlement. Between 1719 and 1727 various proposals were put forward to bring families from the Canary Islands and elsewhere to help occupy the Texas frontier. Finally, in 1729 the first ten families of a proposed 400 set out from the Canary Islands for Texas by way of Havana and Veracruz, then overland to Mexico City and onward to the frontier. The experiment proved so costly, time-consuming, and inefficient that the viceroy later refused to repeat it. The fifty-six Isleños (Canary Islanders) who arrived in San Antonio on March 9, 1731, were a fortunate lot, for the Crown had granted them certain privileges as *hidalgos* (members of the lower nobility) and *primeros pobladores* (first settlers of a new community).

Captain Juan Antonio Pérez de Almazán, commander of Presidio de Béxar and *justicia mayor* (district magistrate), was a busy man in 1731. It must have seemed as if all the world were descending on him as missionaries, Isleños, and military settlers lined up for a piece of the San Antonio River valley. Concerned for the survival of Old World farmers without frontier experience, the captain decided to grant the Isleños farmland and a town site between the presidio and Mission Valero that came to be known as San Antonio de Béxar, or simply Béxar. The decision, although expedient, brought about considerable conflict with the already established military settlers, who lost access to the farmland and irrigation ditch they had helped open to the new arrivals.

Four days before the Isleños arrived, Captain Almazán had begun dealing with the other group of land claimants that had descended on the fertile and well-watered valley, the Querétaro Franciscans from East Texas. The three East Texas missions that had been forced to close as a result of Rivera's inspection tour decided that the San Antonio River was both a safer and a more convenient location. Along with Mission Concepción, which occupied a site between missions Valero and San José, Captain Almazán assigned land and water to missions Capistrano and San Espada.

By the end of 1731 Béxar had evolved from a simple stopover on the trail to the Texas capital at Los Adaes to the province's most diverse settlement. The friars of the five missions that occupied rich farmland on alternating banks of the river were busy planning sophisticated irrigation systems, laying out village compounds, and attempting to transform the region's Coahuilte-can bands of hunter-gatherers into villagers. They relied on *mayordomos* (overseers), usually soldiers and former soldiers, to help train, discipline, and supervise the Indians. Missions Valero and San José, which had been in oper-ation for over a decade by then, both produced surpluses that the friars could sell to the presidios, the proceeds going toward the needs of the missions and the neophytes.

Spanish Texas's First Civilian Community

Similarly, the Isleños, who at first had been housed among the military settlers, were busy putting up their first homes, expanding the *acequia* (ir-rigation ditch) system and agricultural land they had inherited from the mili-tary settlers, and accustoming themselves to running a town government. The king's orders provided for the Canary Islanders to be a self-governing community, with a *regimiento* or *ayuntamiento* (town government) of six *regi-dores* (aldermen), two *alcaldes ordinarios* (municipal magistrates), an *alguacil mayor* (constable or sheriff), a *procurador* (municipal attorney), and *escribano* (public scribe).

The military settlers, a number of whom had retired or were about to retire and hoped for land, water, and house lots, were at first left out of this town-building activity. The presidio, although adjacent to the new town, rep-resented a separate jurisdiction, and its commander continued to exercise exclusive authority over soldiers, their dependents, and any settlers not con-sidered *vecinos* (citizens) of the town. Most Isleños made every possible effort to exclude military settlers, whom they referred to as *agregados* (additional or secondary settlers) and considered competitors, from access to water and agri-cultural land.

Time and numbers were not on the Isleños' side, however. On the one hand, construction projects, supply convoys, and retirements and recruitments at the presidio all brought people to San Antonio, reinforcing the non-Isleño popula-tion. On the other hand, no more Canary Islanders would come to reinforce the initial contingent. Isleño offspring soon began finding spouses among the military families. Lacking business ties and appropriate economic skills, some Isleños formed partnerships with military settlers. A few Isleños even aban-doned civilian life for the financial security of military service. In time, non-Isleños, particularly those allied with Islanders began to participate in town government.

Squabbling between Isleños and agregados was not San Antonio's most pressing problem; that honor went to the continued hostilities with the Lipan Apaches. It was a situation at least in part of the settlers' making, however, or so thought the missionaries. Friar Benito Fernández de Santa Anna complained after a major campaign in 1739 that "the expedition was profitable only to those who had horses and other goods, which they sold at excessively high prices . . . and had greater hopes of a considerable prize of horses, hides, and Indian men and women to serve them." Whether it was the Lipans who retaliated for unprovoked campaigns by the settlers, or the settlers who exacted a measure of retribution from the Apaches for their continual depredations, the result was that everyone was at risk: mission Indians tending herds and flocks, settlers among their crops, muleteers carrying supplies into and out of the province, and Lipan Apache band members in their camps.

Finally, following a major campaign in which the Spaniards pursued the Apaches deep onto the Edwards Plateau, the Lipans agreed to call a truce in 1745. The cease-fire lasted until August 1749, when, at a formal treaty ceremony held at San Antonio, Lipan chiefs, military officers, the missionaries, and town

The Institute of Texan Cultures.

San Antonio's Plaza de las Islas (Main Plaza) commemorates the city's early Canary Islands settlers. What is now the French gothic San Fernando Cathedral started out as the humble San Fernando church, the construction of which began under the direction of Canary Islanders in 1738.

officials literally buried the hatchet. Into a great hole dug in the presidio plaza the participants threw a live horse, arrows, a lance, and a ceremonial hatchet. As the hole was covered, they held hands and embraced.

The Expansion of Spain's Rio Grande Settlements, 1746–1767

The Apache peace at Béxar came just as colonial New Spain underwent its last and most successful colonization effort on the northeastern frontier. For years officials in Mexico City had been concerned about Spain's weak presence along the Gulf of Mexico coast, north of Tampico. The mountains of the Sierra Madre Oriental, the mosquito-infested coastal lowlands, and the semiarid expanses north of the Rio Grande had all contributed to discouraging Spanish interest in the area. As a result, the Seno Mexicano, as the area was commonly called, remained home to hunter-gatherer groups and became a haven for Indians fleeing Spanish domination, who turned around and launched highly destructive raids into Spanish areas. In view of growing tensions between England and Spain over colonial boundaries and trading privileges, English occupation of any portion of the Seno would be a strategic disaster for Spanish interests. The Seno Mexicano had to be settled.

The Spanish Push into South Texas

After considering a number of proposals in the 1730s and early 1740s, José Escandón y Elguera's plan for occupying the remote region emerged as the favorite. Escandón was a Spanish-born military officer who had made a name for himself as an honest and successful Indian fighter. After receiving his appointment as governor of the new province of Nuevo Santander in September 1746, he decided that only by determining the best trails, most fertile and well-watered locations, and the territories of existing Indian groups, could the project achieve quick success.

From the reconnaissance of the area, Escandón came up with a bold plan to gain for Spain complete control of the coastal region. Colonists would enter the Seno from neighboring provinces and occupy strategic locations as far north as the Nueces River. To facilitate contacts with Texas, Escandón ordered the relocation of La Bahía from its Mission Valley site to its present location on the San Antonio River. For his part, Escandón would establish a new town on the Nueces River near present-day Corpus Christi to serve as the northern limit of Nuevo Santander. Although that settlement never materialized, La Bahía flourished at its new location, which had timber and stone for construction, open prairies for farming and grazing, and plentiful water in the San Antonio River.

The missionaries shared the optimism of the military community. At Mission Espíritu Santo the Indian population quickly recovered from the move, and by 1758 the initial wooden church and friary had been replaced with stone-and-mortar structures. Renewed efforts among the Karankawas followed, as Friar Juan de Dios María Camberos gathered hundreds for a new mission. Not waiting for an official reply to his request for permission, he established Mission Nuestra Señora del Rosario nearby in 1754.

Throughout the 1750s and 1760s La Bahía made steady progress despite the advent of Apache and Comanche raiding in 1762. From just a handful of civilians in 1749, La Bahía's population increased to forty-six civilian households in 1767. Marriage among the presidio company added to the nonmilitary population, and by the 1760s the sons of former soldiers were themselves enlisting in the company. At the missions, although the numbers fluctuated, populations numbered in the hundreds, more than enough to perform all the essential functions at the mission compounds and at the outlying ranches. Few Karankawa families entered Mission Rosario, with most bands merely incorporating the La Bahía missions into their annual foraging cycle.

Increased economic activity centered on livestock. Thousands of head of cattle grazed the open ranges of the coast. Mission Espíritu Santo, although it could only count a few thousand branded head, claimed over 40,000 animals between the San Antonio and Guadalupe. The presidio commander's ranch, which occupied thousands of acres on the west bank of the San Antonio River, was so productive that it employed both civilians and enlisted men in its operation. Over time the community's growing prosperity encouraged the appearance of the first merchants and craftsmen.

The Lower Rio Grande Settled

Of importance to the history of Texas was not only the relocation of La Bahía, but Escandón's founding of a series of settlements along the Rio Grande. By the end of March 1749 he had authorized settlements along the south bank of the lower Rio Grande, including Camargo under the leadership of Blas María de la Garza Falcón, a member of a leading stock-raising family from Coahuila. As families continued to respond to Escandón's initial success, new settlements sprang up over the next few years. Finally, in 1755 yet another wealthy stockman, Tomás Sánchez, received Escandón's permission to found the town of Laredo on the north bank of the Rio Grande.

The Rio Grande towns, the villas del norte, were part of the twenty-three civilian settlements, fifteen missions, and two mining camps of Nuevo Santander that Escandón authorized in six years. By his reckoning he was responsible for the settlement of 1,337 civilian and 144 military families, for a total of 6,385 persons. In the fifteen missions there were 2,837 neophytes. The contrast of Nuevo Santander with Texas, where settlement had not successfully expanded beyond the three mission-presidio complexes left behind by the Marqués de Aguayo in 1722, and which contained a Spanish population of only 1,800, could not be starker.

The people of Nuevo Santander, like those of Texas and the rest of New Spain's northern region, were ethnically and socioeconomically mixed. Criollos made up about one-third of the population, castas about half, Christianized Indians approximately 15 percent, and peninsular Spaniards only 1 or 2 percent. Despite a folklore that touts the European and even noble ancestry of the region's Hispanic population, many of the people of Nuevo Santander, as one local official reported in 1757, were poor families that lived off the seasonal employment they could obtain from hacendados. Escandón was blunter, declaring that his recruiting success was a result of colonists fleeing the abuses of local officials and "the slavery in which they lived, having been made debtors to the hacendados." Without a doubt, however, the Nuevo Santander–South Texas frontier offered opportunities for those intrepid enough to face the risks.

Although Escandón had made exceptional progress in making Nuevo Santander secure and productive, there were problems. The missionaries complained that rather than carrying out their primary mission of converting the Indians, Escandón forced them to serve the civilian population, turning them into little more than parish priests. Worse, the *reducción* (gathering of non-sedentary Indians in missions) of the native peoples had become the means by which their labor was exploited by colonists. The friars accused the governor of "having not the slightest interest in the most important and proper matter of the pacification and settlement of the Indians." As a result, peaceful Indian groups had fallen into virtual slavery and aggressive ones had abandoned the missions and started preying on outlying ranches and settlements. Under these conditions, the missions quickly declined; by the 1790s the mission system in Nuevo Santander had completely collapsed. An Indian population in the territory estimated at approximately 25,000 in 1750 stood at less than 2,000 at the end of the century.

Missionaries were not Escandón's only critics. Many settlers, especially those of substantial means, complained that although they had repeatedly been assured of land titles, none had as yet been distributed. Although he could deflect or ignore the missionaries' complaints, the governor did have to account for the unsettled state of land ownership in the province. Escandón's explanation to the viceroy was that his extensive duties kept him from attending to the matter and that he had no qualified subordinate to see that the job was done properly. Moreover, because settlers continued to arrive, some of whom he considered of better quality than the original settlers, he wanted to wait longer and make sure the land went to those most capable of making the best use of it.

Determined not to allow such a promising start to descend into chaos, the viceroy appointed a royal commission to carry out a general inspection and distribution of lands to the settlers of Nuevo Santander in 1767. Conditions along the river created unique problems: abundant water in the Rio Grande, but a scarcity of fresh water away from it, especially on the north bank; an adequate amount of good bottomland available for agriculture, but high flood banks that limited irrigation on the south side and made it impossible on the north bank. What the local experts who worked with the royal commission came up with was a unique solution to the complicated issues. When it came time to distribute grazing land, the experts gave each family access to the Rio Grande. They laid out each tract of approximately 8,000–10,000 acres with a very narrow frontage on the river. These long, narrow lots, which received the name *porciones*, allowed stockmen to move their herds and flocks close to the river during the dry season and graze them away from the stream during rainy periods.

On their departure for Mexico City in fall 1767, the commission left behind a well-settled and quickly expanding ranching kingdom. The commission had issued land grants to over a thousand settlers, most for tracts intended for ranching purposes. Even the territory north of the Rio Grande, the most exposed to Indian attacks and the most arid, saw a steady advance in cattle operations that produced many ranchos measuring in the tens of thousands and some in the hundreds of thousands of acres. These ranchos became the progenitors of the famous Texas ranches of later generations.

The Desert Blooms at Paso del Norte

Hundreds of miles upstream from the developing ranching communities of the lower Rio Grande valley, a very different type of settlement activity had produced a thriving set of communities at Paso del Norte. Located at a crucial juncture of the road between New Mexico and Chihuahua, the residents of Paso del Norte prospered from providing services to travelers and goods to the region. A combination of climate, soil, and the waters of the Rio Grande made the area a desert oasis and ideal viticulture country. By mid-century Paso del Norte's wines, brandies, and raisins were in great demand throughout northern New Spain. Farming extended to the cultivation of wheat in well-irrigated fields that produced substantial surpluses for export to the mining camps to the south. In fact, the use of farmland for grapes and wheat meant that in some years residents did not harvest enough corn to meet local needs.

Economic success brought population growth. Despite increased raiding by Apaches, the population of the district grew from about 1,000 people at the turn of the century to almost 5,000 in 1765. The civil-military settlement located on the south bank of the river, El Paso del Río del Norte, was home to over 2,800 residents. The presidio company of 49 men and their families, 230 persons in all, made up less than 10 percent of the total. Indians and *genízaros* (New Mexico term for detribalized Indians incorporated into Spanish society) made up about 20 percent of the population. The remaining 70 percent consisted of criollos and castas, usually referred to as mestizos, but also including mulattoes. Some of the genízaro families had even managed to gain vecino status, that is, they were considered full citizens of the settlement, an indication that economic and social opportunities on the frontier conspired to downplay the social and racial labels that restricted social mobility elsewhere.

The three mission communities established for area Indians—Guadalupe, Senecú, and Socorro—also prospered, as did Ysleta, the settlement established for the Tigua Indians who fled New Mexico with the Spaniards at the time of the Pueblo Revolt of 1680. Although all three communities had substantial numbers of non-Indians living in them by the middle of the eighteenth century, each retained its distinctive Indian character. As in Nuevo Santander, the Franciscans who supervised these communities also served the area's settlers.

Successful as the Paso del Norte district was, it shared a major problem with Texas, Coahuila, and the other northern frontier provinces: Apache Indian raids. As in Texas, the most important factor contributing to the increase in hostilities was the pressure from the north being put on the eastern Apache tribes (those located east of the Rio Grande) by advancing Comanches. Sporadic depredations took their toll, mostly in lost horses and mules, which the Apaches used both for transportation and for food, but also in the occasional killing of field hands. Given the strategic and developing economic importance of the Paso del Norte district, however, area settlers adapted to the violence.

 ## Spanish Intrusions in Indian Texas

Unlike Nuevo Santander, where José de Escandón directed an essentially civilian colonization effort, or Paso del Norte, which occupied a significant economic niche, much of what is today Texas remained fundamentally a religious-military frontier. Efforts at expansion in Texas during the 1740s and 1750s were tied to the twin objectives of bringing more Indians into the fold of the Catholic church and preventing French penetration of Spanish territory.

Missionary Expansion into Central Texas

For Friar Mariano Francisco de los Dolores y Viana, of Mission San Antonio de Valero, the appearance at Béxar of a delegation from the Ranchería Grande tribes on June 2, 1745, was an answer to his prayers and years of patience and hard work. Representatives of the Ranchería Grande, a composite of Atakapan, Tonkawan, Ervipiame, and other local bands, requested that a mission be established in their territory—a large area of central Texas between the Colorado and Trinity rivers. They insisted that the friars come to them, as San Antonio was too far from allies and hunting grounds. The Ranchería Grande groups may also have wanted to attract Spaniards to them in order to help keep their enemies, the Lipan Apaches, at bay.

Not waiting for authorization from his superiors, Mariano and a small support group headed for the Ranchería Grande. He caught up with the Indians in January 1746 near the junction of the San Gabriel River and Brushy Creek (present-day Milam County). He soon had a mission, San Francisco Xavier de Horcasitas, in operation, describing the land as "much better than that found in San Antonio, and there is an abundance of buffalo, deer, turkeys, fish, persimmons, prickly pears, and other fruits used by the Indians." Although other reports were less optimistic, the viceroy consented to the project, detaching soldiers from Los Adaes and La Bahía for a garrison, and authorizing two other missions.

Despite the missionaries' enthusiasm, the San Xavier experiment was short-lived and tragic. As in other similar situations, mission life proved too alien for the Ranchería Grande's hunter-gatherer people. Disease, drought, shortages of supplies, and lack of discipline among the soldiers assigned to protect the missions drove the Indians away. The May 1752 murder of one of the missionaries and a man, whose wife the friars had accused the presidio's commander of having an affair with, did not inspire confidence among the Indians. By September 1753 the San Xavier presidio-mission complex had completely collapsed and missionaries and the new commander, Pedro de Rábago y Terán, began advocating for the relocation of the missions, which he did without authorization in summer 1756.

With the retreat of the Spaniards from the San Gabriel (its name is a mistranslation of the original Spanish, San Xavier), the Ranchería Grande alliance collapsed and disappears from the records. However, one of its component groups, the Tonkawa, not only survived but became the most prominent native group in the area. For the next thirty years the Tonkawas would alternate between fighting and trading with Lipan Apaches and Spaniards, but eventually settled into a wary peace with Spaniards and war with the Lipans.

Spaniards in Apachería

A number of friars had dreamed for many years of converting the Lipan Apaches. Periodically, individual Apache chiefs approached the missionaries claiming to want the benefits of Spanish civilization, and some had even brought their families or bands into the San Antonio missions; accordingly, the Franciscans blamed the Spanish colonists for ongoing hostilities. Mariano's insistence on the potential for peace with the Lipans if a mission were established for them in their own territory, commonly referred to as Apachería, led to expeditions into the hill country northwest of San Antonio.

In 1756 Friar Alonso Giraldo de Terreros's rich cousin agreed to underwrite the project. The viceroy gave Colonel Diego Ortiz Parrilla, a former frontier governor and soldier, military command of the expedition but gave Terreros independent authority to negotiate with the Indians. The colonel, cynical about the Apaches'

No greater gift could a man give God than to sacrifice himself in the cause of the Faith. So thought the Franciscans who achieved the "Crown of Martyrdom" at Mission San Sabá, when they became victims of an Apache–Norteño struggle for control of western Texas.

intentions, soon quarreled with the missionaries, complaining to the viceroy, "The state in which we have found the Apaches is so different from what I expected that I assure you the method of their pacification is a major concern to me."

Indeed, when in April 1757 the entrada arrived at the site of present-day Menard and pitched camp, the Lipans were nowhere in sight. Construction soon began on a mission and presidio, but each passing day gave another indication that the San Sabá complex was not to flourish. Three thousand Apaches appeared near the mission in June, but soon departed to hunt buffalo and raid their enemies, the Norteños.

The Norteños (northerners), or Nations of the North, represented a new force on the Texas scene. Essentially a Spanish term identifying the Indian nations north and east of San Antonio, specifically the Wichitas, but generally including Caddos, Bidais, Tonkawas, and Comanches, it also represented a broad Indian coalition based on intergroup economic and political interests that pitted them against the Lipan Apaches. While the Apaches had been the preeminent indigenous people of much of the Texas region west of the Hasinais at the beginning of the eighteenth century, by the 1740s they faced considerable pressure from new groups that had been making their way into Texas from the north. Wichita bands moving south of the Red River and Comanches moving southeastward challenged Lipan Apaches for hunting grounds and trading privileges with surrounding peoples. By mid-century Spaniards at San Antonio were aware of the changing intertribal dynamics, but their choice to focus on converting the Apaches unwittingly turned the Spaniards into allies of the one Indian nation at war with just about all others in Texas.

With the Apaches unwilling to settle down and no prospects for attracting other groups, some of the missionaries gave up on the project, leaving Mission San Sabá in the hands of Terreros and two colleagues from the San Fernando College. During the fall and winter of 1757–58 various Apache bands made rest stops at the mission, but all refused to stay. The end came in March 1758. At the beginning of the month a war party attacked the presidio's horse herd and made off with sixty-two mounts. On March 16, a large group of Norteño warriors, including Caddos, Tonkawas, Atakapans, Wichitas, and Comanches encircled the mission compound, many of them bearing French muskets and swords. After ransacking the buildings, the attackers killed friars Terreros and José Santiesteban along with a few of the assistants and soldiers. Unwilling to challenge the military directly, the Norteños approached but did not attack the presidio.

Unable to pursue the attackers, Colonel Parrilla sought revenge in a more deliberate way. Parrilla offered to lead a campaign not only to avenge the deaths of two friars and eight other Spanish subjects, but also to demonstrate to the Norteños that they could not act with impunity. At a January 1759 meeting Parrilla, the governors of Texas and Coahuila, and the region's presidio commanders decided that they would mount a 500-man expedition, including a contingent of Apache allies, against the Wichitas and Tonkawas that summer.

Although it achieved a minor victory against one Tonkawa camp near the Clear Fork of the Brazos, and the allied Apaches overwhelmed another camp, the expedition's encounter with the Wichitas was not so successful. The Wichita village at present-day Spanish Fort was not only fortified but was also flying a French flag. The Wichitas, armed with French muskets, were every bit a match for the ragtag force under Col. Parrilla. The Wichitas repulsed the Spanish assault and their Lipan Apache allies fled. The Spanish suffered only fifty-two casualties, and believing they had made their point withdrew. In the aftermath of the Norteño campaign, the presidio on the San Saba River hung on for another decade before being moved southward, first to support a last effort to settle the Lipan Apaches at the El Cañon missions at the headwaters canyon of the Nueces and eventually below the Rio Grande. However, the failure at what is now called Spanish Fort near Gainesville, Texas, spelled the end of Spain's hopes of expanding into the southern plains from Texas.

The Wichitas encountered by the Spaniards at San Saba and the fort on the Red River were Caddo-speaking agricultural people whom the early Spanish expeditions had encountered in Kansas and Oklahoma. They had been undergoing their own process of cultural reinvention over previous decades. Pressure from the Osages to their northeast and Comanches to the west, access to horses and eventually to firearms and European trade goods from the French, and the effects of disease had brought about a steady southward migration that included the abandonment of dispersed agricultural settlements for more concentrated villages, an increased dependence on bison hunting, and a greater involvement in southern plains trading. By the mid-eighteenth century they had formed an alliance with the Comanches, acting as their commercial intermediaries with the French, and a lasting enmity with the Lipan Apaches, who raided Wichita villages for horses and provisions on a regular basis. Of all of this, Spaniards were only very imperfectly aware. It would take another three decades for them to come to terms with Wichita control of North Texas.

The Effects of French Rivalry on Spanish–Indian Relations

The San Sabá episode therefore illustrated two major problems with Spain's frontier system in Texas: the inadequacy of the presidio-mission complex for expanding Spain's territory and the inability to prevent foreign access to Indians, who were more than capable of asserting their sovereignty over much of the territory claimed by Spain. At San Sabá, as at San Xavier earlier, Spaniards came into contact with Indians bearing French muskets, wearing French clothing, and boasting of their ties to Louisiana. Spanish policy against trading firearms to Indians, making conversion and subordination the paramount objectives in their dealings with indigenous peoples, a dysfunctional political economy that crippled commerce, and an underpaid and undermanned frontier military establishment all worked against Spanish interests. Spanish security along the Louisiana frontier proved so lax that by the early 1750s a small party of Frenchmen under the direction of Joseph Blancpain was able to establish a trading post on the lower Trinity River.

Discovery and arrest of the Frenchmen probably reflected the governor's effort to protect his own pocketbook (he was involved in contraband activities) rather than to defend imperial interests, but it did set off another abortive attempt to expand Spanish control in Texas. In 1756 Viceroy Marqués de las Amarillas authorized a presidio-mission complex for the lower Trinity River. By the end of the year a thirty-man post had been established, named Presidio San Agustín de Ahumada in honor of the viceroy. (Agustín de Ahumada y Villalón, Marqués de las Amarillas holds the distinction of being the only viceroy to have two presidios named for him.) A mission named Nuestra Señora de la Luz had also taken shape near present-day Anahuac in Chambers County.

El Orcoquizac, as the complex was commonly called, proved a disaster from the beginning. The Akokisa and Bidai Indians, for whom Mission Nuestra Señora de la Luz was built, showed as little interest in settling down permanently at this location as they had at the San Xavier missions a few years earlier. The thirty-man garrison at the presidio suffered great privation as flooding and the stifling heat and humidity made it difficult to keep the presidio store stocked and the crops growing well. About the only thing that made life bearable for the garrison was trading in contraband—the very thing they were there to prevent.

Contraband was, in fact, what East Texas was all about. Since foreign commerce was illegal except through the very rigid mercantilist policies of the

Spanish Crown, Natchitoches stood as a monument to Spain's lack of authority in Texas. The garrison and small civilian population in the vicinity of Los Adaes often lacked provisions and supplies to make ends meet, so French Natchitoches supplied the needs of Spanish East Texas. Likewise, the lack of trade goods and official Indian policy meant that even those Indians who had sworn allegiance to the Spanish Crown actually had more interactions with the French across the border. Indians brought horses captured during raids on Spaniards and rival nations in the interior to trade at Natchitoches, whose farms supplied Indians and Spaniards in Texas and beyond with tobacco and whose merchants supplied Indians with firearms and Spaniards with an assortment of manufactures. Fortunately for Spanish policymakers, a solution to the problem of French interference with Spain's Texas Indians was in the making on the battlefields of Canada and Europe.

Conclusion

By the early 1760s there was a marked contrast between Texas and the neighboring provinces of Nuevo Santander and Coahuila. José de Escandón had fired the imaginations of thousands of Spanish frontiersmen with his offers of generous land grants and effective measures against the Indians of the region. Towns, ranches, and mining camps soon dotted the Nuevo Santander countryside from the area just north of Tampico to the Rio Grande valley. Even the least settled part of the new province, the semiarid prairies of what is now South Texas, began to see the expansion of a ranching culture that played a significant role in New Spain's economy. Similarly, in Coahuila, although the progress was slower, the subjugation of the province's Indians led to the founding of new towns and great haciendas. The Apaches remained a constant menace, but the province showed signs of flourishing, especially in the realm of livestock production.

In Texas, however, Spanish civilization was stalemated by Indian cultures capable of successfully fending off both its military might and its religious blandishments. Spaniards were just one among various newcomers—Comanches, Wichitas, Frenchmen, Tonkawas—who altered the economic, political, and cultural patterns of the region as they had existed before 1680. As Wichitas and Comanches asserted themselves as Texas peoples and Frenchmen established themselves as the representatives of European commerce, Spaniards continued to hold on to the idea that they were sovereign. With insufficient resources to enforce that sovereignty, officials played a shell game with the few soldiers and missionaries at their disposal. The successive failures at San Xavier, San Sabá, and El Orcoquisac largely discredited the presidio-mission system of frontier expansion. (California, founded in 1769, seems to have been the exception that proved the rule.) San Antonio, La Bahía, and Los Adaes survived, as did a few missions, but they exercised control over a very limited hinterland. If the Spanish Crown really wanted to fully incorporate Texas into the empire, it would have to try something different.

Suggested Readings

Along with the appropriate chapters in David Weber's *The Spanish Frontier in North America* and John Kessell's *Spain in the Southwest,* those interested in the social history of northern Mexico and the American Southwest at that time can turn to the very readable, though somewhat dated, *Los Paisanos: Spanish Settlers on the Northern Frontier of New Spain* by Oakah L. Jones, Jr. (1979, 1996). Understanding the Spanish frontier military system is vital to an appreciation of colonial Texas history, and the work that does the best job of explaining that system is Max L. Moorhead's *The Presidio: Bastion of the Spanish Borderlands* (1975). The most controversial of Spanish frontier institutions is the mission. Missions were traditionally viewed as the great civilizing force through which the Spanish brought both salvation and enlightenment to the native peoples; see, for example, the introductory chapter in Marion A. Habig, *The Alamo Chain of Missions: A History of San Antonio's Five Old Missions* (1968). A newer generation of scholars has come to focus on the negative effects of the missionary project on the target populations; see, for example, David Sweet, "The Ibero-American Frontier Mission in Native American History," in Erick Langer and Robert H. Jackson, eds., *The New Latin American Mission History* (1995).

The Paso del Norte Corridor, 1598–1554

The various early expeditions and Juan de Oñate's conquest of New Mexico in 1598 are covered in *El Paso: A Borderlands History* by W. H. Timmons (1990), which also traces the seventeenth-century history of the area. Marc Simmons's *The Last Conquistador: Juan de Oñate and the Settling of the Far Southwest* (1991), also discusses Spanish activity in the El Paso area up to 1598. The poetically inclined might wish to look up the Oñate story in epic poem form, *Historia de la Nueva México, 1610,* by Gaspar Pérez de Villagrá (1992), originally published in 1610. A very readable account of the Pueblo Revolt and the Spanish flight to the El Paso area in 1680 is Andrew L. Knaut, *The Pueblo Revolt of 1680: Conquest and Resistance in Seventeenth-Century New Mexico* (1995). Representative of a recent trend to tell the revolt story from the Pueblo perspective is Matthew Liebmann's *Revolt: An Archaeological History of Pueblo Resistance and Revitalization in 17th Century New Mexico* (2012).

La Salle and the Spanish Rediscovery of Texas, 1684–1694

No one has produced more work on La Salle's expedition and its consequences than Robert S. Weddle. His most recent work, *The Wreck of the Belle, the Ruin of La Salle* (2001), is an exhaustive study of the explorer from his early Canadian ventures to his death in East Texas. A four-decade older, but still the best narrative of the Spaniards' efforts to find the French colony is Weddle's *Wilderness Manhunt: The Spanish Search for La Salle* (1973). Another writer who has made significant contributions to our understanding of this period is William Foster. His edition and annotation of Juan Bautista Chapa's *Texas and Northeastern*

Mexico, 1630–1690 (1997), ties the history of Texas to that of Nuevo León and Coahuila. Also of value are Chapters 2 through 5 of his *Spanish Expeditions into Texas, 1689–1768* (1995), in which he tries to pin down the routes of the various entradas of the late seventeenth century.

The French Challenge, 1714–1722

When Louis Juchereau de St. Denis arrived at San Juan Bautista del Río Grande in 1714, the first Spanish missions of Texas had already been abandoned for twenty years. Texas remained a mostly unknown land, despite a few entradas north of the Rio Grande by missionaries and military men. In Chapters 6–9 of *Spanish Expeditions into Texas*, William Foster discusses the expeditions that brought the Spanish back to Texas permanently. Louis Juchereau de St. Denis not only instigated the permanent occupation of Texas by Spaniards, but founded Natchitoches, the story of which is told by H. Sophie Burton and F. Todd Smith in *Colonial Natchitoches: A Creole Community on the Louisiana-Texas Frontier* (2008). Ross Phares, *Cavalier in the Wilderness: The Story of the Explorer and Trader Louis Juchereau de St. Denis* (1952) is a full-scale biography of St. Denis. Essays on "Francisco Hidalgo/Louis Juchereau de St. Denis," "Antonio Margil de Jesús," and "Marques de San Miguel de Aguayo/Pedro de Rivera y Villalón" in *Notable Men and Women of Spanish Texas* by Donald Chipman and Harriett Denise Joseph (1999) provide a good understanding of the backgrounds of the military and religious leaders of early Texas.

Spanish Texas Takes Shape, 1721–1731

Rivera's record of his inspection of Texas in 1727 provides a good description of the province ten years after its founding. His diary and report, along with an assessment, are included in *Imaginary Kingdom: Texas as Seen by the Rivera and Rubí Military Expeditions, 1727 and 1767*, ed. Jack Jackson, annot. William C. Foster (1995). Updating our understanding of Spanish–French rivalry in Texas is David La Vere, "Between Kinship and Capitalism: French and Spanish Rivalry in the Colonial Louisiana–Texas Indian Trade," *Journal of Southern History* (1998). Historical work on colonial Texas has overwhelmingly centered on San Antonio, the province's largest and most diverse community. The story of its founding and early development appears in *Tejano Origins in Eighteenth-Century San Antonio*, ed. Gerald E. Poyo and Gilberto M. Hinojosa (1991) and Jesús F. de la Teja, *San Antonio de Béxar: A Community on New Spain's Northern Frontier* (1995).

The Expansion of Spain's Rio Grande Settlements, 1746–1767

What is now South Texas, from Corpus Christi to Laredo to Brownsville and South Padre, was the northern half of Nuevo Santander during the colonial period. Most of the historical work on this region has been done by Mexican scholars, and remains untranslated although there is a handful of very useful recent works on the subject in English. The colonization and early development of this vast region that became the home to huge ranching estates is told by Armando Alonzo in the early chapters of *Tejano Legacy: Rancheros and Settlers in South Texas, 1734–1900* (1998) and in "José de Escandón y Elguera," Chapter 7 in *Notable Men and Women of Spanish Texas*. A useful synthesis of what is known of the aboriginal peoples of that area is found in *Indians of the Rio Grande Delta: Their Role in the History of Southern Texas and Northeastern Mexico*, by Martín Salinas (1990). The story of La Bahía has yet to receive comprehensive scholarly treatment, but two works, along with the article "La Bahía" in *The New Handbook of Texas*, provide basic information: Kathryn Stoner O'Connor, *Presidio La Bahia, 1721–1846* (1966), and Craig H. Roell, *Remember Goliad! A History of La Bahía* (1994). For developments at Paso del Norte, W. H. Timmons offers a good overview in Chapter 2 of *El Paso: A Borderlands History* (1990).

Spanish Intrusions in Indian Texas

The collapse of Spanish expansion efforts in Texas centers on two pivotal events: the disintegration of the San Xavier mission-presidio complex and the successful Norteño and Comanche resistance to a Spanish punitive expedition following their destruction of Mission San Sabá. Herbert E. Bolton's *Texas in the Middle Eighteenth Century: Studies in Spanish Colonial History and Administration* (1915, 1970) remains the best survey of Spanish activities in the region, except the San Sabá story. That tale, and the follow-up Spanish effort to punish the Indians responsible, is told by Robert S. Weddle in *The San Sabá Mission: Spanish Pivot in Texas* (1964, 1988). The Norteño–Comanche destruction of the San Sabá mission, which the Spanish built for the Lipan Apaches, is also notable for having produced the first artwork with a Texas theme, a large allegorical painting executed in Mexico City in the early 1760s. The painting itself has an interesting story, nicely summarized by Sam D. Ratcliffe in "'Escenas de Martirio': Notes on The Destruction of Mission San Sabá," *Southwestern Historical Quarterly* (1991). For the East Texas–Louisiana connection during this time, see H. Sophie Burton, and F. Todd Smith, *Colonial Natchitoches: A Creole Community on the Louisiana–Texas Frontier* (2008).

New Opportunities, New Rivalries, 1767–1800

In October 1770, Athanase de Mézières, the French-born lieutenant governor for the Natchitoches district of Louisiana, acquired by Spain in 1762, traveled to the Kadohadacho village of San Luis on the Red River to meet with various groups of Caddo and Wichita-related Indians. He brought word to the skeptical chiefs and elders of the new colonial order and the wishes of His Catholic Majesty, King Charles III, to establish a lasting peace:

> Do not forget that there are now no Frenchmen in these lands, and that we are all Spaniards. I have and will keep in mind your promises in order to report them to my chief, to whom they will undoubtedly be pleasing, and he will receive you into the number of his children and of the happy subjects of our monarch. But meanwhile it is fitting, since you have committed so many insults, robberies, and homicides in San Antonio de Béxar and vicinity, that without loss of time you should journey to that city. . . . There you will humble yourselves in the presence of a chief of greatest power who resides there, and whose part it is to ratify the treaty which you seek, since you have established yourselves within his jurisdiction, and to name the light and easy conditions to which you must conform in order not to incur the misfortune of being deprived of so desirable a boon.

Mézières's words reflected the opportunities Spanish imperial authorities saw for a new start on New Spain's northern frontier. Without a European rival on their doorstep and with a cadre of experienced French frontier agents now in Spain's service, colonial officials could explore new ways to gain the respect and loyalty of the large number of tribes that until recently had been under French influence. The elimination of one rival, however, merely set the stage for the appearance of a new one in the form of the increasingly powerful Comanches, who came to regard much of Texas as their domain.

CHAPTER 3 New Opportunities, New Rivalries, 1767–1800	
1766	Marqués de Rubí begins inspection tour of Texas region at Paso del Norte
1772	Reglamento de 1772, intended to reorganize frontier defense system, issued
1773	Presidio Los Adaes and East Texas missions suppressed; San Antonio de Béxar becomes capital of Texas
1774	Refugees from Los Adaes found settlement of Nuestra Señora del Pilar de Bucareli at Trinity River crossing of Camino Real
1777	Comandancia General de las Provincias Internas organized
1778	Commandant General Croix holds war council in Béxar, establishes Mesteña tax on unbranded livestock
1779	Nacogdoches established when Bucareli abandoned following Comanche raids and flooding
1785	Governor Cabello makes peace with Comanches and Norteños
1790	Commandant General Ugalde defeats the Apaches at Sabinal Canyon
1793	Secularization of Texas missions begins with San Antonio de Valero (the Alamo)
1797	La Bahía missions exempted from secularization
1800	First permanent bridge across the Rio Grande in operation at Paso del Norte; Rosa María Hinojosa de Ballí controls ranching empire of 1 million acres

For Charles III and his officials throughout the Spanish Empire, there was much work to do in the aftermath of the Seven Years' War (1756–1763). The defeat of the Spanish military in the Old and the New Worlds revealed the superficiality and inadequacy of the military reforms and rebuilding programs of Philip V and Ferdinand VI, Charles's father and brother. Charles, a son of the Enlightenment, believed in the progressive and absolute power of the monarchy and the value of scientific knowledge and rational thought. Like his fellow Enlightenment monarchs throughout Europe, he was determined to curb the power of the Catholic Church, which remained a useful instrument of government, but represented the old, less rational, less modern way of doing things. Likewise, he turned to Europeans to carry out his wishes, distrusting a *criollo* population that he and his policymakers considered more loyal to the local interests than to the empire. While his immediate predecessors had focused on reforming the political, economic, and social institutions of peninsular Spain, Charles turned his attention overseas, intent on shaking up a colonial system over 250 years in the making.

The most prominent of this new breed of enlightened administrators was José de Gálvez. An accomplished judge with a no-nonsense attitude, in 1765 Gálvez became *visitador* (inspector general) for New Spain, with power to implement immediate reforms to increase revenue, foster government efficiency, and strengthen the colony's defenses. During his six years in New Spain, Gálvez established a number of monopolies and overhauled the tax structure to expand revenues and began designing a new administrative system that, although not implemented until 1786, divided New Spain into eleven large districts called *intendencias*. He also ordered the occupation of Alta California (what is today the state of California) in order to forestall Russian moves in that direction. And, ironically since California was occupied using the mission-presidio model, he began reducing the role of missions on the northern frontier.

Among the greatest challenges on the northern frontier was Texas, where Indian peoples held the upper hand over much of its extent. The Lipan Apache peace of 1749 had merely drawn Spaniards into intertribal warfare. The Comanches, who established themselves as the dominant people of the southern Plains, along with their Wichita allies, seemed to offer the best prospect for a lasting peace, but the negotiations would have to take place as much on the Indians' terms as those of the Spaniards. Coastal peoples, including the Karankawas, finding trade partners in British merchants who periodically sailed into Texas's Gulf bays, had little need of dealing with the Spaniards, even as the Coahuiltecan population between the Rio Grande and San Antonio rivers collapsed, leading to the rapid decline of the San Antonio and La Bahía missions. And, as Mézières's visit to one of the Caddo confederacies' main villages made clear, Spain had very little influence in that region.

As you read this chapter, consider the following questions:

1. How did the Marqués de Rubí's inspection mark a critical turning point in Spanish Indian policy on the Texas frontier?
2. What were the causes for the rapid decline of the Franciscan missions in Texas in the second half of the eighteenth century?
3. Why did the cattle industry prove to be an ideal fit for the greater Texas region's economic development?

Effects of Spanish Louisiana on the Northeastern Frontier

Maximizing royal revenues and streamlining colonial government were not Charles III's only concerns in New Spain: There was the critical matter of the military. The weaknesses of Spain's military had come to light in the humiliating defeats of the Seven Years' War. Having joined the conflict, which in North America came to be called the French and Indian War, as an ally of France, Charles had failed to achieve any of his goals. Gibraltar—which had been lost to the English during the War of the Spanish Succession, the war that brought his father to the throne sixty years earlier—remained in English hands. Not only had the English threat to Spanish claims in North America not been removed, but the English capture of Havana had required that Spain cede Florida to England in 1763. Complicating the matter, England's defeat of France in North America led the French to cede Louisiana to Spain in order to keep the vast territory away from their powerful European rival. The only thing that Spain's acquisition of Louisiana from France did was relieve the pressure on the Texas frontier, which no longer bordered on rival territory.

Much of the problem stemmed from Spain's neglect of colonial defenses. New Spain's military establishment was small, consisting of only a couple of garrisons protecting the major ports; its militias were disorganized and poorly trained, and the navy was outdated and in disrepair. On the northern frontier, no reforms of the presidio system had been undertaken since Brigadier Pedro de Rivera's inspection tour of the 1720s. There was little standardization in anything: uniforms, equipment, or training. Chains of command were confusing, with some commanders reporting to the local governor and others to the viceroy, and there was only haphazard cooperation among units. And, completely outside Spanish control, was the transformation of a vast part of today's Texas into Comanche country.

The Rubí Inspection and Reform Program

The job of reforming frontier defenses in response to the new international situation fell to Cayetano María Pignatelli Rubí Corbera y Saint Climent, Barón de Llinás, and Marqués de Rubí, a career military officer holding the rank of field marshal. Rubí received his orders in August 1765. He was to inspect "all the

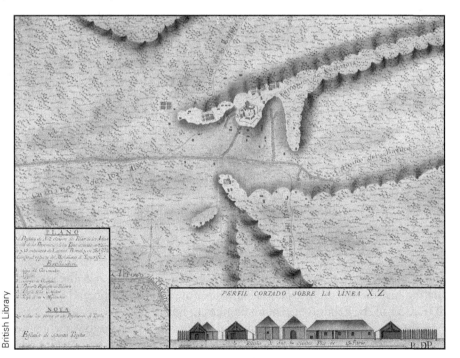

Never a successful settlement, Los Adaes, despite being the capital of Texas from 1720 to 1773, remained an isolated military outpost that was often dependent on nearby French Natchitoches. José de Urrutia's map and elevation of the presidio accentuates both its isolation and its architectural distinctiveness from other Spanish colonial settlements.

presidios of this Kingdom, examine their condition, their location, inspect their troops, review the old price regulations under which they subsist, and . . . propose changes appropriate to the present situation and spell out everything else that for their better government and defense" he considered necessary.

Rubí's inspection tour first reached the vicinity of what is now Texas in August 1766, when he visited Paso del Norte. He found the district, which at the time consisted of a presidio, a civilian settlement, and various *haciendas* (large, well-developed estates) and missions on both sides of the Rio Grande, in a flourishing state. Things were very different at La Junta de los Ríos at the junction of the Conchos River and Rio Grande, where Presidio Nuestra Señora de Belén y Santiago de Amarillas, built on the Texas side in 1760 by future Texas governor Captain Manuel Muñoz, had been abandoned sometime before Rubí's arrival. Intermittent missionary efforts among the local semisedentary bands had failed to produce a stable Spanish presence in the area, and Mescalero Apaches took advantage of the instability. Nevertheless, to Rubí, La Junta seemed a strategic location for one of the presidios in the defensive line he proposed for the northern frontier. The new garrison, Presidio del Norte, built on the south side Rio Grande in 1773 at present-day Ojinaga, Mexico, later became the site of Spain's last effort to pacify the Apaches. In 1779 a so-called peace establishment was opened for Mescalero Apaches willing to settle down, an experiment that lasted about a decade.

It was almost a year later when Rubí made his next Texas stop, missions San Lorenzo (near present-day Camp Wood, Real County) and Candelaria (near today's Montell, Uvalde County), which had opened in 1762 in a follow-up attempt to convert the Lipan Apaches after the disaster at San Sabá. Known as El Cañón, the attempt to place the Franciscans deeper and, hopefully, more safely in Apachería had proved a failure: Mission Candelaria was completely abandoned, there were no Indians at San Lorenzo, and the military detachment from San Sabá was totally destitute. And, moving on to San Sabá, which remained under the direct authority of the viceroy, Rubí's immediate assessment was that the presidio there was about as useful "as a ship anchored in mid-Atlantic would be in preventing foreign trade with America." With its horse herd under constant assault from the Comanches and Norteños and the men poorly equipped and prone to desertion, Captain Felipe Rábago y Terán, who had been exonerated of all charges in the San Xavier murders of a decade earlier, had given up hope of transforming the presidio into a center of settlement and turned to profiteering from his company's payrolls. Rubí rode out of Presidio San Sabá on August 4, 1767, already formulating his final recommendation—abandonment of El Cañón and San Sabá and transfer of the handful of civilian families to Béxar.

Nothing could have prepared Rubí for conditions at San Antonio when he arrived on August 8. In the forty years since Rivera's inspection San Antonio de Béxar had undergone considerable change. The presidio now anchored a settlement containing a formal town and five missions, with a total population of about 2,000 individuals, representing a diverse ethnic mix of criollos, *castas*, acculturated Indians, and neophytes from a dozen or more Coahuiltecan, Karankawa,

and Apache groups. General farming and a limited amount of ranching supported the majority of the population, and textile manufacturing was beginning
at some of the missions. Unlike Paso del Norte, Béxar was still in no position to
defend itself, especially as the mission Indians remained prone to flight, but the
location showed promise in its fertile and irrigated fields, its vast grazing lands,
and its healthy climate.

For all the development in its first half-century, Béxar remained a decidedly
backward place. Rubí found the 22-man garrison ill equipped, undisciplined,
and overextended. The presidio was in disrepair in part because the viceroy had
reduced its size by half to staff San Sabá and only seven men were available to the
captain at any one time; the other fifteen were assigned to mission guard duty.
Captain Luis Antonio Menchaca, more businessman than officer, had his men
uniformed in a colorful mix of lace, silk, and silver, which kept his pockets full
and the men in want of basic necessities.

Rubí found conditions even worse at Los Adaes, the "capital" of Texas, when
he arrived on September 11. Presidio Los Adaes exhibited the scars of the corrupt former governor's neglect: Serviceable weaponry among the company of

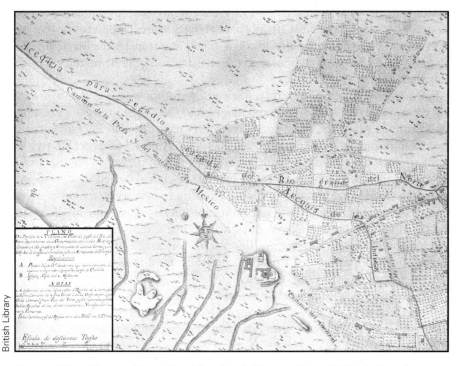

Compare Urrutia's map of Los Adaes (above) and this one of Paso del Norte. Note the
number of structures along roads, the agricultural fields, and extensive irrigation system.
By the time the Marqués de Rubí and Urrutia visited what is now the El Paso-Juárez area,
the missions, presidio, and civilian settlement had a flourishing economy combining
ranching, viniculture, and subsistence crop production.

sixty-one soldiers consisted of two muskets, seven swords, and six shields; the company herd contained only twenty-five horses fit for service instead of the regulation 500–600; a number of soldiers lacked basic items of dress, including shirts, shoes, and hats. The former governor, Angel Martos y Navarrete, had illegally employed the men in his command as cowboys and farmers on his private ranch, had sold back to them part of the crop that they had grown in the company's communal farm, and stocked his store with contraband merchandise from Natchitoches.

Los Adaes, Rubí concluded, did not meet expectations for a Spanish provincial capital. The settlement lacked a substantial civilian population beyond the soldiers' families, although there may have been as many as 100 families living in the forest clearings and at former Hasinai Indian village sites, subsisting on farming, trapping, Indian trade, and contraband commerce with Louisiana. The declining Caddo population, having experienced a series of epidemics as well as the adverse climatic conditions of much of the eighteenth century, had never been converted; the area's three missions contained not a single neophyte yet cost the Crown 450 pesos a year for each of the missionaries staffing them. With Natchitoches in Spanish hands, and with its French residents on good terms with the area Indians, what need was there to maintain Los Adaes? As the inspector's entourage departed, Rubí must already have arrived at the solution to reinforcing San Antonio: close down the Presidio Los Adaes and transfer the local population to Béxar, where farmlands awaited the civilians and genuine military service awaited the soldiers.

Following a circuitous and tortuous route through woods and swamps, it took the Marqués de Rubí from September 28 to October 15 to reach Presidio San Agustín de Ahumada and Mission Nuestra Señora de la Luz del Orcoquisac. Since its founding in 1756 (near present-day Wallisville, Chambers County) to counter French penetration of southeast Texas by way of Galveston Bay, El Orcoquisac had failed by every measure. The garrison itself had turned to contraband and Indian trade in the absence of any opportunity to raise its own food or meet its other needs. The presidio suffered from constant desertions; the mission had failed to attract the local Atakapa-speaking Indians; and no civilian population had established itself in the vicinity. Best for all concerned—the royal treasury, missionaries, and beleaguered soldiers and their families—was the complete abandonment of the site, Rubí decided.

In November 1767, when Rubí reached La Bahía (present-day Goliad) he was in sore need of some good news. Although conditions were not perfect at the presidio, they were better than conditions anywhere else in the province. This was due in large part to Captain Manuel Ramírez de la Piscina, whose seventeen-year tenure had begun when the complex had been moved to the lower San Antonio River by order of José Escandón. Although the old captain, who had died the previous July, had some of the same faults as his contemporaries at the other Texas posts—he overcharged for the goods he sold to his soldiers, who also worked at his ranch—he had kept his command disciplined and relatively well supplied.

Unlike the situation elsewhere in Texas, settlement at La Bahía appeared to be moving in the right direction. The number of families was increasing, from under ten in 1762 to about twenty-five at the time of the inspection. Although there was no formal town as yet, the more than 300 inhabitants of the presidio settlement seemed to be flourishing. Captain Ramírez had successfully come to terms with the Karankawas and Coahuiltecans of the area, and the missionaries at missions Espíritu Santo and Rosario had learned to be patient with these hunter-gatherers, who had refused to adjust to the sedentary life of Spanish colonial society. As far as Rubí was concerned, La Bahía was worthy of serving as the eastern anchor in the presidio line he was about to recommend to the viceroy.

Bypassing Laredo, which did not have a presidio, Rubí and his retinue visited Presidio del Río Grande in November 1767, before arriving in Mexico City the following February. There he prepared a *dictamen* (official opinion) regarding matters on the frontier. The problems he had found in Texas were common throughout the borderlands. To remedy them, Rubí proposed that the entire frontier, from the Gulf of California to the Gulf of Mexico be considered a single unit, so that officials could base their decisions on overall strategic considerations rather than immediate tactical or local interests. Further, he proposed a complete reform of the organization, command structure, and financial management of the presidios to produce cost savings to the Crown and better conditions for the soldiery.

Rubí's recommendations were incorporated into a series of reforms carried out in the 1770s that streamlined not only military policy but political and religious administration as well. The first, known as the *Reglamento* of 1772, called for a complete overhaul of the presidio system. With the exception of Santa Fe and San Antonio (which was to become the capital of Texas) all the presidios would now line up roughly along 30° north latitude, from Altar in Sonora to La Bahía in Texas, so that in the end a string of fifteen presidios, approximately 100 miles apart from each other, could effectively coordinate their activities. In order to curb the abuses of the presidio commanders, who also controlled the purse strings of their individual garrisons, each company was to elect a commissary officer who would be held strictly accountable for his financial dealings. Soldiers' salaries would be reduced in light of reforms certain to lower their expenses, and they would receive part of it in cash. Training and duties were to be standardized, as were soldiers' uniforms, and presidio commanders were to keep regular muster rolls and enlistment papers.

The big winners in Texas were Presidios de Béxar and La Bahía. At San Antonio the Reglamento called for a company commanded by the governor, manned by eighty officers and men and a chaplain. Presidio La Bahía was to be manned by its captain, fifty officers and men, and a chaplain. Not all Tejanos (Texans of Spanish–Mexican descent) were happy with the reforms, however, and the new governor assigned to the province had his hands full attempting to please his superiors in Mexico City and Madrid while placating the disgruntled and dispossessed denizens of East Texas and taking on the growing challenge of the Comanches and their Norteño allies.

The Rise of the Comanches along the Texas Frontier

The Nʉmʉnʉʉ, a branch of the Uto-Aztecan speaking Shoshone peoples, came into history as the Comanches at the beginning of the eighteenth century in New Mexico. Father Agustín Morfi, who accompanied Commandant General Marqués de Croix on his frontier inspection tour of 1777–1778, wrote this brief, but useful description of them:

> Comanches, 5000 men distributed in five tribes with different names. This nation is far superior to all the others in the number of warriors, the extent of the lands they occupy, the modesty of their dress, the hospitality shown to visitors or those they meet, the human treatment of captives, and the valor they display, which is admirable even in their women. But the wandering life they lead mars so many good qualities and forces them to be professional thieves. They have attacked us fiercely in New Mexico and Texas, but nothing can compare with the mortal hatred they feel for the Apaches, with whom alone they are cruel when they succeed in capturing them.

Changing climatic conditions in the sixteenth century, sometimes referred to as the Little Ice Age, brought peoples out of the Rockies, the northern woodlands, and the Mississippi valley out onto the Great Plains, where buffalo herds flourished and increased rainfall made agriculture bountiful. Among the peoples descending on the region were the Shoshone, who soon entered into competition with other nonsedentary buffalo hunters. Pressed by agriculturally inclined tribes on the southeast, and rival buffalo hunters to the east, ravaged by epidemic disease, but having acquired horses in the years following the Pueblo Revolt, the Shoshones divided in two. By the early eighteenth century the major part of the Eastern Shoshones had settled on exploiting the sizeable buffalo herds of the northern Plains while the smaller part, which became the Comanches, gradually migrated southward.

The term "Comanches" comes from the Southern Ute term for them, *kumantsi*, the meaning of which is "enemy" or "stranger." Indeed, shortly after coming into contact, Utes and Comanches, both Uto-Aztecan speakers, formed an alliance that lasted well into the eighteenth century. As the Comanche population prospered and the extent of the territory it occupied grew, it subdivided first into three major divisions: Jupes ("Timber people"), Yamparika ("Root Eaters"), and Kotsoteka ("Buffalo Eaters").

During the late seventeenth and first years of the eighteenth century, the Ute–Comanche alliance operated from the mountainous region of northern New Mexico eastward to the high Plains. As their society evolved into a fully equestrian buffalo-hunting culture, the Comanches began a move onto the southern Plains, successfully displacing local Apache groups. Well fed, mobile, and opportunistic in their absorption of outsiders, particularly captives, into their bands, the Comanche population grew throughout the eighteenth century, despite the occasional epidemic or military reversal. By the middle of the century they had made the Texas high and rolling Plains part of a homeland stretching beyond the Arkansas River that soon came by the name Comanchería. Their conquests checked any idea of Spanish expansion into the region, either from New Mexico or Texas. And, by the late 1780s they had forced Spaniards to accept their sovereignty to the north and west of San Antonio, Texas, and east of the Pecos River valley, extracting regular payments from the Spaniards that have been variously described as bribes, tribute, and extortion.

One reason that the Comanches posed such a challenge for other Indian peoples as well as the Spaniards was their highly decentralized sociopolitical organization. Fundamentally, an adult male warrior who had proved himself capable of supporting a family through his hunting and military exploits was an independent actor in his band. In fact, he could take his property and join another band as he chose. Thus, leadership was based on status and nonbinding. A man who chose not to follow another selected to lead a raiding or hunting party could refuse without repercussions. Likewise, young men who still needed to garner enough property to start a family could ignore the advice of band elders. The more success a male had in warfare, raiding, and hunting, the more prestige and honor he acquired; the more it demonstrated the strength of his *puha*, or medicine. The greater the puha a man had, the more status he held within Comanche society. Comanches could acquire puha from the supernatural through a vision

George Catlin, "Comanche Moving Camp, Dog Fight Enroute," original in the Smithsonian American Art Museum, 1985.66.466

Offshoots of the Shoshone, The Comanches became the most powerful peoples of the southern Plains by the mid-eighteenth century. Their endurance and horsemanship made them formidable adversaries not only for Spaniards, but for other Plains people, in particular the eastern Apaches, the invasion of whose hunting ranges sparked ongoing hostilities that lasted into the nineteenth century.

quest or an unsought dream. They could also obtain puha directly from someone who already owned it. Prestige and status required demonstrations of generosity and hospitality, which prevented social relations among a group's families from becoming too unbalanced.

Wealth and family were thus intricately mixed in Comanche society. The practice of bridewealth governed marriage among the Comanches, requiring a man to pay the bride's family for the loss of a productive member. The more property, essentially horses, that a man owned the more wives he could purchase. The more wives and slaves in the household, the more productive the family was, since women, along with any slaves that the women deemed fit to incorporate into the household, had the responsibility of processing the hides brought back by the man of the house while slaves looked after the warrior's horses. In essence, the household was the domain of a man's wives, who carried out all the household functions as well as directing household members in gathering activities to supplement the fruits of the hunt and the raid.

The Comanches' political economy depended on two principal items: buffalo and horses. Before being introduced to equine stock at the end of the seventeenth century, Comanches and other Plains peoples had hunted buffalo on foot, requiring considerable cooperation among band members and limiting the group's range of movement and the amount of household goods, including the size of tipis, as the only means of transporting things was the backs of people or the pulling capabilities of dogs. After the introduction of the horse among them, not only did the Comanches experience a rapid cultural transformation, they also experienced an economic revolution. With everyone—men, women, children, and slaves—mounted, bands could expand both their buffalo-hunting range and their raiding and trading activities. Accessing Wichita and Euroamerican traders to the east, they could exchange animals and people captured in New Mexico or from the Apaches for French and later English goods from the Mississippi valley. But it was more complicated than that, as Comanches would occasionally show up in New Mexico with animals and captives taken from Spanish areas of Texas. The Comanches found that Spanish frontier communities were good targets for what amounted to pirate raids and good partners for peaceful exchanges. In other words, what Euroamerican observers considered thievery, the Comanches considered the preferred way of building wealth.

Contrary to popular understanding, during the eighteenth century the Spanish communities of New Mexico and Texas were not the Comanches' primary enemies. That place belonged to the Apaches. Since the sixteenth century on the edges of the southern Plains, Comanches and Apaches had confronted each other over control of the region. As the Comanches proved the more resilient of the two peoples, the eastern Apaches began a gradual withdrawal southward, eventually beyond the Edwards Plateau, which became the recognized southeastern end of Comanchería. Unfamiliar with the Comanches in Texas, the Spaniards there had opted for an alliance with the Apaches that lasted through the 1760s but ultimately proved disastrous. Only with the adjustments made to the frontier military and political system begun with Rubí's inspection did the debate over who represented the principal threat to long-term Spanish interests in the far north shift Spanish attitudes in favor of the Comanches and their allies. Spaniards accepted Comanche control of the intervening country between San Antonio and Santa Fe and sought their help in crushing the Apaches once and for all. It was a project that remained incomplete at the end of Spanish rule in Texas.

The Death and Rebirth of Spanish East Texas

The new governor of Texas, Spanish-born Colonel Juan María Vicencio, Barón de Ripperdá, accompanied by his Mexican-born wife, Mariana Gómez de Parada Gallo y Villavicencio, arrived in San Antonio early in 1770, marking the beginning of a new chapter in Texas history. Technically, his command was Presidio Los Adaes, but the pressing needs of reorganizing and strengthening defenses at Béxar, not to mention the perils and inconveniences of taking his new wife to East Texas, led him to take up residence in the *casas reales* (government building).

He and the baroness must have been greatly relieved when late in 1771 Viceroy Antonio María de Bucareli denied Ripperdá's half-hearted request to transfer to Los Adaes with the admonition that because Natchitoches was now in Spanish hands, he should remain where he was. Rubí's inspection had made clear the deplorable conditions at Los Adaes, which despite officially serving as the province's seat of government, was little more than a poverty-stricken appendage to Natchitoches. Previous governors, who also served as presidio commander, had exploited contraband trade with French Louisiana and the labor of their subalterns, with little thought but a quick exit from what seemed like the most remote and least inviting portion of New Spain. Life in Spanish Texas was hard; at Los Adaes it was harsh.

Women in Frontier Society

Although they were members of the elite, the baron and his wife's arrival in Texas was an example of a common occurrence at the time: the migration of families to the frontier. The myth of a European, male-only frontier does not stand up to close scrutiny in the Texas case. La Salle had attempted to establish a well-rounded colony by bringing a number of French women along on his tragic expedition of 1685. The Spanish Crown, always interested in establishing stable colonial communities, had encouraged married soldiers to move to Texas from the time of the Ramón and Alarcón expeditions of 1716–18. One of the viceroy's counselors commented that married soldiers were a double benefit, as "they will be able to fill their presidios with the children that their wives bear them," and they would be less likely to make advances to the neophyte females and take advantage of them. The effort to bring Canary Islanders to Texas had also been predicated on the migration of families, rather than single individuals; of the fifty-six Isleños who eventually made it to Béxar in 1731, only four were single adult males.

Of course, frontier conditions made Texas a male-dominated society, and Spanish females were always in short supply. Women like the Baroness Ripperdá, a high-born criollo, were rare. Most Spanish women in Texas had been born on the frontier, and their "Spanish" status was often based on social convention rather than biological grounds. Beginning with the conquests of the sixteenth century, exclusively male undertakings, many men had found companionship in Indian women, and some took women of African descent as wives. Over the course of generations, if family circumstances improved, the children of such mixed couples might "pass" into the ranks of the "Spanish"; by the late eighteenth century the term "Spaniard" was more recognition of social status than ethnic label, especially on the frontier. In the case of Texas, although the evidence points to considerable ethnic mixing, "Spaniards" were reported to make up a majority of the population. The continued infusion of significant numbers of acculturated Indians (and a smaller number of individuals of African descent) into the Hispanic population kept the reported Indian population consistently at about 25 percent and the mixed-blood population at about 20 percent.

Aside from her relative wealth, the Baroness Ripperdá was fortunate in a number of respects. Her husband lived out his stay in Texas, whereas many other Tejanas could expect to be widowed once or twice if they did not die in childbirth, in one of the periodic epidemics that swept through the province, or during an Indian attack. The baroness delivered six children during her husband's tenure in Texas, at least two of whom died in infancy. Her experience was not uncommon: Most women in Texas, indeed throughout New Spain, could expect to lose half of their offspring in infancy (from birth to two years).

Although the baroness did not have to worry about food or shelter (despite her husband's repeated complaints about their quarters' poor state of repair), the overwhelming majority of her contemporaries faced a life of unremitting toil. With the exception of a few families that had one or more servants— sometimes a hired hand, sometimes a captured Apache or Comanche child who was brought up in the household as a *criado* (literally reared, as distinct from a hired servant or slave)—women worked long hours to maintain their households. The large number of widows meant that many women had to take on the role of sole provider for their families. As heads of households, they engaged in a variety of occupations outside the home such as seamstress, midwife, and shopkeeper. A few women acquired property through inheritance and marriage and became important ranchers and farmers in their communities. For some, economic reversals and lack of other opportunities prescribed a life of servitude or prostitution (an activity that seems to have been grudgingly accepted in colonial Texas). And, of course, there was always the danger of being captured during a raid, thus becoming a commodity in the region's economy, to be either ransomed, enslaved, or married as a secondary wife.

Active public participation in the economic life of Texas required women to have legal rights that afforded them considerable protection in what was a man's world. Thus the Baroness Ripperdá and all women, from the best-positioned Spanish matriarch to the lowliest Indian maid, benefited from a legal system that recognized them as individuals. Women had the right to their own separate property, including those goods and real estate they had acquired before marriage or that had been bequeathed to them. Moreover, after marriage they were entitled to half the property that husband and wife acquired while a couple. The right to defend one's property and honor required that women play a role in legal proceedings, so they could initiate legal actions and give testimony. These rights extended even to slaves, who on a number of occasions successfully petitioned to be removed from the homes of abusive masters. And, as theirs was a Roman Catholic society, women could file for divorce from abusive or runaway husbands, although neither party could remarry before the death of his or her former spouse.

The First Capital of Texas Abandoned

Los Adaes, despite the Marqués de Rubí's dismissive assessment of East Texas and the Ripperdás' dread of having to live there, was the second largest settlement in the province of Texas, and the most ethnically diverse in 1770. Over 500 Spanish subjects lived among the remaining aboriginal inhabitants, members of various Hasinai and Atakapan groups, and a growing number of Louisianans, white and black. In fact, Natchitoches, just across the border, was a thriving community that offered more regular contacts with the outside world for the Spanish population of East Texas than Bexareños and Badeños (residents of La Bahía) had. The death warrant for the fifty-year-old capital of the Provincia de los Tejas y Nuevas Philipinas had long since been signed, however, and it fell to the Baron Ripperdá to execute it. In the process he and the policymakers in Mexico City came to discover just how deep-rooted the local Tejanos' attachment was to their homes in the woods of East Texas.

Ripperdá arrived at Los Adaes in June 1773 with draconian orders. Not only was he to close the existing missions, but he was to see that the two presidios were destroyed and the entire Hispanic population of the area relocated to San Antonio. Resentment and resistance emerged on all sides. Some Adaesanos, as the Los Adaes area residents were known, fled to Natchitoches and others into the isolated woods where they had cleared fields and built their cabins. The Hasinai groups in the vicinity took the withdrawal as evidence that the Spanish had allied with the Apaches and prepared to make war on them. After the governor failed to adequately reassure them, the refugees had to leave two families behind at Nacogdoches in a sign of goodwill toward the Indians.

The overwhelming majority of Adaesano refugees arrived in Béxar on September 26 to a less than enthusiastic welcome. They were instructed to look for house lots and farmlands in the vicinity, but without disturbing the property of Bexareños or missions. This was impossible without moving so far away from the settlement that they would be exposed to Indian attack and lack access to irrigation water. Some families did find places for themselves, either as sharecroppers at the missions, hired hands for some of the better-off residents, or in military service at the presidio. At least half of the refugees, however, were determined to return to East Texas, and soon after their arrival they petitioned for permission to establish a new settlement at the site of the former Mission Nuestra Señora de los Ais (present-day San Augustine).

The Adaesanos' petition had Governor Ripperdá's support. He was not only sympathetic to the plight of the dispossessed Adaesanos, but their return to East Texas would buttress the Indian policy he favored: forming alliances with area Indians through trade. Of particular importance was establishing friendly relations with the Wichita groups that had moved into north central Texas. The Wichitas seemed well disposed toward the Spaniards, but were actively trading with Louisiana. Ripperdá believed that removing the Hispanic East Texas population would not solve the illegal Indian trade problem, but would only serve to undermine the authority and respect officials in San Antonio commanded among the Indians of the region. His opinions were not shared by *Ocónor* or the viceroy, both of whom wished to toe the line in regard to closing Texas off from Louisiana, prohibiting trade in firearms with the Indians, and sticking to Rubí's presidio line of defense. Eventually, Ripperdá's refusal to carry out instructions he regarded as counterproductive cost him his office.

The viceroy did not permit the Adaesanos to settle so close to Louisiana, but did allow them to select an intermediate location. More than 120 families made the decision to move to a site at the Camino Real crossing on the Trinity River, while about sixty or seventy families remained behind in San Antonio. The new settlement, Nuestra Señora del Pilar de Bucareli, required a government and protection. No presidio or army detachment had been authorized for Bucareli so the governor organized a militia, naming Antonio Gil Ybarbo captain of the militia and *justicia mayor*, effectively making him lieutenant governor for the district. It is difficult to imagine anyone better suited to the job of running what was essentially a renegade settlement of smugglers and Indian traders. A native of Los Adaes, Ybarbo was schooled in various Indian languages and French, adept at contraband trade, and skilled in the arts of political survival. His rather loose interpretation of property rights had landed him in jail in New Orleans by order of Governor Ocónor in the late 1760s, when he was caught with horses alleged to have been stolen by Indians from various Texas settlements. Any enemy of Ocónor's was a friend of Ripperdá, and the Texas governor soon obtained Ybarbo's release from jail. The two men saw eye-to-eye on a variety of issues: the need for a continued Spanish presence in East Texas; the need for broad and sympathetic trade relations with the northern tribes; and the need to maintain commercial ties with Natchitoches.

Indian–Spanish Relations Transformed

Under Ybarbo's guidance Spanish East Texas was reborn, even as the settlers were forced to abandon Bucareli for the site of Mission Nacogdoches in early 1779 because of hostilities with the Comanches and flooding on the Trinity River. The settlement of Nacogdoches coincided with administrative changes both at the local and the viceregal level. In late October 1778 Colonel Domingo Cabello y Robles, Governor Ripperdá's replacement, arrived at Béxar. A career army officer like his predecessor, the fifty-three year-old had considerable experience in colonial matters, but none in frontier affairs. He had served in Cuba, displaying conspicuous valor during the English capture of Havana in the Seven Years' War. His gallantry earned him the governorship of Nicaragua, a position he held for almost twelve years before receiving the Texas post.

Cabello must have wondered what he had done to deserve such a posting. Texas had such a bad reputation in New Spain that his cook, "came to believe that the Indians would eat him, for which reason he resigned from my service. And the same thing happened with my manservant and a secretary.... Although I recognize that they did right, because this place is worse than Siberia and Lapland." There were no cannibals in Texas, but Cabello's comments reflect the general perception of the Texas frontier as a savage land. With about 3,500 Spanish residents (including acculturated Indians) to tens of thousands of indigenous inhabitants, Spanish Texas remained very much de facto Indian country.

By the time Cabello assumed office, the most revolutionary of Rubí's reform ideas was underway: the creation of an independent administrative and military jurisdiction for the northern frontier. The Comandancia General de las Provincias Internas represented José de Gálvez's attempt to make frontier government more responsive and efficient. The region, including the entire north of the viceroyalty, from Sonora and Sinaloa to the west to Nuevo Santander and Texas to the east, would be administered by a commandant general, a military official holding both military and political authority independent of the viceroy.

On January 1, 1777, Caballero Teodoro de Croix became the first commandant general of the Interior Provinces. Croix was an experienced army officer who had served in various political capacities under his uncle, a former viceroy. He was acquainted with the situation on the northern frontier and in Texas and did not agree with the policies of either the current viceroy or Inspector General Ocónor. He soon replaced Ocónor, and began to carry out an inspection tour of his jurisdiction that included holding a war council at San Antonio de Béxar.

As far as Texas was concerned, Croix agreed with Ripperdá and Athanase de Mézières: make peace with the Nations of the North and the Comanches, and make war on the Apaches. Athanase de Mézières, a native of Paris and former French army officer and Indian trader, had served at Natchitoches beginning in the 1740s. After the Spanish take-over, Louisiana governor Alejandro O'Reilly appointed De Mézières, who readily accepted Spanish rule, lieutenant governor for the Natchitoches district. De Mézières quickly won over Governor Ripperdá to his ideas on Indian relations and helped the Spanish maintain good relations with the frontier tribes.

Not surprisingly, the war council held by Croix at San Antonio in January 1778 placed blame for Texas's Indian problems squarely on the shoulders of the Apaches, especially the Lipans, and called for all-out war against them. The Nations of the North and the Comanches had not been hostile to Spanish interests until the Spanish had made peace overtures to the Apaches and built missions and a presidio for them. Even worse, because the Apaches refused to keep their word, Spanish Texas had ended up at war against all these groups. The council also approved Ripperdá's agreements with the Nations of the North negotiated through De Mézières. "Although some have groundlessly regarded these treaties as deceitful, all the nations except the Comanches have scrupulously kept them."

Only all-out war against the Apaches combined with concerted diplomacy toward the Norteños and Comanches could bring peace and prosperity to the province. And only Athanase de Mézières had the necessary diplomatic skills to bring the province's Indians into an alliance against the Apaches. However, De Mézières's declining health did not permit him to accept Commandant General Croix's offer of the Texas governorship. He died in San Antonio in November

Portrait of Caballero Teodoro de Croix (1730-92) Viceroy of Peru and Chile (oil on canvas), Spanish School, (18th century) / Chateau Franc-Waret, Ardennes, Belgium / © Paul Maeyaert / Bridgeman Images

For Spanish colonial administrators, including Teodoro de Croix, first commandant general of the Provincias Internas, Texas posed a series of frustrating and seemingly insurmountable problems. Arriving in San Antonio in January 1778 for a council of war, Croix experienced firsthand the penury of the Tejanos, the struggles of the missions, and the neglect of the presidio system in the province. Later he would comment that Texas "did not deserve the name of the Province of Texas . . . nor the concern entailed in its preservation."

1779, having made peace between the Nations of the North and the Spanish and still advocating diplomacy toward the Comanches and war against the Apaches.

The situation was not so clear to Governor Cabello, however. On his arrival he was confronted by Comanche raids on Bucareli and friendly visits from Lipan and other Apache chiefs. From Cabello's brief survey of the situation, De Mézières's insistence that the Comanches were not the problem made little sense. Consequently, at first Cabello decided not to take sides in intertribal affairs. Rather, he focused on getting various tribal groups to accept Spanish sovereignty. For instance, in 1779 he made the Tonkawa leader El Mocho medal chief. (All three North-American European powers gave large ornate medals to Indian headmen who they recognized as a tribe's or band's leader.) The honor did not make the Tonkawa leader compliant. El Mocho refused to gather his Tonkawas in a village or to stop dealing with the Apaches, as Governor Cabello desired. In fact, in 1782 he organized a trade fair in his territory (the territory of the former Ranchería Grande between the Brazos and Trinity rivers) for the Apaches and his tribe, the Hasinais, Karankawas, and the Atakapas. Although the fair was broken up by Wichitas and Comanches who saw the danger to themselves of a revitalized Lipan Apache nation, El Mocho's independence so enraged Cabello that he arranged for the chief's assassination two years later at La Bahía.

In time, Cabello came around to the general consensus that Norteños and Comanches presented an opportunity for peace while Apaches represented menace. Having accepted that the Lipan Apaches, who had relocated in the region between San Antonio and La Bahía from the San Antonio River valley southward, posed an ongoing threat, Cabello now was ready to negotiate with the Comanches. Likewise, for Wichitas and Comanches, the smallpox epidemic of 1781, a devastating drought, and trade disruptions with Louisiana favored reaching some agreement with Texas Spaniards.

In 1785, employing the new policy of gift-giving and diplomacy and making use of experienced translators, Cabello and the Comanches and Wichitas came to terms. The agreements effectively recognized Comanche and Wichita independence to the north and west of San Antonio; trade and gifts replacing raiding. Scholars debate what the regular gifts from the Spaniards might have meant to the Comanches: reciprocal hospitality for the good treatment Spaniards received in Comanche camps, wealth redistribution as a measure of kinship or alliance, or a form of tribute from the Spaniards. From the Spanish perspective, the gift giving, referred to by some scholars as "peace by purchase," might be seen as a way of attaching the favored Indians to Spanish trade goods and services, since only in the Spanish settlements did the artisans exist to repair the firearms and acquire the gunpowder that now became part of the Spanish–Indian exchanges. The Spanish Crown could claim, fanciful as it might be, that the Indian peoples of Texas were its vassals. Until well after the turn of the century only the various Apache tribes and occasional groups of young independent warriors troubled Spanish Texas. It was the longest period of relative peace that the province enjoyed until the end of the Indian wars in late 1870s.

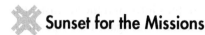 Sunset for the Missions

Reform and change marked the religious realm as well as the military and political spheres of life in late eighteenth-century Texas. The mission system, backbone of Spanish policy on the frontier, had given way to a more secular and economic perspective on Spanish–Indian affairs. In Texas the eastern missions had failed to produce tangible results among the Hasinais in over fifty years of existence, and the mid-century experiments at San Sabá and El Cañón with the Lipans, San Xavier with the Ranchería Grande, and El Orcoquisac with the Akokisas had been disastrous. Even the active missions at Béxar and La Bahía faced new challenges that would prove insurmountable in the long run.

The Mission System in Decline

For all intents and purposes, by the early 1770s the only active missions in Texas were located at Béxar and La Bahía. These missions had made such remarkable progress in physical terms through the early 1770s, that there was considerable animosity between Hispanic settlers and the friars over livestock, land, and water rights. The missions controlled some of the best grazing land in the San Antonio River basin, having established their ranching operations long before the civilian population had begun to venture into the countryside. The Béxar missions had built extensive and sophisticated *acequia* systems. By the 1770s the mission compounds included large stone churches, workshops, granaries, and living quarters. In effect, the missions were independent communities that competed with civilian settlements for both resources and markets.

Despite all these physical advantages the missions had always faced one important hurdle in becoming the ideal Christian Spanish communities the friars wanted them to be: maintaining adequate Indian populations. The Ranchería Grande, Coahuiltecans, and Karankawas on whom the Franciscans of Béxar and La Bahía depended to populate their missions had never been numerous peoples to begin with. Life at the missions often proved detrimental to the health of these hunter-gatherers. Dietary changes combined with different hygiene regimens weakened immune systems already under assault from a variety of pathogens alien to the region. Periodic epidemics of smallpox, measles, and other Old World diseases took a great toll on all residents of Texas, but particularly on the Indians. In addition, the missionaries' efforts to impose European values, particularly in the areas of division of labor, work routines, and sexual relations, contributed to the Indians' frequent flight.

In time the mission system faced a population crisis that the Spaniards were unable to overcome. Although the Béxar missions had averaged more than 200 neophytes each during the 1750s and 1760s, by the mid-1770s there were fewer than 200. At La Bahía, there had been a large number of Indians at Espíritu Santo, and a new station, Nuestra Señora del Rosario, had been constructed for local groups in the 1750s. Neither establishment contained more than fifty families by the 1770s. A Karankawa attack against Rosario in 1778 had led to the mission's abandonment by all its Indian residents. The collapse or flight of neophyte populations forced friars to undertake forays into the countryside to round up runaway neophytes or recruit new ones, but these coercive exercises were increasingly unproductive. The Coahuiltecans were becoming scarce. Coastal Indian groups, which proved particularly well insulated from Spanish encroachment, found that they could incorporate the missions into their annual cycle of seasonal migration without having to accept unwanted aspects of Spanish civilization. The Lipan and other Apaches might flirt with the missions, but as groups they proved unwilling to abandon their independent way of life, even in the face of increasing pressures from their Norteño and Comanche enemies. Missions were never able to attract the most populous tribes of Texas Indians, the Comanches and Wichitas of northern and western Texas. As a result missions came to depend on a small core of acculturated Indians and increasingly larger numbers of non-Indian residents to maintain operations.

Presidio-mission complexes had operated fairly amicably with the community in East Texas and at La Bahía, because for the most part, in East Texas the missions never developed substantial resources and at La Bahía the civilian community remained small. Such was not the case at Béxar, however. From the time of the Canary Islanders' arrival, there had been considerable tension between the civilian and mission communities. There was competition over land, water, cattle, and the sale of agricultural products to the presidio market; the settlers attempted to gain access to the labor of neophytes; and the friars felt that the settlers were corrupting their Indians.

These circumstances combined to increase pressure on the Texas missions to scale down their operations. The first missions to close were the remaining East Texas stations, those among the Hasinais as far east as Los Adaes and the one for the Akokisas on the lower Trinity River. These closures released Zacatecas College friars for duty at the four Béxar missions operated by the Querétaro College, which in 1777 abandoned Texas to concentrate on its more successful operations in Sonora and Arizona.

The pressure mounted with the arrival of Commandant General Croix in 1778. Croix listened to the complaints of settlers and missionaries about each other. He certainly understood the problems, and as a member of the new breed of more secular and regalist officials that the Spanish Bourbons were employing to modernize the empire, his actions favored settler and government interests. As far as the province's livestock was concerned, he strictly enforced the property rights of all parties, including the Crown. As for the dispute over resources between Mission Valero and the townspeople of San Antonio, he ordered the suppression of the mission. Each Indian family would gain agricultural land and a house lot from the distribution of mission property, after which the Adaes settlers and other civilians would have access to the remaining farmland and lots. It was not until the early 1790s that both of these decisions were implemented, however, as lawsuits and reprieves wound their way through the imperial bureaucracy.

Secularization Begins

When the president of the Texas Franciscans, Fray José Francisco López, sat down to make his report on the state of the missions in 1789, there was little positive to say. Nine friars attended to the needs of the province, one at each of the six operating mission communities, another two at the Nacogdoches settlement, and one as a substitute wherever he was needed. Only San José and Espíritu Santo counted more than 100 Indian residents, most of whom spoke imperfect Spanish even after a long time in residence. In fact, the missions had become multiethnic communities, "the Indians," as Fray López wrote about Valero, "having married mulattoes and mestizos." The physical state of the missions varied widely in quality and state of repair, with Valero and the abandoned Rosario in the worst shape, and Espíritu Santo and San José in good condition. Various construction projects had had to be abandoned for lack of Indian labor, including larger churches at Valero (the main part of today's "Alamo chapel") and at Capistrano.

Although the Texas missionary enterprise seemed to have some life left to it in the coastal environs of La Bahía, conditions at Béxar were such that the Zacatecas College could no longer justify operating five stations there. With the college considering Fray Manuel Julio de Silva's ambitious proposal for converting all the coastal Indians from Nuevo Santander to the Mississippi, the college's resources would have to be redistributed. Although the plan ultimately foundered and only the Copano Bay mission, Nuestra Señora del Refugio, was built, the project set in motion the suppression process for the Texas missions.

Governor Manuel Muñoz received a new order for the suppression of San Antonio de Valero in February 1793. Suppression, or secularization, was the final stage in the life cycle of a mission and marked the successful transition of a new Christian community to parish status. Secularization was not a mark of failure, therefore, but of success for the religious, as it marked the formation of a permanent Catholic community. The goods and property of the mission were divided among the Indians, who had farmed communally and, except for a limited amount of self-governance, followed the directives of the friars. They were now considered adult Christians and full citizens in Spanish colonial society. Leftover land and water could be used by the community to attract additional settlers, in this case, the Adaesanos and other worthy San Antonio families, or held in reserve for the children of current families. In the spring of 1793, therefore, San Antonio de Valero became a separate civilian community (although, as far as religion was concerned, it became part of San Fernando parish).

On April 10, 1794, a year to the day from when secularization of Mission Valero began, Commandant General Pedro Nava issued a decree for the secularization of all missions more than ten years old in the Provincias Internas.

The order had two principal objectives. First, it was meant to address the complaints of ranchers, farmers, and mine owners throughout the region that the missions only served the interests of the friars, who had sole access to Indian labor. Suppression of missions would free up valuable and scarce water and land for the expanding civilian population. Second, a reduction in the number of missions would mean a real savings to the Crown, which had to provide each friar with an annual stipend. In addition, with the reduction in the cost of guards, escorts, and incidental expenses, the savings to the royal treasury would be substantial.

In Texas the decree meant closure, not only of the remaining four Béxar stations, but also of Espíritu Santo and Rosario. Typical of the confused and contradictory "enlightened" reform effort of the Spanish Bourbons, the decree gave the mission Indians their freedom, granting them all the rights and privileges enjoyed by *gente de razón* (rational people, that is, competent adults), while at the same time ordering governors to appoint local officials as *justicias* (magistrates) to oversee the activities and property of Indians, so that they would not be victimized or become lazy and debauched. The Indians were no longer under the supervision of the missionaries, who were now limited to looking after their spiritual welfare, yet they were not completely independent either.

Governor Muñoz was skeptical about whether secularization would be successful, particularly in the case of the La Bahía missions, where populations consisted of Indians only recently brought under instruction. Consequently, he decided to start with the four Béxar missions, where he carried out the distribution of property during summer 1794. Beginning at Espada, and moving northward to Capistrano, San José, and Concepción, he distributed land and chattels to the resident Indians, with most of the land set aside for future use. Concerned that there were still a few Indians under instruction, he divided responsibility for the mission residents between the justicias, who had authority over those Indians deemed civilized enough to participate in the new order, and the friars, who remained in charge of neophytes.

Nevertheless, it seems clear that the four missions continued much as they had in the past. The friars continued to exert considerable influence over the activities of the Indian residents. The residents continued to elect a governor and *alcalde* annually. The farming and animal husbandry that went on was mostly on a subsistence basis. Every once in a while a small group of Indians would appear at the gates of the mission compounds and come in for instruction. The one significant change was the steady growth in the number of settlers who occupied farm and ranch land in the vicinity of each mission. By the turn of the century, Concepción, Capistrano, and Espada all had a majority of non-Indian residents.

Having completed his work in Béxar, Governor Muñoz traveled to La Bahía early in the fall of 1794 to inspect the missions there. He found too few of the Indians at Espíritu Santo and Rosario ready for "civilized" life and so petitioned for a reprieve. It took until May 1797 for the commandant general to decide to grant the two La Bahía missions a five-year deferment from the secularization

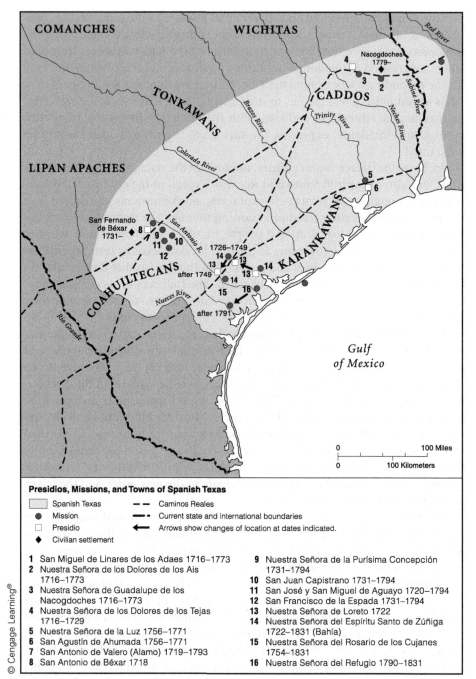

Presidios, Missions, and Towns of Spanish Texas

	Spanish Texas	– –	Caminos Reales
●	Mission	▬▬•—	Current state and international boundaries
□	Presidio	←	Arrows show changes of location at dates indicated.
◆	Civilian settlement		

1 San Miguel de Linares de los Adaes 1716–1773
2 Nuestra Señora de los Dolores de los Ais 1716–1773
3 Nuestra Señora de Guadalupe de los Nacogdoches 1716–1773
4 Nuestra Señora de los Dolores de los Tejas 1716–1729
5 Nuestra Señora de la Luz 1756–1771
6 San Agustín de Ahumada 1756–1771
7 San Antonio de Valero (Alamo) 1719–1793
8 San Antonio de Béxar 1718

9 Nuestra Señora de la Purísima Concepción 1731–1794
10 San Juan Capistrano 1731–1794
11 San José y San Miguel de Aguayo 1720–1794
12 San Francisco de la Espada 1731–1794
13 Nuestra Señora de Loreto 1722
14 Nuestra Señora del Espíritu Santo de Zúñiga 1722–1831 (Bahía)
15 Nuestra Señora del Rosario de los Cujanes 1754–1831
16 Nuestra Señora del Refugio 1790–1831

© Cengage Learning®

Presidios, missions, and towns of Spanish Texas.

decree. In that time Mission Nuestra Señora del Refugio, which had first been founded in 1793 as part of Fray Silva's project for the conversion of coastal Indians, had found a permanent home at the site of present-day Refugio. At the end of the eighteenth century the three La Bahía missions represented the only fully authorized Franciscan missions in the province.

The Birth of the Texas Cattle Kingdom

By the time secularization of the San Antonio missions began in 1793, all of the Franciscan establishments in the San Antonio River basin had long ceased to play an important role in the province's economy. In fact, because they controlled valuable irrigable farmland near Béxar and vast expanses of grazing land as far away as the coast, the missions stood in the way of progress. Although they had been instrumental in establishing the first successful livestock operations in Texas, by the 1780s the missions could no longer train or employ enough Indian herders to maintain themselves or challenge the increasingly aggressive civilian ranchers who were encroaching on mission ranch land.

The First Texas Ranches, 1720–1780

Stock raising had been an important economic activity from the very beginning in Spanish Texas. The early expeditions introduced herds of horses and cattle, and sometimes sheep and goats. In 1720, the Marqués de Aguayo brought thousands of head of stock, not only to supply his army, but also to help seed the presidios and missions he left in the wake of his expedition. One of the wealthiest ranchers in northern New Spain, he might have been using his visit to Texas to scout out the country for potential expansion of his haciendas. In the end, neither he nor any of the other great stockmen—sheep- and cattlemen known as *hacendados*—established operations as far north as Texas.

A few of the early military settlers managed to build up small herds. Mateo Pérez, an early soldier who died in 1748, left over 200 head of cattle and 50 horses in his will. Early soldiers Bernabé Carbajal and Francisco Hernández had herds large enough by the 1730s that they obtained grants of grazing land, but their operations were limited by the threat of Indian attacks and their own meager economic means. In fact, it was the very limitations of livestock raising that influenced use of the term *rancho* (originally a humble, mixed-farming property) rather than hacienda for Texas livestock properties.

It was the missions, particularly those at La Bahía and Béxar, that first developed herds and flocks large enough to require construction of ranch compounds. At first the mission herders, specially trained neophytes with civilians or soldiers acting as overseers, maintained their animals in the vicinity of the missions. As the herds grew, however, it became necessary to move them farther away. Except for Mission San José, which headquartered its operations south of Béxar on the Atascosa River, the other San Antonio missions established their ranches southeast of the settlement. East of these ranches, between the San Antonio and Guadalupe rivers, Mission Espíritu Santo claimed land in what are today Victoria, Goliad, DeWitt, Gonzales, and Karnes counties.

Of all the mission ranches established in Texas, the one that best illustrates the conflicts that arose between the missions, the civilians, and the government is Rancho de las Cabras (Goat Ranch), the livestock enterprise of Mission San Francisco de la Espada, and today a state historical park. By the 1740s the southernmost of the Béxar missions had established its pastures along the south bank of the San Antonio River opposite the present-day Floresville. The ranch was more than a goat ranch, however, as flocks of sheep and herds of cattle and horses also required the attention of a growing number of neophyte ranch hands (making these Indians among the earliest Texas cowboys). In time the operation grew to comprise an impressive complex of structures that were the envy of the area's civilian ranchers. From the extensive archaeological remains, we know that red sandstone walls enclosed a large compound that contained a sturdy stone chapel, dwellings for the ranch families, and utility buildings and corrals. For defensive purposes two *torreones* (towers) served as bastions at the northwest and southeast corners of the compound.

Although its stone walls could protect the residents of Rancho de las Cabras, nothing could protect the open range claimed by the mission from the assaults of both settlers and Indians. Following the 1749 treaty with the Apaches, a number of families with livestock interests moved into the countryside in force, claiming what pastures and watering places the missions had not reserved for themselves, and conflict soon arose. The missionaries charged that the so-called ranchers were moving next to the mission ranches in order to efficiently despoil the neophytes of their livestock. They argued that all the cattle in the countryside, branded and unbranded, belonged to their Indians because the missions had brought the first cattle to the area.

The ranchers responded that their parents and grandparents too had brought cattle and horses into the province. As one San Antonio alcalde reported to a Mexico City judge hearing a complaint from the missionaries: "this so distant Province could be no less populous than that of Saltillo, because its land is pleasingly fertile, with abundant places to take water, and fields and plains sufficient to receive and maintain large populations; but as these waters and lands are only diverted in order for the missions to make ranches, the nonholding vecinos do not benefit nor does His Majesty in that his dominions are not settled."

While the ownership issue slowly made its way through the courts and various layers of bureaucracy, Indian warfare had created a crisis situation. By 1772 only Ignacio de la Peña's ranch and Rancho de las Cabras had withstood the Indian assaults that had resulted in the destruction or abandonment of all the other operations in the area. Construction of a military post, Fuerte de Santa Cruz del Cíbolo, halfway between Béxar and La Bahía on Cíbolo Creek, was ineffective.

The fort was conceived by the Marqués de Rubí as a way to repopulate the area by offering immediate protection against Indian assaults. Governor Cabello, never happy with the location of the understaffed and overextended fort, eventually prevailed upon the commandant general to abandon and destroy it in 1782.

Governor Ripperdá had attempted to mediate the complaints of both camps, only to find himself the subject of complaints. When Commandant General Croix arrived in Béxar in January 1778 to hold his war council, he was forced to listen to days of grievances from governor, missionaries, and ranchers alike. Although the positions of friars and stockmen were similar—the unbranded stock belonged to them—the governor had a larger agenda. Ripperdá pointed out to Croix that the uncontrolled and indiscriminate slaughter and export of cattle from the province was bound to lead to its extinction. Also, here was a public source of wealth being exploited by people who paid no direct taxes to the Crown.

The commandant general responded by issuing what can be considered Texas's first environmental regulation. His ordinance of January 11, 1778, declared all unbranded stock property of the Crown, required licensing of all cattle exports from Texas, established a tax on all unbranded stock captured either for export or slaughter, and imposed heavy fines for the unlicensed slaughter of unbranded cattle. Through this measure Croix hoped to raise revenue from a

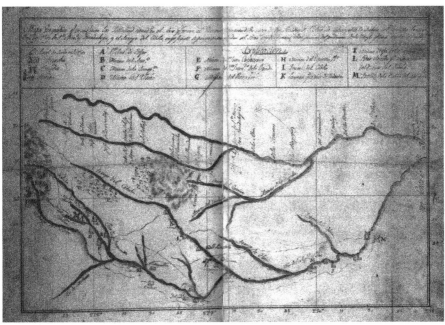

The Bureau of the Chief of Engineers, National Archives, College Park, MD

Governor Domingo Cabello drew up this map of the San Antonio–Guadalupe rivers basin, showing the location of settlements, missions, ranches, and roads between San Antonio and La Bahía.

province that had always been a drain on the royal coffers, protect the cattle population, and end the ownership dispute. The *mesteña* (unbranded stock) fund, as the livestock tax was commonly known, proved extremely controversial, and was challenged by all stock raisers in the province. Efforts by succeeding governors to control the consumption of breeding cows, a particularly detrimental practice, only served to increase animosities. Only in 1795 did one of Croix's successors, Pedro de Nava, reaffirm the measure, forgiving back taxes owed, but granting all legitimate stockmen just one year to gather *mesteño* cattle and horses before taxes were assessed again.

Governmental regulations putting missions on a par with ranchers in regard to unbranded stock contributed greatly to the demise of the Texas mission system. Continued Indian depredations and an inability to recruit neophytes took their toll on Rancho de las Cabras, which, although it still had twenty-six residents when Croix and Fray Morfi passed through on their way to La Bahía early in 1778, was already in decline. The murder of six to eight Espada herdsmen by raiding Indians in 1780–81 was an almost insurmountable loss, especially when hiring civilian cowboys cost one peso a day, the highest wage for any skilled work in colonial Texas. When Governor Cabello ordered a branding roundup in 1780, Rancho de las Cabras was unable to participate. In fact, Valero was the only Béxar mission able to field a roundup and branding crew; the rest of the participants were private ranchers.

Triumph of the Civilian Ranchers, 1780–1800

By the time Governor Cabello managed to negotiate a general peace with the Comanches and Norteños in 1785, the end of the mission ranches was in sight. Cabello's successor, Rafael Martínez Pacheco, who was sympathetic to the plight of all Texas stockmen, crafted a series of roundup agreements in 1787 that allowed the missions and ranchers to round up as many animals as they could within assigned territories. Fray Pedro Noreña, representing Espada, was optimistic that somehow he could field a crew and revive the fortunes of Rancho de las Cabras. Such was not the case, however. When Martínez Pacheco issued his final report on the roundups, neither Espada nor any of the other Béxar missions had managed to capture a single animal. Only Mission Espíritu Santo had branded cattle: 1,418 head, compared to 6,231 cattle and 183 horses branded by the ranchers.

Without neophyte *vaqueros* (cowboys) to maintain the mission's ranching interests, Espada's missionaries, along with the friars at the other missions, had long since begun to make compromises with encroaching stockmen, which led to the eventual transfer of Rancho de las Cabras to civilian ownership. Ignacio Calvillo had occupied land in the vicinity of Rancho de las Cabras as early as 1774, and had gained the mission's approval by 1778. Within three years he was the recognized owner of Rancho Paso de las Mugeres. Similarly, Juan Barrera, a native of Coahuila and tithe collector for Texas, moved into the area during the

1780s. He operated a ranch he called Santa Gertrudis, possibly only renting the land so he could pasture the stock he collected as *diezmero* (tithe collector). Soon after secularization the two men moved to complete their takeover of Rancho de las Cabras, Calvillo taking the upper portion of the mission ranch, including the site of the headquarters compound, and Barrera taking the lower portion, which came to be called Las Cabras Viejas. This process was repeated at the other San Antonio missions.

The return of mission grazing lands to the royal domain that accompanied suppression was the ultimate victory for the *vecino* stockmen of Béxar who had vied with the missions for control of this valuable asset for more than half a century. Ranchers won in two ways. First, they acquired large numbers of un-branded cattle that roamed the prairies of south-central Texas. Second, in the three decades following secularization, civilian stockmen moved onto the former mission ranches and claimed them for themselves.

By the turn of the century, ranching had become the principal economic activity of Texas, despite adverse climatic conditions, severe financial constraints, persistent though greatly diminished Indian raids on herds, and continued reliance on natural reproduction of the semiwild stock on the open range. At Béxar, where there were fourteen recognized ranch owners in 1791, there were thirty-five in 1810. Nacogdoches too saw a boom in ranching, particularly in horse breeding, during the 1790s, as the final collapse of the area's Caddo population left a number of clearings open for the taking. By 1810 there were more than twenty registered ranch owners in East Texas, including a number of Anglo and French Americans who had made their way into the area as authorized Indian traders, government agents, and squatters.

A Ranching Empire in the Lower Rio Grande Valley

By the time secularization of the Texas missions began in the 1790s, Nuevo Santander had become an even more successful ranching region than its neighbor to the north, Texas. No one knew this better than Rosa María Hinojosa de Ballí, matriarch of its most powerful ranching clan. From the various explorations of the region, José de Escandón had come to believe that this part of Nuevo Santander, which is sometimes referred to as the trans-Nueces, was best suited to a stock-farming way of life, and he had encouraged hacendados from Coahuila and Nuevo León to establish sheep and cattle operations in the region. With no missions to stand in the way of occupation, one of these hacendados, Captain Juan José Hinojosa, with his relatives, friends, and a select group of other families, fanned out from the Rio Grande settlements in the last three decades of the eighteenth century to establish ranches as far north as today's Nueces County.

Among these stockmen was militia captain José María Ballí, whose father had brought his family to Reynosa in the earliest days. Like other prominent heads of family, Ballí served as a militia officer as well as alcalde. By the late 1750s, the

Hinojosas and Ballís were two of six families, all interrelated, that controlled the economic and social life of Reynosa. The alliance between the two clans was further cemented through the marriage of Hinojosa's daughter Rosa María to Ballí, and during the 1770s and 1780s father-in-law and son-in-law worked as business partners to build up a ranching empire. The partnership included making joint application for a 37-sitio (166,500-acre) grant along the Rio Grande east of Hinojosa's *porciones* in the Reynosa jurisdiction.

Hinojosa must have seen something special in his daughter from early on. Unlike the vast majority of women in the Spanish world, including many elite women, Rosa María received an education under the direction of a local priest. Later, she received business training from her father and husband. As a result, upon their deaths in the late 1780s she was more than ready to handle the family's affairs. By age 38 she had become matriarch of the Ballí family and was known to many area residents as *la patrona* (the mistress).

Not only did she inherit property from her husband and her father, but she inherited their debts and obligations. Between 1790 and 1803, the year of her death, she reversed the family's financial fortunes and more than doubled its land holdings. In the process she became a pillar of the community, serving as witness to legal proceedings, becoming godmother for dozens of children born to friends and employees, and serving as lender to fellow ranchers and benefactor to the churches in Reynosa, Camargo, and Matamoros.

The Hinojosa–Ballí land empire was Doña Rosa's greatest accomplishment. A shrewd businessperson, she spent much of her time during the 1790s expanding upon the 12 sitios (54,000 acres) she inherited from her husband and her three-sitio inheritance from her father. On behalf of one son she applied for 72 sitios (324,000 acres) to the northeast of other family holdings, a grant known as San Salvador del Tule. As financier for her brother Vicente she obtained 12 sitios out of the 35-sitio Las Mesteñas grant she helped him obtain. In partnership with another son, Nicolás, a diocesan priest by calling, she acquired an interest in the lower portion of Isla de Santiago (now Padre Island). Purchases and other transactions brought tens of thousands of additional acres under her control, so that at the beginning of the nineteenth century the Ballís controlled about 1,000,000 acres of grazing lands in what are now Cameron, Hidalgo, Willacy, Kenedy, Kleberg, and Nueces counties.

These vast holdings were managed principally from Doña Rosa's headquarters on the La Feria estate. Like the other few major ranch owners in the region, she maintained one residence in town (in her case, Reynosa) and another at the ranch headquarters. Although some subsistence farming took place, the primary sources of income came from grazing horses, cattle, and sheep and leasing out pastures to landless or land-poor ranchers.

Despite her impressive accomplishments, Doña Rosa was representative of a society and an economic system that was land-rich, but money-poor. Many ranchers of the trans-Nueces owned little, if any, land at all, and grazed their small herds and flocks on the more marginal and isolated, as yet unclaimed, land

in the area. Others leased land from the better-off stockmen who were able to establish legal title to large tracts that often contained what little permanent water
was available in an area. The marginal quality of most unimproved land meant
that even the major stockmen, such as the Ballís, ran only a few thousand head of
all types of stock combined. With the relatively low prices the ranchers received
for the animals and by-products they produced, few ranchers had the means to
improve their production capabilities. For example, the obstacles to effectively
fencing the trans-Nueces range meant that selective improvement of stock was
impossible. Animals mated in the field, to be rounded up only for branding,
slaughter, or sale. The circumstances created a society made up of a few ranchers who had vast landholdings but limited wealth, a larger population of landless
stock owners who had neither land nor wealth, and an even larger sector of society that worked the land and stock of others.

Consequently, Doña Rosa María and the other leading ranchers were the *patrones* (masters) in a social system in which hierarchical relationships were all-
important. Patrones met the needs of their employees (sometimes referred to
as *peones*), and employees were expected to have unconditional loyalty to their
patrones. Especially at Reynosa, the large ranchers held the local political and
military posts, so their interests and concerns had a better chance of being addressed than those of the majority of the settlers, the *rancheros*, and the mestizos,
mulattoes, and Indians that made up the majority of the population.

Conclusion

In the last third of the eighteenth century Texas and neighboring Mexican provinces made considerable strides toward development. Rubí's reforms and the creation of the Comandancia General de las Provincias Internas reinforced Béxar
and La Bahía and even presented an opportunity for Tejano frontiersmen to
establish a civilian community in East Texas. All three settlements experienced
significant population and economic growth—none more so than Béxar, where
the increasing number of merchants and artisans attested to expanding market
opportunities.

The new policy of making war on the Apaches and accepting the autonomy
of other tribes eventually bore fruit. From the Spanish perspective, the best demonstration of the efficacy of the new policy was the spectacular defeat that Commandant General Juan de Ugalde and his troops and Indian auxiliaries inflicted
on over 300 Lipans, Lipiyans, and Mescaleros at Sabinal River canyon in 1790.
Peace with Norteños and Comanches allowed renewed expansion of the livestock industry, now without the obstacle of mission ranches. In the last third
of the eighteenth century Texas and the trans-Nueces became a cattle empire,
establishing a legacy for centuries to come.

At Paso del Norte, too, the reduction in Indian hostilities was noticeable in
a number of ways. Rapid population growth brought the number of residents in

the district to almost 6,000 by the end of the century. Economic activity on both sides of the river and along the Camino Real between the rest of New Mexico and the interior of New Spain increased to such a degree that the first permanent bridge across the Rio Grande—500 feet long and 17 feet wide—was in operation by 1800.

The birth of new ways to foster the development of the frontier brought the death of old ways. The missions, which had played such an important role in the permanent occupation of Texas, no longer had anything to offer. The Indians of Texas were either friendly to the Spaniards, had concluded that better trade relations and regular gifts from the Spaniards produced better results than raiding, or were sorely weakened enemies. Although young Apache, Comanche, and Norteño warriors sometimes tested their mettle by launching minor raids on cattle and horse herds, mechanisms were in place for resolving conflict without the terror of generations past.

Texas and surrounding areas were headed in the right direction, an observer at the end of the eighteenth century might have concluded. Population and economic growth were evident among both Spaniards and most of its Indian groups, the peace between the Norteños and Comanches and the Spaniards was holding, and the Apache menace seemed be under control. Then it happened: The nineteenth century blew in like a blue norther.

Suggested Readings

In the last third of the eighteenth century, Texas and all of northeastern New Spain again came under the scrutiny of royal officials eager to make the empire more efficient and defendable. The broad outline of this story, and Texas's place in it, is presented in Chapters 8 and 9 of David Weber's *The Spanish Frontier in North America*, and in Chapters 10 and 11 of John Kessell's *Spain in the Southwest*. Works from the first half of the twentieth century remain our best English-language sources for the two most important figures in frontier reform efforts: *José de Gálvez, Visitor General of New Spain, 1765–1771* by Herbert I. Priestly (1916, 1980) and *Teodoro de Croix and the Northern Frontier of New Spain, 1776–1783* by Alfred B. Thomas (1941). The economic expansion of New Spain, from which Texas benefited only marginally, is well covered by David A. Brading in *Miners and Merchants in Bourbon Mexico, 1763–1810* (1971). Donald Chipman continues the story of Texas during this time frame in Chapters 9 and 10 of *Spanish Texas, 1519–1821*.

Effects of Spanish Louisiana on the Northeastern Frontier

Reform had to be based on firsthand knowledge, and so the Marqués de Rubí, on instructions from José de Gálvez, set out in 1766 on an inspection tour of the Indian frontier from the Gulf of California to the Gulf of Mexico. The Texas portion of his travels is covered in Jackson and Foster, *Imaginary Kingdom*.

A second opinion on Texas appears in *The Frontiers of New Spain: Nicolas de Lafora's Description, 1766–1768*, ed. Lawrence Kinnaird (1958). V. A. Vincent discusses the consequences of the Rubí inspired regulations of 1772 in "The Frontier Soldier: Life in the Provincias Internas and the Royal Regulations of 1772, 1766–1787," *Military History of the Southwest* (1992). Among recent works dealing with rise of Comanche and Norteño dominance in Texas, two stand out: *Comanche Empire* (2008) by Pekka Hämäläinen and *The Wichita Indians: Traders of Texas and the Southern Plains, 1540–1845* (2000) by F. Todd Smith. Also valuable for understanding Spanish–Indian relations during this period are the first two chapters of Smith's *From Dominance to Disappearance: The Indians of Texas and the Near Southwest, 1786–1859* (2005) and the second half of *Storms Brewed in Other Men's Worlds: The Confrontation of Indians, Spanish, and French in the Southwest, 1540–1795* (1975) by Elizabeth A. H. John.

The Death and Rebirth of Spanish East Texas

The reorganization of Texas and the restructuring of Spanish–Indian relations fell to a high-born Spanish governor and two frontiersmen, one a native of East Texas and the other a long-time resident of French Louisiana. Although the Spaniard, Governor Barón de Ripperdá, has yet to receive the separate attention he deserves, his role in the abandonment of Los Adaes and establishment of Bucareli is covered well in the chapters on "Athanase de Mézières" and "Marqués de Rubí/Antonio Gil Ibarbo" in Chipman and Joseph, *Notable Men and Women of Spanish Texas*. Ripperdá's successor, Governor Domingo Cabello, does get his own chapter in the same book. On the development of Nacogdoches as the heterogenous center of Spanish East Texas, see Patrick J. Walsh, "Living on the Edge of the Neutral Zone: Varieties of Identity in Nacogdoches, Texas 1773–1810," *East Texas Historical Journal* (1999).

Sunset for the Missions

The secularization of the Texas missions was a drawn-out process that only began in the 1790s. As with other subjects in Spanish Texas history, most work has focused on the San Antonio area. The process of secularization in the context of rivalry between mission communities and the civilian population of Texas is treated in Félix D. Almaráz, Jr., "San Antonio's Old Franciscan Missions: Material Decline and Secular Avarice in the Transition from Hispanic to Mexican Control," *Americas* (1987). A missionary's view of the need for secularization at San Antonio is presented in "Report on the San Antonio Missions in 1792," ed. Benedict Leutenegger and Marion A. Habig, *Southwestern Historical Quarterly* (1974). Although secularized, the San Antonio missions survived as living communities with their own folklore, essential portions of which were gathered by Adina de Zavala early in the twentieth century and published under the title *History and Legends of the Alamo and Other Missions in and around San Antonio* (reprint, 1996).

The Birth of the Texas Cattle Kingdom

Given the state's heritage of cattle-raising, it is not surprising that a number of authors have addressed the Hispanic elements of the Texas livestock industry. An exhaustive narrative history, focusing on political struggles among civilians, missionaries, and royal officials is Jack Jackson, *Los Mesteños: Spanish Ranching in Texas, 1721–1821* (1986). Much shorter and focusing on the practices and institutions is *The Ranch in Spanish Texas, 1691–1800* by Sandra L. Myres (1969). The difficulties of creating a safe environment for cattle operations in Spanish Texas is one of the principal subjects of *El Fuerte del Cíbolo: Sentinel of the Béxar-La Bahía Ranches*, by Robert H. Thonhoff (1992). For South Texas, Armando Alonzo's *Tejano Legacy* and Omar S. Valerio-Jiménez's *River of Hope: Forging Identity and Nation in the Rio Grande Borderlands* (2013) provide the best understanding of the development of society in the region.

New Neighbors, New Challenges, 1800–1821

Benito de Armiñán, interim governor of Texas in the spring of 1814, had an impossible task to perform. In the aftermath of the royalist victory over the latest rebellion in the province, families had been broken up by the death or flight of husbands, fathers, and sons; crops had been destroyed or consumed by the contending forces; and the little commerce the province enjoyed had been subject to disruption by Indian attack. Ill and depressed Armiñán sat down to write his superior, Commandant General Joaquín Arredondo, to explain why he might have to resort to violence to keep his men fed if higher authorities did not see fit to send relief immediately. "They are hopelessly lost in their misery. They have been weakened by their past misfortunes. They are complaining most piteously over the lack of sustenance for themselves and their families. They are lamenting over the crisis and weeping bitterly over their fate—especially when they remember the terrible misery which lies before them." Relief did not come for Armiñán and it did not come for his successors. What did come were American and European adventurers, pirates, and Indian raiders who made life as precarious for Texas's Spanish settlements as it had been at the height of the Indian wars of the 1770s and 1780s. The news that Spain and the United States had agreed on a border that respected Spanish claims to Texas was of little consolation to frontier officials or the surviving Tejano population. A decade of destruction and terror had left them so "hopelessly lost in their misery" that they greeted Mexican independence with no great jubilation. Rather, they began to heal the wounds that had divided families; they began to think about hoping again.

The first two decades of the nineteenth century were marked by a level of violence and destruction in Texas that came close to extinguishing the Hispanic presence there. In 1800, Napoleon Bonaparte forced Spain to cede Louisiana as

Chapter 4 New Rivals, New Challenges, 1800–1821	
1800	Napoleon forces Spain to return Louisiana to French control
1801	Philip Nolan killed during his fourth trip to Texas since 1791 when he resists Spanish efforts to arrest him for spying
1802	Lipans successfully attack a Kotsoteka encampment, Comanches fear Spanish–Lipan alliance
1803	Louisiana Purchase
1805	Baron of Bastrop proposes to colonize Texas with Louisiana families
1806	Neutral Ground Agreement between Col. Herrera and Gen. Wilkinson averts war between Spain and the United States over Texas; town of Santísima Trinidad de Salcedo founded
1808	Town of San Marcos de Neve founded; Wichita and Comanche tribes receive American traders led by Anthony Glass
1810	Father Hidalgo launches revolt against Spanish rule
1811	Casas Revolt in Texas fails; Father Hidalgo executed
1812	Gutiérrez–Magee expedition begins invasion of Texas
1813	Texas independence proclaimed; Gen. Arredondo defeats Republican Army of the North at Battle of Medina
1815	Rebels under Father Morelos declare Mexican independence; insurgents and pirates occupy Galveston Island
1817	Battle of Three Trees drives Karankawas from Galveston Island
1818	French settlement Champ d'Asile fails
1819	Adams–Onís Treaty recognizes Spanish title to Texas; James Long launches first expedition to liberate Texas for the United States
1820	Moses Austin proposes to colonize Texas with Catholic families from the United States
1821	Mexico gains independence; second Long expedition fails; Cherokee chief Duwali's followers establish villages in East Texas

part of his plan to resurrect a French empire in North America. When the plan fell through, he sold the territory to the United States in 1803. While Spain and the United States almost came to blows over U.S. claims to everything east of the Rio Grande as part of the Louisiana Purchase, the outbreak of the Mexican War of Independence led to insurrections in Texas on numerous occasions, including the overthrow of Texas's Spanish governor twice. The bloodiest battle ever fought on Texas soil occurred in 1813 and led to the death or flight of over a thousand Tejanos, leaving Nacogdoches virtually abandoned and San Antonio in ruins. The arrival of pirates and adventurers added to the tense conditions in Spanish Texas.

For the Indian peoples of the region, the opening decades of the decade were also a time of great changes—creating opportunities for some and spelling the demise of others. For the Norteños, and the Comanches in particular, the in ability of Spanish officials to maintain the supply of gifts required by the treaties of the 1780s meant a resumption of raiding. Other indigenous groups that suffered in continuing rounds of epidemics and intertribal warfare, disappeared from much of East Texas, leaving the way open for migrant Indian groups from east of the Mississippi, which hoped to find safe haven from American settlers in Spanish Texas. These new arrivals, like the remaining indigenous tribes, paid scant attention to the international borders that both the Spanish Crown and the U.S. government contested.

Texas governors after Armiñán faced the same insurmountable problems he did, as did Spanish officials along the Rio Grande in Nuevo Santander and New Mexico. The last years of Spain's presence in the region were marked by a desperate bid for survival that failed. The remaining Tejanos, whose homeland was Texas, hunkered down to outlast the evil times as their ancestors had in the previous century. Only the Comanches seemed to thrive in the endemically violent circumstance as Spanish Texas emerged the poorest and most sparsely settled portion of the new Mexican nation.

As you read this chapter, consider the following questions:

1. What made the Louisiana Purchase a critical event in Texas history?
2. What conditions in Mexico contributed to the outbreak of a war for independence and what circumstances contributed to Texas taking part in the struggle?
3. How did conditions in the last years of Spanish Texas contribute to the idea of the region as a "howling wilderness"?

Louisiana Once Again a Contested Frontier

In 1800 no one in Texas or Mexico City, or even in Madrid, could have foreseen the chain of events that left the Spanish Empire in ruins and Texas nominally a part of an independent Mexico. For more than a decade New Spain had fought against U.S. expansionism along the Mississippi River and its eastern tributaries. Although the situation was precarious, it was not out of control.

Spanish officials recognized U.S. expansionism as a dangerous successor to British imperialism and moved to counter the threat with the meager resources at their disposal. Beginning in the 1780s local officials took matters into their own hands and allowed Protestant families to settle in Louisiana. In time they were joined by other Anglo-Americans interested in the economic opportunities available in Spanish Missouri, Natchez, and Louisiana. Spanish officials in Florida and Louisiana also took advantage of Indian dissatisfaction with Anglo-American pioneers to keep the United States at bay. A number of southeastern tribes took refuge on the Spanish side of the border or conducted raids against intruding Anglo-American settlers with the support of local Spanish authorities. Slavery was legal in the Spanish world, but slaves from U.S. territory were granted their freedom in Spanish Florida and Louisiana, an issue that became a particular sore point in Spanish–U.S. relations.

After Spain was drawn into the French Revolution and the Napoleonic wars, it proved impossible to maintain adequate commercial contacts with its American empire or to properly defend it against outside threats. As tensions over trade, Indian relations, and slave flight mounted, Madrid forestalled a direct confrontation with Washington by entering into the Treaty of San Lorenzo in 1795. By the terms of the treaty, U.S. citizens enjoyed navigation rights on the Mississippi River and the right to use New Orleans as a trans-shipment port for their products. In addition, both countries would restrain the Indians on their side of the border from conducting depredations on the other side.

Numerous Anglo-American and European entrepreneurs saw great opportunities in Spain's desperate effort to reinforce Louisiana and Texas in the face of U.S. expansion. Some had big schemes, like Pennsylvania Dutch innkeeper Pedro Paulus, who offered to settle 3,000 families on condition that they have freedom of worship, local self-government, and generous land allotments. (His plan never amounted to anything.) Some had more modest ambitions, like William Barr, another Irish immigrant who became a Spanish subject in Louisiana before moving to Nacogdoches in 1793. Barr established himself as an Indian trader and entered into partnership with Natchitoches merchant Peter Samuel Davenport. The House of Barr and Davenport gained a monopoly on Indian trade in northern Texas. Barr died a wealthy man in 1810. By the last decade of the eighteenth century, then, Texas was becoming a destination for foreign adventurers and businessmen who would leave their stamp on the state's history.

Adventurer Philip Nolan: Horse Trader or Spy?

It was in these circumstances that adventurers like Philip Nolan and the self-styled Baron of Bastrop, made their way to the Louisiana–Texas frontier. The two men could not have been more different. As a young man Philip Nolan had emigrated from Ireland to the western frontier of the new United States, where he became a protégé of General James Wilkinson. The American military man, who maintained very friendly relations with the Spaniards (at one point in his career he was actually employed by the Spanish Crown), soon had Nolan acting as his business agent in New Orleans.

While in the Louisiana capital, the twenty-year-old Irish American learned about the Indian trade opportunities in Texas, which led in 1791 to the first of a number of trips there for him. Officially, commercial contacts between Texas and Louisiana were forbidden under Spain's tightly regulated mercantile system. Despite a series of reforms intended to expand trading opportunities among its various American colonies, Spain's mercantilist policies remained the most restrictive of the European empires—on paper. In reality, an inefficient and corrupt customs and administrative system meant that contraband, graft, and incompetence were rife. At the time of the American Revolution the Spanish Crown had consented to a limited livestock trade between Texas and Louisiana, and it was this authorization that adventurers like Nolan took advantage of in order to trade with Texas Indians. The governor of Spanish Louisiana did not think twice about giving Nolan a passport to gather livestock in Texas.

To Texas authorities Nolan's trading license was not valid. They suspected the Irish-American tradesman of being a spy, a contrabandist, or both, and officials in Nacogdoches confiscated his merchandise. Financially ruined and in no hurry to return to Louisiana, Nolan chose to spend some time living with various Texas Indian tribes, among them the Comanches. Although Nolan claimed that "the freedom, the independence of the savage life was always congenial to my nature," he also admitted that he could not completely "indianify."

Between 1794 and 1799 Nolan made two more successful trading expeditions to Texas. It was not just the province's Indians who welcomed the opportunity to trade for the higher-quality manufactured goods that Nolan's company brought with him: Tejanos also did business—illegally—with the American. (And not just business, as Nolan fathered a son in San Antonio during one of his visits.) He eventually sold the horses, hides, and furs he collected in Texas as far east as Frankfort, Kentucky, attracting even more interest among American frontiersmen in the Texas trade.

Nolan had caught Texas fever, but he had also caught the attention of Spanish authorities. Their suspicions were confirmed when he returned to Texas in the fall of 1800 leading a large body of men despite the Louisiana governor having denied him a new license. A deserter from the expedition, Mordecai Richards, later declared that Nolan "had maps of all the rivers, marked all the distances, and explored everything more attentively than a man would do who had no other ends in view than that of catching horses—that he had told him many times that there were mines in this country, and moreover that he had assured his men that if the Spaniards killed a single one of them he would take a commission as an English general . . . and would take possession of all this country."

It was not one of his men, but Nolan himself who died at the hands of the Spaniards. He had built corrals and begun catching horses and trading with Wichita and Comanche bands in what is now Hill County, but a Spanish patrol caught up with him in March 1801. After Nolan was killed by a cannonball, his men quickly surrendered, claiming that their only goal had been to capture mustangs. Authorities remained unconvinced, however.

Businessman, the Baron of Bastrop: Would-Be Colonizer

Another adventurer who eventually turned to Texas for new opportunities was the Baron of Bastrop. A native of Dutch Guiana, Philip Hendrik Nering Bögel had moved to Holland as a child and had become a tax collector. Accused of embezzlement in 1793, he fled the country, adopting the title by which he would henceforth be known. After arriving in Louisiana in 1795 he undertook a variety of business ventures, including real estate development, all with only minor success.

Bastrop's land schemes began shortly after his arrival in Louisiana, when he received permission from the governor to settle families along the Ouachita River. During a recruiting trip to the United States in 1797, a new governor arrived in Louisiana who opposed settlement by Protestant Anglo-Americans and suspended Bastrop's project. Seeing his land schemes evaporate, Bastrop turned to the Indian trade as a means of recovering his fortunes. Although he obtained a contract to supply the Indians along the Ouachita River with merchandise, the sale of Louisiana to the United States in 1803 brought an end to his monopoly and to his profits.

Bastrop, like a number of other Louisiana land promoters, now turned his attention to Texas. Bearing a letter of recommendation from his friend, the former governor of Louisiana, in the fall of 1805 he arrived in San Antonio, where he proposed to establish a colony between Béxar and the Trinity River. The settlers would be some of the families he had previously brought to Louisiana along with friendly and agricultural Choctaws. Having learned his lesson from the Ouachita project, he pledged to introduce only Catholic families.

Both Texas governor Antonio Cordero and Commandant General Nemecio Salcedo thought the project worth pursuing, as it fit with their plans to expand settlement in Texas to counter U.S. occupation of Louisiana. Immediately after the territory's transfer to the United States, President Thomas Jefferson, basing his position on French documents, had claimed that all the lands as far as the Rio Grande were included in the purchase. Spanish colonial authorities, facing what the baron called the "daring land-hunger of the infamous class of Americans" along with Jefferson's claims, naturally grasped at the colonization proposals of Bastrop and other Louisianians in order to create a first line of defense in Texas. Although Bastrop's initial project fell through, the baron soon settled in San Antonio, where he became a leading member of the community.

Neutral Ground

Whatever disappointment Governor Cordero felt about the results of Bastrop's mission could not have measurably added to the distress he already suffered. In 1805 U.S. troops had arrived in the vicinity of Natchitoches and asserted U.S. claims to the area. By early 1806 both sides were convinced that the other was preparing for war. In March President Jefferson reported to the U.S. Congress: "Some time since, however, we learnt that the Spanish authorities were advancing into the disputed country to occupy new posts and make new settlements."

Jefferson responded by ordering U.S. troops to chase out the Spanish detachment that Governor Cordero had ordered to occupy the Los Adaes district, in response to which the Texas governor ordered the militia to reinforce Nacogdoches.

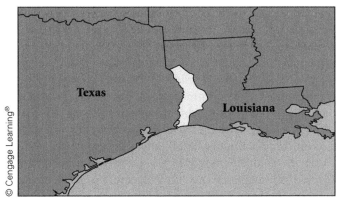

The "Neutral Ground." Following the 1719–1720 "Chicken War" France did not challenge Spain's claim that Texas extended to the Arroyo Hondo. Between 1763 and 1800 the issue was moot, as Spain controlled both sides of the boundary. The agreement reached between commanders in the field James Wilkinson and Simón Herrera laid the groundwork for the Neutral Ground to become part of the Louisiana Purchase under the Adams–Onís Treaty in 1819.

To defuse the situation Commandant General Nemecio Salcedo proposed establishing a neutral ground between Natchitoches and the Sabine River while the boundary between United States and Spanish territory was negotiated.

To these developments were added the complications of the Aaron Burr conspiracy and U.S. reconnaissance of the Red River country. Dissatisfied with his prospects in the United States, Burr, the volatile former vice president, developed a scheme with a number of associates to separate the trans-Appalachian states from the Union and combine them with the Louisiana Purchase and the silver mining region of northern New Spain into a great empire. As soon as rumors of Burr's scheme reached Salcedo, he advised Cordero "it is a very grave matter . . . that some 10,000 men, subjects of the United States, are being prepared in Kentucky with the object of overpowering the uninhabited provinces of this kingdom and our Indian allies, with no respect for the boundaries of Louisiana. You will, therefore, take extraordinary precautions toward putting the country in a good state of defense by bringing up all the auxiliaries."

The commandant general's response to another incident was even more confrontational. In the spring of 1806 an exploratory expedition under Major Thomas Freeman began to ascend the Red River. When he received news of this obvious violation of Spanish territory, Commandant General Salcedo issued orders to stop the expedition from continuing westward. Freeman had managed to travel 600 miles up the Red River before he was confronted by a large Spanish detachment and decided to turn back.

Throughout these months the Spanish had been reinforcing the small Texas garrisons with auxiliary units from other provinces. First to arrive was a light cavalry unit from Coahuila known as the Second Flying Company of San Carlos del Alamo de Parras. The unit arrived in Béxar in 1803 and occupied the abandoned buildings of Mission San Antonio de Valero, lending its name to the site, which would ever after be known as the Alamo. Militia units from Nuevo Santander and Nuevo León brought total troop strength in the province to over 1,000 by early summer.

Despite growing war hysteria along the U.S. frontier and the troop buildup on the Texas side, cooler heads prevailed. Wilkinson arrived unopposed at the Sabine River on October 29 and immediately sent a message to the Texas governor proposing an agreement by which the Spaniards would not recross the Sabine and the Americans would retreat to Natchitoches and not recross the Arroyo Hondo until the boundary had finally been negotiated. While Cordero hesitated, Lieutenant Colonel Simón Herrera seized the moment and on his own authority accepted Wilkinson's terms. On November 5, 1806, at the U.S. Army camp on the Sabine, General Wilkinson and Inspector Francisco Viana signed what came to be called the Neutral Ground Agreement. Cordero could now turn his attention to preparing the rest of Texas for what he was sure would be an inevitable onslaught of Anglo-Americans.

Fortress Texas: Reinforcing against the American Threat

Governor Cordero and his superiors knew that troops alone could not hold the province. Defending the Texas frontier of New Spain from the land-hungry Anglo-Americans would depend on increasing the population. The times seemed propitious for a concerted population drive as Spanish subjects in Louisiana deserted what was now U.S. territory and relative peace reigned between most of Texas's indigenous peoples and their Spanish colonial neighbors. Between 1805 and the outbreak of the Mexican War of Independence in 1810, there was reason for hope among the long-suffering Tejanos that this might be their day in the sun.

Antonio Cordero y Bustamante had been thrown into a difficult situation, but this was not the first time in his long and successful career as a frontier officer. Born in Cadiz, Spain, in 1753, he had come to New Spain as a cadet and soon found himself fighting Indians on the northern frontier. He distinguished himself in campaigns against various western Apache tribes before being assigned to the Coahuila theater of action in 1795. Throughout this time he strengthened presidio defenses and organized new settlements, activities that he continued after becoming governor of Coahuila in 1798. Commandant General Nemecio Salcedo turned to the popular Cordero in the summer 1805 to assume the reins of command in Texas. It would be up to Cordero to make sense of the increasingly chaotic situation.

Challenges and Opportunities for the Development of Texas

The interim governor could see that there was much work to do in Texas. Formal settlement remained confined to San Antonio de Béxar, the capital of the province, the presidio-mission complex of La Bahía del Espíritu Santo, and the village of Nacogdoches. Of these population centers Béxar was by far the largest, containing over 2,000 men, women, and children, the other two having roughly 900 Tejanos each. Also during the 1790s an informal settlement of 100 to 200 persons, at least some of whom were involved in contraband trade, had begun to form at Bayou Pierre in the old Los Adaes district. In addition, in 1803 the Alamo company added considerably to the military population of the province and put Cordero's available fighting strength at about 350 soldiers when he arrived in Texas.

Cordero also inherited the difficult problem of Louisiana émigrés. The Baron of Bastrop was not the only Louisiana subject of His Catholic Majesty who sought to start a new life in Spanish Texas. A number of individuals and families petitioned for Texas land. Commandant General Salcedo, suspicious as a result of the U.S. claim that Texas was part of the Louisiana Territory, allowed the settlement of people who could prove their loyalty to the Crown. Cordero absolutely forbid the admission of Anglo-Americans, as they seemed intent on undermining Spanish–Indian relations on the frontier.

As for the Indian peoples in Texas, Governor Cordero might perceive continued challenges to Spanish sovereignty in some but opportunities in others. Some groups were in decline and facing extinction, others were expanding, and there were opportunities for new arrivals. By the early nineteenth century many Coahuiltecan bands had died out completely as separate culture groups. A similar trend was evident among the elusive Tonkawas of central Texas, who at several hundred tribe members, were at least holding out better than the Bidai and Akokisa, who numbered no more than 100 or 200. The Caddo speakers of East Texas had also experienced drastic drops in number, most tribes consisting of no more than a few hundred individuals. Many villages had been abandoned and their surviving members had moved in with Caddo relatives on the Louisiana side of the frontier. Even in their declining numbers, these groups still posed challenges to Spanish governance, although Cordero had even bigger Indian concerns.

For Cordero the Indians requiring serious attention were the various Apache, Wichita, and Comanche tribes that still ranged freely on the western peripheries of Spanish Texas. The combined pressure of Comanches and Norteños on the Apaches had forced the Lipans southward until, by the end of the eighteenth century, they inhabited a territory south of San Antonio and stretching into northern Coahuila. There Mescaleros and Lipans made peace with each other and, finally, with Spanish colonials, whose main complaints continued to be loss of livestock to young raiding warriors.

More formidable were the Comanches and Wichitas. Their commercial contacts with Louisiana and New Mexico, their large numbers, and their dominance of the southern plains required Spanish officials to deal with them as equals. Governor Cordero continued the successful policy of peace by purchase, but faced a new challenge in Anglo-American tradesmen who moved onto the southern plains in an effort to gain the friendship—economic and political—of these peoples. Numbering in the thousands, mobile and militarized, they represented autonomous societies that belied Spain's assertions of complete sovereignty in the region.

Another type of Indian challenge developed at this time in the form of immigrant tribes from U.S. territory, which for Cordero may well have represented an opportunity to strengthen the border. Spain's rivalry with the United States made Texas an attractive destination for groups seeking to escape Anglo-American control. Small bands of Indians from a number of tribes began making their way into Spanish territory during the 1790s, particularly into the eastern part of the province, where the decline of the indigenous communities had left a considerable amount of land suitable for settlement. Among the immigrant tribes that Cordero had to deal with during his service in Texas were bands of Alabamas, Apalaches, Biloxis, Coushattas, Pascagoulas, and Shawnees. Welcoming such groups, which did not represent a menace to the Tejano population, might help stabilize the border situation in Spain's favor.

Defensive Colonization

Under the circumstance, there was no doubt that Texas also needed reinforcing with Hispanic settlers, and Cordero concluded that settlement should concentrate on the Camino Real between Nacogdoches and San Antonio. Occupation of strategic sites along the road would expedite communications within the province and make it easier for the new settlers to transport their goods. By the end of September 1805 Governor Cordero was requesting permission to found towns on the Trinity and Brazos rivers with a mix of native Tejanos and Louisiana émigrés. In December 1805 five families from Béxar that had been recruited for the project were on their way to the Trinity, where they discovered a group of Louisiana émigrés waiting for them. Early in 1806 they founded the town of Santísima Trinidad de Salcedo, most often referred to as Salcedo, under the supervision of a military officer from Béxar. By late January, titles to house lots and agricultural land were being issued, and construction began on a number of buildings. So successful was this first settlement effort under Cordero that families from Nacogdoches petitioned for permission to relocate to the new town.

Despite Salcedo's approval of Cordero's initial settlement plan, the two men did not see eye to eye on how best to utilize the growing pool of immigrants. In particular, Cordero saw the Louisianians, many of whom wished to remain in the Nacogdoches area, as the only means to populate East Texas in the absence of any significant migration from the interior of New Spain. This was especially important as the Tejano population of that part of the province was unable to supply provisions to the growing number of troops. Salcedo, concerned about the ever-present contraband problem and suspicious of the loyalties of many of the new arrivals, refused to allow them to locate permanently east of the Trinity.

His superior having made clear his hard line on settlement in the Nacogdoches region, Governor Cordero turned his attention to promoting new settlements farther west. He now requested permission to found towns on the Colorado, Guadalupe, and San Marcos crossings of the Camino Real, a request that was granted by the commandant general. The first and only one of the three towns that was actually established was San Marcos de Neve. Cordero worked out a deal with Felipe Roque de la Portilla, a fellow army officer from Spain who had seen service in Nuevo Santander. In return for a large land grant and a sizable subvention to the families he recruited, Portilla gathered a group of followers and a substantial number of animals and brought them to San Marcos in April 1808.

Of the five authorized settlements in Texas only Salcedo and San Marcos were established. Unlike Salcedo, which was made up of Bexareños and Louisianians, San Marcos was settled mostly by families from below the Rio Grande. Whereas Salcedo enjoyed military protection from the beginning, San Marcos had no garrison and was therefore exposed to Indian depredations. Salcedo enjoyed modest growth until its abandonment, but San Marcos attracted no new settlers after the first few months. Both ultimately suffered the same fate, however, falling victim to the warfare that engulfed Texas during the Mexican War of Independence and being completely abandoned by the fall of 1813.

Last Efforts at Reform

In the summer of 1808, much to Cordero's relief, his replacement arrived. The new governor turned out to be none other than Nemecio Salcedo's thirty-two-year-old nephew, Manuel María de la Concepción Josef Agustín Eloy de Salcedo y Quiroga. Despite his young age, Manuel came with considerable experience: he had assisted his father, who had served as the last Spanish governor of Louisiana. To assume his post, Manuel Salcedo and his family had traveled by way of the United States, landing at New Bedford, Massachusetts, going on to New York City, then to Philadelphia and Pittsburgh, Pennsylvania. Riverboat travel down the Ohio and Mississippi rivers brought them to Natchez. From there they traveled by coach to Natchitoches. In Natchitoches, Salcedo met with U.S. government officials before proceeding to Nacogdoches, where he arrived in early October 1808. By the time he reached the Texas capital at Béxar at the end of the month, Salcedo must have been fully aware of the challenges that confronted him.

Manuel Salcedo took over the most exposed province of a colony under assault. Not only had Texas territory been compromised through establishment of the Neutral Ground Agreement in 1806, but the United States continued to claim the Rio Grande as the true boundary of the Louisiana Purchase. Also, various foreign agents had penetrated the province before his arrival. One of these, Zebulon Montgomery Pike, had succeeded in crossing the southern plains to arrive in New Mexico early in 1807. Treated well by the Spaniards, he collected considerable information on the state of Spanish defenses on the northern frontier, including conditions in Texas, through which he passed on his return to Louisiana. A year later another foreign adventurer, the Napoleonic agent Octaviano D'Alvimar, crossed from Louisiana into Texas with instructions to sow insurrection in New Spain. Captured by Texas troops, he was brought before Governor Cordero, who shipped him off to the interior before he could cause much harm to Spanish interests. The presence of runaway slaves and U.S. Army deserters also added to tensions.

The aggressive moves of the United States along the border were only one concern for Salcedo, who also had to consider recent events in Spain and Mexico City. Napoleon had forced the abdication of the Spanish Bourbon King Charles IV and his son Ferdinand VII in favor of his brother Joseph Bonaparte. That move had met with resistance both in Spain and throughout the empire. From Mexico City had come news of an abortive move by the colonial capital's *criollo* elite to take over the government, an effort that had been frustrated by the powerful resident *peninsulares*. The peninsulares replaced a pro-criollo viceroy with one of their own. Eventually word arrived that a revolutionary *Cortes* (parliament) in Spain had declared the empire a constitutional monarchy. Traditional lines of authority were being disrupted, the legitimacy of the Crown was being questioned, and misinformation and disinformation were rife.

Conditions, therefore, were ripe for an Anglo-American move against Texas, and Salcedo pleaded for reinforcements and extensive economic investment in the province. His request was grounded in what he perceived to be essentially a problem of political economy. Like his predecessor, Salcedo considered the government responsible for existing conditions because it had failed to provide the necessary resources with which Tejanos could develop the province.

> The industry of these inhabitants is nonexistent, because neither have they had nor do they have elements for it. And one even marvels at how most of them cultivate their lands without the necessary farming tools by substituting for them as best they can, how some have built houses without artisans and how others suffer the rigorous cold and hot weather in those homes that they have made with sticks and shed-roofs of straw, and lastly at how in this poverty they have been able to dress themselves and their families, since this province has no other port of entry than that of Veracruz distant more than five hundred leagues.

Certainly there was some exaggeration in the governor's description of the situation, but not much. A few families at San Antonio and a few at La Bahía and Nacogdoches were living above a subsistence level, enjoying the meager profits of the livestock trade, an occasional sale of provisions to the local military, or participation in contraband activities. The province's few artisans could not practice their crafts on a regular basis, but relied on subsistence agriculture to make ends meet. If not for the military payrolls, there would have been practically no business for the few legitimate merchants, who themselves combined a variety of economic pursuits and credit schemes to keep their doors open and their families fed.

Texas presidial troops at the beginning of the nineteenth century remained an Indian fighting force poorly equipped to handle a well-armed adversary. Smooth bore carbines and pistols, often in disrepair, were considered less reliable than the lance, short sword, and shield. Added protection from arrows came from a leather jacket with cotton padding.

Governor Salcedo's plans required money and more communication between Texas and the outside world, of course, and Commandant General Salcedo was not in a position to grant the former or allow the latter. A port at Matagorda Bay would only create increased opportunities for smuggling and illegal immigration from Louisiana. The expense of raising, equipping, and maintaining the kind of force Governor Salcedo proposed was impossible. No, Texas would have to get by on what it already had.

Short of resources (his uncle would not even permit him to hire a secretary), Governor Salcedo took up the task of reforming the frontier province in every imaginable way. He issued orders on the proper preparation and filing of legal documents and he attempted to increase the efficiency of the mail system. He re-organized troop deployments, hoping to put soldiers lacking weapons to work on military construction projects for which no labor funds were available. Officials at La Bahía and Nacogdoches were snowed under by Governor Salcedo's constant requests for information and detailed instructions on just about every issue. In particular, they had to adjust to the commandant general's change of heart regarding immigrants, as the governor ordered that former Spanish subjects from Louisiana were to be received openly and warmly in Texas.

At Béxar, Governor Salcedo took a personal hand in bringing order to a people that previous governors had considered unruly and untrustworthy. He issued ordinances on everything from the licensing of midwives to the licensing of ox carts (in effect, the first vehicle registration law in Texas history). He restructured local government and organized the countryside into police jurisdictions. He established a curfew, instituted a noise ordinance, and required owners to keep their properties clean and well maintained. Unfortunately for Manuel Salcedo and the other representatives of the Spanish monarchy, these last efforts at enlightened government could not hold back the tide of rebellion that began to sweep New Spain toward independence.

 ## Insurrection on the Frontier

The urgency of Governor Salcedo's appeals to the loyalty and patriotism of Tejanos intensified as rebellion broke out in the central parts of the viceroyalty. At the beginning of the nineteenth century, New Spain was rife with the social and economic contradictions that have often made for revolution. A tiny percentage of the population lived in opulence in Mexico City, Guadalajara, and a handful of other major urban centers, whereas the overwhelming majority of colonial Mexicans lived in abject poverty. Although the silver mines of the colony remained the driving engine of the economy, most people relied on subsistence agriculture for a living. In the very small manufacturing sector, consisting mostly of second-class textiles and ceramics, as well as on the large agricultural estates, abusive labor practices predominated.

The Causes of the Mexican War of Independence

Spanish colonial institutions were antiquated and corrupt. The church represented the largest and richest property owner in the colony, recipient of a tithe that the government collected for it and beneficiary of innumerable bequests. The church, consequently, served as the colony's principal landlord and lender. Yet, in the countryside many parish priests lived a poor, hand-to-mouth existence that led many to become disaffected. Exploitation of the rural Indian and *castas* (mixed blood) population also came at the hands of an underpaid and, therefore, extremely corrupt local officialdom. Bourbon reform efforts ultimately failed to solve any of these problems, as they only replaced one group of corrupt petty officials with another. Although the *intendentes*, the regional administrative heads who exercised considerable economic and political power, were themselves well educated and well paid, their local subordinates, known as *subdelegados*, were not, and they came to rely on graft and extortion to make a living.

Compounding these problems, which to one degree or another were endemic to most polities of the time, was the complex and oppressive ethnic ordering of society inherent in the *sistema de castas*. Spanish colonial society, which consisted of about 6 million people at the turn of the century, was divided into two large groups, the *república de indios* and the *república de españoles*, with separate codes of law governing each. Mexico's 3.5 million Indians remained perpetual wards of the Crown, with a protective legal structure governing their economic and political dealings. The overwhelming majority lived in ancestral villages, spoke their native languages, and practiced syncretic forms of Catholicism. Local representatives of the Crown took advantage of their authority over the Indians to exploit their labor and monopolize business dealings with them.

The rest of the population, about 15,000 peninsulares, 1 million criollos, and 1.5 million castas—the república de españoles—was governed by a legal code that operated on the assumption that all men were not created equal. Punishment for criminal offenses was based on ethnicity: Spaniards often received fines whereas the castas were subject to corporal punishment of varying degrees. The legal distinctions among the various social groups extended to opportunities for advancement in both the public and private sectors. The late Bourbon push to entrust positions of higher authority such as intendente, bishop, and high court judge to *gachupines* (a derogatory term for European Spaniards) troubled the considerable number of well-educated criollos who saw their prospects limited. Although criollos made up the overwhelming number of hacienda and mine owners and occupied the vast majority of local government posts, they did not run the viceroyalty. Although blacks, mulattoes, and *mestizos* made up the bulk of the non-Indian population, they were denied full opportunities for personal advancement.

At the same time that the Crown and its advisers were consolidating power and "modernizing" the empire in Madrid, they were ignoring the needs and wishes of their colonial subjects. In America, meanwhile, criollos were developing a sense of nationalism. American-born Spaniards began to resent the superior attitude and privileged status of gachupines and advocated a new relationship to mother Spain. Criollo intellectuals began to feel pride in their early civilizations and to regard their accomplishments as no less worthy than those of ancient European societies. They challenged the idea that the New World environment was intrinsically inferior to that of the Old World. The American provinces were no different from, and certainly not inferior to, the European possessions of the Crown, and the American colonies should be governed by Americans.

Added to this long-simmering disaffection, economic and political upheavals in the first decade of the nineteenth century precipitated insurrection. First, often cut off from its American possessions by enemies during the course of the Napoleonic Wars (1792–1815), Spain's normal commerce was disrupted; European and American imports flooded colonial markets, disrupting domestic manufacturing. Second, in 1804, desperate for revenues with which to fund its war effort, the Crown confiscated church assets, eliminating the single largest source of available capital in the viceroyalty. Third, drought late in the decade produced famine and widespread rural unemployment, especially in the Bajío, the colony's most productive economic region.

To these troubles was added the political instability that began in 1808 with Napoleon's usurpation of the Spanish throne. Having entered Spain under the pretense of marching against Britain's ally Portugal, Napoleon took the opportunity to force the abdication of King Charles IV, transferring the Spanish Crown to his brother Joseph Bonaparte. The Spanish people rose in revolt against the French invaders, launching what is known as the War of Spanish Independence. Spain's American colonies also rejected the usurper Joseph Bonaparte, claiming to be loyal to the legitimate heir, Ferdinand. When a meeting of Mexico City's criollo elite declared that New Spain should be governed by *junta* (provisional council) until the monarchy was restored and the sitting viceroy agreed, panicked peninsulares carried out a coup and placed one of their own on the viceroy's throne.

The Struggle Begins

In this atmosphere of political and economic turmoil, groups of discontented criollos and mestizos began to conspire to overthrow the government. One such group, centered at Querétaro, a major agricultural center in the Bajío, included the man who would come to be known as the father of Mexican independence, Miguel Hidalgo y Costilla, parish priest of the small agricultural town of Dolores. Hidalgo, along with the lower-rank military and political officials who made

Banner of Father Miguel Hidalgo y Costilla's insurgent army. The active participation of Texas in the Mexican War of Independence took place during the early years of the struggle. By the time Hidalgo supporter Bernardo Gutiérrez de Lara led the Republican Army of the North into Texas in 1812, Hidalgo and some of his chiefs had been executed.

up the conspiracy, was a criollo of rather liberal bent and broad interests. The conspirators had read the writings of French Enlightenment thinkers and were informed about the political thought behind American constitutionalism. They did not entirely reject their ties to Spain, indeed Hidalgo never declared the outright independence of Mexico from the mother country, but the conspirators did believe that Mexico should be governed by Mexicans rather than peninsulares. Unlike the majority of their fellow criollos, whose fear of the masses kept them allied to the gachupines, the conspirators were willing to gamble on their ability to control the Indians and castas who would bear the burden of fighting.

In the early morning hours of September 16, 1810, the bells of his church signaled to townspeople and nearby peasants that something was wrong. Hidalgo stepped out on the front steps of his church and made an impassioned speech to the gathering crowd. He is said to have ended it by uttering his famous *grito* (cry): "Long live Religion! Long live our Blessed Mother Guadalupe! Long live Ferdinand VII and death to bad government!"

News of the revolt made its way northward within days, where at first there seemed to be little support for expanding the insurrection. The north did not have large numbers of disgruntled and hungry Indians and had only a few peninsulares, so discontent in the region appeared to be under control. However, the same class of disaffected criollos and castas that existed in the more central portions of the colony also existed in the northeastern provinces. In addition, the large number of frontier troops, overwhelmingly locals serving either in the frontier presidio companies or in militia units, had conflicted loyalties. Unlike regular army troops these men had been recruited from the frontier population to serve as a sort of home guard. They were accustomed to fighting Indians to protect their homes. How would they respond to their Spanish officers' efforts to employ them against insurgents?

The answer to that question was alarming to royal authorities, as they discovered in December 1810. The military units in Nuevo Santander revolted against the royalist government when told to prepare to march on the rebels farther south. Early in January, the entire command of the well-liked but royalist Antonio Cordero defected when confronted by a rebel force of 7,000–8,000. When insurgent envoys arrived in Nuevo León soon thereafter, that province too allied itself with the insurrection. Of the northeastern Interior Provinces only Texas remained under royal control.

Texas Joins the Revolt

In Texas, Governor Salcedo desperately attempted to retain the loyalty of the inhabitants of the province. Arrests of suspected instigators (both Tejanos and outsiders), speeches on the need for loyalty to king and God, and assurances of the safety of the population from Indian attack did little to quell a growing unrest. From Natchitoches, American agents reported to the U.S. government that substantial numbers of Tejanos, including members of leading San Antonio families, were preparing to overthrow the royalist authorities. The troops stationed in Béxar were uneasy about the possibility of being marched south to confront the insurgents, in the process leaving their families exposed to Indian attack. This unease only increased with news of the revolt's spread through neighboring provinces.

Texas, however, was awash in disaffection. Some Tejanos were upset with the Crown's lack of responsiveness to the needs of the province. For all of Governor Salcedo's efforts, there were few signs that the necessary investment in money and people were coming any time soon. At San Antonio, where the reforms of Governors Cordero and Salcedo had most affected traditional patterns of leadership, there was resentment. There was also resentment among those whose economic interests had been hurt by the military's efforts to curtail contraband. Even more critical was the anxiety that Salcedo had created among the troops when he announced that the entire garrison at San Antonio might have to march south against the insurgents.

The man who led Texas's first revolt against Spanish rule, Juan Bautista de las Casas, was himself a retired criollo militia officer. He later claimed he was a loyal subject of Ferdinand VII and that his sole purpose in deposing Governor Salcedo had been to prevent the province from falling into anarchy, but his actions indicated otherwise. Although his motives may never be known, much weighed against him: the participation of a number of known Hidalgo sympathizers and disgruntled citizens of San Antonio in his coup, his constant communications with the insurgency's leadership in the interior of Mexico, and his orders for the arrest of all gachupines in the province as well as anyone who did not recognize him as governor.

The Casas Revolt, which took place on January 21, 1811, was on shaky ground almost from the very beginning, however. Many among the province's leading families had stayed on the sidelines, unwilling to risk alienating a government that, although it might not be as responsive as they wanted, still paid for the defense of Texas against enemy Indians. News of Hidalgo's defeat at Guadalajara on January 17 and the flight of the insurgent leadership toward the frontier contributed to the sense of unease among prominent Tejanos. Casas's own arbitrary rule antagonized members of San Antonio's elite families who rallied instead around Father Juan Manuel Zambrano, a native of Béxar with aspirations of his own.

On March 17, not three months after his assumption of power, Casas was overthrown by Zambrano and his supporters. Most of his followers quickly switched allegiance and royalist officials throughout the province soon took up their posts again. Restored to the governorship, Manuel Salcedo now governed a province that was very different from the one he had lost the previous January. The Comanches and Norteños resumed large-scale raiding, dissatisfied that Spanish officials no longer had the gifts and merchandise that had been the basis of the peace that had existed for a quarter century. Salcedo considered the 1,136 men who formed the province's military defense largely untrustworthy. They had already mutinied once, and they continued to be exposed to the revolutionary rhetoric of disloyal kinsmen and ever-present foreigners. Every day shortages mounted: Paper, clothing, candles, even horses, were all in short supply. But, most troubling of all were reports filtering in from Louisiana of preparations for an invasion of Texas by a force of insurgents and Anglo-American mercenaries.

Rebellion Turns into Struggle for Independence

The reports were not rumors. Mexican insurgents had fled to the United States at the time of Hidalgo's debacle and were attempting to enlist U.S. support for their cause. In the aftermath of the royalist capture and execution of Hidalgo on March 21, 1811, leadership of the war against Spanish rule devolved upon another cleric, Father José María Morelos, a mestizo whose more realistic grasp of the situation and better organizational skills brought him considerable initial success. Under his leadership a revolutionary congress finally declared independence from Spain, abolished slavery, and drafted a constitution for Mexico.

On the frontier, José Bernardo Gutiérrez de Lara took up the cause of independence. He was a criollo and a native frontiersman. He had been born in the Rio Grande valley town of Revilla (now Guerrero Viejo, Tamaulipas) in 1774, the son of pioneer settlers in Escandón's colony. By 1810 he was a family man, a petty merchant, blacksmith, and, like many settlers of the area, a landowner. He was also disaffected. When the Hidalgo Revolt erupted, he immediately embraced the cause. As a result he played a prominent role in helping the insurgents achieve early success in Nuevo Santander.

The defeat of the rebellion in the early months of 1811 did not discourage Gutiérrez de Lara. Claiming to have been assigned to seek assistance in the United States, he traveled to Washington, D.C., in July. Although he failed to obtain overt assistance from the U.S. administration, Gutiérrez de Lara received tacit approval for his plans. Back in Louisiana by the spring of 1812, he met with local authorities and began recruiting what eventually became the Republican Army of the North. His most important collaborator in organizing the invasion was a U.S. Army officer, Augustus Magee. The West Point graduate resigned his commission to take up military leadership of the Anglo-American volunteers in the army, which came to consist of about equal numbers of Anglo-Americans and Mexicans.

In the meantime, Governor Salcedo had been restored to power and was attempting to implement political reforms coming from Spain. In their resistance to Napoleon, Spaniards had set up a Cortes, or parliament, to legislate, and a regency to govern in the name of Ferdinand, the Bourbon heir to the throne. The Cortes, meeting in Cadiz, called for a constitutional convention with representatives from throughout the empire. The product of the convention's work, the Constitution of 1812, was a liberal document that created equality among all citizens of the empire, established a constitutional monarchy, and divided the empire into provinces, each of which was to be represented by a legislative body called the provincial deputation. It proved impossible for Texas to find someone competent and wealthy enough to serve as its representative to the Cortes and so relied on the representative from Coahuila. When in June 1814 the provincial deputation was formed for the Eastern Interior Provinces, of which Texas was part, the unsettled situation in the province also prevented it from sending a delegate to Monterrey. The experiment was short-lived, however, as once he assumed the throne, Ferdinand abolished the constitution and dismissed the provincial deputations. Although they existed only for a few months, the provincial deputations had established a precedent for republican government in Spanish America.

In August 1812, the Gutiérrez de Lara–led expedition crossed the Sabine River. It is doubtful Gutiérrez de Lara was aware or interested in the turn of events in Spain. The expedition arrived in Nacogdoches to find the local troops unwilling to fight. In September, now grown to 300 effectives, the Republican Army of the North took Santísima Trinidad de Salcedo. Discovering that Governor Salcedo had marched to the Guadalupe River to obstruct their advance on Béxar, Gutiérrez de Lara and Magee turned southeast to La Bahía, where they occupied the presidio in early November. Between November 1812 and February 1813 the royalists besieged La Bahía, but were unable to dislodge the insurgents, who finally went after Salcedo's army as it retreated to Béxar. The royalists made one last stand about nine miles southeast of San Antonio on March 29. At the Battle of Rosillo about 1,200 men under Colonel Simón Herrera met the approximately 800-man Republican Army of the North. Having lost hundreds of men, more than a thousand horses, all of his field artillery and most other equipment, Salcedo had no choice but to surrender. On April 1, 1813, the Republican Army of the North, under the command of Gutiérrez de Lara and Samuel Kemper, Magee's successor, took San Antonio.

The First Independence of Texas

The process of nation building began with bloodshed. On the evening of April 3, Salcedo and his subordinates, a total of 14 gachupines, were assassinated a few miles outside of Béxar as they were being "escorted" out of the province. Kemper and a number of other Anglo-Americans were outraged by the brutal action. A declaration of independence adopted on April 6 and a constitution that the Mexican insurgents drew up in the following days completed the alienation of many Anglo officers, who took their leave and returned to Louisiana. According to the Constitution, the state of Texas, as part of an independent Mexico, was to be governed by a "president-protector," whose power would be shared only with a junta of five men that enjoyed a merely advisory role. Catholicism remained the established religion. If anything served to partially appease some of the Anglo-American participants, it was the constitutional provision for land grants of approximately 4,500 acres to each volunteer.

In short order, factionalism overwhelmed the republicans. Gutiérrez de Lara and his supporters, mostly Mexican insurgents and sympathizers, faced off with the Anglo-American volunteers and U.S. government agents, who perceived Gutiérrez de Lara as an arbitrary and divisive leader. Pressing for the removal of Gutiérrez de Lara was William Shaler, a U.S. State Department representative who championed José Álvarez de Toledo as the solution for the problems of the insurgent government. In the days following his arrival in Béxar on August 1, 1813, Toledo and Gutiérrez de Lara fought over control of the government. In the end, Toledo won and Gutiérrez de Lara withdrew to Louisiana.

By this time it was clear that Viceroy Calleja was determined not to allow the murders of Salcedo and the other Spaniards to go unavenged or to have Texas remain in the hands of insurgents and foreigners. The man he charged with recovering control of the errant province was General Joaquín Arredondo, who had recently been promoted to commandant general for the eastern Interior Provinces. Arredondo had considerable experience fighting insurgents in the north, having served as military governor of Nuevo Santander and having put down the rebellion in that province in 1812. With an army of over 1,800 men, Arredondo moved north toward San Antonio in early August for a final showdown with the Texas insurgency.

GACETA DE TEXAS.

No. 1.]   NACOGDOCHES, 25 de Mayo, de 1813.   [Vol.

The "First Texas Newspaper." Actually, the Gaceta de Texas, or Texas Gazette, which has a publication date of May 1813, was printed in Natchitoches, Louisiana, by José Álvarez de Toledo, who later replaced José Bernardo Gutiérrez de Lara as the leader of the Texas insurgency against Spanish rule in the summer of 1813. This copy was sent back to Washington by U.S. State Department special agent William Shaler, who was monitoring and surreptitiously assisting the independence movement in Texas.

On August 18, 1813, Arredondo's royalist army fought Toledo's 1,400-man Republican Army of the North a few miles south of the Medina River, near the Laredo–San Antonio road. The daylong Battle of Medina was a complete disaster for Toledo's army of Mexicans, Anglo-Americans, and Indians. Colonel Ignacio Elizondo, the man who had captured Hidalgo, was now turned loose on the fleeing insurgents. With a 200-man force he pursued what remained of the Republican Army of the North northward and by September had reached Nacogdoches. He reported having executed 71 rebels and taken over 100 people captive, mostly women and children. Arredondo, meanwhile, had executed hundreds more and imposed martial law in San Antonio. He began his final, and rather inflated, report on the campaign: "The ever victorious and invincible arms of our Sovereign, aided by the powerful hand of the god of war, have gained the most complete and decisive victory over the base and perfidious rabble commanded by certain vile assassins ridiculously styled a general and commanders." Texas was again in the royalist fold.

Meanwhile, in Mexico, Father Morelos, had taken over as the leader of the independence movement. A better military tactician than Hidalgo, he managed to establish control over a considerable portion of the country south of Mexico City and organized a congress that formally declared Mexico's independence from Spain. Unfortunately, he proved unable to convince enough criollos to back the cause. In November 1815 Father Morelos was captured and executed. By that time Texas had experienced a second failed insurrection and was teetering on the brink of utter devastation.

A Howling Wilderness: The Last Years of Spanish Texas

Spanish Texas in the fall of 1813 was a land devoid of hope. From across the border in western Louisiana, Juan Martín Veramendi, Francisco Arocha, Vicente Travieso, and Francisco Ruiz, all Tejanos who had participated as local leaders in Gutiérrez de Lara's republican experiment, heard the news that they were not included in the general amnesty granted to contrite rebels. Yet others, such as Erasmo Seguín, were caught between loyalties. The one-time Béxar postmaster and leading member of Zambrano's revolt against Casas had been accused of providing letters of introduction for insurgents, for which crime all of his property had been confiscated. It took years for him to clear his name. Some unrepentant Tejano insurgents continued to work actively against Spanish rule. One such rebel was Vicente Tarín, a former officer in the Alamo Company who had joined the Gutiérrez–Magee expedition. He organized a small company of like-minded men and roamed throughout northern Texas, bartering with the Indians and inciting them against the Spaniards. For the general population of Texas, even those who had remained steadfastly in the royalist camp, the abandonment of crops, the sequestration of property, impressment into military or other public service, and the constant menace of Indian attack meant a precarious existence.

Indian Texas

Even as insurgents and royalists struggled for control of San Antonio and the other Tejano settlements, Texas remained very much an Indian country. Despite the general peace established in the first years of the nineteenth century, young Lipan, Comanche, and Wichita warriors occasionally raided Tejano horse herds or committed thefts in outlying ranches. Tejanos retaliated, sometimes indiscriminately, leading to the death of unrelated Indians. Early in the decade the Comanches also suspected a renewed Spanish–Lipan alliance, with rumors circulating that Spanish troops had assisted in a Lipan raid on a Comanche encampment. At the same time, the various Wichita tribes were divided between those closer to the Americans, who favored the United States because of the higher quality and cheaper goods the North American provided, and those closer to Spanish settlements, who advocated continuing the Spanish alliance. Only concerted diplomatic efforts between 1804 and 1806, including a reinforcement of trade contacts and gifts, by governors Elguézabal and Cordero on the Spanish side and Lipan chiefs Canoso and Morrongo, Kotsoteka Comanche leaders Chihuahua and Yzazat, and Tawakoni Wichita chiefs Quiscat and Daguariscara kept the peace structure in place. A separate agreement in1805 between Chief Cuernitos of the Tonkawas and Governor Cordero broke down almost immediately, as the Spaniards were unable to supply the goods promised in the agreement and the Tonkawas resumed their raids against Spanish herds.

In effect, those tribes with direct access to American goods adopted a similar strategy to that of the Caddos during much of the eighteenth century of playing Spaniards off Frenchmen. Kadohadacho chief Dahauit, who had assumed de facto leadership of the region's remaining Caddos, clearly expressed this attitude when he confronted a Spanish official who threatened to confiscate any American goods the Kadohadachos brought back to Texas from Natchitoches on the Camino Real. The road, Dehahuit claimed, "had always been theirs, and if the Spanish prevented them from using it as their ancestors had always done, he would soon make it a bloody road."

The Caddos and Wichitas were encouraged in their aggressive attitude toward the Spaniards by John Sibley, Thomas Jefferson's Indian agent on the Louisiana–Texas frontier. Part of Sibley's job it was to line up as many Indian tribes in the region on the American side for the coming war that many in the American administration and the Spanish government felt was inevitable as a result of the dispute over the boundary of the Louisiana Purchase. Although war did not come, Americans continued to penetrate ever westward, giving the region's Indians increasingly less incentive to work with the Spaniards. For instance, in summer 1808 Anthony Glass led a group of American Indian traders to the Wichita and Comanche settlements in the Red River region, which Spanish officials were informed about but were unwilling to stop for fear of antagonizing the tribes.

The outbreak of the Mexican War of Independence, which spelled the end Spanish–Indian trade, let alone annual gifts, further eroded Indian ties to the

Spaniards. Although most tribes—both indigenous and migrant—stayed out of the escalating Mexican rebellion against Spanish rule in the early stages, once Lipans, Tonkawas, and the most anti-Spanish Wichitas perceived that the Republican Army of the North had gained the upper hand in the Texas insurgency, they threw in their lot with the rebels. Lipans under Chief Cuelgas de Castro and other Indian auxiliaries participated in the Battle of Rosillo, as a result of which the republicans forced Governor Salcedo to surrender. By the time of the Battle of Medina, approximately 100 Indians, including Lipans, Wichitas, and Tonkawas, were part of the Republican force. Their commitment to the insurgents was not deep; however, and they abandoned the field shortly after the battle began. The Indians did not entirely escape Arredondo's wrath, as he sent a small force as far as Nacogdoches to attack an encampment of suspected Lipan rebel sympathizers.

Between the Battle of Medina and Mexican independence eight years later, the Indians of Texas became dependent on American trade goods, looking to Spanish Texas and the Rio Grande country for the horses and mules that increasingly formed the basis of exchange. In addition, captive-taking increased, particularly among the Comanches, who had suffered declines as a result of epidemics and a drought that had reduced the number of buffalo on the southern plains. The reversals, in fact, led to the disappearance of the Kotsoteka and Yamparika tribal divisions and the emergence of the Penateka Comanches, just as changes among the Wichitas led to the emergence of a new Tawakoni tribe named Waco, whose large principal town was located at the site of the present-day downtown Waco. Divisions among the Lipans resulted in Chief El Cojo's band of Lipans striking a separate peace with the Comanches and Wichitas, which meant that San Antonio, La Bahía, and Spanish settlements below the Rio Grande often faced joint raids by members of all three tribes.

In general, the smaller tribal groups and migrant Indians proved friendlier to the Spaniards. Biloxis, Alabamas, and Coushattas, for instance, had come to Texas fleeing American settlers, and although they had no choice but to trade with Americans, they appreciated the hands-off approach of the Spanish government. As long as Spain maintained its title to Texas, they would be safe from further displacement by land-hungry American frontiersmen. Consequently, although they did not directly involve themselves in Spanish affairs, they did keep royal officials informed of foreign activities in the southeast Texas area where they built their villages. Moreover, while they reached agreements with the few remaining Bidais and Akokisas of the coastal region, they drove out the Cocos tribe of Karankawas, making clear their intention to establish their hunting grounds in the area.

While the Cocos were forced to move south by the migrant tribes, the other Karankawa tribes faced attack from the Lipans, Comanches, and outsiders. Skirmishes between Jean Lafitte's freebooters and Cocos on Galveston Island led to the 1817 Battle of Three Trees, in which 30 Karankawas were killed and the rest fled across the bay; the end of an Indian presence on Galveston Island. Cujanes who had converted to Christianity and settled at Mission Refugio abandoned the

Among the Indian tribes from east of the Mississippi River that sought the protection of Spanish authorities in Texas at the beginning of the nineteenth century were the Alabamas and Coushattas. In time the two small bands joined together on a single reservation in Polk County, where they remain today. This water color by Lino Sanchéz y Tapia of Coushatta warriors captures the degree to which southeastern Indians had adopted Western dress and technologies.

station the following year after Comanche and Lipan raids. They joined other Karankawa groups close to the coast, where they could better defend themselves against increased attacks from enemy tribes. Shipwrecked sailors along the middle Texas coast were routinely killed by the Karankawas, not out of loyalty to the Spaniards but in defense of their territory.

Pirates and Insurgents

By the time Antonio Martínez arrived in Texas to take over as governor in May 1817, things had reached the breaking point. Agriculture in the province had completely broken down and grain shipments from Coahuila were unreliable and inadequate to meet Texas's needs. Norteño and Lipan raids had left a considerable number of Tejanos dead with others taken as captives, not to mention the destruction to herds. With Ignacio Pérez and most of the other able-bodied men in the province impressed into active militia service, cultivation of even subsistence crops proved extremely difficult and dangerous.

The situation had become critical as Texas faced a new wave of invasions from the United States and beyond. In late 1815 a former U.S. military officer and member of the Gutiérrez–Magee expedition, Henry Perry, organized a successful though minor invasion of Galveston Bay and occupied the mouth of the Trinity River. He was joined in the area in September 1816 by Louis Michele Aury, a pirate who had sold his services to a group of New Orleans conspirators intent on turning the Mexican War of Independence to their own advantage. Setting up headquarters on Galveston Island under the authority of Mexican rebel agent Manuel de Herrera, Aury was soon joined by other pirates, the brothers Jean and Pierre Lafitte. Spanish authorities, aware of these activities, could do little but stay informed and bide their time.

An abortive invasion of Mexico agreed upon by Perry, Aury, and the newly arrived insurgent Francisco Xavier Mina in April 1818 became the basis of the first of a number of expeditions intended to bring about the separation of Texas from Mexico. After a falling out among the three leaders, Perry decided to lead his men to La Bahía. When Governor Martínez received word of Perry's arrival at Matagorda Bay, he transmitted the information to Commandant General Arredondo, along with a general assessment of how things stood:

> The pitiful condition of [La Bahía commander] Castañeda's few forces—in addition to his lack of supplies for subsistence, they are unmounted and barefooted— does not permit him even to select parties to go out on observation duty and those whom he does send in this condition go at full risk, and I am almost in the same situation. Now I cannot furnish him any kind of assistance. In regard to the forces, I have fifty men at Río Grande to transport corn, as I have already told you, and 100 men commanded by Lieutenant Colonel Don Ygnacio Pérez have had to go out to punish large bands of Indians who raid us quite frequently. I am alone in this capital with thirty or forty men, most of whom are ill, and I cannot count on those who are not because they are on foot and the arms they have are useless. My sole protection depends on the few citizens who without exception are in exactly the same condition I have said the troops are in.

Fortunately for the royalists, on June 18, one of Martínez's subordinates caught up with Perry and his forty-three men north of La Bahía and defeated the intruders.

Despite the problems, and his limited ability to carry out any consistent reconnaissance beyond the vicinity of Béxar and La Bahía, Martínez was resourceful enough to confront the major challenges that presented themselves in the last three years of Spanish rule from 1818 to 1821. Certainly the presence of the Lafitte brothers, who had usurped Aury's position in Galveston, was not a critical issue for the Texas governor. The pirates were interested in maritime conquests and Texas was receiving no seaborne traffic that might be affected. The Indians were an intractable problem, but they had been so for a century. No, the challenge that concerned Martínez was the one posed by foreign invaders who might seize Texas.

One such challenge arose in 1818, when a large group of Napoleonic exiles attempted to establish a French outpost on the Trinity River. Charles Lallemand, a general in Napoleon's armies, led more than 150 men and a few women and children to a spot near the present town of Liberty, where they built a fort called Champ d'Asile. Although Lallemand claimed that his followers were peaceful agricultural colonists, the military nature of the encampment—with 600 muskets and 12,000 cartridges—and the failure of the colonists to clear land and plant crops points to other purposes. From the Spanish ambassador to the United

States came word that Lallemand's intention was to occupy part of New Spain in order to proclaim Joseph Bonaparte king of Mexico.

Martínez could do little but send out scouting parties during the months following initial word of the arrival of the French. It was only in mid-September that Captain Juan de Castañeda, former commander at La Bahía and now in charge of the Alamo company, set out for the Trinity with 240 men. His orders, beyond expelling the French intruders, included driving out squatters and Indian traders, punishing the local Indians who had sided with the foreigners, and destroying the abandoned settlement of Nacogdoches. Fortunately for Casta-ñeda, when he arrived at Champ d'Asile, he found that the French had already abandoned the fort and taken refuge on Galveston Island. Although he sent an ultimatum ordering them to immediately depart or surrender, he had no boats to cross the bay and was in no position to attack. Neither was he in a position to carry out a punitive campaign against East Texas Indians or even to drive out squatters and illegal Indian traders. Castañeda had to be content to tear down the French fortifications and cabins and head back to Béxar.

The Close of the Spanish Era

The good news that Captain Castañeda brought back from Galveston Bay marked a temporary improvement in Spanish fortunes in Texas. U.S. interests in the last remaining vestige of the Spanish Empire in eastern North America brought more good fortune to Spanish authorities in New Spain the following spring. Although the United States had continued to claim Texas as part of the Louisiana Purchase, General Wilkinson's acceptance of the neutral ground in

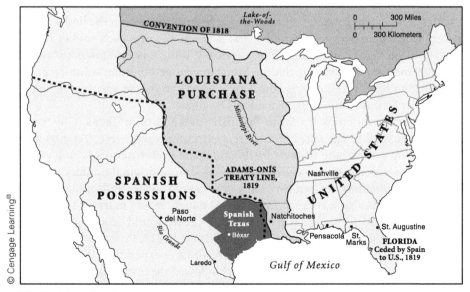

The Louisiana Purchase.

1806 had weakened the U.S. position. During and after the War of 1812, in which the Spanish Crown tacitly supported the British against the United States, Spanish Florida had become a haven for Creek and other Indians hostile to the United States, leading to two invasions of the province by Andrew Jackson's army. Expediency demanded that U.S. secretary of state John Quincy Adams and Spanish ambassador Luis de Onís reach agreement. In February 1819, they concluded a compromise: Spain would keep Texas but give up Florida.

Perhaps Secretary of State Adams and President James Monroe concluded that Spain would not long be in control of Mexico and that Texas would naturally fall to the United States soon thereafter. Whatever the case, the Adams–Onís Treaty (also known as the Transcontinental Treaty) did not win the approval of western political interests, who had long been advocating Anglo-American expansion in that direction. Certainly the speculators who had backed Perry, Aury, and Mina would not sit still for the Yankee secretary of state giving away American rights to Texas. Meeting in New Orleans in May, the group began organizing an expedition to "liberate" Texas from Spain. At Natchez too, irate citizens of the West organized to bring about a proper resolution to the situation. The conspirators found the man to lead the liberation of Texas in James Long, a Natchez merchant and veteran of the War of 1812.

What has come to be known as the first Long expedition began in June 1819, when an advance party of 120 men crossed the Sabine and occupied Nacogdoches. Long arrived later in the month and immediately organized a government that declared the independence of Texas on June 23, 1819. The document, drafted by Long and a group of Anglo-American supporters, presumed to declare, "The citizens of Texas have long indulged the hope, that in the adjustment of the boundaries of the Spanish possessions in America, and of the territories of the United States, that they should be included within the limits of the latter." One of the new government's first acts was to grant each soldier in the army 6,400 acres as compensation for service. Within a month, Long had more than 300 men at his service, including Mexican insurgent Bernardo Gutiérrez de Lara, Tejano rebel Vicente Tarín, the Anglo-American Indian agent John Sibley, and former Spanish–Indian agent Samuel Davenport.

To counter this new threat to Spanish sovereignty in Texas, Governor Martínez turned to Ignacio Pérez. Dire as circumstances were, Tejanos had not given up on the land of their birth, and some even rose to a high level of prominence; among these was Pérez. Descended from original military settlers and Canary Islanders, he had become a prominent rancher and militia officer at Béxar. He was also a staunch loyalist (his daughter was married to former governor Cordero). Among his services to the Crown would be an eight-month stint as interim governor of Texas between 1816 and 1817. Promoted to lieutenant colonel for his service against the Gutiérrez–Magee expedition, Pérez became a trusted field commander in the chaos that followed the insurgency.

Now, with Martínez unsure of the size of the threat—reports filtering in ranged from several hundred to several thousand invaders—he could find no better man in whom to entrust the mission than Lieutenant Colonel Pérez. Mustering 550 men, two cannons, 425 pack mules, and enough horses to provide each man with two or three remounts, the small army left Béxar on September 27, 1819. Pérez's instructions were not only to drive out all foreigners from East Texas, but to punish any Indians in the area who had supported the intruders.

By the time Pérez and his now reinforced command of 650 men reached Nacogdoches, Long and most of his men had withdrawn to Louisiana. A few stragglers were captured, but the danger seemed to have passed. Pérez pardoned some of the remaining residents of Nacogdoches on the grounds that they had joined the rebels only because they could not resist. The expedition returned to San Antonio by February 1820, a resounding though not total success, having captured forty-four Anglo-American adventurers and Mexican rebels and having expelled a large group of squatters he had allowed to cross over into the Neutral Ground.

After fleeing to Natchitoches, the president of the Supreme Council of the republic of Texas proceeded to New Orleans. There he met with another Mexican insurgent, José Félix Trespalacios, a native of Chihuahua who had recently escaped a royalist dungeon in Mexico and was now preparing his own invasion of Texas. The two men decided to join forces and by early 1820 Long had established new headquarters at Point Bolivar. There he remained until September 1821, when he marched for La Bahía. He captured the presidio on October 4, but was forced to surrender to Pérez, who was now in the service of the new Mexican nation.

The writing on the wall that Long had failed to see or had chosen to ignore had been clearly visible for some time. A revolt by a Spanish army waiting to sail for Spanish America to put down independence movements had forced Ferdinand VII to restore the liberal Constitution of 1812. For criollos, many of whom had lost faith in the legitimacy of the Spanish government, the changes merely symbolized the continued instability of royal authority. One of these criollos was a royalist officer named Agustín de Iturbide. Sent into the field to crush the leading rebel, Vicente Guerrero, Iturbide instead reached an agreement with him for the separation of Mexico from Spain. The Plan of Iguala, signed by the two men on February 24, 1821, consisted of three important clauses: (1) the continued special status of the Catholic church in Mexican society, (2) the independence of Mexico as a constitutional monarchy, and (3) equality between peninsulares and criollos.

Hesitant to appear rebellious after carefully cultivating their royalist connections since August 1813, Béxar's leaders waited until the very last moment to endorse independence. Only on July 19, two months before Iturbide's triumphant Army of the Three Guarantees entered Mexico City did civilian and military officials take the oath to the new nation. A few days later, word arrived from La Bahía that its officials had also taken the oath. Spanish Texas was no more.

 Conclusion

In the second decade of the nineteenth century the progress of the previous century had been almost totally undone. The extent of the damage done by adventurers, insurgents, royal armies, and enemy Indians made Texas appear to be a "wild, howling, interminable solitude," to Stephen F. Austin as he traveled from the Sabine toward San Antonio in summer 1821. Austin's father Moses, one of the Anglo-Americans who had settled in Spanish Louisiana, had lost everything during the Panic of 1819 and had looked to the green pastures and rich bottom lands of Texas to restore his fortunes. He had come to Béxar in December 1820 with a proposal to settle 300 Anglo-American Catholic families on the Brazos or Colorado River. And, Governor Martínez and Commandant General Arredondo had been so desperate to do something for the forlorn province that they had agreed to the plan.

In early 1821, Texas consisted of little more than the San Antonio River valley settlements of San Antonio de Béxar and La Bahía del Espíritu Santo, with a population of about 3,000. Ranches throughout the area were largely abandoned and most crop land lay fallow. The settlers of La Bahía were able to reap only a meager harvest that could not possibly meet even subsistence needs. The presidio company had no horses and remained barefoot. Conditions at San Antonio were equally bad. A major flood in July 1819 had added to the local misery, as had field fires intentionally set by enemy Indians. As a result, harvests were poor or nonexistent and the towns found themselves at the mercy of whatever convoys of corn and flour could make it up the road from Río Grande and Laredo.

Former royalists and former republicans were now all Mexicans. Surprisingly, they seemed to put aside previous differences and begun the rebuilding work. It would take all their energies and talents and a large amount of outside help to rebuild what was now Mexican Texas. The new government negotiated with the Indians who had helped bring Spanish Texas to its knees and who controlled the vast majority of Texas.

In 1821, then, Texas remained an abstraction that meant different things to different people, and nothing at all to others. To Tejanos, the Hispanic population with roots in a century of frontier survival, it represented a homeland whose potential would not be realized until the Indian problem was solved and immigration fostered economic development. To Mexican national officials, Texas represented the inheritance from Spain of a border region the control of which required resources well beyond the reach of the new nation. To many American frontiersmen, Texas represented the unredeemed portion of the Louisiana Purchase, while to others it was a natural extension of the quickly expanding Cotton Kingdom. Finally, to those Indian peoples who had migrated to Spanish Texas fleeing land-hungry American frontiersmen it was a last hope to live as free and independent people; while to the indigenous peoples who persisted there was no Texas at all, only the hunting grounds and village fields and the trails that ancestors had carved out of the brush and forests generations before, and that they would defend against all comers.

Suggested Readings

Texas was no longer an isolated and backward Indian frontier province after 1800. Events over which colonial officials and Tejanos had no control thrust the poor and underpopulated province into the thick of international politics and revolution. The literature on the major international events of this period—the Louisiana Purchase, the Aaron Burr conspiracy, the War of 1812, and the Napoleonic Wars—is too voluminous to discuss adequately here. Some understanding of the processes by which the Spanish Empire collapsed, particularly in Mexico, can be gained from *The Independence of Latin America*, ed. Leslie Bethell (1987). For Mexico specifically, a good survey is Timothy J. Henderson, *The Mexican Wars of Independence* (2009). In Chapter 10 of *The Spanish Frontier in North America*, however, Weber provides a useful summary of events along the Spanish borderlands, as does John Kessell in Chapter 13 of *Spain in the Southwest*. U.S. foreign policy toward Spanish North America, with Chapters 4 and 5 focusing on Texas, is the subject of J. C. A. Stagg's *Borderlines in Borderlands: James Madison and the Spanish American Frontier, 1776–1821* (2009). Donald Chipman surveys the era from the Texas perspective in the aptly titled chapter 11 of *Spanish Texas*, "The Twilight of Spanish Texas, 1803–1821." As well, David La Vere's *The Texas Indians* continues the history of Texas emphasizing the Indian side of the story.

Louisiana Once again a Contested Frontier

Just as Spanish Texas had its beginnings in the French occupation of what eventually came to be known as Louisiana, so too is the end of Spanish Texas tied to its eastern neighbor. For the story of the most representative of the early intruders, see Maurine T. Wilson and Jack Jackson's *Philip Nolan and Texas: Expeditions to the Unknown Land, 1791–1801* (1987). Although Charles A. Bacarisse's doctoral dissertation on the Baron of Bastrop was never published, he did prepare an article summarizing his research: "Baron de Bastrop," *Southwestern Historical Quarterly* (1955). Extensive accounts of Spanish efforts to stop Anglo-American penetration of Texas appear in *Jefferson & Southwestern Exploration: The Freeman & Custis Accounts of the Red River Expedition of 1806*, by Dan L. Flores (1984), and Jack D. L. Holmes, "Showdown on the Sabine: General James Wilkinson vs. Lieutenant Colonel Simon de Herrera," *Louisiana Studies* (1964).

Fortress Texas: Reinforcing against the American Threat

The Opening of Texas to Foreign Settlement, 1801–1821, by Mattie Austin Hatcher (1927; reprint 1976) remains unsurpassed in telling the story of Spain's desperate efforts to hold back the tide of Anglo-American westward expansion. Spanish policy in Louisiana, which helped shape attitudes in Texas, is the subject of

Gilbert C. Din's "Spain's Immigration Policy in Louisiana and the American Penetration, 1792–1803," *Southwestern Historical Quarterly* (1973). The colorful and competent Governor Antonio Cordero still awaits a biographer, but his successor has received much closer scrutiny in *Tragic Cavalier: Governor Manuel Salcedo of Texas, 1808–1813* by Félix D. Almaráz (1971). The problems these officials had in keeping undesirable people and ideologies from taking hold in Texas is the subject of Odie Faulk's "The Penetration of Foreigners and Foreign Ideas into Spanish East Texas, 1793–1810," *East Texas Historical Journal* (1964).

Insurrection on the Frontier

No period of Texas colonial history has received more attention than that of 1811–13, when the province was caught up in the whirlwind of the Mexican War of Independence. Julia Kathryn Garrett's *Green Flag over Texas: A Story of the Last Years of Spain in Texas* (1939) remains a very readable narrative of the entire period. The most recent work to deal with insurgency, *A World Not to Come: A History of Latino Writing and Print Culture*, by Raúl Coronado (2013) takes a novel intellectual and literary history approach and offers new insights into Gutiérrez de Lara's motivations. A number of more specialized studies add to or provide a different perspective on events. An essay appearing in *Tejano Journey, 1770–1850*, edited by Gerald E. Poyo (1996), "Rebellion on the Frontier," by Jesús F. de la Teja, discusses local political conditions, especially in San Antonio, and how these contributed to partisanship during the war of independence. A very interesting collection of documents related to the first revolutionary episode was translated by Frederick C. Chabot in *Texas in 1811; the Las Casas and Sambrano Revolutions* (1941). The story of how San Antonio's elites restored royal government is told by J. Villasana Haggard in "The Counter-Revolution of Béxar, 1811," *Southwestern Historical Quarterly* (1939). A good summary of the Gutiérrez–Magee expedition that is also a detective story about the author's efforts to pin down the site of the Battle of Medina is Ted Schwartz, *Forgotten Battlefield of the First Texas Revolution: The Battle of Medina*, August 18, 1813, edited and annotated by Robert H. Thonhoff (1985). In addition, in a series of newspaper articles in the 1850s, José Antonio Navarro published an extensive version of events from his personal experiences as a teenage participant: *Defending Mexican Valor in Texas: José Antonio Navarro's Historical Writings, 1853–1857*, edited by David R. McDonald and Timothy M. Matovina (1995).

A Howling Wilderness: The Last Years of Spanish Texas

The history of the last years of Spanish Texas has been given over to stories of pirates and adventurers. The classic study in the field is Harris G. Warren, *The Sword Was Their Passport: A History of American Filibustering in the Mexican Revolution* (1943). Other useful readings include Fane Downs, "Governor Antonio Martínez and the Defense of Texas from Foreign Invasion, 1817–1822," *Texas Military History* (1968), and Ed Bradley, "Fighting for Texas: Filibuster

James Long, the Adams–Onís Treaty, and the Monroe Administration," *Southwestern Historical Quarterly* (1999). A very good summary of Texas from the Indian perspective during this period can be found in Chapters 2–4 of F. Todd Smith's *From Dominance to Disappearance: The Indians of Texas and the Near Southwest, 1786–1859*. For a somewhat different reading of the Indian story, see Chapter 5 of *The Lipan Apaches: People of Wind and Lightning* by Thomas A. Britten. The story of French exiles who made a brief, unsuccessful attempt to establish themselves on the lower Trinity River is told by Kent Gardien in "Take Pity on Our Glory: Men of Champ d'Asile," *Southwestern Historical Quarterly* (1984). On the ever popular Jean Laffite, Jack C. Ramsay, Jr's, *Jean Laffite, Prince of Pirates* (1996) makes entertaining reading. The anticlimactic change of sovereignty is the topic of Félix D. Almaráz's *Governor Antonio Martínez and Mexican Independence in Texas: An Orderly Transition* (1979).

Mexican Texas, 1821–1835

He had been unsure of the venture at first, so much so that his father had written, "I hope and pray you will Discharge your Doubts, as to the Enterprise." Trusted friends had been enthusiastic, and all the arrangements had been made. In Natchitoches, Louisiana, a delegation headed by Erasmo Seguín met twenty-seven-year-old Stephen Fuller Austin and in July 1821 escorted him across the Sabine into Spanish Texas, where he was to meet his father Moses and commence their colonizing work. Barely had the traveling party started, though, when word came of Moses's death in Missouri. Now it would be up to Stephen F. Austin himself to found the Anglo colony that had been his father's dream. As the party moved deep into the interior of Texas, to the Brazos River and beyond, he encountered few settlers; aside from the reduced settlement of Nacogdoches through which he had passed, most of the Tejano population was concentrated along the San Antonio River. He saw no Indians. Austin noted with enthusiasm the abundant wildlife, the fertile soil, the clear-running rivers, the pleasing way in which woodland alternated with prairie. He was bound for San Antonio, hoping and trusting that the Mexican officials there would allow him to carry out his father's deathbed wish that his son replace him in the Texas enterprise. Outside the town, an advance party returned with the news that Mexico had declared its independence and Texas was no longer under Spanish rule. This news posed another complication for Austin, but by now he was fully committed to the vision of an Anglo-American colony flourishing in Texas. His work toward that end would prove crucial to the reshaping and redefining of Texas.

How to explain the welcome that Stephen F. Austin received from the Tejano leadership and even from many within Mexico's postindependence elite? Looking back from the early twenty-first century, it seems illogical for Mexicans

134

Chapter 5 Mexican Texas, 1821–1835	
1821	Mexican independence under the Plan de Iguala; Stephen F. Austin arrives in Texas and proceeds with his father's colonization plans
1822	Agustín de Iturbide becomes constitutional emperor; Texas sends representative to the Imperial Congress
1823	Imperial Colonization Law allows Austin to proceed with colonial project; Emperor Agustín I abdicates, a federal republic is declared
1824	Texas and Coahuila merged into a single state; National Colonization of 1824 enacted; federal Constitution of 1824 takes effect
1825	State Colonization Law enacted
1826–27	Empresario Haden Edwards and his supporters stage the Fredonian Rebellion
1828–29	Gen. Manual Mier y Terán travels in Texas and reports back to Mexican government; President Guerrero abolishes slavery in Mexico—Texas exempted; Presidential succession in Mexico undermined by Federalist revolt
1830	Centralists overthrow Guerrero government; Law of April 6 seeks to greatly restrict U.S. immigration into Texas
1832	First Anahuac disturbance; Convention of Anglo-American communities declares for separation from Coahuila; Federalist revolt ousts Bustamante regime; San Antonio *ayuntamiento* sends petition to state legislature in support of colonists' reform demands
1833	Santa Anna elected president of Mexico; second colonists convention convenes and appoints Austin to carry reform requests to Mexico
1834	Austin arrested for sedition; Santa Anna deposes vice president Gómez Farías and Centralists begin dismantling Constitution of 1824
1835	Second Anahuac disturbance; Centralist–Federalist power struggle in Coahuila intensifies; Austin returns to Texas

to have supported a colonization project that would bring a culturally alien people to a land that Mexicans had yet to fully control. Mexicans, in fact, were well aware of their neighbor's expansionist activities. Between 1803 and 1819 the United States had absorbed one piece of Spain's North American domains after another. In some cases, for instance in what are now known as the Florida parishes of Louisiana, the acquisition had been accomplished through the introduction of settlers who waited until the right moment to declare independence. Quickly asking for annexation, the area had been incorporated into the United States at the start of the War of 1812. Now, here came American settlers into a region that had been Spanish territory but which until recently had been claimed by the United States as part of the Louisiana Purchase. Why did Mexicans not see the American annexation through settlement process beginning all over again in Texas?

In part the answer lies in the few options open to Mexicans, whether frontier Tejanos or Mexico City statesmen. A decade of insurgency and Indian warfare had undone decades of work to bring even a modicum of Hispanic civilization to what, despite Austin's first impressions, very much remained American Indian country. Where would the resources come from to rebuild what had been and to develop what might be? The nascent nation of Mexico, as you will see, suffered mightily in its first years; its political, economic, and social travails led to wild swings in government and to neglect of the economic fundamentals of territorial integrity. For Tejanos, then, Anglo-Americans represented a possible way out of the abyss into which the province had fallen the previous decade. For Mexico City, Anglo-Americans represented an inexpensive way of settling a frontier it otherwise was unprepared to develop or even properly defend. Both Tejano and Mexican elites at first believed that the partnership with the North Americans could be managed, and men like Stephen F. Austin said all the right things. They could not see that the overwhelming force of what soon would come to be called Manifest Destiny, already had some Americans coming to Texas with a very different agenda.

As you read this chapter, consider the following questions:

1. How did conditions in postindependence Mexico contribute to Texas's forced union with Coahuila?
2. How did reliance on empresarios to foster development of the region prove a blessing for Texas but a curse for Mexico?
3. Who were the Centralists and Federalists and why did both Anglo and Mexican Texans tend to be in the Federalist camp?

The New Nation, 1821–1824

When Agustín de Iturbide marched into Mexico City to a triumphal reception in September 1821, little had been settled with regard to Mexico's future. While some leaders advocated for a complete break from Spain, others worked to retain a monarchical form of government. There were also questions about race, status, and the relationship between far-flung jurisdictions and Mexico City, which from the beginning was regarded as the new nation's capital. For Texas all these questions were particularly relevant as the few thousand who could be considered Tejanos (Mexican Texans) shared the vastness of Texas with many more thousand indigenous peoples who could not. How would Texas and Texans fit into the new scheme of things?

Political Instability Following Independence

The decade-long struggle for independence had devastated Mexico. Aside from the hundreds of thousands dead, silver mining, the engine of the economy, was in ruins. Agriculture, the livelihood of the bulk of the population, was in shambles. Some parts of the country were governed by military strongmen of

The pomp and circumstance—and expense—of a viceroy's entry into Mexico City, the capital of the viceroyalty for the previous 300 years, was accorded to Agustín Iturbide on his ascent to the throne of the very short-lived Mexican Empire. Within months such profligate spending contributed to the collapse of independent Mexico's first monarchical scheme.

uncertain loyalties, despite the restoration of local governing bodies, the provincial deputations, which had existed briefly under the Constitution of 1812. In other parts, the links to Mexico City were so tenuous as to raise questions almost immediately about continued union with Mexico.

Among Mexico's problems was the formation of a national government. Iturbide quickly named a provisional governing *junta*, which turned around and named him its presiding officer. The junta then named a five-man regency to manage day-to-day affairs, and Iturbide became one of its members. The junta and the congress that replaced it were both dominated by men supportive of Iturbide. However, when the congress began to take steps to cut back on the size and power of the military Iturbide intervened. Arranging for street demonstrations in which he was hailed as "Agustín I, Emperor of Mexico," he *humbly* accepted the will of the people and on May 19, 1822, became constitutional emperor.

The farce lasted less than a year. Perhaps a more gifted man might have made a convincing monarch, but Iturbide was petty and self-serving. With unemployment rising, debt mounting, and little sign that the government had any idea of how to fix the country's problems, Iturbide's support waned. At the end of October he dissolved congress, after protests against his censorship and arrest of opposition members had turned the majority against him. To create a façade of representative government, he selected a small group of congressmen to serve as a *junta instituyente*, or governing council.

In early December, the commander of the port of Veracruz, Brigadier Antonio López de Santa Anna began his career in political meddling by declaring himself against Iturbide. In February 1823, anti-Iturbide conspirators issued the Plan de Casa Mata calling for the end to Iturbide's reign. Support for the Casa Mata plan spread quickly and on March 19, 1823, Agustín I abdicated. In short order, he was on board a ship bound for exile in Italy. An ill-considered attempt to return to Mexico a year later led to his arrest and execution the following July.

In the course of 1823 the country moved from a centralized monarchy to a federal republic. In July the Central American provinces abandoned Mexico and no one tried to stop them. The restored provincial deputations demanded a new national compact, and so elections for a Constituent Congress took place in the fall. When the new congress met in November 1823, its composition and goals were very different than the Imperial Congress. Unlike the majority of monarchical representatives in the first congress, the majority now espoused republican ideology. As more representative of the provincial deputations and local elites who selected them, most delegates were supporters of a system of government promoting strong states' rights.

In effect, between 1821 and 1823 the ideological lines were drawn for Mexican politics for the next half century. On one side were the Centralists. They consisted of much of the hierarchy of the Catholic Church, a considerable portion of the army's command officers, and most of the business community tied to Mexico City's leading commercial houses. They argued that Mexico lacked experience in self-government and needed a strong central government to keep the country together. Some were monarchists; some were conservative republicans. On the other side were the Federalists. They maintained that the provincial deputations, which represented the will of Mexico's regions, had already established local rule and that decentralized power would prevent the rise of new dictators. Some were professionals and local elites, and some were members of the lower clergy and junior military officers. As political parties failed to form, like-minded men used masonic lodges as the venues for their meetings, the Centralists gathering under the Scottish Rite and the Federalists under the York Rite.

Not surprisingly, the federal Constitution of 1824, which would come to play a prominent role in Texas's struggle for independence, reflected aspects of American, French, and Spanish political thought. To the U.S. Constitution it owed a government structure with separate executive, legislative, and judicial branches. Rejecting the awkward idea of a plural executive, it called for the separate election of a single president and vice president by the legislatures of the respective states. Congress was to be bicameral, with a lower house representing the population and a senate representing the states equally. Reflecting its Spanish heritage, and in concession to the Centralists, the constitution declared the Catholic faith thc only religion of the country and granted the clergy and military their *fueros*, that is, judicial autonomy that made them subject only to the legal structures of their respective institutions.

Texas in the New Order

When Father Refugio de la Garza, San Antonio's parish priest and a native of the town, arrived in Mexico City in 1822 as Texas's delegate to the Imperial Congress, he came with a wish list reflecting Texas's desperate needs. Texas needed a military campaign against hostile Indians; it needed a string of presidios to provide a barrier against both Indian and foreign encroachments; it needed large numbers of settlers from the interior of the country; it needed final decommissioning of the remaining missions to open up productive land for development.

Father De la Garza had some success. The colonization and secularization laws he supported passed, but most of his other efforts came to naught. He could not even get the government to address the needs of the troops already in Texas, let alone provide for the military expansion necessary to properly control the frontier. He especially lamented the wasted time and energy of Iturbide's reign and was glad to see it go. In May 1823 he wrote an optimistic letter to San Antonio's *ayuntamiento*, or town council, that reflected the self-government aspirations of so many:

> To repeat what I have written in my previous letters: Arbitrariness is ended as are oppression, despotism, and tyranny. Today Texas enjoys unlimited freedom, without obstacles or hindrances. Texas may dispose of everything which prodigal nature has bestowed upon it, land and sea, without regard to any laws other than those that the province may itself liberally impose.

Back in Texas, local elites took up the cause of home rule with enthusiasm. Within a month of Iturbide's abdication they set up a *junta gubernativa*, or governing council, with seven representatives from San Antonio and one each from La Bahía and Nacogdoches. In the fall of 1823, Tejanos elected their own provincial deputation. The deputation in turn selected Erasmo Seguín, a long-time public figure and friendly to U.S. immigration, as Texas delegate to the Constituent Congress. Having acquired a taste for local governance, Tejanos would be reluctant to give it up.

Seguín spent almost a year in Mexico City, often suffering the privations of someone representing the poorest portion of the new nation. At one point he wrote to his wife, "I have no money, but I am not hungry. And, were I hungry, I would not ask for help from my province, for she is more fit to receive help than to give it." His agenda was much the same as Father De la Garza's had been. Soon after his arrival, he realized that keeping the four northeastern provinces of Tamaulipas (Nuevo Santander's new name), Nuevo León, Coahuila, and Texas together as a single political entity was unworkable. It was also clear that Texas, with its small population and underdevelopment, would not be accepted as stand-alone state. In time, Seguín came to see that the national government's dysfunction militated against territorial status. As he wrote to the Barón de

Bastrop in April 1824, "The situation is bad, very bad. Every day the number of conspiracies increases, and everyone is out to undo the government's orders." Finally agreeing to union with Coahuila, he had included in the decree a provision that gave Texas the option of petitioning for separate statehood when its population grew enough to warrant the move.

Seguín also saw himself as an advocate for Anglo-American immigration, on which he and other Tejano oligarchs were pinning their hopes for Texas's prosperity. Fortunately, he served on the committee that produced the National Colonization Law of 1824, which left most of those matters in the hands of the states. To assuage the concerns of those suspicious of U.S. intentions, the law reserved to the national government approval of all foreign settlement within a twenty-league (fifty miles) reserve along international borders and ten leagues (twenty-five miles) along the coast. Seguín also worked on behalf of the preservation of slavery as necessary to attract Americans of substance rather than just poor farmers. Congress settled on a vague prohibition of the slave trade. On the issue of freedom of conscience, Seguín advised that "there shall be no other cult than the Christian Catholic," but that the provision applied only to public worship, "as even under the old government religious toleration was permitted."

Texas never warmed to its relationship with Coahuila. With the new capital located at Saltillo, at the southern end of the state, the reins of power were far from Texas. San Antonio saw an immediate demotion in status; it now became the seat of government for the Department of Texas, with a *jefe político*, in effect a deputy governor, appointed by the state governor. As Anglo-American immigration changed the face of Texas, tensions with both Saltillo and Mexico City rose, making the union with Coahuila one of the principal grievances in the coming decade.

Political and Economic Development on Mexico's Northeastern Frontier

The Federalist reordering of Mexico also brought change to the Mexican communities along the Rio Grande. Paso del Norte, which had been part of New Mexico during the colonial period, was transferred to the jurisdiction of the state of Chihuahua. During the early independence era, Paso del Norte continued to grow and prosper, despite increasing Apache attacks. Much of the growth was the result of booming commerce brought about by the Santa Fe trade. As American merchants opened up commercial links between Missouri and New Mexico along what has come to be known as the Santa Fe Trail, there was a corresponding increase in trade along the Camino Real between Chihuahua and New Mexico.

The new trade and accompanying growth created economic opportunities for men such as Juan María Ponce de León and Hugh Stephenson. Ponce de León received land grants from the ayuntamiento of Paso del Norte on the north side of the Rio Grande in 1827 and established farming and ranching operations in what is now downtown El Paso. Hugh Stephenson, an American fur trapper and teamster, also acquired land in the area in the mid-1820s and by 1828 had married the daughter of a prominent Paseño merchant. Even the devastating floods of 1829, which cut a new channel for the Rio Grande and left Ysleta, Socorro, and San Elizario on what eventually would be the Texas side of the border, did not halt the area's development.

Political and economic changes also came to the settlements of the Lower Rio Grande valley, where ties to Texas were more immediate. In 1825 Tamaulipas, which during the colonial period had been the province of Nuevo Santander, passed a colonization law modeled on the one from neighboring Coahuila y Texas hoping to draw a similar type of settlement to the vast expanse between the Rio Grande and Nueces rivers. Although no Anglo-American colonization projects materialized, the generous provisions of the land law led to the founding of numerous ranching estates as far north as the Nueces by the mid-1830s.

The expansion of the livestock industry in northern Tamaulipas, always a risky proposition because of the environment, had come to a halt in the decade of independence struggle when Indian raids and insurgent warfare had disrupted ranching operations. For instance, Matamoros resident Enrique Villarreal, a royalist army officer who fought at the Battle of Medina, was forced to abandon his ranch at Rincón del Oso on Corpus Christi Bay in 1817 because of the raids. He reestablished the ranch in 1824 and acquired a title to over 40,000 acres from Tamaulipas in 1831.

For men such as Villarreal the growing markets for livestock, especially hides and wool for export and horses and mules for domestic use, made the risks worthwhile. So did smuggling. Although much of the new trade at first took place through the port of Matamoros, which had opened to international trade in 1823, by 1828 an increasing amount of goods was coming in by way of Corpus Christi and then overland into the interior. High Mexican import tariffs on manufactured goods that competed with national manufactures drove the smuggling. As in the case of the Chihuahua-Santa Fe-Missouri trade, Mexican exports consisted largely of silver, although hides and wool also headed out to American ports.

The growing shipping between Matamoros and New Orleans in time created a commercial center that, as in the case of Paso del Norte, drew young entrepreneurs from Europe and the United States, such as eighteen-year-old Connecticut native Charles Stillman, who arrived from New Orleans in 1828 and became involved in a broad range of business activities in Tamaulipas and Nuevo León. American businessmen such as Stillman, who established themselves in Matamoros in the 1820s and 1830s, eventually turned their attention to the American side of the border, where during the 1840s and 1850s they acquired, sometimes in quite shady ways, title to much of the land granted by Spain and Mexico in the previous century.

For Paseños, as the residents of the Paso del Norte area were known, developments in far off Texas were little more than news of mild interest, but of little direct consequence. For Tamaulipecos, that is the residents of the country below the lower Nueces River, events in Texas were of great consequence. Many of the residents of the river towns, from Laredo to Matamoros, had participated in military actions in Texas during the Mexican War of Independence. Many, too, had suffered from raids by Indians from Texas and had an interest in developments in the neighboring state that might make life more peaceful. Increasingly, Tamaulipecos had business contacts with Texans, both Tejanos and Anglos. And, of course, there were many Anglo-Texans and Americans who saw everything north of the Rio Grande as part of Texas, and no part of Tamaulipas at all. It is no surprise that when the Texas Revolution began, some of the Texan adventurers hoped to conquer Matamoros for Texas.

The Age of the Empresarios, 1821–1830

By the time that the political reorganization of the Mexican north under the Constitution of 1824 took place, the transformation of Texas into an extension of the American cotton kingdom had begun. This transformation was abetted and facilitated by Mexican policymakers, particularly Tejanos, who saw in a settlement program under officially sanctioned promoters—empresarios—the best hope for attracting productive farmers and planters. Not all settlers who came did so under the auspices of an empresario and not all empresarios had the best of intentions, however. By 1830 Mexican reservations over the wisdom of the experiment would lead to the first efforts to stop immigration from the United States.

Austin's Colony

The first and most successful of the empresarios was Stephen Fuller Austin, or Estevan as he soon started signing his name. Having grown up in a family of frontier entrepreneurs, having received a good basic education, and having acquired some military and public service experience, Stephen was well prepared for the challenge ahead. In December 1820 he was in New Orleans beginning an apprenticeship in law when he received a letter from his father explaining the Texas colonization project and asking for his help.

Austin's first trip to Texas in summer 1821 went well enough to convince him of the project's potential. The lands he inspected along the bottoms of the Brazos and Colorado rivers were perfect for an agricultural settlement. After visiting with Governor Antonio Martínez one last time to work out the details of individual grants, Austin left for New Orleans to recruit colonists, the first of whom arrived in December 1821. Unfortunately, when in early 1822 Austin returned to Béxar to report on the colony's progress, Martínez informed him that he was acting outside the law. Austin must obtain the approval of the new government in Mexico City.

Austin's time in the new nation's capital might have discouraged a less determined man. Although he presented the order from the provincial deputation authorizing his father to establish the colony and the agreements that he and Governor Martínez had made regarding the location of the colony and the

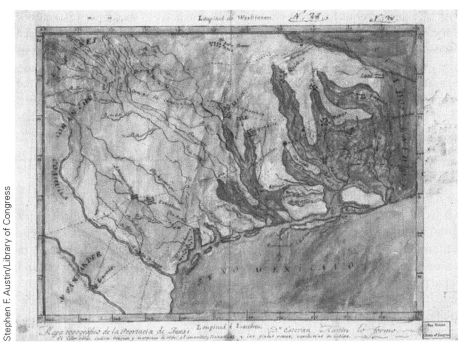

The first map of Texas made after Mexican independence was compiled in 1822 by Stephen F. Austin, whose interest in agricultural lands is demonstrated in the dark coloring of bottom lands along the province's eastern watersheds. Note that Texas clearly ends at the Nueces River.

Stephen F. Austin/Library of Congress

size and terms of individual grants, little happened. In fact, Austin experienced the waste of time and effort that marked the first Mexican Empire. In August he even wrote out a scheme of government (never presented) that he prefaced with a reproach:

> As a citizen of this Empire I should be wanting in my duty did I not feel that anxiety for the common welfare of my Country which ought to animate the bosom of every good man. I have therefore viewed with great interest the political agitations of the nation, and particularly of this Capital for the last two months; and believing that the evils which now embarrass the operations of Government arise solely from a defect in the organization of the Legislative department; I have taken the Liberty to offer my ideas on the subject.

After Iturbide dissolved congress at the end of October, Austin lamented, "These people will not do for a Republic."

Out of the turmoil, however, came the Imperial Colonization Law of 1823, which set up an empresario system that surpassed Austin's initial expectations. It offered a square league, or *sitio*, of 4,428 acres to each family involved in stock raising and a *labor* (unit of cropland) of 177 acres for a family's farming operation (not surprisingly, all settlers claimed to be stock raisers). It provided other inducements as well, such as a seven-year moratorium on import duties, and the ability to pay the minimal costs of the land in installments. Empresarios would not receive payment for their colonization efforts from the government until they had settled at least 200 families, at which point they would receive choice lands of their own. The law made clear that the land included in the colony contract was not the empresario's and that a commissioner representing the government would be responsible for issuing titles. Until then, the law allowed the empresario to charge moderate fees to offset surveying and administrative costs. As it turned out, although there were a number of individuals in Mexico City lobbying for empresario deals, the only contract issued under the imperial colonization law was Austin's first.

During the period from 1821 to 1824, Austin exceeded the 200-family requirement for his own land, and by 1827 he approached the projected number of settlers, with 297 families, later referred to as the "Old Three Hundred." By the terms of settlement laid out in 1823, they were to be "of unblemished character, good Morals, Sobriety, and industrious habits." They were also supposed to be Catholics; for the overwhelmingly Protestant settlers, this was a conversion in name only. As a group, Austin's colonists had high literacy rates for the era and were people of some means. Of those who had settled by the fall of 1825, sixty-nine families possessed slaves, who made up 25 percent of the colony's population of 1,800. Jared Groce of Alabama, the wealthiest colonist, brought with him ninety bondsmen whose labor quickly helped him consolidate his wealth and position in their new location beside the Brazos.

Austin ran his colonial project from the town of San Felipe de Austin, perhaps the last Texas town intentionally named for a Catholic saint, as the name was proposed by Commandant General Felipe de la Garza to honor both his patron saint and Stephen F. Austin. It was the first Anglo-American town to be granted an ayuntamiento and it was the first to have a formal militia. The empresario was responsible for everything, including justice and defense, until suitable civil institutions were authorized. Fortunately for Austin, in overseeing the colony's governance he had the able assistance of Samuel May Williams, a Rhode Island native who had learned Spanish in South America. Williams was not only Austin's secretary, he managed the colony's affairs while Austin was away on business and also served as secretary of the ayuntamiento at San Felipe, which in effect was the capital of Austin's Texas.

Other Colonizing Efforts

Even before he had completed the terms of his first contract, Austin set to work to obtain the right to introduce yet more settlers. Those contracts, as well as those made to most other would-be empresarios, were made under the state colonization law of 1825, the features of which generally followed the provisions of the imperial law of 1823 and adhered to the strictures of the national law of 1824. The most important provision of the state law was the elimination of the separate 177 farming allotment, making the maximum size of a family grant 4,428 acres. It would be the responsibility of the governor to appoint a commissioner to issue titles to the settlers in the name of the state, and colonists could not dispose of the land for six years.

Among the early empresario contracts issued by the government of Coahuila y Texas, the most significant after Austin's was that of Green DeWitt. In 1825 DeWitt, a former Missouri sheriff, with the help of Austin and the Barón de Bastrop (who had become commissioner for Austin's first contract) was awarded a grant bordering Austin's on the west and was authorized to locate 400 families on the Guadalupe. The seat of the colony became the town of Gonzales, which was originally founded in 1825 but after Indian attacks was relocated to its present site in 1827. Unfortunately, in the confused circumstances of the early stages of land distribution, the boundaries of DeWitt's contract overlapped with those of Martín De León, the lone successful Mexican empresario.

De León had received his authorization to establish a settlement from the provincial deputation in early 1824, before the merger of Coahuila and Texas. Therefore, it was granted after Austin's contract with Iturbide's empire but before DeWitt's contract with the state. In fact, De León, a native of Tamaulipas, had petitioned the Spanish government as early as 1807 to settle in South Texas. With the onset of the Mexican War of Independence, he had withdrawn below the Rio Grande, but in the early 1820s decided to make another go at establishing a ranching operation in Texas. In 1824, he received a contract to locate forty-one Mexican families on the lower Guadalupe River. A settlement named in honor of the first president of Mexico, Nuestra Señora Guadalupe de Jesús Victoria, soon known simply as Victoria, served as the colony's seat of government. Despite boundary and other disputes with DeWitt's colony, De León established a prosperous ranching-based community that eventually totaled over 150 grants.

Between 1825 and 1829 the state awarded various empresarios contracts covering most of Texas and, because of imperfect knowledge of the interior, well beyond what were supposed to be the state's borders (although Texas would claim those lands as late as 1850); only a handful produced results. James Power and James Hewetson, Irish businessmen who had located in Coahuila after independence, in 1828 received a contract to settle both Mexican and Irish families in the coastal area between the Lavaca and Guadalupe rivers. John McMullen and James McGloin, also Irish merchants in Mexico, took over a failing empresario contract in 1828 and brought Irish settlers to their colony in the brush country of South Texas just north of the Nueces River. By 1834, about 250 Irish families had settled in Power and Hewetson's colony centered at Refugio and in McMullen and McGloin's at San Patricio.

Most empresarios, however, had little success in attracting significant numbers of settlers. In 1822 Sterling Robertson, a Tennessee plantation owner, joined other stockholders in a "Texas Association" planning a settlement in Mexican Texas. In 1825 his colleague Robert Leftwich secured a contract to settle 800 families in what is now central Texas but was unable to follow through. Robertson continued his attempts to recruit settlers in Tennessee and Kentucky but was not able to advance the colonization under his own name until the 1830s. By the

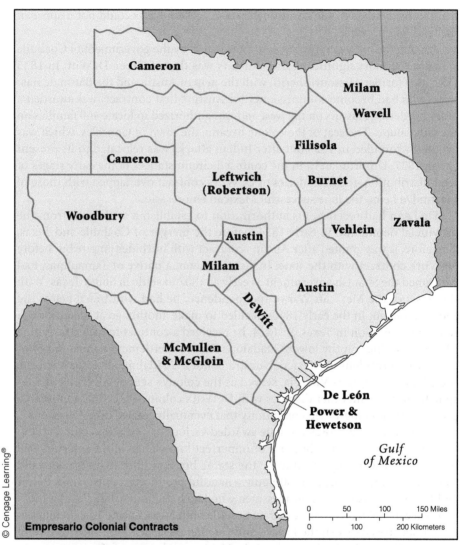

Empresario Colonial Contracts

While the national government issued Austin's original contract under the Imperial Colonization Law of 1823, and Martín de León obtained his contract under special terms from the Texas Provincial Deputation in 1824, more than a dozen other empresario contracts were issued up to 1829 under provisions of the State Colonization Law of 1825 of Coahuila and Texas. Because of conflicting claims and accusations of fraud, litigation over some of the contracts extended into the statehood period.

time he did, Samuel May Williams had gotten the state government to turn the contract over to him and Austin, and a protracted legal battle ensued that lasted beyond Texas independence.

The sordid tale of the Galveston Bay and Texas Land Company reveals the unscrupulous behavior of some empresarios and the American land speculators who hoped to take advantage of what appeared lawless conditions in Mexican Texas. In 1826 David G. Burnet, a New Jersey native, Ohio lawyer, and Louisiana trader with the Comanches on the Brazos, and Joseph Vehlein, a German merchant in Mexico, received contracts to settle 300 families each in East Texas. In 1828 Vehlein received an additional contract for 100 families south of the first one. In 1829 Lorenzo de Zavala, one of Mexico's most prominent statesman of the independence period, obtained an empresario contract for 500 families between Vehlein's and the Sabine. Failing to find the means to carry out their projects, in 1830 the three men signed over their contracts to the New York–based Galveston Bay and Texas Land Company, but the transaction was a clear violation of their contracts with the state government. Worse, the company then turned around and started selling land scrip (certificates for blocks of land) instead of locating settlers within the colonies. Not only was the sale of scrip illegal, since the company did not own the land, but it did so after the Mexican congress had passed the Law of April 6, 1830, which voided all empresario contracts not substantially fulfilled. Yet, the actions of the Galveston Bay and Texas Land Company were not the most egregious actions by an empresario.

The Fredonian Rebellion

That dubious honor belongs to Haden Edwards and to his unofficial partner in the contract, his brother Benjamin. Empresario Edwards, a wealthy former U.S. senator from Kentucky, had obtained authorization to locate 800 families around Nacogdoches. Unlike Austin's contract area, however, Edwards's boundaries included a sizeable and mixed population. There were the "old settlers"— both Mexican and Anglo—who had held on to their homesteads through the turbulence of the previous decade, some possessing grants from the Spanish government. Also in the area lived approximately sixty Cherokee families that had crossed the Sabine in 1820 and attempted to gain land titles north of Nacogdoches. Squatters had also established themselves in the area, gambling on gaining title to land at some point.

The Edwards' high-handed behavior antagonized the old settlers and even the squatters, some of whom had lived in the vicinity for a number of years. In September 1825 the Edwards posted notice that everyone occupying land within the contract area had to produce a valid title or pay him for it. In December, Haden upheld what was obviously a rigged *alcalde* election of his son-in-law Chichester Chaplin, who had recently arrived from Louisiana. When the old-settler supporters of defeated opponent Samuel Norris claimed vote fraud, political chief José Antonio Saucedo in San Antonio overturned the election and ordered that Norris be installed as alcalde.

So intolerable was the empresario's behavior that in June 1826 President Victoria annulled Edwards's contract and ordered his expulsion from Mexico. Lacking the resources to carry out the president's orders, Saucedo hesitated, giving the Edwards faction an opportunity to escalate the situation. In November a group of Edwards supporters took captive a number of the key players in the political struggle, including Norris and Edwards himself. Edwards was quickly released, but members of his faction tried and convicted Norris and others of "oppression and corruption in office" and installed their own alcalde. On December 21 the conspirators took the next step and declared the independence of the Republic of Fredonia.

In doing so, they enlisted the support of the Texas Cherokees. These migrant Indians had planted crops, constructed homes, and integrated themselves into the life of an area partially within Edwards's contract. Frustrated in their repeated efforts to negotiate a land title from the government in Mexico, the Cherokees feared that they would again be forced out as more U.S. immigrants arrived. Consequently, leaders Richard Fields and John Dunn Hunter fell for Benjamin Edwards's offer of the land they currently occupied and much more land to the west if they would join the rebellion. The Fredonian Declaration of Independence, then, claimed to speak for "the White and Red emigrants from the United States of North America" in their resistance to "an imbecile, faithless, and despotic government, miscalled a Republic."

The rebellion unraveled within the month. On January 4 a skirmish between Edwards supporters and loyalists took place in Nacogdoches. Soon the Cherokees, led by Big Mush and Chief Bowl, also known as Duwali, withdrew their support of Edwards, going so far as to have Fields and Hunter executed in an attempt to reassure Texas authorities that they had no wish to foment trouble. Knowledge that Mexican troops and a militia from Austin's colony were on the way led many settlers who had supported the rebellion to reconsider. By the time Colonel Mateo Ahumada's force, accompanied by Saucedo and Austin, arrived in Nacogdoches on February 8, Haden Edwards and the other ringleaders had escaped to Louisiana.

The conflict demonstrated to Mexican officials some of the dangers of allowing colonization from the United States, but the situation was not yet dire. The Edwards faction had failed to recruit many settlers, and many others had opposed the rebels. Austin and his colonists responded in a way that demonstrated their commitment to Mexico and the rule of law. The Cherokees' reversal of their position meant that the government still had a chance to reach a peaceful and permanent solution to at least some of Texas's Indian issues.

Indians in a Changing Texas

On his initial surveying expedition, Austin had encountered a band of Cocos, a branch of the Karankawas. Their meeting was peaceful, and Austin hoped to avoid conflict, but he anticipated that "there will be no way of subduing them but extermination." The dwindling Karankawas did not have a strong enough presence to challenge the part of Austin's colony that infringed on their traditional grounds. Instead, they moved in and out of the colony boundaries, quickly coming to be considered a nuisance and a threat because of occasional raids they made on solitary colonists or small parties. The death of two Austin colonists and the wounding of two others in early 1823 led to a retaliatory attack on a

Karankawa camp by an ad hoc company of settlers led by Robert Kuykendall. At least nineteen Indians were killed and scalped and their possessions taken. John H. Moore, one of the participants in the Skull Creek massacre, reasoned

> We all felt it was an act of justice and self-preservation. We were too weak to furnish food for Carankawaes, and had to be let alone to get bread for ourselves. Ungainly and repugnant, their cannibalism being beyond question, they were obnoxious to whites, whose patience resisted with difficulty their frequent attacks upon the scanty population of the colonies, and when it passed endurance they went to their chastisement with alacrity.

As more settlers arrived in the Austin colony, the plight of the northern Karankawas worsened. In the fall of 1825, heeding the demands of colonists, Austin authorized a campaign of extermination in which settlers from the DeWitt and De León colonies participated. The war came to a temporary end on May 13, 1827, when Karankawa leaders Antoñito, Delgado, and Soldado met with empresarios Austin, De León, and DeWitt, as well as the commander of La Bahía and missionaries. In return for safe conduct for any remaining Cocos within Austin colony boundaries and the release of any Indian captives, the Karankawas agreed to remain west of the Lavaca, where they could live in peace as long as they left Anglo Americans and Tejanos at peace. Unable to reestablish secure fishing and hunting grounds, and decimated by hunger and disease, some Karankawas raided Tejano cattle herds to survive, leading to further violence. The expulsion of the Karankawas from Texas would continue into the 1850s.

Unlike the Karankawas, the other Texas indigenous people whose range overlapped with Austin's colony boundaries, the Tonkawa, were not subject to what some scholars have referred to as ethnic cleansing. Austin and DeWitt considered the Tonkawas as a nonthreat and, in fact, useful as a barrier to Comanche encroachments into the colonies. The Tonkawas had also made overtures to the Mexican government to serve as allies against the Comanches, so peace prevailed between the tribe and Tejanos and Anglos. The Tonkawas, blocked from direct access to American trade goods by Comanches and Norteños to the north and by the migrant tribes to the east, took to bringing their hides and pelts into the Austin colony to trade. When Tonkawas stole livestock or damaged crops, Austin worked through tribal leaders he trusted to have the guilty punished. Consequently, incidents of violence between Texans and Tonkawas were few during the years of Mexican rule.

The same could not be said for the Comanches and Apaches, as old patterns reemerged. A treaty with the Lipans in 1822 restored a semblance of peace between Tejanos and Apaches, who were now free to resume their hostilities against the Comanches. Absent a restoration of an effective gift policy after a Comanche delegation visited Mexico City in 1822, the Comanches resumed their raids against Tejano ranches and as far as the Rio Grande country in Coahuila and Tamaulipas.

Finally prodded to take the offensive, Mexican presidio forces organized a campaign for fall 1825. The Lipans, who continued to hold a grudge against the

Comanches, were enthusiastic participants in the campaign. Presidio troops from both La Bahía and Rio Grande and their Lipan allies inflicted defeats on Comanche raiding parties in Texas and Tamaulipas, bringing about a decline in the number and intensity of Comanche raids. So effective was the employment of Lipans in these campaigns that government officials made sure to keep them supplied with guns and ammunition. By 1827 new peace initiatives undertaken after Commandant General Anastasio Bustamante, who served as the Mexican army commander in the northeastern states, threatened war against the Wichitas and Comanches began bringing Penateka bands into negotiations that resulted in yet another general peace that endured through the Texas Revolution.

The Wichita tribes of Texas also took Bustamante's threat seriously and agreed to peace negotiations that reduced Taovaya, Tawakoni, and Waco raids to manageable levels. Like the Comanches, the Wichitas had increased their raids in the early 1820s. Austin had attempted to establish a separate peace with them in 1824, but by the following year their incursions within his colony's boundaries led Austin to order hostilities against them in support of the beleaguered Tejanos. In 1826 a large militia force under Captain Aylett Buckner marched against the Wichitas' Brazos River towns, which the Indians evacuated, but in retaliation Wacos and Tawakonis carried out raids against San Antonio and Gonzales. Only after being warned by General Bustamante did Waco and Tawakoni leaders sit down to negotiate with Nacogdoches commander Francisco Ruiz and Indian agent Peter Ellis Bean, a member of Philip Nolan's last expedition who subsequently settled on the Texas frontier.

In the negotiations, Bean also extended an olive branch from the Cherokees to the Wichitas. The Texas Cherokees had calculated that their participation in the campaigns against the Wichitas would lead the government to grant them the land titles they so desperately wanted. Similar reasoning led the other migrant tribes of Texas, Alabamas, Coushattas, Shawnees, Choctaws, and Chickasaws to side with Tejanos and settlers against hostile tribes. Having built villages, cleared crop lands, and established trade networks in eastern Texas, they were eager not to be pushed off their lands as had happened to them in the United States. Unfortunately, in the political maneuverings between empresarios, land speculators, and government officials, the pleas for clear land titles went unheeded. Even an 1833 trip to Monclova by Duwali and other Cherokee leaders to petition the state directly proved fruitless. Except for the Alabamas and Couchattas, who eventually merged into a single tribe, the aspirations of the migrant Indians would be dashed by the anti-Indian attitudes and policies of Texans following independence.

Life in Mexican Texas

Beyond the chronic menace posed by the still powerful independent Indian groups, Euroamerican Texans faced a number of challenges in what was still very much a frontier environment. Despite a century of settlement at San Antonio and La Bahía, Tejanos there and in East Texas still lived a frontier life of isolation and crude living conditions. The decade of instability that preceded independence had led to deterioration in agriculture, the collapse of ranching, and the drastic decline even of the contraband trade that had supported a considerable portion of the province's economy. Mexicans were not attracted to a frontier that could be described in no better terms than it had been fifty years earlier. Consequently, San Antonio's and La Bahía's populations, about 1,500 and 500 respectively in 1824, were slow to grow, and in the Nacogdoches area growth came from immigration by Anglo Americans and American Indians. The only bright spot on the Tejano frontier was the development of a thriving ranching-based community at Victoria, where the few hundred settlers, mostly from Tamaulipas, dominated the area by the early 1830s.

Tejanos, then, remained trapped in an essentially subsistence economy, isolated from the development of the cotton economy that was transforming Texas to the east. San Antonio remained the administrative capital for the department, but with the scope of government limited to a few basic functions, the office of the political chief did not contribute much to the local economy. The ill-paid and maintained troops that garrisoned the city in the early years of independence were actually a burden on the population, as they turned to theft and pawning their equipment to help their families survive. The garrison at La Bahía experienced much the same conditions. The situation improved only slowly over the course of the decade.

The Anglos who settled in Austin's colony did not have it much better in the early years. Mary Crownover Rabb, who in 1823 arrived in Austin's colony from Arkansas with her husband John, first settled in the LaGrange area. Soon they moved near relatives in the small community of Indian Hill, further upriver, but John grew impatient with the constant Indian depredations. The couple moved from one isolated farming location to another, camping out or creating rudimentary log shelters. In the U.S. colonial tradition, they produced what they needed at home: John constructed a loom and Mary sat under a tree weaving mosquito netting before their cabin was constructed. Often left alone with her children for long periods, Mary dealt with her loneliness and Indians ranging nearby by working late into the night and sprinkling shelled corn on the floor for the pigs, noting "by the time I got in the bed, all them little pigs would be in the house cracking corn until I would be asleep and the Indians gone and the pigs gone."

In other colonies, conditions were even more precarious. Noah Smithwick visited DeWitt's colony two or three years after its founding and found a dozen families living huddled together for fear of the Indians. Smithwick provided a particularly vivid picture of the lives of the women, who did not share the men's excitement about hunting and exploring: "They had not even the solace of constant employment. . . . There was no house to keep in order; the meager fare was so simple as to require little time for its preparation. There was no poultry, no dairy, no garden, no books, or papers. . . . no schools, no churches—nothing to break the dull monotony of their lives."

In frontier Texas, the natural environment often provided challenges to travelers. With this illustration from an 1834 book titled *A Visit to Texas*, J. T. Hammond conveys the size of the thick cane breaks through which travelers found and forged routes.

Still, they came. By 1830 more than 7,000 Americans, not including slaves, already outnumbered Tejanos 2 to 1 or more. Many lived solitary lives because the grants they claimed, tracts of 4,428 acres for a family unit, meant considerable distances between neighbors, and the villages that began to appear were few and far between. Roads remained little more than ruts in the prairies or trails in the forests. But these conditions were those that the parents, grandparents, and great grandparents of many colonists had faced. To them the "wilderness" was to be conquered, the native peoples being little more than yet another obstacle to be overcome. And soon, Mexicans would also come to be seen as obstacles to progress, to the personal liberty and local autonomy that was their American birthright.

Tensions, 1830–1833

In many ways Mexico had been accommodating to the Americans. Not only had the federal government and the government of Coahuila y Texas encouraged immigration with generous land grants, but despite general Mexican opposition to slavery, exceptions were made for U.S. immigrants. Even when President Vincente Guerrero officially abolished slavery in 1829, an exemption was made for Texas. Yet political problems mounted between the government and its citizens in Texas, particularly the newcomers from the United States.

The Law of April 6, 1830

Mexican policymakers had opened the doors to Anglo-American settlement in Texas to solve a set of intractable problems, including underdevelopment and Indian hostilities. Tejanos themselves had been among the first to ask for a rational and enforceable immigration policy and to complain about the lack of assimilation among the immigrants. In their instructions to Father De la Garza as representative to the imperial congress, they asked him to request that Anglo Americans only be allowed to settle in Texas with the government's permission, "under the specific condition that they be Catholics, have property, [and] a craft or useful profession." In 1826 Rafael Manchola, one of Martín De León's sons-in-law and local public figure in Goliad, commented on the Anglo colonists' lack of respect for Mexican law:

> No faith can be placed in the Anglo-American colonists because they are continually demonstrating that they absolutely refuse to be subordinate, unless they find it convenient to what they want anyway, all of which I believe will be very detrimental to us for them to be our neighbors if we do not in time clip the wings of their audacity by stationing a strong detachment in each new settlement, which will enforce the laws and jurisdiction of a Mexican magistrate which should be placed in each of them, since under their own colonists as judges, they do nothing more than practice their own laws which they have practiced since they were born, forgetting the ones they have sworn to obey, these being the laws of our Supreme Government.

Nevertheless, the majority of Tejano oligarchs supported immigration from the United States, because, as future signer of the Texas Declaration of Independence Francisco Ruiz put it in 1830, "I cannot help seeing the advantages which, to my way of thinking, would result if we admitted honest, hard-working people, regardless of what country they come from . . . even hell itself."

What Tejanos thought and did was one thing, what the federal government should do about a situation like the Fredonian rebellion was another. In 1827 the Victoria administration decided to act by sending General Manuel Mier y Terán at the head of a commission, ostensibly to set the border between the United States and Mexico as originally called for in the Adams-Onís Treaty of 1819, but also to check on the situation in East Texas. Writing from Texas in 1828, he cautioned President Victoria: "I am warning you to take timely measures. Texas could throw the whole nation into revolution." In Nacogdoches, in particular, he found a lack of necessary authority and order. New immigrants from the United States were streaming in and simply appropriating plots of land, many of them "fugitives from our neighbor republic and bear[ing] the unmistakable earmarks of thieves and criminals," although he noted that some of these "have reformed and settled down to an industrious life."

On one issue, however, he found most Texas residents in agreement, from Austin's colony northward: the need to separate Texas from Coahuila. Mier y Terán cited reasons such as the impracticality of having to seek recourse from a state capital in Coahuila "so distant and separated from this section by deserts infected by hostile savages" and the friction resulting from "the mixing of [Texans'] affairs with those of Coahuila." Governance on the frontier was inadequate and, consequently, the new citizens lacked respect for the country's institutions. Mier y Terán's recommendations that the government expend more effort in recruiting Mexican and European settlers, develop trade with the Mexican interior, and encourage foreign trade along the gulf coast served as the basis for the measures that the Centralist administration of Anastasio Bustamante began to adopt after seizing power in early 1830.

Unfortunately for Mexico, a tradition of orderly transfer of power did not develop under the new constitutional order. Guadalupe Victoria, who served from 1824 to 1829, was the first and only president who took office during the first federal period (1824–1835) without military intervention. Dissatisfied that their favorite had not won the 1828 election, Santa Anna and Zavala threatened an uprising, allowing congress to void the election. In a new election the correct results were a forgone conclusion: Vicente Guerrero became the nation's second president, but managed to serve less than a year. The constitution required a separate election vice president, and Centralist general Anastasio Bustamante won the post. He, in turn, led a revolt that overthrew Guerrero at the beginning of 1830.

Bustamante quickly set to work to implement Mier y Terán's recommendations. The result was the Law of April 6, 1830, a decree that attempted to restrict and control American immigration into Texas. Among other provisions, the legislation voided empresario contracts that had not been completed, theoretically halting immigration from the United States. The most objectionable provision was Article 11, which welcomed future U.S. immigrants to settle in the interior of Mexico but not in border states, that is, Texas. The law banned the importation of slaves into Texas, reinforcing President Guerrero's emancipation decree of the previous year from which Texas had been exempted. The legislation also called for a national commissioner of colonization, encouraged immigration from the interior of Mexico, and opened coastal trade to foreigners for four years. To enforce the law, military posts and customs houses would be reinforced or established along the border and gulf coast.

Early Troubles at Anahuac and Nacogdoches

Austin, who was acquainted with Mexico's leading men, certainly had an advantage over the other empresarios, who found themselves on the wrong end of the new law. He obtained an exemption for his own colonial enterprise and that of DeWitt by claiming that their terms had been substantially fulfilled. He was fortunate that filling the new commissioner of colonization office was none other than Mier y Terán, who as a member of congress had worked with Austin on the Imperial Colonization Law eight years earlier and who appreciated Austin's trustworthiness. But Austin's loyalty had limits, as he indicated July 1830: "As to my colony I can say that we have been true and religiously faithful in our acts and in our views, to Mexico—and so we will remain—but I also say that Mexico cannot oppress us alive—we may be overwhelmed & anihilated [sic]— but we cannot be treated like children nor like slaves."

Early grumblings over the Law of April 6 erupted into open resistance in two events that came to be known as the Anahuac Disturbances. Anahuac, near the mouth of the Trinity River on Galveston Bay, was established by order of General Mier y Terán as a military post to assist in the enforcement of the Law of April 6. He appointed John (or Juan) Davis Bradburn, a Virginian who had become a Mexican military officer, as commander of Anahuac. The problems began with the arrival in early 1831 of José Francisco Madero, special commissioner from the Federalist governor of Coahuila y Texas, who issued land titles to area residents. Bradburn, citing the National Colonization Law of 1824, argued that Madero had no authority to act within the ten-league coastal reserve. Madero, briefly jailed by Bradburn, nonetheless issued about three dozen land titles and also formed an ayuntamiento, Santísima Trinidad de la Libertad, which was quickly shortened to Liberty by area residents. Although Bradburn suspended the ayuntamiento, area residents resisted the action.

Friction between southeast Texans residents and the national government increased when late in 1831 Bradburn was joined by customs collector George Fisher, a Hungarian-born émigré from Mississippi to Mexico. He quickly antagonized Texans and American ship captains by attempting to collect customs duties and by ordering that all vessels doing business in Texas had to obtain permission to sail at Anahuac.

Tensions reached the boiling point when Bradburn imprisoned law partners William Barret Travis and Patrick Jack. An Alabama lawyer, Travis like many new immigrants was both fleeing the past—in his case, an apparently unhappy marriage—and seeking an opportunity to distinguish himself economically, socially, and politically in the new environment. Jack, a Georgian, was another young man seeking his fortune on the frontier. They quickly ran afoul of Bradburn when they organized a citizens' "militia," ostensibly for defense against Indians but in reality in opposition to the Mexican garrison. When the pair, hired by a Louisiana slave catcher, tried to trick Bradburn into giving up runaway slaves, Bradburn arrested them.

Resentful settlers, already upset that the government had garrisoned troops among them, protested the actions taken by Bradburn, a military official representing the national government, against the two Anglo colonists. On June 9, 1832, a group of about 200 colonists reached Turtle Bayou, about six miles from Anahuac, where they decided to wait on a cannon from Brazoria to use against Bradburn's post. When the commander at Velasco, Domingo de Ugartechea, attempted to stop the ship carrying the cannon, the Battle of Velasco ensued. Between 100 and 150 Texans fought 90–200 Mexicans, with about twenty killed and wounded on each side. Ugartechea had to surrender when his troops ran out of ammunition.

Gen. Manuel de Mier y Terán worked diligently to address problems for the Mexican government as American colonization in Texas—legal and illegal—continued, but he despaired of maintaining effective frontier control.

American Colonization in Texas

Meanwhile, the insurgents produced the Turtle Bayou Resolutions, in which they represented themselves as supporting the Federalist cause by opposing Bradburn, the Centralist commander at Anahuac. In couching their actions as support for the latest political uprising in Mexico, the Federalist revolt against Bustamante's Centralist administration, the framers pledged their "lives and fortunes" in support of "the highly talented and distinguished Chieftain—General Santa Anna." Their sole purpose, they declared in the Resolutions, was to support the military campaign to restore the Federalist Constitution of 1824, which the Bustamante administration had undermined. Even as the first Anahuac disturbance was coming to an end, General Mier y Terán, deeply depressed over the death of his wife and the country's state of affairs, particularly what he now clearly foresaw as the loss of Texas, took his own life. On July 2, the day before he fell on his sword, he wrote presciently, "How could we expect to hold Texas when we do not even agree among ourselves. . . . As it is, we are lost. . . . Texas is lost. . . . What will become of Texas? Whatever God wills."

Although the controversy at Anahuac ended—temporarily—when Bradburn's military superior, Colonel José de las Piedras, replaced him and released the prisoners, tensions did not immediately die down. At the end of July, Piedras, fearing a repeat of the troubles at Anahuac, ordered the East Texas settlers to surrender their weapons to the garrison at Nacogdoches. Area settlers quickly organized a "national militia" led by James Bullock, an "old settler" from Attoyac Bayou, which reached Nacogdoches on August 2, and demanded that Piedras adhere to the Federalist cause. When Piedras refused, two days of fighting broke out—the bloodiest fight between Texans and the Mexican army prior to the outbreak of the revolt in late 1835. In the Battle of Nacogdoches, Piedras suffered over eighty men killed and wounded, while the Texans had only eight casualties. A mutiny within the Mexican column led to its surrender on the afternoon of August 3. Piedras, who was taken prisoner to San Felipe, was soon paroled and left Texas while his 300-man battalion was marched to San Antonio and disbanded. With the defeat of the Nacogdoches garrison and the relocation of the Anahuac garrison to the Rio Grande, eastern Texas was cleared of Mexican forces, easing tensions but giving the appearance that the colonists lacked respect for Mexican rule.

Growth of Political Opposition

Not all colonists supported Travis and Jack. In fact, many colonists were indifferent to the political turmoil, being determinedly individualistic and concerned with building their own fortunes in the demanding but bounteous regions of eastern and southeastern Texas. And overall, despite the Law of April 6 and the furor surrounding Bradburn, the Mexican government had imposed only intermittent and limited controls on their presence.

Many Texans, however, were frustrated and impatient with the government's continued political shifts and its attempts to exercise authority even as it failed to provide for the safety and well-being of its citizens. Most Tejano elites, firmly in the Federalist camp, were as frustrated with the turn of events as Austin and the colonists. Political Chief Ramón Múzquiz protested against Guerrero's 1829 emancipation decree as shortsighted since it undermined the progress that Texas was finally making. The two Texas representatives to the state legislature, José María Balmaceda and Rafael Manchola (who had previously cautioned against unsupervised Anglo-American immigration), found themselves censured and the former expelled in fall 1830. The difference between the Tejanos and the Anglo-American colonists was in the former group's respect for the legalities of the state constitution.

The Anglo settlers, coming from a constitutional tradition embracing freedom of assembly, gathered to discuss action without thought to Mexican legal principles. In October 1832, fifty-five representatives of the settlers met at San Felipe and petitioned the Mexican government for a repeal of the Law of April 6 and separate statehood for Texas. To the delegates, the convention was a way of democratically advancing political agendas, but to Political Chief Múzquiz it was illegal, as only ayuntamientos could petition the government.

Béxar leaders favored reform but, given the political turn of events in Mexico, where the Federalist revolt against the Centralist government hung in the balance, they wished to act within the law. Working through the ayuntamiento, in December 1832 they sent a memorial to the state legislature citing the same complaints raised by the convention, and early in 1833 the ayuntamientos of Goliad and Nacogdoches sent their own memorials in support of San Antonio's.

All of them included references to possible separation from Coahuila if reforms did not materialize. As the Goliad Tejanos bluntly put it, "Let's be republicans, let's be men, let's defend our rights, or let's not exist at all." Austin, working hard to maintain the Tejano-colonist alliance, commented that the Tejano elite "are as anxious for separation [from Coahuila] as we are, but wish to show to the world that they are right and stand on just ground in case force must ultimately be resorted to."

Even as news of the Federalist victory and Santa Anna's elevation to the presidency of the republic arrived in Texas, impatient colonists called a new convention to begin on April 1, 1833. Political Chief Múzquiz also disapproved of this new gathering, but did not have the means to prevent it. Once again, the delegates called for the repeal of the Law of April 6, for frontier defense, for tariff exemptions, and for more effective and efficient handling of criminal acts and legal disputes. It petitioned that the union of Coahuila and Texas be severed, with Texas residents "authorized to institute and establish a separate state government, which will be in accordance with the federal constitution." This time delegates went so far as to prepare a provisional state constitution.

The convention appointed Austin, Erasmo Seguín, and physician James B. Miller to take the petition to Mexico City. Miller, tending victims of a cholera epidemic, was unable to make the trip, and Seguín, although sympathetic, declined to participate. Thus, Austin made the journey by himself. Nearing Mexico City, through a countryside still ravaged by Civil War, with a revolt against Santa Anna's new Federalist government already in progress, he pledged, "So soon as I am convinced that there is no hope of success I shall return as quick as possible by water." Austin was right in his assessment of the seriousness of the situation, but he would be unable to follow through on his pledge. He did not see Texas again until late summer 1835.

Toward Revolution, 1833–1835

In 1835 there were approximately 30,000 new Texas residents most of whom had migrated from the United States. They had brought some 5,000 African-American slaves with them. Many of the immigrants were committed settlers, others were young male adventurers who might or might not settle down. Most were drawn by the potential of Mexican Texas for farming, trade, town-building, and land ownership and speculation. Many were "pushed" from the United States, not necessarily fugitives from the law, but people trying to leave financial burdens and other failures behind. One visitor from Louisiana noted, "When a new-comer averred that he had *ran away from his creditors* ONLY, he was regarded as a gentleman of the *first water.*" Rarely making contact with the approximately 4,000 Tejanos, or other Mexicans, other than the occasional government official, they were coming to see Texas as their own; battle lines were being drawn.

The Selling of Texas

When Austin left for Mexico City in 1833, families and adventurers from the United States continued to cross the Sabine illegally, disregarding the Law of April 6. Some were drawn by an 1833 book on Texas by Austin's Connecticut cousin, Mary Austin Holley. The cultured Holley had made an initial tour of Texas in 1831. Her travel account provided a detailed picture of life in the Anglo colonies. Among other observations, she noted the work necessary to establish one's family in the colonies, and the lack of ready and regular supplies. Despite the constant need to create whatever one wanted or needed, Holley noted that "even privations become pleasures" as "people grow ingenious in overcoming difficulties." She characterized the Texans she met as "kind and hospitable," finding them generous with what they did have. And she spoke glowingly of the natural abundance of the country.

Undaunted by the Law of April 6, speculators large and small looked upon Texas as a reservoir of land wealth. Jane McManus Storm Cazneau is an example. Daughter of a New York congressman, she arrived in Texas in December 1832 with Galveston Bay and Texas Land Company scrip and a recommendation from former U.S. vice president Aaron Burr stating that she could "send out one or two hundred substantial settlers in less time . . . than any man or half a Dozen men whom I this day Know." At San Felipe she was designated a Mexican citizen and received the transfer of an eleven-league grant through the approval of the San Felipe alcalde. Stymied in her own efforts to settle a colony of Germans, she sought to act as an agent providing immigrants to Austin's colonies. She also speculated in Texas lands for many years.

The provision in the Law of April 6 that favored European and Mexican settlers led to a new colonization scheme. James Grant, a Scotsman who had established himself in the political hierarchy of Coahuila and Texas, and Englishman John Charles Beales, a Mexico City–based surgeon, received the blessings of the Mexican government to establish a settlement in 1832. They obtained a contract to settle 800 European families far to the west of the settled colonies, between the Nueces and the Rio Grande. The colony, located in a desert landscape near the Rio Grande, quickly foundered. The German and English colonists found little game, heat too intense for unirrigated agriculture, and a scarcity of timber suitable for construction. Comanches regularly passed through the area and harassed its occupants. Although they built irrigation works, a mill, and other buildings, crop failures, harassment by Indians, and the outbreak of the Texas Revolution soon brought the colony to an end.

No one except the Comanches would contest Grant and Beales for their chunk of South Texas desert. However, by 1834 empresarios and others clashed over claims of land ownership in the more desirable areas. Over the years since the grants had begun, some settlers had moved outside the perimeters originally determined. Others had established settlements under competing authorities. DeWitt's and De León's colonists continued to argue over boundaries. To the south and west, long-term Mexican residents and newer immigrant residents occupied a checkerboard of grants issued by ayuntamientos and empresarios. Thousands of immigrants, including migrant Indians, were squatting on the lands east of Austin's colony now claimed by the Galveston Bay and Texas Land Company. Eleven-league grants to Mexican citizens from the Mexican government had passed into the hands of speculators in Texas and the United States. And in 1833 and 1834, the state legislature in a desperate bid for revenue had sold 400 leagues (almost 1.8 million acres) to one group of investors and authorized the exchange of another 400 leagues for the raising and equipping of a 1,000-man Indian defense force, moves that the national government declared illegal.

Texans of African extraction also found themselves hard-pressed. Despite the variety of laws and orders calling for an end to the slave trade, for abolition, and for emancipation, the colonists continued to consider their African servants as bondsmen. After the state outlawed the further introduction of slaves in 1828, a loophole had been created by allowing for indentured servant contracts made in the United States to be legal in Coahuila y Texas. In consequence, African Americans continued to be bought and sold in Texas. Afro-Mexicans, meanwhile, were fully accepted members of Mexican society; President Guerrero was himself of mixed ancestry, having both African and Indian roots. It is not surprising, then, that the colonists and Mexicans were far apart on issues of race and slavery, a problem that would grow following independence.

Many of the immigrants arriving in the early 1830s, particularly in 1833 and after, had little patience with Indian or even Mexican land claims. Neither did they feel allegiance to the Mexican government; whether they settled in Austin's colonies or other areas, they were more likely to align themselves with the likes of Travis and Jack. They saw the empresarios and land speculators as having made corrupt bargains with state politicians, threatening access to good farmland. They were inclined to be contemptuous of slow diplomatic efforts when their freedom to settle where they pleased and do what they pleased was at issue.

The Federalist Triumph Promises Reforms

The triumph of the Santa Anna–led Federalist uprising against Bustamante appeared to offer the first real chance for Texas to finally achieve the reforms that its overwhelming Federalist Tejano leadership and the colonists had been clamoring for. In a bid to reestablish constitutional order, in early 1833 a new presidential election was held that Santa Anna won. Valentín Gómez Farías, an ardent Federalist won the vice presidency, and when Santa Anna, who never enjoyed the work of president as much as the title, retired to his country estate, Gómez Farías took charge and began to implement reforms targeting the privileges of the church hierarchy and the military.

The Federalist administrations, both at the national and state levels, were supportive of the Texan cause—up to a point. With Austin lobbying in Mexico

City, the national government made key concessions, including reinstatement of voided empresario contracts and resumption of U.S. immigration into Texas, beginning in May 1834. The Coahuila y Texas legislature, also in Federalist hands, passed reforms advantageous to the colonists, including approval of English as a legal language, establishment of trial by jury and a circuit court for Texas, and expansion of legislative representation for Texas by dividing the department into two in 1833 and three in 1834. For a time, the state was even under the governorship of a Texan, Béxar native Juan Martín Veramendi (who unfortunately perished with most of his family in the cholera epidemic sweeping through North America at the time).

In the colonies, the reforms gave the upper hand temporarily to a "peace party" that opposed an emerging "war party" consisting of younger, brasher, less-established immigrants such as Travis, as well as more-established settlers disillusioned with controversies over land speculation and the general state of the region under Mexican rule such as William Wharton. Land speculator A. C. Allen of Nacogdoches noted, however, "The people generally appear to be satisfied with what has been done for the present [and] are willing to defer the state question. They consider their pro[s]pects truly cheering."

Both national and state officials remained opposed to the idea of statehood for Texas, however. Finally, in October 1833, deeply frustrated by the lack of progress on the statehood issue, Austin informed Vice President Gómez Farías "that Texas must be made a state by the Govt. or she would make herself one." He also wrote a fateful letter to the ayuntamiento of San Antonio calling for the Texas ayuntamientos to "unite in a measure to organize a local government independent of Coahuila, even though the general government withholds its consent."

In December 1833, Austin started home, feeling that he had made some progress. In January, however, when he reached Saltillo, he was arrested by the commandant on orders from Mexico City. Austin's remark to Gómez Farías had raised suspicion, and his letter to San Antonio appeared to call for revolt. Imprisoned for a time and then kept from leaving Mexico City until summer 1835, Austin was sidelined as the Centralist–Federalist struggle intensified. By the time he returned to Texas at the end of August 1835, he had abandoned the idea that Texas could work with either Centralists or Federalists and would espouse armed revolt.

Shortly after Austin's arrest, Gómez Farías dispatched Colonel Juan N. Almonte, the New Orleans educated son of Mexican independence hero Morelos, to inspect the situation in Texas. His public report noted some of the issues that Mier y Terán had raised five years earlier, but highlighted the progress being made in meeting the needs of the colonists. His secret report also made clear, however, just how quickly Texas was slipping away from Mexico. The Department of Béxar, centered at San Antonio, had become an economic backwater: "At present the only export commerce is reduced to 8 to 10 thousand skins of all kinds and the importation of some goods from New Orleans." Economic activity in the Department of Brazos, which included the Austin and DeWitt colonies,

East Texas Research Center, Stephen F. Austin State University

On the campus of Stephen F. Austin University in Nacogdoches sits a reconstruction of the "Old Stone Fort." Antonio Gil Ibarbo built his *casa de piedra* shortly after founding Nacogdoches in 1779. For more than a century the building served as home, store, and saloon, until demolished in 1902. In 1834–1836 it served as the government building for the Department of Nacogdoches. In 1936, the stones from the original structure were used in construction of the replica, which today serves as a museum of early East Texas history.

was an entirely different matter, amounting to 600,000 pesos annually. The department expected to export 5,000 bales of cotton that year. The situation was much the same in the Department of Nacogdoches, which had just been formed and included East Texas. It expected to export 2,000 bales of cotton, 90,000 pelts, and 5,000 head of cattle. All of this commerce was with the United States—such that Mexico was economically irrelevant to Texas.

The Centralist Resurgence and Texas Resistance

The anticlerical and antimilitary reforms promoted by acting-president Gómez Farías immediately led to Centralist opposition, which eventually led Santa Anna to a political transformation. Although he vaguely shared the liberal ideals of Gómez Farías, Zavala, and Federalists in general, Santa Anna was at heart a cautious individual. He had warned the liberal ideologues in 1833 that he could not support radical change, and when like-minded individuals pointed out the chaos that the radical Federalists were inflicting on the country, Santa Anna returned to office and began dismantling his vice president's reform efforts. Operating under the Plan de Cuernavaca, which was drawn up by a group of Santa Anna supporters headed by José María Tornel and which carried the slogan "*Religión y Fueros*" (Religion and Judicial Autonomy), Santa Anna closed down congress, fired Gómez Farías and his cabinet, took on emergency powers, and rescinded the Federalist reforms. He claimed to be acting on behalf of the nation and above politics: "I have not joined any party that may have as its main aim to destroy the mother country, nor will I ever cooperate [with one] as a blind instrument; without abandoning that independence that characterizes me, and consulting the true interests of the mother country." True to form, as soon as the new congress that he helped orchestrate took office in January 1835, Santa Anna again retreated to his hacienda, leaving the government in the hands of his new vice president Miguel Barragán.

Whatever Santa Anna's true intentions, the result of his actions was to set off Federalist resistance to the new government. When congress severely restricted the state militias in March 1835, Zacatecas governor Francisco García, who had allied with Santa Anna in the 1832 uprising, declared his state's rejection of congress's usurpation of a state power. Santa Anna, not one to brook defiance, took personal command of an army to put down the Federalist revolt. On May 11, 1835, he crushed the governor's underprepared militia and subjected the city of Zacatecas to a horrific sacking that Texans would recall a few months later when they began preparing their own resistance to Santa Anna's campaign against them.

Zacatecas was not the only state where Federalists challenged the new order. In Coahuila y Texas, Governor Agustín Viesca and the Federalist-leaning legislature for a time sheltered Gómez Farías, who was now under an expulsion order from the national government. The legislature also addressed a memorial to congress, remonstrating that

> the state of Coahuila and Texas lawfully represented by its legislature, protests in the most solemn manner that, having joined the confederacy by virtue of the fundamental pact, and on the basis therein established, it neither does, nor ever will, recognize the acts and measures emanating from the general congress, should they not conform to the plain meaning of the aforementioned articles: It will admit no other amendments of the constitution than those effected conformably to the steps and requisites provided in the same.

Clearly believing that Texas offered protection for the Federalist state authorities, the legislature authorized the governor to move the government to any point in the state he found convenient when it recessed on May 21, 1835. Although Viesca managed to leave the capital on May 25 escorted by 150 militiamen, including a contingent from Texas that had been organized by Juan Seguín and Ben Milam, he changed his mind a day later and returned to Monclova, where he disbanded the militia, wishing to avoid bloodshed. A few days later he again attempted to flee the city with a small cadre of supporters but was captured on June 5, 1835, by General Cos's forces.

Texas residents, confused and anxious over the latest shifts of power, were divided in their responses. The previous November Seguín, political chief of the Department of Béxar, had attempted to organize a meeting of Texas ayuntamientos, but had gotten no response from the political chiefs of the departments of Brazos and Nacogdoches, an indication that the Federalist–Centralist struggle had little relevance for the vast majority of colonists. In part, the lack of support resulted from the legislature's corrupt and profligate land transactions. At the same time, some Anglo settlers counseled "union, concert, and moderation." In June, when Travis again emerged at the center of resistance to the government's latest effort to restore the customs post at Anahuac, the action sparked no rebellious unity among Texas colonists. In fact, many rushed to disassociate themselves from Travis in this second Anahuac disturbance. Anglo settlers seemed to wish to adjust to the new government and go about their business.

There were disturbing—and true—rumors, however, of a Mexican military force on its way to Texas to subjugate a rebellious populace swollen and agitated by people from the United States who were not Mexican citizens. Hints of this impending punitive action sparked renewed talk of concerted opposition in Texas. Public meetings were held across the frontier communities, and people began to talk of a convention, or consultation, to address the governmental threat. Both those who wanted to move cautiously but purposefully and those who breathed open defiance saw the need for a convention.

So did Stephen F. Austin, who had been released from his extended detention in Mexico City and had returned to Texas via New Orleans. In that city, he called—defiantly now—for new immigrants, asserting "I wish a great immigration this fall and winter from Kentucky, Tennessee, every where . . . any how." Austin was ready to declare with other members of the former "peace party" that "Texas shall be effectually, and fully, Americanized."

Both firebrand orators and respected leaders warned that Centralist forces would disrupt and destroy the settlements—particularly the Anglo settlements—and deny the rights of their citizens, all in violation of the overturned federal Constitution of 1824. Federalists, both Mexican and Anglo-American, viewed events as an ideological struggle over constitutional order. Instigators of rebellion argued that the Centralist government, not the residents of Texas, had abrogated Mexican liberal principles. For an increasing number of Anglo Americans, this argument was a way to sidestep the question of whether it was right and moral for Anglo Americans to seize control of Texas from Mexico. But this was the implicit agenda for many as Anglo-Texas communities in particular galvanized into military preparedness against the oncoming army. At the end of September 1835, Texas was teetering on the edge of revolution.

Conclusion

In 1820 and 1821, Spanish and Mexican officials saw Anglo-American colonization efforts as an opportunity to strengthen Mexico's devastated northern frontier and to offset the threat of U.S. expansion. When Stephen F. Austin first entered Béxar, this seemed a feasible course to follow in Texas: And what did Mexico have to lose? Either the colonizers would do their work well and reinforce Mexican claims by occupying and cultivating the land and by building towns and trade networks, or they would forfeit the grants, and the officials would devise another remedy for the problems of maintaining the northern frontier.

Yet by 1830 it had become clear that the immigration from the United States was spiraling beyond Mexico's control. The new Texas residents perceived their relationship with the Mexican government differently than did the officials in far off seats of power. Their attitudes toward issues like taxes, slavery, and the administration of justice clashed with developing Mexican norms. From Texans' vantage point, both Tejano and Anglo-American, their needs had been neglected, due to the constant political upheavals of the new nation. They struggled at the local level with disputes over land titles, troubles with hostile Indians, and lack of a stable economic system. In a way, the isolated life had suited them, for most residents demanded considerable autonomy, but this demand was constantly undercut by Texas's position as part of a larger Mexican nation state.

Who, then, would have the power to define Texas in the future? In the following months, that question was to be fought out from Béxar to the South Texas plains to the coastal marshes and bayous bordering the San Jacinto River.

Suggested Readings

A comprehensive survey of Texas during the Mexican period remains to be written. For much of the twentieth century the pioneering work of Eugene C. Barker was central to understanding the period. Gregg Cantrell's *Stephen F. Austin: Empresario of Texas* (1999) supersedes the Barker biography and provides a more balanced account of the empresario's role in the transformation of Texas into an extension of American southern society. Recent scholarship has also explored Mexican self-government and experience in Texas in this period. The most prominent work is Andrés Tijerina's *Tejanos and Texas under the Mexican Flag, 1821–1836* (1994), which in part argues that Mexican Texans had already established many frontier government forms adopted by emerging Anglo leaders. Other aspects of the Tejano experience during this period include Timothy M. Matovina's *Tejano Religion and Ethnicity, San Antonio, 1821–1860* (1995), Raúl A. Ramos, *Beyond the Alamo: Forging Mexican Ethnicity in San Antonio, 1821–1861* (2008), and Jesús F. de la Teja, ed., *Tejano Leadership in Mexican and Revolutionary Texas* (2010). For the origins of American-imported slavery in Texas, a key source is Randolph B. Campbell's *An Empire for Slavery: The Peculiar Institution in Texas, 1821–1865* (1989). Of course, just about all the people and events mentioned in this chapter have individual entries in the *Handbook of Texas*.

The New Nation, 1821–1824

The complexities of Mexico's first years as a nation are the topic of Timothy E. Anna's *Forging Mexico, 1821–1835* (1998) and Stanley C. Green, *The Mexican Republic: The First Decade, 1823–1832* (1987). Of the numerous biographies of Antonio López de Santa Anna, the man that both Texans and Mexicans love to hate and the pivotal figure of Mexican history from independence to the U.S.-Mexican War, the best is Will Fowler's *Santa Anna of Mexico* (2007). Still very much on target for understanding Texas in the context of Mexico's northern frontier is David J. Weber, *The Mexican Frontier, 1821–1846—The American Southwest under Mexico* (1982). A detailed overview of the political history of Texas during the Mexican period can also be gained from "Texas as Viewed from Mexico, 1821–1834," by Nettie Lee Benson, in *Southwestern Historical Quarterly* (1987). The best summary of the politics behind the union of Coahuila and Texas remains Charles Bacarisse's "The Union of Coahuila and Texas," *Southwestern Historical Quarterly* (1958). The opening chapters of *River of Hope: Forging Identity and Nation in the Rio Grande Borderlands*, by Omar S. Valerio-Jiménez (2013), provide considerable insight into the development of the Lower Rio Grande region during this period. A basic understanding of developments at Paso del Norte can be gained from chapter 4 of *El Paso: A Borderlands History*, by W. H. Timmons (1990).

The Age of the Empresarios, 1821–1830

Aside from Cantrell's biography *Stephen F. Austin: Empresario of Texas*, a good summer of the empresario process can be found in Chapter 9 of Weber's *The Mexican Frontier, 1821–1846*. A still useful survey of the colonization contracts issued by the state beginning in 1825 can be found in Mary Virginia Henderson, "Minor Empresario Contracts for the Colonization of Texas, 1825–1834," *Southwestern Historical Quarterly* (1928). While there is no recent scholarly treatment of Green DeWitt's or most of the other empresarios' efforts, Ana Carolina Castillo Crimm has told the story of Martín De León and his colony in *De León: A Tejano Family History* (2003). The story of the Irish colonies of South Texas is the subject of *Land! Irish Pioneers in Mexican and Revolutionary Texas* (2002). For a detailed look at Sterling C. Robertson's colonization effort, see Malcolm D. Maclean, ed., *Papers Concerning Robertson's Colony in Texas*, seventeen volumes published between 1974 and 1991.The best recent treatment of the Fredonian Rebellion can be found in Jack Jackson, *Indian Agent: Peter Ellis Bean in Mexican Texas* (2005). Dianna Everett's *The Texas Cherokees: A People between Two Fires, 1819–1840* (1990) chronicles the Cherokees' attempts to establish a home in East Texas, while Kelly F. Himmel tells the story of Indian expulsion from the Austin colonies in *The Conquest of the Karankawas and the Tonkawas, 1821–1859* (1999). A controversial look at the process by which the native peoples of Texas came to be removed from the state is *The Conquest of Texas: Ethnic Cleansing in the Promised Land, 1820–1875*, by Gary Clayton Anderson (2005). For early Anglo women's experiences, part 1 of Jo Ella Powell Exley's *Texas Tears and Texas Sunshine: Voices of Frontier Women* (1985) provides three early first-person accounts.

Tensions, 1830–1833

There is no specific work on the Law of April 6, 1830, but essays by Josefina Zoraida Vázquez, "The Colonization and Loss of Texas: A Mexican Perspective," and Jesús F. de la Teja, "The Colonization and Independence of Texas," in *Myths, Misdeeds, and Misunderstandings: The Roots of Conflict in U.S.-Mexican Relations*, ed. Jaime E. Rodríguez O. and Kathryn Vincent (1997), combined with Nettie Lee Benson's article "Texas as Viewed from Mexico, 1820–1834" provide a fairly comprehensive treatment of the issues. For a balanced treatment of the event of and surrounding the first Anahuac disturbance, see Margaret S. Henson, *Juan Davis Bradburn: A Reappraisal of the Mexican Commander of Anahuac* (1982). There is no recent stand-alone study of the conventions of 1832 and 1833, but they are discussed in detail from Austin's perspective in Cantrell's *Stephen F. Austin: Empresario of Texas.*

Toward Revolution, 1833–1835

Continuing empresario attempts are chronicled in such works as Linda S. Hudson's *Mistress of Manifest Destiny: A Biography of Jane McManus Storm Cazneau 1807–1878* (2001). Louis E. Brister tells the story of the failed colonization effort by Grant and Beales in *John Charles Beales's Rio Grande Colony: Letters by Eduard Ludecus, a German Colonist, to Friends in Germany in 1833–1834, Recounting His Journey, Trials, and Observations in Early Texas* (2008). Almonte's inspection of Texas is at the heart of *Almonte's Texas: Juan N. Almonte's 1834 Inspection Secret Report and Role in the 1836 Campaign,* ed. Jack Jackson (2003). Unfortunately not available in English, but offering a detailed discussion of political affairs during this period from the Coahuila perspective is Vito Alessio Robles, *Coahuila y Texas desde la consumación de la Independencia hasta el Tratado de Paz de Guadalupe Hidalgo* (2 vols., 1945).

II

DEFINING TEXAS

n 1821 the Mexican government, newly independent from Spain and seeking ways to populate its northern frontier, permitted a colony of families from the United States to settle on the coastal and blackland prairie lands of southeastern Texas. This officially sanctioned effort soon turned Texas into a beacon for poor farmers across the South. Word spread quickly, and the cheaper land in Texas drew thousands of them to emigrate during the 1820s and 1830s. In 1844, a Matagorda newspaper editor claimed that "It has been the fate of Texas to attract the attention of the world to a greater extent than was ever done by the same number of the human family in any age."

The large Anglo-American immigration—perhaps 30,000 by 1836—led to differences with the Mexican government, to revolution in 1836, and to independence and the Republic of Texas later that year. Spurred by "Texas fever" that swept up the Mississippi Valley and driven by the financial Panic of 1837, immigrants continued to arrive, anticipating quick annexation to the United States. But powerful antislavery forces prevented even recognition, much less annexation, and Texas had to go it alone as an independent country. It proved to be a trying time, but those who stayed the course developed an esprit de corps that some have described as the beginning of Texian character, of Texian nationalism. It was about this time that an article appeared in the *Telegraph and Texas Register*, a newspaper that began publication in San Felipe de Austin in the fall of 1835, observing that an appropriate name for the people of Texas had been the subject of some debate. After considering *Tejano*, or *Texano*, the writer concluded that, "We believe that, both by the Mexican and American residents of the country, the name commonly used is Texians." Perhaps it was an effort to foster a spirit of unity among the people, and many of those who recoiled against Santa Anna's political and military threat would soon claim that name, "Texian," as an independent—and revolutionary—identity. "May you live always," one old Texian wrote another. "I would not write you as I have, if we had not been raised together on the Colorado, in the dark days of the Republic."

Sam Houston, the hero of independence and the first president of the republic, set the tone with an 1837 speech to the Texas Congress: "While reflecting upon the dispensations of an Almighty Being . . . ," Houston began, "it is but gratitude . . . to render to him our most devout thanks, and invoke his kind . . . providence, that he will preserve and govern us as a *chosen people*." "No longer were Americans to be found on the land extending from the Sabine to the Rio Grande," a French visitor wrote in 1839: "People began to refer to themselves only as Texians." A British visitor noted that same year, "the Texians are at present Americans but more in customs, manners, habits, than in feeling." And as University of Texas anthropologist William W. Newcomb later concluded, indeed, "They came to see themselves as a breed apart."

This "feeling," nurtured during the almost ten years of the Texas republic, did not disappear with statehood and is still experienced in intangible ways today. Victory in the war with Mexico only confirmed to Texans that their cause was just and that it was their "manifest destiny" to possess this land. The defeat of the Confederacy was a bitter blow to most Texans, but the four years of radical Republican Reconstruction after the war largely failed in its attempt to "reconstruct" Texas society and political life, and the Texas esprit lived on. Southern migration continued, gins overflowed with "King Cotton," and the planter class once again wielded political, social, and economic power. The tradition of the Texas Rangers grew as the famous Frontier Battalion played a significant role in defeating the Comanches and Kiowas. And while this esprit leads many Texans to believe that our historical experience is unique, we must also realize that it did not include large portions of the population. Whites held African Americans in slavery, then, after federally enforced emancipation, offered them meager prospects as tenant farmers or sharecroppers shackled with "black codes." Tejanos were pushed to the periphery of public life, cut off from economic opportunity, and, in many cases, driven from their property. Women were denied equal political rights, and the Indians were killed or driven onto reservations.

These were the decades that nurtured the Texas identity. The bitterness of the war and Reconstruction and the exhilaration of Democratic victory further enhanced the Texas esprit. The whites invoked it, in the form of racial solidarity, in their bid to unseat the "black Republicans" in 1874 and repeated similar appeals to white voters for decades, warning of what would happen to them should there be a return to Republican rule. Years later, former Governor Oran M. Roberts, one of the first law professors at the new University of Texas and a former Confederate, crafted the interpretative approach that most Texans accepted throughout much of the twentieth century—that the Democrats had "redeemed" the state "from the ignominy and ruin with which it was threatened by the continuance of such Republican rule."

Today, through the lens of time and historical research, we have a clearer understanding of these pivotal years and can evaluate them for their positive as well as their negative aspects. The result, nevertheless, is as geographer Donald W. Meinig later explained, "Texans had strongly asserted and the nation had in some degree readily accepted the idea of Texas as a highly individual place and Texans as a distinctive people."

Revolution, 1835–1836

By September 1835, Juan Seguín had become convinced that the time for revolution was "close at hand." The twenty-eight-year-old political chief in San Antonio had been baptized as an infant in the community, as had his father, Erasmo, and his grandfather, Santiago. The Seguíns had successfully navigated a number of Spanish and Mexican political shifts that affected their community. Juan had his father's example of befriending and partnering with the new Anglo immigrants to Texas. The Seguíns had even taken in Stephen F. Austin's younger brother, James, and introduced him to the Spanish language and Mexican culture.

Now the younger Seguín wanted to take a stand against Santa Anna. In the spring his militia had been the only one from Texas to respond to Coahuila y Texas governor Agustín Viesca's call for resistance to Santa Anna's imposition of centralist control in Mexico. When that attempt failed in Monclova, Seguín and his company returned in June, as he wrote in his memoir, "pledg[ing] to use all our influence to rouse Texas against the tyrannical government of Santa Anna." Yet both within his own native community and among the settlements made up primarily of U.S. immigrants, people either tried to avoid actions that would affect their private fortunes and daily lives, or they remained confused and divided on what actions to take in response to the centralist control and the looming threat from Mexican troops.

On September 27, Seguín traveled to his friend Salvador Flores's ranch to convince the Mexican ranch owners along the San Antonio River that they should arm themselves against the current Mexican government. He was to play an active role in the upcoming struggle. The participation of Seguín and other Mexican residents with deep Texas roots reminds us that the revolution was not a simple battle between Anglo colonists and Mexican troops. It was a complex redefining of Texas carried out—often with much tension and confusion—by people with different experiences of and expectations for the region.

Chapter 6 Revolution, 1835–1836	
SEPT. 1835	General Martín Perfecto de Cos reaches the Texas coast
OCT. 1835	Texians refuse to give up Mexican cannon in incident near Gonzales; Cos arrives in San Antonio de Béxar; Texian volunteers march on San Antonio and camp at nearby creek; colonists' "Permanent Council" attempts to devise a revolutionary government
NOV. 1835	"Consultation" continues work of Permanent Council; Texians remain camped outside San Antonio
DEC. 1835	The Texian volunteer siege force takes San Antonio; small volunteer force remaining in San Antonio fortifies the Alamo for siege
FEB. 1836	Provisional Texian government has fallen apart; Santa Anna begins siege of Alamo; General José de Urrea begins his march northward along the coast
MARCH 1836	Texian convention meets at Washington-on-the-Brazos, declares independence, and sets up new interim government; Alamo falls; Texas residents flee Santa Anna's troops in the Runaway Scrape; James Fannin and his troops are captured by Urrea and most are executed (Fannin Massacre)
APRIL 1836	Sam Houston's troops defeat Santa Anna's at San Jacinto and Santa Anna is captured

As Stephen F. Austin approached the mouth of the Brazos River on board the schooner *San Felipe* on September 1, 1835, he saw an armed Mexican naval schooner, *Correo de México,* under attack by an American merchant brig, assisted by a small Texian steamboat, the *Laura.* The *Correo* had been patrolling the Texas coast, seizing ships suspected of avoiding customs duties. The clash showed Austin how close Texas was to rebellion. "I fully hoped to have found Texas at peace and tranquility," Austin told a large crowd that gathered at Brazoria a week later to welcome him home, "but regret to find it in commotion; all disorganized, all in anarchy, and threatened with immediate hostilities." He pleaded for "peace and a local government," but concluded that it was "impossible" to "remain indifferent, when our rights, our all, appear to be in jeopardy." He called for a "consultation of the people" to decide whether to yield to the centralism of the Mexican government or to demand their rights under the Constitution of 1824.

Austin was a changed man as he addressed his fellow citizens in Brazoria that evening: sick and weak from his imprisonment, but angry. The following week, as the San Felipe Committee of Correspondence and Vigilance began coordinating plans for the upcoming consultation, Austin learned that General Martín Perfecto de Cos was en route to Texas "to destroy and break up the foreign settlements in Texas." He now concluded that "WAR is our only resource." Texas was about to embark on a course that, in retrospect, appears foreordained, but, in fact, was anything but assured.

As you read this chapter, consider the following questions:

1. Could Mexico have done anything to keep Texas from rebelling?
2. Why did many Texians not support the rebellion?
3. What is the significance of the battle of the Alamo in the Texas Revolution? In Texas history?

The Rebellion—Early Months (September–December)

As Juan Seguín rode to the Mexican ranches to encourage revolt, and Austin labored with the committees of correspondence to organize the Consultation, others left San Antonio on a different mission: Domingo de Ugartechea, military commander of Texas, had sent a company of 100 dragoons under Francisco de Castañeda to retrieve a cannon provided to the citizens of Gonzales in 1831 for Indians defense. Given the charged political climate, Ugartechea felt it was dangerous for the colonists to possess the cannon.

The First Shots

The town of Gonzales, the center of Green DeWitt's colony on the Guadalupe River, had been vulnerable to raids by bands of Indians, and its citizens had gratefully accepted the gift of a six-pounder cannon from the Mexican government. Unlike other American colonists, they had not succumbed to the revolutionary

Texas State Library and Archives Commission

Juan Seguín, like his father Erasmo, a San Antonio native and political leader, sided with the Anglo newcomers in the fight for Texas's independence from Santa Anna's centralist government. Painting by Thomas Jefferson Wright.

fervor circulating through the colonies since 1832. Yet a Mexican soldier had attacked a colonist in September, and there was concern that the government might be as harsh and uncompromising as some in the so-called "war party" were claiming.

This was the situation Ugartechea sought to address by sending the dragoons, with orders to retrieve the cannon peaceably. Reaching the outskirts of Gonzales, however, the soldiers found that they could not cross the rain-swollen Guadalupe because the colonists had removed the ferry. On the other side of the river stood eighteen colonists led by Albert Martin, a local storekeeper. The settlers buried the cannon tube in a peach orchard, and it soon became a symbol of resistance to the Mexican government rather than the Indians. A Mexican courier swam across the river, but Martin informed him that the dragoons must remain on the other side of the river until the local *alcalde,* Andrew Ponton, returned to Gonzales. Ponton, meanwhile, was, directing the Gonzalez Committee of Safety as they sent letters requesting assistance to neighboring settlements.

Camped on a high mound across the river, Casteñada vainly repeated to the colonists that he had not come to fight and was eager to talk with their representatives. But volunteer forces from Fayette and Columbus had arrived and applauded rhetoric that likened their resistance to that of the patriots of the American Revolution. They unearthed the cannon and loaded it with metal scraps, as cannonballs were not available.

The Texians, now 180 strong, crossed the river during the evening of October 1 and approached the Mexican camp in the early hours of October 2. They were soon discovered and, following a short burst of gunfire, both sides scrambled to defensive positions. As daylight arrived, the two sides skirmished again, the settlers falling back from a forty-man Mexican cavalry charge. Casteñada and John Henry Moore of the Fayette contingent then parleyed, with Casteñada protesting that he, too, was a supporter of the Constitution of 1824 and that he had no order, and no desire, to force the cannon issue.

With a makeshift flag made from Naomi DeWitt's wedding dress—white with an image of the disputed cannon and the legend "Come and Take It"—the Texians began firing the cannon and their Kentucky rifles as well. Castañeda withdrew rather than "compromis[e] the honor of Mexican arms," for his carbines were no match for the Texians' rifles. The Mexicans had suffered only one or two casualties, the Texians none. Thus ended the first "battle" of the revolution, significant not for its scope but for its effect: Texians were now in open defiance and had shown they would fight.

An Army and Government Form

Meanwhile, the rumored military force sent to enforce Texas allegiance to the Mexican central government had arrived on Texas soil. On September 20, General Cos had sailed into Copano Bay with 500 soldiers and every intention of imposing military control over Texas. His goal was to disarm colonists and arrest the leaders of the recent attack at Anahuac and land speculators who had attempted to obtain choice land for themselves at the spring legislative session in Monclova. To help him in this endeavor, he had a well-trained cavalry and twenty cannons. He scoffed at the insurgents' motives, writing, "[I]t is quite useless and vain to cover them with a hypocritical adherence to the federal constitution."

Cos quickly moved his troops to the presidio of La Bahía at Goliad. A volunteer Texian force, made up primarily of Anglo men from Matagorda but including Mexican *vaqueros* (cowboys) and African American freedman Samuel McCulloch, hurriedly gathered to storm La Bahía, but Cos had moved on to San Antonio, leaving only a small guard at the presidio. Just eight days after the confrontation at Gonzales, these Texians took the inadequately defended presidio and Goliad with the support of some of the area's Mexican population.

Volunteer forces began to gather in Gonzales, an army bent on driving Cos and the Mexican army out of San Antonio de Béxar and Texas. But this was no well-defined, disciplined fighting force; it was a volunteer enterprise, with no commander-in-chief. Companies voted on their commanders and changed their minds as new combinations of militias formed. Enlistment periods were unclear or unenforceable, and troops came and went as they pleased. In many cases, the volunteers—especially young, single men with little to lose—were just looking for a good fight, and almost all militiamen remained fiercely independent and individualistic. They distrusted the military profession, placing their faith instead in the "natural" abilities of the "common man."

Several of the volunteers realized that they needed someone who could unite them and implored Austin "earnestly to come on *immediately,* bringing all the aid you possibl[y] can." Others realized that Texas also needed a trained, regular, uniformed, and disciplined army to defeat the Mexicans, among them Austin's friend Lorenzo de Zavala, the Mexican empresario and liberal politician who cast his lot with the revolutionaries in Texas. The experienced Mexican revolutionary warned Austin that although there was "individual patriotism," a "unified patriotism" did not exist: "They will defend their private rights until death; but still they do not realize the necessity for cooperation." Austin was convinced and advised the Consultation of the "absolute necessity of organizing a *regular army* and inviting a Military man of known and tried Talent to command it."

Nonetheless, he accepted the role of commander-in-chief when those present in the Gonzales volunteer camp elected him on October 11. He was not a military man, and not in good health, but he was the one person on whom the volunteers could agree. Noah Smithwick, a twenty-seven-year-old blacksmith who had joined the army to repair guns, vividly remembered the march to Béxar: "Buckskin breeches were the nearest approach to uniform," he recalled in his later years, "and there was wide diversity even there." Some wore military caps, others beaver hats, still others a Mexican sombrero. There was even an occasional "coonskin cap, with the tail hanging down behind." Some were well mounted, others walked. Many carried a Kentucky long rifle, others shotguns, and some had no firearms at all.

Along the way, other volunteers joined. Twenty-eight-year-old Juan Seguín, Austin's long-time friend, arrived with thirty-seven men and joined up; Austin promptly made him a captain. Along with the forces of Plácido Benavides, alcalde in Victoria, Seguín brought Tejano contingents to the insurgent army to 135 men. Other late arrivals included the hard-drinking former slave trader James Bowie, the land speculator who made infamous the knife that bears his name, and Erastus "Deaf" Smith, a forty-eight-year-old native New Yorker who was tough, fiercely independent, and an excellent scout. By October 19, this rag-tag force drew near to San Antonio de Béxar and camped on Salado Creek.

As the volunteers set up camp, other Texians struggled toward a rude governing system. Almost 100 delegates had been elected to the Consultation that Austin had planned for October 15, but, with all the military activity and confusion, most were slow in arriving. In the meantime, a so-called "Permanent Council" made up of representatives from San Felipe and a few other communities met and dispatched supplies to Austin's army. They also directed that the land offices be shut down to reduce the tension and turmoil over conflicting land claims, as requested by the volunteers who feared that land speculators would snap up all the best land, and began the effort to raise funds in the United States for the revolution.

The Permanent Council was anything but permanent, however, for on November 1, the planned Consultation took over. With only fifty-eight of the delegates in attendance, this assembly wrestled to establish the direction they should take, whether to insist on a return to the Constitution of 1824 with Texas as a separate Mexican state or complete independence from Mexico. The majority surely favored independence, but they still hoped for support from Mexican federalists, who favored the Constitution of 1824. Thus, they concluded that, while Santa Anna's actions had given them the right to revolt, they pledged to create a separate state government that would be loyal to the Constitution of 1824. Austin was happy with the compromise, thinking that it was the best policy at that moment.

The Consultation also hammered out the structure for an independent provisional government, which they called the Organic Law. This law established a General Council made up of representatives from each municipality and a governor. In theory, these representatives were to aid the new executive, sharing his duties and even extending his powers if and when they deemed it necessary. In reality, the plan would prove troublesome, with the council and governor disagreeing on most issues. It was complicated even more with the mistaken selection of cantankerous and uncompromising Henry Smith of Kentucky, a member of the war party, as governor. More immediately, however, was the blunder they committed with regard to the authorization of a regular army: they appointed the popular Sam Houston commander-in-chief, but they undercut his role by refusing to give him authority over the volunteer forces already in the field. Houston, in other words, was a general without an army.

Houston was about to become one of the major figures in Texas history, but he was already a figure of some renown in the United States. A native of Virginia, he had a colorful past, which included a three-year sojourn with a Cherokee band as a teenager and notable service in the 1814 battle of Horseshoe Bend during the War of 1812. The latter brought him to the attention of General Andrew Jackson. As Jackson's political star rose in the 1820s, Houston became a leading "Jacksonian Democrat," loyal to the frontier war hero who envisioned an egalitarian American republic, at least for Anglos, and who seemed to represent the common man against privileged interests. Living in Tennessee after the war, Houston rose to become state governor in 1827 and acted as unofficial campaign manager in Jackson's successful bid for the U.S. presidency a year later.

Soon thereafter, Governor Houston married nineteen-year-old Eliza Allen, but the marriage ended quickly, mysteriously, and disastrously. Ruined both socially and politically, and personally humiliated, he resigned the governorship and left Tennessee, rejoining the Cherokees (who were now living near Fort Gibson in what is today Oklahoma) with whom he had lived as a boy. Eventually, Houston again traveled to the East Coast on a mission for the Cherokees, but became involved in another incident that hastened his departure for Texas. In Washington, D.C., in April 1832, he learned that an Ohio congressman had insulted him in a speech on the floor of the House of Representatives. When he encountered the congressman on the street, Houston beat him with a cane. Tried and reprimanded by the House, Houston looked to Texas for a new start. He hoped to become an agent for the Galveston Bay and Texas Land Company but when that did not work out, he determined to go anyway.

Houston did, however, have a mission, one provided by his old friend President Jackson: to parley with the Comanches and to assess the Indian situation in Texas in general. Jackson also encouraged Houston to keep him advised of the events in Texas. There is also a possibility that he hinted to Houston that, should a revolution begin, the United States would assist Texas by sending troops as far as the Neches River in East Texas. Jackson considered the area between the Sabine and Neches Rivers disputed territory.

In Mexican Texas, Houston had set up a law practice and immediately become involved in the political unrest. He served as a delegate to both the Consultation of 1833 in San Felipe and the current Consultation that named him major general of a nonexistent regular army. In late October, he had visited the volunteer army camped outside Béxar, finding the men divided as to when to attack the town. He suggested that they wait until they had obtained more cannons and were more fully trained, but Austin was still the commander, and, although he was so sick that he was hardly able to sit on his horse, he replied that he felt that it was important that the army remain at San Antonio "because the salvation of Texas depends on the army being sustained."

The Siege of Béxar

Upon arrival in San Antonio, General Cos had fortified the old Alamo mission complex with more than twenty cannons and almost 650 troops. His cavalry was well-trained, and he expected reinforcements within a few days, but many of the other soldiers were conscripts and convicts who had been given the choice of

James Bowie, shown here in an 1832–1833 portrait by American artist G. P. A. Healy, decided, with Travis, to defend the Alamo and, like Travis, he died there.

going to Texas or to jail. Austin decided that a frontal assault was out of the question and opted for a siege, hoping to force Cos to surrender.

About a week after the siege began, the first engagement of any note occurred when Austin dispatched a ninety-two-man contingent under famed frontiersman James Bowie to locate a site closer to Cos's defenses. Bowie, too, had traveled to Texas with a messy past and an eye on opportunity. Known as a scrapper in his native Kentucky, he was already renowned for his use of the "Bowie knife" in a Natchez duel. He had engaged in apparently fraudulent land speculation and "slave running" (taking captured slaves from the Caribbean and illegally selling them in Louisiana). Turning to entrepreneurial opportunities in Texas, he had applied for Mexican citizenship in 1830 and married Ursula de Veramendi, member of a leading San Antonio family. Veramendi and her influential father, Juan Martín de Veramendi, died in an 1833 cholera epidemic; but Bowie continued to try to build his Texas holdings while advocating for war.

As night approached on October 27, Bowie's contingent dug in at a bend in the San Antonio River near the Mission Concepción. This would allow the volunteers to fight in a manner more natural to them—from behind the riverbanks and trees rather than on an open prairie, if the Mexicans were to attack. Recognizing that Bowie had only a small group, General Cos dispatched 100 infantry and 300 dragoons to drive them from their camp. The Mexicans advanced with muskets and belching cannons, but they proved ineffective against the well-sheltered Texians. The fire from their long rifles, accurate at a greater distance than the muskets, and their "snipe-and-hide combat" tactics carried the day. Only one Texian was fatally wounded. Approximately seventy-six men in the Mexican force were killed or wounded, and Cos withdrew.

Worried that his army might become separated and be defeated piecemeal, Austin had been busily moving the rest of the volunteer army forward and came upon the scene shortly after the Mexican soldiers had retreated. He was not a military man, but his instinct told him that he should immediately follow up on this apparently easy victory and attack the city itself. Cooler heads prevailed, however, reminding him of the significant defensive fortifications into which the Mexicans had retreated. Again, the volunteer army made camp, this time at the bend in the San Antonio River.

Now the opposing forces sat and waited—Cos for reinforcements, Austin for reinforcements and for a siege gun or guns that would breach Cos's entrenched defenses. The Texian Army of the People began to disintegrate as some men left, impatient with the lack of action. Others drank heavily. Many fell ill, without medication or treatment available. A lack of strong, decisive leadership and a shared understanding of what they were trying to accomplish contributed to the discipline problems. On November 2, Austin wrote Philip Dimmitt, commander of the Goliad garrison, "Whether the army can be kept together long enough to await the arrival of reinforcements, and the necessary supply of heavy battering-cannon and ammunition, I am sorry to say is somewhat uncertain."

The Texians cheered when a number of artillery pieces arrived and promptly wheeled them into action against the Mexican fortifications, although with little effect. The arrival of the Greys, a volunteer company formed in New Orleans, further lifted their spirits, for they brought visible support from the United States, a development that galled Mexican officials and proved to them that the United States had designs on Mexican territory. Volunteer companies from Kentucky, Mississippi, Georgia, and Alabama would later join in the Texian fight, as well as additional "deserters" from the General Edmund P. Gaines's U.S. troops who had been stationed east of the Sabine under the ruse of preventing "Indian troubles."

On November 22, hearing that the Mexican force was demoralized and suffering from desertions, Austin ordered his troops to prepare to attack. But his officers told him that the troops were disillusioned with his command and that no more than 100 men would obey this order. Some historians believe that Houston was behind some of the dissatisfaction, as he had made no secret of his concerns about the wisdom of the siege. Reluctantly, Austin rescinded his order and acknowledged that he could better play a diplomatic role. He decided to accept an appointment as commissioner to the United States. He assembled the troops on November 24 and told them of his decision. About 400 of his troops agreed to stay and fight and immediately elected Colonel Edward Burleson as their leader. On November 25, Austin left the camp for San Felipe.

Despite the men's vote of confidence (and recognition by the provisional government on December 1), Burleson inherited a fractured and debilitated fighting force, one ready to strain at any rumor. Thus, when a scout entered camp on November 26 with a report of 100 men in a large pack train headed toward San Antonio, word quickly spread that it was a company of dragoons returning with pack mules loaded with silver to pay the garrisoned Mexican soldiers.

Texas State Library and Archives Commission

When Stephen F. Austin left to advocate for the Texas cause in Washington, D.C., Colonel Edward Burleson took command of the troops besieging San Antonio.

Burleson sent James Bowie with 100 mounted men to survey the pack train, warning him to refrain from engagement. But, on finding the train beside a creek south of town, the pugnacious Bowie immediately attacked it. With little bloodshed on either side, the Mexican column, at a disadvantage with their muskets, abandoned the pack train for the safety of the Béxar fortifications. The Texian volunteers found only grass in the packs; the train had been a foraging party trying to supply the hungry horses in the garrison, evidence that the Mexican garrison was indeed in difficult straits. The incident became known to history as the "grass fight." Burleson, who had been considering withdrawal, began to think seriously about ordering an attack.

Divided Opinion over Rebellion

Further confirmation of the Mexican garrison's plight came when Cos released two Anglos living in San Antonio, John Smith and Samuel Maverick, on the condition that they return to the United States. Instead, they made their way to the ranch of José Antonio Navarro, a revolution-minded Tejano. They brought encouraging reports of the garrison's vulnerability, and Burleson gave the order to attack, but his officers responded with further arguments, and Burleson, like Austin before him, rescinded the order. Those who had finally been preparing to fight responded with anger. An estimated 250–300 men left camp, and the others sank into gloom.

Burleson decided that his only recourse was to give up the siege and retreat to Goliad to establish winter quarters. Many of the troops responded to his announcement of this decision on December 4 with palpable frustration and anger. Why had they marched to the outskirts of Béxar, and stayed there for as long as seven weeks on short rations and rumors, only now to leave?

The indecision of the beleaguered insurgency leaders reflected division within Texas and the United States over the issue of whether to support the rebellion. Southern slavery advocates were too involved in their own political battles in the United States to send significant aid to Texas. And even within Texas, the rebels found significant lack of interest among many residents. Insurgent leaders despaired when Anglo settlers—including some prominent ones—remained loyal to Mexico: they did not aid the war effort in any way; they did not share their food or other resources; and the men did not serve in local militias.

The response was uneven from other groups as well. Although some Tejanos joined the war effort, those in the Nacogdoches and Goliad-Victoria areas were already divided. In Nacogdoches, Anglo immigrants were suspicious of all Mexicans, and the Tejanos had reason to be wary of a rebel effort that could leave them even more at the mercy of the newcomers. Local rebel leaders formed a militia, with prominent area landowner Vicente Córdova as its commander. But Córdova and his fellows carefully distanced themselves from the war and focused on defending Tejano rights and participation in the local power structure. In the meantime, Irish settlers had fought alongside the Mexican military when, in a side action in late October, Goliad commander Dimmitt had sent a small force to take the Mexican post of Lipantitlán on the Nueces River. The Irish of San Patricio shared allegiances as well as the Catholic religion with their Mexican neighbors, who had assisted them in getting settled. Carlos de la Garza, whose family had settled on a ranch near Goliad, offered the services of about eighty *Guardias Victoriana* to serve as scouts for General José de Urrea when he swept through the area in the spring of 1836, while his in-laws Silvestre de León and Plácido Benavides fought on the Texian side, as did the Irish residents of Refugio. No wonder Houston was having little luck recruiting for his regular army.

Despite the work of the Permanent Council and the Consultation, efforts to resist allegiance to Santa Anna's government or to declare outright independence remained confused, piecemeal, and diffuse. Meanwhile, the sullen, ragtag volunteer army camped outside San Antonio was, for better or worse, the most united, potent force the Texas insurgents had. And this army was about to move the conflict to a new level, to make it indisputably a revolution.

From Rebellion to Revolution—Victory and Defeat (December–March)

Benjamin Rush Milam had a more checkered past in Texas than most of his fellow volunteers at the Siege of Béxar. A veteran of the War of 1812, by 1818 he was in Texas trading with the Comanches. In New Orleans the following year, he had joined James Long's first filibustering expedition, traveling to Vera Cruz and Mexico City. Although he spent time in jail in the capital, after the Constitution of 1824 introduced republican government, he became a Mexican army colonel. As an unsuccessful empresario in Texas, he took his case for land titles to Governor Viesca in Monclova, just as Viesca declared against Santa Anna, and was captured and jailed with Viesca. Escaping, he had made his way northward to the Goliad area. Here the Texian detachment sent to take Goliad had found him hiding under a tree, weary and alone. Milam, who joined the volunteer army, refused to accept Burleson's order to retreat, thereby providing the spark for the next series of revolutionary events.

The Storming of Béxar

Milam returned to camp from a scouting mission on December 4 to find his compatriots packing up. Milam got Burleson to agree that, if he could convince enough of the remaining men to storm the village, Burleson would stay with the others as a reserve force to cover a possible retreat. Milam emerged from the meeting shouting the legendary question, "Who will follow old Ben Milam into San Antonio?" Three hundred of those remaining—about six out of ten—stepped forward.

Milam sent J. C. Neill, an experienced artilleryman, with a small group of men, to distract Cos's troops with a feint on the Alamo, while he and Colonel Frank Johnson led two columns of rebel troops into the city. At least a few dozen Tejanos joined in the assault, while others, such as Erasmo Seguin, provided grain from his ranch. The Texians fanned out and rushed down the streets, getting within 200 yards of the central plaza before being discovered. Then the Mexicans began firing their artillery, loaded with canister, down the narrow streets, forcing the Texians to take refuge inside nearby homes and sending men, women, and children out in the middle of the night. The easy part of the battle was over. Now it became a slow advance from house to house, and the Texians had a decided advantage in that their Kentucky long rifles were much more accurate than the muskets that the majority of the Mexican troops had. On the second day of fighting, a Mexican sniper, firing a much more accurate British Baker rifle, killed Milam as he surveyed the defenses through a field glass. Infuriated at the loss of their leader, the Texians renewed the assault. Their slow progress forced General Cos to try a desperate measure. Thinking that the Texian camp might be poorly defended, he ordered a daring attack on their base, but J. C. Neill's artillery quickly turned them back.

Cos was running out of supplies and workable defense plans. When Ugartechea finally arrived with a relief column on the afternoon of December 8, most of the men he brought with him were shackled convicts and reluctant participants who proved not only resistant to taking orders but disruptive and violent, even attacking Cos himself. The heavy artillery fire from both sides had created a landscape of "blackened tree-stumps, battered walls, smoldering ash heaps." Over the objections of some of his men, on the morning of December 9, Cos had a white truce flag unfurled and asked for terms of surrender. Milam was one of only four Texians who died in the fighting, along with an estimated fourteen wounded. Mexican losses were estimated at 150 dead and wounded.

Burleson and Johnson granted liberal terms to Cos, allowing him time to remove his wounded and supplying him with "such provisions as can be obtained" for his retreat to the Rio Grande. In turn, Cos promised not to take up arms against the rebel forces again. As he directed the removal of his troops, residents of San Antonio who had been forced to flee the fighting returned. Juan Antonio Chávez remembered, "We found the house badly shattered with shot and shell. The doors were riddled with bullets and grape shot from the cannon and escopetas [muskets] and the rifle balls."

The men who took San Antonio felt that they had sent a decisive message in favor of a return to the Mexican Constitution of 1824 that would serve as a rallying signal for a general Mexican revolt against Santa Anna. At the same time, many Anglos clearly favored complete independence, either long term or as a means of transferring the region to the United States. A couple of weeks after the Texians' victory at Béxar, the Goliad garrison proclaimed its independence from Mexico. A Texas official in New Orleans collecting supplies for the Texians expressed his sense that "a very large majority of the people wish to come into the Union with Uncle Sam." Yet in general, Anglo leaders remained cautious about advocating a full break from Mexico.

That hesitation was apparent in the Texians plan to attack Matamoros. While Austin was laying siege to San Antonio, he endorsed the idea of a Matamoros expedition, which he and others hoped would attract support from Mexican liberals, who also favored the Constitution of 1824. But the effort suffered from uncoordinated leadership and floundered when Mexican General José de Urrea arrived to defend the city. Colonel James Fannin, who was one of the several commanders assigned to the expedition, settled in Goliad, where he bolstered the defenses of La Bahía, which he deemed crucial to the defense of Texas.

Preparing for War

After brutally crushing the rebellion in Zacatecas in May 1835, Santa Anna had returned to his estate at Manga de Clavo near Veracruz, leaving the work of establishing the centralist government to his cohorts, Interim President Miguel Barragán and Minister of War José María Tornel y Mendívil, one of the persons responsible for the Law of April 6, 1830. They abolished the federalist Constitution of 1824 by legislative decree in October 1835 and began work on a new centralist constitution. As the Texas situation deteriorated, Santa Anna returned to Mexico City to take personal charge of the Texas campaign, bragging to the British and French ambassadors that if he found that the American government was fomenting rebellion in Texas, he would march his army all the way to Washington, D.C., and "place upon its *Capitol* the Mexican *Flag.*"

Even as a group of headstrong volunteers in the Goliad garrison was declaring its independence from Mexico, an action that surprised the council, because it had been careful not to break with the Tejano and Mexican federalists, Santa Anna reached San Luis Potosí on December 5 and began efforts to raise money

Antonio López de Santa Anna, pictured here in a daguerreotype portrait that has been reversed, had appeared to be a strong federalist leader for Mexico, but his switch to centralist policies and his authoritarian presidency greatly fed unrest in Mexican Texas.

and troops for the Texas expedition. He ultimately mobilized an army of more than 6,000 men, with over 2,500 camp followers, more than 1,800 mules and 200 oxcarts to haul their equipment and supplies across more than 500 miles during the coldest months of the year. By the end of the month, they marched toward San Antonio.

Santa Anna planned to encircle the Texians in a giant pincer movement. Two roads led to Texas from the Mexican interior, the Atascosito Road from Matamoros along the coast through San Patricio, Refugio, Goliad, Victoria, and on to San Felipe de Austin; and the Old San Antonio Road, the old *Camino Real,* which crossed the Rio Grande at Guerrero, near present-day Piedras Negras, and proceeded northeastward across desolate territory to San Antonio, Bastrop, Nacogdoches, San Augustine, and on into Louisiana. Two forts protected these entrances into Texas: Presidio La Bahía at Goliad, where Colonel Fannin commanded more than 400 men, and the Alamo in San Antonio, where Colonel James C. Neill held forth with a smaller force.

As the confrontation loomed, both sides of this fledgling rebellion had their own problems: Santa Anna managed to raise money for the expedition only by pledging his own fortune as collateral. Many of his recruits had only minimal training and inferior weapons, and many others were draftees who would welcome a chance to bolt; the officers relied on outdated tactics of warfare; there was a serious lack of basic supplies and medical treatment for widespread illness the word should be illnesses; there were periodic Indian threats; and the cold was bone-chilling, which proved especially hard on the recruits from tropical Yucatán.

The Texian army also faced problems of almost farcical proportions. In November, the Consultation had elected the pro-independence Henry Smith as provisional governor. He and the council had quickly split, in part over a possible Matamoros expedition, which Mexican federalists advocated. There was strong federalist sentiment in the city, and they felt that an attack would spread the revolution into the state of Tamaulipas. Some volunteer army leaders, including Frank Johnson and empresario James Grant, favored the idea as well. The council supported the enterprise, but Smith stood adamantly against it, considering it a brazen gamble with limited forces even as Santa Anna was preparing to invade Texas.

The council appointed Johnson and Fannin as commanders of the expedition. Fannin was another veteran of the siege of Béxar and an ardent revolutionary. He had attended West Point, which gave him an added cachet in revolutionary war circles, but he had never led troops in battle. Governor Smith insisted that, if there were to be an attack on Matamoros, Houston should be the commander and dispatched him to Goliad, the rallying point. There Houston found empresario Dr. James Grant claiming to be acting commander-in-chief, so he simply joined the enterprise and bided his time.

Soon word came that the council had rescinded Houston's appointment as commander-in-chief and deposed Governor Smith after he tried to dissolve it. The council appointed Fannin to be the commander, but Houston continued taking orders from Smith. As the expedition began to fall apart, Houston left to attempt to persuade the Cherokees in East Texas to remain neutral. If the Mexican government had guaranteed the Cherokees title to their lands at this moment, the Indians could have had a devastating impact on the Texian effort, but Houston mollified them with promises of title to their lands, promises that he would be unable to keep, because many Texians wanted the Cherokee out of Texas.

Defending Béxar

Back in San Antonio, Colonel Neill was directing a concerted effort to prepare for Santa Anna's arrival. Neill was an able artilleryman whose cannons had provided a significant distraction as the storming of Béxar began. In the wake of that victory, the council had given him a regular army commission as lieutenant colonel of artillery and had left him in command of the volunteers remaining in San Antonio. But, despite the fact that everyone expected Santa Anna to attack San Antonio, the council had permitted the Matamoros expedition leaders to strip Neill of men and much-needed supplies. Volunteers who "had not been in the army more than four days," according to Neill, commandeered the clothing sent by the council for those who had "endured all the hardships of winter and who were not even sufficiently clad for summer." With only 100 men left, he still chose to fortify the old Alamo mission.

In this effort, at least, he had plenty of weaponry—all the artillery Cos had left. Neill and his men mounted the guns on the walls and made other preparations for a siege. As they did so, Houston, who had set up his headquarters in the village of Washington-on-the-Brazos, issued a call for volunteers for the regular army and encouraged the formation of an interior line of defense from Gonzales to Goliad and Refugio and Copano, on the gulf coast. Guessing Santa Anna's strategy, Houston would have abandoned San Antonio: He felt that the city's residents largely supported the centralist government, and he could not raise enough men and armaments to defend a site that he considered militarily unimportant. He ordered James Bowie to Béxar reportedly with instructions to destroy the Alamo and withdraw the troops, but to use his discretion depending upon what he found.

When Bowie arrived on January 19, he found Neill's improvements compelling justification to maintain the Alamo. He notified Smith that he and Neill were resolved to stay and defend the position. In agreement, Smith ordered William Barret Travis, now a regular-army lieutenant colonel of cavalry, to raise volunteer reinforcements for the post, but Travis complained when he could raise only thirty poorly armed men. "I am willing, nay anxious, to go to the defense of Béxar," he replied, "but sir, I am unwilling to risk my reputation (which is ever dear to a soldier) by going off into the enemy's country with such little means, so few men, and with them so badly equipped." Nevertheless, Travis led his meager contingent into the Alamo on February 3.

They were joined on February 8 by a small volunteer force from Tennessee, including one of Tennessee's most famous sons, David (Davy) Crockett. As a frontier character, Crockett was already the subject of popular literature. A former frontier militiaman and U.S. congressman from Tennessee, he had lost a congressional reelection campaign, and Texas had beckoned as a new avenue for his political and economic aspirations. Like other enthusiastic volunteers, he judged the region the "garden spot of the world. . . . a world of country here to settle." Furthermore, he anticipated "being elected a member to form a constitution for the province" while "making a fortune yet for myself and family."

At the Alamo, Crockett did not press for a leadership position, which was just as well, as there was already dissension between the regular army and the volunteers over who would be in command. When Neill was called home by family illness on February 14, Travis, with his regular army commission, technically succeeded him. But the volunteers lobbied for Bowie, an elected colonel, and the vote split along predictable lines: the regulars for Travis, the volunteers for Bowie. After a drinking bout, Bowie sobered up and suggested that they share the command. Travis agreed, and none too soon. Santa Anna crossed the Rio Grande on February 16, approaching San Antonio from the west. The next day, General José de Urrea crossed as well, moving up the coast to recapture Goliad. At about the same time, Jesse Badgett left the Alamo garrison as its delegate to a new convention called by the council at Washington-on-the-Brazos for March 1; the other garrison-elected delegate, Samuel Maverick, remained.

The convention was a desperate necessity. The provisional government had dissolved in squabbling, leading one citizen to write Sam Houston, "I sincerely hope the Convention will remedy the existing evils and calm the Public since if not Texas must be lost." And a dispute had occurred over who was allowed to elect delegates. Many of the Anglo revolutionaries looked upon the Tejanos with suspicion, although it was finally decided that Tejanos who were against the Mexican government could vote. Two natives of Texas, José Antonio Navarro and José Francisco Ruiz, who had been elected by the people of Béxar, along with relative newcomer Lorenzo de Zavala, who had resigned his appointment as the first minister of the Mexican legation in Paris to protest the shift to centralism, represented the Mexican Texan population. Brash recent arrivals, including a group of Kentucky volunteers who vociferously protested their exclusion from voting at Nacogdoches, forced a place for themselves at the ballot box and influenced the election in favor of pro-independence candidates unconcerned with a return to the Mexican Constitution of 1824.

When Badgett left to join the other elected delegates, the Alamo defenders still felt that Santa Anna would not be able to reach San Antonio before mid-March. They were wrong. On February 22, a messenger reported that an advance Mexican force was camped only eight miles south of town, but that did not prevent the men from staging a *fandango* that evening to celebrate George Washington's birthday. The next morning, even more Béxar residents left hastily. That afternoon, garrison members still drowsy from the all-night celebration watched from their parapets as hundreds of Mexican troops settled into and around the town.

The Siege and Fall of the Alamo

Santa Anna marched into Texas intent upon driving all the rebellious colonists out of Texas and killing any who were captured, a policy that he and Tornel had enunciated as early as December 1835. As he arrived in San Antonio, he ordered the blood-red flag, signaling that no quarter would be given, raised on the tower of San Fernando church. He informed the rebels that if they would surrender and "place themselves immediately at the disposal of the Supreme Government from whom alone they may expect clemency after some considerations are taken up," they would be allowed to live. Travis responded with a defiant cannon shot aimed at the tower. The Mexican artillerymen then began shelling the Alamo walls. Travis was not being suicidal in defying Santa Anna, for he was confident that reinforcements were coming.

Everyone knew that the old mission walls would give at some point. But the Mexicans' heavy siege guns had not yet arrived and their attempts to position their small cannon close to the structure were met with witheringly accurate fire from the rebels' long rifles. The Texians had placed their artillery at strategic points, but with only about 150 men, they could not hope to cover the entire sweep of the Alamo's perimeters. Even the cannons were exposed to enemy fire. The Texians' only real hope lay in the arrival of reinforcements.

On February 24, Travis sent Gonzales resident Captain Albert Martin out to raise volunteer reinforcements. Martin rode to his hometown with Travis's famous "Victory or Death" letter addressed "To the People of Texas & All Americans in the World": "*I shall never surrender or retreat.* Then, I call on you in the name of Liberty, of patriotism & everything dear to the American character, to come to our aid with all dispatch." At Gonzales, Martin recruited

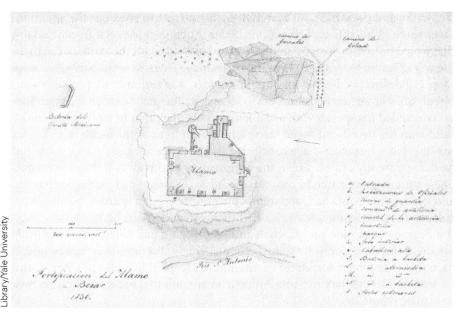

Naturalist Jean Louis Berlandier visited Texas several times, first as a member of the 1828 Comisión de Límites. This is his drawing of the Alamo in 1836 as the Texians prepared to defend themselves against Santa Anna.

the Gonzales Ranging Company of Mounted Volunteers, two dozen or so men who were joined by a few others on the seventy-mile ride to the Alamo's defense, where they arrived on February 29.

Yet these were the only reinforcements the besieged garrison would receive. Fannin had started toward Béxar, then turned around, citing as his reasons an oxcart breakdown on the road and the warnings of his officers, who argued that he needed to defend Goliad, as Santa Anna had targeted it, too, and "Both places are importent [*sic*]." Travis had suspected that Fannin was not coming, and courier James Butler Bonham confirmed it on March 4. In the meantime, the Mexicans extended their batteries so close to the north wall that every volley blasted further into it. In the meantime, Travis had written his letter "to the People of Texas & All Americans in the World." The Alamo was besieged by more than 1,000 Mexican soldiers under Santa Anna, he explained, and he anticipated that the number would increase daily. The garrison had food for the moment, but they were surrounded and supplies had been cut off. Although he had lost no men, it was only a matter of time. The Mexican artillery was closing in, relentlessly battering the old mission's walls. He concluded his letter: "If this call is neglected, I am determined to sustain myself as long as possible & die like a soldier who never forgets what is due to his own honor & that of his country VICTORY OR DEATH."

As the end drew near, on March 4, each side met to consider the situation. Over some of his officers' objections, Santa Anna decided on a frontal assault that would bolster the troops' morale instead of waiting for the artillery fire to do the work. Travis, too, called a meeting of his men. There were probably few more than 250 defenders. Bowie, his co-commander, was seriously ill, probably with pneumonia or advanced tuberculosis. Some writers have contended that Travis concluded his speech with a challenge to his men, that he drew a line in the sand with his sword and asked those who would fight to the death to step over the line. Later historians have concluded that this story is just that—a story. But he did apparently offer his men the opportunity to slip away if they chose, and one—a Frenchman named Louis Rose—did so. Couriers had managed to come and go, as Santa Anna had, apparently purposefully, left a sparsely guarded corridor to the east. Samuel Maverick had finally departed for the Washington-on-the-Brazos convention on March 2; and Juan Seguín had taken Travis's appeals for aid to the settlements. By some accounts, Travis also promised the remaining men that they would surrender or attempt to escape if help did not arrive, and he sent an intermediary to Santa Anna in an attempt to discuss surrender terms, only to be rebuffed.

On that fatal morning, March 6, Santa Anna ordered four columns to position themselves for attack, one from each direction, with the commander himself overseeing the reserve troops. At the head of one column was General Cos, who had been persuaded by Santa Anna that a promise given to rebels was not binding. Mexican soldiers marched silently into position and waited through the cold night. They began their attack at 5:30 A.M. while the Texians were asleep, their dozing sentinels easily dispatched by an advance guard of light infantry. A few in the Mexican ranks, however, could not resist rallying cries, which woke the Alamo defenders to the sight of the columns of soldiers already drawing near.

There followed a bloodbath. The Texian cannons quickly began spitting grapeshot and followed it with nine-pound iron balls. The metal shards ripped through the tight columns, the iron balls adding to the general destruction. At the same time, Texians were being picked off the wall at close range by the Mexican Baker rifles, British arms with great short-distance accuracy. Although they had only a few ladders, the Mexican soldiers found enough footholds on the north wall that some men were able to slip over and open the gate. Ironically, the long rifles that had served the Texians so well proved a poor defense at this point, for the troops poured through the breach as the Texians tried to reload. The invaders then turned the captured cannon on the doors through which the defenders were firing.

Travis fell early in the fighting, with a bullet in the forehead. Some Texians tried to surrender by waving white cloths, but most fired on the advancing troops and then engaged in hand-to-hand fighting. The chapel was overrun last. Bowie was killed in his sickbed. James Butler Bonham and Almeron Dickenson died beside the cannon they had manned. The battle had lasted a mere ninety minutes.

Various accounts state that a few of the defenders fought to the last and were taken prisoner. Among those captured, it was rumored, was David Crockett. The memoir of Mexican officer José Enrique de la Peña confirmed these accounts. In de la Peña's reporting, several officers, including General Manuel Fernández Castrillón, wanted to spare the six or seven captives, but Santa Anna reacted in indignation, insisting that they be executed. When the guards hesitated, some of his staff officers, seeking to curry his favor, set upon the captives with their swords. Surveying the carnage, Captain José Juan Sánchez Navarro y Estrada remarked, "With another such victory, we will all go to the devil."

San Antonio resident Eulalia Yorba and her children had gone to the home of a Spanish priest to get some food and watched from there as the shooting began. Yorba related that a Mexican colonel came and asked those in the house to minister to the dying Mexican soldiers. When she emerged to do so, she found "The roadway. . . thronged with Mexican soldiers with smoke and dirt begrimed faces, haggard eyes and wild, insane expression." In the Alamo itself, she observed doors "splintered and battered in," floors "crimson with blood," the air "dark with powder smoke" and "hot and heavy." Tending to the wounds of some of the Mexican soldiers, she saw dead Texians lying "singly and in heaps of three or four, or in irregular rows here and there all about the floor of the Alamo, just as they had fallen."

Santa Anna summoned Béxar alcalde Francisco Antonio Ruiz to identify Travis, Bowie, and Crockett. Then he ordered Ruiz to see to the interment of the dead Mexican soldiers, estimated at 600, or one-third of the attack force. But Ruiz did not have the resources to bury so many, and his workers threw many of the bodies in the San Antonio River, where they jammed up on snags and bends. Pablo Díaz, a young man at the time of the battle, remembered that the sight and their stench made him ill, "for they lined the river's course and banks all the way from Crockett Street to more than a mile below." The Alamo defenders met a different fate, as Santa Anna ordered two funeral pyres built for them. According to Díaz, "Grease of different kinds, principally tallow, was melted and poured over the two pyres," he remembered. "I saw ashes, as well as the blackened chars of the different anatomical fragments. They emitted an odor even more sickening than did the corpses of those who had been thrown into the river. . . ."

The only Alamo defender to receive burial was Gregorio Esparza, who had served under Juan Seguín in the siege of Béxar and had stayed in his command. Esparza's brother Francisco had served under General Cos. Francisco got permission from Cos to take his brother's body. "I proceeded to the Alamo," Francisco would relate, "and found the dead body of my brother in one of the rooms," with "a ball in his breast and a stab from a sword in his side."

Not everyone in the Alamo died. The old mission had also sheltered a number of noncombatants, most of whom survived the carnage. Most famous in Anglo annals are Susannah Dickenson, wife of Almeron, and their child Angelina. There were also African Americans and members of Tejano families, including Gregorio Esparza's wife and children. One of the children, Enrique, later related his mother's courage and pain. When confronted by her captors as she began searching for food for the children and the other refugees, "[s]he told him she did not care whether she was under guard or not, she was going to have something to eat for herself, her children, and her companions whom she intended to feed if Santa Anna did not feed his prisoners." Enrique noted, "[a]fter our release we went back to our home and my mother wept for many days and nights."

In his official report, Santa Anna greatly inflated the statistics of battle to enhance his reputation, claiming that more than 600 Americans died in the battle and that he lost only about seventy men killed. Along with the report, he sent the captured flag of the New Orleans Greys to Mexico City as proof of American interference in Texas. In this he was largely correct; there were few old Texians at the Alamo, for many of them did not support independence until the slaughter at the Alamo convinced them that they had little choice. But the several days that Santa Anna spent at Béxar—he did not depart until mid-March—would permit the rebel convention to organize a revolutionary government and draft a constitution.

A small contingent of men had come together at the Alamo—natives and immigrants, Mexicans, Anglos, and Europeans, a few old settlers, more recent immigrants, and newly arrived adventurers. They had all sensed opportunity—for land, for glory, for a return of republican principles, for a separate Mexican state of Texas or a Texas as part of the United States. Now their deaths would provide a rallying point for the Texian cause.

The Revolution—The Winning of Independence (March–April)

While anxiously awaiting news of the Alamo defenders, delegates to the independence convention were at work at Washington-on-the-Brazos. On March 2, while they still thought that Fannin was headed to the Alamo's aid, they adopted a Texas declaration of independence, decisively breaking with the idea of continuing as part of a federalist Mexico. They framed their argument in terms that Americans would recognize from their own Declaration of Independence: freedom of worship, the right to bear arms, billeting of troops "among us," citizens imprisoned, "mercenary" armies. "The necessity of self-preservation," they concluded, ". . . now decrees our eternal political separation. . . . the people of Texas do now constitute a FREE, SOVEREIGN, and INDEPENDENT REPUBLIC." "It is indisputable that the Texas revolution and the American revolution of 1776 stand on the same basis," wrote the editor of the *Telegraph and Texas Register*. "If the American revolution was a just and glorious cause, so is the cause of the Texas revolution."

At the Independence Convention

When there was no word from or of the Alamo by March 13, lawyer William Fairfax Gray, a land agent traveling in Texas who kept a diary describing the events at the convention, wrote, "The anxiety begins to be intense."

Despite the desperate atmosphere, the fifty-nine delegates who had assembled by March 11—primarily from the American South, with only one in six residing in Texas before January 1830—set about creating a constitution modeled on the U.S. Constitution and fulfilling as much as possible the functions of a government.

At Washington-on-the-Brazos, delegates worked hurriedly to define laws and the governmental structure of a new republic. They followed some Spanish and Mexican precedents, for example, in laws on homestead exemptions and debtor relief. The delegates tried to address the thorny issue of land claims by voiding some eleven-league claims and questionable titles, noting that "one of the great duties of this convention" was "the protection of the public domain from unjust and fraudulent claims, and quieting the people in the enjoyment of their lands."

The governmental structure devised by the convention reflected the American system: executive, legislative, and judicial branches; a Senate and a House of Representatives; and supreme, district, county, and justice courts. Convention members used a definition of citizenship that included Tejanos but excluded "Africans, the descendants of Africans, and Indians" and affirmed the practice of slaveholding, returning all blacks who had been slaves before coming to Texas to that status. The republic Congress would not "have power to emancipate slaves," and an owner who desired to do so would either need Congress's approval or have to "send his or her slave or slaves without the limits of the Republic." Congressional approval would be required for a freedman or woman to reside in the state.

On March 17, members approved the document in an atmosphere of continued anxiety and uncertainty. They settled on an interim government that included empresarios David G. Burnet as president and Lorenzo de Zavala as vice president, with Samuel P. Carson as secretary of state, Robert Potter as secretary of the tiny Texas navy, David Thomas as attorney general, Bailey Hardeman as treasurer, and Thomas Jefferson Rusk as secretary of war.

Further Setbacks: The Runaway Scrape and the Fannin Massacre

Houston, who had again been named military commander-in-chief by the convention, had not hurried to the Alamo's relief. By one account, Houston doubted the reports from Travis and Fannin, considering them political grandstanding. He had just begun to put together a new force composed of both volunteers and militia, and even if he had gone to their defense, he would have been too late. News of the Alamo's fall reached him at Gonzales on March 11, which took on a horrified mourning with so many of their kinsmen and fellow townsmen dead at the Alamo. Houston, resolving not to be trapped by Santa Anna's and Urrea's advancing forces, added to townspeople's misery by ordering Gonzales burned. Retreating to Burnam's Crossing on the Colorado, near present-day La Grange, he ordered Fannin at Goliad to join him, with plans to combine Fannin's volunteer army of about 400 with his own force of about the same size.

A general panic now swept the settlements with the news of the Alamo's fall and Houston's retreat. Families began a pell-mell rush eastward and southeastward in what became known as the Runaway Scrape. "Deserters were constantly passing us on foot and on horseback," remembered Rosa von Roeder Kleberg, who had settled outside San Felipe. "The old men who were with the families laughed at them and called to them, 'Run! Run! Santa Anna is after you!'" Frances Meneffee Sutherland, mourning the loss of her son, William De-Priest Sutherland, in the Alamo, recalled, "We went to the Colorado, forty miles, but after some time, [Houston] thought proper to retreat farther and of course we had to go, too." At the Brazos River, they stopped for a few days, her husband leaving to join the Texian army. But news came that the Mexican army was drawing near, and the settlers continued their confused flight. "I wish you could know how the people did as they kept going about trying to get somewhere," Sutherland wrote, "but no person knew where they were going to get to."

Families suffered greatly. Dilue Rose Harris, almost eleven years old when the Alamo fell, would later remember her family's desperate flight: "We left home at sunset, hauling clothes, bedding and provisions on the sleigh with one yoke of oxen." At the Lynchburg ferry on the San Jacinto River, they found "fully five thousand people trying to get across." For some, however, the advancing Mexican troops evoked a quite different response. Santa Anna and General Urrea had made it known that Mexican law forbidding slavery would now be enforced in Texas, and a number of slaves rushed to meet the troops, gaining protection and freedom.

As many Texians scrambled, wondering if they would ever be able to return to their frontier homes, Houston continued to fall back—and Fannin still failed to appear. By this time, Fannin had his own troubles. He had ordered a company to Refugio to evacuate settlers there, only to have them run into a detachment of Urrea's troops. Departing from Matamoros, Urrea had been successful in a sweep northward through the coastal prairies in February and March, crushing what was left of the Matamoros Expedition at San Patricio. His troops now bested the Goliad company and the Georgia battalion sent to reinforce it. Loyal Tejano residents of the Refugio–San Patricio area, some of whom had received highhanded treatment from the Texian volunteers, provided Urrea with crucial assistance.

The Goliad garrison consisted almost entirely of recent newcomers to Texas; a few might still have worn the pants of U.S. Army regulars, for a number of "deserters" from the Third and Sixth Infantries stationed along the Sabine River showed up on the rolls of the Texas army. Fannin was an exception, having been resident in the state for about a year and a half. He was also unusual because of his formal military training, although it did not serve him well. He delayed in following Houston's order to retreat because he had not wanted to leave his troops at Refugio, but even when he received word of their defeat on the afternoon of March 17, he still failed to retreat. Ignoring Houston's order to dump the nine cannons in the river, Fannin was burdened by underfed oxen with both baggage and artillery, and when the troops finally started, the oxen proved agonizingly slow. Garrison member Herman Ehrenberg remembered that "disgust at the creeping pace of our column induced us finally to abandon all our equipment."

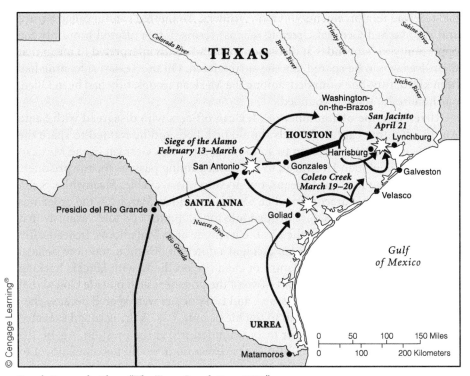

Revolutionary battles—"The Texas Revolution, 1836."

In perhaps his most inexplicable move, after only six miles Fannin halted the column for a rest break in the middle of a prairie. Some of his men protested, urging him to push on to the relative safety of a distant tree line, but he apparently felt that the Mexican troops would not attack a 400-man contingent. The men rested without incident, but soon after resuming the march, they looked back to see Mexican cavalry spilling from the timberline two miles away.

Again, Fannin rejected the idea of trying to reach the tree line ahead, despite the protestations of his officers that it would be a better defensive position even if they suffered casualties along the way. Fannin ordered the men to form a hollow square, with the artillery posted at the corners. In the early afternoon, the Mexican dragoons began the attack. Fannin's men were able to direct withering rifle, musket, and artillery fire on the advancing troops, but Mexican sharpshooters picked off the Texian gunners. Fannin, to his credit, bravely led the defense, but the Texian force ran out of water, and the Mexican sharpshooters had killed the oxen, making it impossible to move the baggage and the wounded. The fighting ceased at nightfall, but the Texians knew that Urrea's troops had them surrounded.

The only possible escape seemed to be a stealthy nighttime retreat, but Fannin agreed that they could not abandon the wounded. They tried through the night to erect breastworks, but when the morning dawned, they saw that Urrea had received reinforcements and more artillery. An injured Fannin called a truce and approached General Urrea to discuss terms. Urrea offered him only the opportunity to "surrender at discretion," which Fannin interpreted to mean that their lives would be spared, and he surrendered. On the Texian side, nine had been killed, fifty-one wounded; among the Mexican troops, fifty had been killed, one hundred and forty wounded.

Urrea was one of a number of Mexican officers who disagreed with Santa Anna's edict that captured rebels should be killed, and he wanted to spare the men. He even allowed Fannin to go to the coast with a German in the Mexican service, Colonel Juan Holsinger, to see about gaining passage for the prisoners on a ship bound for New Orleans, but no ship was available. Meanwhile, Santa Anna reiterated his draconian edict. On Palm Sunday, March 27, the order was carried out. The Texians were divided into four columns and told variously that they were being marched to the coast to go home or to Matamoros. Instead, after a short march, with each column going in a different direction and now isolated from each other, Mexican infantry opened fire on them, with lancers backing them up. Three hundred and forty-two of the prisoners died outside Goliad that day; twenty-eight managed to escape, and two doctors were spared because they were desperately needed to tend to the Mexican troops. A firing squad executed Fannin and then killed another forty wounded still at the presidio. Again, the Mexicans burned the Texian dead. These executions would become known to Texians as the "Goliad Massacre."

Sam Houston and San Jacinto

Meanwhile, Secretary of War Thomas Jefferson Rusk, a South Carolinian who had joined Burnet's colony in 1835, had moved the interim government to the relative safety of Harrisburg and tried to rally various militias to defend against the oncoming Mexican forces. He also found himself in the unenviable position of trying to coordinate with and direct General Houston. Despite grumblings from his army, Houston had retreated again on March 19, judging the Burnam's Crossing location indefensible and a poor strategic location to keep Santa Anna from striking the settlements. He moved his new camp at Beeson's Crossing, near present-day Columbus, where he welcomed a sizable number of fresh volunteers, many of them residents of the settlements who had tried to stay out of the conflict but now had been galvanized by news of the Alamo's fall. He also had time to begin to teach them how to march and to fire by companies.

Santa Anna, meanwhile, had split up his forces to search for Houston's army. He sent General Antonio Gaona with instructions to occupy Bastrop and continue along the Old San Antonio Road to Nacogdoches, and he ordered General Joaquín Ramírez y Sesma to Beeson's Crossing with a large force. On March 21, Ramírez y Sesma drew up on the west side of the Colorado opposite Houston's army but could not cross because recent spring rains had swollen the river. Meanwhile, Urrea had also reached the mouth of the Brazos at Matagorda and was similarly stymied. His position effectively kept the Texians from any port except Galveston.

In a little publicized action, however, the fledgling Texas navy had kept open communication between Galveston and New Orleans and prevented the Mexican troops from being resupplied by sea. The General Convention had granted letters of marque and reprisal to several privateers until the four small schooners that they had purchased in January 1836 were fitted out for war. Under the command of Commodore Charles E. Hawkins, the Texas navy captured several ships that were loaded with supplies and munitions intended for Santa Anna.

Houston now realized that he was about to be trapped. Gaona could swing down on his right flank and Urrea on his left, with Ramírez y Sesma in the center. Then, on March 23, he received the shocking news of the massacre of Fannin's command. That intelligence, along with his precarious position, forced him to retreat again, this time to San Felipe, which brought him further censure and even the desertion of some troops who resented his apparent lack of courage. Historians, however, have generally concluded that an engagement at Beeson's Crossing would have been a tactical error.

To the dismay of many of his troops, meanwhile, Houston ordered a further retreat, from San Felipe to Jared Groce's plantation twenty miles away. He left a small rear guard to defend the San Felipe and Fort Bend crossings on the Brazos and departed with the rest of the army, now numbering about 500. "We foundered through mud and water, pelted by the storm," Private J. H. Kuykendall recalled. By the time Santa Anna arrived at San Felipe, nine days after Houston's departure, the Texians had burned the town and disappeared. Santa Anna, who in addition to driving the colonists from Texas intended to secure the border at the Sabine River, continued eastward, crossing the Brazos in early April. It appeared that Houston was, in fact, trying to lure Santa Anna into East Texas, although he denied it at the time.

The size of Houston's army continued to grow—to 900, including more "deserters" from the American army on the Sabine—and the two weeks at Groce's plantation allowed them to rest and recuperate from a host of ills brought on by hard camp living and relentless rains. They also had additional time to drill in some of the rudiments of warfare. When they crossed to the east side of the Brazos River, further good fortune arrived in the form of two six-pounder cannons, a gift from the people of Cincinnati. The troops immediately dubbed them the "Twin Sisters."

Then, Santa Anna discovered that the Texian government was in nearby Harrisburg, to the east. With Houston's force to the north, he realized that this might be his opportunity to seize the rebel government and at the same time cut off their conduit to the United States, Galveston Bay, ending the rebellion in one stroke. He dashed forward with only about 900 troops, sending word to the armies behind him to rendezvous at Fort Bend to complete the sweep of East Texas.

With the headstrong and independent-minded volunteers chafing at Houston's inaction, Secretary of War Rusk arrived in camp on April 6 with a stern message from ad interim President David Burnet: "Sir: The enemy are laughing you to scorn. You must fight them. You must retreat no further. The country expects you to fight. The salvation of the country depends on your doing so." Burnet had authorized Rusk to seize command from Houston if the general still refused to fight, and some of the troops clearly wanted Rusk to do so. But, in a private conference, the secretary listened to Houston's explanations for his actions and responded by joining the army. Surely Houston had taken Rusk into his confidence with regard to Gaines's army waiting at the Sabine. On April 12, Houston started the troops eastward again.

The defining action seemed destined to take place near the Lynchburg Crossing of Buffalo Bayou near Harrisburg, where the Mexican army, in pursuit of the Texas government, and the Texas army in pursuit of the Mexican army, were all headed. An advance force under Colonel Almonte got close enough to the fleeing rebel government to shoot at their boat as they rowed toward a steamer in the bay, but the presence of Burnet's wife among the rebels led him to hold fire. At this point Santa Anna believed he had the Texians on the run.

Historians remain divided on whether the Texian army's decision to stand and fight at San Jacinto was Houston's or his army's. Having come to a literal fork in the road, marked by a giant oak that came to be called the "Whichway Tree," a decision was needed on whether the Texians would push into East Texas and force Santa Anna to pursue them in the direction of the Sabine or, as much of the rank-and-file wanted, they would turn in the direction of Harrisburg, where the Mexican army awaited. Some now believe, however, that Secretary Rusk had taken the decision out of Houston's hands the previous evening, ordering him to fight. With Houston lagging toward the rear of the column as the army approached the Whichway Tree, the army surged toward Harrisburg. Perhaps Houston was following orders from his superior officer, but the army would fight.

As the Texians forced marched toward Harrisburg, documents from a captured courier revealed that Santa Anna was headed toward Lynchburg with only 660 men. Leaving the baggage and sick at Harrisburg, Houston determined to reach the crossing first and gain the upper hand. The Texians did arrive first and established themselves in a tall oak grove with Buffalo Bayou at their back, a position particularly well suited for their riflemen. Perhaps overconfident, Santa Anna took a relatively risky position, to the dismay of his officers, with the San Jacinto River on his right and a swampy area called Peggy Lake at his back. His only route of escape was to the southwest across a small bridge over Vince's Bayou. There was a slight rise in the plain between the two camps, so that they could not actually see each other without climbing a tree. Santa Anna immediately sent men to test the Texians' defenses. The Texians greeted them with fire from the Twin Sisters. The Mexicans responded with their own twelve-pounder, and then pulled back into a wood.

Some Texians wanted to attack immediately. Houston said no, although he did allow the hotspur Sidney Sherman to reconnoiter with a group of mounted riflemen. Sherman immediately disobeyed orders and charged the Mexican cavalry. When he was cut off and asked for infantry assistance, Houston refused, but once again, the Texian army took the decision out of his hands. A whole infantry regiment deliberately ignored Houston's order to turn around and assisted Sherman in returning to safety.

Both armies settled down for the night. The Mexicans continued building breastworks to shore up their relatively vulnerable position and eagerly awaited reinforcements under General Cos, who arrived with about 540 men at 9:00 A.M. the next day, April 21. This, of course, shifted the numerical advantage: Houston had 910 men, Santa Anna now had about 1,200.

Again Houston hesitated as he met with his officers from noon to 2 P.M. But, finally, as the afternoon wore on, Houston himself ordered the men into battle positions and to advance in two lines over the rise that had separated them from the Mexicans' view. He also permitted "Deaf" Smith to destroy the bridge over Vince's Bayou, the only escape route, which emphasized to his men that this was a battle to the death. Houston had at first denied Juan Seguín's detachment a place in the battle line because many of the other soldiers had demonstrated considerable animosity toward Mexicans in general, and Houston was afraid that they might be shot by their own compatriots if not the Mexicans. But Seguín and his men argued for the opportunity to fight, reminding Houston of their unflagging commitment to the cause.

Santa Anna had kept a close watch through most of the day but had grown complacent in the afternoon. Houston had not mounted an attack yet; why should he now, just after the Mexican force had built breastworks and received reinforcements? Thus, the Texians' artillery unit advanced within 200 yards of the enemy without being detected and opened fire. This was immediately followed by a Texian cavalry charge. At about that time, a four-piece band began playing a popular ballad, "Will You Come to the Bower?" and then, according to some sources, "Yankee Doodle." Houston had the infantry hold their fire, but after the first volley, he lost control of them, and they fell to hand-to-hand skirmishing with knives, swords, and rifles as clubs.

The Mexican officers, surprised and confused, struggled to organize their frightened troops, but without success. Santa Anna emerged from his tent, but could do nothing to bring order to the "bewildered and panic-stricken herd." With Texians scaling the barricades, the battle was over in eighteen minutes— then it became a rout, a bloodbath. The Texians were bent on revenge, and they killed indiscriminately and often brutally. Even the Tejano volunteers proved ruthless. Many Mexican soldiers jumped into Peggy Lake, calling desperately "Me no Alamo—me no Goliad!" but they were easy targets for the Texian gunners. The water soon ran red with their blood.

Six hundred and fifty Mexican soldiers were killed, most of them after the brief battle, and most of the rest were captured. The victory for the Texians was decisive but not complete. They had subdued only a part of the Mexican army. At first, they even feared that Santa Anna had escaped them, but he was apprehended the next day after finding the bridge burned out at Vince's Bayou and spending the night hiding in tall grass. Even with the dictator as a prisoner, Houston still feared that the bulk of the Mexican army under generals Vicente Filisola and Urrea might arrive at any moment, and he knew that his disorganized, bedraggled force would be unable to fend them off. Under terms of his surrender, Santa Anna ordered his second-in-command, Filisola, to retreat to Béxar, but Filisola and Urrea had no intention of abandoning the war. They agreed to retreat west of the Colorado and await orders from the government.

Then, the rain began to fall. An already soaked soil turned to sticky mud, a bog, and the retreat of the Mexican army was marked by abandoned cannonballs, wheels, carts, rifle balls—finally even some of their weapons as nature vented its ferocity on the exposed troops. Then came sickness and dysentery. By the time they reached the Colorado, where recent archaeology has found various insignias, buttons, and belt buckles as well, *el Mar de Lodo* (the Sea of Mud) had defeated them as surely as if Houston had attacked with 5,000 fresh troops. Finally, in May they received orders from the government to hold all conquered territory, but by then the army was already south of the Nueces River on its way to Matamoros and in no condition to carry on the fight.

Houston, who had had two horses shot from under him and had been wounded in the ankle during the battle, soon headed to New Orleans to receive treatment. Ad interim president Burnet and the civilian government, now established at Velasco at the mouth of the Brazos, took charge of Santa Anna and negotiated two treaties: one public (calling for a ceasefire, repatriation of prisoners, return of Texian property, and safe conduct for the Mexican army, which was to retreat beyond the Rio Grande) and one private (promising Santa Anna immediate freedom in return for his influence in getting the Mexican government to recognize Texas independence, with the Rio Grande, its southern and western boundary).

Stephen F. Austin was in New Orleans on June 10, on his way back from his unsuccessful mission to Washington, D.C., to try to raise money and support for Texas when he learned of Santa Anna's capture at the battle of San Jacinto. He realized that citizens would be suffering the ravages of war and arranged for a shipload of food and other necessities to be sent to Texas. Then he headed home.

Conclusion

The volunteer army had made the independence declared at Washington-on-the-Brazos a reality. Texas was now a nation born in conflict—not only the conflict between the Mexican government and its recalcitrant Texas citizens, but conflict among those citizens as well. There had been the war and peace parties, and within the war party those fighting for recognition of a separate Mexican statehood stood apart from those fighting for separation from Mexico. There had been those who simply wanted to be left alone but were drawn unwillingly into the conflict. There had been tensions between newcomers and established

Texians, with the roles constantly shifting. Newcomers did not have the perspective of residents of a year or two; residents of a year or two did not have the perspective of Austin's Old Three Hundred; and Austin's Old Three Hundred did not have the perspective of the Tejanos. There had been tensions between Anglos and Tejanos, even as some of them had worked and fought well together. There had been tensions among the Anglos dominating the new military and the new government, with pro- and anti-Houston factions, pro- and anti-Smith factions. And continued rumors of Indian warfare, inspired by Mexican agents, spread throughout the Texas frontier.

Somehow, in part because of Santa Anna's harsh and arrogant conduct of the war in Texas, all of this had added up to a victory for the revolutionaries. But there were still many conflicts to be resolved. The Mexican government refused to recognize Texas independence; Mexicans were bitter about losing a large part of their territory so early in their own history as an independent nation, with many struggling to maintain republican principles that they shared with the United States. The United States would see the developments in Texas as both a blessing and a curse: With possible annexation, Texas provided an opportunity for westward expansion of the United States, but it would also be a catalyst for further problems between the slaveholding South and the North. Texas slaves themselves saw any hope of an improvement in their status and for freedom disappear. With Anglos from the American South overwhelmingly in positions of power, racial and ethnic differences would become more significant. Juan Seguín would find post-revolution Texas more difficult to endure than the sieges of Béxar and the Alamo and the battle of San Jacinto, until he became, as he said, "a foreigner in my native land."

But he was indisputably one of the most prominent revolutionary veterans, and he would continue in the service of the republic. To him was given the task of burying the remains of the Alamo defenders. Shortly before the first anniversary of the Alamo's fall, he located the heaps of ashes from the cremation and interred them after a sober procession, with "three volleys of musquetry . . . fired over the grave by the whole Battalion." Seguín did not have enough powder to fire the larger guns, "but every honor was done within the reach of my scanty means." The Alamo would ever loom large in Texians' memory, but, in many ways, the battle had only begun.

Suggested Readings

The Texas Revolution—particularly the defense of the Alamo—has generated copious scholarship and dramatic conjecture. A classic scholarly work is Amelia Williams's "A Critical Study of the Siege of the Alamo and of the Personnel of Its Defenders" in *Southwestern Historical Quarterly* (1932–33). Paul Lack's *The Texas Revolutionary Experience, A Political and Social History, 1835–1836* (1992) is a key scholarly source for understanding the events of the revolution. Another key source is Stephen L. Hardin's clear and informative

Texian Iliad: A Military History of the Texas Revolution (1994). A good brief overview is provided in "Colonization and Revolution," Chapter 1 of Richard Bruce Winders's *Crisis in the Southwest: The United States, Mexico, and the Struggle over Texas* (2002). The *New Handbook of Texas* (1996) has a detailed "Texas Revolution" entry and helpful entries on the key events and participants. See also, Jack Jackson, ed., *Almonte's Texas: Juan N. Almonte's 1834 Inspection, Secret Report & Role in the 1836 Campaign* (2003).

Despite the debates as to its veracity, José Enrique de la Peña's *With Santa Anna in Texas: A Personal Narrative of the Revolution* (1974) is an important source for the period. For other primary sources, consult *Documents of Texas History* (1994), eds. Ernest Wallace, David M. Vigness, and George B. Ward; *The Papers of the Texas Revolution* (1973), compiled by John H. Jenkins; and "Revolutionary Texas, 1835–1836," in Sam Haynes and Cary D. Wintz's *Major Problems in Texas History* (2002).

The Rebellion—Early Months (October–December 1835)

In addition to the works above, Gregg Cantrell's *Stephen F. Austin, Empresario of Texas* provides good secondary material on the early months of the war. Alwyn Barr focuses on the siege of Béxar in his *Texans in Revolt: the Battle for San Antonio, 1835* (1990). Interesting primary accounts are included in Noah Smithwick's *Evolution of a State* and Herman Ehrenberg's "The Fight for Freedom in Texas," included in Natalie Ornish's *Ehrenberg: Goliad Survivor, Old West Explorer* (1997). Graham Davis's "Models of Migration: The Historiography of the Irish Pioneers in South Texas" in *Southwestern Historical Quarterly* (1996) includes an analysis of how one ethnic group split in its loyalties between the Mexican government and the revolutionaries.

From Rebellion to Revolution—Victory and Defeat (December 1835–March 1836)

The classic account of the battle of the Alamo is Walter Lord, *A Time to Stand* (1961). William C. Davis's *Three Roads to the Alamo: The Lives and Fortunes of David Crockett, James Bowie, and William Barret Travis* (1998) examines in detail the three men's paths to the Alamo and provides a brief account of the Alamo's fall. *A Line in the Sand: The Alamo in Blood and Memory* (2001), by Randy Roberts and James N. Olson and *The Blood of Heroes: The 13-Day Struggle for the Alamo—and the Sacrifice that Forged a Nation* (2012), by James Donovan, examine both the events at the Alamo and the myths surrounding them. See also James E. Crisp, *Sleuthing the Alamo: Davy Crockett's Last Stand and Other Mysteries of the Texas Revolution* (2005). Primary accounts of the period leading up to the Alamo battle and the Alamo's fall appear in Bill Groneman's *Eyewitnesses to the Alamo* (1996), Ron Jackson's *Alamo Legacy: Alamo Descendants Remember the Alamo* (1997), Timothy M. Matovina's *The Alamo Remembered: Tejano Accounts and Perspectives* (1995), and Alan C. Huffines, *Blood of Noble Men: The Alamo*

Siege and Battle (1999). For Santa Anna's actions, see Will Fowler, *Santa Anna of Mexico* (2007).

The Revolution—The Winning of Independence (March–April 1836)

Good primary accounts are included in Jackson's *Alamo Legacy*, in editor Paul Lack's *The Diary of William Fairfax Gray from Virginia to Texas, 1835–1837* (1997), in Crystal Sasse Ragsdale's *The Golden Free Land* (1976), and in the reminiscences of Dilue Rose Harris, included in Jo Ella Powell Exley's *Texas Tears and Texas Sunshine*. Juan Seguín's story from this period is told in *A Revolution Remembered* (1991), edited by Jesús F. de la Teja.

Sam Houston comes to prominence in this portion of the revolutionary story; there have been numerous biographies of this leading Texas figure. Two good ones include Randolph B. Campbell's *Sam Houston and the American Southwest* (1993) and James L. Haley's *Sam Houston* (2002).

Texas Independent, 1836–1845

Pleasant and Margaret Rose brought their young family home to their farm in Austin's colony near the Gulf Coast, when the Runaway Scrape was over, with independence still a fragile reality. The family arrived after dark and camped, having heard that Mexican troops had vandalized their house. When morning dawned, they found hogs exiting its front door, floorboards pulled up, and their possessions scattered. Pleasant immediately began plowing, while Margaret shocked daughter Dilue by veering from religious observance and doing the family wash on a Sunday. Neighbors filtered back, tired and threadbare. Bread was hard to come by. Across the settlements, homes had to be restored or rebuilt, cattle reclaimed or replaced, food provisions renewed. "Mother was very despondent," Dilue would write, "but father was hopeful. He said Texas would . . . become a great nation."

The challenges were immense. Mexico refused to recognize Texas's newly won independence, and other nations—including the United States—would be slow with official recognition. The populace lived under continued threat of a renewed attack from Mexico, as well as from the Comanches and other hostile tribes to the north and west. All of the old problems of living on a frontier had been exacerbated by the losses and disruptions of the war. Many residents now openly advocated annexation to the United States, both because most of the population had strong American roots and because of the need for stability and security. Yet annexation would be long in coming, and when it finally occurred, new struggles over identity would stress and eventually fracture the state.

By the end of 1836, Texas was a sprawling and vastly underpopulated territory of perhaps 30,000 Anglo-Americans, 5,000 slaves, 3,500 Tejanos, and between 10,000 and 15,000 Indians of various tribes, 8,000 of them belonging to the

Chapter 7 Texas Independent, 1836–1845	
1836	Sam Houston becomes first elected president of Republic of Texas
1837	United States recognizes Republic of Texas but rebuffs Texas's attempts to win annexation
1838	Mirabeau B. Lamar succeeds Houston as Texas president; Vicente Córdova leads Córdova rebellion
1839	Cherokees are forced from Texas
1842	Houston again becomes Texas president; Mexican troops twice invade Texas, which Mexico refuses to recognize as independent; Somervell and Mier expeditions are mounted in retaliation
1844–46	German stock company Adelsverein transports thousands of German immigrants to Texas
1845	Mexico offers to recognize Texas if the republic will not annex itself to another country, but Texas wins annexation to the United States

so-called "civilized tribes" that had migrated or been driven from the United States. A recent immigrant from Connecticut lamented to his family that, "The war has entirely broken up every kind of business in Texas. Thousands have been ruined in all but their land. In fact you can scarcely conceive of the suffering that this war has occasioned. All of the country west of the Brazos has been deserted and overrun and pillaged by the enemy."

As the interim leaders set about organizing the new country, old antagonisms and factions resurfaced, with men jockeying for positions of influence and power in the new order. The disarray developed in the absence of a strong, well-established governmental structure and was intensified by the unpredictable mix of newcomers who had arrived during the revolution. Revolutionary veteran Mirabeau B. Lamar spoke for many when he worried that Texas was "upon the verge of anarchy."

As you read this chapter, consider the following questions:

1. What problems did Texas face in establishing a stable government and economy?
2. Did Mexico make a serious effort to reconquer Texas?
3. Why did immigrants settle near the Indian lands?

Annexation or Empire, 1836–1845

For many, an independent Texas was simply a prelude to annexation to the United States, and, as Interim President David G. Burnet struggled to get the government on a solid footing, he set national elections for September 1836, including on the ballot the proposition that Texas seek annexation. But for others, like Lamar and Thomas Jefferson Green, this was the opportunity to establish a new North American empire that would stretch to the Pacific Ocean. The resulting conflict between annexation and empire would destabilize the new nation for all of its existence. The first president of the Republic of Texas, Sam Houston, would lead the efforts to achieve annexation while revolution veteran and second president of the Republic of Texas Mirabeau B. Lamar entertained grandiose visions of Texas as an independent nation.

Sam Houston's First Term, 1836–1838

Henry Smith, the volatile former provisional governor, promptly announced his candidacy for president, but he was not a viable candidate because he had made too many enemies during his governership, and Texas could ill afford another period of such divisiveness. Thomas Jefferson Rusk, the popular commander-in-chief of the postwar army, declined to run. Some of the old Texians promoted Stephen F. Austin, and he agreed to serve if elected—but many, especially newcomers and those who had served in the army, saw him as too vested in the empresario system, still tied to old ways of relating to Mexico, and severely tainted by the Monclova land speculations of his business partner, Samuel May Williams.

Saying that "the crisis requires it," Sam Houston entered the race on August 20, just eleven days before the election. Houston had strong critics throughout the revolution, and the victory at San Jacinto had not silenced them. But he brought more to the table than just the glory of victory. He had a strong public identity and presence and a background in both political and military affairs. The republic was fortunate to have a unifying figure of such stature.

In the election that followed, both Houston and the annexation proposal won by landslides, with Houston polling 5,119 votes to only 587 for Austin. Even more

Daughters of the Republic of Texas Library, San Antonio, Texas

Perhaps the earliest known photograph of President Sam Houston, dressed as he might have been at the inauguration of Mirabeau B. Lamar, the second president of the republic.

humiliating to Austin was the fact that 743 voters favored Smith even though he had withdrawn from the race when Houston entered. Lamar was elected vice president. Voters also approved the new constitution at the same time that they enthusiastically cast their ballots for annexation. But the new republic started with a public debt of over a million dollars and had little hope of doing anything but adding to it, and most citizens yearned for identity with the United States and the security and definition that being part of the larger nation would provide.

The two representatives that Interim President Burnet had sent to Washington, D.C., that summer had already begun to appeal to the U.S. government for annexation by the time Houston took office in October 1836. Houston also committed himself to annexation in his inaugural address, saying, "The appeal is made by a willing people. Will our friends disregard it? . . . We are cheered by the hope that they will receive us to a participancy of their civil, political, and religious rights, and hail us welcome into the great family of freemen."

Despite Houston's optimistic plea, the U.S. government hesitated to provide even diplomatic recognition of the new republic. During the summer of 1836, President Jackson had sent a special agent to Texas, who reported in August that Texas "may still be considered a mere experiment upon independence which the loss of friends or of a single battle may disperse to the winds." In December, Jackson, also wary of the powerful antislavery forces in Washington, D.C., opposing annexation, told the U.S. Congress that the United States should delay recognition, because acknowledging Texas's shaky independence would only deepen the Mexican government's anger and convince it that Americans had plotted the entire affair to gain Texas annexation. Texians were disappointed. As one observer wrote, the prospect was grim for a "Texas independent, and compelled to fight her own battles and pay her own debts." Yet this was the reality. Annexation was beyond their control and would not occur for longer than many expected or hoped. That quest would color the decade that Texas spent as a republic, especially the politics, even as new Texians and new developments altered the social and economic landscape.

Relations with Mexico

In an attempt to bring order to this rowdy assemblage of old Texians, newcomers, and Tejanos, President Houston appointed a unity cabinet, with members of both the war party and the peace party—no political parties yet existed—but members of the Tejano community were notably absent. Austin reluctantly accepted Houston's offer to serve as secretary of state, for he was mentally and physically exhausted; in fact, in mid-December, he caught a cold that rapidly developed into pneumonia and died at the age of forty-three. Houston responded with a proclamation: "The Father of Texas is no more! The first pioneer of the wilderness has departed." He was buried near his sister's home at Peach Point with all the ceremony that the new republic could muster. In 1936, the year of the Texas centennial of independence, Austin was disinterred and his body moved to the State Cemetery in Austin.

Interim President Burnet had tried to release Santa Anna in June, 1836, as he had promised in one of the treaties of Velasco, but recent newcomers such as Thomas Jefferson Green of North Carolina, who had served as brigadier general during the revolution and had returned to the United States to raise money, volunteers, and ammunition, led some bellicose factions of the army in demanding that Santa Anna be made to pay for the atrocities at the Alamo and Goliad. Burnet saved Santa Anna from the mob by moving the government further up the Brazos to Columbia, but it was clear to all that the army was virtually out of control. In October, Burnet finally resigned early in the hope that Houston would be able to quell the unruly volunteers.

Houston first dealt with Santa Anna, finally releasing him in November 1836, with the understanding that he would visit American President Andrew Jackson before returning home. In January 1837, the deposed dictator arrived in Washington, D.C., where he was given a warm welcome by Northerners who believed that the whole Texas affair was a slave owner conspiracy to add another slave territory to the Union. In a cordial meeting, President Jackson proposed that Mexico sell Texas and northern California to the United States for $3.5 million, but he was well aware that a defeated Santa Anna could not bargain on behalf of his country and, thus, sent Colonel Anthony Butler to Mexico to negotiate the purchase of Texas. The Mexican Congress would have none of it, and there matters remained as Santa Anna made his way back home. Upon his arrival in Veracruz, the people welcomed him with "innumerable manifestations of happiness," and Secretary of War Tornel ordered the black bows mourning Santa Anna's capture removed from all Mexican flags.

With Santa Anna off his hands, Houston turned to the disruptive army. Morale was low, because the troops were poorly equipped and supplied. Their main ration was beef, and one soldier complained that he had not seen any bread in months. Now various members of the army wanted to invade and plunder Matamoros. To save money and prevent them from provoking another Mexican invasion, in March 1837, Houston furloughed all but 600 of the troops while commanding General Felix Huston was away from camp.

Organizing the Government

Meeting in Columbia for its first session, the Texas Congress identified twenty-three counties, based primarily on the Mexican municipalities already in existence, and set up a Supreme Court with a chief justice and four associate justices, as well as a county court system. Congress authorized an army, a navy, a small force of mounted rangers, a militia, and a series of frontier forts and trading posts. Economically, the republic was bankrupt throughout its existence, a situation made more difficult by the Panic of 1837, which brought depression to the U.S. economy as well. The republic had no banks and imported far more value in manufactured goods than it exported in raw material, thereby drawing all the hard money (silver and gold, the only legal currency in the republic) out of the country. In 1837, "to avoid the absolute dissolution of the Government," Houston authorized the issue of $500,000 in promissory notes, which were to be redeemed twelve months from the date of issue at 10 percent interest. Other forms of paper money also circulated—"schinplasters," which were promissory notes from private firms or municipal corporations, and "redbacks" (promissory notes not bearing interest issued by the Lamar administration), for example—and the result was monetary disorder, with all the various forms of paper notes traded at steep discounts.

In December, Congress formally claimed that the southern and western boundary of Texas was the Rio Grande, from its mouth in the Gulf of Mexico to its source and thence a line due north to the forty-second parallel, in what is now southern Wyoming. The eastern boundary had been established by the Adams–Onís Treaty of 1819, which had set the boundary between the United States and Spanish Texas as the Sabine River and the Red River westward and northward to the Arkansas River. But the territory between the Sabine and Red Rivers had not been surveyed; in fact, this was the boundary that Santa Anna had expected to confirm had he defeated the rebels.

Even as Texas leaders grandiosely claimed an extensive domain, most of them still looked to the United States for annexation and were encouraged when Jackson, in his last official act as president, recognized the republic's independence early in March 1837. Mexican officials, of course, had rejected the treaties that Santa Anna signed at Velasco and were not prepared to accept any borders between Mexico and an independent Texas.

Also in one of their initial acts, in October 1836, the Texas Congress accepted an invitation from Augustus and John Allen, two enterprising developers who had established the new town of Houston, which they named after the president, on the southern bank of Buffalo Bayou. The town had a population of twelve people and only one log cabin on January 1, 1837, but the Allen brothers promised land and buildings for the government if it agreed to move the capital there. By the time Congress convened there in April, it boasted almost 1,500 settlers and immigrants and 100 structures.

It was at this time that one of the most famous Americans of the era visited the village. The naturalist and artist John James Audubon was about to finish his great book, *The Birds of America*, and was looking for the last few specimens that he would be able to incorporate into his already famous work. He and his son arrived at Galveston Island in April, 1837, witnessing the poor conditions under which the Mexican prisoners from the battle of San Jacinto were held. As they headed up Buffalo Bayou, they paused to survey the site of the recent battle and collected artifacts from the field. They arrived a few days later at Houston, where the residents had just celebrated the first anniversary of the battle. After being soaked in a rainstorm, Audubon wrote, "We amused ourselves by walking [in ankle deep mud and water] to the capitol, which was yet without a roof, and the floors, benches, and tables of both houses of Congress were as well saturated with water as our clothes." He later met President Houston, who "was dressed in a fancy velvet coat, and trowsers trimmed with broad gold lace; around his neck was tied a cravat somewhat in the stile of seventy-six." Of Houston Audubon recalled, "Our talk was short; but the impression which was made on my mind at the time by himself, his officers, and his place of abode [a dog-trot log cabin], can never be forgotten."

It was soon apparent that the village not only lacked housing and amenities, but it had also been built on a swamp. Mrs. William Fairfax Gray, wife of one of the city's notable lawyers, said that she "never saw anything like the mud here. It is a tenacious black clay which can not be got off of anything without washing— and is about a foot or so deep." Add to the mud the carcasses of dead animals that lay where they fell and decayed along with the other refuse, horse droppings, and raw sewage. No wonder that Dr. Ashbel Smith, surgeon general of the Texas Army, asked a New Orleans friend to send him a good "pair of Indian Rubber overshoes."

But the mud was only one of the problems in building a city on the banks of Buffalo Bayou, as the new residents soon discovered. During the summer, the swarms of flies were constant and carried the germs of dysentery; mosquitoes carried malaria. Typhus, influenza, cholera, and tuberculosis were common, and yellow fever seemed to strike every year. But newcomers immediately noticed the fleas, which "were as thick as the sands of the sea," according to C. C. Cox, a clerk in one of the new stores. And the rats might have been worse. Gustav Dresel, a young German immigrant, reported in 1838 that "Thousands of these troublesome guests made sport by night, and nothing could be brought to safety from them. . . ," that there were so many that even the best rat dogs grew tired of chasing them. Cox confirmed Dresel's comments. "I cannot convey an idea of the multitude of Rats in Houston at that time," he wrote. "They were almost as large as Prairie dogs . . ."[1]

From this "city in embryo," shortly after Audubon's visit, President Houston began to implement his grand diplomatic strategy. He knew that the United States saw Texas as an unstable entity and feared that Great Britain and/or France might take advantage of the uncertainty to gain influence on America's southwestern border. In hopes of strengthening Texas's diplomatic hand, he opened negotiations with Britain and France, seeking further recognition and political and economic alliances, while at the same time formally asking the U.S. government for annexation. The administration of Martin Van Buren answered that such a move would violate U.S. treaty agreements with Mexico. Yet the stronger factor behind American reluctance probably was resistance in the North to adding another slaveholding state to the Union. Benjamin Lundy and other abolitionists such as John Quincy Adams in the U.S. House of Representatives had made sure that Northerners were well aware that the admission of Texas would mark a major expansion of slave territory in the United States. The request languished until the following summer, when Houston appointed Anson Jones minister to the United States and instructed him to withdraw it.

One of the main concerns of the Houston administration was to improve relations with the various Indian tribes. He had promised the Cherokees title to their lands as a result of their neutrality during the revolution against Mexico; now he wanted to send agents among the other tribes to negotiate treaties and seek trading agreements with them. His task was complicated by the continual arrival of new tribes pushed westward by U.S. Indian policy, by activities of Mexican agents among the Indians, and by private land companies that steadily pushed their surveys into territory that the Indians claimed. Ultimately, the republic abandoned Houston's conciliatory policy for Lamar's aggressive, warlike policy.

Mirabeau B. Lamar's Term as President, 1838–1841

The new constitution prohibited the first president of the republic from seeking a second consecutive term, and the election of Houston's vice president, Mirabeau B. Lamar, to the presidency in November 1838 brought major changes. A native of Georgia, Lamar had been a Georgia state senator before two failed attempts at a congressional seat. After arriving in Texas and participating in the revolution, he had briefly and unsuccessfully acted as major general and commander-in-chief of the chaotic Texas army, but he had emerged as one of the heroes of San Jacinto, and that enabled him to win the election.

Lamar differed from Houston in many ways. He was a horseman who fenced, painted in oils, and wrote poetry. He shared with Houston his southern origin and romantic proclivities, but had a significantly different vision of the future of Texas and the Indians' role in it. Where Houston sought annexation and believed that the future of Texas depended on joining the Union, Lamar dreamed of a Texas empire that stretched to the Pacific Ocean. Where Houston had lived for several years with the Cherokees, believed that they had a right to land, and had negotiated a treaty guaranteeing their lands early in the revolution, Lamar opted for strength and outright aggression and worked to defeat the Cherokee treaty in the Texas Senate and repudiated it as president. Houston's antics at Lamar's inauguration assured that the two men would remain political and personal enemies. Houston showed up to make his farewell speech dressed as George Washington and occupied the podium for three hours, throwing Lamar into such a snit—"unable on account of indisposition," according to a reporter at the event—that the secretary of the senate had to read his speech to the exhausted audience.

Lamar was quick to have his revenge. In one of his first acts, while Houston was out of the country, he adopted a new flag for Texas—the familiar red, white, and blue with a lone star—discarding Houston's favored gold star on an azure field. He also set out to move the capital from Houston to a spot near the village of Waterloo, about eighty miles northeast of San Antonio, which he had discovered while hunting buffalo along the Colorado River. A committee appointed for the purpose endorsed his recommendation and acquired more than 7,000 acres of land to accommodate the envisioned broad avenues, public squares, capitol

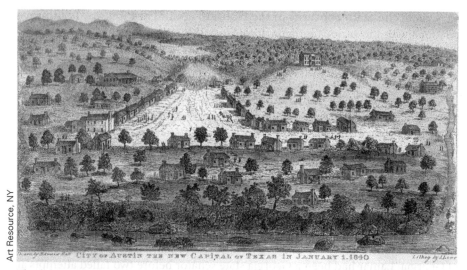

This lithograph of Austin, the new capital of Texas in 1840, appeared in an 1840 emigrants' guide. It shows a rudimentary settlement, with Congress Avenue stopping at the site of the future state capitol.

hill, and a new two-story executive mansion. It is a beautiful site, and Lamar hoped that it would encourage settlers to move further west. But at the time it was on the frontier, and many feared that it was vulnerable to both Indian and Mexican raids. Nevertheless, within ten months of taking office, Lamar had moved the capital to the interior and renamed it Austin in honor of the recently deceased Stephen F. Austin.

Lamar had an intense interest in education and the arts and became known as the "poet-president" of Texas. In his first message to Congress, in December 1838, he stated that, a "cultivated mind is the guardian genius of Democracy, and while guided and controlled by virtue, the noblest attribute of man" (which in an abbreviated form and translated into Latin later became the motto of the University of Texas at Austin). Early on he succeeded in passing a land act for public education that set the stage for the development of public schools and two universities that became Texas A&M University (founded in 1876) and the University of Texas at Austin (founded in 1881). It would be decades before the school system was established, but Lamar predicted that the republic would develop into "Roman firmness, and Athenian gracefulness and wisdom" as a result. That foresight earned for him the epithet "father of Texas education."

In an effort to build on what he perceived as the Texian spirit, Lamar also encouraged use of the term "Texian" to describe the citizens of Texas. When William Kennedy, British chargé d'affaires, published his highly acclaimed, two-volume *History of Texas* in 1841, he used "Texan" throughout, much to the chagrin of an unnamed author whose review was later published in the *Texas Almanac*. "The inhabitants of Texas, literate and illiterate, have almost universally adopted the term *Texian* to define their political individuality, and we are not apprised of any rule of language that is violated in doing so," the writer advised. Texians furthered that spirit by celebrating April 21 as San Jacinto Day and March 2 as Texas Independence Day.

Foreign Relations under Lamar

Much of the diplomatic work begun by Houston continued under Lamar. In September 1839, France, embroiled in the Pastry War with Mexico, recognized the independence of Texas, and the Netherlands soon followed. Great Britain had also become more receptive to the republic's request for recognition, as Britain faced a possible war with the United States and wanted to assure the continued flow of cotton, which Texas could provide. It also did not want France to gain the upper hand in trade and negotiations with Texas, so British and Texian representatives signed three treaties in 1840 acknowledging Texas's independence and setting trade and navigation guidelines.

Lamar also hoped for a $5 million loan from a European country, but that desire came to naught. He proposed a national bank to try to deal with the Texas's financial woes, but instead the Texas Congress authorized additional issues of paper money in the form of "redbacks," which were handsomely engraved but virtually worthless by the end of his administration.

Lamar had no success in his dealings with Mexico. Santa Anna had returned to power after repulsing a French invasion of Veracruz in the so-called Pastry War (in which the French demanded compensation for damage inflicted on several French shops, including a bakery). In 1839, Lamar sent attorney Bernard Bee, a former South Carolinian, to Mexico with the authorization to offer up to $5 million if Mexico would recognize Texas's independence and accept the Rio Grande as the boundary between the two nations. Santa Anna refused even to meet with Bee. Two other envoys that Lamar sent in late 1839 and in early 1841 met with similar rebuffs.

Lamar then looked to other means to establish Texas's claims to the plateaus, prairies, and plains to the west and to increase trade, which was essential if the republic ever were to become solvent. "Gen. Lamar may mean well," Dr. Anson Jones, who at the time was chair of the Senate Foreign Relations Committee, confided to his diary, "But his mind is altogether of a dreamy, poetic order, a sort of political Troubadour and Crusader, and wholly unfit by habit or education for the active duties, and the every-day realities of his present station. Texas is too small for a man of such wild, visionary, 'vaulting ambition.'" Out of this misguided groping for destiny, the Santa Fe Expedition of 1841 was born.

The Santa Fe Expedition

Located on the eastern side of the Rio Grande, Santa Fe fell in the area claimed by the republic in 1836. In a bid to increase trade and expand into New Mexico, Lamar enlisted three citizens of Santa Fe as commissioners for Texas in 1840 to inform Santa Fe residents that other representatives of the Texas government would soon arrive to discuss a plan for trade and for the incorporation of Santa Fe into the Texas Republic.

The Texas Congress had appropriated money for a commercial expedition, but, recognizing that the expansionist nature of this proposed undertaking would provoke Mexico, refused to authorize the scheme. Convinced that the citizens of Santa Fe would welcome the opportunity to join Texas, Lamar proceeded on his own authority. He promised merchants that they would have transportation and protection for their goods as they crossed the prairie and called for volunteer troops to accompany the expedition.

In June 1841, more than 320 men started out from a fort north of Austin with twenty-one ox-drawn wagons loaded with supplies and perhaps $200,000 worth of merchandise. The expedition included four civil commissioners, merchants, teamsters, and a large volunteer military contingent of six companies under command of twenty-six-year-old Hugh McLeod, a Georgian who in 1836 had resigned his U.S. Army lieutenant's commission to cast his fortunes with Texas. McLeod had quickly become a leader in Indian warfare and risen to the rank of brigadier general. George Wilkins Kendall, editor of the New Orleans *Daily Picayune*, and Thomas Falconer, an English jurist and adventurer, went along as guests and would later write best-selling books about their experiences.

With "not a single map of the route among them," the expedition headed north into unsettled territory, planning to reach the Red River and follow it westward toward Santa Fe. "At Austin we left the last tokens of a settlement," Kendall would later write, "beyond, all was in a state of wild, uncultivated nature." They cut their way through the dense timberlands of the Western Cross Timbers rather than detouring around them. Upon reaching the Wichita River, they mistook it for the Red River and began traveling along its valley. With Comanches and Kiowas threatening them and water and provisions running low, they tried to correct their course, again striking northward for the Red River, but the Caprock Escarpment that divides the rolling plains of West Texas from the High Plains proved daunting for the heavily loaded wagons.

With progress agonizingly slow, McLeod authorized about one-third of the expedition members to ride ahead. After many hardships, in September the advance group arrived in the Mexican settlements of New Mexico, expecting to be welcomed by the New Mexicans. Instead, Governor Manuel Armijo met them with troops. One of their members turned traitor and convinced his comrades to lay down their arms. Armijo then sent him to meet the main group, and he persuaded them, in their desperate condition, to surrender as well. Without firing a shot, Armijo had taken the entire Texian force prisoner and began them on a harrowing forced march to Mexico, where they were eventually jailed in Perote Castle near Veracruz. The expedition was a complete failure, and the fate of the prisoners became the subject of an intense diplomatic controversy between the United States and Mexico, and the resulting publicity stimulated further interest in Texas and the Southwest.

Houston's Second Term, 1841–1844

As the Santa Fe prisoners entered Perote in December 1841, Houston was re-elected president of Texas, and Santa Anna was planning the reconquest of Texas. In March 1842, Colonel Rafael Vásquez with approximately 700 troops invaded and captured San Antonio. He quickly returned to Mexico, his expedition considered little more than a plundering party, but it exposed Texas, and especially the new capitol at Austin, as vulnerable to attack. That summer, Adrían Woll, a French soldier of fortune in the service of the Mexican government, entered Texas with 1,500 troops and easily recaptured San Antonio on September 11. This time the citizens were better prepared, however, and an armed party under Captain Mathew Caldwell approached San Antonio and lured Woll into a battle near Salado Creek. Woll retreated back into the city, then evacuated two days later, and returned to Mexico with a number of captives. A number of Tejano families also accompanied him, afraid that if they remained in San Antonio they would be victimized by irate Anglo volunteers intent upon revenge. They relocated to villages on the south side of the Rio Grande.

Houston, meanwhile, had convened the government further to the east at Washington-on-the-Brazos and immediately sent a company of rangers to get the archives. But the citizens of Austin, realizing that the removal of the archives would mean the loss of the capital, organized and overtook the rangers at Brushy Creek. The archives were returned to Austin and have remained there ever since. The incident became known as the Archives War.

The Mier Expedition

Houston preferred diplomatic maneuvering to fighting, but the Mexican incursions had aroused the fighting spirit of the Texian volunteers, who rallied in San Antonio. Houston sent Brigadier General Alexander Somervell to control the bellicose troops, many of whom remained undisciplined and hungry for revenge and plunder. In late November, Somervell led 700 men south and seized Laredo, which was located on the eastern side of the Rio Grande, but whose citizens had remained loyal to Mexico. One hundred and eighty-five members of the expedition turned back at that point, but Somervell led the remainder across the river to capture the village of Guerrero. When it became apparent to him that they could not hope to further the campaign, he ordered the army to disband.

But many of the volunteers refused to quit and elected revolutionary war veteran William S. Fisher as commander. On December 23, 1842, more than 300 men crossed the river, occupied the village of Mier, and demanded supplies as plunder. They took the *alcalde* hostage and retreated across the river to wait for delivery of the goods. Meanwhile, the Mexican military arrived and stopped the delivery. Most of the volunteers recrossed the river on Christmas Day and engaged the Mexican soldiers. Although they suffered heavy losses, the Mexican force prevailed and took most of the Texians prisoner. It was Mexico's most important victory in the effort to reclaim Texas and a blow to Houston's hope of annexation. Within little more than a year, Santa Anna's forces had captured the men of the Santa Fe Expedition, occupied San Antonio twice, and defeated an invasion attempt.

On the march to Mexico City, the Texian prisoners overcame their guards at Hacienda del Salado, south of Saltillo, and escaped, but the mountainous desert of northern Mexico proved too much for them, and 176 of them were recaptured. This incident provides the context for the infamous "black bean" episode. Santa Anna ordered that the prisoners be executed, but, because of the intervention of the British and American ministers, changed the order to the effect that one in ten be shot. Each of the prisoners was required to draw a bean from an earthen jar, which had been filled with 159 white beans and seventeen black beans. Those who drew the black beans were shot. A month after the executions, as the remaining prisoners approached Mexico City, Santa Anna ordered that Ewen Cameron, who had drawn a white bean, also be shot because he was the leader of the escape attempt. The other members of the expedition gradually won their freedom. The Mier expedition thus came to a tragic end. Amazingly, one of the members of the expedition was an artist, Charles McLaughlin, and he documented their experiences, including drawings of the prisoners drawing the beans and the executions, which were

Artist Charles M'Laughlin was a member of the Mier expedition and depicted the fateful ceremony in which men of the expedition drew beans from a jar to determine who among them would be executed by Mexican troops. Seventeen of the 176 prisoners were shot to death.

published in Thomas Jefferson Green's firsthand account of the episode, *Journal of the Texian Expedition Against Mier*, in 1845.

The Texians suffered another setback on their northwestern frontier. In January 1843, Colonel Jacob Snively, the assistant quartermaster of the republic, proposed to President Houston that he be permitted to retaliate for the recent insults at the hand of Mexico by raising and outfitting a force to raid Mexican caravans traveling along the Santa Fe Trail in territory that Texas claimed. Any booty that they captured would be split between the government and Snively and his men. Houston approved this plan because he wanted the United States to see that Texas was actively claiming its territory. Unfortunately, the expedition came to an inglorious end when Snively and his men were disarmed by an American force escorting a Mexican caravan along the trail.

These failures made clear the unrealistic nature of Lamar's expansionist dreams for the republic. The nation's debt now totaled more than $8 million, and most Texians agreed with Houston that the only solution for the nation's woes was annexation to the United States.

Challenges and Opportunities in the Republic of Texas

The unsettled state of affairs and the remoteness of the republic remained two of its foremost problems. At a time when no one traveled faster than a horse, simply getting to Texas was an ordeal, because the new nation was three weeks travel, at best, from the East Coast of the United States, and traveling within it was even more difficult. Some observers judged transportation within the country to be one of "the chief obstacles to prosperity."

Transportation

The Indians had blazed a network of trails across Texas over centuries of occupation and trade. With their explorations of the sixteenth and seventeenth centuries, the Spaniards had established two royal roads (*caminos reales*) in Texas, one from the Rio Grande to San Antonio and on to Nacogdoches, and another from Chihuahua to El Paso to Santa Fe, New Mexico. The old San Antonio road, as the first *camino real* became known, overlaid some Indians trails but ultimately formed its own network of roads through the settled portions of Texas. It was over this road in the early nineteenth century that immigrants fought choking dust at times and oceans of sticky mud at others as oxen hauled heavily laden wagons from Natchitoches in Louisiana to Nacogdoches and on into other parts of the colonies. By the late 1830s those who came by sea to the coastal settlements could travel in impressive steamboats, although most couldn't afford the cabins and crammed into steerage or took deck passage, but most new arrivals came overland. Within Texas, despite the advent of a few stagecoaches, the standard modes of transportation continued to be horseback, wagon, and ox cart.

The Texas rivers initially seemed to offer a transportation network, but ultimately proved a disappointment in terms of moving people and goods. Sometimes shallow-draft steamboats could ply the Colorado and the Trinity, but river transport was unreliable because of frequent low water. Even steamers designed for shallow rivers could not navigate the San Jacinto, the Guadalupe, the San Antonio, or the Nueces. The Brazos was barely navigable on its lower reaches, between Washington-on-the-Brazos and the gulf. And the republic was far too poor to clean up the periodic rafts of logs and brush, dredge the sand bars, or mount railroad and canal projects. Only Buffalo Bayou between Houston and Galveston developed into an important commercial waterway during the republic period, and, although it had some natural, canal-like qualities, it, too, was difficult to navigate. All of this meant that the settlements of the Republic of Texas were a series of remote sites and, except along the gulf coast, difficult to reach and particularly difficult to supply with goods.

These new arrivals were mainly victims of the Panic of 1837 from the American South, poor but hardworking Anglo-Americans, a significant minority of them slaveholders. Austin had insisted that settlers in his colony be of a good moral character, but other empresarios were not as demanding, and many immigrants simply arrived on their own and settled where they could. Perhaps having failed in business or matrimony, thousands of settlers migrated to Texas to get a a new start, and, as early as 1825, the phrase "gone to Texas" (and abbreviated GTT) had found its way into the popular press of the United States as a synonym for having "taken French leave," as a writer for the *Louisville Public Advertiser* explained.

The immigrants came despite the initial lack of recognition by the United States and the uncertainties that plagued the Texas economy. But, because of the threat of further hostilities with Mexico, which still claimed sovereignty over the region, and with hostile Indian tribes, particularly the Comanches, along the western and northwestern frontiers, Texas agents still found it impossible to establish credit and secure loans from the United States or any European nation. Nevertheless, the white, slave, and Hispanic population of Texas had grown to approximately 40,000 by 1836, with an additional perhaps 15,000 Indians. While there was no census of the republic in 1845, the vote that year suggests a total population might have reached 125,000.

Land, the Only Asset

Common to virtually all the emigrants was the hope for economic opportunity. In the American South, from whence most of them came, economic opportunity was tied up with the ownership of land for farming, ranching, and/or speculating and colonizing. And Texas had plenty of land—more than 250 million acres of public domain as the republic era began. One early traveler remarked that "on some of the prairies, when near the middle, it resembles being on the ocean, the scene appears boundless. . . ." More than 26 million acres had already been granted through a hodgepodge of Spanish, Mexican, and empresario claims, but the new government was more than ready to use much of the rest as an inducement to settlers. The constitution liberally allowed for a league and a labor (a league is approximately 4,428.4 acres; a labor is approximately 177.1 acres) for every head of household in Texas at the time of independence and for one-third of a labor for every single man (excluding African Americans and Indians). The Texas Congress followed up with a series of grants for new arrivals in the period from March 1836 through December 1841. The grants were generous, and the newcomers only had to live in Texas for three years to gain clear title to the land.

As a further inducement, on January 26, 1839, the Texas Congress passed a homestead exemption act to protect debtors from seizure of their homes. Although this act had its origins in the Mexican period, when the legislature of Coahuila y Texas had enacted a similar statute, it was a first in American jurisprudence, stating that each citizen or head of family was protected from the seizure of his or her homestead—"fifty acres of land or one town lot . . ., and improvements not exceeding five hundred dollars in value"—in the event of bankruptcy. When even the homestead measure did not stimulate enough migration, in 1841 the Texas Congress authorized the president to implement another empresario contract system. The following year, a colonization law stipulated that the new empresarios would receive "ten premium sections, each to be settled by one hundred families," with the government holding on to alternate sections to sell after the original sections were settled.

As with previous empresario efforts, the results were uneven at best. In 1841 William Peters, an English musician and businessman, established a colony in the vicinity of present-day Dallas, with the assistance of both English and American investors, thrusting settlement far northward, close to the Red River. Henry F. Fisher and Burchard Miller failed in their effort to introduce a large number of German immigrants to Texas, but others picked up the challenge, and the resulting colonies extended the western frontier into the Hill Country west of San Antonio and Austin. The republic made arrangements with Henri Castro, a French banker who tried to help the republic gain a loan, to settle Catholic Alsatian families in what became the Castroville area, on the Medina River southwest of San Antonio.

Visitors and immigrants continued to be excited by the agricultural potential of the lands they saw in traveling through the settlements. Many newcomers agreed with David Crockett, who wrote in his last letter that, "I must say as to what I have seen of Texas it is the garden spot of the world. The best land and the best prospects for health I ever saw, and I do believe it is a fortune to any man to come here. There is a world of country here to settle." Cotton cultivation in particular was developing, and with it a planter class that depended heavily on slave labor. In 1845, a Texian wrote, "All are land-hunting, seeking sugar, cotton and stock farm lands, but are as much at a loss in their selection as children in a toy-shop."

Other Opportunities

Merchandising might have been a lucrative field but for the lack of cash, which complicated the exchange. Merchants or traders would buy items on credit and then sell them to farmers, planters, townspeople, even to other merchants, often taking crops in place of cash. Many merchants suffered because of the financial instability of the republic, with its paper money worth only twelve cents in exchange of the U.S. dollar, and because of the global economic Panic of 1837. Adolphus Sterne, a merchant who had been in business in Nacogdoches since 1826, would complain in May 1842, "[T]imes have never been so hard in Texas, like they are now, I have never known the want of two bits until now,—!!!!!"

Sterne was also a land agent, and many like him tried to seize the opportunities to make money in land speculation. Land agents and land lawyers bought and sold and took commissions, "organiz[ing] the land market in the new territories" and serving as "critical intermediaries" between the Tejano elite who owned much of the most desirable land and those who wanted their own parcel. In a well-established American tradition, speculators bought up whatever lands they could in hopes of realizing vast profits, but many bought on credit and then saw the acreage drop in value.

Some used the fledgling towns both as objects of speculation and as bases for it. A visitor to Houston in 1837 found "the spirit of speculation . . . afloat," with lots "selling at enormous prices, in some instances as high as four and five thousand dollars apiece." Few of the towns could be said to be flourishing, however, and some would even decline during the republic years: By 1844, Brazoria was looking distinctly rundown. Texas entrepreneurs, like their government, lacked a vital trade system, a stable currency, and the ability to attract outside investors.

Texas as Opportunity—or Not

Anglos and Europeans Seize Power

In these challenging times, those who most often found the opportunity they sought in Texas were Anglo men of some means from the American South, men who had previous experience with American forms of economic and/or political power. They resembled—and in many cases were—the architects of the late revolution, men who knew their way around a cotton farm and a courtroom, a plantation, and a political office. They had migrated primarily from the Lower South—Alabama, Louisiana, Mississippi—bringing with them strong proslavery views. Many had experienced failure—business reverses, lost political elections, fractured personal lives—yet they maintained a sense of unbridled optimism and entitlement. Ira Ingram of Matagorda wrote in 1834: "I did not, for one, invade the wilderness of Texas, to speculate in cents, piccons, shillings, nor yet in dollars. I came here for a fortune. . . ." In the United States, only white males could exercise that most basic right of citizenship, the vote. These men had absorbed the concept of Manifest Destiny, although it still did not yet have a name: They saw themselves as representatives of a culture and a race destined for greatness and inheritors of the American continent.

Other Texians, whatever their location and pursuits, still could expect to have at least rudimentary homes. Anglo settlers usually lived in log cabins, known as "dog-trot" cabins because they were designed with a room on either side of a central "dog-trot" breezeway. The floors were clay or dirt. Food was equally simple—beef, bacon, cornbread, coffee. Wheat flour proved so scarce throughout the period that most families relied on cornmeal instead. "Raising corn," one German settler recalled, "was a matter of life and death, since upon it depended the existence of the colony." Others grew their own wheat. Many were happy to get a cow; as one young woman who arrived shortly after the republic period explained to her father: "[F]or over three months we had neither a scrap of butter or a drop of milk, but we got by nicely and oh how wonderful did the first cup of coffee with milk and the first piece of cornbread with butter taste to us!"

European men, too, found opportunities, although most of them were new to the continent and had to adjust to American ways as well as to the presence of Mexicans and Indians. To a great extent, the immigrant European groups initially stayed together, setting up their own small German, Alsatian, Irish, and French enclaves; however, the men moved about freely and engaged in farming and business along with their American counterparts. The largest European immigrant group by far was the Germans, whose numbers would be estimated at more than 11,600 by 1850. Germans had migrated to Texas as early as the 1820s. With the advent of industrial production and population growth, merchants and craftsmen began losing economic ground in Germany and found it increasingly expensive to maintain even a small business. And land was a powerful allure, especially after the failed German revolution of 1848, when many political dissenters came to Texas looking for freedom. These new arrivals became known as the "Forty-Eighters."

The 1842 Fisher and Miller contract to bring German colonists to Texas was expanded in 1844, but the two men soon sold it to a German organization called the Adelsverein, or Society for the Protection of German Immigrants in Texas. In exchange for a flat fee, the Adelsverein, a joint-stock company, promised to transport German colonists to America and then to Adelsverein lands in Texas. Because the Fisher–Miller grant was so remote, located between the Colorado and Llano Rivers, the Adelsverein purchased a site on the Guadalupe River, closer to the edge of Anglo settlement.

Prince Carl of Solms-Braunfels, the first commissioner-general of the Adelsverein, selected a site on the Texas coast southeast of Victoria as a landing area for the colonists. It was initially called Karlshafen, but later took the name of the small town of Indianola, established nearby. The first colonists arrived before Prince Carl had adequately prepared Karlshafen as a staging area for the long inland journey. Already weary from the long sea voyage, the travelers now faced a

German immigrant Carl G. Von Iwonski titled this painting *Log Cabin, New Braunfels*. It provides one picture of antebellum Texas farm and frontier life.

wilderness trek to their Guadalupe River homesites as they struggled with illness, incessant rains, and oxcarts constantly mired in mud. They established the town of New Braunfels in 1845, and 5,200 German immigrants arrived between 1844 and 1846.

Prince Carl cut quite a swath through Texas frontier society. A tireless worker in the colonization effort, he was nonetheless best remembered for his aristocratic and eccentric ways. Diarist Mary Maverick, the wife of Samuel Maverick, reported that his two attendants lifted him into his trousers each day, and the members of his entourage wore cock feathers in their hats—characteristics hardly destined to survive on the frontier. Following him in the role was Otsfried Hans von Meusebach, who in Texas became John O. Meusebach and established a second center of settlement, Fredericksburg, some sixty miles northwest of New Braunfels.

In the ideology of that era in America, women were to stay at home, to maintain the "private sphere," while Anglo and northern European men engaged in the business and politics of capitalistic empire building. This division of labor was reinforced by women's frequent pregnancies and, in Texas as on frontiers elsewhere, by the very real work of maintaining a self-sufficient frontier home whose residents had to rely to a large extent on their own inventiveness rather than on nonexistent or erratic supply networks.

Yet the same frontier conditions also gave Anglo and European women some autonomy. They ran farms and businesses as well as homes in the absence— sometimes frequent and prolonged—of their men. They operated boarding houses, participated in a frontier bartering economy, hunted and harvested as need dictated, and worked to establish schools and churches. Women also had more rights under the Hispanic-influenced community property laws than did their counterparts in the United States, for economic gains in a marriage belonged to both the woman and the man. They could also expect some court protection against abusive or wayward husbands; recognizing the isolation and vulnerability of many frontier wives, the 1841 divorce act established standards penalizing abandonment and cruelty. State lawmakers would follow with anti- cruelty standards said to be "among the most liberal found in the antebellum South." Nonetheless, political opportunities remained off-limits, economic opportunities meager; and women could not legally accumulate property or sell it without the permission of their husbands.

If women of the increasingly dominant Anglo and European American cul- ture faced restrictions, members of different ethnic groups found their opportu- nities even more constrained. Stephen F. Austin had become convinced by the summer of 1835 that "Texas should be effectually, and fully, *Americanized*—that is—settled by a population that will harmonize with their neighbors on the *East,* in language, political principles, common origin, sympathy, and even interest. *Texas must be a slave country. It is no longer a matter of doubt.*" That destiny would not bode well for any of the racial minorities in the republic. Increasingly, African Americans, Tejanos, and Native Americans found far more challenges than opportunities in the Republic of Texas.

The African American Experience

In a land of rough conditions, slaves experienced the worst. Most Texians probably would have agreed with John S. ("Rip") Ford, a physician, newspaper editor, and former Texas Ranger, who believed that, "Slavery came to the Southern man authorized by the Supreme Law of the Land. . . . The assumption in the Declara- tion of Independence that 'all men are created equal' was not intended to include the African race, or was a falsehood on its face." And, if ever there was a terri- tory economically suited for slavery, surely it was the fertile bottomland along the lower Brazos and Colorado Rivers of Texas. The land was ideal for cotton, but a large workforce was necessary to till the huge acreage, and, for most Texians, that workforce had to be black. William Bollaert, who surveyed the Texas coast for the British admiralty, stated the commonly held but mistaken belief that the climate in Texas, especially along the riverbanks in southeast Texas, was too harsh for white people to perform the hard work necessary to raise cotton or sugar. So, the number of slaves in Texas increased rapidly. There are no actual counts until the census of 1848, after Texas joined the Union, but all indications are that the number of slaves more than doubled to perhaps as many as 11,323 by 1840 and to 23,624 in 1845.

Most Texas slaves arrived with their masters, although a fair number were brought in by slave traders from other states, and a few came via the African trade, although it was universally outlawed by then, including in the Texas constitution. Whereas most slaves in the southern states lived on large plantations, in Texas most lived on small isolated farms. Even in 1860, more than half of the slaveowners in Texas held four slaves or fewer with only 1.5 percent claiming to own more than fifty.

Of course, slaves lived the most circumscribed of lives. William Fairfax Gray recalled that some of the slave homes he saw in the midst of a chilling norther in 1837 were "more open than the log stables in Virginia." But rough living conditions were not all they faced. The Republic of Texas government meted out harsh punishments for any crimes or even perceived crimes committed by slaves. "Insulting or abusive language" directed at a white person earned twenty-five to a hundred lashes. White owners could hire out slaves at will and controlled all their transactions, as it was forbidden for anyone to buy something from a slave without written permission from his or her master. There were harsh penalties, too, for anyone harboring an escaped slave or in any way encouraging or abetting his or her escape, although that did not prevent slaves from running away, many to Mexico, which had outlawed slavery in 1829.

Marriage between African Americans and whites was simply against the law, and the few liberties a slave might enjoy depended upon the temperament of his or her owner: Would the owner, for example, allow the slave to marry someone on a neighboring plantation, or even to visit him or her? Even under a relatively lenient master, slaves could not choose their own marriage partners, learn to read, or escape arbitrary punishment. And there was no guarantee that their families would remain intact, for the owner could choose, for whatever reason, to sell one or more of them.

Free African Americans were restricted as well. The punitive legal codes that applied to slaves also applied to them, and the Constitution of 1836 required them to receive special permission to live in the republic. In 1837 Congress qualified this requirement, allowing those in Texas at the time of independence (approximately 150 people) to remain in the republic. One of those affected by these laws was Samuel McCulloch, Jr., who had fought in the revolution as a member of the Matagorda volunteer company. After passage of the 1836 law, he had petitioned for citizenship and land grants; the 1837 law had automatically granted him citizenship but left his land grant request in limbo. In 1840, Congress again reversed itself, passing a law barring the immigration of free blacks to Texas and stipulating that all free men and women must leave within two years or be sold into slavery. Although this draconian plan was not fully implemented—for example, McCulloch and four relatives won exemption—free African Americans faced an uncertain existence at best.

While the abolitionist movement gained strength nationally, there were few active abolitionists in Texas. One of the few was Stephen Pearl Andrews, a Houston lawyer and real estate developer, who argued that slavery was bad for economic development. He suggested that money be raised to purchase the slaves' freedom, thereby abolishing slavery in the republic, and even made a trip to Britain in 1843 in an attempt to raise the money. The effort failed when Ashbel Smith, the Texian chargé d'affaires in London denounced it. Many slaveholders blamed Andrews for stirring up trouble among the slaves and, that same year, mobbed his home, forcing him to flee the state.

The lives of African Americans in Texas reflected the long-lasting effects of the slave system in the South. Blacks coming to Texas, usually through no choice of their own, knew all too well the ways in which their lives could and would be limited. In the republic era, however, many Tejanos were just beginning to comprehend the implications of the growing Anglo presence for their own future.

The Tejano Experience

Immediately after the revolution, Tejanos were pushed, prodded, and deprived of opportunity in a variety of ways. Members of the Tejano elite who had worked with Anglo leaders were increasingly excluded from or moved to the margins of the developing power structure of the republic. The cooperative spirit that had seen José Antonio Navarro and José Francisco Ruiz as members of the convention to establish a government and Lorenzo de Zavala named the first vice president of the republic fell apart. Tejano settlers near the Anglo colonies often found themselves, their homes, and their livestock targeted by former soldiers who were bitter toward Mexicans. It did not matter whether the Tejanos had actively aided the revolutionary effort, remained loyal to the Mexican government, or maintained their neutrality. Many were driven from their homes, particularly those who lived near the Austin and DeWitt colonies and in the Nacogdoches area, as immigrants swarmed onto accessible lands with little or no regard for Mexican land titles. Juan Seguín, one of the heroes of the revolution and mayor of San Antonio in 1840–42, recalled that "the American straggling adventurers . . . were already beginning to work their dark intrigues against the native families, whose only crime was, that they owned large tracts of land and desirable property."

The area between the Rio Grande and the Nueces was a disputed territory that soon became a no-man's land. While claimed by both Mexico and Texas, most of this area was, in fact, dominated by various Indian tribes, except for the relatively intact Mexican enclaves such as Laredo, which was still considered a part of the Mexican state of Tamaulipas even though it was on the east side of the Rio Grande. Emboldened by a pernicious decree that declared Mexican livestock public property, former Texas soldiers raided south of the Nueces and took cattle belonging to Mexican residents, many of whom had sought refuge in the towns along the Rio Grande during the revolution.

Far to the east in Nacogdoches, tensions between Tejanos and Anglos continued after the revolution. By the end of the war, emigrants from the United States decisively outnumbered Tejano residents and showed little interest in or respect for Mexican social and political structures and culture. Tired of the intimidation, some Tejano residents rallied around Vicente Córdova, the Nacogdoches-area landowner and former *alcalde* and militia commander, who had opposed independence for Texas. Encouraged by General Vicente Filisola, the Mexican commander at Matamoros, in August 1838 Córdova rallied several hundred followers from the local Tejanos and Indians from different tribes and conducted raids along the upper Trinity River on land claimed by the Cherokees. Major General Rusk called out the militia and quashed the affair that became known as the Córdova rebellion. Córdova left for Mexico, but intimidation of the local Tejanos continued. Thirty-three men of Mexican heritage faced treason charges in the Nacogdoches and San Augustine district courts. Only one, a former Nacogdoches official, was found guilty and sentenced to hang. He eventually received a pardon, but the Nacogdoches troubles resulted in more than a hundred Mexican families leaving the country the following year.

In San Antonio, as in Nacogdoches, the old cooperative structures were crumbling, with land and power rapidly shifting into Anglo hands. But, despite conditions elsewhere, the Tejanos of San Antonio had preserved their heritage through religious practices, nationalistic and religious celebrations, and schooling for their children. Increasingly, Anglos paid little attention to or ignored this heritage. Some newcomers voiced suspicion of the Mexican population and doubted their loyalty, but others acknowledged their plight. Many of the elite Tejanos, in particular, were caught between economic, political, and even personal ties with Anglos—as daughters of leading Tejano families married prominent or soon-to-be-prominent Anglo men—and their Catholic, Spanish, and Mexican identity and heritage.

To be sure, Seguín remained an influential figure, an indisputable war hero who was able to speak with authority to both the Mexican and Anglo communities. He was repeatedly elected to the senate of the republic, where he was the only Tejano, and when he returned to San Antonio, he was elected mayor in late 1840. But, as mayor, he found that "[a]t every hour of the day and night my countrymen ran to me for protection against the assaults or exactions of those adventurers."

Rumors soon engulfed Seguín, who had connections with Mexico through his continued support of the federalists there. He found himself suspected of collaborating with the Mexican government by providing information about the ill-fated Santa Fe Expedition. He denied the charge and won reelection as mayor, but the rumors continued. Seguín requested permission from General Vásquez, the commander of the Mexican frontier, to travel to Mexico to get some livestock, and the manner of Vásquez's reply led Seguín to surmise "that an expedition against Texas was in preparation for the following month of March." He reported his suspicion to the secretary of war, but, without further credible information, the secretary took no action. Seguín did not think he could defend the town without help, so he, his family, and a number of other Tejano residents left town for outlying ranches as Anglos in San Antonio tried to set up a defense.

The Mexican troops arrived as predicted, but occupied the town for only two days in March 1842, then returned to Mexico. Seguín even served in one of the companies that pursued them, but when he returned he found "reports about my implausible treason were spreading widely." He heard threats daily: "All the parties of volunteers en route to San Antonio declared 'they wanted to kill Seguín.'" He resigned as mayor in April and reluctantly prepared to move to Mexico to escape the "constant wretchedness" his family was experiencing. He had become, in his own words, "a foreigner in my own country."

The Cherokee and Comanche Experience

If Seguín had been caught in a cultural and political crossfire in San Antonio, the same could be said of Chief Bowl, or "Duwali," the elderly leader of the Cherokee Indians in East Texas. The agent that Andrew Jackson had sent to Texas in the summer of 1836 estimated the Indian population to be 10,000 to 15,000, with 8,000 of them members of the tribes that the United States had forcibly removed from the American Southeast, probably about 400 of them Cherokees. The Cherokees were beset by conflicting appeals to their loyalties, by factionalism within the tribe, and by possible alliances with other Indians. During the revolution, Chief Bowl, at Sam Houston's urging, had signed a treaty with the republic pledging loyalty to the independence movement in return for a clear land title. Now, after the war, Lamar and others had scuttled the treaty, and the Cherokees faced increased suspicion and hostility from their Anglo neighbors. They still had no title to the land they had cultivated since before Austin's colonists had arrived in Texas. In addition, Mexican agents continued to sow discord in Texas, attempting to recruit the Cherokees and other Indians in their effort to disrupt the new government, and some of Chief Bowl's young warriors had grown impatient and were ready to listen.

Indian policy was at the head of Houston's agenda for several reasons. One was the attack of some 500 to 700 Caddo, Comanche, Kiowa, and Kichai Indians on Fort Parker, a private fort near the headwaters of the Navasota River, in May 1836. Five men were killed and two women and three children taken captive. One of the children, Rachel Plummer, would later write vividly about her captivity in a book published in Houston in 1838, while another of them, Cynthia Ann Parker, would make her life with the Comanches, later giving birth to the last chief of the Quahadi Comanches, Quanah Parker.

New settlers pushing onto the Indian lands exacerbated the situation. Houston tried to reach out to the Cherokees by marking the boundaries of the land they claimed, but even as the surveyors finished their work, General Rusk led the Texas militia through the Cherokees' region in a show of force. Lamar's election to the presidency had effectively sealed the Cherokees' fate. For Lamar and many other frontiersmen, Indians were either hostile or potentially hostile nuisances to be removed without compunction by whatever means necessary. He would later sum up his view to the fourth Congress of the republic: "The white man and the red man cannot dwell in harmony together. Nature forbids it." The great photographer of Indians Edward S. Curtis would later characterize the Texas policy as, "Go elsewhere or be exterminated."

The tragic end to the Cherokees in Texas came in July 1839, when Lamar sent Rusk, at the head of 500 troops, to remove the Cherokees from the republic. Rusk informed the Cherokees that they would be paid for their improvements and their crops, but that they would have to remove the gunlocks from their weapons and the militia would escort them from the republic. Rather than subject themselves to this indignity, the Indians left on their own, closely pursued by the militia. On July 16, near the site of present-day Tyler, the militia caught up with the Cherokees and allied Delawares, Shawnees, and Kickapoos. The elderly Chief Bowl was shot and killed, and the Indians scattered, some to Arkansas, some to Mexico, and others to various tribal groups. Land speculators, including Burleson and Burnet, quickly claimed the Cherokee lands, and Burleson crassly sent Chief Bowl's tricorn hat to Houston, who was then serving as a member of Congress representing San Augustine district. The Cherokees' fate vividly demonstrates the limits of opportunity in Texas for those who were perceived as a threat or a nuisance by members of the dominant culture.

The Comanches, who perceived the surveyor's compass as "the thing that steals the land," posed a much larger threat, and the campaign against them was even more costly. The worst incident occurred, ironically, when the southernmost band of the Comanches, the Penatekas, buffeted by a smallpox epidemic and fights with the Cheyenne and Arapaho to the north and the Texas Rangers to the east, sent messengers to request a peace council. Widely thought to be the least warlike band among the Comanches, the Penatekas agreed to come to San Antonio with their white captives in March, 1840, and brought their women and children with them as a sign of their peaceful intentions. But they only brought one white captive, Matilda Lockhart, who, according to diarist and San Antonio resident Mary Maverick, had been "utterly degraded." The Comanches said that Matilda was the only white captive they held, that the others were held by different bands over whom they had no control, but Matilda told the Texians that the Indians still held several more. Once the chiefs had gathered in the council room of the local jail, the Texians informed them that, because they had not brought all their white captives, they were to be held hostage while the warriors returned to their camp to get the others. Soldiers filed into the room to back up the threat, and chaos ensued. The troopers opened fire, and a dozen chiefs fell in the council room. At least eighteen men, three women, and two children were killed outside. The Texians sent one woman back to the Comanche camp to explain that the remaining women and children were being held to exchange for the remaining Anglo captives. A few captives were exchanged over the next few months, but the massacre at the Council House would not be forgotten.

Comanche honor required that the dead be avenged, and an all-out war ensued. The Penatekas went into New Mexico and as far north as Bent's Fort in what is today southern Colorado in the search of allies and weapons, and, in August, Buffalo Hump, the highest surviving Penateka chief, led an estimated 500 Comanches and Kiowas in a vengeful raid into south Texas all the way to the gulf. Although such encouragement was probably not needed, Mexican agents among the Indians probably incited violence as well. Accompanied by a number of women to gather up and haul the plunder, the raiders passed through the Guadalupe Valley wreaking havoc as they went; they hit Victoria on August 6, then two days later they arrived at Linnville on Lavaca Bay. There citizens sought safety in a steamboat anchored in the bay or rowed out to sea in their own boats, from where they watched as the Indians looted the warehouse, pulling gloves, umbrellas, top hats, and coats from recently delivered goods intended for San Antonio shops. They set the town on fire and retired across a nearby bayou and camped for the night. The next morning, wearing topcoats and hats and waving umbrellas, they began their retreat, weighted down by hundreds of thousands of dollars' worth of goods and more than 3,000 horses—an immense treasure for nomadic Indians.

Help was not long in arriving. A group of hastily assembled settlers attacked the raiders as they left Linnville, but the warriors formed a rear guard as the women fled with the booty. The Texians could gain no ground on them because the Indians frequently changed to fresh mounts. Finally, San Jacinto veteran Ben McCulloch went ahead to Lockhart and assembled another group of volunteers. They ambushed the Comanches on Plum Creek, a tributary of the San Marcos River near Lockhart, killing perhaps as many as eighty warriors. The defeat of the Penatekas was completed that fall when another ranger group attacked their camp on the upper Colorado, killing another fifty or so warriors. Lamar's campaign against the Comanches had momentarily settled the frontier, but it ensured enmity between the two peoples for decades to come and, at a cost of $2.5 million, had greatly increased the debt of the fledgling nation.

In his second term as president, Houston tried to restore peace to the frontier. In 1844 his representatives negotiated a treaty with the Caddo and Tonkawa Indians and a number of their allies near what is today Waco. The Treaty of Tehuacana Creek declared that "the tomahawk shall be buried, and no more blood appear in the path" between the whites and the Indians. It did not specify a boundary line between the two nations, but the de facto boundary became the string of trading houses that the Texians had established on the middle Brazos and lower San Sabá Rivers and at Comanche Peak, where the Indians could buy and sell goods and obtain blacksmith services to repair their guns. The Comanches later came to an agreement, because they had found a new source for their plunder, the ranches of northern Mexico. The Texians even gave Comanche raiding parties passports so they could travel unmolested through Texas on their way to Mexico. But the grievances on both sides endured, especially as settlers continued to push westward into territory that the Comanches considered theirs, and Houston remained convinced that only annexation to the United States would solve the republic's frontier problem.

George Barnard was a clerk at the Torrey trading post near Tehuacana Creek, where Texas agents signed treaties with the Caddo, Tonkawa, and a number of other tribes in 1844.

Larry T. Jones III Collection, Austin, Texas

The Quest for Annexation Succeeds, 1841–1845

Houston's return to the presidency in 1841 again brought the issue of annexation to the fore. Lamar's campaign against the Indians had been costly, and Dr. Ashbel Smith, the Texas minister in Paris, deplored the "ill advised" expeditions against Mexico that, he said, "have done our national standing infinite harm." The republic was sinking even deeper into economic distress, with government debts spiraling and vast amounts of virtually worthless paper money from the Texas treasury in circulation. Nor could the republic's leaders effectively develop trade and settlement or protect the citizenry. Dr. Jones had lamented to his diary that the personal animosity between Houston and Lamar had reached the point that, "Gen. Houston, I fear, does not care how completely L---r ruins the country, so that he can . . . say, 'I told you so; there is nobody but old Sam after all.'" Enthusiasm for an independent Texas was waning, and the influx of thousands of newcomers, most from the American South, had even lessened the use of "Texian" to identify residents of the region. "Texan" was being used more frequently. Thus, Houston again quietly began trying to build support for Texas annexation to the United States.

The real issue behind U.S. rejection of Texas annexation was surely slavery, which had been a divisive issue since the inception of the American Republic, and the acquisition of the Louisiana Purchase territory in 1803 kept the issue current. Neither President Thomas Jefferson nor the U.S. Congress had made any stipulations regarding slavery in this vast tract of land west of the Mississippi, and when Missouri, one of the first areas in the region to be settled by U.S. emigrants, applied for admission to the Union as a slave state in 1819, much bitter wrangling ensued. Proponents of slavery and aggressive expansion of the slave system (mostly in the Lower South) debated the abolitionists (mostly in the North) and those with more tentative or limited proposals in the middle (mostly in the Upper South). These different views reflected different economic and political realities and visions, pitting the North with its growing emphasis on free labor, industrialization, and republicanism against the Lower South, with its burgeoning cotton economy supported by a large, enslaved work force and defined by old paternalistic models of privilege and responsibility. The Missouri Compromise that ultimately emerged in 1820 preserved a balance between slave and free states for the moment by admitting Missouri as a slave state at the same time that Maine was admitted as a free state. The compromise further stipulated that slavery would not be permitted in the Louisiana territory north of Missouri's southern boundary, with the exception of Missouri. At the time it seemed like a solution, but, in fact, it only postponed resolution of the dilemma.

Changing Climate for Annexation

Houston effectively courted the British, and they were eager to talk. Forty-one year old Captain Charles Elliot, a veteran diplomat and member of a prominent family, arrived in 1842 as the British chargé d'affaires, eager to build a viable commercial trade with Texas to arrest U.S. westward expansion in the Southwest. Elliot was also an abolitionist and hoped, indirectly at least, to exert some influence over slavery and tariff issues. He soon became acquainted with the republic's leading figures and ingratiated himself into Galveston society with elegant dinner parties, which he used to lobby actively against Texas annexation. Pointedly ignoring American diplomats, Houston worked through Elliot and the British minister in Mexico City to try to gain release of the Texas prisoners captured in the cross-border battles. Houston's gambit worked, and a worried President John Tyler, who shared southern attitudes on slavery, reopened communication with Houston on the subject of annexation.

Houston deftly played American authorities off against the British, and James Pinckney Henderson, whom Houston had sent to Washington, D.C., to assist Texas chargé d'affaires Isaac Van Zandt in the negotiations, reported in February 1844, "All things prove now the *very great* desire of the U.S. to annex us." In an effort to influence opinion in the United States, the Tyler administration began a propaganda campaign to convince the public that the British were playing a dangerous game in Texas that could lead to the emancipation of Texas slaves, "the darling policy of England," that would, in turn, destabilize the institution in the South. Finally, former President Jackson came out in favor of the "reannexation" of Texas (he had long claimed that Texas should have been included as a part of the Louisiana Purchase).

Negotiations limped along until Tyler's representative, the energetically pro-slavery Secretary of State John C. Calhoun, signed a proposed treaty of annexation with Henderson and Van Zandt. Houston was concerned about reactions from Mexico and wanted U.S. troops in Texas before any news of impending annexation leaked out, but he need not have worried. In his enthusiasm, Calhoun wrote a strongly worded letter to the British foreign minister, warning that the United States would oppose any British interference in Texas, and then proceeded to instruct the minister on the benefits of slavery. Calhoun probably reacted out of a genuine concern that the British were trying to block U.S. interests in the Caribbean, Mexico, and the West, but his blatant appeal to sectional interests aroused a furor in the North, and Northerners who had been prepared to vote for the treaty backed off. In June 1844, the U.S. Senate, which seemingly had been prepared to approve the treaty by a two-thirds vote, rejected the document by more than a two-to-one margin. Henderson wanted to remain in Washington, D.C., and continue working for annexation, but Houston ordered him to return to Texas.

Annexation at Last

Five months later, expansionist and Jackson protégé James K. Polk of Tennessee won election as U.S. president, in part through advocating "reannexation" of Texas, adding weight to Tyler's fumbling efforts to bring Texas into the Union. At about the same time, Dr. Anson Jones, Texas Secretary of State and a strong Houston supporter, succeeded Houston as president. Jones sensed that Polk's election gave Texas renewed bargaining power and refused to renew the annexation request without assurance that the U.S. Senate would approve it.

Meanwhile, lame-duck President Tyler switched tactics and, on March 1, 1845, Congress approved a joint resolution to annex Texas, which only required a majority in both houses of Congress rather than two-thirds approval in the Senate. The agreement allowed Texas to enter the Union as a slave state and hold onto "all the vacant and unappropriated lands lying within its limits," but keep its public debt. Some protested that an independent nation could not be added to the Union in such a manner and that a treaty, which would have required the approval of two-thirds of the Senate, was required, but the argument soon became moot.

Nevertheless, Britain and France continued to try to stave off annexation. Their representatives convinced Jones to delay a response to the American offer and belatedly pressured Mexican officials to recognize the still shaky republic rather than confront the specter of a strong United States on their border. In late April 1845, Mexican officials tentatively recognized the independence of the Republic of Texas provided Texas would not annex itself to another country.

Thus, Jones was able to offer the Texas Congress, meeting in special session in June, both the annexation agreement and an alternate: continuation as an independent republic with Mexican recognition. Congress unanimously chose

In "The Republic of Texas Is No More," illustrator Norman Price envisioned the annexation ceremony of February 19, 1846, with President Anson Jones leading in the lowering of the republic flag.

annexation. Then, on July 4, by a vote of 55 to 1, representatives led by Rusk, as president of the convention, resolved that the territory of the republic "may be erected into a new State, to be called the State of Texas . . . in order that the same may be admitted as one of the States of th[e] Union."

The Convention then proceeded to create the Texas Constitution of 1845, providing for election of a governor, a lieutenant governor, and a legislature, as well as the appointment of other state officials. On October 13, Texas voters overwhelmingly approved both the document and annexation. In a special election they elected James Pinckney Henderson as the first governor. Meanwhile, the U.S. Congress also approved the state constitution, and on December 29 President Polk signed the act making Texas the twenty-ninth state in the Union.

On February 19, 1846, with the first meeting of the state legislature in Austin, Dr. Jones turned over the reins of government to Henderson in a noon ceremony in front of the capitol. With the republic flag lowered and the American flag raised to fly over it, Jones proclaimed to the gathered crowd, "The lone star of Texas . . . has . . . become fixed forever in that glorious constellation . . . the American Union." According to a newspaper report, many in the crowd wept, but few of them would have wished for a different course for Texas, given the American origins of most of the citizenry and the experiences of the previous ten years. "Thank God, we are now annexed to the United States," Mary Maverick wrote in her diary, "and can hope for home and quiet."

With annexation, the struggles over Texas's identity seemed to recede into the past, and new state officials busily worked to bring Texas into the federal system. Two prominent leaders of the revolution and the republic, Thomas Jefferson Rusk and Sam Houston, headed to Washington, D.C., as the first U.S. senators from Texas.

 ## Conclusion

The republic period was essential in defining Texas's identity. Governor Peter H. Bell would later claim that "the days of the Republic were 'the days of our glory'. . . deeds of devoted patriotism and daring chivalry were then performed which would have graced the heroic pages of Greece and Rome . . ." But the difficulties of maintaining an independent republic, much less trying to build an extended empire, had proved more than formidable; in the near decade of independence, the fledgling nation had fallen deeply into debt and remained an uncertain frontier plagued by external threats and internal divisions. So most Texians were glad to become a part of the United States, and the San Augustine *Red-Lander* seemed to speak for them when it headlined, "GLORIOUS NEWS! TEXAS ANNEXED! WELCOME INTELLIGENCE!" But, as a harbinger of events to come, Texas naturally aligned itself with the other states that championed slavery, for it was a state in which cotton remained "king" and slavery was increasingly to be defended at all costs.

Suggested Readings

The republic era stands as a very distinct period of almost a decade in Texas history, a period in which Texas leaders struggled to create a stable government and economy and to withstand challenges from Mexico while residents struggled to survive and thrive under continued frontier conditions. Readings that focus on this period include William Ransom Hogan's classic *The Texas Republic: A Social and Economic History*, first published in 1946, Stanley Siegel's *The Political History of the Texas Republic, 1836–1845* (1956), and John Edward Weems's *Dream of Empire: A Human History of the Republic of Texas 1836–1846* (1971). The *New Handbook of Texas* (1996) has a good "Texas Republic" entry and entries for various events and biographies of the era.

On the subject of Texas annexation, Frederick Merk's *Slavery and the Annexation of Texas* (1972) is considered a classic. Subsequent works have built on and challenged Merk, significantly William W. Freehling's *The Road to Disunion: Secessionists at Bay, 1776–1854* (1990) and Sam W. Haynes's "Anglophobia and the Annexation of Texas: The Quest for National Security" in *Manifest Destiny and Empire: American Antebellum Expansion* (1997). See also Haynes, *Unfinished Revolution: The Early American Republic in a British World* (2010).

Much of the scholarly research on the early statehood period, from annexation to the Civil War, as well as in the republic period, focuses on ethnic groups or individual families; some of these are noted below under "Challenges and Opportunities in the Republic of Texas" and "Marginalized Groups in the Republic." A useful source for understanding gender and ethnicity issues is Mark M. Carroll's *Homesteads Ungovernable: Families, Sex, Race, and the Law in Frontier Texas, 1823–1860* (2001). The *New Handbook of Texas* contains many useful entries for the early statehood period—for example, on the Mexican War and the "Cart Wars."

For primary documents of the republic and the early state, see *Documents of Texas History* (1963, 1994), edited by Ernest Wallace, David M. Vigness, and George Ward. For primary accounts, see *Rip Ford's Texas* (1963, 1987), edited by Stephen B. Oates; *Texas Tears and Texas Sunshine: Voices of Frontier Women* (1985), edited by Jo Ella Powell Exley; and Crystal Sasse Ragsdale's *The Golden Free Land* (1976).

Randolph B. Campbell's *Sam Houston and the American Southwest* (1993) provides an accessible overview of the first Houston presidential administration. Because Sam Houston was such an important Texas figure throughout the periods covered in this chapter, the Campbell work is also more broadly useful, as is James L. Haley, *Sam Houston* (2002), and Sam W. Haynes's "Sam Houston and His Antagonists" in *Major Problems in Texas History* (2002). For a detailed account of the Santa Fe Expedition, see Paul N. Spellman's *Forgotten Texas Leader: Hugh McLeod and the Texan Santa Fe Expedition* (1999). For the Mier Expedition, see Sam W. Haynes, *Soldiers of Misfortune: The Somervell and Mier Expeditions* (1990).

Challenges and Opportunities in the Republic of Texas

In addition to the general works on the republic, individual family fortunes are traced in Margaret Swett Henson's and Delolece Parmalee's *The Cartwrights of San Augustine: Three Generations of Agricultural Entrepreneurs in Nineteenth-Century Texas* (1993) and Paula Mitchell Marks's *Turn Your Eyes toward Texas: Pioneers Sam and Mary Maverick* (1989). Two good sources for German immigration and settlement are Terry Jordan's *German Seed in Texas Soil: Immigrant Farmers in Nineteenth-Century Texas* (1966) and Walter Struve's *Germans & Texans: Commerce, Migration, and Culture in the Days of the Lone Star Republic* (1996). A good source on women is Fane Downs's "Tryles and Trubbles: Women in Early Nineteenth Century Texas," *Southwestern Historical Quarterly* (1987).

Marginalized Groups in the Republic

Sources on African Americans include Randolph B. Campbell's *An Empire for Slavery: The Peculiar Institution in Texas, 1821–1865* (1989), Elizabeth Silverthorne's *Plantation Life in Texas* (1986), and Alwyn Barr's *Black Texans: A History of African-Americans in Texas, 1528–1995* (1996). Sources on Tejanos include

Timothy M. Matovina's *Tejano Religion and Ethnicity, San Antonio, 1821–1860* (1995), Jesus F. de la Teja's *A Revolution Remembered* (1991), David Montejano's *Anglos and Mexicans in the Making of Texas, 1836–1986* (1987), and Andrés Tijerina's *Tejano Empire: Life on the South Texas Ranchos* (1998). Dianna Everett's *The Texas Cherokees: A People Between Two Fires, 1819–1840* remains the best source of information on the Cherokees' tragic end in East Texas.

The Annexation Quest Continues

The annexation sources cited above prove useful for understanding the final movements toward annexation within and outside Texas as well. See also David M. Pletcher, *The Diplomacy of Annexation: Texas, Oregon, and the Mexican War* (1973), and Joel H. Silbey, *Storm Over Texas: The Annexation Controversy and the Road to Civil War* (2005).

Statehood and Civil War, 1845–1865

Texas Congressman Sam Maverick faced a decision in 1860. Decades earlier, he had left his home in South Carolina, in part because he disagreed with the widely held states' rights and secessionist views in that state. Now, after a quarter-century as a Texan, he once again found himself surrounded by calls for states' rights and secession. As the presidential election of 1860 approached, Maverick found that secession advocates dominated the state Democratic convention in Galveston, some arguing for Texas to become an independent nation again. Meanwhile, at the national Democratic convention, the party split. Northerners nominated Stephen A. Douglas, the U.S. senator from Illinois who had argued that territories could not be compelled to pass laws protecting slavery. White Southerners held a separate convention and nominated Kentuckian John C. Breckinridge, who espoused their strong proslavery views.

The Republican Party had grown rapidly in the past decade, largely around opposition to the extension of slavery. Delegates to its convention in Chicago now nominated lawyer Abraham Lincoln, a leading Illinois Republican, for president.

Maverick had strong feelings about maintaining the Union and had also judged that a curse seemed to hang over a slave country, but had determined "to use without abusing the institution." He held a few slaves and as a lawyer and land speculator was included among the wealthy southern elite of Texas. But, like all Texans, he could not avoid a fateful decision and became "a good Breckinridge man," still hoping that secession could be averted. It was not to be, and the peace and security that Texans had gained by joining the Union was once again at risk—but this time from within.

Chapter 8 Statehood and Civil War, 1845–1865	
1846	On February 19, Texas officially became the twenty-eighth state in the Union
1846	War between Mexico and the United States begins; Baylor University opens at Independence
1848	Treaty of Guadalupe Hidalgo cedes Mexican holdings in American Southwest and West to United States
1850	Compromise of 1850 limits Texas boundaries but permits the state to pay off its debts and keep its public lands
1859	Indians on West Texas reservations are expelled to Indian Territory; Juan Cortina leads insurrection in South Texas
1860	Texas slave owners make up just over a quarter of the population but hold three-fourths of the wealth; Texas is strongly identified as a southern state
1860	Republican Abraham Lincoln is elected U.S. president
1861	Texas joins other southern states in seceding from the Union
1862	Federal troops make inroads on Texas gulf coast; suspected Unionists are executed in the "Great Hanging at Gainesville"
1863	Confederates retake or defend key points on Texas gulf coast
1865	War ends with South's defeat; on June 19, in Galveston Gen. Gordon Granger declares slaves in Texas to be free, providing basis for the Juneteenth holiday; President Andrew Johnson begins mild presidential Reconstruction

As you read this chapter, consider the following questions:

1. What concerns did men like Samuel Maverick have as Texas moved toward secession?
2. Why did most Texans favor slavery and secession when a majority of the population did not own slaves?
3. Do you think that Texans and the Southerners adequately understood the risks of secession and civil war?

 ## The New State

Most Texans sighed with relief once the American flag was raised over the capitol in February 1846. It meant greater stability and a healthy economy. It meant that the U.S. Army would take up the substantial problems of border and frontier security. And it meant that Texas would at last have a stable currency—the U.S. dollar. For most Texans, it meant that they had been reunited with their home country; for the Tejanos, it meant that they had been divorced from theirs.

The new state grew rapidly, with more than 70,000 persons arriving within the first five years of statehood. The population, excluding Indians, grew from an estimated 142,000 in 1847 to 212,295 in the census of 1850 and to 604,215 in

1860, the large majority of them from the states of the Old South. The German population had increased to about 20,000 by 1860, with a scattering of other European immigrants, such as Irish, Polish, Czech, Swedes, and Norwegians. There were perhaps as many as 14,000 Tejanos in the state in 1850, a growing number of individuals but a declining percentage of the entire population, with the large majority of them settled in South Texas.

This dramatic growth, however, contained within it the seeds of destruction that would split the Union and deliver a devastating blow to Texas and the nation. The slave population grew at an even more astounding pace: 12.9 percent from 1836 to 1847, 50 percent from 1847 to 1850, and 213.8 percent from 1850 to 1860, with the overall total reaching 182,566 in 1860 and accounting for almost one-third of the population. Like many Texans, John H. Reagan, a future postmaster general of the Confederacy, realized that slavery was a particularly "bad inheritance," but "did not see how they were to be relieved" of it. And, as the situation worsened in 1861, and the Civil War became unavoidable, Governor Sam Houston told Reagan that, "Our people are going to war to perpetuate slavery, and the first gun fired in the war will be the knell of slavery."

The War with Mexico

In 1845, however, Texans had a different problem: Most assumed that the United States would soon be at war with Mexico and welcomed the opportunity to gain revenge for perceived wrongs dating back to the revolution. Mexicans, on the other hand, regarded annexation as proof positive that the United States had been behind the Texas rebellion from the beginning.

As the United States offered annexation to Texas, President Polk ordered General Zachary Taylor to station his army "on or near" the Rio Grande and be prepared to defend American interests. In June 1845, Taylor landed nearly 4,000 troops, almost half of the American army, at Corpus Christi, at the mouth of the Nueces River, which Mexico considered the traditional boundary between Texas and Coahuila. Meanwhile, President Polk had sent John Slidell of Louisiana to Mexico with instructions to resolve the diplomatic issues between the two countries. The most pressing one, of course, was the Texas boundary. Polk supported Texas in its claim of the Rio Grande, while the Mexicans insisted that it had always been the Nueces. Other issues included $2 million in claims that American citizens had against Mexico and President Polk's desire to purchase California. Polk had thought that the Mexican government might be persuaded to recognize Texas's boundary claims in return for the United States dropping the claims of its citizens, but President José Joaquín de Herrera refused even to see Slidell when he learned the purpose of his mission. Slidell left Mexico with the opinion that, "we can never get along well with them, until we have given them a good drubbing."

President Polk apparently agreed and ordered Taylor to move his army from Corpus Christi to the Rio Grande, where the Americans established Fort Texas on the site of present-day Brownsville. At the same time, General Mariano

Paredes y Arrillaga overthrew the Herrera regime in Mexico with the announced goal of reconquering Texas. During the stalemate, President Polk was thinking of asking Congress for a declaration of war against Mexico, but the day before he was to send his message to Congress, he received a dispatch informing him that the conflict had already begun. In April, a Mexican army of 600 troops had crossed the Rio Grande upriver from Fort Texas and had ambushed a detachment of sixty-three American soldiers, killing or wounding sixteen and capturing the rest. In fact, the first substantial battles of the war, the battles of Palo Alto and Resaca de la Palma near Brownsville, had already occurred, on May 8 and 9, as American troops attempted to resupply the Fort Texas (later Fort Brown) from Port Isabel on the gulf coast, and Mexican troops maneuvered between them and the fort. Polk delivered his amended war message to Congress on May 11, claiming that Mexican soldiers had "invaded our territory and *shed American blood on American soil,*" and ignored the fact that the hostilities had occurred in the disputed territory. Mexico had never agreed that the Rio Grande marked the border. Congress responded two days later with a declaration of war.

There was serious opposition to the war in the United States, especially among prominent members of the Whig political party, which had organized in the 1830s to oppose President Jackson and the Democrats. Many felt that Polk, an expansionist Democrat, had provoked the conflict. Opposition to the war and to slavery led author and abolitionist Henry David Thoreau to refuse to pay his taxes. As a result, he spent a night in jail and wrote one of the most famous statements on civil disobedience entitled *Resistance to Civil Government* (1849). But in Texas, public sentiment among the Anglo-American majority was decidedly pro-war, with resentment and bitterness against the Mexican government still lingering.

Texans played a major role in the fighting. Governor Henderson asked the legislature to release him to command the Second Texas Regiment, and he led his unit in the capture of Monterrey in September, along with Colonel John Coffee ("Jack") Hays and the Texas Mounted Rifles. Major Benjamin McCulloch's spy company contributed to the American victory at the battle of Buena Vista in February 1847, and Hays, now leading a company of Texas rangers, supported General Winfield Scott on his march to Mexico City. General Taylor paid tribute to the Texans, saying that, "On the day of battle I am glad to have Texas soldiers with me for they are brave and gallant, but I never want to see them before or afterwards, for they are too hard to control."

With the fall of Mexico City in September 1847, the United States claimed victory. In the 1848 Treaty of Guadalupe Hidalgo that followed, Mexico ceded to the United States a great swath of the West, including California, New Mexico, and Arizona, and portions of Utah, Nevada, and Colorado, in return for $15 million. The United States also agreed to guarantee the property rights of people living in the ceded territory and to prevent hostile Indians north of the border from raiding into Mexico. (This last clause proved to be unenforceable and was negated in the Gadsden Treaty of 1854.)

The New State Takes Shape

The Treaty of Guadalupe Hidalgo resolved the southern border for Texas, but the Rio Grande north of El Paso now fell in federal territory, so Texas had to deal with the federal government with regard to its claim to a large portion of New Mexico and Colorado including Santa Fe. During the war, Colonel Stephen W. Kearny had taken Santa Fe without a fight in August 1846 as his "Army of the West" marched toward California. He had set up a temporary territorial government without the consent of the Texas government or acknowledgement of its claim. Texans pointed out that the joint resolution by which Texas entered the Union contained a clause to the effect that if Texas were ever divided into more than one state, slavery could not exist north of the Missouri Compromise line of 36°30′. This resolution constituted a tacit acknowledgment of the Texas claim to territory north of that line, that is, to the source of the Rio Grande. Within six weeks of the signing of the Treaty of Guadalupe Hidalgo, Texans tried to further their claim by creating Santa Fe County. The Texas governor sent a judge to Santa Fe to organize the county and serve as judge, but the American military commander in Santa Fe refused to recognize his authority.

Following the 1848 inauguration of President Zachary Taylor, a Whig, Texas Governor Peter Hansborough Bell, a veteran of both the Texas Revolution and

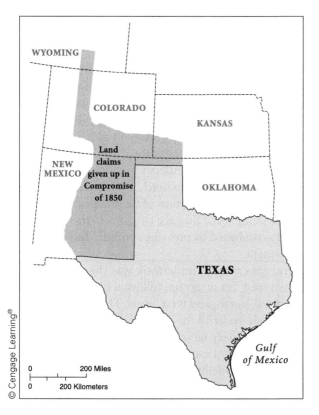

Compromise of 1850

© Cengage Learning®

the war with Mexico, tried again to assert the Texas claim to part of New Mexico territory. In early 1850, Bell sent Robert Simpson Neighbors, a former volunteer ranger and the first Indian agent for Texas, to organize four counties in New Mexico territory. Neighbors succeeded in El Paso County but faced "a bitter anti-Texan feeling" in Santa Fe, which by this time was pursuing separate statehood for New Mexico.

Texas won an advantageous resolution to this matter in September 1850. As a part of the Compromise of 1850, Texas relinquished all of its New Mexico claims except for the El Paso region. In exchange, the federal government offered the state $10 million. Voters overwhelmingly approved the agreement, and in November 1850 Bell signed the compromise, fixing the present boundaries of Texas and giving the state a tremendous economic boost. The federal government retained half of the $10-million award to settle revenue debt owed to those holding Republic of Texas securities. But with the other half, state officials were able to pay off the state's debts and establish an endowment for public schools and would later provide loans to railroads to develop rail lines in Texas. They also remitted most county taxes for a number of years, enabling the counties to use their tax money for development. Although the money brought stability to a government just a few years removed from the financial ruin of the republic, Texas was not yet able to attract viable railroad projects, and the lack of fast, efficient transportation remained an obstacle to economic growth.

The Frontier

One of the primary tasks for the federal government as it took control of security for the state was the establishment of peace with the various Indian tribes. The government followed its usual policy by negotiating treaties to regulate trade and land claims. However, this process was complicated in Texas because the state had retained title to all its public lands. The federal government did not have the authority to provide Texas land to the Indians, and the State of Texas did not recognize any Indian land claims. At the same time, settlers were moving west into traditional Indian hunting grounds, and the buffalo herds, which sustained the nomadic natives, grew smaller through a combination of bovine disease, white hunters, and the Indian practice of killing breeding age cows for their soft hides and tender meat. All these factors combined to provoke sporadic Indian raids and killings along the line of settlement.

A second task that the federal government undertook was the exploration and blazing of trails across the vast west Texas terrain, followed by the establishment of a line of forts through central, north, and west Texas. These served both to protect the frontier and to provide security for immigrants as they moved onto the plateaus and plains of the region (see table showing Forts of Texas).

During the 1850s, the federal government established a second group of forts along the frontier, from the Rio Grande northward to the southern reaches of the Llano Estacado, or "Staked Plains," to protect both the upper and lower trails

Year	Fort	Location
1846	Fort Brown	The southern tip of Texas
1848	Fort Ringgold	Rio Grande City
1848	Fort Bliss	Along the Rio Grande near El Paso
1849	Fort McIntosh	Laredo
1849	Fort Duncan	Eagle Pass
1849	Austin and Fort Worth	At the junction of the Clear Fork and West Fork of the Trinity River
1851	Fort Belknap	Northwest of Fort Worth
1858	Fort Quitman	Along the Rio Grande near El Paso

Rush Rhees Library/ University of Rochester

Capt. Arthur T. Lee painted this picture of Fort Davis, which was established in far West Texas in 1854 to protect the San Antonio–El Paso road.

between San Antonio and El Paso. Although settlement would not reach to most of these forts in the 1850s, it did push westward into the Texas Hill Country and northward through the eastern Cross Timbers.

Soldiers partnered with merchants and others intent on finding the best routes through the vast and often forbidding stretches to the west. In 1848, a civilian expedition under the command of Jack Hays and financed in part by San Antonio merchants teamed with a small military force under Captain Samuel Highsmith to map a trade route between San Antonio and El Paso. The Hays–Highsmith expedition helped spur more explorations in the following years. In the meantime, Captain Randolph B. Marcy of the U.S. Army explored a wagon route across the Texas Panhandle to Santa Fe. Noting the desert-like characteristics of West Texas, the army even experimented with camels for transportation. Thirty-three camels arrived at Indianola in 1856 and were sent to Camp Verde, northwest of San Antonio. Forty-one more camels arrived the following year. The army used them to explore the Big Bend region and on treks across the New Mexico and Arizona deserts to California. The experiment might have been judged a success, but it was interrupted by the Civil War. Some of the camels were left to wander the southwest, while others were sold to civilians; still others wound up in circuses in Mexico.

Pressures on Indians and Tejanos

All of this activity, of course, periodically incited Comanches and their allies on the southern plains in the late 1840s and the 1850s. Neighbors served in the legislature from 1851 to 1853 and sponsored legislation that enabled the establishment of reservations in Texas. Appointed Texas Indian agent again in 1853 under a new federal administration, Neighbors oversaw the transfer of twelve leagues of vacant land to the federal government for the use of Texas Indians. The law required that all tribes not native to Texas be removed. An East Texas reservation was established in 1854 for the Alabama and Coushatta Indians who had migrated from Alabama to Spanish Texas beginning in the 1780s. Then Neighbors set up two western Indian reservations in 1855.

About half of the Penateka Comanches, who had suffered severely from a cholera epidemic in 1849, agreed to occupy the reservation on the Clear Fork of the Brazos River in Throckmorton County; the other western reservation, on the Brazos in what is today southeastern Young County, became home to what remained of a hodgepodge of tribes, including Waco, Caddo, Anadarko, and Tonkawa. Neighbors labored tirelessly to get the Indians onto these reservations and to protect them once they were there. Settlers pressed unmercifully, however, contending that Indians from the reservations were responsible for depredations against them. Rather than blaming nonreservation Indian bands or even Anglo outlaws who conducted raids, settlers hoped that the Indians on the reservations would be blamed and sent out of state, thus opening up the reservations to settlement. Neighbors had to employ federal troops to protect the western reservation Indians, many of whom had helped frontier volunteers and the military in campaigns against hostile bands of Indians.

The situation finally deteriorated to the point that Neighbors requested permission to move the reservation Indians across the Red River to Indian Territory. In late summer 1859, Neighbors accompanied his charges across the river to Indian Territory. En route home, he stopped at Fort Belknap and was shot in the back and killed by one of the Anglo raiders. Neighbors' murder led to a complete breakdown in relations with the Indians and to a new wave of violence as hostile Comanches and Kiowas conducted severe raids along the Texas frontier. But they were virtually the only Indians left in Texas, other than the few hundred

Alabamas and Coushattas occupying their reservation deep in the woods of east Texas. Almost all the friendly tribes had been driven from the state.

The hostility that many of the new arrivals to Texas felt for the Indians was often matched by their disdain for residents of Mexican heritage as well. As cities such as San Augustine, Marshall, and Nacogdoches grew, white settlers' tolerance of Mexican Texans diminished. Frederick Law Olmstead, a journalist and an abolitionist who visited Texas in 1855, reported that most Tejanos had voting rights but few used them. If they did vote in a place such as San Antonio, where they might be able to prevail in an election, he surmised that it could result in a "revolution" among the Anglos, who "constantly distinguish themselves as 'white folks,'" superior to Tejanos as well as to African Americans and Indians. In San Augustine, Olmsted observed that all the Tejano residents had left; "we could not find a trace of them," he reported.

Many Tejanos were pressured into leaving. In September 1854, Seguin residents tried to ban Mexicans "of the peon class" from visiting or living in Guadalupe County, and in Austin a similar movement forced out all except "those vouched for by 'respectable citizens.'" Others were forcibly expelled. According to a committee of investigation, in 1856, citizens of Colorado County accused a Mexican of being one of the leaders of a slave plot that called for the slaves to overthrow their masters and fight their way to Mexico and freedom. The whites arrested all the Mexicans in the county and expelled them. Three slaves were hung, two whipped to death, and 200 lashed.

In San Antonio, conflict between Anglo and Tejano cartmen required the state's intervention. Between the coast and San Antonio, Tejano haulers monopolized the transport of food and merchandise by offering lower prices. Anglo teamsters began to terrorize the cartmen in an effort to drive away the competition. As early as 1855, accounts circulated in Guadalupe County that the Committee of Vigilance had destroyed some Mexican carts. In the late summer of 1857, attacks on the cartmen became common, and by November, Governor Elisha M. Pease announced, "It is now very evident that there is no security for the lives of citizens of Mexican origin engaged in the business of transportation, along the road from San Antonio to the Gulf." There was some sympathy for the cartmen, because merchants were not anxious to pay the higher prices that the Anglo haulers were charging. Because of a complaint from the Mexican minister in Washington, which was relayed to the state, the legislature approved a militia to protect the freighters, but the pattern was clear. Economic opportunity and any kind of power—economic, political, and social—were to be the hegemony of the Anglos. Not only did the Mexican freight business suffer, but the remaining Mexican elite in San Antonio were now relegated to lower-level positions.

South and west of the Nueces, where Tejanos were the great majority of the population (especially in Laredo), some families managed to hold onto their land and some of their power, but many of the greediest and most prejudiced newcomers tried to uproot the populace and in many cases successfully laid claim to their land. To forestall such confiscations—and to subvert a nascent separatist movement by a motley assortment of Anglos and *rancheros*—the legislature established a special commission in 1850 to confirm legal land titles in South Texas. The commission completed its work in 1852, having conformed more than 250 titles. Other questions about land titles were left to the courts. But the commission did not resolve all the difficulties the state faced. In El Paso, Anglos assumed control of the town while Tejanos held sway in the countryside. Resentments festered among the Mexican Texans in South Texas until an incident on the streets of Brownsville crystallized these resentments into a challenge to Anglo hegemony.

Juan Cortina had grown up the eldest heir of the second family of José Narciso Cavazos, who owned a large grant in the Brownsville area. Although Cortina and his family held legal title to the grant, his father's first family had sold the portion of it on which Brownsville was located to Charles Stillman, who with two partners had established the town of Brownsville in 1848. Cortina opposed the illegal sale of his land and that of other Mexican Texans in the area as well. Then, on July 13, 1859, he watched as the Brownsville City marshal arrested and abused a former Cortina employee. Cortina shot the marshal and departed with the former employee. A few months later, he returned with an armed group of men and took over the town. Persuaded to abandon the occupation by a Mexican

DeGolyer Library, Southern Methodist University, Dallas, Texas, Lawrence T. Jones III Photography Collection

Juan Cortina led his South Texas neighbors in resisting the Anglo-American appropriation of large amounts of land in the Rio Grande Valley.

official from Matamoros, he retreated, but he produced a manifesto detailing the wrongs committed against Mexican Texans. He also petitioned Governor Houston to protect the rights of Mexican Texans. In October, an Austin official wrote President James Buchanan to inform him of the affair, an outrage "so flagrant and astonishing that I would not believe it possible, if the information were not on undoubted authority."

Neighboring Mexicans rallied to Cortina, and his force reportedly grew to 400 men. He engaged in repeated skirmishes with Texas rangers and the U.S. Army under Major Samuel P. Heintzelman before retreating into Mexico. "Our object," Cortina insisted in a proclamation, ". . . has been to chastise the villainy of our enemies," who had robbed and harassed with impunity "without any cause, and for no other crime on our part than that of being of Mexican origin." Seaman William A. Tennison from Point Isabel put the situation more bluntly in a letter to Governor Houston: "the original difficulty is nothing more or less than a land rob[b]ing affair which is carried on in a very extensive scale." Cortina would mount a second challenge to Anglo hegemony in South Texas during the Civil War, a reminder that the situation on the border was far from resolved.

Texas as a Slave State

In the years 1845–1860, the Texas economy became more tightly intertwined with the production of cotton as the plant's cultivation expanded from the older settled areas into central Texas. Texas farmers produced more than 58,000 bales in 1849–1850 and more than seven times that only ten years later. At the same time, the number of slaves jumped from 30,505 in 1846 to almost 183,000 in 1860, one-third of the Texas population. In thirteen counties, slaves accounted for over half the population. The 27 percent of the population that owned slaves held almost three-fourths of the wealth in Texas by 1860, the bulk of which was concentrated among the elite—the approximately sixty planters who owned more than 100 slaves. Jared Ellison Groce, who arrived in Texas in 1821 with 100 slaves, was one of the wealthiest men and largest landholders in the colony. By 1840, Groce's son, Leonard Waller Groce, owned 180 slaves. Texas's identity—economic, political, and social—had become intricately tied to the "peculiar institution." Ironically, however, throughout this period, most Texas citizens did not own slaves, and, of those who did, most owned only one to four.

It is not hard to see how Texas developed an identity as a slave state. Stephen F. Austin had won concessions from the antislavery Mexican government as Anglos began to stream in to the state. The largest group of newcomers came from the American South with proslavery attitudes. National events also pushed Texas toward the southern slave-state camp. As the nation expanded, it divided over whether new states could outlaw slavery. The Missouri Compromise of 1820 had outlawed slavery north of 36°30′ latitude, but in 1854 the Kansas–Nebraska Act repealed the Missouri Compromise by allowing white settlers in Kansas and Nebraska to decide by popular vote whether slavery would be legal. This act opened

Caricaturist Edward W. Clay depicted Texas as a cruel slave master in this late 1840s era lithograph.

YOUNG TEXAS IN REPOSE.

the possibility that slavery could be legal in the new territories north of 36°30′ latitude. It also doomed the people of Kansas to violence and near anarchy after vote fraud there gave the election to the proslavery forces. In "bloody Kansas," the situation remained volatile through the late 1850s, feeding national tensions and southern intransigence. Sam Houston had voted against the Kansas–Nebraska Act in the Senate, but many Texans felt that he had faltered in his loyalty to slavery and to Texas, and the legislature officially condemned his vote.

Southerners justified slavery on a number of grounds, primarily the sheer necessity of having a large labor force and their feeling that the slaves, as an inferior, childlike people destined for servitude, benefited from the benevolence of their masters and the material conditions they provided. John Salmon ("Rip") Ford argued that the institution was in harmony with natural law: "it was sanctioned by the Bible, and it had all the authority of time to uphold it." Preachers extolled it from their pulpits and editors from their newspaper columns, and the Texas legislature actually discussed reopening an African slave trade. As fanciful and morally reprehensible as these arguments are, they were accepted tenets of southern thought. Those in the South who questioned them usually knew to keep their mouths shut; those who did not quickly learned. "We are abstractly opposed to slavery," wrote James P. Newcomb, speaking for himself and his partner, J. M. West, editors of the *San Antonio Herald*, but "we look upon it as one of those evils that must be left to root itself out, which it will do, as soon as free labor becomes as cheap and reliable, and not until then." As in the Lower South, then, Texas institutions reflected the acceptance and promotion of slavery.

The conditions of slavery as it developed in Texas varied. Some slaves were brutalized, forced to work incessantly, kept hungry and ragged, even whipped to death. Former Texas slave Lulu Wilson recalled that the master and mistress "nearly beat us to death," working their slaves incessantly from early childhood on and feeding them poorly: "For years all I could get was one little slice of sow-belly, a puny little piece of bread and a tater. I never had enough to stave the hongriness out'n my belly." Although Lulu was able to stay with her mother, the owner spirited other children away and sold them when Lulu's mother was working in the fields. For others, life was not as harsh. A fair number of slaves were allowed to hire themselves out, despite an 1846 state law prohibiting it. Some gained limited protection from juries against cruel treatment. But none of them were free.

To Anglo and European Texans, who overwhelmingly shared a sense of racial superiority, the slavery of African Americans was an accepted means of pursuing economic opportunity in the state: The growing of cotton. And most defended that course with vehemence. For example, in 1854, when German "Forty-Eighters" called a political convention at San Antonio and denounced slavery as an "evil," the outcry was instant and vitriolic, even though the Germans had also argued for the right of the state to decide without federal intervention whether to perpetuate slavery. In 1855, Galveston lawyer and legislator Lorenzo Sherwood received encouragement for his plan for economic development of the state, which involved making banking and railroad building "semipublic enterprises." But, because Sherwood also viewed slavery as a "temporary institution" incompatible with democracy, a view long held by many in the Upper South as well as the North, he was driven from office, faced censure by the House, and threatened with death if he should continue to speak out. The *Galveston Weekly News* announced in 1857 that, "Those who denounce slavery as an evil, in any sense, are the enemies of the South. . . ."

This public reaction did not represent the feelings of the full voting populace, as evidenced by the fact that in 1859 Sam Houston, still an ardent Jacksonian Democrat after the legislature had replaced him in the Senate, defeated the incumbent governor, Democrat Hardin Runnels. Runnels had signed a bill encouraging free blacks to enslave themselves by selecting a master. For much of Texas's brief history, the main distinction in politics had been those who supported Sam Houston and those who didn't. The Whigs had made inroads in Texas in the early 1850s, as had the nativist Know-Nothing party, an unabashedly anti-Catholic and antiforeign organization. But both of these parties had quickly faded from the Texas scene, leaving the Calhoun, or states' rights, Democrats as the only organized political party. There was, however, a Unionist branch of the party, as represented by Sam Houston, and there were others like him. In 1859, an audience at a public debate near Paris, Texas, left after the Union speaker's talk, despite his urgings that they stay to hear the secessionist. He was told that, "no damned Secessionist could speak there, or if he did, he would speak to an empty house."

But by the end of the 1950s, the "Calhoun Democrats," staunchly in favor of states' rights, were in ascendance. "Vigilance committees" sought to stamp out any signs of slave uprisings or attempts to encourage slaves toward freedom. Called "the *most* southern State" by the *Dallas Herald*, Texas was a former Spanish and Mexican province, a former republic, a state with a strong Mexican heritage, a state with thousands of European immigrants, a state that was made up of people from all over the American South and North, and a state that was coming under the dominance of the slaveholders. It had matured as a southern state aligned with the other states that championed slavery, a state in which cotton was "king," and slavery was increasingly to be defended at all costs. The state was headed into another crisis of identity, one that would prove to be both extended and costly. The architects of antebellum Texas—Southerners invested culturally, emotionally, and, for many, financially in the slave system—were ready to take a stand.

Secession and War, 1861–1865

In the summer of 1860, much of Texas simmered with unrest and suspicion. A series of mysterious fires in North and East Texas during that scorching season, with temperatures hitting 114 degrees, put everyone on edge. Parts of downtown Denton and Dallas went up in flames. Proslavery agitators began attributing these fires to slaves and their northern sympathizers, rumors of slave uprisings were in every newspaper, and slaves were coerced into "confessions" as a panicked vigilantism mounted. Vigilantes killed at least thirty people. Even in September, as the panic was subsiding, a posse chased down and hung Anthony Bewley, an antislavery Methodist minister suspected on questionable evidence of provoking the arsons. The "Texas Troubles," as they came to be called, were both a sign and a cause of the Texas secession that was to follow. Although several of the fires were subsequently determined to have been the result of high temperatures and the spontaneous combustion of new phosphorus matches, the proslavery propagandizers manipulated racist fears to influence Texans who strongly identified with the South.

Secession

In the election of 1860, the Democratic Party split. Southerners and Texans alike strongly insisted that the platform pledge the party to the protection of slavery in all the territories, but Northerners opposed to the guarantee prevailed. Delegates from the Deep South states walked out, later meeting in Richmond to nominate John C. Breckinridge of Kentucky. The remnant of the Democratic Party nominated Stephen Douglas, who had sponsored the Kansas–Nebraska Act, and endorsed popular sovereignty. An ad hoc organization calling itself the Constitutional Union Party nominated John Bell, a wealthy slaveholder from Tennessee.

The Democratic split assured the election of the Republican candidate, former Illinois Congressman Abraham Lincoln, and his running mate, Hannibal Hamlin of Maine. Southerners felt that the northern states had prevailed in electing, in the words of Texas's subsequent declaration of secession, "two men whose chief claims to such high positions are their approval of . . . long-continued wrongs, and their pledges to continue them to the final consummation of these schemes for the ruin of the slave-holding States." As Southerners, Texans viewed Lincoln as an archfiend and his party as responsible for "Texas Troubles."

Texas secessionists began to clamor for a state convention that would declare a complete break with the U.S. Governor Houston remained adamantly pro-Union, but, on December 17, he reluctantly called the legislature into session for January 21, hoping that moderates in that body would prevail and that no secession convention would be called. In the meantime, South Carolina seceded from the Union. When the Texas legislature met in the new year, delegates had already been elected to a Texas secession convention to meet a week later. The legislature simply voted to authorize the scheduled convention. As a member of the House, Sam Maverick of San Antonio reluctantly cast his vote for this convention, unwittingly placing himself in the middle of yet another struggle for the identity of Texas.

On January 28, the convention met, with O. M. Roberts, Texas Supreme Court judge and avid secessionist, presiding. Members moved speedily to vote in favor of breaking away from the United States, insisting that "the governments of the various States . . . were established exclusively for the white race,

Oran M. Roberts, supreme court justice and avid secessionist, presided at the secession convention.

for themselves and their posterity," with "the African race . . . rightfully held and regarded as an inferior and dependent race." Governor Houston did all that he could to slow the process, but he was powerless under the circumstances. When his old acquaintance John H. Reagan invited his cooperation, Houston declined. And when a committee from the convention called on him, hoping to convince him to go along with their decision, Houston advised that they should settle their differences with the Union peaceably. "I know what war is," he said, baring his shoulder to show them the fresh bandages on his 1814 wounds that had never healed. "I have been in it often and do not want any more of it. War is no plaything and this war will be a bloody war. There will be thousands and thousands who march away from our homes never to come back."

Houston and others favoring federal union and compromise had insisted that the people of Texas certify the convention's action. With this vote set for February 23, both supporters and opponents of secession took their arguments into the voting districts and to the newspapers of the state, printing and distributing copies of the ordinance of secession in English, Spanish, and German. In the meantime, the convention appointed a Committee of Public Safety to authorize volunteer troops and force the U.S. military to turn over the 2,700 federal soldiers, twenty-one forts, and weapons stores in Texas. On February 16, Texas volunteer troops arrived in San Antonio and accepted the surrender of federal military personnel, sites, and stores. Even Colonel Robert E. Lee, who had recently commanded the San Antonio garrison but would soon cast his lot with the Confederacy, was shocked at the surrender of more than $3 million worth of federal property. Approximately 2,000 troops were given safe pass to leave Texas.

A week later, Texas voters approved secession by a vote of 46,129 to 14,697. To understand why Texas voters so overwhelmingly approved secession, it is important to remember that those Texans who could vote—overwhelmingly, white southern males—favored a southern economic system based on cotton cultivation, and, by extension, on slave labor. They also favored a caste system that valued white over black. And they valued states' rights over continuing in a Union controlled by people who opposed the continued growth of a slave system.

Eighteen counties in Northeast and Central Texas and one in East Texas, however, actually voted to remain in the Union. Counties with significant numbers of Germans or immigrants from the Upper South—primarily former residents of Missouri, Arkansas, and Tennessee—and from the North were far less likely to ratify secession. But despite the opposition—which would continue during the war—the convention had its mandate and made the break with the Union official on March 2. Texas quickly joined the Confederacy, requiring everyone in office to take a loyalty oath to the new confederation. When Sam Houston and his secretary of state, E. W. Cave, refused to do so, they were removed from office, with Lieutenant Governor Edward Clark replacing Houston. Less than a month later, the Civil War began when soldiers of the Confederate states fired on federal troops in Fort Sumter, South Carolina.

Where was Sam Maverick as all of this transpired? As one of the three members of the Committee of Public Safety charged with appropriating federal troops and stores, he became a leading Confederate official, taking the loyalty oath and voting that those who did not should be deposed. His wife Mary, who would join in the war effort herself by leading the Ladies Aid Society and the women's wing of the Southern Defense Aid Society in San Antonio, offered an explanation: "At last he came to believe the quarrel was forced upon us, and that there was before us an 'irres[i]s[t]ible conflict' which we could not escape, no matter where we turned." That decision would cost them dearly.

Texans in the Confederacy

Even before the citizen vote for secession, Texas had dispatched seven delegates to a convention to organize the Confederate government in Montgomery, Alabama. Once Texas entered the Confederacy, it was obliged to acquiesce to central Confederate authority in such matters as conscription laws, use of slave labor, and cotton trade with Mexico. At the same time, it had its own representatives and influential men in the Confederate government: Texans Louis T. Wigfall and W. S. Oldman became members of the Confederate Senate, and John H. Reagan, Texas lawyer, judge, and legislator, became postmaster general of the Confederacy.

There were occasional tensions between the state and Confederate government over policy and procedure, such as when to give men exemptions to Confederate service so as to retain a defense force in Texas. And throughout the war, both governments had to contend with deserters and evaders of the conscription laws. But in the recruiting of fighting men, Texans by and large answered the call. Within ten months of the firing on Fort Sumter, 25,000 Texans were enlisted in the Confederate army. Two-thirds of them were in cavalry units; eventually, almost 59,000 Texans would serve in the cavalry. Although Governor Francis Lubbock's November 1863 estimate of a total of 90,000 Texans in Confederate service has been dismissed as too high for any one time, historians say that the figure probably has validity for the whole war effort—this from a fighting-age population estimated at 100,000–110,000.

Texans were well represented, too, in the Confederate officer corps, with numerous brigadier generals and colonels. The highest-ranked officer was General Albert Sidney Johnston, a veteran of the Texas Revolution and the Mexican War, who assumed command of the Western Department of the Confederacy but died leading troops at the battle of Shiloh in 1862. John Bell Hood was a native of Kentucky who had served in the U.S. Army on the Texas frontier, but declared himself a Texan because he was displeased with his native state's neutrality, and rose from captain to colonel to brigadier general in charge of Hood's Texas Brigade in Robert E. Lee's Army of Northern Virginia. A promotion to major general followed and then one to lieutenant general. Hood commanded the Army of Tennessee in the later months of the war.

The highest-ranking Tejano in the Confederate army was Santos Benavides, a descendant of the founder of Laredo, county judge of Webb County in 1859, and colonel of the Thirty-Third Texas Cavalry. Benavides, aided by his brothers Refugio and Cristóbal, led efforts to protect the Mexican border, pushing back both Union guerillas and Juan Cortina, who in 1861 again tried to rally supporters on the Texas side of the border. The Thirty-Third built an impressive record, but Tejanos also served throughout the Texas Confederate forces. More than 300 enlisted in the Eighth Texas Infantry, and there are estimates that at least 2,500 Tejanos served as Confederate soldiers in encounters from Virginia to New Mexico.

Not all Texans who fought or commanded did so for the Confederacy. Many who opposed Texas's stance joined Union troops. Judge E. J. Davis had resigned rather than take the Confederate loyalty oath and traveled to New Orleans, where he organized the First Texas U.S. Cavalry to fight against the Confederacy. The Second Texas Cavalry comprised Tejanos and Mexicans from the Rio Grande, drawn by the bounty money they received for enlisting but also propelled by grievances about their treatment by Texas officials and by opposition to slavery.

About two-thirds of the Texas Confederate troops remained in the western theater, or west of the Mississippi, many serving in the Louisiana and New Mexico campaigns. In fact, Texas became the base for two attempts to extend the Confederacy westward in an echo of previous Texan attempts to claim New Mexico. In the first attempt, John Baylor, lieutenant colonel of the Second Texas Mounted Rifles, expanded upon his orders to protect the overland route to El Paso by invading New Mexico. Baylor had raised a volunteer force of almost 1,000 men to fight the Comanche Indians in northwestern Texas a few years before, and in the Mesilla Valley he proclaimed himself the military governor of the new Confederate Territory of Arizona and began a campaign against the Apaches. When he ordered one of his subordinates to exterminate the hostile Apaches in his area in March 1862, Confederate President Jefferson Davis removed him from command.

Meanwhile, Brigadier General Henry Hopkins Sibley proceeded along similar lines. He had convinced President Davis that he could take a group of Texas volunteers, arm them from the federal forts and arsenals now under Confederate control, and seize New Mexico in what would become the western front of the Civil War. The Confederacy would then be in a position to take Colorado and the Southwest all the way to southern California. This would bolster the rebel economy and enhance its chances of being taken seriously as a viable republic by European nations. Sibley, a West Point graduate who had five years of military service on the Texas frontier, began recruiting in San Antonio in August 1861. By late October, he had more than 3,000 men organized in three regiments and in supply and artillery units. They marched westward along the San Antonio–El Paso Road in detachments, their numbers staggered to make use of the limited water holes. Following Baylor's steps—and incorporating some of Baylor's volunteers—in January 1862 Sibley made Mesilla his base of operations.

To meet the Confederate threat, Colonel Edward R. S. Canby, commander of the federal Military Department of New Mexico, had massed federal troops and

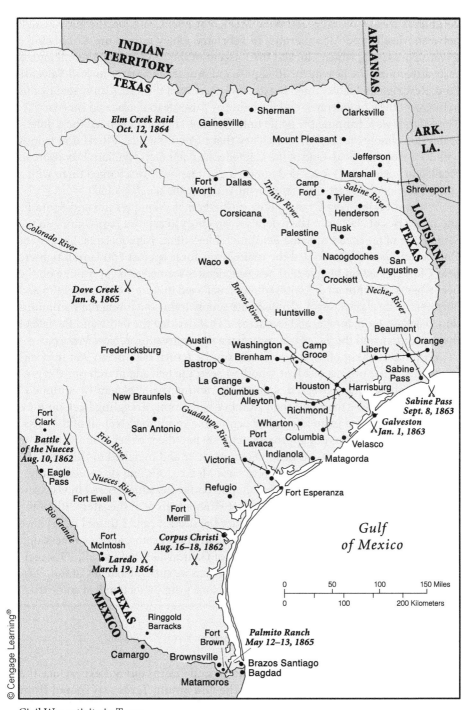

Civil War activity in Texas

volunteers from Colorado and New Mexico at Fort Craig, on the Rio Grande between Mesilla and Albuquerque. In February, Sibley moved most of his force toward Fort Craig, which blocked their ascent of the Rio Grande, then detoured eastward around the heavily fortified post and proceeded upriver toward Valverde Ford. Realizing that Sibley intended to cross the river at the ford, Canby sent troops to intercept the Confederates, and the battle of Valverde took place on February 21. The federals were winning the battle until Colonel Thomas Green led the Confederates in a charge on the Union artillery that turned the tide. The Union troops withdrew from the field. One of the Confederate volunteers, William Davidson, to recalled in verse that, "We heeded not their great renown/We charged them with a yell/We turned their tactics upside down/And gave the regulars hell."

Without taking Fort Craig, Sibley pushed on to Albuquerque and Santa Fe and to a series of clashes in the federals in an effort to capture Fort Union, on the Santa Fe Trail northeast of Santa Fe. With Sibley still in Albuquerque, Lieutenant Colonel William R. Scurry led the main Texas force against 850 Union fighters near Glorieta Pass on March 28. The Confederates seemed to be prevailing on the field when a detachment of Union soldiers managed to skirt the Confederates and burn the entire eighty-wagon Confederate supply train containing their ammunition, baggage, food, forage, and medicines. That decided the battle and the fate of the expedition, and the Texas troops began a slow retreat from New Mexico.

Without their supplies, the suffering on the return trip to San Antonio was intense. A San Antonio resident who had seen the brigade march out the previous October, "finely dressed, splendidly mounted and elegantly equipped" now observed fewer than half their number had "come straggling back on foot, broken, disorganized in an altogether deplorable condition." Not all of the missing were accounted for, but approximately 500 had died, either from wounds or disease, and another 500 had been taken prisoner and marched to Illinois. Like previous Texas attempts to expand into New Mexico, this one also ended badly.

In the eastern theater, as battle piled upon battle, casualties soared in ways few could have anticipated. Texan W. R. Bell of Blossom wrote of the aftermath of the battle of Franklin, Tennessee, "I helped bury the dead . . . and I think I could have walked all over the battlefield on dead men." Battlefield deaths, injuries, illness, and desertion all took their toll; B. F. Carpenter of Gainesville would recall, "Our regiment went out of Texas with 1,180 men and when we surrendered at Canton, Mississippi, there were 240 at roll call." Sam Houston's grim prediction had come true.

The War in Texas and Its Impact

There were few and limited battles in Texas, and Texans did not experience the invasion and destruction visited upon the Old South. Texas was spared from experiences like the Union General William Tecumseh Sherman's burning of the city of Atlanta and punishing "March to the Sea." The war did reach Texas, however, and it affected the state and its citizens in very important ways.

In the wake of the Confederates' firing on Fort Sumter, Union naval vessels began blockading southern ports, quickly including Texas. Confederates tried to strengthen the Texas coastal positions, but in the fall of 1862 Union ships shelled the sites. The bark USS *Arthur,* the yacht *Corypheus,* and the steamer *Sachem* harassed trade and routed Confederate positions on the Texas coast, seizing Confederate sloops and schooners. In August, the *Arthur*'s commander tried to follow up by taking the town of Corpus Christi but was repulsed in two engagements by a Confederate force of 700, a combination of local volunteers and four companies of the Eighth Texas Infantry battalion.

Despite this victory, the Texas coast remained vulnerable as the war seesawed in the East. The Battle of Antietam in September put an end to Robert E. Lee's attempt to press into Union territory in Maryland. That same month, a federal blockade patrol shelled the Texas coast at Fort Sabine, constructed by local residents to protect the community of Sabine Pass, near the juncture of the Sabine River and the Gulf of Mexico. Damage to the fort and an outbreak of yellow fever caused local militia and Texas infantrymen to abandon the post. In October, a squadron of Union ships sailed into Galveston harbor, and their commander demanded the surrender of the island. Confederate Brigadier General Paul O. Hébert, in charge of the Confederate District of Texas, judged the island to be indefensible and removed his troops to the mainland.

This military abandonment of the Galveston dealt a blow to the spirits and fortunes of many Texans. Galveston had developed as a significant commercial and transportation center. Its steamers carried people and goods to Houston and back through Galveston Bay and Buffalo Bayou. A railroad company had even built a bridge to the island in 1860 and constructed a short railroad line. Now this vital coastal artery had been severed.

Major General John Bankhead Magruder, a Virginian and Mexican War veteran, followed Hébert as commander of the district on November 29 and immediately began planning to retake the island. On New Year's morning 1863, the Confederates struck with infantry, cavalry forces, and two river steamers, with cotton bales stacked on deck as defensive armor, for a naval attack. The troops crossed over the railroad bridge, and the two "cottonclads" opened fire from behind the Union ships. Twenty-six Confederates were killed and 117 wounded, whereas the Union suffered about 150 casualties. The federal ships departed. Magruder had retaken Galveston and captured a number of Union infantrymen who were abandoned when the Union ships headed out to sea.

This victory was followed by news of Lee's December victory over the Army of the Potomac near Fredericksburg, Virginia, and by the January 21 with the retaking of Sabine Pass. On January 30, Mary Maverick, busy with relief efforts for soldiers and their families, reflected the thoughts of many when she wrote to her son in Confederate service, "With all our grand victories & all their losses, won't we have peace soon think you?"

But the war was far from over, the southern independence far from secured. In the summer of 1863, the biggest single battle of the war occurred at

Gettysburg, Pennsylvania, where Lee's southern troops were pushed back and combined casualties—dead, wounded, or missing—topped 43,000. Further Union victories in the South positioned the federal forces to take control of the Mississippi River and freed Major General Nathan Banks to look toward the conquest of Texas. Banks' first attempt came at the previously contested Sabine Pass, from which he planned to capture Houston, recapture Galveston, and gain entrance to the state's interior. He sent 4,000 troops by ship, and the U.S. Navy dispatched four gunboats to cover their landing.

At Sabine Pass, the Davis Guards, Company F of the First Texas Heavy Artillery Regiment, had been busy fortifying the site and preparing for an attack by sea. When one of the four gunboats, the *Clifton,* appeared and began shelling from a distance on the morning of September 8, the Confederates bided their time. Lieutenant Richard W. Dowling, a genial Houston saloon owner from Ireland, and his men had rehearsed for this moment by placing stakes in both channels of the river so they could judge the accuracy of their cannons. The other three ships joined the *Clifton* in the afternoon, advancing on the pass. Dowling and his forty-seven-man Confederate force held their fire until the Union ships were within range of their cannons, and then they opened up, firing more than 100 times in a thirty-five-minute battle. The small Confederate force turned back the invasion, and the federal troops returned to New Orleans. The Confederates captured two of the gunboats and more than 300 Union soldiers.

General Banks, however, maintained pressure on Texas. In particular, he was eager to capture Brownsville, which had become a key import/export center for the western Confederacy, with southern cotton going to Europe through Matamoros and war supplies and other essentials coming in to Texas. In November, Banks took Brazos Santiago Island, at the mouth of the Rio Grande near Brownsville, forcing Confederate troops to abandon defense of the town. Banks's occupation of Brownsville and disruption of trade there was temporary, but federal soldiers worked their way along the Texas coastline, occupying the port of Indianola as well. Eudora Moore, a fifteen-year-old resident of the port town, later recalled the federal soldiers "digging rifle pits and building forts on the prairie back of town" and appropriating the family's cattle. Soon Galveston and Sabine Pass were the only ports remaining in Confederate hands, and residents as far inland as San Antonio prepared to flee. Meanwhile, the cotton trade moved further up the river to the Eagle Pass–Piedras Negras area.

In yet a third thrust, Banks and General Frederick Steele planned a two-pronged attack into East Texas, Banks from Louisiana and Steele from Little Rock, Arkansas. But in spring 1864, Steele was halted by Confederate troops—including Texas brigades—at Camden, Arkansas. Banks's troops met the Confederates at the battles of Mansfield and Pleasant Hill in Louisiana but then fell back east of the Mississippi. One Texan, John Howard King of Gilmer, remembered of Pleasant Hill: "Here was the wildest shooting that I saw during the war. They shot the tops of the trees all to pieces. . . ."

As the war dragged on for another year, Texas troops retook Brownsville and other points along the coast. But the Army of the South was faring badly elsewhere. In September 1864, Sherman took Atlanta in a terrible blow to the Confederacy. By the end of the year, John Bell Hood's Army of Tennessee had been devastated, and southern manpower and resources had been strained to the breaking point. The greatest blow to Confederate hopes came in the East on April 9, 1865, when Lee surrendered the army of Northern Virginia to Grant at Appomattox Courthouse, Virginia. Nine days later, Joseph E. Johnston surrendered one of the last major Confederate armies.

The war was essentially over, but in early May Lieutenant General Edmund Kirby Smith, commander of the Confederate Trans-Mississippi Department, announced that his western Confederate forces would continue to fight. In the meantime, the Union commander on Brazos Santiago Island was negotiating unsuccessfully for a Confederate surrender at Brownsville. This continued resistance resulted in the last engagement of the Civil War—the Battle of Palmito Ranch.

Learning of the surrenders in the East, many soldiers in the Brownsville area left for home, but others continued to occupy and hold the town. They skirmished twice with Union forces before Colonel Benavides and Colonel John Salmon ("Rip") Ford appeared with Confederate reinforcements. Ford was one of the more ubiquitous and colorful characters in this era of Texas history. He had arrived in Texas immediately after the revolution and had worked as a medical doctor, Texas military officer, state senator, Texas ranger, and newspaper editor. His nickname stemmed from his dispatches reporting deaths of American troops during the Mexican War; he would use "RIP" as shorthand for "Rest in Peace." He, too, had engaged in extensive border service during the war.

At Palmito Ranch, the Union and Confederate forces were now nearly even. With their field artillery firing, Ford and Benavides attacked the Union troops from the left, the right, and the center, forcing them into a rout. The federal troops hurried back toward Brazos Santiago Island with the Confederates in pursuit, the four-hour battle ending when the federal troops reached reinforcements near the island.

Even as the battle raged, Kirby Smith and other western Confederate officials acknowledged the futility of a continued Confederate resistance. Federal officers entered Brownsville to arrange a Confederate surrender. On June 2, Smith formally turned over the Confederate Trans-Mississippi Department to General Canby, who had stopped the early Confederate advance into New Mexico.

After four years of conflict, the loss would rankle those Texans who had embraced the identity of Texas as an extension of the American South. But whatever one's political stance, the war in Texas had had a significant impact, in spite of the fact that invasion had been confined to the coast. There is no accurate estimate of how many Texans died in battle or from disease, but it would, no doubt, number in the thousands. The war effort had drained manpower and resources, stymied development, and created division and new uncertainties about Texas's identity.

Wartime Conditions

During the war years, more and more men were conscripted into Confederate service. At first, the call was for men aged 18–35, but by war's end, with Confederate losses mounting, conscription acts included men from 17 to 50. The unpopular Conscription Acts of 1862 allowed those overseeing twenty slaves or more an exemption from Confederate service, but the great majority of Texas men either volunteered or were conscripted. Some of the youngest and oldest recruits served in the "Home Guards," or "heel flys" as they were better known, because they spent much of their time tracking down those who deserted or otherwise avoided military service. Farming, ranching, and businesses naturally suffered with the absence of men of fighting age. But many women, following the American colonial tradition of women as "deputy husbands," took over the management of farms, plantations, ranches, and businesses during this period.

Union blockades and the disruptions of war meant that Texans learned to make do or do without. Texans learned to use coffee substitutes such as peanuts, corn, barley, okra, or even the "horrid decoction of burnt wheat" that was served to Kate Stone, a twenty-two-year-old southern belle from northeastern Louisiana who had to abandon her plantation home because of the fighting around Vicksburg. After arriving in Lamar County, Kate wrote in her diary that,

> I am already as disgusted as I expected to be. This part of the land . . . is a place where the people are just learning that there is a war going on, where Union feeling is rife, and where the principal amusement of loyal citizens is hanging suspected Jayhawkers. Hoops are just coming in with full fashion. . . . Have not seen a hoopless lady since entering the state. Shoes are considered rather luxuries than necessaries and are carefully kept for state occasions. As for bowls and pitchers, Oh no, they never mention them. . . . And oh, the swarms of ugly, rough people, different only in degrees of ugliness. There must be something in the air of Texas fatal to beauty.

When they reached the Tyler area, Kate concluded that she and her mother had indeed found "the dark corner of the Confederacy." When items previously in good supply did appear, they commanded exorbitant prices. In early February 1864, Mary Maverick squeezed into the crowded Mutual Aid store in San Antonio, getting for her efforts and $180 a bolt of domestic cloth, a pair of shoes, and a dozen candles. Every now and then medicine or tobacco supplies would be available, having arrived through Mexico.

Homespun and handwoven clothing became a symbol of patriotic pride; Governor Francis R. Lubbock was inaugurated in a homespun suit in 1861, and the chorus of the Confederate song "Bonny Blue Flag" noted "My homespun dress is plain I know/My fan is homemade too/But then it shows what Southern girls/For Southern rights will do." Eudora Moore recalled her mother constructing a pair of pants from a "parlor table cover." Despite the severe shortages at home, girls and women also worked hard to clothe the soldiers and provide them with medicine and food, as the Confederate and state governments struggled to provide them with the most basic necessities.

Texas did enjoy an important trade advantage over other southern states in its proximity to Mexico. At Matamoros, on the Rio Grande across from Brownsville, and at Bagdad, a small Mexican village at the mouth of the Rio Grande, the Texas cotton trade had reached "enormous proportions," according to the U.S. consul in Matamoros, with "all kinds of army goods going back." John Warren Hunter, a youth of only fourteen when the war started, graphically described the route through South Texas to Matamoros. "Ox trains, mule trains, and trains of Mexican carts, all laden with cotton coming from almost every town in Texas," traveled what became known as the "cotton road." This 125-mile stretch of road between the King Ranch and the border, with bits of cotton snagged on the dense mesquite and prickly pear cactus and looking like snow, was "a broad thoroughfare along which continuously moved two vast, unending trains of wagons; the one outward bound with cotton, the other homeward bound with merchandise and army supplies." The trains converged on Brownsville, he later recalled, making it the "greatest shipping point in the South" and "Matamoros . . . a great commercial center." The cotton was transported to the village of Bagdad, which grew from "two or three board shanties" in 1861 to a bustling town of more than 4,000 by 1864, with first-class hotels, boarding houses, stores filled with merchandise, and any number of saloons. There Lt. Col. Arthur J. L. Fremantle, a member of the British Coldstream Guards who toured the border area during the war, counted "seventy vessels . . . constantly at anchor" off the coast, with "their cotton cargoes being brought to them . . . by two small steamers." And "for an immense distance" along the shore he saw "endless bales of cotton" awaiting shipment. Mexican, Tejano, and Anglo merchants operating on the Rio Grande made fortunes in trade during the war years as blockade-running vessels and those sailing from Mexican ports evaded the Union ships in the gulf.

Nonetheless, the war greatly hurt economic and community development in Texas. The state was just beginning to establish the transportation arteries necessary for increased trade and growth when the conflict broke out. For example, railroad projects of the 1850s, although limited and short-lived, had already made a difference in Texas travel. A thirty-six-mile trip northwest from Houston to the Hockley area took a day and a half by stagecoach (through mud) in 1854; the same trip over the same ground took an hour and forty minutes by rail in 1857. The war played havoc with the fledgling railroad efforts. Although a few short railroad lines in Texas were actually completed and put in service during the war years, others had to shut down. In some cases, their rails were dug up and used as military fortifications or laid elsewhere as part of the military supply effort. Meanwhile, many railroad construction efforts simply stopped midway through.

Work ground to a halt on other community development efforts as well. Since her arrival in San Antonio in 1838, Mary Maverick had longed to worship in an Episcopal church, practicing the faith in which she was raised. Construction on

St. Mark's Episcopal Church finally commenced in the midst of the statewide agitation over secession, but was suspended with the advent of the war.

At its most extreme, the war pushed Texans back into uncertain frontier conditions, not only in terms of supplies and community development but in terms of safety. During the early statehood period, American and European immigrants had moved westward through the Texas Hill Country, pushing settlement onto the Edwards Plateau. To the north, they had moved onto the grand prairies and into the western cross timbers of north central Texas, pressing westward to the prairies beyond. In both cases, they were approaching the rolling plains still occupied by embattled Comanche and Kiowa Indians. Although the early months of the war were relatively quiet on the western frontier, with men and resources being drained for the fighting, the free-roaming Comanches, in particular, began to use the situation to their advantage. They mounted punishing raids on the outlying western settlements, hitting hard in Cooke, Denton, Montague, Parker, and Wise counties. Texans "forted up," as they had in earlier days, with families coming together and stockading for protection.

From the outset of the war, the state government had tried to address the need for frontier protection, from Indians as well as other threats. In December 1861, the Texas legislature authorized a Frontier Regiment to replace a Texas Confederate regiment briefly assigned to home-front protection. Led by Colonel James M. Norris, the new force of more than 1,000 men established a frontier defense line a short distance west of the settlements, from the Red River on the north bordering Indian Territory southward to the Rio Grande, with a string of sixteen forts bisecting the state, north to south. A Confederate regiment patrolled the border area along the Rio Grande.

In the spring of 1862, Confederate President Jefferson Davis responded to complaints about lack of protection by Texas Governor Francis R. Lubbock and Missouri's governor by establishing a Trans-Mississippi Military Department with Edmund Kirby Smith commanding. But the Confederacy's military attention and resources remained in the east. At first, Norris's troops patrolled regularly from fort to fort, but the Comanches and their allies from other tribes, discerning the pattern, stepped up their attacks on temporarily exposed areas. In 1863, Governor Lubbock reorganized and expanded the regiment. It abandoned the patrol system in favor of an aggressive series of scouting parties beyond the line of defense.

As the frontier force sought to quell the Indian threat, state officials and President Davis sparred over its status. State officials wanted the regiment to be a Confederate force, but to remain under state control to respond quickly and knowledgeably to Indian threats. Davis wanted the regiment to be subject to all Confederate rules and regulations, which meant that its members could be pulled from the Texas frontier and used elsewhere. In an agreement that became official in March 1864, the regiment was switched to Confederate service and divided, some of the companies moving elsewhere in Texas. On the western frontier, those remaining were joined by more than 4,000 local militia men. Like other "Home Guard" units, older men and teenage boys too young for the regular military filled its ranks.

Indian depredations continued, the most prominent of which was the Elm Creek raid of October 1864. Comanches and Kiowas rode into the Elm Creek Valley in Young County and raided the settlements, killing eleven residents and five Confederate troopers and capturing seven women and children.

Dissent within Texas

In the waning months of the war, the Comanches and their allies shifted their attentions away from the Texas frontier, a move that should have ensured a much-needed peace. But the frontier—and much of North Texas—remained chaotic and strife-filled, the remaining companies chasing outlaws, deserters, and those who refused to serve in the Confederacy or Home Guard. In October 1864, General Edmund Kirby Smith noted, "The frontier counties . . . are . . . a grand city of refuge where thousands of able-bodied men have flocked to escape service in the Confederate Army." The conscription evaders and the deserters were called "brush men" because they hid in the scrub country in the northwest part of the state. All attempts to corral and control them ended in failure. Henry McCulloch, commander of the northern sub-district, offered the deserters an amnesty in the fall of 1863 and organized those who responded in the "Brush Battalion," charged with chasing down other deserters and protecting against Indians. But the members of the battalion were so troublesome, and prone to desert, that McCulloch disbanded it in March 1864.

McCulloch's experience reveals an important aspect of the war in Texas: Increased divisiveness. Not only had some Texans chosen to fight for the Union, but some of those who stayed refused to commit to the war effort, or actively opposed it. At first, many Texans excused immigrants from Europe. But as the casualties began to mount, and as it became apparent that the Confederacy was fighting for survival, dissent or even neutrality was viewed as suspect at best, traitorous at worst. In San Antonio, as one resident noted, "It was like living in an asylum where every one was crazy on one especial subject; you never knew what dangerous paroxysms were about to begin."

Secessionists perceived opposition to the southern cause among the Germans of central Texas and the immigrants from the Upper South living in frontier north Texas. Although members of both groups enlisted and fought for the Confederacy, their numbers did include staunch antislavery contingents that felt that slaveholding provided an unfair advantage in an agricultural society and was at odds with the principles of democracy. While in Texas, Kate Stone visited a friend "in the famous Union neighborhood, Honey Grove, where they say there is only one Confederate family. There, everyone you talk to says of course we will be conquered." Further, there were avowed Unionists in both groups; many of the North Texans were rumored to be members of a Union League formed during the war as a means of pledging continuing fidelity to the United States.

In fact, many Germans had left their home country disappointed by its failure to reach unification. Many immigrants from the Upper South, whether or not they favored slavery, also felt that the issue should be resolved without secession. Some Upper Southerners moved on to Kansas or California, and some Germans left for Mexico. One such group of German Unionists, en route to Mexico and camped beside the Nueces River in Kinney County, were set upon by Confederate troops in August 1862. Of the sixty-plus members of the traveling party, nineteen were killed in the "battle of the Nueces," along with two Confederates. Confederates executed nine wounded Germans as well.

Many Upper Southerners in North Texas felt secure and well established in their independent views. After all, they lived in an area of the state where slavery had only a tentative foothold, and many had arrived in the 1830s and 1840s. Yet immigrants from the Lower South, especially those holding slaves and with more wealth, in general, had arrived in the 1850s. Some of these representatives of antebellum southern culture, spurred in part by stories of the Union League, in part by tales of North Texans collaborating with Kansas abolitionists and Indians across the Red River, began to form vigilante groups to ferret out Union sympathizers. This atmosphere led to a series of vigilante killings of suspected or known Union sympathizers in Cooke, Grayson, Wise, and Denton counties. The most notorious killings occurred in Cooke County and became known collectively as the "Great Hanging at Gainesville."

Suspicions had been provoked when a number of Cooke County citizens signed a petition protesting the Conscription Acts of April 1862 because the acts exempted men in charge of at least twenty slaves. The acts had caused grumbling statewide, but resistance was stronger and more vocal in the northern counties, where dissenters were unhappy about being drafted or seeing their sons drafted. When rumors began to circulate of a Unionist plot to seize the militia arsenals at Sherman and Gainesville, the commander of the Gainesville-area militia district authorized the arrest of any able-bodied men who failed to respond to a call to arms. Colonel James G. Bourland, a former state senator and plantation owner, led state troops in arresting more than 150 men on October 1. They were to be tried by a "citizens' jury" organized by Bourland and Confederate colonel and fellow slaveholder William C. Young, who happened to be home on leave.

None of the accused owned slaves, but seven of the twelve jurors did. The jurors proceeded to convict seven leading Unionists of "conspiracy and insurrection" or "disloyalty and treason." These seven men were summarily hung, but the jury was in the process of exonerating the others when a mob arrived and demanded more convictions. Fourteen more men were turned over to the vigilantes, escorted by Bourland's troops, and hung from a large elm tree on the banks of Pecan Creek just east of Gainesville.

In Gainesville, it appeared that the rest of the prisoners would be released, but then William Young and another man were ambushed and killed by unknown assailants. Many of the prisoners were immediately retried, and nineteen more were executed. In all, forty men were hung and two killed while trying to escape before the troubles in Gainesville came to an end. A family member of one of the executed men charged that most of the dead "were old settlers in this county, and had fought the Indians from their doorsteps. And they did not want to be crowded back on the back seat by a few newcomers that was [*sic*] trying to take the lead and run the country."

The war left a palpable bitterness between those who had wholeheartedly embraced the cause and those who could not and would not do so. In San Antonio, as people like the Mavericks struggled to comprehend and accept the defeat of a cause to which they had given time, energy, money, and sons, Confederate veterans raided and looted, defending their actions on the grounds that San Antonians had not fully supported the war effort.

 ## Conclusion

Even without the internal enmities, the military and political loss festered. "Our humiliation in defeat . . . is harder to bear, than all the exposure, hunger and wounds during the war," former Confederate soldier J. L. Greer of McKinney wrote. "It rankles me in my heart still. . . ."

The war left many Texans exhausted, disheartened, and divided, with not only the plantation system but their towns and farms in disorder and decay. Galveston's population had declined, and a local newspaper reported that even Confederate troops had "torn [fine residences] to pieces merely for fuel during the whole war, and that too while there has been an abundance of wood at the head of the bay." Beaumont had been growing in promise and prominence as a sawmill and ranching town and a railroad transportation hub before the war, but after the war the sawmills sat deteriorating, the railroad bridges and roadbeds untended and unused. In the countryside, much farming land lay uncultivated, its cash value diminished and the farms deteriorated.

If any group had reason to rejoice at the South's capitulation, it was African Americans, most of them slaves. Texas had more slaves than ever at war's end—an estimated 250,000—because many Southerners had sent their slaves to Texas to place them beyond the reach of the Union army. The feeling of freedom was sweet to people who had lived so long without it; Annie Hawkins would remember, "We was the happiest folks in the world when we knowed we was free."

Nevertheless, former slaves had reason to be uneasy. General Gordon Granger had arrived in Galveston on June 19 and proclaimed enforcement of the Emancipation Proclamation in Texas, an event that would later spark the creation and observance of "Juneteenth" celebrations among African Americans. But even the wording of the proclamation seemed to send mixed messages. It demanded "an absolute equality of rights and rights of property between former masters and slaves," yet also suggested that the slaves "remain at their present homes and work for wages" and warned that "they will not be allowed to collect at military posts" or be "supported in idleness, either there or elsewhere." Some even had to overcome the deception of their owners; Lulu Wilson's owner told her stepfather that adults had been freed, but children had to remain with masters until they reached adulthood.

Many of Texas's leaders and voting citizens had defined Texas as part of a southern Confederacy built on cotton culture; its most powerful citizens were those who managed large-scale cotton cultivation with slaves. They had separated Texas from the very Union it had sought to enter in the 1830s and 1840s. Now Texans were going to have to redefine themselves and their relation to that Union, including expanding definitions of citizenship—or accept definitions imposed from outside.

Suggested Readings

Good primary sources for the Statehood and Civil War periods can be found in Ernest Wallace, David M. Vigness, and George B. Ward, *Documents of Texas History* (1994) and in Chapters 8 and 9 in Sam W. Haynes and Cary D. Wintz, *Major Problems in Texas History* (2002). Because these are two very distinct crisis-ridden periods, the sources for each are specified below.

The War with Mexico

The best overall history of the war is K. Jack Bauer, *The Mexican War: 1846–1848* (1974). A good source on Texas and the Mexican War is Richard Bruce Winders's *Crisis in the Southwest: The United States, Mexico, and the Struggle over Texas* (2002). For the Compromise of 1850, see Mark J. Stegner's *Texas, New Mexico and the Compromise of 1850: Boundary Dispute and Sectional Crisis* (1996). For Indians, see Brian DeLay, *War of a Thousand Deserts: Indians Raids and the U.S.–Mexican War* (2008).

The New State

For an overview see Ernest Wallace, *Texas in Turmoil, 1849–1875* (1965). For slavery, see Campbell, *An Empire for Slavery* (1989) and Campbell and Richard G. Lowe, *Planters and Plain Folk: Agriculture in Antebellum Texas* (1987). For Tejanos, see Arnoldo De Leon, *The Tejano Community, 1836–1900* (1982). To place Texas's movement toward secession at the end of this period into a national context, an excellent resource is William W. Freehling's *Road to Disunion* (2 vols., 1990).

The Frontier

See Robert Wooster, *Soldiers, Sutlers, and Settlers: Garrison Life on the Texas Frontier* (1987); Robert M. Utley, *Lone Star Justice: The First Century of the Texas Rangers* (2002); Jerry D. Thompson, *Cortina: Defending the Mexican Name in Texas* (2007); Thomas T. Smith, *The U.S. Army and the Texas Frontier Economy, 1845–1900* (1999); Pekka Hämäläinen, *The Comanche Empire* (2008); and

Gary C. Anderson, *The Conquest of Texas: Ethnic Cleansing in the Promised Land, 1820–1875* (2005).

Secession and War, 1861–1865

The *New Handbook of Texas* has a number of useful Civil War–related entries, including one on the "Texas Troubles" and entries on various military units, battles, and campaigns. A good source for understanding Texas's decision to secede from the Union is Walter L. Buenger's "The Roots of Texas Secession" in Haynes and Wintz, *Major Problems in Texas History,* pp. 230–237, and Buenger, *Secession and the Union in Texas* (1984). For general Civil War information, readers are encouraged to look at the work of Clayton E. Jewett, *Texas in the Confederacy: An Experiment in Nation Building* (2002), and Ralph A. Wooster: *Texas and Texans in the Civil War* (1996) and *Lone Star Generals in Gray* (2000). For the story of the Confederacy's thrust into the Southwest, see Donald S. Frazier, *Blood and Treasure: Confederate Empire in the Southwest* (1995) and Jerry Thompson's *Civil War in the Southwest: Recollections of the Sibley Brigade* (2001). Thompson has also written about Mexican Texans in the war: *Mexican Texans in the Union Army* (1986) and *Vaqueros in Blue and Gray* (1976). Evault Boswell's *Texas Boys in Gray* (2000) offers reminiscences by Confederate soldiers.

The War in Texas and Its Impact

For the Union efforts to conquer Texas, see Stephen A. Townsend, *The Yankee Invasion of Texas* (2006). For firsthand descriptions of Texas during the war, see B. P. Gallaway, *Texas, the Dark Corner of the Confederacy: Contemporary Accounts of the Lone Star State in the Civil War* (3rd ed., 1994). For African Americans' experience in the war, see the accounts in Haynes and Wintz and Randolph B. Campbell's *An Empire for Slavery* (1989). Jo Ella Powell Exley's *Texas Tears and Texas Sunshine* (1985) contains some women's accounts of the period; Paula Mitchell Marks in *Turn Your Eyes toward Texas* (1989) charts the Maverick family fortunes during the war. David Montejano's *Anglos and Mexicans in the Making of Texas, 1836–1986* (1987) deals briefly with the war years.

Dissent within Texas

For dissent in Texas, see L. D. Clark, ed., *Civil War Recollections of James Lemuel Clark and the Great Hanging at Gainesville, Texas in October 1862* (1997); Richard B. McCaslin, *Tainted Breeze: The Great Hanging at Gainesville, Texas, 1862* (1997); David Pickering and Judy Falls, *Brush Men & Vigilantes: Civil War Dissent in Texas* (2000); and David Paul Smith, *Frontier Defense in the Civil War: Texas' Rangers and Rebels* (1992).

Reconstruction, 1865–1874

Although Texas had not been successfully invaded, and had suffered little of the calamity that befell the other Confederate states, the Civil War nevertheless brought enormous changes to the state. Most important, the approximately 250,000 slaves in the state had been freed. Former slave Felix Haywood remembered the moment when he learned that freedom had come when he was interviewed in his San Antonio home in about 1937:

> *Hallelujah broke out—*
>
> *Abe Lincoln Freed the nigger,*
>
> *With the gun and the trigger,*
>
> *And I ain't going to get whipped no more.*
>
> *I got my ticket,*
>
> *Leaving the thicket,*
>
> *And I'm heading for the Golden Shore.*

Soldiers, all of a sudden were everywhere—coming in bunches, crossing, and walking, and riding. Everyone was singing. We were all walking on golden clouds.

> *Hallelujah!*
>
> *Union forever.*
>
> *Hurrah, boys, hurrah!*
>
> *Although I may be poor,*
>
> *I'll never be a slave—*
>
> *Shouting the battle cry of freedom.*

Everybody went wild. We all felt like heroes, and nobody had made us that way but ourselves. We were free. Just like that, we were free. It didn't seem to make the whites mad, either. They went right on giving us food just the same. Nobody took our homes, but right off colored folks started on the move. They seemed to want to get closer to freedom, so they knew what it was—like it was a place or a city.

We knew freedom was on us, but we didn't know what was to come with it. We thought we were going to get rich like the white folks. We thought we were going to be richer than the white folks, because we were stronger and knew how to work, and the whites didn't, and we didn't have to work for them any more. But it didn't turn out that way. We soon found out that freedom could make folks proud but it didn't make them rich.

Chapter 9 Reconstruction, 1865–1874	
1866	New state constitutional convention meets as a condition of Texas's reentry into the Union
1867	First Reconstruction Act of U.S. Congress ushers in congressional Reconstruction
1868–1869	Another constitutional convention meets under requirements of congressional Reconstruction
1870	Under Republican governor E. J. Davis, Texas gains readmittance to the Union and home rule
1872	State elections favor resurgent "Old South" Democrats
1873	Democrat Richard Coke is elected governor over Davis
1875	Another constitutional convention meets and produces the Texas Constitution of 1876, still in use (with multiple amendments) into the twenty-first century

By December 1863, President Lincoln had begun to ponder how to bring the Confederate states back into the Union. On December 8, he issued the Proclamation of Amnesty and Reconstruction, which specified that all Southerners except the highest political and military leaders of the Confederacy would receive a full pardon and restoration of property, new state governments would be formed as soon as 10 percent of the citizens swore allegiance to the United States, and the states themselves would devise a plan to deal with the former slaves so long as their liberty was not constrained. By the time General Edmund Kirby Smith surrendered the western Confederate forces, however, Lincoln had been assassinated, and his vice president and successor, Andrew Johnson, a Unionist Democrat who had served as the military governor of Tennessee, was left to proceed with Lincoln's "ten-percent plan" or propose his own program for the "reconstruction" of the rebellious states.

An anonymous caricature of Texas as the state came back into the Union following Reconstruction.

New-York Historical Society, New York City

Thus began the arduous process of reuniting the country, a process that had as its high-minded goal the establishment of equal rights and self-rule for all Southerners. To simply say that such a principled agenda failed, however, is to underestimate the revolutionary impact that transforming the slaves into free laborers and equal citizens would have had on the social and political lives of all Texans. Race and class were too deeply ingrained to be brushed aside in such a short period of time. And when the "Redeemers," as the Democrats called themselves, returned to power in 1873, they did so with a vengeance.

As you read this chapter, consider the following questions:

1. Were the goals of congressional Reconstruction realistic?
2. Did the federal government deal properly and realistically with Texas during Reconstruction?
3. What motivated the "Redeemers" in writing the Constitution of 1876 and what political goals did they achieve in ratifying the constitution?

Reconstruction

Although he had owned slaves, Johnson was a staunch Unionist whose public record seemed to place him among the Radicals. "Treason must be made odious, and traitors must be punished and impoverished," he had said in 1864. He argued that because secession had been null and void, the states remained in the Union, and that his goal was to establish constitutional governments in them as quickly as possible. In May 1865, he announced his Reconstruction program, which offered amnesty and pardon, including restoration of all property except slaves, to former Confederates who would take an oath of allegiance to the United States and support emancipation. But, at the same time, he listed fourteen classes of important Confederate officials and persons who owned more than $20,000 in taxable property who would be required to apply individually for presidential pardons. These conditions were quite different from those that Lincoln had proposed, and many in the North expected that, by this latter policy, especially, Johnson intended to end the political and economic dominance of the plantation elite and provide the yeomen farmers opportunities to have a voice in the new governments. But, as it turned out, Johnson gave pardons liberally—7,000 by 1866—revealing a less noble rationale for the exclusions: They could be used to insure the planter elite's political loyalty in the next presidential election. Further, in choosing provisional governors in the South, with the exception of Andrew J. Hamilton in Texas and William W. Holden in North Carolina, Johnson picked men who were acceptable to a broad majority of the white population, and not all of whom could take the Ironclad Oath (that they had never "borne arms" against the United States). The southern states quickly accepted Johnson's terms and prepared to draft constitutions and hold elections in 1865. Thus, the old southern power structure began to reassert its hold on political and economic power.

The big issue that split the electorate, both North and South, was black suffrage. The Radicals in Congress wanted to make it a requirement for the former Confederate states to regain their status in the Union. They argued that because the southern states had given up their statehood, Congress, as the arbiter of admitting new states, should direct their return. Congress took control of Reconstruction in 1867 and, through military occupation of ten of the eleven rebel states and the assertion of Republican principles, set out to win equal political and civil rights for the freedmen. The resulting turmoil lasted for decades as Texans sought to address the many political, economic, and social problems wrought by the Civil War. In Texas, as elsewhere in the South, some sought to establish a new order while others sought to reclaim the old one.

Presidential Reconstruction in Texas

While Texans suffered less than their fellow Confederates, the war destabilized agriculture and ranching, mainstays of the state's economy. The same was true of the political traditions among the elite. The war had opened irreparable breaches among them, and they now faced the prospect of trying to unite to govern the state and reinvigorate the economy. The most devastating blow was the number of men sacrificed to the war. Probably more than 90,000 Texans had served in the war, including 2,000 in the Union army. While there are no accurate records on casualties, thousands were killed and wounded, and the war affected virtually every family in the state and left thousands physically and mentally crippled.

Following his Reconstruction plan, President Johnson ordered a convention "to restore [Texas] to its constitutional relations to the federal government." To be eligible to serve, delegates only had to take the loyalty oath, so Johnson allowed all but the most prominent Texas Confederate leaders to participate in the political process. This was but one decision that seemed to favor former members of the Confederacy and fall short of the rehabilitation of the region that many Northerners felt was required. Indeed, Southerners soon came to view Johnson as an ally in their resistance to compliance with his announced policies, such as full civil rights and political equality for freedmen, and it appeared that the political and economic elite would soon reassert their control over the emerging social order.

Johnson appointed Andrew J. ("Colossal Jack") Hamilton provisional governor of Texas on June 17, 1865. The controversial Hamilton embodied many of the political dilemmas of the era. He proved to be one of Johnson's more radical appointments and, for many Texans, the most dangerous kind of turncoat. For others, however, he was a hero. A native of Alabama, he was an Austin lawyer and former slave owner who had been among those moderate Democrats who tried to fight the secessionist tide in the 1850s. His popularity was such that he won a U.S. congressional seat in 1859 and a special election to the Texas Senate early in the war. But by mid-1862, he felt so harassed for his views that he left Texas and spent several months in the Northeast and in occupied New Orleans lecturing on the inevitable conflict between slavery and a democratic society, the slave-owning elite's suppression of the rights of yeomen, and the strong Union sentiment in parts of Texas. With the North anticipating the occupation of Texas, Lincoln had appointed him military governor of the state, and he participated in the Union invasion of South Texas in the fall of 1863. He waited out the later stages of the war in Union-occupied New Orleans.

One of the first problems that the provisional governors throughout the South faced was the control of the labor force. Planters were concerned that the freedmen would not work as hard as they had before emancipation, and that they would fail as free laborers. Initial experiences with the occupying military led many former slaveowners to think that they would be permitted to maintain control of the freedmen with restrictive laws, and news from Washington of a growing split between President Johnson and Congress encouraged the planters' resistance. In such an environment, it was difficult to secure full political equality for the freedmen. Years later, Christopher G. Memminger, who had served as the first secretary of the treasury of the Confederacy, agreed that Southerners should have followed a "different course" with regard to black suffrage, but, as he explained, Johnson "held up before us the hope of a 'white man's government,' and . . . it was natural that we should yield to our old prejudices." When John H. Reagan, the Texan who had served as postmaster general in Jefferson Davis's cabinet, wrote from a Union prison in Boston to "the People of Texas" in August 1865 urging that they "accept the present condition of things, as the result of war," including limited black suffrage, as the only way of regaining "the blessings of local self-government" and banishing military rule, he was widely denounced.

John II. Reagan, who served as Postmaster General for the Confederacy, counseled Texans from his prison cell in Boston to accept the results of the war, including black suffrage.

Hamilton and other Unionists encountered intense opposition as they began to implement some of the provisions of Reconstruction. Hamilton believed that men who had opposed secession should make up the new state government and tried to place only staunch Unionists in district, county, and precinct positions; he denied positions to even the most nominal Confederates. The state's Unionists, after all, had their own list of wrongs to avenge, and even under Johnson's lenient policies, former Confederates often felt the wrath of those whom the secessionists had silenced and marginalized. James W. Throckmorton, who opposed secession but then supported the Confederacy, lamented that they "keep up past issues—keep open old sores—and inflame old wounds that ought to be allowed to heal." Minyard H. Harris of Kirvin, for example, reported himself to be "in constant danger of being caught and shot or hanged" for his actions as a "heel-fly" (chasing down deserters and forcing them back to their units) during the war.

Hamilton called for an election to name delegates to a convention to create a constitution for the state that would bring it into conformity with national laws. Minimal requirements included the establishment of full political liberty and civil rights (although only limited suffrage) for the freedman, acceptance of the Thirteenth Amendment (outlawing slavery), recognition that the ordinance of secession was null and void from the beginning, that Texas had no legal or constitutional right to secede from the Union, and the repudiation of the debt that the Confederate had accumulated.

As 1866 began, it was clear that Governor Hamilton wanted to implement major changes and that would set Texas on a course for quick readmission to the Union. Of course, unreconstructed Confederates opposed his plans, but moderate Democrats also opposed him because they felt that he was pushing racial issues too quickly. They especially felt that the freedman's independence had to be constrained in some manner, and the mixed signals coming from Washington encouraged their foot-dragging. Seeing some Union men going over to the conservatives because the federal government had failed to intervene, Hamilton feared that the Unionists would lose the peace after winning the war. "The sternest and strongest only have been able to weather the storm and keep the faith," he wrote.

In most parts of the state, the old order managed to reassert itself fairly quickly, in part thanks to Johnson's lenient pardoning policy and to his ignoring the Ironclad Oath in favor of the "amnesty oath," which required only that a person swear that he would support the Union in the future. But, after Hamilton had been in office only a month, a wave of violence further hampered his efforts. The price of cotton had been high in the summer of 1865, because the Civil War had created a global scarcity. Planters had borrowed money to get their crops in the ground and had signed expensive labor contracts with freedmen. By the time the crops reached market, however, the price had tumbled because British and French textile manufacturers had found other suppliers in India and Egypt. Buyers in Galveston offered only half of what they had paid earlier in the year, leaving planters owing their loans as well as their contracted labor costs. Some absconded without paying the workers while others simply refused to pay them. But some tried to drive the workers away so they could claim that the blacks had violated their contracts, and neither Hamilton nor the military had the troops to stem the violence. Other acts of violence were less focused. "The war has educated a class of men into idleness and into a familiarity with deadly weapons," wrote Ferdinand Flake, the Republican editor of *Flake's Bulletin* in Galveston, "that prompts them to resort to the revolver whenever it suits their drunken vag[a]ries."

In this atmosphere of uncertainty, voters went to the polls to elect delegates to the federally mandated constitutional convention in early 1866. The Unionists, who supported Hamilton, claimed that they understood the mood of Northerners and were the only party that could bring Reconstruction to a successful end. The conservatives opposed the expansion of civil rights for the freedman and argued that President Johnson would prevail with his lenient Reconstruction plan. They maintained that those who had served Texas loyally, even as Confederates, were the most trustworthy to represent the people at this critical hour. In a modest turnout, the conservatives carried the election. The delegates generally fell into three groups: diehard secessionists, conservative Unionists, and radical Unionists. More than a third of the delegates had been officers in the Confederate army and perhaps another third had served as enlisted men. That did not mean that they would all oppose Hamilton, for some Unionists such as James W. Throckmorton, a conservative Tennessean from Collin County who was elected president of the convention, had served the Confederacy. But it did mean, as Hamilton telegraphed President Johnson, that there were some "violent & impractical men" at the convention.

The results deeply disappointed Hamilton. Members agreed to nullify the Texas act of secession, but not to do so *ab initio* (from the beginning) as this would mean that they had had no right to secede in the first place and would nullify all laws and transactions made in Texas since 1861. They avoided ratification of the Thirteenth Amendment, arguing that it was not necessary because it had already become a part of the U.S. Constitution, which they had agreed to support in their oath. They repudiated the war debt and acknowledged certain freedman rights, including protection of person and property, but they rejected any idea of freedmen voting or holding public office. The delegates approved the 1845 state constitution with amendments on secession, the war debt, and freedmen and called for a June 25 election to approve the entire document. None of this was likely to satisfy Radical Republicans in Congress.

Texas voters approved the constitution and elected their first postwar governor in a contest between two moderates: the constitutional convention's chair, Throckmorton, and former Texas governor Elisha M. Pease. The Unionists had first asked Governor Hamilton to head their ticket, but he refused, explaining that he could not support the proposed constitution. Then they turned to Throckmorton, a member of the Texas legislature before the war who had held out against secession until it was accomplished, but had promptly enlisted in the frontier defense, then in the Sixth Texas Cavalry. A former surgeon and soldier in the Mexican War, he had fought in various Civil War engagements, eventually serving as General Kirby Smith's commissioner to the Indians. The Union Party made only a half-hearted effort on behalf of Pease, who had been an able governor during the 1850s, had participated in the writing of the constitution of the Republic in 1836, and had served in a variety of government roles since that time. Like Throckmorton, he had opposed secession, but, unlike Throckmorton, he had remained loyal to the Union and had quietly adhered to his principles.

Throckmorton emerged the victor, in part because Pease, while he did not actively favor black suffrage, agreed that he would accept it if Congress required it for readmission to the Union. Nor did Hamilton campaign for the ticket, departing instead for Washington, where he lobbied against Johnson's policies and for Congressional intervention in former Confederate states. With the power structure of the Old South reasserting itself, even many moderates refused to support some of the most basic citizenship rights for African Americans.

The Freedman's Bureau

In truth, African Americans found precious little freedom or independence after the war and much hostility to their assuming any role but a variation of slavery. Because they remained landless, they had few choices but to labor for whites as tenants. Indeed, General Granger had encouraged them to do so in the June 19 proclamation declaring slavery abolished in Texas. The freedmen's best hope became an agency established in March 1865 to be administered by the U.S. Army; the Bureau of Refugees, Freedmen, and Abandoned Lands, commonly known as the Freedman's Bureau, came to Texas in September of that year.

Agents of the bureau—including military men, Northerners, and some Texans—were charged with helping former slaves make the transition into citizenship. This included ensuring that blacks had the same protections under the law as whites, helping them set up schools and providing teachers, monitoring the freedmen's labor contracts to insure fair terms, and helping former slaves unite with scattered family members. At its peak, the bureau had agents in fifty-nine districts in Texas. Because the bureau was a branch of the army, many of the agents were former army officers. Others were northern citizens (commonly called "carpetbaggers"), and a few were Texans (whom many considered traitors to the South and called "scalawags"). Most of these agents worked hard to achieve two goals: the establishment of a fair and workable agricultural system and good schools for the freedmen. While they made some progress, the size of the state, the difficulties of travel and communication, and white hostility made their job a hard and dangerous one. General Oliver Otis Howard, commissioner of the bureau, noted in his autobiography that he considered Texas "at the time . . . to be the post of greatest peril." Because most of the agents were former army officers, white Texans viewed the bureau as a branch of the occupying force sent to punish them by the victorious North. Even though Andrew Johnson in late August 1866 declared "the insurrection which heretofore existed in the State

Texas State Library and Archives Commission, Austin, Texas

New Yorker George T. Ruby was a traveling agent for the Freedman's Bureau in Texas and later served as Collector of Customs in Galveston and as a member of the Texas State Senate.

of Texas is at an end," violence—especially violence directed against African Americans and representatives of the federal government—was all too common.

One of the most active agents was George T. Ruby, a freeborn native of New York who had traveled extensively before moving from Louisiana to Galveston after the war. Here he served as a *New Orleans Tribune* correspondent, started his own Galveston newspaper, became active in politics, and taught school. Soon he was administering bureau schools in a number of counties. Within a few months of its establishment in Texas, the bureau was operating sixteen schools serving just over 1,000 black pupils. The schools were the bureau's most successful program. By the end of its tenure, in July of 1870, it operated 150 schools enrolling 9,086 black students, but that was only a small percentage of the potential enrollees.

The Fourteenth Amendment

In Washington, moderate Republican Lyman Trumbull, one of the most influential men in Congress, concluded that the bureau needed to be strengthened. He proposed two bills early in 1866. The first would have extended the bureau's life and, for the first time, provided direct funding for its activities. It also would have enabled its agents to take jurisdiction in cases where state officials had denied freedmen their civil rights and to punish state officials. Far broader was the Civil Rights bill, which defined every person (except Indians) born in the United States as a citizen and specified his or her rights of equality without regard to race, rights that could not be denied by any state law or custom. Congress passed both bills with strong Republican support, but Johnson surprised everyone by vetoing them. He explained that the bureau was an "immense patronage" that the country could ill afford at the moment and that he did not deem the protection of black civil rights to be a federal responsibility. This set up a confrontation between Johnson and a divided Congress that many observers initially thought Johnson would win. Even such a prominent Unionist as John Hancock, an attorney and politician who had served in the legislature and refused to take the oath of allegiance to the Confederacy, concluded that Johnson would prevail and that Texas, therefore, did not need to go as far as Hamilton had proposed.

Congress also grappled with another difficult problem, which Maine Congressman James G. Blaine labeled the "somewhat startling result" of emancipation: how freedmen would be counted in calculating each state's congressional and Electoral College representation. Before the Civil War three-fifths of the slaves had been counted, as prescribed in the Constitution. Counting them all would greatly increase the representation of the southern states. No political party, not even the Radical Republicans, fully and publicly espoused giving the vote to freedmen at this time; nor could they accept the possibility of increased southern political power. Radical Congressman Thaddeus Stevens of Pennsylvania proposed a compromise that would have based representation on the number of qualified voters in each state rather than the total number of people. This elegant solution had the advantage of leaving the qualification of voters to the states. If Southerners wanted to increase their representation at the federal level, they could permit blacks to vote. Of course, it also proved problematic for some northern states as well. Would states like Rhode Island agree to eliminate literacy and naturalization requirements that were then in place in their quest to find more voters? And, because the westward migration of males had left the New England states with a majority female population, would they accept female suffrage rather than permit their political clout to decline? (The answer to that question was no, leaving feminist leaders feeling deeply betrayed and realizing that they needed an independent movement to accomplish their goals.)

Out of this difficult situation, the Fourteenth Amendment emerged, but it would not be ratified until after the presidential election of 1868. It proposed that no state could abridge an individual's rights, that representation would be reduced by an amount equal to the percentage of male citizens twenty-one years old, or older, who were denied the vote, that those who had voluntarily aided the Confederacy could not vote in national elections, and that the Confederate debt be repudiated. The Republican majority in Congress pushed it through on a strict party-line vote. President Johnson, who had been in favor of the Stevens proposal, rejected the amendment. He was not the only one. Even abolitionists such as Wendell Phillips and William Lloyd Garrison opposed it: Phillips because southern states, if they chose, could deny suffrage based on race, and Garrison because he felt confident that whites would find a way to take it away. In one of his most eloquent statements, Stevens explained his vote: "Do you inquire why . . . I accept so imperfect a proposition? I answer, because I live among men and not among angels." Thus, as the congressional elections of 1866 approached, the battle lines were drawn between the president and the Congress around the Freedman's Bureau bill, the Civil Rights bill, and the Fourteenth Amendment. Reconstruction in the southern states hinged on the results.

Texas Resists Change

As Governor Throckmorton and the new legislature took office in August 1866, they could have charted a course similar to Tennessee's that would have quickly led to Texas's readmission to the Union, but they were distracted—and encouraged—by the developing conflict in Washington. With regard to the more controversial issues of the Thirteenth and Fourteenth Amendments and a labor system, Throckmorton, therefore, took a conservative position, much as he had during the constitutional convention. "Never in the history of any people . . . was so much prudence and discretion required," he wrote. "We must court harmony and good feeling" and repel "the bitter abuse of those who would oppress us." Throckmorton sought, according to one historian, "a rapid, painless restoration of Texas's rightful place in the Union, only a mild restructuring of southern race relations, and magnanimity toward former Confederates."

Throckmorton's recalcitrance on these major issues seemed justified when President Johnson declared in late August that the insurrection in Texas was over. The governor asserted that civil authority was now restored and clashed with bureau agents who tried to protect the freedman in labor contracts and make sure that they received their pay, claiming that the agents were interfering with civil authority. Neither the governor nor the courts did anything to help the freedmen. Devious planters employed various subterfuges to cheat the workers, such as employing a middle man who might abscond without paying the laborers. The planters, of course, would feign innocence in any such scheme. The bureau tried to help, but it was overwhelmed, and the civil courts seemed only to help the planters gain further dominance over the workers.

In the fall of 1866, the Eleventh Legislature convened and not only rejected the Fourteenth Amendment but also appointed a leading secessionist, Oran M. Roberts, to the U.S. Senate and established laws similar to the "black codes" passed in other southern states. One provision placed a lien on one half of a farmer's crop to insure that workers would be paid and permitted workers to break a contract in the event of harsh treatment. But other provisions were nothing more than an effort to control the labor force. Youths between the ages of fourteen and twenty-one could be apprenticed if the parents agreed; wages could be reduced for a myriad of reasons (sickness, unsatisfactory work, and damage to equipment); employees could be fined for a number of acts including "impudence"; and workers had to get permission from the employer to leave the home workplace. Vagrancy laws permitted anyone without a job to be arrested or fined and forced to work on public projects until the fine was paid. The Throckmorton administration, in short, failed to guarantee the rights of freedmen.

Prejudice against the freedmen even in the North greatly influenced efforts to remake southern society. Even staunch Unionists preferred to maintain their political power by disenfranchising former Confederates rather than expanding their political base by extending voting rights to the former slaves. And, while Johnson had initially talked of destroying the planter's economic and political control, his desire to keep blacks as an orderly labor force prevented any real economic reform and ultimately led him to accept the return to power of the planter class.

In Congress, meanwhile, a consensus was emerging. Texans got warning of it when Congress refused to seat Roberts and other members of the Texas delegation, mostly ex-Confederates, when they arrived in Washington in November 1866. None could take the required oath of office. In reflecting upon his experience, Senator-elect Roberts recalled that "the vanguard of the radical party" was the "one body of men who had any positive affirmative ideas. They knew exactly what they wanted to do, and were determined to do it."

Congressional Reconstruction

The 1866 elections proved disastrous for Johnson. Although he actively campaigned on behalf of his programs, his manner offended many. Meanwhile, bloody racial riots broke out in Memphis and New Orleans, further discrediting his policies and appointments. Republicans won a huge victory, garnering enough seats in both houses to more than override a presidential veto. By 1867 Johnson had lost almost all support, and the following year, the House of Representatives impeached him over his attempt to remove the secretary of war. Johnson survived conviction by one vote. The Radical Republican victory was complete. As one observer put it, "The President has no power to control or influence anybody and legislation will be carried on entirely regardless of his opinion or wishes." The attempted return to power of so many ex-Confederates had frightened Southern Unionists, who finally realized that their salvation required the empowerment of freedmen. Congress assumed military control of the southern states and with a series of Reconstruction acts forced them to do what most had failed to do under presidential Reconstruction: involve African American men in the reconstruction of state government and grant freedmen voting rights.

The first Reconstruction Act, passed on March 2, 1867, essentially reestablished military rule in the South. It declared that governments in the former Confederate states were not legal and that the current governments were provisional; it divided the South (except Tennessee, which had approved the Fourteenth Amendment) into five military districts; it required a new state constitution that conformed to the U.S. Constitution and included universal male suffrage; and it required that the first state legislature elected after adoption of the new constitution approve the Fourteenth Amendment, which penalized states for denying adult male citizens the right to vote ("except for participation in rebellion, or other crime").

Two more acts followed, specifying who was disqualified from voting, authorizing military commanders to "suspend or remove" and replace any officeholders in their districts, and making it more difficult for former Confederates to gain a pardon. General Charles Griffin, who had risen to major general as a Union commander during the war, now had federal authority over the Department of Texas and pursued an ambitious agenda of voter registrations, black and white. He repeatedly clashed with Governor Throckmorton, the governor charging that the military was usurping civil authority and Griffin responding that the governor was an obstructionist who refused to use his authority to check the violence against blacks and Unionists. Griffin complained to his superior, General Philip H. Sheridan, and on July 30 Sheridan removed Throckmorton from office. Although Sheridan appointed the seasoned and respected Pease in Throckmorton's stead, this transparent use of military power only hardened many Texans against the occupation.

Like provisional governor Hamilton, Griffin also replaced former Confederate officeholders with Union men. He enforced the congressional voting restriction by which officials, candidates, potential jury members, and even voters had to take the Ironclad Oath. Radical Reconstructionists reasoned that these exclusions were necessary, at least temporarily, to significantly change southern society. Congressman Thaddeus Stevens of Pennsylvania advocated even more radical measures, including disenfranchising large numbers of Southerners and confiscating their land, which might have been distributed to the freedmen.

Such acts would be "intended to revolutionize their feelings and principles," he explained. "This may startle feeble minds and shake weak nerves. So do all great improvements." Such an initiative never gained momentum, however.

Given these major changes, it was no surprise when the February 1868 elections for a new constitutional convention yielded a distinctly different set of delegates from previous conventions. Many Democrats were adamantly opposed to the new convention and simply stayed away from the polls or were barred from voting by the loyalty restriction. For the first time, African American men voted, and voted in large numbers, spurred on by the voter registration campaign administered by the military. Later reports showed that approximately 89 percent of the registered blacks voted, while only 31 percent of the white voters turned out. Ten of the ninety delegates elected were African Americans, the most prominent of whom was probably George T. Ruby. In addition to his work with the Freedman's Bureau, Ruby had served as president of the Union League, an organization effective in involving African Americans in politics. Although a few Democrats were elected, most of the delegates were Republicans who had opposed the old southern leadership in one way or another. Former Governor Hamilton, in something of a shift, now led the moderate Republicans loyal to Pease. Another contingent consisted of Radical Republicans intent on forcing Texans into line with federal mandates and keeping all former Confederates out of power. This group was led by Hamilton's brother, Morgan, and Edmund J. Davis, who was elected president of the convention.

Born in Florida in 1827, Davis had moved to Galveston with his family in 1848. He was admitted to the bar in 1849. In 1853, he became the first district attorney in Brownsville. Governor Pease appointed him district judge in 1856, and Davis served in that capacity until the Civil War began. He supported Sam Houston and took a principled stand against secession in 1861; he fled the state the following year. After visiting with President Lincoln in Washington, Davis received a commission as a colonel in the Union army and recruited the First Texas Cavalry (U.S.). Described by a contemporary as a "tall, gaunt, cold-eyed, rather

Edmund J. Davis, shown here in his federal uniform, was elected governor of Texas after Congress took charge of reconstruction.

commanding figure," he participated in the occupation of Galveston in 1863 and was a member of General Nathaniel P. Banks's unsuccessful Rio Grande campaign, winning the undying hatred of many Confederate Texans in the process. Promoted to brigadier general, Davis commanded General Joseph J. Reynolds's cavalry in the Division of Western Mississippi and was one of those present when Kirby Smith surrendered the Confederate forces in Texas in June 1865.

When the constitutional convention convened in Austin on June 1, 1868, the new Republican Party, a coalition of so-called scalawags, carpetbaggers, conservative Unionists, and African Americans, was clearly in charge. But that did not mean that they all agreed on what to do. In addition to supporting the Fourteenth Amendment, Congress expected the delegates to revisit the *ab initio* question and nullify the original secession decision and any laws that followed from it. Congress also expected them to support the Thirteenth and Fifteenth Amendments, the latter a flat statement that voting rights could not be denied "on account of race, color, or previous condition of servitude." With Davis elected as presiding officer, questions on the *ab initio* issue received most of the attention: Should nullification extend to the initial act of secession? This was more than just a theoretical question: Should the railroads have been permitted to pay off their debt to the state school fund in Confederate money, for example. The radicals favored *ab initio*, while the moderates feared its economic and political consequences and wanted to leave intact all laws that did not conflict with U.S. laws.

Another question that divided the delegates was whether Texas should be split into two states, east and west. Governor Pease said no, that the population could not sustain two governments. But there were delegates from both regions who favored this move as a means of addressing the fact that East Texas remained, in many ways, an extension of the South, whereas West Texas—represented most vocally by the Radical Republicans—had a more iconoclastic population and less reliance on the cotton culture.

When General Ulysses S. Grant, who had led the Union to victory in the war, won the presidency, the Radical Republicans felt affirmed in their vision of a reconstructed Texas, which would have included a new state of West Texas as well as delayed statehood for East Texas because of the continuing hostility there against Reconstruction. The delegates had done some visionary work, particularly in the area of education, setting aside monies from the sale of public lands for a permanent school fund to educate Texas children irrespective of race and color. But they had only a partial draft of a constitution, and that one signed by only half the delegates. General Joseph J. Reynolds, who had replaced General Griffin as commander of the Department of Texas, appointed a committee to take the records of the convention and complete the work.

The document that went before voters in November 1869 both softened the restrictions against former Confederates and, finally, affirmed universal male suffrage irrespective of "race, color, or former condition." It contained the far-reaching public education plan under a state superintendent of public instruction. Perhaps most important was its vision of a centralized government, which was at odds with the Jacksonian democratic ideal that had underpinned Texas politics to this point: That the "common [Anglo] man" had a right to be involved in governmental decisions. The constitution gave great powers to the governor, who would have a longer term—four years—and would now appoint district judges and some key state officials who had previously been chosen by election. As part of the centralization, elections were to be held at the county seats, not in precincts, and county commissioners were eliminated, with justices of the peace taking over county court functions. On the whole, the document embodied the feeling of most Republicans that some controls were still needed to establish a loyal government in Texas and guarantee freedom and equality to the freedman.

At the same time that voters were asked to approve the new constitution, they also voted for new state and county officials. The race for the governor was crucial to the next stage of Reconstruction. Former provisional governor Hamilton announced as a candidate, continuing along the more conservative course that he had adopted during the convention. He opposed the radicals' attempt to form a state of West Texas and even declined to support black suffrage. Davis represented the radical branch of the party and received the support and assistance of General Reynolds, whose cavalry Davis had commanded in the later stages of the war. Continuing to exercise his power over even local appointments, Reynolds saw to it that Davis supporters filled the voter registration boards, which so angered Governor Pease that he resigned in protest in September.

With leading Democrats disenfranchised or disaffected and divided on how to oppose the Republicans, voters approved the document in the November election. For the first time, black candidates appeared on a number of ballots, and two won places in the Texas Senate—Ruby and Matthew Gaines, a Baptist preacher who had been born a slave in Louisiana—and twelve in the Texas House. Charges and countercharges of voter fraud tarnished the elections, but Davis emerged the victor by a narrow margin, helped along by the heavy turnout of African Americans, who recognized in him a champion of a new Texas in which blacks could play roles previously denied them.

Conditions in Texas during Reconstruction

"Times are awful hard now in Texas," according to a young Englishman who had immigrated in 1869. "Money is scarce, land is worth almost nothing . . . things generally are in a state of stagnation." A year later, the census recorded 818,579 people in the state, 93 percent of them living in rural areas in the eastern half of the state. Most famers lived on small plots averaging about thirty acres in size, with the goal of self-sufficiency rather than cash crops. If he produced any surplus tobacco or cotton, he could exchange them for necessities such as salt, cloth, or plowshares, or a luxury such as coffee. Planters faired well after the war. They had lost considerable wealth when the slaves were freed, but most of them had maintained their land and employed their former slaves to work it. Studies of individual counties show that one-third to one-half of the upper 5 percent of the wealthiest residents remained in the elite following the war. The small farmer had prospered in the years before the war, but after the war droughts, depressions in the 1870s and 1890s, and continually low commodity prices kept the farming sector depressed. During this same period, tenant farming and sharecropping increased significantly.

In the absence of railroads, shipping to and from the interior of the state was by wagon or stagecoach, except for the area of northeast Texas around Jefferson. Because of the Red River raft, a massive logjam, the water level in Cypress Bayou had risen to the level that steamboats were able to run between Jefferson and Shreveport and New Orleans on a regular schedule for several years, making Jefferson the sixth largest city in the state (population 4,180 in 1870) and second only to Galveston in total commerce. Steamboat traffic ended soon after 1873, when the Army Corps of Engineers cleared the raft.

These were the circumstances as Davis took charge—Texas was still scarred, battered, undeveloped, divided, and reliant upon the fluctuating price of raw materials. Cotton prices had dropped by almost half since 1866, causing a subsequent drop in land values. There were, however, encouraging signs: The rate of population growth was higher in Texas than in the nation as a whole, largely because thousands migrated from the stricken South; industry was developing; key towns were growing again, with Galveston and San Antonio leading the way; and the 1870 census showed that 60 percent of employed Texans were property-holding farmers, businessmen, professionals, or skilled tradesmen. Merchants and bankers were beginning to take their places among the state's economic elite.

Intensified Violence

But there were also discouraging signs. The continuing violence of the era seemed to intensify. Local and regional feuds erupted, the most extended and murderous being the Sutton–Taylor Feud in DeWitt County. There were also outlaw gangs to contend with, such as that of Cullen Baker, a resident of northeast Texas whose murderous tendencies were well documented before the war. After the conflict, in which he served intermittently as a Confederate soldier, he and his band turned their ire against African Americans and Reconstruction representatives, killing a number of people, including Freedman's Bureau agents in Arkansas and Texas. Other outlaw bands roamed northwest Texas near the Red River and in the Big Thicket country, where desperate men fleeing Confederate conscription had joined them. The resulting violence probably was worse than the Indian raids along much of the frontier.

Meanwhile, the Ku Klux Klan, first formed by Confederate veterans in Tennessee in 1866, had spread to Texas by spring 1868. This secret association, loosely organized in Texas, had among its goals resistance to Reconstruction and restoration of white supremacy. Members throughout eastern Texas—particularly the northeastern region—targeted African Americans, carpetbaggers, scalawags, and Republicans in general. They destroyed crops, stole horses, burned houses, beat and murdered victims, and intimidated local authorities. Some forced former slaves into registering to vote as Democrats. Similar secret organizations arose, promoting a rhetoric of white superiority, the Knights of the Golden Circle, for example, pledging to "maintain and defend the social and political superiority of the White race on this Continent; always and in all places to observe a marked distinction between the White and African races. . . ."

A committee for the 1868–1869 constitutional convention had determined that of the 939 murders reported by county officials between 1865 and 1868, almost half were committed by whites against other whites and 40 percent were committed by whites against blacks. Documentation for the years 1865 to 1871 show that, while 4,425 crimes were reported, there were only 588 arrests and even fewer convictions. Military commander Reynolds had been at least partially effective in prosecuting some of the more flagrant lawless acts, but many other murders and crimes went unreported.

Republicans in Charge

When Davis and Radical Republican legislators took office, they had four goals: return Texas to the Union (which involved assuring civil and political rights for the freedmen), promote public education, encourage railroad construction, and restore law and order. The Twelfth Legislature acted quickly to pull Texas out of Congressional Reconstruction, in part by ratifying the Fourteenth and Fifteenth Amendments. On March 30, 1870, Texas officially returned to the Union. It now had home rule, although there were still many "unreconstructed" Confederates who did not feel that the government represented them.

Railroad construction resumed after the war. The Houston and Texas Central Railway had laid eighty-one miles of track when the war began and it had to suspend construction. It resumed in 1867, building all the way to Red River City (Denison) by 1873, where it connected with the Missouri, Kansas, and Texas, which opened a railroad route from Galveston all the way to St. Louis.

The immediate result was the spread of cotton cultivation into the interior and westward; much of Central and East Texas was capable of cotton production, and only the lack of transportation had limited its spread. Livestock raising and grain cultivation in the counties along the Brazos River valley gave way to cotton production after the arrival of the railroad. Prior to the war, cotton was cultivated mainly on plantations, while the small farmer achieved self-sufficiency by growing wheat, corn, rye, and many different garden crops. Improved transportation meant that the small farmer could raise cotton as a cash crop and buy more of the products that he needed. By 1874, production of cotton had almost reached prewar levels, despite bad weather and the arrival of the cotton worm, which devastated crops during the late 1860s. The growing dominance of cotton was good in prosperous years, but ruinous in bad years, and increasingly linked the state's economy to a single crop.

One of the most far-sighted accomplishments of Davis and the Republican-dominated Twelfth Legislature was the public education system. In 1870–1871 they passed laws establishing a free and compulsory public school system, to be supported with an adequate tax base. Citing the need to bring state and congressional election dates in line, advocates delayed the regular election until November 1872. Because it added another year to their terms, this looked to Democrats and disgruntled Republicans like a power play for Davis and the radicals.

The State Police

A part of Davis's plan to stem the violence was the passage of a militia bill authorizing the governor to declare martial law and order able-bodied males between the ages 18 and 45 into state service, and the establishment of a State Police force in July 1870. The legislation placed the police under the direction of the adjutant general, who reported to the governor. Many of the police were veterans of the war, both North and South; they were white, Mexican, and black. Some had experience as lawmen and, alas, some as criminals. Most all of them were Republicans. Although the legislation authorized a force of 257, there were never more than 200 troopers.

Much to the dismay of the Democrats, Governor Davis immediately sent the police into areas where he proclaimed martial law—to deal with gangs of outlaws in Hill County, Huntsville, and Lampasas. According to one estimate, there were more than 1,500 documented cases of white on black violence from 1865 to 1868. In their first month the police arrested 978 suspects, 109 for murder and 130 for attempted murder. By 1872, arrests totaled 6,820: 587 for murder, 760 for attempted murder, and 1,748 for other felonies. In 1871 alone they arrested 3,602 suspects and recovered $200,000 in stolen property. Despite this laudable record, they became one of the most hated—and misunderstood—organizations in the state. Detractors called them "the Governor's hounds." Many accused them of supporting the Davis military dictatorship, but as Matthew Gaines, one of two black senators during Reconstruction, remarked, the real problem was not the "idea of placing such a great power in the hands of the executive," but the "idea of gentlemen of my color being armed and riding around after desperadoes."

To add further fuel to the fires of resentment, Davis often called out the militia to protect African Americans, mostly against real threats, but at times the Democrats charged that it was for the purpose of political of intimidation his enemies. And the Democrats, with many of their number no longer excluded from voting and holding office, were gaining in power. They continued to resist citizenship rights for African Americans and saw Davis's presence in the governor's mansion as yet another feature of federal Reconstruction. In the elections of 1872, they would be ready.

Black Texans

The growing population, the increased cultivation of a desirable cash crop, the steady growth of cities and towns, and the decreased violence assured that Texas recovered from the war more quickly than the other southern states. While conditions for the black man did not keep pace, there were significant improvements. Of course, the most important change was freedom itself. The modest and conflicting goals of President Johnson's Reconstruction plan encouraged the planter class to hope—and in some cases, assume—that the economic and social conditions would change little and that some form of slavery, such as gradual emancipation, would be coupled with a system of compulsory labor. Even though that was not the case, most blacks took General Granger's advice to remain with their former masters and engaged in agricultural pursuits, either working for wages or as sharecroppers. Perhaps as many as 25 percent left their masters. A smaller percentage farmed their own land in several cotton-belt counties. Some went to work on ranches and on the trail drives; George W. Saunders, a legendary South Texas cattleman, estimated that freedmen constituted 25 percent of the cowboys and drovers in post–Civil War Texas. In East Texas they worked in the burgeoning lumber industry. Others moved to towns, where they sought work as policemen, soldiers, railroad workers, and domestic servants. Although they faced resistance from white artisans, who feared that they would drive wages down, some blacks went into trades. They took jobs on the dock in Galveston and formed their own union in 1870.

A number of black youths attended the Freedman's Bureau schools, but even more attended school after the Twelfth Legislature established a free statewide education system, segregated, but with compulsory attendance for children between the ages of five and eighteen. One estimate concluded that 129,542 students enrolled in school in 1872–1873, approximately 56 percent of all the school-age children in the state, and that one-fourth to one-third of them were black students. The African Methodist Episcopal Church in Austin established Paul Quinn College in 1872 as an elementary and secondary school, and the following year the Texas Conference of the Methodist Episcopal Church founded Wiley College in Marshall.

Perhaps most important, freedmen began immediately to establish their families, which had been virtually impossible under slavery. The Constitution of 1868–1869 recognized their marriages and their parental rights. By 1870, more than three-quarters of blacks lived in a traditional family situation headed by a father, about the same percentage as whites. The freedmen also established their own churches, despite the opposition of many whites, who saw the churches as nothing more than organizations to nurture discontent. Embracing the evangelical style of worship so popular in Texas, most blacks attended Baptist or Methodist churches, often associated with the denominations where they had worshiped as slaves. Their congregations were separate, but they sometimes shared a building with a white congregation. The black churches quickly became the center of the black community, providing social, educational, and political activities.

 **Indian Policy**

When the U.S. military withdrew from the West Texas forts as the war began, one resident predicted that the "Indians will run rough shod over this country." Some settlers immediately left their homes and moved to the relative safety of more settled areas; others moved closer to their neighbors. Governor Francis R. Lubbock quickly organized Frontier Regiments in an effort to replace the military, and the Confederacy sent a representative, Albert Pike, to negotiate a peace treaty with the Comanches in August 1861. Pike asked only that the Comanches "prepare to support themselves, and live in peace and quietness" in return for annuities and permission to hunt in the west, which, some historians have pointed out, would have required that the Comanches cease being Comanches.

The annuities were important, for a long-running drought had reached its sixteenth year as the treaty was signed, the bison herds had diminished, and a smallpox epidemic in 1862 killed many members of the tribe. Caught between Confederate Texas and Union New Mexico, the Comanches maintained the appearance of neutrality and adroitly played one off against the other while continuing to collect provisions from both sides. The following year, the U.S. Senate rejected a proposed treaty with the Comanches and Kiowas that sent them raiding once again. They had learned from a few probing forays that there were fewer soldiers and rangers on the frontier than there had been. They stole large numbers of horses and cattle along the Texas frontier, which they sold to Union contractors in New Mexico. Governor Lubbock appealed to the Confederacy for aid, but Brigadier General John B. Magruder, commander of the Department of Texas, saw little Indian threat and continued to divert troops to the eastern theater. Meanwhile, the state defense units, the Frontier Regiment, and later, the Frontier Organization, maintained the peace at least as well as the antebellum army had.

Postbellum Negotiations

With the collapse of the Confederacy in 1865, U.S. peace commissioners met with eleven Comanche chiefs on the Little Arkansas River in present-day southern Kansas and signed the Treaty of Little Arkansas. The commissioners were willing to sacrifice Texas land to pacify the frontier and promised the Comanches a vast swath of territory including western Oklahoma, the panhandles of Oklahoma and Texas, and a triangular patch of western Texas below the Panhandle. In return, the Indians were to live in peace, return all captives, and allow military forts to be established on their land. It was the first time that the government had recognized a Comanche claim to land.

With the treaty in place, U.S. officers stationed most of their troops in the populated areas of Texas and along the Rio Grande, where the French invasion of Mexico had created some concern. As a result, the frontier forts were not reoccupied until the late 1860s—only two cavalry regiments were assigned to the Comanche frontier—and many Texans had not yet returned from the war. This seemed to create the perfect situation for a Comanche resurgence as herds of unprotected cattle roamed free with only a depleted workforce to defend them. By 1867, Texans estimated that 162 people had been killed and forty-three abducted and that they had lost 4,000 horses and 30,000 cattle, many of which the Comanches had traded to the Comancheros, Hispanic traders, in New Mexico. The Comanches once again extended their raids into Mexico and eastward into New Mexico. Governor Throckmorton watched in dismay as the entire western frontier seemed to collapse. Federal authorities refused to respond because they thought he was exaggerating the situation. "The murders that have been committed on our frontier are so frequent that they are only noticed by their friends and acquainted as they would notice ones dying a natural death," one official explained.

Other well-publicized incidents—the San Creek Massacre in 1864 and the Fetterman Massacre in 1866, among others—helped bring about a reconsideration of U.S. Indian policy and created a split between the army and the Bureau of Indian Affairs. Perhaps daunted by the bloody Civil War, the public now seemed to support a more humanitarian policy toward the Indians, and Congress created the Indian Peace Commission, which met with representatives of five Plains tribes at Medicine Lodge Creek, sixty miles south of Fort Larned, Kansas, in October 1867. The commissioners offered cash and the usual gifts and annuities but wanted to limit the Comanches and Kiowas to a 5,500-square-mile reservation, rather than let them roam the western frontier of Texas. The Indians were furious, for they were being asked to give up more than 140,000 square miles of territory that been awarded to them in the Treaty of Little Arkansas, which also had prohibited white settlement on these lands. Eventually, all five tribes signed the agreement, but the question of land ownership remained ambiguous. The commissioners understood that the Indians had given up their claim to the land, but could still hunt there "so long as the buffalo may range thereon in such numbers as to justify the chase." The Indians left with the understanding that they could roam their traditional hunting grounds and still use the reservation more as a seasonal supply base. To them being able to hunt on land was tantamount to what the U.S. commissioners thought of as owning it.

With little help available from the federal government, the Twelfth Legislature created a frontier force of 1,200 men to be divided into twenty ranging companies to protect the frontier. Because Davis had not sold the bonds to pay for the force by the end of 1870, his administration disbanded the ranging companies and organized, instead, twenty-four companies of minutemen who could be called up when needed. They were to be employed against the Comanches, Kiowas, and others in northwest Texas and the Kickapoos along the Rio Grande, who raided across the international boundary, then retreated to their reservations in Mexico, where they had the protection of the Mexican government.

While results are hard to measure, the frontier defense seemed to discourage raids on frontier communities.

In 1869, the new Grant administration brought further change to Indian policy. The new Peace Policy emphasized Christian education over force and employed Protestant missionaries as Indian agents. Lawrie Tatum, an Iowa Quaker, took charge of the Comanche and Kiowa agency at Fort Sill, just north of the Red River. The Indians took this new policy as confirmation of their traditional habits. They hunted, traded, and raided on the Plains during the year, and in the winter returned to the reservation. The Peace Policy considered the reservations to be demilitarized zones where no arrests could be made, although, had Tatum been able to identify any raiders, he would have at least withheld their rations. The military quickly became disenchanted with this policy. General Sheridan explained, "If a white man commits murder or robs, we hang him or send him to the penitentiary; if an Indian does the same, we have been in the habit of giving him more blankets."

Sherman's Investigation

The Indian raids had grown to the extent that Governor Davis accused the army of failing to protect the Texas frontier and organized seven new ranger companies. The secretary of war called for an investigation, and William T. Sherman, who had succeeded President Grant as commanding general of the Army, decided to conduct it himself. Sherman still tended to discredit reports of Indian raids, believing that many were the work of white men disguised as Indians. With a small, seventeen-man escort, he followed the Butterfield Overland Mail route to Fort Richardson, near Jacksboro on the northwest Texas frontier. Arriving on May 18, he learned that more than 100 Indians had attacked a twelve-man wagon train that had followed him by only a few hours. The details were gruesome. They had killed seven teamsters, chaining one to a wagon wheel and setting him on fire.

Sherman was furious. The Indians had let his party pass, choosing to attack the more poorly defended freighters. He immediately dispatched Colonel Ranald S. Mackenzie, commander of the Fourth Cavalry at Fort Richardson, to search for perpetrators. With new respect for marauding Indians, Sherman left Fort Richardson on May 20 for Fort Sill, riding in his ambulance with a Winchester rifle on his lap.

When Sherman arrived at Fort Sill, he learned that the Kiowa Satanta had bragged of the attack to Tatum. Sherman interviewed the Indian himself and arrested him on the spot, along with Satank and Big Tree, whom Satanta had implicated in the attack. A fourth leader, Big Bow, got away. Mackenzie took the three Indians to Jacksboro to be tried in a civil court, but Satank was killed en route when he pulled a knife and injured one of the guards in an escape attempt. The other two were tried and sentenced to be hanged. President Grant and other federal officials, including Tatum, appealed to Governor Davis to commute their sentence, arguing that holding the two chiefs hostage might do more to quell the violence than executing them. After visiting with Tatum and tribal leaders at Fort Sill, Davis agreed and sent the chiefs to prison in Huntsville. Two years later, he bowed to federal arguments that Texas had no jurisdiction over the two Indians because they were not citizens and pardoned them.

In the fall of 1871, Sherman, now convinced of the seriousness of the reports, ordered Colonel Mackenzie to lead the battle-hardened troops of the Fourth Cavalry and the Eleventh Infantry into the Llano Estacado and stop the raids. Mackenzie marched through Blanco Canyon into the eastern Llano, pushing the Comanches deep onto the Plains until winter weather forced him to interrupt the operation. He was back again the following spring, avoiding major engagements, yet disrupting the Indians' seasonal activities. In September 1872, he ambushed a large village on the North Fork of the Red River, forcing the Indians back to the reservation.

The Slaughter of the Buffalo

Meanwhile, an equally effective assault of another kind was underway. The transcontinental railroad, completed in 1869, had divided the great American bison herd into two huge groups, one north of the railroad and the other south. The southern herd ranged deep into Texas, coming into contact with the advancing cattle and farming frontier—and with white hunters, the deadliest killers that the bison had yet encountered. J. Wright Mooar, a Kansas buffalo hunter, glimpsed the potential of the buffalo trade in 1871 when he sent fifty-seven hides to relatives in New York with instructions to try to sell them. A Philadelphia tanner purchased the lot for $200. When the hides proved to make fine leather, he gave the Mooar brothers an order for 2,000 more, and by the mid-1870s there

Texas State Library and Archives Commission, Austin, Texas

Photographer George Robertson of Austin accompanied several buffalo hunters into Taylor County in 1874 and documented the hunt.

were, perhaps, 3,000 buffalo hunters roaming the Texas Panhandle in search of what was left of the once great southern herd. The slaughter that would bring the American bison almost to extinction had begun.

Previously, the Plains Indians depended upon the bison for every aspect of their lives, and white men had killed them for sport and food, primarily for the crews building the transcontinental railroads. Now, the hunters slaughtered them for their hides, which could be quickly converted into cash. They left the carcasses on the ground to rot. "No mercy was shown the buffalo," plainsman and Indian fighter Billy Dixon recalled of his 1874 hunt. "I killed as many as my three men [skinners] could handle, working them as hard as they were willing to work. This was deadly business, without sentiment; it was dollars against tender-heartedness, and dollars won."

The buffalo hunters were engaged in an unprecedented slaughter of what General Sheridan had called the "Indians' commissary," and he concluded that they had "done more in the last two years and will do more in the next year to settle the vexed Indian question than the entire regular army has done in the last 30 years."

After the hunters came the "bone pickers." Northern industries had been using buffalo bones for buttons, combs, and knife handles for some time, but they soon realized that the bones could also be ground into meal or charred and used to remove the color from sugar. Fresh bones also provided calcium phosphate ash for bone china furnaces. By the mid-1870s, bone pickers got from $7 to $9 per ton for bones and $12 to $15 for hooves and horns. And the prairie was littered with the bleached bones of the millions of animals that the hunters had killed and left to rot. Pickers hauled wagonloads of bones to the railroad right of way and stacked them to be shipped, some of the mounds reaching a height of sixteen feet and stretching for half a mile. Looking from the window of his Dallas office in 1877, forty-two-year-old attorney John M. McCoy saw "great loads of Buffalo Hides and cotton constantly coming in." Texas led the world in bone production for a brief period during the early 1880s, and prices got as high as $22 to $23 per ton. Within a few years, however, the bone pickers had gathered virtually all of the bison skeletons, and by the turn of the century, industries returned to using cow bones.

In the spring of 1874, the Comanches found the Plains littered with the skinned, rotting carcasses and bones of thousands of buffaloes. The spring hunts, carried out in the midst of dozens of white hunters, yielded few kills, and the Plains Indians faced starvation. Inspired by the charismatic medicine man Isa-tai, various tribes gathered on Elk Creek near the North Fork of the Red River, to consider their future. They concluded that they must drive the hunters from the Plains, and on June 27 more than 700 Comanche, Cheyenne, and Kiowa warriors under the leadership of Quanah Parker, the son of the kidnapped Cynthia Ann Parker and Chief Peta Nocona, and Isa-tai attacked a camp of buffalo hunters at Adobe Walls, northeast of what is today Borger. The well-armed hunters repelled the Indians, who then laid siege, but Quanah was wounded and when a stray shot killed Isa-tai's horse, the Indians lost confidence in him and gave up the siege.

Indians of all three tribes fled their reservations and took refuge on the Staked Plains of the Texas Panhandle, the heart of the remaining Comanche

Chief Quanah Parker and the Comanches were defeated in the Red River War of 1875 and forced to move to reservations in Indian Territory.

domain. Army columns advanced from five directions. Because the Indians were elusive and would fight only under favorable conditions, the army fought few battles, but resorted to brutal tactics such as slaughtering their horses, ravaging their villages, and confiscating food and weapons—anything the Indians needed to survive. The worst blow was Colonel Mackenzie's surprise attack on a camp in Palo Duro Canyon in September. Few Indians were killed, but Mackenzie captured 1,400 horses and most of the Indians' winter food supply. He gave several hundred horses to his Indian scouts and then ordered the others slaughtered. So relentlessly the army harassed the Indians through the winter of 1874–1875 that most returned to their reservations and surrendered. The Red River War ended Indian hostilities on the southern Plains and brought to a close the conflict that had raged along the Texas frontier for more than fifty years. West Texas was now open to ranchers and farmers, which set the state on a different course from the other southern states.

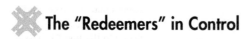 The "Redeemers" in Control

In preparation for the congressional elections of 1871, when all four Texas congressmen were on the ballot, the Democratic Party in Texas reorganized itself, hoping to lure former supporters back into the fold as well as appeal to the many recent immigrants. The Reconstruction amendments and black suffrage were no longer issues, and they no longer felt the need to seek the support of conservative Republicans. At their January convention, they emphasized traditional Democratic issues such as states' rights and the alleged corruption and centralization of power of the Davis administration. They noted with approval that the Hamilton and Pease wing of the Republican Party was splitting away from Davis.

The Democrats focused on the school system, perhaps because it was the largest item in the state's budget. The Davis administration had organized a totally new system in one year at a cost of $1.2 million; the most the state had spent on education in prior years was $100,000. The Democrats criticized the system itself, claiming that compulsory attendance was a violation of personal freedom and that the Republicans used the new administrative and teaching jobs as bribes for party loyalty. The culmination of the campaign was a Taxpayers' Convention held in Austin in September 1871, two weeks before the election. Former governor Pease presided as the Democrats accused Davis of exercising "despotic power" and perpetrating a "violation of nearly every private right of the citizen." In sum, the delegates concluded, "The . . . people of the State no longer govern themselves, but are governed by E. J. Davis, as completely as if there were no Constitutions, State or Federal." The new Democratic newspaper in Austin, the *Democratic Statesman,* kept the charges before the public.

The Republicans also realized that they needed to appeal to the recent immigrants, especially since the "Ironclad Oath" was no longer required for voters. Most of these recent arrivals had come from southern states, so the Republicans had to change their strategy. They claimed that they were the party of the common man; they no longer talked of social and political equality and largely took the freedmen's vote for granted in their effort to attract the new voters. They took credit for quelling the violence, establishing order, and opening public schools, which provided education and opportunity for all. They admitted that they had to raise the taxes of wealthier people in the process, but, in the words of Governor Davis, who campaigned for the party in a last desperate effort, "if you have public schools and law and order, you must pay for it." Executive committee chairman James G. Tracy invoked the common man again when he explained that, even if some landowners had to sell their property because they could not afford the taxes, it would "equalize the possession of the soil which God intended not for a few but for all mankind."

The Democrats, who had managed to greatly increase their constituency, won overwhelmingly. White men again resorted to violence and intimidation in several counties. The editor of the *Neches Valley News* in Beaumont crowed,

"[T]he people of Southeast Texas have done handling political issues with gloves and intend to do their share in tearing down and uprooting the government policy implemented by Eastern fanatics." The greatest outbreak occurred in the Third District, and Davis declared martial law in Limestone and Freestone counties, but the election was so devastating to Republican hopes that, when the Twelfth Legislature convened for its last session in September, they began to undo their own programs. They cut back on the frontier force, trimmed the public school budget, and abolished the county's authority to raise certain special taxes.

Davis's Defeat

Democrats prepared to "redeem" the state, and Davis struggled to keep the Republican Party from collapsing. The fall 1872 elections completed the rout: Democratic candidate Richard Coke, a Waco lawyer, Confederate veteran, and district and state judge under Presidential Reconstruction, decisively defeated Davis. The Democrats won a majority in the House and overwhelming election victories throughout the state. Where the Republicans had held fifty-five seats in the House, they now held only twelve. Where they had a thin majority in the Senate, they were now in the minority. The Democrats did not win enough Senate seats to override a gubernatorial veto only because two-thirds of the seats were not up for election. In part, the election reflected the disenchantment of former Davis supporters, some of whom had participated in the Taxpayers' Convention.

No doubt, intimidation of black voters continued to play a role, but there was a more sinister element that crept into the campaign. As it became apparent that the old elite had maintained control of the Democratic Party, poor whites objected to the party's generous support of the railroads and even proposed organizing a "people's movement" to represent their interests. In response, Democratic spokesmen argued that Davis was the black man's candidate and that whites must sacrifice their economic interests for the sake of racial unity. The success of this argument clearly reflected the continuing and growing southern sentiment among Anglos, both those who were in Texas before the war and those new immigrants who arrived after the war.

But the governor still had supporters, and they quickly identified issues on which they felt they could challenge the elections. They argued before the state Supreme Court that the constitution required that elections should be held at the county seats "until otherwise provided by law; and the polls shall be opened for four days." The constitution had been violated because the legislature had ordered that the polls be open for only one day. On January 5, 1874, the Court agreed with the Davis supporters that the election was illegal, thereby voiding results not only in the governor's race but also of all the other races and opening the door to legal challenges to any actions the new slate of elected officers might take.

Davis had not been involved in the court challenge, but he felt obliged to uphold the rulings of the attorney general and the Supreme Court even as the

Democrats proceeded with plans to convene the legislature and inaugurate Coke. The Democrats rejected the attorney general's opinion and openly defied the court decision, forcing Davis to acquiesce or use force. Although Davis called up units of the state militia, he did not have the military power to stop the Democrats and telegraphed President Grant to request military intervention to keep the peace until the political situation could be resolved.

The president replied that domestic violence as defined in the Constitution did not exist, that the elections had been conducted with the approval of the governor and both political parties, and that it would be "prudent, as well as right, to yield to the verdict of the people as expressed by their ballots." Without support from the federal government, Davis had no choice but to vacate the office.

The scope of the Republican defeat was apparent when the Thirteenth Legislature convened on January 13, and the Republicans joined the Democrats in abolishing more of Davis's agenda. They eliminated the state police force, which had a mixed record but did a great deal to defend the rights of the former slaves. They changed some of the governor's appointive offices to elective and repealed his power to declare martial law. They permitted voting to be moved back to precincts, and broke up the school system, shifting much authority to local school boards. By the elections of November 1873, virtually the only Radical Republicans still in office were the remnants of radical home rule serving out their terms.

As a political player and as governor, Davis had been punitive and controlling, but he had also been genuinely concerned with the law, with the problems of post–Civil War Texas, and with the rights of freed African Americans. He befriended several black leaders, including Norris Wright Cuney of Galveston, who much later became the chair of the state Republican executive committee. Even his moderate detractors acknowledged what they called "the unseemly advances of the Negro" under his administration. Their racist rhetoric and their desire to overturn progressive Reconstruction policies were apparent, yet they were sincere in their embrace of a theoretically more balanced and less centralized government.

Coke and his supporters lost no time in consolidating their power, placing Democrats in district judge positions and all five positions on a new state Supreme Court. The revision or replacement of the Republican-dominated Constitution of 1869 would take more time. In particular, Democrats wanted to abolish the centralized powers that the Republicans had established; they wanted to limit the governor's and the legislature's authority and to do away with the voter registration provisions that had kept many of them from the ballot box.

The Constitution of 1876

It is surprising that it took the "Redeemers" until 1876 to rewrite the 1869 constitution that many considered the tool of the Radical Republicans. The Fourteenth Legislature assigned a commission to write a new constitution by making a few key changes to the Constitution of 1869, but that smacked too much of the

Republicans' centralization of power, and the draft failed to pass either house of the legislature. The reason Governor Coke gave for the delaying a constitutional convention was that the state did not have enough money, which portended the mood of the ninety delegates who gathered in Austin in September 1875. The majority agrarian population was represented by forty-one farmers, the largest bloc at the convention, almost all of whom belonged to a newly formed organization, the Patrons of Husbandry, or the "Grange," a cooperative to protect and improve the lives of farm families who were feeling threatened in their livelihoods and increasingly marginalized after the economic Panic of 1873. Twenty-one lawyers also served in the convention. Seventy-five of the delegates declared themselves as Democrats, while there were fifteen Republicans, six of whom were African Americans. A number of the delegates had served as officers in the Confederate army; there were also a few U.S. Army veterans.

The Democrats, who valued the Jacksonian philosophy of limited government and low taxes, considered the Republicans to be spendthrifts, for they had left the state $2,418,626 in debt when Davis left office, a total that was inflated by bonds issued to cover expenses after the taxpayer revolt cut anticipated revenues. The Democrats patterned the new document after the Constitution of 1845, but imposed even more restrictions on the power of the governor and returned to local governments many functions that the Republicans had centralized. The delegates reduced the governor's term from four years to two, removed the power to declare martial law, and to fill vacancies without the approval of the Senate. Nor did the governor have any constitutional control over five of the other six members of the executive branch. The convention made the lieutenant governor, comptroller, treasurer, commissioner of the land office, and attorney general elective offices. Only the secretary of state remained an appointive office.

The delegates mandated biennial sessions of the legislature; members of the House of Representatives served the usual two-year terms, but the convention reduced Senate terms from six years to four and made all judicial offices elective rather than appointive. They included a homestead exemption protecting family homes and limited acreage from forced sale, reflecting both Mexican precedent and the "pro-debtor, anti-bank" attitudes long held by Texans. The delegates showed their distrust of corporate power by a ban on state-chartered banks and in attempts to regulate the railroads by declaring them "common carriers," delegating authority to the legislature to set limits on freight and passenger rates.

Perhaps most significant, the new constitution dismantled the public school system that the Republicans had established. Arguing that parents should be responsible for the education of their children, delegates abolished the office of state superintendent and returned authority for the schools to the local communities, but provided them with no authority to tax to pay for them. In part, white landowners, who resented the idea that they would have to pay taxes to educate black children, joined with agrarians who objected to taxes in general and to required attendance in specific because their children engaged in seasonal farm work. Thus began a tradition of inadequate funding for public schools. The convention did set aside public lands to establish a permanent school fund, but it revoked an 1858 grant of 3 million acres given for the establishment of the University of Texas and replaced it with 1 million acres of unclaimed land in West Texas. (Fortunately, in 1923 this land would prove to contain some of the largest oil fields in the state.)

The constitution is probably a fair reflection of the feeling of most Texans in 1876. It mirrored their distrust of a central government and placed such severe restrictions on the government that, even today, changes to almost any aspect of government or legislative power require an amendment to the constitution. It was a reaction to the recent experience of Reconstruction, but ultimately, it also reflected an old agrarian outlook, with vestiges of the old plantation South, depending for its definitions on a rather homogenous population engaged primarily in independent farming. It is still in force today, but has been amended more than 470 times and is considered to be one of the most confusing and disorganized documents of any state.

Ironically, the new constitution did not stir much interest on the part of the voters—perhaps because its adoption was a foregone conclusion—and not even the state Democratic convention officially endorsed it. Still, voters approved it by a more than two-to-one margin. The electorate subsequently defeated the only two serious attempts, in 1919 and 1975, to adopt a constitution more attuned to the needs of a modern state.

Conclusion

Congressional Reconstruction had two goals: to bring the former Confederate states back into the Union, and to assure equal political and civil rights for the freedmen. Southerners met the first goal, but failed in the second. As a state—as a southern state—Texas had cast its lot with the Confederacy and on the wrong side of history. The resulting war had temporarily drained the state of much of its manpower and, despite the Rio Grande trade, retarded growth and development. It had also fed serious divisions, both between the North and South and among Texans. The extent of these divisions became abundantly clear in the troubled decades following the war. As the federal government sought to "reconstruct" the southern states, first with fairly mild measures, then with more stringent ones, Texans had to deal with circumstances outside the familiar conditions of antebellum life. For the first time, African Americans as a group sought opportunity as free men, but found little, as the old elite viciously reasserted a racial caste system. In the words of historian and civil rights leader W. E. B. Du Bois, "The slave went free; stood a brief moment in the sun; then moved back again toward slavery."

As modernizing influences began to alter old understandings, many Texans became concerned about a future in which agriculture, which had been their livelihood, no longer seemed to offer the prosperity of the prewar years. Cotton prices slid downward during the Panic of 1873, and entire families of blacks as well as poor whites found themselves locked into the pernicious system of share-cropping. A few Texans were beginning to move into the drier areas of the state, areas that initially seemed less suited to agriculture and that called for a different identity, a western one.

As Texas came out of Congressional Reconstruction, railroad construction took off, linking Texas markets and culture with other parts of the nation, especially the burgeoning Midwest, while sea routes from Galveston connected the state with traders and merchants in New Orleans and the Northeast. Manufacturing began to develop in the state, most of it initially connected to farming, but sawmills, textile mills, and iron smelters and foundries constituted the initial stages of industrialization. Towns were becoming cities, the largest, Galveston, boasting not only colleges, banks, theaters, and concert halls, but such modern amenities as street cars and gas lights. More and more, Texas would become firmly linked culturally and economically to the rest of the nation. But it continued to carry the burden of its southern legacy, reinforced by the Reconstruction experience, in attitudes toward government, political parties, and race well into the twentieth century.

Suggested Readings

Reconstruction

The best general work on Reconstruction is Eric Foner's *Reconstruction: America's Unfinished Revolution, 1863–1877* (1988). General works on Reconstruction in Texas start with the Charles W. Ramsdell conservative classic, *Reconstruction in Texas* (1910), but there are various reassessments, including Carl Moneyhon's *Republicanism in Reconstruction Texas* (1980) and *Texas after the Civil War: The Struggle of Reconstruction* (2004) and Randolph B. Campbell's *Grass-Roots Reconstruction in Texas, 1865–1880* (1997). The *New Handbook of Texas* has an excellent entry on Reconstruction and useful entries on the constitutional conventions and constitutions produced in this period. For biographies of the period, see John L. Waller, *Colossal Hamilton of Texas* (1968); Kenneth Wayne Howell, *Texas Confederate, Reconstruction Governor: James Webb Throckmorton* (2008); and Moneyhon, *Edmund J. Davis of Texas: Civil War General, Republican Leader, Reconstruction Governor* (2010).

African American Leaders

For information on African American leaders in Reconstruction, see Alwyn Barr and Robert A. Calvert, *Black Leaders: Texans for Their Times* (1981); James M. Smallwood, *Time of Hope, Time of Despair: Black Texans during Reconstruction* (1981); Merline Pitre, *Through Many Dangers, Toils, and Snares: The Black Leadership of Texas, 1868–1900* (1985); Carl Moneyhon, "George T. Ruby and African

American Politics during Reconstruction" in Haynes and Wintz, pp. 260–269; and Lawrence D. Rice, *The Negro in Texas, 1874–1900* (1971).

Indian Policy

Information on the Indian wars may be found in Rupert Norval Richardson, *The Comanche Barrier to South Plains Settlement: A Century and a Half of Savage Resistance to the Advancing White Frontier* (1933); William H. Lecke, *Military Conquest of the Southern Plains* (1963); Robert Wooster, *Soldiers, Sutlers, and Settlers: Garrison Life on the Texas Frontier* (1987); Pekka Hämäläinen, *The Comanche Empire* (2008); and S. C. Gwynne, *Empire of the Summer Moon: Quanah Parker and the Rise and Fall of the Comanches, the Most Powerful Indian Tribe in American History* (2010). For the battle of Adobe Walls, see T. Lindsay Baker, Billy R. Harrison, and B. Byron Price, *Adobe Walls: The History and Archaeology of the 1874 Trading Post* (2001).

Life in Texas during Reconstruction

An interesting view of Texas life in this period is provided by Robert J. Robertson, *Her Majesty's Texans: Two English Immigrants in Reconstruction Texas* (1998). The endemic violence is discussed in Barry A. Crouch's "White Violence in Reconstruction Texas" in Haynes and Wintz, pp. 252–260; William L. Richter's *Overreached on All Sides: The Freedmen's Bureau Administrators in Texas, 1865–1868* (1991); and Crouch's *The Freedmen's Bureau and Black Texans* (1992). Ralph A. Wooster's "Wealthy Texans, 1870" examines economic, political, and social power in Wooster and Calvert's *Texas Vistas*, pp. 75–186. See also William L. Richter, *The Army in Texas during Reconstruction: 1865–1870* (1987).

A good study of the end of Radical Reconstruction is Carl H. Moneyhon's "Edmund J. Davis in the Coke–Davis Election Dispute of 1874: A Reassessment of Character" in *Southwestern Historical Quarterly* (1996).

Creating an Infrastructure, 1876–1898

In July 1873, the *North Texas Epitomist* published what became known as the "tarantula map," which showed Fort Worth, a former army post on the Clear Fork of the Trinity River, as a regional center with rail lines (spider legs) extending in every direction. Cattle buyers, professional people, and merchants moved to the city with the understanding that it would soon become a railhead. As Texas began to recover from the economic impact of the Civil War and Reconstruction, the cattle drives up the Chisholm Trail brought thousands of Longhorns through Fort Worth, and the "cow town" began to grow. In the spring of 1873, 116 new buildings were erected, and forty new stores opened within one week.

Then came the Panic of 1873, one of the worst economic depressions that the country had seen. It began when one of the most respected firms on Wall Street, Jay Cooke and Company, failed. The New York stock market closed for ten days in September; a month later trail drivers arriving in Kansas either found no market for their herds or had to sell at a considerable loss. As the shock waves spread across the country, the Texas & Pacific (T&P) Railway, which had expected to reach Fort Worth that year, stopped construction at Eagle Ford, six miles west of Dallas, and Fort Worth's overnight boom turned just as quickly into a bust. Dozens of businesses closed and hundreds of economic refugees flooded the wagon road east to Dallas as Fort Worth's population dropped from an estimated 4,000 to approximately 1,000. One of the apparently bitter defectors, newly arrived in Dallas, told the editor of the *Dallas Daily Herald* that Fort Worth was so desolate that "a panther . . . wandered at his own sweet will during the night through the streets" and that the "terror-stricken natives" found the monster's tracks the next morning, where he had slept undisturbed in the business district, which was as quiet as a cemetery.

Refusing to accept defeat, Fort Worth citizens took matters into their own hands. In 1875 they formed the Tarrant County Construction Company to grade the railroad bed so that the T&P could lay the track, and the city gradually began to recover its confidence. The T&P track had to reach Fort Worth by the time the legislature adjourned the following spring in order to receive the 15-million-acre land grant that the state had promised. As the deadline drew near, Tarrant County employed 100 laborers to prepare the roadbed and called for volunteers to assist in the effort; the T&P sent 300 mule teams and 1,000 men to lay the track. The legislature extended the deadline thirty days past adjournment, but Fort Worth did not need it. The track was finally completed on July 18, and the first train arrived the next day, to be greeted by a huge crowd, a twelve-piece band, and a photographer to document the occasion.

Most people in the city had pitched in to meet the deadline, and now they were ready to celebrate. As businesses returned—many boasting the word "panther" in their names as a proud response to the Dallas newspaper article—Fort Worth became a shipping center for cattle, buffalo hides and bones, lumber, cotton, and groceries and a supply depot for the cattle trade as well as expansion into West Texas. As the railroads expanded during the last quarter of the nineteenth century, they brought similar economic benefits to every region of the state, adding essential framework in the infrastructure of a developing state.

CHAPTER 10 Toward Modernization, 1876–1898	
1870s	Windmills in widespread use in West Texas
1874	Invention of barbed wire
1874–75	Indian wars end
1875	Scott Joplin moves to Texarkana with his family
1876	State adopts present constitution; the Agricultural and Mechanical College (now Texas A&M University) opens
1877	The Compromise of 1877 ends Reconstruction; Texas Farmers Alliance established
1883	Cowboy Strike in the Panhandle; University of Texas opens in Austin
1885	Open range trail drives decline
1888	New Texas state capitol inaugurated
1891	Texas Railroad Commission established
1898	Spanish–American War; Texas public domain exhausted

Although the last quarter of the nineteenth century was dominated by agrarians, who constituted the large majority of the state's population and controlled the writing of the 1876 constitution, it also saw the beginnings of industrialization and the birth of the modern state. During these years, the large majority of people in Texas still earned their living from the land, and many joined organizations such as the Patrons of Husbandry, or the Grange, and the Farmers' Alliance. But these years also witnessed a tripling of the state's population, a huge increase in industrial output, the birth of labor unions, and unprecedented growth in railroads (pushing the state from twenty-eighth in miles of track in 1870 to first in 1904), and the return to power of the old elite as represented in the Democratic Party. This was what economic historian Walt Rostow called the "take-off" phase of industrialization that occurred between 1843 and 1900 in the United States but several decades later in Texas, and constituted the framework for the infrastructure of the developing modern state.

The one development tool that Texas had in 1870 was the same one that it had in 1836—millions of acres of land. To populate this sparsely settled domain, the state established the Texas Bureau of Immigration in 1871 to encourage new settlers. The bureau was abolished in 1876, but only after its generous land grant policies had a significant impact. Immigrants—blacks as well as whites—poured in, mostly from the southern states, such as Arkansas, Alabama, Mississippi, and Tennessee that had been devastated by the Civil War. By 1900 the population had grown to 3,048,710, with almost 83 percent still living in rural areas, but the state's established cultural patterns remained largely intact.

At the same time, however, Texas began to industrialize. The value of the state's manufactured items increased from one-fourth of the gross farm income in 1870 to one-half in 1900. But more people probably were involved in nonfarm sectors of the economy than the raw census data would suggest. In 1860, for example, although 89 percent of the people lived in rural areas, only 59 percent of all Texans considered themselves to be involved in agricultural pursuits. Ten percent claimed to be involved in manufacturing, and 11 percent pursued one of the professions, owned or worked for a business, or worked in transportation. By 1870 the average sawmill was larger, and a number of them had begun to specialize, for example, in planing lumber. This chapter will examine how these transformations took place.

As you read this chapter, consider the following questions:

1. Why did the cowboy become such a popular American figure?
2. Were the railroads a positive or negative influence on the Texas economy?
3. Why did the Populists fail to capture the governor's office in 1894 or 1896?

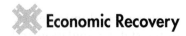 Economic Recovery

Three major changes occurred in the 1870s that greatly influenced the economic development of the state. The first was the adoption of the agrarian-dominated constitution in 1876, which enabled, but did not necessarily encourage, Texans to create the infrastructure for industrialization. Reeling from what they considered an abusive and dictatorial Republican government under Reconstruction, the agrarian Democrats and ex-Confederates did all they could to ensure that taxes would remain low and the government weak. The delegates took advantage of the huge public domain that the state possessed to continue the cheap land policy that the state had been following.

The second major change that occurred in the 1870s was expansion into West Texas. The invention of barbed wire and the windmill and the displacement of Native American population enabled settlers to claim and farm public lands. Preemption (whereby an individual already living on a tract of land is permitted to purchase it from the state) and homestead grants and cheap land policies made acquisition of land relatively easy until 1898, when the Texas Supreme Court declared the public domain to be exhausted.

Finally, during this period, Texas was able to accumulate enough capital to accommodate huge projects such as the construction of railroad tracks, the improvement of port facilities, and the growth of large businesses, including the state's first multimillion-dollar corporation.

The End of the Indian Wars

The railroad was bringing change to Texas at an exhilarating rate, but it could not be extended into the western portions of the state until the hostile Indians on the northwestern and western frontiers had been subdued. Comanche chief Quanah Parker's defeat in the so-called Red River War in 1875 was the beginning of the process. The final defeat of Texas Indians occurred in the summer of 1880, when units of "buffalo soldiers" of the Tenth Cavalry stationed at Fort Davis in far West Texas confronted the wily Apache chief Victorio and his band. The Indians called the black troops, who served in both the Ninth and Tenth Cavalry and the Twenty-fourth and Twenty-fifth Infantry, buffalo soldiers, probably because the texture of their hair reminded the Indians of the buffalo. The black troops realized that the Indians regarded the buffalo as sacred and accepted the term as a compliment.

One of the ablest Apache leaders, Victorio had rejected as intolerable life on the reservation, and he and his band left, raiding ranches on both sides of the border as well as stagecoaches and travelers on the San Antonio–El Paso Road. In August 1880, Colonel Benjamin H. Grierson and his buffalo soldiers drove the Apaches from West Texas by establishing impregnable positions around the seasonal water holes, which effectively cut the Indians off from the few sources of water that enabled them to ride through the dry desert country with seeming immunity. Victorio and his band fell back into Mexico, and there, in

October, Mexican troops assaulted them on the rocky slopes of Tres Castillos in Chihuahua, wiped out nearly all of his followers, and killed the dynamic chief himself.

The human suffering and drama on both sides of the Indian wars were deplorable and poignant. "The Indian loves to live as well as the white men," Buffalo Good, a Wichita, had said in 1871, "and can't help being there." But, as anthropologist W. W. Newcomb observed, "the obliteration of Texas Indians was but a small part, a footnote really, to the nineteenth-century development and emergence of a new, and in technological terms, a tremendously powerful nation-state."

The Impact of Barbed Wire

At the same time, another product of the industrial state hastened the closing of the frontier and changed settlement patterns in West Texas. Fencing had always been a challenge. In East Texas, where timber was plentiful, most fences were made of board, split rail, or, in some cases, rock. On the plains, with no timber or rock, ranchers used hedges, with bois d'arc being the favorite because the scrubby trees could be planted along a line and bent and shaped into an almost impenetrable barrier. In fact, export of bois d'arc seeds was a minor enterprise for a few years.

That changed when Joseph F. Glidden of Illinois invented barbed wire in 1874. Meeting with only limited success in Illinois, Glidden's agents moved to Texas. Barbed wire was controversial when it was first introduced: People thought that it would not restrain wild cattle or horses, or that the animals would be severely injured in throwing themselves against it. After Glidden's agents made their first sale in Gainesville in the fall of 1875, however, barbed wire soon proved to be a huge success. Some called it "the devil's hatband," but it was relatively cheap and effective in fencing livestock. Various factories produced about 600,000 pounds of barbed wire nationwide in 1875. Just six years later, in 1881, production had risen to 120 million pounds. In only a few years it changed the nature of western agriculture. Now ranchers could keep livestock out of farmlands and selectively breed their animals by controlling access. The demand for Longhorn cattle, the breed best suited to the open range, fell precipitously. With all these conditions in place, the stage was set for accelerated growth in West Texas.

Expansion into West Texas

While the vast Plains west of the 100th meridian beckoned thousands of eager settlers, water limited their opportunities, as historian Walter Prescott Webb described in his epic, *The Great Plains* (1931). Most new settlers were used to East Texas or the South, where rainfall was much more plentiful than on the Plains. Instead of thirty to fifty inches per year, West Texas usually received just ten to twenty inches. Nor were the few springs useable, because gypsum rendered most of the stream water undrinkable. European-style windmills were impractical because they were large and bulky and required constant maintenance, but by 1875, a Connecticut inventor named Daniel Halladay had provided the solution in the form of a smaller, functional windmill. Halladay constructed a mill with wooden blades that rotated around a horizontal shaft to produce enough power to draw water from a deep well. He attached a vane, or "tail," as the cowboys called it, so that the wheel would turn to face the wind. His invention was simple and operated unattended, and improved, all-metal models were soon on their way to West Texas. Evenly spaced along the railroad track, windmills harnessed the power of the ever-present West Texas wind to tap the vast Ogallala Aquifer, a natural underground reservoir that stretched from the High Plains of Texas to South Dakota that seemed an endless source of water for the locomotive boilers, for the rancher's cattle, and the settlers who would soon follow. One manufacturer considered the windmill the "prime mover" of settlement in the arid regions. Then, in the late 1880s and early 1890s, farmers developed several dry-land techniques that enabled them to produce even more. With the railroad providing easy access to markets, the number of acres devoted to cotton climbed steadily throughout the last quarter of the century.

Another factor contributing to the increase in cotton production was the proliferation of tenant farmers. Tenant farming—whether the farmers are renters or sharecroppers—although usually perceived in a negative way because it often left the farmer in deep debt, can enable people with no savings to get a start. As long as inexpensive or free public lands were available in West Texas, those who were not tied down by debt had the option of settling a homestead there, and the line of settlement moved rapidly westward. It reached the northern Panhandle, the South Plains, and the Trans-Pecos region in the 1880s.

The number of acres under cultivation skyrocketed—from 36,292,000 in 1880 to 51,407,000 in 1890, and 125,807,000 in 1900. It would be thirty-five years before that total was exceeded. Additional counties were organized until, by 1900, all but twenty-four of Texas's 254 counties had been established. An "almost unprecedented tide of immigration," according to an Agricultural Commission report, had brought the Texas frontier to a close. And, at the same time, immigrants to East Texas—in many cases, African Americans from other southern states—had more than replaced the population that had moved west.

The expansion of cotton farming into ranching areas was not always harmonious. The newcomers always sought land near streams and rivers and often fenced the water off from the cattlemen, who had in some instances been grazing their livestock on public land for years. The ranchers' practice was to buy the land with the water and use adjoining public domain. Most ranchers felt they were entitled to free use of the state's land because they had suffered the risks and hardships of settling the frontier. But the increased use of barbed wire—by

The eclipse windmill, one of the most popular models, made settlement of the plains possible. This one was located on the XIT Ranch.

1883 almost $1 million worth was sold in Texas annually—resulted in extensive fencing, even in West Texas. This precipitated such widespread fence cutting that the Texas Rangers had to be called in. The farmers were not always the catalyst in these cases, nor the rancher always the perpetrator, for competition between ranches sometimes produced similar lawlessness. The episodes, according to the *Galveston News*, inspired a "spirit of agrarianism among the poorer classes."

Following a heated debate, the legislature passed a law in 1884 declaring that fence cutting and setting grass fires were felonies punishable by one to five years in prison. Knowingly fencing public lands, or lands belonging to others, without permission became a misdemeanor. And, if a fence blocked access to a public road, the builder was required to place a gate every three miles and to keep the gates in repair.

Production of all the major crops—wheat, corn, oats, and cotton—increased during these decades, but, abetted by tenant farming, cotton far outpaced the others with a more than fourfold increase, from 805,284 bales produced on

Acreage in Texas Farms, 1850–1960

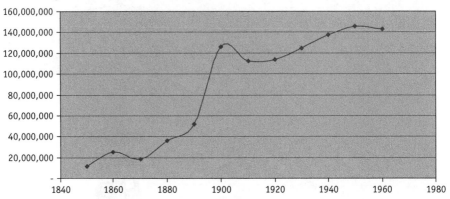

Acreage in Texas Farms, 1850–1960. Taken from *Historical Statistics of the United States, Colonial Times to 1970.*

2,178,435 acres in 1879 to approximately 3,500,000 bales produced on 7,178,915 acres in 1900, making Texas the leading producer of cotton and cotton seed in the nation. The expansion of railroads into the cotton-producing areas helped to make this possible, but Robert S. Munger of Mexia also made significant improvements in the ginning process (separation of the seed from the fiber). Farmers, who had lived in a barter economy and maintained subsistence farms that supplied virtually all of their family's needs, now turned almost wholly to cotton.

Despite these innovations, there were those who warned against dependence upon a single crop. "Plant cotton," the editor of the *Albany News* counseled, "not all cotton, but some cotton." But the most common method of financing for a farmer, the crop lien, also dictated that he grow cotton. The farmer would pledge his future crop to a bank or merchant, who might be the landowner as well, to gain financing for the year. The merchant covered his risk with high interest rates and by charging more for goods purchased against the lien, which reduced the farmer's buying power and prevented him from buying or securing credit elsewhere. Even if the farmer did not want to grow cotton, the lender usually influenced him to do so. This pernicious credit system, according to one historian, "sprang out of the ruins of the old regime, and spread, like Jimson weed, a curse to the soil." The logic of the Albany editor's warning became apparent when the price of cotton declined in the 1890s, and all farmers were hurt, especially the tenant farmers and sharecroppers, who found themselves deeper in debt. This was not the American dream. Would-be entrepreneurial farmers did their part: They occupied a piece of the public domain in West Texas, bought their tools, worked hard, and produced more crops, only to wind up in debt and working as tenant farmers. As farming continued to move toward commercialized agriculture, organizations like the Patrons of Husbandry and the Farmers' Alliance proposed different solutions for their problems, and many farmers were ready to listen.

The Growth of Ranching

The open range of South Texas seemed made for cattle, and from the eighteenth century on they bred and multiplied in the wild as well as under the care of the mission priests and on the *rancheros*. It was here that the Spanish *vaqueros* developed the techniques and costume that later spread throughout the American West and that the famous Longhorn, a random mix of Spanish cattle with the English breeds that Anglo settlers brought with them, developed. Anglo-Americans and African Americans contributed their own sets of skills to the handling of cattle when they began to arrive in large numbers in the 1820s.

The cattle industry of South Texas, the home of the Ballí, King, Kenedy, O'Connor, and other large ranches, grew rapidly during the postwar period. Led by Gail Borden's invention of the meat biscuit (made of dehydrated meat and flour) in 1849, Texas boasted fifteen factory-size meatpacking plants in 1870. After the Civil War, as the U.S. Army moved the line of defensive forts farther westward, the cattlemen followed and sometimes preceded them. By 1876 ranchers like Charles Goodnight had passed the 100th meridian all the way from Kimble County in the Edwards Plateau to Childress County in the eastern Panhandle, and Goodnight installed his first windmill in 1886.

Ranchers had already begun to address another serious concern—how to get their cattle to market. Because it was cheaper to walk the beeves to market, feeding them on free grass and water, than to slaughter and pack them in Texas, the number of packing plants declined to three by 1880; throughout the heyday of the trail drives (1867–1885), the second most lucrative part of the business, after raising and selling the cattle, was the service that the drovers provided in getting them from ranch to market. Men like Goodnight, Thomas S. Bugbee, and C. C. Slaughter pushed into West Texas, New Mexico, and Colorado to occupy the newly cleared land. By the mid-1880s, Texas-style ranchers had extended their operations as far north as Alberta and Saskatchewan to take advantage of the free grasslands.

The American Cowboy

Out of these trail drives came the most popular folk character in American history: The cowboy. The Texas cowboy was usually a young, small, wiry character with a knack for herding animals, hardly a hero in the normal sense. The highlight of his year was the spring and summer cattle roundup and drive to one of the Kansas railheads. Except in the way the Texas cowboy practiced it—cowboys usually were hired specifically for the trail drive, as opposed to ranch hands who remained on the ranch and worked year-round—the trail drive itself was not unique. His cow-handling predecessors in Europe and colonial America had driven cattle to market, but the cowboy lived with the cattle, camped out for the three months of the drive, and slept on the ground nightly. He began work before the sun rose and did not turn in until it had set. In between he stood his turn at watch, losing two or three hours of sleep. Throughout the drive, the

Colorado Historical Society

A Texas cowboy. Photograph by William Henry Jackson.

cowboy ate only the chuck that the cook had on his wagon. The day was filled with hard, difficult work, for a herd of 3,000 cattle required constant supervision.

The cowboy is personified by Charles A. Siringo, who was born to an Italian father and an Irish mother in Matagorda County in 1855, became a cowboy at the tender age of fifteen, and thirty years later wrote the first cowboy autobiography, *A Texas Cowboy; or, Fifteen Years on the Hurricane Deck of a Spanish Pony—Taken from Real Life,* which proved to be immensely popular, particularly among cowboys themselves. But there were many other representative types; one historian has estimated that perhaps as many as one-third of the drovers were Hispanic or black.

Sometimes the experience was more than hard work, because the trail drive was often dangerous. In *Lonesome Dove,* a fictional treatment of Goodnight and Oliver Loving's experiences, among others, Texas novelist Larry McMurtry has enshrined the water moccasin attack in the river as one of the dreaded events of the trail. But becoming unhorsed in midstream was equally perilous, for few of these dry land laborers could swim. One of the main advantages of the Chisholm Trail was the absence of large rivers. One also stood a good chance of getting caught in a thunderstorm or a stampede and had to endure blistering sun that dried up the streams and turned the cattle into thirst-crazed creatures that might stampede at the slightest whiff of water. Rain and bone-chilling cold wind were equally certain to make the trip north as miserable as possible.

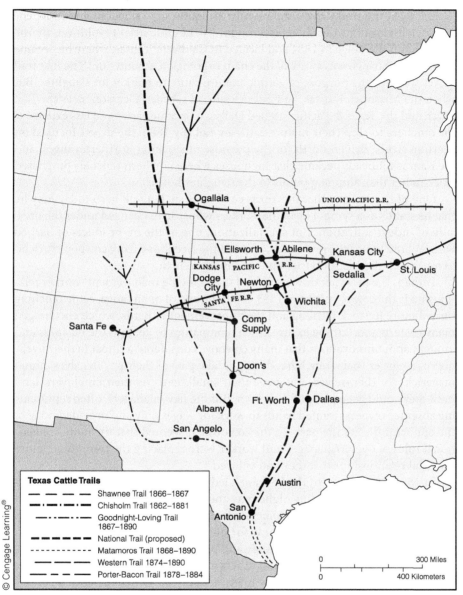

Texas Cattle Trails.

The trail drive was not just a character-building experience for ambitious wanderers, but also an original piece of Americana. In many ways it resembled a military expedition, as the boss gathered his crew, rounded up the cattle, and maintained tight control over them as they set out for Dodge City, Abilene, Sheridan, or one of the other small cattle towns that dotted the Kansas Pacific and Union Pacific railroad lines. Most drovers only made the trip once, then set out for Montana, or some other newly opened ranch land to try to locate their own spread.

But even the trail drives, supposedly the epitome of freedom and independence, fell victim to the changes wrought by the industrial revolution. By the time he quit the range in 1884 and located in Caldwell, Kansas, where he became a merchant, Siringo was aware of the changes going on around him. The first trail drives were for the purpose of getting mature cattle to market for slaughter. But when the Missouri, Kansas, and Texas Railroad reached Denison, near the Red River, and the Texas & Pacific reached Dallas, it became easier and less expensive for ranchers to ship their mature cattle by rail. By 1880, the drives focused on yearling steers, driven north for the purpose of stocking northern ranges, and the Kansas railheads became clearinghouses where northern ranchers purchased stock rather than shipping points to the slaughter house.

One of the reasons that the Texas cowboy is such a folk hero today may be that he stands as a symbol of all the workers whose lives changed under the pressure of industrialization. But specialization, one of the by-products of barbed wire and the industrial revolution, affected the freedom-loving cowboy every bit as much as it did the sodbuster and the longshoreman.

Perhaps the most famous example of the changing management–worker relationship is the cowboy strike of 1883. With the end of open range, cattle ranching turned more to stock farming and the improvement of herds, which encouraged many eastern and European investment companies to get into the business and brought about innovations that many cowboys considered a threat to their livelihood. In earlier years, ranch hands might take part of their pay in calves, brand mavericks for themselves, and graze their small herds on their employers' land until they could get a place of their own. But the new managers, often representing absentee owners, wanted hands to work for wages only and provided none of the opportunities of the past. To the cowboys, it seemed that the more conventional roles of owner/manager and worker were replacing the traditional, more fraternal relationships that they had enjoyed.

In 1883 Tom Harris of the LS Ranch led a small group of cowboys in drafting an ultimatum demanding higher pay and threatening a strike against several ranches, which they believed to be controlled by corporations or individuals who were involved in ranching only for quick profit. Twenty-four men signed the document, which set a strike date and promised limited assistance to strikers who needed money. Harris and others attempted to recruit all the cowboys in the area, but no one knows how many actually participated. With a combination of temporarily higher wages for those who defied the strike, immediate firing of those who participated, and rumors of violence on the part of the strikers, the stockmen defeated the fledgling union within two and a half months, and the spring roundup occurred without incident. But the failed strike was a clear indication that modernization and industrialization had changed ranching. Many of the old-timers like Siringo had gone into ranching themselves or into some other line of work, and the new breed of ranch hand represented the working class more than the undisciplined, freedom-loving character of popular culture.

Historians disagree as to whether this strike was part of the larger labor movement in Texas, but the fact that it seemed to share some of the same causes as other labor unrest—growing anonymity on the job, changing worker–employer relationships—has invited such speculation, especially because it occurred at the same time the large national union of working men, the Knights of Labor, was enjoying its greatest successes in Texas.

Texas Industries Develop

The leading industries in the state in 1870 were what economic historian John S. Spratt called "migratory," meaning that the owners had little capital invested and they could easily move from one community, source of raw materials, or market to another. Water-powered flour and grist mills were the leading industry, and virtually every community was home to a mill of some kind. But only about 1 percent of the population—fewer than 8,000 wage earners—was employed in all of the 2,400 manufacturing shops in the state. The value of all manufactured goods produced in the state was less than $12 million, less than 25 percent of the value of agricultural products. By 1900, however, the value of manufactured items had jumped to more than $92 million, which was one-half the value of the state's agricultural products.

The Timber Industry

The first big change came in the timber industry. East Texas was a veritable woodland of yellow pine, extending westward from the Louisiana border across perhaps 20 million acres of heavily timbered terrain but concentrated in what is known as the Big Thicket, now a national preserve. By 1870 only about 100 million board feet of lumber were being cut annually in Texas, less than 1 percent of the total U.S. production, and that primarily by commercial mills in Orange, Beaumont, and Houston. More of the early settlers undoubtedly would have cut timber, had their routes to mills and markets not been limited to the Neches and Sabine rivers and to rough wagon roads.

Another initially limiting factor was the wood itself, for most lumbermen considered the Upper Midwestern white pine superior to the Texas yellow pine. But as supplies of white pine began to run short, entrepreneurs looked again at East Texas, encouraging the construction of railroad lines into timbered areas. Indeed, as railroad expansion increased in the 1880s, the subsequent demand for wooden rail ties further stimulated the industry, with the T&P ordering 500,000 crossties in 1880 alone. The railroads provided the inexpensive transportation needed to propel lumbering into the forefront of Texas industry by the end of the century, and Texas into one of the top ten lumbering states in the nation.

Lack of capital initially hindered development, but the arrival of entrepreneurs like Henry J. Lutcher and G. Bedell Moore from Pennsylvania in 1877 marked a change in the East Texas industry. Lutcher and Moore built sawmills near Orange, and established both a domestic and an international trade. John Henry Kirby and Nathaniel D. Silsbee, who acquired more than a quarter of a million acres of pine forests, built large corporations that brought order to the industry. Entrepreneurs constructed company towns that often included churches, schools, stores, and homes and virtually controlled the life of their employees, one-third of whom were African Americans. The lumber industry employed more than 8,000 persons by 1880. By the turn of the century, although individuals still owned half of the lumbering plants, corporations so dominated the industry that they employed three-quarters of the workforce, produced three-quarters of the industry's total value, and were growing at an accelerated rate. The Kirby Lumber Company, chartered the following year, became the state's first multimillion-dollar company.

The same kind of concentration occurred in the flouring and gristmill industry. Although the industry had slipped to third in the state, behind cottonseed mills, in overall value by 1900, and the number of mills had decreased by almost 50 percent, total capital investment had increased significantly. No longer was every town required to have its own mill; larger mills ground grain more cheaply than the small mills and shipped it by rail. These developments helped fuel the growth of urban areas.

The Growth of Texas Cities

The largest and most productive city in the state in 1870 was Galveston, with a population of 13,818 and more than $1.2 million in total value of manufactured products. Second was Jefferson, the state's leading river port, at the head of Big Cypress Creek in Marion County. But the city that benefited most from the developing East Texas lumber industry was Houston, by virtue of its location at the edge of the thick forests to the east and north. Timber fueled the industrial revolution nationwide, providing power for railroads, steamboats, and city-based factories, and Texas was no exception. As the nearby supplies were depleted, Houston's business leaders organized and built a narrow-gauge railroad into the Big Thicket to ensure a continual supply of wood. The city's population grew from 9,382 in 1870 to 27,557 in 1890, despite the fact that it lacked a reliable source of coal, which had become the fuel of choice in the Northeast. Still, the growth continued, with Houston's population reaching 44,633 in 1900 and the total value of manufactured products $13 million, making Houston the top producer in the state.

Dallas was the state's second largest manufacturing city in 1900, followed by El Paso, San Antonio, and Fort Worth. Galveston, focusing its efforts on obtaining a deepwater port and solidifying its position as the major Texas trade center, had fallen to sixth in manufacturing value. The completion of the railroad lines to Marshall, Longview, Texarkana, and other cities in Jefferson's economic sphere ended that city's dominance of Northeast Texas because rail transportation was more reliable than the untimely steamboats, which had problems navigating Big Cypress Creek during periodic droughts. East Texas cotton began to flow toward St. Louis, an important rail center, rather than the gulf port of New Orleans.

As Texas cities grew, citizens expressed their civic pride in public architectural monuments. The new state capitol in Austin, designed by Michigan architect Elijah E. Myers and completed in 1888, was the most important new public building. Inspired by the nation's capitol, the new Texas state capitol is some 562 feet long by 287 feet deep. The star that the Goddess of Liberty holds in her hand is 311 feet above the ground. The imposing, new red granite capitol building opened in the spring of 1888 with a gala party, marred only by a huge leak in the roof that drenched the celebrants during a typical Texas thunderstorm. Restored and greatly enlarged with an underground expansion during the 1990s, the structure still serves as the seat of the state's government.

At the same time, the state continued to promote itself to would-be settlers with an avalanche of handsomely illustrated railroad guides and dozens of lithographic bird's-eye views of Texas cities. Part of a national fad that included the publication of almost 5,000 views of American cities during the century, the Texas images ranged from the largest cities in the state—Houston, Galveston, San Antonio, Dallas, Fort Worth, and El Paso—to some of the smallest, such as Wolfe City, Flatonia, and Clarendon. Chauvinistic residents apparently constituted a ready market for the handsome pictures, which depicted the cities from an imaginary point high in the air—a sort of combination of a panoramic view and a map—and merchants and city fathers used them to advertise the communities as well as individual businesses. And the fact that almost seventy different views of Texas cities were produced between 1871 and 1900, along with dozens of guides to the state, suggests the enthusiasm with which Texans promoted their communities.

The Impact of Railroads

The most important element of industrialization—and the catalyst for so much of the economy—was the expansion of railroads into almost every region of the state by 1900. As the nation slowly recovered from the Panic of 1873, Texas entered its greatest era of railroad building and one of the greatest in the nation. As Houston began to overtake Galveston as an industrial and shipping center, Galveston businessmen organized the Gulf, Colorado, and Santa Fe Railway Company in 1873 to build a line from Galveston, around Houston, through the fertile Central Texas cotton belt. The Galveston sponsorship of the line is reflected in some of the towns created along its route—Temple, Heidenheimer, Rogers, Moody—that were named after Galveston leaders.

The state had only 1,650 miles of track in 1875, all in East Texas, but more than half of the total railroad construction in Texas occurred during the next decade. In part, this was because the constitution of 1876 authorized land grants to railroads to encourage their construction, as in the case of Fort Worth. The state awarded sixteen sections of land for every mile of track laid, and Texas rail companies collected 32,153,878 acres of land in return for 2,928 miles of track; the Texas & Pacific Land Trust is still one of the largest landowners in the state.

In 1877 Texas led the nation in miles of track built, and in the following year railroads laid more track in Texas than in all the other states and territories combined, but still ranked twenty-fifth in manufacturing because of the state's largely agrarian nature. The era of land bonuses came to an end in 1882, when state officials were embarrassed to discover that they had awarded 8 million acres of land that they could not supply.

Although such a vast state had a genuine need for economical transportation, and construction of the railroad lines clearly spurred development, the spurt in railroad building also resulted from outside factors, including competition between two of the most powerful railroad moguls of the Gilded Age: Jay Gould, one of the leading New York developers of, and speculators in, railroads, who acquired the Texas & Pacific Railroad in 1879, and California-based Collis P. Huntington, one of the "big four" of western railroading, who owned the Southern Pacific. Together, they owned or controlled more than half the track mileage in Texas. With the joining of T&P and Southern Pacific at Sierra Blanca, eighty miles east of El Paso in 1881, another transcontinental route across America was completed. By 1900 Texas had almost 10,000 miles of track, approximately 5 percent of the total railroad mileage in the United States, and every city of significant size had service, with cities such as Denison, Texarkana, Dallas, Fort Worth, San Antonio, and Houston being served by multiple lines. "Railroads are the great civilizers and soon bring the country in lively competition with the older and more advanced portions" of the nation, Dallas attorney McCoy had predicted in 1872. "A very few years now will change northern Texas into one of the most flourishing portions of the U.S."

Texans had seen the railroads as the answer to the state's economic problems and had invested considerably in their construction through massive land grants. But, when the promised prosperity did not immediately follow, disillusionment quickly set in, especially in the agricultural sector. Then came news of widespread corruption within the railroad industry: Fraudulent stock manipulation, inflated construction costs, incompetent management, and questionable business ethics. Rather than continue to compete with each other, Gould and Huntington reached a pooling agreement in 1882, which slowed the construction of new tracks and fixed interstate shipping rates. Three years later, a group of intrastate lines created the Texas Traffic Association to set intrastate rates. Farmers had initially been enthusiastic about railroads, but following the Panic of 1873 they were caught between low commodity prices and steadily increasing shipping rates, which characterized the latter part of the century. At the same time, railroads began vigorously marketing the millions of acres of land that they had received from the state, creating even more agricultural competition. Farmers, had taken the precaution of designating the railroads as "common carriers" (a common law term meaning that the railroads would transport any goods or people and be responsible for any losses incurred during the process) in the constitution of 1876, and they now began calling on the state to regulate them.

The Growth of Labor Unions

Another response to the growing industrialization of the state was the establishment of labor unions. Before the Civil War, Texas unions were, for the most part, limited to typographers, who worked mainly for newspapers and printers, and carpenters, because most workers lived in widely separated rural areas, which was not conducive to the organization of unions. Following several attempts to organize black workers, the National Labor Union (Colored) established a branch in Houston in 1871. The following year the International Workingmen's Association organized an affiliate in Houston, but it fell apart when it became clear that it would include black workers as well as whites. If "the colored man is to be taken into full fellowship in this society, socially and politically," said member Bernard Lochrey, "I must decline to become a member." Galveston, however, remained the most fertile area for union memberships, with small organizations for carpenters and joiners, hack-drivers, painters and plasterers, longshoremen, bricklayers, and typographers.

Public sentiment initially seemed to be neutral or sympathetic toward unions, but that changed as the unions began to engage in what many regarded as bothersome if not "revolutionary" activities. The first large-scale strike in Texas occurred in 1872 when workers for the Houston and Texas Central Railway objected to an agreement that the company demanded to the effect it not be held responsible for any injury or death on the job. Calling the agreement a "Death Warrant," the workers, even though they were not officially unionized, maintained their strike for several days, and a number of newspapers editorialized in their favor. The strike ended when Captain L. H. McNelly and the state police arrived to make sure that the situation remained calm. The company fired perhaps half of the strikers, but it also withdrew the "Death Warrant."

Violence finally turned public opinion against labor unions. In 1882, the Knights of Labor, a successful national union, began organizing in Texas and by 1885 had more than 30,000 members in the state. The flashpoint was an 1886 strike that the Knights called against Jay Gould and the T&P over the firing of a foreman in Marshall. Thousands of men, many of whom had hoped to improve their lot by moving west with the railroad but who had been caught in the squeeze of economic depression and declining wages, walked off the job, seriously affecting service in North and West Texas. Public opinion initially seemed to be on the side of the workers, but when Gould refused to compromise, an armed clash occurred in Fort Worth, and Governor John Ireland sent the Texas Rangers and the state militia to restore peace. The affair was settled when the T&P passed into the hands of a federal receiver, and the court held the strikers in contempt. The Knights' power declined rapidly thereafter, but they still played a role in the successful boycott of the contractors building the new capitol in Austin, who had imported Scottish granite cutters in violation of the Alien Contract Labor Law.

African Americans were usually barred from white unions, although some were members of the Knights of Labor, including David Black, who served on the union's state executive board. Concentrated in East Texas and in the coastal cities, blacks were able to establish their own unions, such as the Negro Longshoremen's Association in Galveston. Most Mexican Americans, by virtue of their residence in South Texas, were not involved in unionizing activities, although some of the mutual aid societies (*mutualistas*) in Laredo engaged in activities similar to unions. Because the state was largely rural and the electorate increasingly suspicious, Texas labor unions remained weak as the nineteenth century drew to a close, a period in which national unions struggled as well.

The Redeemers' Program, 1876–1898

During the last quarter of the century, politics increasingly came to reflect the economic realities that Texans faced. Supporters of the new governor, Richard Coke, elected in 1874, represented what they called the New South and proposed to industrialize Texas by enticing railroads, lowering taxes, holding down government expenses, and creating an inexpensive labor supply. Largely ex-Confederates, these men felt that Republican "misrule" during the years after the Civil War had destroyed Southern prosperity by upsetting the traditional relationship between the races. Although they represented the party of slavery, secession, and defeat, they now cast themselves as the redeemers of the Democratic Party of their forebears and the true South, and the 1876 constitution, still in effect today, was only their first effort to erase all traces of the Republican regime.

Path to Financial Stability

Because per capita income in Texas was only 63.2 percent of the national average in 1870, more than 5.5 percent lower than the average personal income in the adjacent states of Louisiana and Arkansas, and because of a nationwide depression in 1873, Democrats felt that their only option was retrenchment. Coke resigned the struggle in 1876 to accept appointment to a seat in the U.S. Senate. Richard B. Hubbard replaced him, but was denied the 1878 nomination because critics claimed that he had not done enough to reduce the state's debt. Instead, the Democratic convention nominated ex-Confederate Oran M. Roberts, of Tyler, the "Old Alcalde" who had served as chairman of the secession convention of 1861 and was now chief justice of the state supreme court.

A native of South Carolina, Roberts was educated at the University of Alabama and moved to San Augustine in 1841, where he opened a successful law practice and taught law at the University of San Augustine. A bearded legal scholar who spoke softly and precisely, he was elected to the Texas Supreme Court and, after helping to raise a Confederate regiment in East Texas, returned to Austin and the Court until he was deposed along with the other Confederate office holders. He spent a little time in Mexico, but after the Democrats returned to power in 1874, Roberts returned to the Supreme Court. With Roberts leading the way, the Democrats trounced both the Republicans and the new Greenback Party in 1878.

The Greenback Party, like the Grange and the Farmers' Alliance, was largely backed by farmers who were feeling the brunt of the extensive societal changes as well as the economic downturn. They advocated for an inflated currency through the issuance of paper money (greenbacks) not backed by gold, among other things, in the hope that more money in circulation would make it easier for them to repay their debts.

Instead, Roberts began to cut taxes, instituting what many considered extreme measures to restore the state's financial stability. He also wanted the state out of the land business and led efforts to dispose of public land as quickly as possible. Such policies hurt the big landowners, the railroads, and the Capitol Syndicate, a group that had accepted land in return for building additional railroad tracks and the new state capitol. Under the law, the railroads had to dispose of their land within eight years of receipt, but when they tried to sell it, they found that the state became their main competitor, forcing prices down.

The Syndicate, which had ultimately received more than 3 million acres of Panhandle lands for building the new capitol building, had initially hoped to subdivide its land and sell it to settlers at a profit. It established the famous XIT Ranch instead, which was at one time the largest piece of fenced property in the world, with 6,000 miles of single-strand wire fence ringing its ninety-four pastures and outer perimeter.

Roberts compiled a formidable fiscal record during his two terms. In addition, the legislature established the University of Texas in Austin during his second term. By the time he left office to take a professorial position with the new University of Texas Law School, he had balanced the state's budget, reduced the debt by $500,000, and accumulated a treasury surplus of $300,000. Roberts had even published a book, *A Description of Texas, Its Advantages and Resources, with Some Account of Their Development, Past, Present and Future* (1881), touting the state's opportunities for would-be immigrants. Almost unnoticed, however, was the rising number of Texas farms that were worked by tenants rather than by owners.

The Temperance Movement in Texas

Consumption of alcoholic beverages had been a concern for many Texans for years, but became a political issue during the late 1880s. Roberts's successor, Governor "Oxcart John" Ireland (1883–87), who had earned his nickname by opposing land grants to the railroads when he was a member of the legislature, continued the pro-business policies that he inherited. Nevertheless, German-Texans and other ethnic groups were suspicious of him because he was rumored to favor the prohibition of alcohol. Lawrence Sullivan Ross (1887–91), who succeeded Ireland, was one of the state's best known former Texas Rangers and military heroes, who in 1860 had returned the white captive Cynthia Ann Parker from the Comanches against her will, but prohibitionists called him "a saloon stump speaker" and demanded that a prohibition amendment to the state constitution be submitted to the people. The Women's Christian Temperance Union, United Friends of Temperance (the first statewide prohibition organization), and other groups had been preaching prohibition for decades; now the message began to resonate, especially among fundamentalist Protestants, and found supporters among such esteemed politicians as U.S. senator John H. Reagan. The state constitution authorized local option elections, but prohibitionists now called for a statewide ban on the sale of alcoholic beverages and convinced the legislature to put a constitutional amendment on prohibition before the electorate in 1887. Even though it carried only thirty-two counties and failed by a vote of 220,627 to 129,270, the prohibitionists vowed to continue the fight.

The Marginalization of the Republican Party

Another reality on the political scene was the decreasing importance of the Republican Party. Known as the party of African Americans ever since its organization in 1867, the Texas Republican Party had not recovered from the devastating defeat it had suffered when the Democrats returned to office in 1873 and 1874. With the percentage of African Americans in the state's population decreasing from 31 percent in 1870 to 20 percent by 1900, the Republicans realized further losses when the "lily-whites" split from the party and joined with the Democrats to disenfranchise African Americans through the organization of white men's political clubs, the legal process, and intimidation. It is likely that as many as 300 to 500 African Americans were lynched during the last quarter of the century.

Briscoe Center at the University of Texas at Austin

Norris Wright Cuney served as Collector of Customs in Galveston and was an able politician.

Norris Wright Cuney, an able black politician from Galveston, became head of the party when former governor Davis died in 1883. As sergeant-at-arms during the Twelfth Legislature (1870–71), Cuney was skilled in the use of political patronage, especially after President Benjamin Harrison appointed him collector of customs in Galveston in 1889. He even survived various modifications in the election code, such as the elimination of the use of colored paper ballots to aid illiterate voters, and was resourceful enough to continue to get Republicans elected to office in a few counties in East Texas and along the gulf coast. But he could not prevent the passage of such Jim Crow segregation laws such as the one offered in 1889 by the state senator from Marshall, William H. Pope, requiring railroads to provide separate coaches for African Americans and whites. As the Republican Party became increasingly marginalized, Cuney tried to maintain his power by allying with a Democratic Party faction or with a third-party movement.

Populism Challenges the Status Quo

As their economic situation worsened, farmers turned for help to various organizations such as the Grange, or the Patrons of Husbandry, Greenback clubs, and the Farmers' Alliance. But it took several years before these concerns would coalesce into the Populist protest movement of the 1890s, the People's Party, one of the most vigorous third-party movements in American history.

Salado farmers organized the first Grange in Texas in 1873. The Grange had begun as a secret social, educational, and nonpartisan society, but soon began to advocate political and cooperative solutions to agrarian problems. By the mid-1870s, it had circulated two colorful posters to help educate the public on the role of farmers. One was entitled "I Feed You All," and the other was a little more pointed: "I Pay for All!" Other agrarians belonged to Greenback clubs, which had reached Texas in 1876 with the assistance the national Greenback Party. They wanted "greenbacks," paper money issued during the Civil War, to be declared full legal tender and to be exchanged for specie. By the 1880s, however, the Texas Farmers' Alliance had become the dominant agrarian group in the state. From its beginning in Lampasas in 1877 as the Knights of Reliance, organized to protect a group of farmers from nearby ranchers, the alliance was more political and more activist than the Grange. As the name suggests, these farmers supported the militant tactics of the Knights of Labor.

Claiming that the goal of a family homestead had been, in the words of historian Henry Nash Smith, "aborted by the land speculator and the monopolist," the alliance demanded wholesale economic changes rather than modest reforms. The alliance shared many goals with the Greenback Party, advocating for abandonment of the deflationary gold standard in favor of free coinage of silver (the inflationary issuance of silver coins at a ratio of sixteen to one to gold), the establishment of a subtreasury system (whereby the government would store farmers' crops, lend the farmer money against the future sale of the crops, and sell the crops at a more advantageous time and price), the abolition of the national banking system and the "serfdom of the lien system," adoption of an income tax, an eight-hour workday, direct election of senators, the Australian (secret) ballot, and referendum and recall, but it made fewer and less radical demands than its counterparts in other states with regard to issues such as government ownership of the railroads and the establishment of a new political party. Alliance lecturers—"whirlwinds of zeal"—were quick to place blame for the farmer's problems: "the capitalist holds your confidence in one hand, while with the other he rifles your pocket," S. O. Daws repeated to enthusiastic crowds across the state. By 1885, more than 600 delegates attended the alliance's state convention. Seeing no place for themselves in the evolving economy, many of these have-nots of society rallied first under the banner of one of these farmer-oriented organizations before moving on to form the People's Party, which gathered all these causes under its political umbrella.

Although these agrarian movements attracted many voters, the person who most effectively voiced their concerns in Texas was Democrat James Stephen Hogg, a crusading East Texan, who had served as attorney general under Governor Ross and in 1891 became the first native-born Texan to be elected governor. As attorney general, Hogg had zealously defended the public lands, regaining over 1.5 million acres for the state. He demanded that out-of-state insurance companies comply with Texas law and drove from the state those who did not. He sought to regulate railroads under the constitution of 1876, which had declared the railroads "common carriers." He broke up the Texas Traffic Association and helped to write the second state antitrust law in the nation. But he soon realized that neither the legislature nor his small office could deal effectively with the railroads and campaigned for governor in 1890 on a platform that included passage of a constitutional amendment that would enable the establishment of a railroad commission.

A tall man who weighed more than 250 pounds, Hogg was an energetic campaigner with a common touch, a love of the homespun language, and a native understanding of people. He easily ingratiated himself with rural audiences, who seemed immediately to identify with a man named Hogg. It is difficult to imagine the task that campaigners faced in addressing the huge outdoor crowds in those days. When Hogg opened his campaign for the governorship at Rusk in April 1890, for example, perhaps 3,000 people gathered in a shady grove outside of town for the event. Without the benefit of the public address systems we have today, Hogg's strong and intelligible voice gave him a big advantage over his opponents in such situations; even the men and boys in the trees near the edge of the crowd could hear him. Once he tore into the railroads and others who took advantage of farmers, he could hold an audience for hours. As the temperature rose on a hot summer afternoon, he would fling off his coat, loosen his suspenders, and gulp water to refresh his throat and maintain his strength. At times his plain speech may have offended the ladies, but still they came to hear him even though they could not vote. His zeal and personality earned him a long list of enemies by the time he decided to run for governor, but, fortunately for Hogg, he had many more friends.

Reformer James Stephen Hogg served as attorney general from 1886 to 1891, then as the first native son to be elected governor, 1891–95.

Hogg's Reforms

Hogg called for a number of policies in the 1890 campaign, such as reform of the state's land policy, longer school terms, an endowment for the University of Texas and the A & M College, a home for disabled Confederate veterans, and, regrettably, separate railroad coaches for African American and white passengers. At the head of his list, however, was the need to regulate the railroads, and he focused on passing a constitutional amendment to grant the state that power. In doing so, he appropriated one of the main tenets of the Farmers' Alliance and the People's Party and appealed to them to join his campaign. Five Democrats announced against him. The railroads helped finance Hogg's opponents and resorted to such practices as laying off engineers and canceling planned new construction in certain areas. But the agrarians remained with Hogg, whom they saw as their defender even though he did not endorse a subtreasury, and he had only token opposition. He swept into office, and the constitutional amendment permitting an intrastate railroad commission also passed handily.

Hogg quickly established the Railroad Commission as an appointive body and convinced John H. Reagan, who as a member of the U.S. House of Representatives had shepherded the Interstate Commerce Act (ICA) through Congress in 1887, to resign his new seat in the U.S. Senate to become the chair. Many other states had already enacted regulations of various kinds, but the ICA, due to railroad lobbying, was rather vague, calling for "reasonable and just" interstate rates as well as prohibiting rebates, "drawbacks," and pools. While Reagan's appointment drew widespread praise, the alliance was unhappy because it had wanted an elective commission, and Hogg added fuel to the flickering fire by declining to appoint any of their supporters to it. The People's Party, or the Populists, formally organized into a third national political party in St. Louis in April 1892, leading conservative Democrats, who had opposed the establishment of the commission, to believe that their more liberal colleagues might desert the party, enabling them to unseat Hogg in the next election.

Hogg's election represented a rebuke to the Bourbon, or conservative, wing of the Democratic Party, leading them to bolt in the 1892 election. Hogg might not have survived had his campaign not been masterminded by one of his close friends, who later became one of the most unusual, mysterious, and influential figures in American politics. Edward Mandell House of Austin had enjoyed a privileged youth as the son of a wealthy Houston merchant, banker, and landowner and had moved to Austin in 1885 to escape the heat of Houston and to be closer to his cotton plantations. There he befriended a number of political leaders, including Governor Hogg. He admired Hogg, especially his reform efforts, and learned politics from him. A reporter later described House as "one of the small wiry men who do a great deal without any noise. His is a ball-bearing personality; he moves swiftly, but with never a squeak or a rasp. He cannot be classified because there never has been any one quite like him." House explained his role as aiding the underdog: "When I found out that the railroads and the entire corporate interests of Texas were combined to defeat Hogg," he later wrote, "I enlisted actively on his behalf." It would be largely through House's guidance and organizing skills, both at the state and national levels, that Hogg would gain reelection and that Texas would later gain influence in the federal government more quickly than the other states of the Confederacy.

As the Democrats gathered in Houston in August 1892 for what would become known as the "street car barn" convention (because the barn was the only structure large enough to hold all the delegates), the Hogg forces were in control. More or less according to plan, the conservatives bolted, held their own convention, and nominated Waco attorney George W. Clark, a staunch supporter of the railroads. The race soon became a three-way contest with the entry of Thomas L. Nugent of Fort Worth as the Populist candidate.

African American leaders such as John B. Rayner of Calvert, meanwhile, hoped that they could bring Republican Party chair Cuney and other African Americans into the Populist fold, but Cuney had other plans. Thinking that the liberal votes would be split between the Democrats and the Populists, he formed a coalition with Clark. However, the coalition abetted a split that was already under way in the Republican Party. Objecting to continued African American domination of the party, the small faction known as the lily-whites held their own convention and nominated A. J. Houston, Sam Houston's youngest son.

Hogg also made a serious appeal to African American voters. He campaigned vigorously on the issues, including his opposition to lynching, which he eloquently expressed in a Brenham speech in June. He pardoned several African American prisoners in an obvious attempt to impress blacks, and African American speakers volunteered to campaign for him and organized "Hogg clubs" throughout the state. This was the first election in which large numbers of African American voters deserted Cuney and the Republicans to vote for the Democratic candidate.

The Populist campaign, meanwhile, took on the aura of a religious crusade. They used biblical rhetoric to tell familiar stories and substituted political slogans for the words of well-known hymns. Hoping to challenge the Democrats with a biracial coalition, they promised equal protection under the law as well as guaranteed suffrage, regardless of race.

Ultimately, Hogg won the bitter race, but only by a plurality—190,486 votes to Clark's 133,395 and Nugent's 108,483. Populist candidates drew even more support at the congressional level, finishing second in ten of thirteen races. The election served notice to the Democrats that a Populist alliance with the Republicans based on the concerns of blacks and poor whites could be a real threat, especially if they were unable to heal the breach in their own party. And it proved to the Populists that they would have to appeal to more than economic self-interest to get the black vote.

Now wary of the Populists, Hogg continued his reform program. He had already begun to incorporate many of their issues into his own platform—making the railroad commission elective rather than appointive, for example—but he refused to go so far as to endorse a subtreasury system. He signed the Perpetuities and Corporations Land Law with the intention of keeping companies "whose main purpose of business is the acquisition or ownership . . . of lands" from owning lands, but it missed its main targets, the great land and cattle companies, because they defined their primary activity as cattle-raising. He signed legislation in 1893 to prevent the railroads from issuing "watered," or overvalued, stock and another law restricting the amount of indebtedness that counties or municipalities could incur. He established the Board of Pardon Advisors to review the hundreds of clemency pleas and make recommendations to the governor, extended the public school term from four to six months, and increased the appropriation for the new University of Texas.

House became Hogg's closest advisor. He visited with the governor virtually every day and was the man to see if one wanted a political appointment or to petition the governor on any subject. He also continued his correspondence with his far-flung network of friends and confidants that he began to refer to as "our crowd." Although Hogg offered him several political positions, House refused them all, finally accepting the honorary title of lieutenant colonel, which the press quickly shortened to colonel. House had begun to perfect the behind-the-scenes political machinations that would ultimately take him to Washington as a personal advisor to President Woodrow Wilson in 1912.

Women and Minority Rights

Hogg was also more active than any other governor in trying to bring an end to lynchings in Texas. He called those who would lynch a fellow citizen "bands of murderers" who had "no respect for constitutional guarantees or the stability of government or the lives of human beings." When a mob seemed about to threaten the life of an African American man arrested for murder in Bastrop County, Hogg notified the sheriff that he had posted a $1,000 reward for the arrest and conviction of each member of the mob if a lynching occurred; the mob dissipated. Then, responding to the horrible torture and burning death of Henry Smith at Paris in 1893, Hogg called the affair a disgrace to Texas and unsuccessfully petitioned the legislature to pass an antilynching bill. By comparison, Nugent, who espoused a strict and pervasive segregation, claimed that the white lynch mobs had acted out of "a frenzy of grief and rage" and, therefore, were not responsible for their acts.

Neither Hogg nor the Populists made an effort to do anything about the disenfranchisement of more than half the population, that is, women's suffrage. It had been an issue for a number of years, but both constitutional conventions, in 1868–69 and 1875, had refused to take any action. Rebecca Henry Hayes of Galveston led in the establishment of the Texas Equal Rights Association at a Dallas meeting in May 1893, but the effort to get the three major political parties to include a suffrage plank in their platforms failed the following year. She and others were successful in arousing interest in the cause as auxiliaries spread to a number of cities, and newspapers began to take notice of their efforts. But the organization split after it failed to get the state House of Representatives to recommend a constitutional amendment in 1895.

Mexican immigration had begun to increase before the American Civil War and continued to grow into the 1890s. Mexicans were not so much attracted to Texas as they were driven from Mexico by the developing social chaos, the increased population, the collapsing economy, and the spread of entrepreneurs who drove the village farmers from their *ejidos* (common lands) in the name of government-approved development. The state census of 1887 counted only about 83,000 Hispanics, about 4 percent of the population, and they lived mostly along the border. The newcomers were generally limited to hard labor such as grubbing and picking cotton, sheepherding, and ranch work, but because they constituted a large majority of the population in the counties along the Rio Grande, they were generally able to keep their culture intact, including language, religion, holidays, foods, folk medicine, and family structures. The 1900 census showed that there were perhaps as many as 165,000 Mexican Americans in Texas, some 71,000 of them born in Mexico. There was similar growth in the Anglo population, but with far fewer foreign-born among them.

Although he could easily have won a U.S. Senate seat, Jim Hogg, who had no means of support except his job, announced at a "harmony meeting" in Dallas in January 1894 that he would not be a candidate for political office. In debt and feeling that he should tend to his family's needs, he entered into what became a lucrative legal practice in Austin, serving the same corporations and railroads that he had attacked while in public office. After the discovery of oil at Spindletop in 1901, he moved his practice to Houston and became involved in the oil business, helping to organize the Texas Company, which ultimately became Texaco. Some ten years after his death, oil was discovered on property that he had purchased near West Columbia, making his three children "oil rich."

The Rise of Business-Oriented Democrats

Hogg's 1892 reelection was only the beginning for Colonel House, who controlled the state Democratic Party machinery for the next decade, orchestrating the elections of a series of business-oriented Democrats to the governorship. Each of the Democratic factions fielded candidates again in 1894, the most reputable of whom was former U.S. Senator and railroad commissioner John H. Reagan, the "old Roman," whom Hogg favored. But Charles Allen Culberson, a reformer who had supported Hogg's platform and as attorney general had enforced the laws that he passed, entered the race with House's assistance and won the nomination.

In the general election, Culberson faced an invigorated People's Party that had increased its influence by taking over most of the Farmers' Alliance structure in the state and was making its best showing to date in Texas. Nugent was again their candidate, and he had the support of John B. Rayner, who agreed with Nugent on segregation and reasoned that blacks had much in common with poor whites. The Populists had also added a plank to their platform promising black trustees for black public schools. Realizing that he had lost a number of voters both to the Populists and to Hogg in 1892, Cuney and the Republicans fielded their own candidate in this election, as did the "reform" Republicans (lily-whites) and the Prohibitionists. Culberson won by a plurality, 216,373 votes to 159,676 for Nugent, again the Populist candidate, and 57,147 for the "regular" Republican, W. K. Makemson. Although the Populists did not win any major elections, they took hundreds of local offices and twenty-four of their number won seats in the legislature. The growing Populist totals—over 35 percent of the vote in this election—did not bode well for the Democrats.

Unfortunately, no one will ever know what the actual vote might have been, for both the Democrats and the Populists had honed a number of techniques to sway the African American vote. White sheriffs intimidated African Americans with guns or courted them with whiskey. In some counties, the parties paid influential African American men to pressure their friends and neighbors. In others, they sponsored all-night parties with lots of food and drink; the next morning mounted and armed white men escorted the African Americans to the poll, supplied them with ballots, and paid them twenty-five or fifty cents. Such practices gave credibility to the Greenback and Farmers' Alliance charges of vote fraud and to their campaigns for the Australian (secret) ballot and an honest count.

House's organizing genius was needed even more in Culberson's reelection bid in 1896, because the feared union between the Populists and the Republicans became a reality and marked the high tide of Populism. In the midst of a national depression, Culberson was an easy target. Nugent had died the previous year, and the Populists chose as their candidate Arkansas-born Jerome C. Kearby, a charismatic Dallas lawyer who was reputed to have been the youngest enlisted man in the Confederate army at age fifteen. But Kearby and the Populists were greatly disenchanted when the great Populist orator and champion of free silver, William Jennings Bryan of Nebraska, accepted the presidential nomination of the Democratic Party as well as that of the Populist Party. The executive committee of the Populist Party urged "fusion" with the Democrats, but Populist orator James H. "Cyclone" Davis warned that the Populists would be "swallowed bag and baggage" by the Democrats, and most Texas Populists refused to go along. No doubt Bryan's decision hindered the state's Populist ticket.

Kearby polled 44 percent of the vote, the largest total that the Populists would ever receive in Texas, but he still lost to Culberson by an official count of 298,528 to 238,692. Many of the local Populist candidates went down to defeat because voters had stayed at home because of the fusion with the Democrats. The Democrats claimed that 47 percent of the African Americans voted for them, but the election is generally considered one of the most corrupt in the state's history, with the widespread use of "influence" men on both sides, and there is no way to verify the claim. The coercion that occurred in Franklin, the county seat of Robertson County, is representative of many of the incidents, as armed white Democrats patrolled the streets all day, turning away African American would-be Populist voters. In Hearne, white men stood in front of the polls and fired pistol shots into the air to break up a crowd of African Americans who were attempting to vote. Some historians think that an honest election might have resulted in a Populist victory.

Following the 1896 election, the Populist coalition in Texas broke up. "The opportunity was lost." Kearby told a reporter. "I trust it may appear again; I fear not." One reason for the Populist failure was the national Democratic Party's adoption of several of the most important Populist positions after Bryan became its candidate for president. Race was an issue in some precincts, particularly in East Texas, and a genuine conflict with Republican ideology left other voters no choice but to return to the Democratic Party, the emerging Socialist Party, or other organizations.

Colonel House, meanwhile, continued his influence over the state's politics by allying himself with a long-haired, smooth-talking southern orator named Joseph Weldon Bailey. Originally from Mississippi, Bailey had come to Texas in 1885 and settled in Gainesville, where he practiced law. His outgoing personality and flair for spinning yarns in the Jim Hogg fashion soon won him many friends, who urged him to run for Congress. Elected in 1890, he became a spokesperson for the silver Democrats and by 1897 had become the House minority leader.

Colonel House enjoyed the feeling of power that he gained by manipulating other men, and his Texas experience proved valuable preparation for the role that he would soon play on the national scene.

 Conclusion

Some of the men who served in office during these years are among the most popular and capable Texans in the state's history. Oran M. Roberts, although generally faulted for viewing government in narrow, legalistic terms, returned the state to financial solvency. After leaving office, the "Old Alcalde" served for ten years as professor of law at the University of Texas and became the founding president of the Texas State Historical Association in 1897. Lawrence Sullivan Ross's two terms were so peaceful and prosperous that historians have often referred to his tenure as an "era of good feeling." The people revered the "Old Roman," John H. Reagan, to the point that Jim Hogg felt that only Reagan could imbue the new railroad commission with the credibility it needed to succeed. Colonel House will forever be regarded as the cagey Texas kingmaker who would go on to succeed in the same low-key and personal manner at the national level. And most historians still consider Jim Hogg, who personified the reform movement in Texas, one of the best chief executives the state has ever had.

Nevertheless, these men left unresolved some of the most troubling and complex issues of the day, including prohibition, segregation, civil rights, and women's suffrage. An issue ever since the days of the republic, prohibition drew particularly strong support in most rural areas of the state. It would recover from its resounding defeat at the polls in 1887 to become a virulent political issue as the twentieth century dawned. Although legally prevented from voting during this time, women used voluntary organizations to address legal and social problems; when supporters of these two issues—prohibition and women's suffrage— merged, beginning with the state branch of the Woman's Christian Temperance Union in 1883, the issues become even more compelling to Texas voters. The abolition of segregation and the expansion of civil rights would require more time.

The last quarter of the nineteenth century brought tremendous change and the infrastructure of a modern state to Texas. We still live under the 1876 constitution. Although the population was still largely rural in 1900, it had increased by more than 370 percent. Railroads had spread throughout the state, encouraging immigration, urban growth, and labor unions, exhausting the public domain through land grants, helping to close the hostile frontier of more than half a century, and engaging in excesses that required governmental regulation. Although industry now accounted for half as much production as agriculture, farmers had greatly increased their output through commercialization, used the expanded railroad network to ship their produce greater distances, and responded to national and even international markets. And the Democratic Party reestablished its hegemony in the state and would maintain it well into the second half of the twentieth century.

Although some would argue that Texas was well on its way to fulfilling the destiny that its founders had envisioned, it is also important to remember that these two and a half decades witnessed the renewed subjugation of African Americans, exploitation of Tejanos and increased Mexicans immigration, impoverishment of tens of thousands of tenant farmers and sharecroppers, virtual extinction of the buffalo, the climactic end of the bloody Indian wars, overgrazing of West Texas rangelands, and the first large-scale lumbering in the East Texas timberlands. Indeed, many of the challenges of the ensuing twentieth century would revolve around civil rights and the state's use of and/or protection of the environment and natural resources as Texas became even more populous and urban and industry became more exploitative.

Suggested Readings

The best overviews for the latter part of the nineteenth century are Billy Mac Jones, *The Search for Maturity* (1965), and Alwyn Barr, *Reconstruction to Reform: Texas Politics, 1876–1906* (1971).

Economic Recovery

For the beginnings of industrialization, see John S. Spratt, *The Road to Spindletop: Economic Change in Texas, 1875–1901* (1955); Robert S. Maxwell, *Sawdust Empire: The Texas Lumber Industry, 1830–1940* (1983); Thomas L. Miller, *The Public Lands of Texas, 1519–1970* (1972); and S. G. Reed, *A History of the Texas Railroads* (1941).

Expansion into West Texas

There are literally hundreds of studies on the ranching industry and the cowboy, but the most helpful are Ernest S. Osgood, *The Day of the Cattleman* (reprint, 1957); William C. Holden, *Alkali Trails, or, Social and Economic Movements of the Texas Frontier, 1846–1900* (1930); Jimmy M. Skaggs, *The Cattle-Trailing Industry: Between Supply and Demand, 1866–1890* (1973); and Joe B. Frantz and Julian Ernest Choate, *The American Cowboy: The Myth and the Reality* (1955).

Information on the close of the Indian wars may be found in Kathleen P. Chamberlain, *Victorio: Apache Warrior and Chief* (2007), and Dan L. Thrapp, *Victorio and the Mimbres Apaches* (1991); William H. Leckie, *Military Conquest of the Southern Plains* (1963); and Robert Wooster, *Soldiers, Sutlers, and Settlers: Garrison Life on the Texas Frontier* (1987).

For the settlement of West Texas, see Frederick W. Rathjen, *The Texas Panhandle Frontier* (1975).

Political Recovery

Useful biographies for the period include Robert Cotner, *James Stephen Hogg* (1951); Ben H. Procter, *Not Without Honor: The Life of John H. Reagan* (1962);

Gregg Cantrell, *Kenneth and John B. Rayner and the Limits of Southern Dissent* (1993); John Anthony Moretta, *William Pitt Ballinger: Texas Lawyer, Southern Statesman, 1825–1888* (2000); and Rupert Norval Richardson, *Colonel House: The Texas Years* (1964).

For information on the agrarian movement, see Roscoe C. Martin, *The People's Party in Texas* (reprint, 1970); Gregg Cantrell, " 'A Host of Sturdy Patriots': The Texas Populists," in David O'Donald Cullen and Kyle G. Wilkinson (eds.), *The Texas Left: The Radical Roots of Lone Star Liberalism* (2010); "The Roots of Southern Progressivism: Texas Populists and the Rise of a Reform Coalition in Milam County," in Richard B. McCaslin, Donald E. Chipman, and Andrew J. Torget (eds.), *This Corner of Canaan: Essays on Texas in Honor of Randolph B. Campbell* (2013); and Marion K. Barthelme (ed.), *Women in the Texas Populist Movement: Letters to the Southern Mercury* (1997). For the larger picture, see Charles Postel, *The Populist Vision* (2007).

For information on minorities and women, see Alwyn Barr's *Black Texans: A History of African Americans in Texas, 1528–1995* (reprint, 1996); Arnoldo De León, *Mexican Americans in Texas: A Brief History,* 2nd ed. (1999); and Ann Patton Malone, *Women on the Texas Frontier: A Cross-Cultural Perspective* (1983).

The *Southwestern Historical Quarterly* and the *New Handbook of Texas,* both published by the Texas State Historical Association, contain dozens of useful articles relating to the period. The *New Handbook* is available free of charge on the Internet at www.tshaonline.org.

TEXAS
DEFINED

irt. Cotton. Rain. Sun. Boll weevils. Texans at the turn of the nineteenth into the twentieth century lived and died according to the productivity of the soil. Most Texans lived a rural existence and depended directly or indirectly on agriculture for their sustenance. Categories of race, class, and gender mediated how exactly the rural population lived. Landowners fared better than renters, and renters often earned more than sharecroppers. Small town merchants and bankers rose and fell in proportion with the profits of nearby farmers. Women and children typically lived in dependence on male heads of household. For African Americans and ethnic Mexicans de jure and de facto segregation and discrimination added further challenges. Blues music about the penitentiary, the electric chair, and the hangman suggested just how vulnerable this population was not only to the whims of nature but also to the brutality of an Anglo-run justice system that was anything but just for people of color.

The advance of modernity, though, could not be halted. Indicators that Texas would not remain rural and poor became commonplace in the early decades of the twentieth century: Spindletop, the Houston Ship Channel, new railroads, and the emergence of powerful Texans on the national political stage. Changing economic, social, and political mores meant that Texans could leave aside unpleasant reminders of the Civil War era.

State leaders took the opportunity in 1936 to throw a six-month-long party in Dallas, ostensibly to celebrate the centennial of Texas's independence from Mexico. The live show "Cavalcade of Texas" described four centuries of Texas history in documents and maps and artifacts, recalling the halcyon days of the Texas Revolution and republic, Stephen F. Austin's "Old Three Hundred," and Sam Houston. The real theme of the centennial, however, was the modernization of the state. With futuristic glimpses of automobiles, television, and air conditioning, the centennial organizers suggested that opportunity awaited in Texas. They hoped to attract tourists by marketing the state in a different way—as part of the new West rather than the Old South—and adopted the cowboy and a more western look as the theme for the celebration.

By the late 1930s, Texas was on the threshold of a new, modern, industrial age, but how did the state move beyond a rural one-crop economy with a slaveholding, confederate past?

Oil. Defense contracts. Highways. Air and space. Technology. Cities. Suburbs. These are some of the more important concepts defining Texas and implicitly the way Texans came to live in the second half of the twentieth century. A Texan today may well wear cowboy boots and drive a pickup truck, but odds are he or she would not know what to do with a tow sack, what was used to pick cotton by hand a hundred years ago, or let alone ever have to scrape cow manure off those boots. The identity, economy, society, and politics of the state have evolved in tandem with the new urban and modern place that is Texas in the early twenty-first century. Modern Texas is as remote as it can be from its rural past; it is diverse, multiracial, and on an economic juggernaut, placing it second only to California in population and with a gross national product (GNP) greater than that of most European nations. Here is the story of that transformation.   ■ ■ ■

A Contradictory Movement: Texas Progressivism, 1900–1929

Jim Ferguson was a virtual unknown when he stepped up to the makeshift outdoor podium on the main street of the small Central Texas town of Blum, northwest of Hillsboro. Almost 600 men and perhaps a dozen women stood for two hours in the "penetrating cold and raw, damp chill" on March 21, 1914, to hear the first speech of his campaign for governor. Backed by fluttering American flags and red, white, and blue bunting draped from a storefront awning, Ferguson used vernacular language that would appeal to his audience—"I have caught the black cat tail of superstition and I intend to twist and pinch it until I am inaugurated Governor of this great State"—and argue for modernization and reform. "Our great state shrieks out in agony for a chance to develop its grand and glorious resources," Ferguson stressed.

Ferguson was a handsome forty-three-year-old banker from Temple, Texas, looking like "the substantial business man of farm origin that every town in Texas knows well." He was a political neophyte but not an innocent. He had some formal education, including a working knowledge of the classics, which he revealed from time to time, quoting Adam Smith in his Blum talk, but he also reverted to "country talk" to emphasize his points. Prohibition was the overriding social and political concern of the day, but Ferguson rejected it, telling the farmers, "If I am elected Governor, and the Legislature puts any liquor legislation up to me, pro or anti, I will strike it where the chicken got the ax."

Instead, he addressed a greater evil, one that kept the majority of white farmers economically prostrate and threatened the political system. The amount of rent that many landlords were now charging tenants, Ferguson shouted, amounted to usury, which was against God's law and man's. It had led to statewide poverty and the rise of the Socialist Party. "As long as the tenant was treated fairly and equitably," he reasoned, "the claims of the Socialist were a matter of fine spun theory. Take away the abuses of the present rent system, and the Socialist would not have a leg to stand on." No other politician in the Democratic Party proposed such a radical measure. To the *Dallas Morning News* reporter at the scene, he was "frank and outspoken," but a neighbor recalled that Ferguson could "electrify and sway audiences to the near frenzy of a wild mob." The Socialists would claim that he had stolen their thunder; farmers thought they had found their champion.

Chapter 11 The Early Twentieth Century	
1900	Galveston hurricane
1901	Oil discovered at Spindletop
1902	Poll tax enacted
1903	Terrell election law disfranchises blacks
1904	Texas ranks first in railroad track mileage
1913	Sixteenth (income tax) and Seventeenth (direct election of U.S. senators) Amendments to the U.S. Constitution ratified
1914	Houston Ship Channel opens
1915	*Plan de San Diego* discovered
1917	United States enters World War I
1918	Legislature ratifies Eighteenth Amendment (prohibition) to the U.S. Constitution
1918	Armistice signed, ending World War I
1918	Legislature grants women the right to vote in Texas primaries
1927	The U.S. Supreme Court overturns the white primary in *Nixon v. Herndon*
1929	Value of crude oil production in Texas exceeds the value of the cotton crop, and Texas is the world's leading supplier of crude oil

The first two decades of the twentieth century, give or take a few years, are generally known as the Progressive Era in American history. Although this is an unsatisfactory, and in many ways misleading, term, it has been used historically to embrace the social and political reforms that a rising middle class and agrarian and social reformers proposed during the early years of the twentieth century. Progressivism must be understood as a constellation of political and social movements, some with conflicting goals. Reformers of varying stripes championed its rhetoric and methodology—those wanting economic regulation, woman suffragists, activists in the National Association for the Advancement of Colored People (NAACP), white supremacists, eugenicists, health and safety reformers, and good government activists to name a few. Progressives tackled a wide variety of issues. Who should and should not vote was a dominant question in the first two decades of the century. Reformers advocated both social control and social betterment during the entire thirty-year period with emphasis on prohibition; health and safety reforms for workers, women, and children; and they debated whether to codify segregation or implement integration. Economic reform took two forms in the era: prior to World War I government regulation of business was advocated but in the 1920s the state-sponsored measures to improve business efficiency and productivity dominated.

Progressivism in Texas emerged during the state's drive toward modernization in the opening decades of the twentieth century. During these years, Texas experienced economic growth, rooted in ranching and cotton production and greatly bolstered in January 1901 by the discovery of what was, at that time, the world's largest oil deposit at Spindletop. This growth gave rise to demands for new roads, better schools, and more efficient city government. The political and cultural climate—with its emphasis on one-party control—permitted and at times even encouraged the reforms; indeed, one historian of the era even refers to the state as a "bastion of reform." Furthermore, the federal government's role in state politics and the role that Texans played nationally changed as Texans looked to Washington, D.C. for assistance.

As you read this chapter, consider the following questions:

1. Compare and contrast the modernization of the Texas economy and Texas politics during the Progressive Era. Who benefitted and who did not?
2. Define and evaluate the goals of Progressive Era reformers in Texas. How did their concerns and their tactics shift between 1900 and 1929? To what degree were they successful? To what degree were they not? Were there issues they neglected?
3. In what way or ways should the war years and the 1920s be viewed as continuing the themes of the Progressive Era? In what way or ways should they not?

The Texas Economy in 1900

Agriculture—farming and ranching—still fueled the state's economy in 1900. Since the mid-1870s, Texas farmers had led the South in the production of cotton. By the turn of the century, the state produced more than 3.5 million bales on 7,178,915 acres of land, and there was still arable land yet to bring under the plow.

Cotton production, however, dipped when the boll weevil, a native Mexican insect, began to make its way northward from South Texas, where it was discovered in 1894. The weevil flourished in the semitropical warmth of much of South and East Texas and proved resistant or immune to most known insecticides and poisons. In 1904, the small weevil destroyed more than 700,000 bales of cotton. By 1921, the weevil had ruined 34 percent of the annual cotton crop, costing farmers millions of dollars. Railroad construction and the use of barbed wire spurred the migration of farmers to West Texas and the High Plains, where cotton production flourished, but the weevil did not because of the colder climate.

Even as late as 1927 the value of the state's cotton crop was still more than three times the value of its oil production. Texas farmers, however, did not earn as much as their counterparts in other regions of the country. Texas led the South in farm income per family during these years by a wide margin, but it trailed the Midwest and much of the rest of the nation, largely because of the high percentage of tenant farmers and sharecroppers in the state.

Tenant Farmers

Despite the state law that declared that every Texan was entitled to a homestead of 160 acres, little tillable land remained to be distributed by 1880, and tenants operated about 37 percent of Texas farms. The continuing population increase and the devastating depression of the 1890s drove up the number of tenant farmers. After the state supreme court declared in 1898 that unappropriated public lands were exhausted, the percent of tenant farmers in the state jumped to more than 49 percent in 1900, and to nearly 52 percent by 1911.

Some were "share tenants," who furnished their own tools, plows, work animals, seed, and food, and bargained over the percentage of the crops that they paid the landowner. In a common arrangement, a tenant farmer would provide the landlord with one-third of the cotton crop and one-fourth of the corn crop ("third and fourth" renters). But others—"halfers" or "croppers"—simply worked for the landlord, providing nothing but their labor in return for the proceeds from one-half of the crop, less any debts they might have accumulated during the year. As one would have expected in a segregated state, most of the share tenants were white, whereas most of the "halfers" were African Americans and ethnic Mexicans.

The fate of sharecroppers and tenant farmers in Texas worsened because of the regional decline of semi-subsistence yeoman farming communities in which neighbors sustained one another in bad years. The emergence of cotton as the dominant and sometimes only crop grown contributed to this decline. Rather than growing a variety crops to sell in local markets, farmers sold only cotton, a national commodity, and thus became dependent on cotton brokers and the large landowners. When the price of cotton fell, these semi-subsistent farmers often lost their rights to live on and work their land, and they raised questions about capitalism and how property rights should be determined.

"The poverty of propertylessness," argued historian Kyle E. Wilkison, pushed these rural folk to join multiple rural protest movements: the Greenbackers, the Grange, the Populists—all in the late nineteenth century—and the Socialist Party of America by the early twentieth century. A minority of Texan farmers voted Socialist in the early twentieth century. Others simply stopped voting. One Lamar Country sharecropper explained that he had quit voting because "it did not look like it done any good. It seemed like it went their way, anyhow."

As agricultural prices dropped, farmers and their supporters attempted to organize to improve their conditions. The Renters' Union of North America established more than 200 chapters throughout the state and tried to set rules for tenancy and improve the marketing of agricultural products. Originating in Emory, Texas, in 1902, the Farmers' Union became the 140,000-member Farmers' Educational and Cooperative Union of America (ECUA) by 1914, with a Colored Farmers' Union providing services for African Americans. The ECUA constructed some 1,300 cotton warehouses and marketing cooperatives throughout the state and operated more than 100 cotton gins. In 1908, the ECUA launched the "plowup campaign," in which it tried to create a shortage of cotton by destroying one-third of the crop. The effort was not repeated in subsequent years.

The most successful of all the organizations was the Farm Bureau, more conservative than its forebears and focused on landowners rather than tenants or sharecroppers, but also dedicated to getting more credit for the farmer and helping to sell the crops at the highest prices possible. Ultimately, in terms of the average farmer of the 1920s, they all failed.

The Lumbering Bonanza

With the huge East Texas forest at its disposal, the state's lumbering industry reached its zenith in 1907, cutting 2.25 billion board feet (a board foot is a square foot of lumber one-inch thick), the third highest production rate in the United States. Entrepreneurs changed the industry by establishing complete plants and company towns in remote parts of East Texas—Camden, Fostoria, Kirbyville, Diboll—that received the logs from the forest and delivered finished lumber to the railhead. The work was long, difficult, dangerous, and low-paying. The workers averaged about ten hours a day on the job between 1900 and World War I and then nine hours a day until World War II. Only the most skilled employees earned more than a common laborer's pay. In many cases, these poor conditions persisted until companies, following a "cut out and get out" policy and expecting the cleared land to become farms, exhausted their timber holdings. The industry declined in the 1920s.

Despite the status of agricultural and lumber workers, most people view the 1920s as good economic years. The average Texan's income was almost three-quarters that of the average American, and World War I had increased the demand for lumber (for wooden ships) and boosted the price of cotton to 20.9 cents per pound in 1919. But the relative economic position of the farmer slowly sank during that decade and many forests were destroyed.

The Discovery of Oil

Like other places in the United States, Texas had been home to a modest oil industry for decades before the legendary discovery at Spindletop in 1901. The state's first producing field came in at Corsicana in 1894, and the real estate developers who owned it recruited several Pennsylvania oilmen—including

J. S. Cullinan—to help them develop the field. By 1900, the field was producing 836,000 barrels a year. Cullinan built the first refinery in the state there in 1898 to produce kerosene primarily. Still even in 1900, if a Texan drilled a well, he or she was looking for water, a far more precious substance than oil, especially in the western part of the state.

That began to change on January 10, 1901. The Gladys City Oil, Gas, and Manufacturing Company had been drilling for oil on Spindletop Hill near Beaumont ever since 1893, but they had been foiled by their out-of-date cable-tool drilling rig and the tricky sands of the salt dome formation and had run out of money. Anthony F. Lucas, the leading American expert on salt dome formations, leased the rights from the company and joined in the search in 1899.

A new rotary drilling technique, combined with Lucas's experience in drilling in salt domes and money from the Mellon banking interests in Pittsburgh, brought success. On January 10, shortly after mud began bubbling from the well, the newly released pressure blew six tons of four-inch drilling pipe from the hole. Everyone watched, stunned, as the well seemed to settle down for a few minutes, then a geyser of mud, gas, and, finally, oil burst out of the hole. The oil spewed more than 100 feet into the air at an estimated rate of 100,000 barrels a day for nine days—until the workers finally managed to cap it. By the time it was brought under control, a huge pool of oil surrounded the well, along with hundreds of oilmen, speculators, and onlookers. Inspired by the Spindletop discovery, wildcatters—individuals not associated with a major company who gambled on their instincts—rushed into every part of the state looking for oil.

The first genuine oil boom in the state ensued. Texas had produced approximately 1,000 barrels of oil in 1896; that figure jumped to 21 million in 1902.

Oral History of the Texas Oil Industry Records, e_enr_072, The Dolph Briscoe Center for American History, The University of Texas at Austin

Merry Xmas 1901, Spindletop. Eleven months after the Lucas gusher at Spindletop, the oil boom in Texas had begun.

Thousands of people moved into the area from Houston to Beaumont to Port Arthur, and real estate became more expensive—prohibitively so in some cases. Related manufacturing companies such as machine shops and distribution facilities relocated to the gulf coast. Industry boosters hoped that construction of a ship channel in Houston would increase commercial trade in the region. To get funding for the project, Texans lobbied the federal government in Washington, D.C. Augmenting the facilities at Galveston, the Houston Ship Channel opened in 1914, the same year that the Panama Canal opened, and Texas began to attract shipping from around the world.

The industry produced new terms and personalities to take their place alongside the cowboy in the pantheon of Texas characters: the "go-for-broke" wildcatter, the hardworking, hard-playing roughneck, and the "get-rich-quick" oilman. These characters were firmly established by the 1920s, but Edna Ferber gave them stereotypical expression in the fictional persona of Jett Rink, a merging of the cowboy and the get-rich-quick oilman, in her popular novel (which became a motion picture) *Giant* (1952).

Wildcatters drilled cheek by jowl with other rigs in boomtowns because there were no laws preventing it; more than 200 derricks rose within the city limits of Breckenridge, with several thousand more in the immediate area. Oil overflowed storage tanks and spilled into streams and polluted the air. There were shortages of food and fuel. Heavy rains and constant oilfield traffic turned dirt roads into mud bogs. When torrential rains fell in Desdemona in 1919, influenza and typhoid quickly reached epidemic proportions. Violent crime took place alongside the gambling houses and brothels, and law enforcement officials chained prisoners to trees when jails became overcrowded. When the onslaught overwhelmed city and county services, the state intervened. The governor dispatched the Texas Rangers to Desdemona in 1920; Borger in 1927; and Wink in 1927, 1928, and 1929; and the state militia to Mexia in 1922 and Borger again in 1929.

Creation of the vast petrochemical complex on the gulf coast, today one of the world's largest, began soon after the discovery at Spindletop as dozens of small refineries located in the vicinity. In 1902, Guffey established a large refinery there (renamed Gulf Oil Corporation in 1907) to produce kerosene. That same year he and the Texas Company (later Texaco, a company that more recently sold its name to Chevron but parts of its operations to Shell) connected the pipelines between Spindletop and their Oklahoma field. By 1916 Gulf's production capacity reached 50,000 barrels of crude oil per day. Sun Oil Company, Houston Oil Company, and Security Oil Company (a subsidiary of Standard Oil Company, later Magnolia Petroleum Company, one of the forebears of Exxon-Mobil Corporation) also established sizable installations on the gulf coast.

The state began taxing oil production at the rate of 1 percent of the value of the product in 1905, collecting $101,403 during the first full year of taxation. But by 1919 tax revenues from oil exceeded $1 million, and in 1929 they had reached almost $6 million. The state would become increasingly dependent upon this source of revenue.

The Push to Modernize

The modernization of Texas took place during a changing political and cultural climate. Conservative Democrats developed a one-party system that ensured their dominance and the disenfranchisement of African Americans. Distinguishing themselves from other southerners, Texans began to take pride in their unique heritage and identity. This new self-image made cooperation with the federal government easier, which aided the state's push to modernize.

Abandoning the "Lost Cause"

As the twentieth century dawned, a cultural transformation celebrating the state's unique history, heritage, and values occurred as Texans threw off the emotional shackles of the "lost cause," took a positive outlook, and accepted modernity in the form of new ideas, including increased participation in and assistance from the federal government.

This process was not simple. Vestiges of the "bloody shirt," the southern penchant for recalling Yankee horrors committed during the Civil War, remained as dozens of Confederate monuments overlooking courthouse squares, parks, and cemeteries were installed throughout the state. Sculptors such as Pompeo Coppini, an Italian who first moved to Texas in 1901, earned their living from commissions celebrating the Confederate past, including the John H. Reagan Memorial in Palestine (1911) that features a personification of the "lost cause," a Roman soldier sitting pensively at Reagan's feet, contemplating defeat.

Historian Walter Buenger, however, explains that Texans shifted from an allegiance to the South to an allegiance to Texas itself. This perspective resembled the American dream in that it contained neither the burden of slavery nor the defeat of the Civil War. The fact that Texans successfully resisted Union invasion during the Civil War enabled many to persist in the belief that they had not been conquered. The commemoration of Texas uniqueness had begun as early as 1886 when orators throughout the state celebrated the fiftieth anniversary of the state's independence, comparing Stephen F. Austin and Sam Houston to George Washington and Thomas Jefferson rather than Robert E. Lee and Jefferson Davis. By 1900 the state had acquired more than 330 acres of the San Jacinto battlefield as a memorial; by 1905 it had purchased additional parts of the Alamo and turned it over to the Daughters of the Republic of Texas to administer as a shrine. And in 1901 artist Henry McArdle loaned his two large paintings of significant moments in Texas history, *Dawn at the Alamo* (1905) and *Battle of San Jacinto* (1895), to the state for exhibition in the new capitol. Today, they hang in the Senate chamber and have been reproduced in Texas history books for decades.

At the same time, the Texas State Historical Association, founded in 1897, had begun to publish heroic stories of early Texas in its journal. In 1906, *Dallas Morning News* editorial cartoonist John Knott personified the state in a character that became famous as "Old Man Texas," known for his belief in fiscal responsibility, low taxes, and honesty in government, just as the character of Uncle Sam represents those values for the country as a whole. In addition, generations of schoolchildren learned the history of the state from an enormously popular comic strip, *Texas History Movies*, first published in the *Dallas Morning News* beginning in 1926. The blatantly racist comic strip presented minorities in an unflattering light, for example calling Mexican Americans "tamale eaters."

The result, according to Buenger, is that Texans like novelist Walter Humphrey grew up reenacting the battle of the Alamo in their childhood games instead of the battles of Bull Run and Gettysburg. This developing "Texanness" led the state's residents to associate themselves with victory at San Jacinto rather than defeat at Appomattox. The roots of "Texanness" go back to the period of the republic, though, when President Mirabeau B. Lamar encouraged residents of the state to assume a Texian identity. The twentieth-century identity culminated in the state's centennial celebration in Dallas in 1936, by which time cowboys, cowgirls, and the Big Bend mountains had officially replaced planters, southern belles, and East Texas cotton fields as the state's symbols. Although the cult of Texas exceptionalism had negative effects, it did provide the intellectual underpinning for a newer and more positive culture in Texas than in the other southern states.

Demographic Changes

Texas society became increasingly diverse during these years. In the mid-1880s, a writer for the *Indland Printer* noted, "Texas is a curious state. It is so cosmopolitan that the governors' messages are printed in four different languages. About 30,000 are printed in English, 10,000 in German, and 5,000 each in Spanish and Bohemian." Almost 200,000 Mexicans immigrated to Texas between 1890 and 1910, for example, producing a more than 300 percent increase in the number of Mexicans in Texas, whereas the state's overall population grew by only 75 percent. This represented the largest expansion in the ethnic Mexican population in Texas since the Mexican American War. Moreover, the increased Mexican population occurred alongside a proportionate decline of the African American population in the state. The state had mixed identity as western and southern, causing one writer to observe in 1940: "more southern than western is the state's approach to most political and social questions; more western than southern are the manners of most of its people."

The Conservatives Take Charge

With the breakup of the Populist movement in the late 1890s, the last significant opposition to the Bourbon Democrats (conservative southern Democrats who advocated for business interests) faded. The back-to-back elections of Joseph D. Sayers (1899–1903) and Samuel W. T. Lanham (1903–07) as governor and Charles A. Culberson as senator (1899–1923) confirmed their hold on power. Supported by political operative Colonel Edward M. House, Sayers and Lanham were both former members of the U.S. Congress and were the last two Confederate veterans to serve as governor. Neither Sayers nor Lanham (1903–07) was as reform-minded as Hogg. They were sophisticated men but lacked his transforming zeal. They believed that the modernization of Texas depended on the vast oil reserves at Spindletop and the continued exploitation of the East Texas timberlands. In a political party divided by factions, House had virtually negotiated their nominations, implying that their administrations would be "caretaker" administrations rather than proactive ones. As House bluntly put it, "the people wanted no disturbance" in 1902 and Lanham "managed to say nothing in a most convincing and masterly way." A decline in the proportion of farmers in the legislature reflected a friendlier business climate.

Yet state-level antitrust prosecutions continued unabated. Texas brought more cases than the federal government prosecuted in the entire nation during the same period.

It was also during their administrations that the Bourbon Democrats, with mixed motives, overhauled the state's election laws, which admittedly were a confusing mélange of local laws. Block voting and ballot stuffing were endemic, and the state needed a good system of voter registration. Disturbed by the fact that the combination of African American Republicans and Populists almost won a victory in 1896, the Democratic legislature moved in 1902 to institutionalize the one-party rule and to solve the registration problem. The legislature first recommended a constitutional amendment that would permit a poll tax (which passed with a 65 percent majority). Then in 1903, the legislature enacted a series of "reforms" that encouraged the counties to continue the all-white primaries (which, in this case, was interpreted to include Mexican Americans as well, to accommodate the South Texas political bosses), made third-party competition more difficult, and established a poll tax that had to be paid six months before the primaries and nine months before the general election.

A majority of middle- and upper-class whites favored the poll tax, as did reformers who reasoned that it would be an efficient way of registering voters and discouraging block voting and manipulation of voters. Former legislator Alexander Watkins Terrell was one of those who had advocated a poll tax for years, and he made clear his intention to prevent "the thriftless, idle and semi-vagrant element of *both races*" from voting. Politicians, however, continued to buy the votes of large blocks of workers, tenant farmers, railroad employees, and opponents of prohibition.

The poll tax was effective in reducing the number of people who voted. Political scientists estimate that at the high tide of Populism, 1896, more than 80 percent of those eligible to vote actually did so. That figure dropped to approximately 35 percent in 1904, the first year the poll tax was enforced, and to less than 25 percent in 1906.

Terrell returned to the legislature in 1903 to offer further reforms that would, at the same time, make it even more difficult for minorities to vote. The stated intent of the laws that bear his name was to standardize voting across the state and eliminate fraud. They required, for example, that all counties hold their conventions on the same day, preventing manipulators such as Colonel House from scheduling early conventions in favorable counties. An even more pervasive law enacted in 1905 required primary elections for those parties that had received at least 100,000 votes in the previous general election (later raised to 200,000, then to 20 percent of the vote) and defined the process by which candidates would be nominated for office as well as who would be permitted to vote. Known collectively as the Terrell election laws, these statutes culminated the Bourbon Democratic effort to institutionalize one-party rule. A disgruntled Republican realized as early as 1912 that "the primary election law . . . [is] so effectual . . . that today, a nomination in the Democratic primaries is tantamount to election."

This revamping of the election law, however, did not include women. The Texas Woman Suffrage Association organized in Houston with the intent of establishing chapters throughout the state, but the group's activities stopped when one of its main leaders, Annette Finnegan, left the state in 1905. A small group in Austin carried on the fight. In the meantime, women took pride in the fact that the concerted action of many groups, including the Texas chapter of the Woman's Christian Temperance Union, the Grange, the Texas Federation of Women's Clubs, and the Texas Woman's Press Association, led to the establishment of Texas Woman's University in Denton in 1903.

Half a Dozen Fights

With its newfound dominance, the Democratic Party became the only serious venue for discussion of the state's social and economic problems. It also became home to a number of factions, that, although based on such strong characteristics as class, race, and ideology, moved in and out of the party from time to time and followed one or another of the charismatic leaders who vied for center stage. Powerful orators such as Senator Joseph W. Bailey and Governor Oscar B. Colquitt attempted to persuade the faithful with regard to issues such as voting, workers' and women's rights, tenancy and land ownership, political corruption, railroad law, regulation of insurance companies, penal and tax reform, antitrust legislation, education, conservation, and creation of a highway system, with no one faction gaining dominance. The astute Jim Hogg had helped the party find a middle ground between the conservative, pro-railroad wing, and the more radical Populist demands, and Colonel House had negotiated between various factions of the party for another decade. But no such passionate and domineering a figure as Hogg appeared.

To Thomas B. Love of Dallas, speaker of the Texas House of Representatives in 1907, and Thomas H. Ball of Houston, prohibition was a sincere motive, but they also recognized it as an issue that motivated voters. The railroads had submitted to the regulating authority of the Railroad Commission, and other "foreign" corporations had either fled the state or reconciled themselves to Texas's parochial commercial interests. Lacking a genuine corporate bully, urban abuses, or corrupt political bosses (outside of South Texas) to rally against, Texas re-formers soon united around the prohibition question. Most, like Love and Ball, were fervent in their conviction, but it was also good politics. The state's voting population, was white, male, ethnocentric, conservative, and had roots in the South. Most also lived in a rural area, farmed, and espoused traditional values, as opposed to the sinful vices associated with the growing cities. That also made them naturally suspicious of racial and ethnic minorities who consistently opposed prohibition.

With no threat to their power, the Democrats could afford an intraparty struggle over prohibition, which inspired endless debate, with Bible-quoting evangelists on one side and on the other the majority of Roman Catholics, members of less evangelical Protestant sects, African Americans, Mexicans, urban dwellers, and Democratic conservatives. "We have only one political party in Texas," Governor Colquitt told a Dallas audience in 1911, "but there are enough political fights in that one for half a dozen."

Texas and the Federal Government

Even as the Democratic Party in Texas reorganized and strengthened itself, Texas politicians rose to national prominence. The presidential election of 1912 ushered the Democrats back into the White House and a number of Texans into significant positions in the federal government. Part of this resurgence resulted from Colonel House's personal friendship with the new president, Woodrow Wilson of New Jersey, but an equal part of it was the team of talented officeholders that the state sent to Washington, including Morris Sheppard, the author of the constitutional amendment implementing prohibition; future vice president John Nance Garner; and future Speaker of the House Sam Rayburn.

Although House played no role in Wilson's nomination, the Texas delegation to the Democratic convention in Baltimore did. In a close ballot—and through forty-six roll calls—the Texas delegation, or the "immortal forty," as they became known, remained loyal to Wilson and lobbied others to join them, and Wilson did not forget the Texans. With Colonel House as one of the president's closest advisors, the state found itself in an ideal position to play a major role in the new government.

Wilson left Colonel House to come up with nominations for his cabinet and other appointments while he took a much-needed vacation. After House recommended a number of Texans, the Lone Star State also found itself in an excellent position to influence federal legislation and programs at the same time as the political changes within the state had led Texans to expect more of their government. Texans were pleased to see a Treasury Department that took more interest in the South, and they welcomed the Federal Reserve Act (1913), the Federal Farm Loan Act (1916), aid to agricultural education, lower tariffs, and increased military appropriations in the state as World War I loomed. The coming war in Europe provided the ideal opportunity for Texas to exercise its influence, as army bases were established throughout the state, and Texas oil began to play an important role in the national economy.

 ## Texas Reforms

Aware of the national campaign to reform government and industry, Texas reformers, lacking a political base during the years between governors Hogg and Thomas M. Campbell, began at the grassroots level. A new labor group, the State Federation of Labor, organized in 1898, joined with the even newer Farmers' Union to develop a legislative program and to lobby for its implementation. The Texas Federation of Women's Clubs, founded in 1897 and with more than 230 clubs and more than 5,000 members by 1903, took on other aspects of the Progressive agenda, such as better schools and libraries. The Texas Local Option Association organized in 1903 to defend the state's local option laws, but its members also concerned themselves with moral issues of the day as well as labor and agriculture reforms.

The various reformers worked toward improving government; ending political corruption; curtailing the influence of large, particularly out-of-state, corporations; and improving all aspects of life, from the farm to the city and from schools to prisons and charitable institutions. They believed that such social goals could be achieved through efficient bureaucracies, the application of scientific research and training, and public education.

But prohibition was, in fact, the dominant issue in Texas politics for much of this period. It cut across political factions and classes and gained additional support when women won the right to vote. Progressives believed that "demon rum" would corrupt a democratic society and the fact that most Germans, Mexicans, and other ethnic groups opposed prohibition only seemed to reinforce the point that it would benefit the Anglo-Saxon society. Having failed in previous attempts at statewide prohibition in 1887 and 1911, antiliquor forces concentrated on local-option laws, vowing to dry up the state one precinct at a time.

The "wets," as those who were against prohibition were called, responded with similar propaganda and organization. Although the wets had prevailed, 237,393 to 231,096, in a statewide election in 1911, they now faced an aroused nation and state. On February 28, 1918, the state legislature ratified the Eighteenth Amendment, a prohibition amendment to the U.S. Constitution that outlawed the sale of alcoholic beverages, and immediately enacted a statewide prohibition law.

Government Reform

The first signs of Progressivism in Texas emerged with the efforts of local women's groups, in Dallas, Galveston, and other cities around the state, to reform local governance. These initiatives grew out of women's church work; their benevolent work; club work in entities such as literary, gardening, musical, and patriotic organizations; and civic work. Seeing the faults in the communities where they lived women petitioned for poor relief, childhood nutrition programs, free kindergartens, civic beautification, improved public health, sanitation, and the like. As both Elizabeth Hayes Turner and Elizabeth York Enstam have shown in their respective studies of Galveston and Dallas women proved to be effective politicians even before gaining the right to vote. They convinced local governments to implement these "municipal housekeeping" reforms, and in doing so they reconfigured the artificial boundaries between private and public spaces. Their efforts highlighted deficiencies in urban governments and the need for more efficient, less corrupt structures.

Then the devastating hurricane that struck Galveston Island on September 8, 1900, a most tragic event and the greatest natural disaster to strike North America, hastened the implementation of municipal reform. Galveston had been engaged in an all-out civic struggle with Houston for dominance in gulf shipping, but the hurricane tipped the balance decisively in Houston's favor. Nevertheless, the people of Galveston struggled back heroically. A group of wealthy businessmen feared that the city would never recover its prosperity with the current city council. This oligarchy devised a plan to elect commissioners at large, rather than from specific wards or precincts. The commissioners would then elect the mayor from among their number, and the commission would be both a policy-making and administrative body. Individual commissioners would also serve as heads of specific departments. Architects of the plan wanted to bring increased expertise and efficiency to the rebuilding of the city. Progressives did not object to the elite running the city as long as they made the correct decisions.

Courtesy of the Rosenberg Library, Galveston, Texas

Walking along the Galveston beach after the storm, with some of the devastation apparent in the background.

The effective and businesslike manner in which Galveston recovered from the storm—including building a seventeen-foot seawall on the gulf side of the island, raising the grade level of the city, and building an all-weather bridge to the mainland—caught Governor Campbell's attention, and he encouraged other cities to implement the commission form of government. Houston adopted it in 1905. Dallas, Fort Worth, Denison, Greenville, and El Paso followed in 1907, and by 1920 seventy other Texas cities had implemented the plan along with more than 400 cities nationwide. The Galveston Plan, or the "Texas Idea" as it was known outside the state, continued to spread across the country, but it further eroded minority representation. The at-large elections meant that a majority population could determine the makeup of the entire commission.

Educational Reforms

One of the most important Progressive goals, second in importance only because of the tragedy at Galveston, was educational reform. In general, there were two types of schools at the turn of the century: common schools, which were usually rural and independently governed by trustees who hired the teacher and operated the school, and independent districts that usually resembled the present-day school system. Critics of the common schools usually argued that the one-teacher, one-room rural schools offered an inferior education and proposed consolidating these schools and transporting students to the regional schools at no charge. Progressives, further, insisted upon compulsory attendance, an increase in the tax base, increased teacher qualifications, and free textbooks. They wanted all school districts to use the same books, offer similar courses, and have the same requirements for graduation and teacher certification. They created the new State Board of Education to oversee the curriculum and textbooks.

Because of the state's relative poverty, only a few of the changes could be implemented. A newly created Normal School Board of Regents began oversight of teacher-training schools. The Progressives advocated making education more relevant to students' lives, and they also supported curriculum changes that introduced the new social sciences of psychology and sociology. Schools took on additional duties, including supervised recess periods, supervised athletic and academic competitions (under the University Interscholastic League at the University of Texas, 1910), and improved health care. The goal of public schools significantly changed from imparting technical skills to improving the social order. By 1930, white Texans had a wide range of choices for higher education at a relatively low cost, and student enrollment increased more than tenfold from 2,148 in 1900 to 23,134 in 1929.

Social Reforms

The initial success of the Galveston Plan seemed to indicate that Progressives were right in their contention that science and training could lead to efficiency. They sought further governmental reforms in the areas of prisons, where they hoped to end inhumane treatment, improve health and sanitation, and regularize paroles. They favored segregated facilities so that women would not be housed with men, juvenile offenders with adults, those who had committed minor violations with murderers. The legislature addressed the problem in 1911, ending contract leasing of prisoners in 1912. It established the Gainesville School for Girls in 1917, and transferred the Gatesville School for Boys to the State Board of Control in 1919, with instructions that the school emphasize reform and education. It replaced hanging as the preferred method of execution with the electric chair, thought to be more humane, in 1923, and established the Texas Prison Board in 1927 to reorganize the system. But Progressives and most Texas citizens wanted the prison system to be self-supporting, so further solutions had to be found.

In the early twentieth century, responsibilities for welfare provisions remained with state and local entities. As such, other Progressive efforts focused on establishing county poorhouses and hospitals for the indigent and improving conditions in state asylums, and all such organizations were placed under the State Board of Control. Not all the reforms were carried out. Most citizens felt that the state was too poor to support such programs. Other reforms, such as women's suffrage, continued to be defeated at the ballot box.

Good Roads

Although many national issues, such as urban political machines, did not really apply to Texas, others did. In addition to prohibition and women's suffrage, Progressives in Texas also campaigned for good roads and conservation of timber. The demand for good roads emerged around 1910 as the number of automobiles increased. Because the Texas constitution relegated road upkeep and maintenance to the counties, the state had no network of roads and those that did exist were in appalling condition, often being little more than rocky trails that followed along old Indian routes, circled around hills, large trees, and boulders, forded creeks, and zigzagged in right-angle turns along property boundary lines. Some stretches of flat road developed a ripple pattern known as the "washboard" and there were no barriers to keep motorists from skidding into ditches along the road or signs to warn of upcoming hazards such as a dip. During the seasonal torrential rains, dirt roads became quagmires and often held water or flowed like a creek on the rise. A publicity-shrouded trans-continental drive sponsored by five southern newspapers, including the *Dallas Times Herald* and the *Houston Post*, almost came to a halt in 1913 when the automobile became mired in the impassable black gumbo soil of Hill County, en route from Waco to Dallas. The first modern road from Austin to San Antonio was built only when Travis, Hays, Comal, and Béxar counties each agreed in 1914 to pay their share of the $140,000 required to convert the old wagon road to a sixteen-foot wide roadway covered with a foot of gravel. Governor Colquitt "plowed the first furrow for the great highway" behind a "big road plow drawn by six restless mules," according to a reporter for the *New Braunfels Herald*, and the Austin–San Antonio Post Road was completed a year and one-half later.

Advocates of good roads began working in various parts of the state as early as 1903. They organized auto tours, encouraged volunteer road work, and posted directional signs for travelers. In 1910 they met at the state fair to promote the idea of a central authority to oversee and maintain a statewide network of roads. Hoping to overcome the traditional objection to centralization of power and to educate both the legislature and citizens of the growing need, they formed the Texas Good Roads Association in 1911. In 1916, the first year of automobile registration, 194,720 Texans registered cars and trucks. But the good road enthusiasts faced formidable opposition, because the county commissioners' courts did not have the money to finance the roads and did not want to give up their authority.

The national Progressive agenda came to their rescue, however, as Congress enacted the Federal Aid Road Act in 1916, offering matching funds to all states that created a central planning authority and joined the national highway network. The following year, the legislature created the Texas Highway Department (THD), now the Texas Department of Transportation, overseen by a three-member commission appointed by the governor.

Conservation

Texas Progressives were not as successful with conservation as were its advocates elsewhere in the country. Their primary focus was East Texas, where the timber industry had enjoyed outstanding years during the first decade of the century with an average cut of more than 2 billion board feet a year. As World War I came on, lumbering grew to the point that it threatened the very existence of the vast pine forests. W. Goodrich Jones, a Temple banker, led the effort to regulate the timber industry and implement a program of reforestation.

After attending President Theodore Roosevelt's White House Conference of Governors on Conservation in 1908, Jones returned to Texas and organized the Texas Forestry Association, which espoused a statewide program of forest conservation that called for prevention of fire, selective cutting, sustained yield, and reforestation. Because of the association's encouragement—and Jones's lobbying of fellow Temple resident Governor Jim Ferguson—the legislature established the Texas Department of Forestry as a part of the Agricultural and Mechanical College. Despite much good work on the part of the agency, however, the legislature failed to follow through in other ways. By the 1920s, the intensive lumbering had virtually destroyed the great virgin forests of East Texas, and the boom came to an end. The Progressives got their agency, but it had little power, and by 1932 Texas timber production had decreased to its lowest point since 1880.

Reformers in Charge

Despite the factionalism, all of the candidates in the 1906 gubernatorial campaign identified themselves as reformers who called for antilobby, antitrust, and protax legislation and support for the state's educational and charitable institutions. With no Colonel House to orchestrate the results, Palestine lawyer Thomas

M. Campbell returned to the fray and swept his three primary opponents aside. Although the electorate remained divided on key issues, Campbell's administration, along with the Thirtieth Legislature, became the most reform-oriented government in the state's history. Together, they enacted a number of laws characteristic of reforms throughout the South such as several antirailroad laws that former Governor Hogg supported, an antinepotism law, prolabor laws, antitrust laws, and insurance regulations. During his four years in office, Campbell created a department of agriculture and a library and historical commission and encouraged prison and public school reforms. The Robertson Insurance Law (1907) required insurance companies to invest their policy reserves in the state. Campbell's administration also stopped the contract lease system for prisoners and implemented more humane treatment. Under his administration, the legislature even passed a law taxing the intangible assets of corporations, thereby doubling the value of assets on the tax roll. Although he failed in his effort to enact an income tax, Governor Campbell's efforts led to the only notable increase in state revenue before oil began to play a major role in the state's economy.

The more conservative Oscar Branch Colquitt (1911–15) continued some of the progressive reforms, such as regulation of child labor, factory safety standards, women's work hours, and the state's first workers' compensation law, when he was elected in 1910. But, unlike Campbell, he was against prohibition and that, along with his pro-German sentiments as World War I approached, alienated many Democrats. Ultimately, Governor Colquitt had to spend most of his time dealing with two problems. One, the tax system, was chronic. As the progressive governors increased spending on the state's institutions, it became apparent that Texas did not have a broad enough tax base. Colquitt had inherited a $1 million debt from Campbell and, although he had campaigned on the basis of lowering taxes, he soon had to increase them to pay for growth in public education, prisons, and bureaucracies.

The second problem related to the disturbances along the Rio Grande border resulting from economic chaos and revolution in Mexico. Increased numbers of Mexican refugees had been arriving for some time, and events such as the so-called Garza War of 1891, in which journalist Catarino E. Garza became a folk hero by using a base in Texas to launch a rebellion against Mexican president Porfirio Díaz, did nothing to calm the furor. Governor Hogg had called for assistance from the U.S. Army and had sent a small Texas Ranger force to deal with the matter. Garza finally slipped away into exile in Central America, leaving his followers to return to their South Texas and northern Mexican *ranchos*.

Colquitt never felt that the federal government did enough to protect Texas citizens or to keep Mexican insurgents from using Texas as a safe haven to arm themselves and plan their assaults. He sent the Texas National Guard to join the small Ranger force in an effort to maintain control, but the problem flared into open warfare when U.S. troops invaded northern Mexico on at least two different occasions. These incidents resulted in long-standing disputes and hard feelings between Anglos and Mexicans in South Texas.

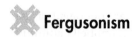 **Fergusonism**

Two of the state's most famous governors, James E. Ferguson and his wife, Miriam Ferguson, the first woman governor of Texas, defied easy political categorization. They appealed to the impoverished rural voters in the state with protest rhetoric, but they also made corrupt deals benefitting their political donors. The "farmer's friend," James "Pa" Ferguson was a self-made man who aimed his message at the long-suffering rural population of the state. Having been born to a central Texas farm family and found his early employment in the fields and work gangs of backcountry Texas, he understood the problems of country folk. Ferguson combined a law practice with real estate and banking, escaping poverty and learning about the needs of an evolving economy. Despite their shortcomings, the Fergusons tended to represent the modern ideals of greater economic opportunity for most Texans.

Ferguson's Rise to Power

In shunning prohibition as a rallying cry, Ferguson did not give up the ability to excite voters, for he focused on what he considered to be a greater societal ill and, at the same time, a greater source of support in a state where the political system was still dominated by rural voters. Farm tenancy had occupied the attention of academics and agricultural journals for a number of years, but it had been ignored by state and national governments, despite the organization of the Land Renters' Union of North America in Waco in 1911. Rising land prices and high interest rates made it difficult for tenants to become landowners and move up the economic ladder, and their children toiled in the fields rather than attend school, dooming them to the same fate. "There is something rotten in Texas when over 50 per cent of our farm families are homeless renters," the *Houston Chronicle* editorialized in 1912. The number was 10 percent higher in the state's richest cotton-growing area, the Blackland Prairie, where Ferguson grew up. "One of these days" the editor argued, "this issue is going to fly up and hit our lawmakers slap in the face."

Ferguson knew the plight of the tenant farmers, although his bank was apparently not forgiving of their debts. His campaign persona belied that heritage, which also included study at Salado College and passage of the bar exam, especially when he lapsed into the dialect that his wife, Miriam, the daughter of a well-to-do Bell County farmer, called "country talk."

And he was good at it, an orator who purposely maligned his opponents with a unique mix of bad grammar, acerbity, libel, and wit: "He spoke the language of the corn rows and the vernacular of the country stores," a veteran Austin newspaper editor recalled. His record of opposing local option prohibition in Bell County quickly brought him to the attention of the brewing interests. Like Jim Hogg before him, he embraced some radical proposals, such as limiting the amount of rent that a landowner could charge a tenant. But in keeping with the white supremacist politics of the era he did not address the challenges of ethnic Mexican and African American croppers, who fared far worse than white tenants.

Ferguson's second major campaign issue targeted what he considered to be the next most difficult problem that the state faced: a poor educational system that ranked thirty-eighth nationally and lagged in such categories as teacher salaries, spending per student, length of school year, and percentage of school-age children in school. His desire to improve the schools stemmed, again, from his own rural heritage as well as an understanding of his constituency and a conviction that education was one of the skills that could most quickly improve people's lives. In his campaign announcement, he declared that Texans should "buy all the education that we can pay for," beginning with "the little schoolhouse on the country road."

Ferguson used props like a gourd and a wooden water bucket in his appearances, and relentlessly attacked the prohibitionist candidate, Thomas H. Ball, who had served in Congress, practiced law in Houston, and seemed the early favorite to win the race. Ball accused Ferguson of being under the influence of the Catholic Church because he had received the endorsement of a priest in his hometown, Temple, Texas, and not being genuine in his rhetoric regarding tenant farmers.

Drawing support from rural, white voters, the brewing interests, South Texas, and the German district of Central Texas, Ferguson handily defeated Ball with more than 55 percent of the vote, and his charismatic personality would flavor Texas politics for the next two-and-a-half decades. Ferguson's first term was relatively harmonious. He fulfilled his campaign pledge by getting a farm tenant bill through the legislature, but it was soon declared unconstitutional and little else was done for the problems of tenant farmers during the Progressive Era. He also followed up on his other main platform pledge with continued educational reform, increased appropriations for higher education, and the creation of a State Department of Forestry.

Trouble on the Border

There were early rumors of malfeasance on Ferguson's part, but they took a back seat to the continuing disturbances on the border. Reports from South Texas noted an increase in raiding as early as January 1915. The local authorities continued to see the raids as nothing more than "bandit activity" until officials arrested one of the insurrection organizers and discovered the *Plan de San Diego*, a revolutionary charter that called for ethnic Mexicans on both sides of the border to rally in a combined revolution and race war. Their goal was to seize the territory that Mexico had lost to the United States in 1848 and to establish an independent republic. The South Texas area was fertile ground for such a movement because it had absorbed literally thousands of Mexican immigrants in the preceding decade as well as an influx of Midwesterners who engaged in citrus farming. South Texas was also experiencing a wrenching transition from a pastoral, ranching economy to commercial agriculture. Racial tensions increased as new landowners brought with them discriminatory practices against Mexicans and Tejanos. A way of life had changed, and many Tejanos were displaced in the process, sometimes now working for wages on property that they or their family had once owned. This tragedy was complicated by the revolution in Mexico and World War I, which had begun in Europe in August 1914, and included the threat of German activity in a disrupted Mexico.

The sporadic raids increased in July of 1915, and a number of Americans were killed in both Texas and Mexico. Ferguson sent the entire Texas Ranger force to the valley and called for additional U.S. troops. There were probably no more than fifteen or twenty Regular Rangers on the border, but they served as leaders, role models, and participants in the events that followed, supplemented by Ferguson's patronage appointment of many "Special" Rangers. The raids peaked on August 8 when sixty Mexicans carrying a red flag emblazoned with the slogan "*Igualdad e Independencia*" ("Equality and Independence") attacked Las Norias Division of the King Ranch. The Rangers and local law enforcement officials immediately retaliated with a "systematic manhunt," callously killing more than 100 people of Mexican heritage. Ferguson called out the Texas National Guard the following year to supplement federal forces under General John J. Pershing, who ultimately invaded Mexico in an effort to capture Pancho Villa, the Mexican rebel leader who had raided Columbus, New Mexico, on March 9, 1916. Virtually the entire combat-ready American army, almost 50,000 troops, was assigned to the border. As the Mexican Revolution drew to a close, and the United States recognized the Carranza government, the raids came to an end. This suggests, of course, that the raiding was directly related to the situation in Mexico, but the raiders would not have been as successful if conditions in South Texas had not been ripe.

These were tragic years on the border, with much of the Anglo community traumatized by the raiders and the Mexican American community brutalized by the lawless Rangers, Special Rangers, local officials, and vigilante groups. This reign of terror on the Rio Grande came to an end in 1919, when both a U.S. Senate investigating committee and a state legislative committee led by Brownsville representative J. T. Canales documented so many atrocities committed by the Rangers—some sources claim that as many as 5,000 murders—that the force was reorganized, or "purified," to use Canales's word, and reduced to four regular companies of seventeen men each.

"Pa" Ferguson's Impeachment

By contrast, Ferguson's escalating conflict with the University of Texas during his second term might seem trivial, but surprisingly, it, rather than the bloodbath in the valley, led to his impeachment and conviction. As early as 1915, the governor had disagreed with acting university president William J. Battle over the university's budget, wanting to control spending from the governor's mansion.

San Antonio Express newspaper headline, August 14, 1915, depicting the one-sided Anglo view of the border disputes without a balanced description of Anglo brutality toward Mexican Americans and Mexicans.

San Antonio Express newspaper

Battle, of course, was appalled by the governor's charges of duplicity and resented his micromanagement. Ferguson, during his 1916 reelection campaign, called for the university budget to be listed line by line.

The evolving conflict probably could have been prevented had Ferguson and Battle managed to overcome the initial problem, but it would have been difficult to find two more opposite personalities. The erudite Battle did not mix with Ferguson, a rough-and-tumble politician who had far more in common with the masses who had elected him than he did with a Harvard-educated classicist.

Ferguson won reelection in 1916 over a surprisingly strong candidate, Charles H. Morris of Winnsboro, and then stepped up his charges against the university, demanding the immediate dismissal of six professors whom he accused of forming an "oligarchy." To the board of regents, he described the faculty as "tenants at will," and, in answer to a question about why the president of the university and certain faculty members should be fired, he replied, "I don't have to give any reasons, I am Governor of the State of Texas."

A group of ex-UT students led by Will C. Hogg of Houston, son of the former governor and a member of the board of regents, ably defended the university and charged that Ferguson was financially corrupt, especially because he took a loan of over $150,000 from brewing interests. The Texas Equal Suffrage Association, led by Minnie Fisher Cunningham, and women's clubs all over the state joined in because Ferguson opposed woman's suffrage.

On July 27, 1917, the Travis County grand jury indicted Ferguson and some of his aides on charges of embezzlement and misuse of public funds. The legislature assembled in a special session and considered impeachment charges against the governor. Ferguson resigned rather than submit to impeachment, but the Senate rendered its decision anyway, removing him from office and banning him from holding any future state offices.

Ferguson's arrogance in office thoroughly provoked the growing urban, industrial, educated, and more progressive segment of the population. The trends that would shift the residual political power of agrarians to the urban dwellers were already in evidence by 1917. Thus did thirty-nine-year-old William P. Hobby, former journalist and editor from Houston and the sitting lieutenant governor, become governor of Texas on August 25.

"Before the time of Ferguson," wrote the political scientist V. O. Key, Jr., in *Southern Politics*, "elections were contested on issues that held deep meaning for the people of Texas. How the state was to protect its citizens from organizations of wealth, what the state was to undertake by way of public services for its citizens, for what citizens these services were intended, and who should pay the tax bill—these are ultimately the great concerns of democratic government, second only to maintenance of the democratic processes themselves in their importance to the citizenry." "Fergusonism" remained an issue into the 1950s, despite the governor's impeachment.

From World War I to the Jazz Era

World War I Brings Change and Reform

After Europe went to war in the summer of 1914, Texans divided over whether the United States should prepare for possible entry into the war. Anglo support for the war intensified in March 1917 after the release of the Zimmerman telegram. Alfred Zimmerman, the German foreign secretary, had instructed the German minister in Mexico City that, in the event of war with the United States, the minister should promise Mexico it would regain all its lost territory in Texas and the Southwest in exchange for a successful alliance with Germany. The British had intercepted the message and given it to Wilson. Many Texans interpreted the telegram as confirmation that Mexico had inspired the recent *San Diego* insurrection in South Texas, and it solidified the president's support across the country. Less than a month later, President Wilson called on the United States to enter the war to make the world "safe for democracy."

Almost a million Texans registered for the draft, including 449 women who served as nurses; 197,789 Texas men actually served, and approximately 25 percent of these were African American. More than 5,000 Texans died in the conflict, many as the result of the Spanish influenza epidemic in 1918, and many more were injured. Most of the Texas troops trained at four large camps that the federal government established in Fort Worth, Houston, Waco, and San Antonio. Other training sites in the state as well included a basic flight instruction school at the University of Texas; training facilities for fledgling aviators, the primary one at Kelly Field in San Antonio; and Randolph Field, which became "The West Point of the Air."

On the home front, the legislature provided compensation to soldiers for economic losses while on active duty and forbade the sale of a serviceman's property until one year after he had been discharged. Another act eliminated the poll tax for servicemen, and the Texas Council of Defense was organized to oversee the efforts of the more than 15,000 county and community defense councils. Unfortunately, some of them also became vigilante groups, harassing people with German names, especially if they refused to purchase war bonds or displayed pictures of the Kaiser in their home. The Socialist newspaper, *The Rebel*, which had attained a circulation of 23,000, was also shut down by government order.

Although welcome for many reasons, the vast infusion of federal resources also had an adverse effect in that it set off an inflationary spiral that greatly outpaced incomes and more than doubled the cost of some of the new state programs, such as the improved school system. The legislature also acted to limit the negative effects of the large military installations on communities—bars and prostitution—but did nothing to stem the racial tensions that existed. The intersection of racial tension with military service was not new to World War I era Texas. In 1906 African American soldiers stationed at Fort Brown in Brownsville, Texas, had been subjected to bigotry. A local bartender was shot dead on

August 13 and a police officer was wounded that night. White townspeople blamed black soldiers from the base for the shooting. The white commanding officers swore the soldiers were all in the barracks at the time of the crime, but the men were all discharged from the military without honor per President Theodore Roosevelt's orders. Several of the 167 men discharged were very near twenty years of military service and retirement with pensions, benefits they lost because of this incident.

During World War I, a white mob in Huntsville killed an African American man and six members of his family when he was accused of evading the draft. Then in Houston in 1917, the federal government had brought in the Third Battalion of the African American Twenty-fourth U.S. Infantry to guard two military installations near the newly opened Houston Ship Channel. Upon their arrival, the troops received racist treatment from the Houston Police Department, in part for challenging Jim Crow segregation. On August 23, following a summer of growing tensions and the arrest and pistol whipping of one black soldier earlier that day for interfering with the arrest of a local black woman, a riot broke out with more than 100 armed and mutinous African American soldiers marching on the Fourth Ward police station. Fifteen whites, including five policemen, died, and eleven others were seriously wounded. Four African American soldiers also died, two accidentally shot by their own men. The army quickly removed the troopers to New Mexico, where, under wartime conditions, the military courts handed down harsh punishments: Nineteen soldiers were hanged and sixty-three sentenced to life in prison.

The war revived prohibition efforts in Texas. Prohibitionists called for a ban on alcohol within ten miles of military bases or schools and attacked its manufacture as wasteful in a time of war, its brewers as agents of the German Kaiser, and its effect on military personnel as unhealthy. When Secretary of War Newton D. Baker let it be known that the government would continue to send large numbers of soldiers to Texas bases if they insured "conditions of cleanliness and wholesomeness" nearby, Hobby submitted these new rules to a special session of the legislature in February 1918. Both houses of the legislature, responding to the drys, approved a bill relating to military bases and then ratified the prohibition amendment (the Eighteenth Amendment) to the U.S. Constitution, which went into effect in 1919.

Finally, the legislature amended the election law to require a runoff in primaries if no candidate received a majority and to extend the right to vote in primaries to women. Supporters of suffrage typically also were supporters of prohibition, and as with the liquor issue, they used the war for their own purposes. The drafting of large numbers of men for World War I helped the woman's suffrage movement nationwide. With so many men in the military, numerous home front jobs opened up for women, and their new wartime responsibilities gave the movement impetus, even eliciting President Wilson's less than ardent support. As Judith N. McArthur has argued, "homefront mobilization completed middle class women's conquest of public space, fatally weakening the old separate spheres argument against female voting." After the legislature extended women the right to vote in primaries, Annie Webb Blanton won election as state superintendent of

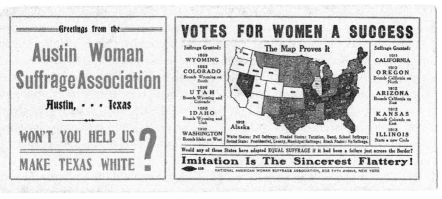

Woman Suffrage Broadside, produced after 1913. The U.S. map denotes those western states that had granted women full suffrage in white. States that were shaded provided voting rights to women in certain local elections while the states that were dotted had liberalized suffrage for presidential elections as well as some local contests. States colored in black denied women the right to vote in all elections. The use of the word "white" in the broadside's caption was a not so subtle rejoinder to critics of voting rights for women who argued that suffrage would harm white supremacy by making it possible for African American women to vote.

education, but women would have to wait until the Nineteenth Amendment to the Constitution was ratified, in 1920, before they could vote in general elections.

Voting rights for women had an immediate impact on state politics as did the war. In 1918, Hobby defeated Ferguson, who despite his impeachment and conviction had secured a place on the ballot in the gubernatorial election. Using his wartime authority, Governor Hobby had appointed almost 1,000 Special Rangers, whose primary duty, it seemed, was to ensure Hobby's election in 1918. With prohibitionists and suffragists strongly behind him, Hobby received a total of 461,479 votes to Ferguson's 217,012. No runoff was necessary.

Postwar Conformity and Conflict

The war came to a close a couple of months later, on November 11, when the Allies and the Germans signed an armistice. The hostilities had brought a measure of prosperity to Texas, as cotton production soared, but it had also brought a growing cultural conformity as the drive to unite a heterogeneous population for war continued long after the peace. The legislature made it a crime to criticize the U.S. government, the flag, the war effort, or soldiers' uniforms, and required that schools teach patriotism, fly the American flag, and teach all classes except foreign language classes in English. In 1919, Hobby vetoed the appropriation for the German department at the University of Texas, and most high schools dropped the language from their curriculum. The 1917 Russian Revolution highlighted the supposed Bolshevik threat, and many Texans believed that union and civil rights activists were evidence of the menace at home. Oil producers rumored that a 1917–18 oilfield workers strike in Louisiana and Texas was inspired by the Industrial Workers of the World, and a violent and prolonged dock strike in Galveston led Governor Hobby to place the city under martial law. Lynchings and intimidation of African Americans continued as well; there was a race riot in Longview and an official of the NAACP was beaten by a white mob in Austin during what became known nationwide as the "red summer" of 1919.

By 1920, the population shift from rural to urban areas was becoming apparent. Meanwhile, the economic difficulties of farmers were temporarily obscured by two years of abundant crops that helped make up for the falling postwar prices. Though Governor Hobby favored urban growth and economic development, he declined to advocate such measures because of a reluctant legislature and a "leave well enough alone" public attitude.

The decade of the 1920s soon became known throughout the nation as the Jazz Age, which was defined by the rise of cities, the decline of religion (coupled with the teaching of evolution), bootleggers and speakeasies, the growth of the Socialist Party and the "red scare," increased European immigration, and the advent of the "New Woman." And perhaps the prototypical Jazz Age flapper was Gordon Conway, born in Cleburne and reared in Dallas. An extremely productive commercial graphic artist and costume designer for stage and film in New York, London, and Paris, Conway produced paintings and drawings of the New Woman for *Vogue, Vanity Fair, Harper's Bazaar*, and many other publications, including her hometown newspapers, from World War I into the Depression. Conway's New Woman was, in many ways, a parody of New York society women involved in charity work, but the new type caught on. The New Woman and the flapper became icons of the 1920s.

Nevertheless, social and economic problems persisted. Lynching had declined but not disappeared, and economic refugees were arriving from Mexico in ever-increasing numbers, with perhaps as many as 126,811 settling in Texas between 1910 and 1920. The burgeoning oil and gas industry had spawned some swindlers and the usual lawlessness that, on occasion, required the intervention of the Texas Rangers and the Texas National Guard; the Volstead Act of 1919, which implemented the new prohibition amendment, caused most of this crime. In Texas, the Jazz Age was characterized by a new lawlessness that accompanied the oil boom. The oil boom only hastened the migration from rural to urban areas, and Texans were quick to display the decline of moral values that was supposedly going on throughout the nation. Less than a year after passage of prohibition, bootlegging was so widespread in Texas that a still with a 130-gallon capacity was found on the Austin-area farm of U.S. senator Morris Sheppard, the author of the Eighteenth Amendment.

The Elements of Jazz

From the hard-scrabble cultures of the cotton farms and lumber mills of East and Central Texas came one of the truly American forms of music, jazz, which, because of its varied folk roots, has been called a true expression of democracy. One strand of jazz can be traced to Texarkana in the 1880s, when Scott Joplin, a young son of a former slave, learned music from a German teacher and began to perform in medicine shows and vaudeville. Joplin, composer and pianist, known as the "father of ragtime," performed in the saloons and brothels of St. Louis, Missouri.

Blues music appeared in East Texas as early as 1890 and is represented by two of its most famous practitioners, Blind Lemon Jefferson (1897–1929) and Huddie "Leadbelly" Ledbetter (1888–1949), who were active in the 1920s and actually played together for a while in the Deep Ellum district of Dallas. A third strand was "barrelhouse-style piano," perhaps better known as boogie-woogie; it probably came out of the lumber camps of East Texas. Because of the rural nature of the state, many of these performers and composers moved to Kansas City, where they were among the first generation to compose, perform, and record jazz.

Segregation and the Rise of the Ku Klux Klan

The Progressive and Jazz Eras also saw the continued rise of racism. During the early part of the twentieth century, the rights that African Americans had gained after the Civil War were systematically taken away. Shocked by the near-success of the Populist Party coalition of poor African American and white farmers, the Bourbon Democrats had embarked upon a campaign to divide the poor by claiming that African Americans were inherently inferior and a threat to society. Their goal was to segregate African Americans into a separate society, divided by law and custom and governed by leaders for whom they could not vote. They largely succeeded, and they did so using the rhetoric of Progressive reform.

There were 670,722 African Americans in Texas by 1900, and 854,964 by 1930, most of them living in rural areas and working as tenants and farm laborers. But others had attempted to escape the racial and economic conditions of rural life by moving out of the state—to northern cities and to Louisiana and Oklahoma—or to Texas cities such as Houston and Dallas. The urban African American population increased from 19 percent in 1900 to 32 percent in 1930; the number of African American males employed in nonagricultural jobs increased from 57,000 to almost 115,000 during that same period, most still in manual labor or servant jobs. Ministers and teachers made up most of a small African American bourgeoisie that also consisted of doctors, dentists, lawyers, and undertakers. There were more than 1,700 African American–owned retail stores in the state in 1929, most of them mom-and-pop operations such as grocery stores, drugstores, and restaurants. Hobart Taylor, Sr., of Houston, who invested in insurance and taxicabs, may have been the first African American millionaire in the state. Prairie View A&M offered courses for African Americans at both the high school and college level, with emphasis on technical, agricultural, and educational training. A few other colleges and universities taught African Americans during this era: Paul Quinn College, Texas College, and Wiley College.

The first step toward racial segregation had occurred when the Redeemers won control of the state government in 1876. The second step was African American disenfranchisement, accomplished by the Terrell election laws. When the Supreme

Court, in *Nixon v. Herndon* (1927), agreed that all-white primaries violated the Fourteenth Amendment, Texas responded by defining political parties as private organizations that could select their own qualified voters. The Court agreed, and African Americans remained effectively shut out of the electoral process.

Next came the segregation of public facilities. Passenger trains had been segregated by race as early as 1891. In 1910 and 1911, the legislature required the establishment of separate waiting rooms in railroad stations and separate public drinking fountains and restrooms. Several cities adopted residential segregation laws after 1910, but the U.S. Supreme Court invalidated them. Cities got around the Court by resorting to zoning regulations. That led to a degradation of health and recreational services and city services such as utilities, paving, and police protection in the African American areas. By the 1930s, African Americans could no longer attend sports or cultural events, eat at restaurants, or stay in hotels unless those facilities provided separate accommodations. Although these laws were not passed with the Mexican population in mind, community cultural mores often denied Mexicans many services and opportunities.

Where laws did not sufficiently enforce segregation, vigilante action often did. The Ku Klux Klan moved into Texas in 1920. It was both a relic of Reconstruction and also the culture of extra legal violence that had developed in central Texas since independence from Mexico. Historian William D. Carrigan has shown how the intersection of the frontier experience, racial slavery, minority resistance to the white power structure, and government tolerance of extralegal violence facilitated a lynching culture. The Klan was a part of this larger structural framework.

William Joseph Simmons, an ex-Methodist minister near Atlanta, Georgia, reorganized the Klan in 1915 as an antidote to what he perceived as moral deterioration and a lack of patriotism. He sent field representatives (kleagles) to organize new chapters (klaverns) throughout the nation and by 1922 the Klan had more than 700,000 members, by 1925 perhaps as many as 5 million. Its militant fundamentalism and anti-Catholicism appealed to many in the South and the Midwest, including Progressive reformers in the urban areas, where the new middle class, usually with rural values still intact, identified with the Klan's goals. With issues such as prohibition foremost in society, the Klan attracted Progressive reformers who did not object to enforcing a moral code so long as it was theirs. Thomas B. Love of Dallas, who had supported Wilson for the presidency, characterized the Klan as "made up almost wholly of misled and misguided good people who are on the moral side of moral questions and on the progressive side of economic questions" who would quickly grow tired of the effort.

The Klan gained many adherents in North, East, and Central Texas. Membership was not nearly so high in heavily Catholic South Texas. Despite the fact that the Klan resorted to such extralegal practices as flogging, tar-and-feathering, and branding to enforce its will (there were more than fifty cases of Klan violence during 1921 alone), many prominent citizens, including Governor Pat M. Neff, refused to speak out against it. With oil boomtowns bursting out of control on occasion and the Mexican Revolution troubles on the border, the Klan claimed that unparalleled lawlessness forced it to act, and Governor Neff seemed

The Ku Klux Klan reached a membership of approximately 90,000 in Texas during the 1920s. Here, the Klan is shown parading in Beaumont on November 10, 1922.

to agree. By playing on fears aroused by race riots, labor disruptions, and rumors of Bolshevik influence, the "invisible empire" gained many members; by 1922 these members included a sympathetic U.S. senator, Earle B. Mayfield, who triumphed over "Farmer Jim" Ferguson in a bitter contest.

The Klan supplanted prohibition as the main issue in Texas politics during the early 1920s, as major newspapers in Dallas, Houston, and El Paso attacked it. Wright patman, a member of the state house, introduced several anti-Klan bills in 1921 as Progressive reforms, but he also pushed for anti-miscegenation legislation. As Imperial Wizard of the Klan, Hiram W. Evans of Dallas instituted a policy of political action rather than violence and intimidation. The Klan denied responsibility for any of the lynchings that took place during these years, but it is likely that the emotionalism and moral passion of its rallies incited them, at the very least. Miriam Ferguson's victory in the 1924 governor's race over the Klan-backed candidate for governor, Felix D. Robertson of Dallas—the choice between "a bonnet or a hood"—marked the end of significant Klan influence in Texas politics.

The Fergusons Return

The "business progressivism" of Governors Hobby and Neff had provided Texans with a respite from "Fergusonism." When Miriam Ferguson ran for governor in 1924, she brought a return to the populism of her husband.

Ferguson won the election because the cult of personality continued to control the Democratic Party in 1924, and the dominant personality of the last decade had been her husband, "Farmer Jim" Ferguson. Ferguson had continued to publish his newspaper, the *Ferguson Forum,* claiming that the major newspapers had "submarined the truth." Still able to energize a rural audience but unable to get his name on the Democratic primary ballot in 1924, he came up with the ruse of running his wife, Miriam. The main issues of the campaign became prohibition and the Klan. He stumped the state on behalf of his wife, proclaiming "two governors for the price of one" and referring to Imperial Wizard Evans as the "Grand Gizzard." Miriam Ferguson, a middle-age, middle-class woman who enjoyed the fashions of the day, showed her own political savvy when she refused to be photographed during the campaign wearing anything but a bonnet and a gingham dress, the attire common to Texas farm women. She understood Texas voters did not want a New Woman in the governor's mansion. The prohibition and Klan candidate was no match for the crafty veteran, and Ferguson won the primary runoff by almost 100,000 votes.

Once in office, and with her husband at her side, Ferguson struck back at the Klan, securing passage of a law that prohibited the wearing of masks in public. She vetoed a number of line items in the University of Texas appropriation and

Historical/Corbis

Miriam Ferguson, the first woman to be elected governor of Texas.

granted more than 2,000 paroles, pardons, and extensions, many of which went to prohibition violators. She lamented the fact that most of those convicted were poor whereas the wealthy continued to have access to drink in their private clubs; she offered a $500 reward for the arrest and conviction of any liquor-law violator who had property worth more than $5,000. But her term was also tainted by charges of graft and scandal. "Pa," it seems, acted as attorney for many of the successful pardons that she granted and saw to it that state contracts for school textbooks and highway construction were awarded to those who bought ads in the *Ferguson Forum*. A final irony may have been the fact that most people who supported the vote for women expected them to clean up corruption in politics, but Miriam Ferguson's election put her cunning and scandal-plagued husband back in power.

Attorney General Dan Moody successfully brought suit to cancel a number of highway contracts that Ferguson friends and allies had received. This initiative secured his victory over Ferguson in the 1926 gubernatorial election where the main issue was corruption.

With his business-progressive point of view, he set about reorganizing several government departments. He led an ostensibly prosperous and increasingly urban state for four years as it sank, along with the nation, into the worst depression that the country has ever known. Few noticed that 1929, the same year that the New York stock market crashed, was also the first year in which the value of crude oil production in Texas ($322,520,000) exceeded the value of the cotton crop ($315,200,000).

 ## Conclusion

In 1929, Texans seemed about to enjoy the rewards of more than two decades of reform and progress. Farming and ranching had certainly suffered during the 1920s, but that was largely disguised by the booming economy nationwide and the growing influence of oil on the state's economy. Prohibition was now a national law, thanks, in part, to platoons of righteous women reformers. The "business progressives" had apparently beaten back the Fergusons, and the state seemed to be coming of age in other ways. Progressive historians at the University of Texas led the way in investigating the state's past with the founding of the *Southwestern Historical Quarterly* in 1897. George Pierce Garrison began teaching the first course in Texas history that year, and two-and-a-half decades later, his protégé, Eugene C. Barker, published his classic biography of Stephen F. Austin. At the same time, Paris-trained Dallas artist Frank Reaugh was leading his students on summer expeditions into West Texas and extolling the virtues of interpreting the Texas landscape. Most Texans were outraged at the publication of Dorothy Scarborough's novel, *The Wind* (1925), because of its haunting and inhospitable portrait of West Texas. They took pride, however, in the work of one of the state's most distinguished writers of fiction, Katherine Anne Porter, who grew up in Kyle and San Antonio, but whose Texas-based short stories gained her international fame. Texas drew strength from its unique heritage and culture and its progress toward modernization as the country headed into the worst economic crisis it had known.

Suggested Readings

Useful general studies of the first three decades of the century include Lewis L. Gould, *Progressives and Prohibitionists: Texas Democrats in the Wilson Era* (1992); Walter L. Buenger's *The Path to a Modern South: Northeast Texas Between Reconstruction and the Great Depression* (2001); and Seth S. McKay and Odie B. Faulk, *Texas After Spindletop* (1965). Biographical essays on Edward M. House, Morris Sheppard, John Nance Garner, Tom Connally, and Sam Rayburn are included in Kenneth E. Hendrickson, Jr. and Michael L. Collins, Eds., *Profiles in Power: Twentieth-Century Texans in Washington* (1993).

The Texas Economy

Works on economic history include Donald E. Green, *Land of the Underground Rain: Irrigation on the Texas High Plains, 1910–1970* (1973), and Diana Davids Olien and Roger M. Olien, *Oil in Texas: The Gusher Age, 1895–1945* (2002). For discussion of farmers and political protest, see Kyle G. Wilkison, *Yeomen, Sharecroppers and Socialists: Plain Folk Protest in Texas, 1870–1914* (2008).

Texas Reforms

A useful work on politics and reform is Evan Anders, *Boss Rule in South Texas: The Progressive Era* (1982). The best work on the Galveston storm of 1900 is Erik Larson, *Isaac's Storm: A Man, a Time, and the Deadliest Hurricane in History* (2000). Excellent works on urban history include David G. McComb, *Galveston, A History* (1986); McComb, *Houston: A History* (1986); David C. Humphrey, *Austin, an Illustrated History* (1985); and Patricia Everidge Hill, *Dallas: The Making of a Modern City* (1996). Important discussions of gender and reform are in Elizabeth York Enstam, *Women and the Creation of Urban Life: Dallas, Texas, 1843–1920* (1998) and Elizabeth Hayes Turner, *Women, Culture, and Community: Religion and Reform in Galveston, 1880–1920* (1997).

Fergusonism

Norman D. Brown, *Hood, Bonnet, and Little Brown Jug: Texas Politics, 1921–1928* (1984) contains an excellent discussion of much of the Ferguson era. A more recent treatment by Carol O'Keefe Wilson, *In the Governor's Shadow: The True Story of Ma and Pa Ferguson* (2014), proves the corruption in the Fergusons' administrations. For information on the border troubles, see Don M. Coerver and Linda B. Hall, *Texas and the Mexican Revolution: A Study in State and National Border Policy, 1910–1920* (1984); David Montejano, *Anglos and Mexicans in the Making of Texas, 1836 1986* (1987); Benjamin Heber Johnson, *Revolution in Texas: How a Forgotten Rebellion and Its Bloody Suppression Turned Mexicans into Americans* (2005); Arnoldo de León, ed., *War along the Border: The Mexican Revolution and Tejano Communities* (2012); and Douglas W. Richmond and Sam W. Haynes, eds., *The Mexican Revolution: Conflict and Consolidation, 1910–1940* (2013). For information on the Texas Rangers, see Robert M. Utley, *Lone Star Justice: The First Century of the Texas Rangers* (2002).

From World War I to the Jazz Era

Works on women include Judith N. McArthur, *Creating the New Woman: The Rise of Southern Women's Progressive Culture in Texas, 1893–1918* (1998). Treatments of race and the culture of segregation include Alwyn Barr, *Black Texans: A History of African Americans in Texas, 1528–1995* (1996); William D. Carrigan, *The Making of a Lynching Culture: Violence and Vigilantism in Central Texas, 1836–1916* (2006); Bernadette Pruitt, *The Other Great Migration: The Movement of Rural African Americans to Houston, 1900–1941* (2013); Arnoldo De León, *Mexican Americans in Texas: A Brief History,* 2nd ed. (1999); and Neil Foley, *The White Scourge: Mexicans, Blacks, and Poor Whites in Texas Cotton Culture* (1999).

Depression and War, 1929–1945

"In 1929, my father was employed as a locomotive engineer," recalled Robert Ozment of the years just before the Great Depression struck. Ozment and his family lived in Temple, a Central Texas farming and railroad center. "We had a new Overland Whippet auto, were buying a home, had money in the bank, and plenty of food and clothing. By 1933, all this was gone except the Whippet. We were living in a rent-free house which bordered the Negro section of Temple. We often had little to eat but oatmeal, we were without electricity, and had few clothes. I remember this house well because it had no coverings on the splintery old floors. My one pair of shoes had to be saved for winter use, and during the summer my feet were constantly bandaged from the . . . splinters.

"I also remember the Whippet. We had no money for either gas or tires so it just sat in the shed. It became a kind of physical symbol of the times to me because, like some of the humans, it was waiting [for] a chance to go to work and did not understand why it could not. All it could do was to waste away its productive years waiting and hoping until the inexorable end should arrive. We sold it for five dollars in 1939 . . .

"I once asked my mother what had caused the depression they talked about so much. Considering the fact that neither we nor any of our family were farmers, her answer may seem a bit peculiar. She said: 'The bottom fell out of the cotton market.' To a person living in Bell County, it was just that simple: the bottom fell out of the cotton market. I was just old enough to remember the physical deprivations which my family suffered," he concluded, "but none of the psychological trauma."

Chapter 12 Depression and War, 1929–1945	
1929	New York stock market crashes; League of United Latin American Citizens founded
1930	East Texas oil field discovered; price of oil falls to 8 cents per barrel
1931	Price of cotton falls to 5 cents per pound
1933	Eighteenth Amendment is repealed
1933	The New Deal begins
1935	Texas repeals its prohibition law
1936	Texas Centennial
1937	Soil Conservation Service recorded 72 dust storms on the plains
1938	U.S. congressman Martin Dies becomes the first chair of the Special Committee on Un-American Activities (later the House Committee on Un-American Activities)
1941	Japan attacks Pearl Harbor, United States enters World War II
1942	Bracero program adopted
1943	"Big Inch" pipeline completed
1944	"Little Inch" pipeline completed; Texas's all-white primary held to be unconstitutional by the U.S. Supreme Court
1945	World War II ends with the Allies victorious

As the presidential election of 1928 approached, many Texans reflected on the good economic times of the Roaring Twenties, when the state's population had increased by almost 25 percent, to more than 5.8 million and cotton, lumber, truck and citrus farming, livestock, and oil and gas fueled the economy, apparently more efficiently than ever. By 1929 the state was the world's leading supplier of crude oil, having produced more than 2 billion barrels, and the development of the Houston Ship Channel had made that city the state's busiest port. Electrical appliances, lights, radios, telephones, and plumbing facilities had greatly improved urban life, and several Texas cities—Dallas, Houston, and San Antonio—were among the most rapidly growing in the country. The number of automobiles, which facilitated the move to urban areas, increased to the point that Texans owned one car for every 4.3 residents. Such affluence led to talk of "Coolidge prosperity," after President Calvin Coolidge (1925–1929), and the general feeling that a permanent cornucopia had emerged in the years after World War I.

The two economic dynamos—oil and agriculture—continued to propel the state forward, from 1930 to 1945. During these years, however, Texas and the nation faced two of their greatest challenges—the Great Depression and World War II—and the state's inability to act forcefully to combat the ravages of the depression required the federal government to play an even more significant role than it had in the Progressive Era. But another force, almost as powerful as the economy, according to some, was the sense of Texas chauvinism and modernism that strengthened in the midst of the Great Depression of the 1930s. Texans celebrated both at the centennial of Texas independence in 1936. This chauvinism all but ignored dependence on federal coffers for surviving the depression and war years.

As you read this chapter, consider the following questions:

1. What social and economic impact did the Great Depression have on Texans?
2. How did federal involvement in Texas differ during the New Deal and during World War II?
3. Why did Texas leaders appropriate a new, western image for the state separate from its southern heritage? Was this effort at rebranding more or less inclusive of all Texans than the identity of the state as southern? Why?

The Great Depression

But the economy had a soft underbelly. Texas farmers, like those of other states, had suffered hard times throughout the seemingly prosperous decade. Farmers had not adjusted their production at the end of World War I and quickly accumulated surpluses that brought a sharp decline in prices in 1920–21. Instead of reducing production, they increased it. The number of Texas farms increased from 436,038 to 495,489, and the amount of cultivated land grew by 3.5 million acres. At the same time, printed notices of sheriff's sales, business failures, and bankruptcies became characteristic of the farm country, and newspaper editors resorted to homilies—"many a family that has lost its car has found its soul. . . ."

Few people were aware of the nation's deeper economic problems. Inequitable distribution of wealth, with a mere 2 percent of the population controlling 28 percent of the wealth whereas the bottom 60 percent controlled only about 24 percent, was only one of the harbingers of the coming difficulties. Agriculture was an industry in trouble with severe overproduction and skewed distribution of wealth. In Texas, the heavy reliance on sharecroppers and tenant farmers embodied this problem. Texans experienced other signs of the depression: bank failures, job losses, and industrial chaos.

But economic crisis was hardly on the minds of Texans as they went to the polls in 1928 to elect a president. Texas had its political coming out party that summer when southern, largely un-air-conditioned Houston hosted the Democratic National Convention, the first time a major national party held a convention in the South since the Civil War. Southwestern booster, financier, banker, and newspaper publisher Jesse H. Jones orchestrated the efforts to locate the convention in Houston. Texas Democrats, like their counterparts throughout the South, cleaved to one version of the divided Democratic Party, support for prohibition and a protestant, traditional culture, but the delegates that year nominated New York governor Alfred E. Smith for the presidency. Catholic, opposed to prohibition, and from an urban background, Smith represented everything about modernity that troubled white Texans. Moreover, he sympathized with the large immigrant population. Said one Texas delegate to the convention of the celebration following Smith's nomination: "I sat by the central aisle while the parade passed following Smith's nomination and the faces I saw in that mile-long procession were not American faces. I wondered where were the Americans." In November, Texans voted *en masse* for Herbert Hoover, the first Republican presidential candidate to carry the state. The choice was less about changing partisan identity and more about preventing cultural conflict and continuing economic prosperity.

The Stock Market Crash

Before Hoover had completed his first year in office, however, the failing economy grabbed the nation's attention in a spectacular way: The New York Stock Exchange crashed. Since the mid-1920s, the steady advance of the market encouraged many investors to speculate by purchasing stocks on margin (with borrowed money). Then, suddenly, in September and October 1929, the market fell. "Black Thursday," October 24, was bad, but the worst occurred on October 29, when 16 million shares of stock, more than ever before, changed hands and the *New York Times* industrial average dropped nearly forty points. A coalition of New York bankers tried but could not stem the tide, and by November exchange listings had declined an average of 37.5 percent. Because relatively few people in the state owned stock, Texans felt insulated from the troubles of the market. They seemed to agree with the editor of the *Taylor Daily Press,* who said that his concern was "Jim Rural" and "Joe Normal," whom he expected would continue to do business as usual. The editor of the *Houston Post-Dispatch* added, "the changes in stock prices are purely an affair of and for stock speculators." Governor Dan Moody finished his term in office without feeling the full force of the coming depression or taking any action to prepare for it.

Nor was the economy the chief concern of voters in the gubernatorial election of 1930, a contest that drew eleven Democrats to the race. Citing his need to enter the private practice of law to pay his debts, Governor Moody declined to run for a third term, and Ross S. Sterling, a founder and former president of Humble Oil and Refining Company, carried the business-progressive mantel in the campaign. Former governor Miriam Ferguson challenged Sterling.

Sterling called for prison reform, better roads and labor conditions, and more support for education. His service as Moody's able chair of the State Highway Commission led him to champion a $300–$350 million bond issue for state highways. James Ferguson, who did most of the campaigning for his wife, initially did not take seriously the heavy-set Sterling, who had once been introduced to an audience as "your fat boy from Houston." Miriam Ferguson led Sterling in the primary by more than 70,000 votes. But personalities came to the fore as she and Sterling met in the runoff where Fergusonism was the issue. Said one Sterling insider: "The issue now was HONEST AND RESPONSIBLE GOVERNMENT VERSUS DISHONEST AND PROXY GOVERNMENT." The added influence of former governor Moody and other officials, who announced for Sterling and began making speeches on his behalf, pushed him to victory.

The Depression Deepens

The election was, however, a sideshow to the main event, as cotton prices continued to fall and unemployment soared. The Hoover administration offered little more than the appearance of action—an endless series of meetings, each of which seemed to culminate with hollow statements of confidence that "prosperity is just around the corner." The optimism continued into 1931, with the *Fort Worth Star-Telegram,* for example, claiming that Texans did not "know what hard times are," and pointing to increased construction, railroad traffic, and oil production, and stable cattle and poultry sales. Even as late as 1933, Jones, the Houston banker whom President Hoover had appointed to the board of the Reconstruction Finance Corporation, told a Dallas audience, "The most important thing before the nation today is to balance the budget."

In Temple, meanwhile, the impact of the Wall Street crash came in 1930— sooner than anyone had expected—when the local banks began to lay off experienced employees. Banks throughout the state struggled with bank runs and closures. As in the rest of the United States, the majority of bank failures occurred in small towns. For example, in December 1931, there were 113 fewer banks operating in Texas than in the year previous; deposits declined by over $200 million. Between Black Thursday and 1932, more than 5,000 banks failed and 100,000 businesses closed nationwide, and the national income was halved— from $80 billion to $40 billion.

The human cost was tremendous, with an increase in the murder rate, the suicide rate, and the number of hospitalizations for mental health treatment during the depression years. Lost bank accounts translated into lost homes and businesses and changed modes of living.

As early as January, 1930, labor union officers asked San Antonio officials to vote bonds to provide work for the growing number of unemployed construction workers. In Houston, a local news vendor reported that his business was up because people who "don't look like they have much more than the price of a newspaper in their pockets . . . are buying them now to read the want ads." By 1931 over 350,000 Texans were unemployed. The results of the crash for women and people of color were worse than for white men.

New oil softened the blow in a few places such as Taylor and Kilgore, but in Midland oil prices crashed because of overproduction in the East Texas field, which led to declining leases and drilling and rising unemployment. The population of Midland dropped by approximately 1,000 between 1930 and 1932.

By 1933, more than 7 percent of Texas families were on relief, compared to 10 percent nationally. The rate in Texas increased to about 13 percent the following year. Some historians have suggested that rural Texans did not suffer as much as city dwellers because they had gardens and continued to raise much of their food. But, as the economy faltered, the average wage paid for the back-breaking labor of picking cotton dropped from $1.21 per 100 pounds in 1928 to 44 cents in 1931. By then farmers had other concerns as well. "I did not go to . . . [church tonight]," William G. DeLoach of Crosby County in the Texas Panhandle recorded in his diary in 1931. "I am afraid to go. That is[,] all of us go away at night. Some people are losing their canned goods. We have quite a lot of foods of different kinds canned up, can't afford to take a chance on some road tramp coming here and getting it, so I stayed home."

Family and friends initially rallied to help those who fell victim to unemployment, and when their resources were expended, private charities helped out. When charitable funds were depleted, only the local and state governments remained to help. Some cities established public works programs to offer temporary aid to the unemployed, but usually tried to limit it to local residents. Midland and other cities sent police officers to train stations to make sure that transients got back on the train. Houston, meanwhile, denied relief to African Americans and Mexican Americans prior to 1933.

Mexicans and Mexican Americans suffered from the federal government's policy of repatriation—which began in 1928 and increased during the Hoover administration—a misleading term since many of the Mexican heritage people returned to Mexico during the depression were American-born U.S. citizens. Approximately 500,000 Mexican heritage people were repatriated to Mexico during the Great Depression with half from Texas. In Texas, the peak year of the repatriation initiative was 1931. Though some repatriates came from urban Texas, the depression in agriculture was the most important reason for this movement. Ironically, many of the repatriates left with substantial resources.

Because many policymakers saw Mexican heritage residents of the United States as temporary—then congressman John Nance Garner said Mexicans were like "homing pigeons" and would readily return to their home country—they saw nothing wrong with the repatriation policy. Actually, repatriation was just as temporary, for it provided only a brief halt to the movement of Mexican migrants into the United States.

Anglo-Texans sometimes behaved violently toward the Mexican heritage population remaining in the state. The headquarters of the Society of Mexican Laborers, located in Malakoff, Texas, was bombed, and the Mexican Consul General in San Antonio told Governor Sterling, "There is intense excitement and fear among Mexican Nationals of serious bodily injury."

The depression had multiple meanings for Texas women. In 1930 one-third of Texas women worked outside the home, typically in jobs designated for women. The modernization of the state and the nation encouraged farm women, especially girls coming of age, to move off the farm and into the cities. Historian

Rebecca Sharpless noted, "Once a family member left home, she often developed into a different person, shedding her old rural appearance and taking on new urban values." The intrusion of the depression exaggerated this process while also forcing urban Texas women to learn new modes of survival.

Anglos used the depression to mitigate against the efforts of minority women to improve their economic circumstances. Historian Monica Perales notes, "El Paso's elites were able to counter the unionization efforts of Mexican American domestic workers by either hiring Mexican women from across the border or structuring relief requirements in such a way that American-born Mexicans had no choice but to accept the miserable paying jobs as maids."

Middle-class women became the target as local business and political leaders implicitly and explicitly suggested women's behavior and choices had exacerbated the depression. For middle-class women, a typical "buy at home" campaign such as the one in Austin urged women to "talk Austin, write about Austin, work for Austin, and live for Austin." Some school districts refused to employ single women and, on the assumption of only one breadwinner per family, fired married women if their spouse had a job. The school board in San Antonio ordered that married women with husbands earning over $2,000 a year should be fired.

In some communities, there simply was no more money. In such circumstances, school districts and retail merchant associations issued scrip as a circulating medium. The depression became so severe that only the federal government stood between the country and complete collapse.

The Dust Bowl

Even if the depression did take longer to arrive in Texas than in other parts of the country, it was no less devastating. Conditions on the farm got even worse as a combination of poor land maintenance and a devastating drought created what became known as the Dust Bowl on the Great Plains. Growing numbers of enthusiastic young farmers had moved onto the plains since the turn of the century, and in just a few years, through cattle raising and row-crop agriculture, they had destroyed most of the native grasses that held the dirt in place. Between 1925 and 1930, with the new gasoline tractors, entrepreneurs plowed up the vegetation on millions of acres of the Southern Plains in what one writer has called "the great plow-up."

The rain stopped abruptly in late 1931, and one of the periodic droughts that plague the semiarid region set in and lasted through 1934. But this was not an ordinary drought. With almost 33 million acres of plains land bare and open to the characteristically high winds, the phenomenon known as the Dust Bowl began. The onset of a polar air mass that might, in an ordinary year, have produced common "sand blows" now incited "black blizzards" that were sometimes accompanied by fantastic displays of lightning. Atmospheric electricity lifted the windblown dirt as high as 7,000–8,000 feet—until it looked like a winter blizzard or a huge thunderstorm. In 1932 the Soil Conservation Service counted fourteen dust storms on the plains. That number increased to thirty-eight in 1933, fell to

Rothstein, Arthur/ Library of Congress Prints and Photographs Division Washington, DC 20540/ LC-DIG-fsa-8b27277

Arthur Rothstein photograph for the Farm Security Administration, a New Deal program, taken in March 1936 of heavy black clouds of dust rolling over the Texas panhandle.

twenty-two in 1934, rose again to forty in 1935, sixty-eight in 1936, and seventy-two in 1937, the worst year on record.

The storm of April 1935 was the worst. As it blew in on April 9, William DeLoach recorded that visibility fell to 200–300 yards. His family remained in the house for several days. On Sunday, while the rest of the family was at church and he sat reading, the worst of the storm hit: "One could hardly get breath," he wrote. "I thought I would choke when I went to bed." Even in Austin, legislators and staff wore gauze face masks in the Capitol.

Thousands of tenants and sharecroppers, and even some landowners, gave up and left. Many joined the exodus to California, a trek that John Steinbeck made famous in his novel *The Grapes of Wrath* (1939). But a large number of the Dust Bowl migrants were not victims of drought, windstorm, and grasshoppers. A number of them were tenants who had been forced off the land by tractors and wage laborers; others had been replaced by Mexican laborers (those not returned to Mexico under the repatriation policy) who had been immigrating northward in increasing numbers since the turn of the century and were willing to work for less. The net result was a reduction of almost 200,000 in the number of people living on farms in Texas between 1930 and 1940.

Even in the face of such tragedies, Governor Sterling apparently agreed with the Hoover administration that his first responsibility as governor was to reduce the state's expenses. He vetoed a number of bills passed by the forty-second legislature, usually because they did not provide taxes to cover their costs. Despite the fact that the legislature met for 131 days, little was done to assist in the state's crisis during what was characterized as a "do-nothing session." This pay-as-you-go approach was traditional in Texas.

Chaos in the East Texas Oil Field

Sterling's greatest concerns were the state's two largest economic engines—oil and agriculture—and, ironically, overproduction was the problem in both cases. By 1930, oil had been discovered all over Texas, and the new wells in the Yates field in West Texas were so productive that many industry experts began to warn of overproduction. Then, in October 1930, Columbus Marion (Dad) Joiner brought in the Daisy Bradford No. 3 near Kilgore and the East Texas boom was on. The East Texas field was even bigger than Spindletop. Within two years, it boasted more than 10,000 producing wells, and the price of oil fell from a little over a dollar a barrel in 1930 to eight cents a barrel in 1931. In the peak year of 1933, the East Texas production reached 204,954,000 barrels of oil, more than the rest of the state combined.

The East Texas field was an anomaly for at least two reasons. The first was its sheer size. Within a few months of Joiner's discovery, successful wells had been drilled into this huge reservoir in five counties spread over 140,000 acres. Experts estimated that it contained about 5.5 billion barrels of oil, approximately one-third of the nation's then-known oil reserves.

The second anomaly—the absence of major oil companies—brought a new element into the industry. This field became known as "the promised land of independent producers and small royalty owners," and they, along with entrepreneurs, swindlers, prostitutes, hustlers of all kinds, gathered around the oil field workers in Kilgore, the center of most of the activity. When the wildcatters realized that they were not drilling in separate fields,

Prints and Photographs Collection, e_enr_182, The Dolph Briscoe Center for American History, The University of Texas at Austin

C. M. "Dad" Joiner and the geologist A. D. "Doc" Lloyd shake hands after the discovery of the East Texas oil field, the largest field discovered in the continental United States, 1930.

as they had thought, but into one giant pool, the frenzy began in earnest. The rule of capture—the law governing the development of oil fields ever since a Pennsylvania Supreme Court decision in 1889—meant that the person who pumped the oil owned it, even if it had migrated from an adjoining lease. Landowners began to sell leases that were measured in feet rather than acres, and, ultimately, one city block in Kilgore contained forty-four wells. The massive overproduction soon forced the price of oil down, and kept it down, as the unusual circumstances of this particular field ensured that everyone would continue to drill and pump as fast as they could. No one would agree to limit production unless they all did.

Governor Sterling first suggested that the Railroad Commission act, under the authority granted by the legislature in 1917. This small state regulatory agency, though, did not have the capacity to control the massive East Texas field, and the problem was not easily resolved. Conservationists and the major oil companies criticized unrestrained production as wasteful of natural resources and as a threat to the very existence of the East Texas field by reducing the internal pressure that made the oil flow. The independent producers refused to stop pumping, because their survival was at stake. Most of them were operating on a shoestring budget or on borrowed money, and slowing down or stopping would have meant bankruptcy. Second, they suspected the motives of the major producers, whose reserves would diminish significantly in value if the price of oil remained low. The independents argued that such restrictions were not for the sake of conservation, but were, in fact, illegal price fixing.

The Railroad Commission initially ordered production limited to about 1,000 barrels per day at each well, but a federal court struck down the order on the grounds that it was price fixing. Through three special sessions in the summer of 1931, the legislature was unable to reach a solution. In the meantime, the major producers, who owned the refineries, stopped buying East Texas oil, claiming that they did not need it. The independents established "teakettle" refineries and their own gasoline stations. Finally, with more than a million barrels of oil a day pouring from the East Texas field, and agreement among the operators apparently not possible, Governor Sterling declared martial law in four counties and sent in the National Guard. The fact that he was a former president of Humble Oil and that the National Guard commander in the field, General Jacob F. Wolters, was an attorney for the Texas Company gave the independents grounds to doubt the state's objectivity in the matter.

The "hot" oil, that is, oil produced in violation of the Railroad Commission's orders, continued to flow, and the secrecy required to circumvent the National Guard also made it extremely difficult to determine the amount of oil produced, who owned it, and whether correct royalties were being paid. In another special session, in the fall of 1932, the legislature authorized the Railroad Commission to prorate production according to market demands and in 1932, at the request of Ernest O. Thompson, chair of the Railroad Commission, the governor sent a force of Texas Rangers to stop the flow of hot oil.

The chaos in the East Texas field was the immediate impetus for Roosevelt's secretary of the interior, Harold Ickes, to propose federal control of the oil industry. As he saw it, the price of oil needed to be higher in the interest of the country's financial recovery, so the unchecked flow of hot oil constituted a problem for the country as well as the industry. His efforts at federal control were met with fierce resistance, particularly among the independent oil producers whose point of view was well represented by the Texas congressional delegation. Because the state had retained title to its public lands upon joining the union, Texas had a credible argument to make against interference by the federal government. Ultimately a begrudging Texas accepted as little federal assistance as it could get away with to adjudicate the lawlessness in the East Texas field only because the Texas Railroad Commission could not alone control the situation.

By 1933, the Rangers had restored some measure of order to the East Texas field, and in January 1934 a federal court upheld the Railroad Commission's right to prorate oil production. But it was not until later that year, with the establishment of a federal oversight board and the threat of prison, that the flow of hot oil declined sharply. When the Supreme Court declared unconstitutional the National Recovery Administration, under whose auspices the federal government had acted, Texas senator Tom Connally sponsored the Connally Hot Oil Act of 1935 specifically to make interstate transportation of hot oil illegal.

Within a few years, most of the small independents had sold out to the stronger, better-capitalized major producers, who owned 80 percent of the East Texas field by the time World War II broke out. Later in the century, when the Organization of Petroleum Exporting Countries (OPEC) nations were struggling to control their own overproduction, they found their model for stabilizing the international price of oil in the Texas Railroad Commission. Sterling had dealt successfully with the East Texas oil crisis, but in doing so he had alienated large numbers of East Texas voters.

Agricultural Overproduction

Sterling's other problem grew out of the continuing agricultural depression. The price of cotton, already low at 9–10 cents per pound in 1930, fell drastically in 1931, bottoming out at around 5 cents per pound that fall. The prices of other commodities fell as well, but not as much. The net result was that farmers' purchasing power was about one-third of what it had been before World War I.

The problem would not have been as severe if Texas farmers had been more diversified or had voluntarily limited production. They had tried several different marketing cooperatives, including the Federal Farm Board and the Texas Marketing Association, both of which failed in the face of the 1931 crop of more than 17 million bales of cotton nationally (5.32 million in Texas), the second largest in history.

Any action to limit Texas cotton producers would have collapsed without the cooperation of the other cotton-producing states, so, in response to a joint resolution of the legislature, Sterling called a governor's conference for the summer

Dorothea Lange image of an African American sharecropper working in the Brazos riverbottoms near Bryan, Texas. This man earned eight cents a day for hoeing cotton on twenty acres of land.

of 1931 to try to come up with a plan for unified action. Five states sent representatives, who agreed to limit cotton production if Texas would. During one of the special sessions of 1931, the legislature passed a law limiting the 1932 cotton acreage to 30 percent of the 1931 crop. A few days later, the courts held it to be unconstitutional. The 1932 yield in Texas alone was 4.5 million bales.

Fergusonism Revived

James Ferguson, an astute and veteran observer of the political scene, concluded that 1932 could be a good "Ferguson year," and Miriam Ferguson filed to run against Sterling, along with seven other candidates. As always with the Fergusons, personalities rather than issues seemed to inspire the voters. The Fergusons accused the wealthy Sterling of trying to buy the election, of misusing the highway fund, and employing political allies in the highway department. Sterling alleged they committed voter fraud, and probably with reason. The Ferguson strongholds of East Texas issued only 359,667 poll tax receipts, but reported that 397,386 votes were cast in the July primary. Sterling lost the runoff by fewer than 4,000 votes. Efforts to investigate vote tampering were thwarted; Ferguson gained a second term as governor.

Miriam Ferguson accomplished little during her second term because the legislature was wary of all proposals that she presented, and because the efforts of newly elected president Franklin D. Roosevelt to deal with the depression overshadowed and preempted state actions. She did support the new president, telling him after he took the nation off the gold standard: "I congratulate you upon the idea to abolish the gold standard. Your action is fully justified because the shylocks have sought to collect a dollar which they did not loan. I mean that they loaned a bank check and now seek to collect a gold dollar."

Ferguson resumed her policy of liberally pardoning prisoners and turned the Texas Rangers into a form of political patronage by appointing 2,344 "Special Rangers." Plans to consolidate state agencies and reorganize the state's higher education system failed. The Twenty-first Amendment to the U.S. Constitution, which repealed the Eighteenth Amendment and once again left the management of alcoholic beverages up to state and local officials, was ratified in December 1933, but Texas did not repeal its prohibition amendment until August 1935. Essentially, the depression had overwhelmed local, state, and private efforts, and, with the election of Roosevelt in 1932, Texas, along with the rest of the nation pinned its hopes for recovery on the federal government.

The New Deal

We know in hindsight that no president could have prevented the depression or quickly returned the nation to prosperity, but President Hoover's lackluster personality and political ineptness made him a scapegoat, and Texans were ready to return to the Democratic fold in 1932. "Truly, I have been hit hard," one penitent voter wrote, "but I deserve no sympathy, I voted for Hoover." When speaker of the U.S. House of Representatives John Nance Garner of Uvalde accepted second place on the ticket with Roosevelt, that sealed the deal as far as Texans were concerned: More than 88 percent of the state's voters supported Roosevelt and Garner in their call for a "New Deal for the American people."

Texas in Washington

With Garner as vice president and de facto head of the Texas delegation, the state was well positioned within the federal government. Some historians consider Garner to have been the most powerful vice president in history, because, as a former speaker of the House who knew virtually every legislator personally, he wielded enormous influence. Sam Rayburn, the congressman from Bonham and Garner's long-time associate and protégé, headed the Interstate and Foreign Commerce Committee. Rayburn shepherded through Congress important legislation to regulate Wall Street. Roosevelt elevated Hoover-appointee Jesse Jones to the chair of the Reconstruction Finance Corporation (RFC), which soon became one of the most powerful agencies in Washington.

Congress structured the RFC as an independent agency, but in reality it was a government bank that made loans, received repayment of loans, and earned interest, and, from time to time, added to its capital. The RFC funded some of the most significant New Deal agencies, but perhaps the most important thing it did was save the banking system itself by purchasing preferred stock in threatened banks. Of course, Jones gained support in Congress by funding a pet project on occasion, but his real source of power was Garner and the Texas delegation, who usually stood united on the important issues. By January 1936 the RFC had disbursed more than $8 billion, received $3.2 billion, and earned $294 million in interest.

The Federal Emergency Relief Administration provided funds for direct relief as well as work relief. Because of the requirement that the state governments share the burden, Texans had to amend the 1876 constitution so that the state could provide $20 million in matching "bread bonds" to feed the hungry. Other programs provided jobs: The Civilian Conservation Corps; the National Youth Administration (NYA), directed in Texas for awhile by the young Lyndon B. Johnson; the Public Works Administration; and the Works Progress Administration (WPA) employed thousands of Texans. Johnson's NYA was one of the more progressive in the nation, employing over 19,000 young African Americans in ways that did not attract publicity or criticism. Aubrey Williams, the national director of the NYA, said Johnson "did a beautiful job" and rated the Texan's efforts as "one of the very best in the country. He fought for those kids to get them all he could, he even fought me to get things and money for them." His efforts helped encourage African Americans to shift political loyalties away from the Republican Party and toward the Democratic Party even though other New Deal agencies were much less helpful to minorities.

The federal dollars went for relief, civic construction projects, and culture. Interviewers paid by the federal government documented the lives of literally thousands of Texans—former slaves, old cowboys, Indians, and pioneer residents in all parts of the state—and federally funded artists painted and sculpted historically based public art works for courthouses and post offices throughout the state. Over sixty-five Texas post offices became home to almost 100 murals in the massive public art project unleashed during the New Deal. The great Mexican muralists, including Diego Rivera, inspired these paintings, which depicted settlement narratives, industrial development and ranching culture, folk heroes, cowboys, and American Indians. All told, the federal government, through public works and relief programs, invested some $351,023,546 in Texas between 1933 and 1936. State and local funds provided another $80,268,595 in assistance.

Unfortunately, many of the poor received little help. Programs that encouraged lower production in an effort to forestall sinking prices for the farmer drove up the cost of food for the consumer, making it difficult for those below the poverty line to maintain an adequate diet. Mexican American and African American families were among those who suffered the most. Programs that rewarded owners for taking land out of production and mechanizing their farms drove tenants off the land. Meanwhile, although a higher percentage of African American workers were on relief than white workers, African Americans in Houston received 25 percent less per month than whites under New Deal programs. Some relief agencies placed African American workers only in unskilled jobs, and others would not hire them at all. These agencies also denied ethnic Mexicans work on the grounds that they were not citizens.

In 1934, Texas attorney general James V. Allred campaigned for governor by identifying with Roosevelt and the New Deal. Although conservative criticism of the president and his programs had begun to surface, Roosevelt still had the support of a huge majority of Texans. And Allred, who had come to public attention as an opponent of out-of-state monopolies and political lobbies, probably had better name recognition than any of his opponents after Miriam Ferguson declined to run, as she said, because of the two-term tradition. The evangelical Allred attracted attention, one Houston reporter likening him to an actor with expert political and oratorical skills. Nevertheless, his call for a Public Utilities Commission, restrictions on lobbies, and a modest tax on chain stores to limit out-of-state competition did not rouse large numbers of voters. A reporter for the *Austin Statesman* claimed that most voters had responded with a "wide yawn." Allred still won the race, defeating his main opponent Tom Hunter, an independent oil man, who, he charged, had made a corrupt bargain to gain the Fergusons' support.

A New Image for Texas

One of Allred's more enjoyable duties as governor was to preside over the Texas Centennial in 1936. The main celebration took place in Dallas, but the centennial was acclaimed all over the state. It became a watershed event, marking the state's modernized economy.

The primary goals of the centennial included introducing Texas to the world and bringing out-of-state tourists to Texas. To succeed organizers concluded that the state needed a public relations makeover. Believing that most people thought of Texas as a primitive, frontier area, or as an extension of the culturally and economically backward South, the organizing committee decided to take advantage of the state's romantic history and myth. It was then that, in the words of centennial historian Kenneth B. Ragsdale, "ten-gallon hats, six-shooters, high-heeled boots, Texas Rangers, bluebonnets, and sex" became the icons of the celebration. The committee's success was assured when Texan Janice Jarratt, the model regularly seen throughout the nation in newspaper and magazine ads as the Chesterfield cigarettes girl, agreed to be the "Sweetheart of the Texas Centennial." A picture of her dressed in western style and waving the official centennial hat on the patio of the Spanish governor's palace in San Antonio was displayed all over the state.

The centennial itself opened on June 6 and carried out this theme in its most popular attraction, "*The Cavalcade of Texas,*" a historical pageant depicting four centuries of Texas history. Children who had grown up playing the battles of the Alamo and San Jacinto and cowboys and Indians now had a fully articulated historical myth

Janice Jarrett was the poster girl for the Texas Centennial celebrations of 1936. Cover of "Pictorial Parade of Texas," published by the Texas Centennial Committee.

of their own to celebrate. That image was further popularized in what was probably the best-attended attraction outside the main centennial celebration, the Billy Rose–produced extravaganza in Fort Worth, featuring the "Frontier Follies," the "Winning of the West," and the stripper Sally Rand. "Let Dallas . . . educate the people," the always-quotable Rose told reporters. "We'll entertain them in Fort Worth."

Nor did the focus on Texas history and legend fade away with the passing of the centennial. The Texas Centennial Commission placed a marker in every county indicating the date of its establishment and the source of its name. The centennial personified the new Texas identity as a part of the West, and scholarly publications such as Walter Prescott Webb's *The Great Plains* and *The Texas Rangers* lent academic credibility to it. The Texan producer and director King Vidor made a popular movie, *The Texas Rangers,* in 1936.

These commemorations of Texas history, though, did not acknowledge the role of African Americans, Mexican Americans, or women in the making of the Lone Star State, but instead projected a white male, Western identity for Texas. The centennial did provide some coverage of African American issues in the Hall of Negro Life. There the murals of Harlem Renaissance painter Aaron Douglas, depicting the history of African Americans in the United States, were on display. African Texans used the centennial's Negro Day as an occasion to discuss strategies to upend segregation in Texas.

The efforts of African Texans in the making of the state are richly documented in the WPA's Slave Narratives. They provide an alternative and

overlooked history of the iconic Texas cowboy, always depicted in literature and film as white. More black cowboys worked in Texas than anywhere
else in the United States. Expectations for African American cowhands included subservience to whites and performance of the most difficult, dangerous jobs. These realities conspicuously are absent from the myth of the
Texas cowboy created in the 1930s. Tom Mills, a black cowboy from Texas,
described his life: "When I got to workin' for myself, it was cow work. I done
horse back work for fifty years. Many a year passed that I never missed a day
bein' in the saddle. I stayed thirteen years on one ranch. The first place was
right below Hondo City."

The Knights of Columbus, a Catholic fraternal order founded in Connecticut
in 1882 to provide mutual aid, offered its own answer to the centennial. It fostered a "Spanish" as opposed to a "Mexican" heritage for the state. For example,
it helped erect historical markers noting the location of early Spanish missions
in Texas. Also, historian Carlos Castañeda wrote about the Catholic Church in
the borderlands; he first published *Our Catholic Heritage in Texas* in 1936. The
Knights of Columbus commissioned the work.

Rising Lawlessness

Another problem was the violence that sprang from a society in turmoil. It seems
to have begun with the agricultural slump of the 1920s, prohibition, the revival of
the Klan, labor and industrial conflict, and the wild and lawless oil boom towns
like Kilgore, Desdemona, Mexia, Wink, and Borger, followed by a nationwide
depression. There were bootleggers in every county, gambling in most Texas cities, and a series of bank robberies and other crimes throughout the state. Addi-
tionally, the Special Rangers—"a contemptible lot by any standard," according to
one historian—that Governor Ferguson had appointed soon became more a part
of the problem than the solution.

With the exploits of John Dillinger, Pretty Boy Floyd, and others making
headlines throughout the Midwest, Texas too seemed plagued by an epidemic of
such infamous criminals as George "Machine-Gun" Kelly, Raymond Hamilton
(who made two successful prison breaks), and Clyde Barrow and Bonnie Parker
in the Dallas–Fort Worth area, and the Whitey Walker gang in Central Texas,
who robbed and murdered apparently at will. State and local authorities seemed
outwitted and outgunned, and most Texans were aware of the problem: "A
Ranger commission and a nickel can get you a cup of coffee anywhere in Texas,"
one newspaper editor sardonically remarked. The situation was so bad that in
May 1934 Governor Ferguson was forced to go outside the Texas Rangers, to Senior Captain Frank Hamer, who had resigned in protest when she was elected, to
find a man to track down Bonnie and Clyde. The infamous couple was gunned
down in Louisiana in 1934.

The Texas Centennial did not aid law enforcement officials either. As Dallas geared up for the celebration, newspaper publisher and civic leader Amon

Carter, Sr. of Fort Worth allegedly reached an accommodation with the liquor control board that would permit the open sale of liquor at the well-publicized "Frontier Follies," which he and others in Fort Worth had organized to compete with the official centennial in Dallas. Not wanting to be upstaged, Dallas officials decided to "open up" their city so they could compete with "Cow Town."

When Allred took office in early 1935, he understood that reorganization of the state's law enforcement agency was one of his most urgent tasks. He immediately proposed a bill creating the Texas Department of Public Safety, which would consist of a new three-person Public Safety Commission to oversee the Texas Rangers, the Highway Patrol, and the Headquarters Division in Austin, which was to be a new, modern scientific crime laboratory. The Fergusons had left the Rangers in complete disarray, and one of the first acts of the new commission was to rehire the Rangers who had been fired and give them tenure. The commissioners also established standards for the operation of the agency.

Recovery from the Depression

On the political front, Allred had to face the grim realities of the depression. He fulfilled one of his campaign promises when the legislature approved the chain store tax in 1935 during the first of three special sessions, but the primary problem with his initiatives was that the state lacked sufficient money to fund them. Another problem was that many of the New Deal programs that offered assistance—such as the Social Security Act of 1935—required matching state funds, which meant that the federal government dictated much of the governor's tax agenda. The act established the Social Security program that we know today, funded by both the employee and the employer, as well as federal-state programs to cover unemployment insurance, care of dependent mothers, children, disabled and blind persons, public health services, and a pension to assist persons over age sixty-five.

Recovery from the depression continued to dominate Allred's agenda after he was reelected in 1936. An Allred-backed state constitutional amendment permitting establishment of an old-age pension passed handily that fall, so one of his first goals was to get the pensions funded. The state had estimated that there might be about 63,000 people eligible for pensions, but by the fall of 1936, 81,000 applications had already been filed, and the commission administering the program estimated that number might go as high as 125,000. The state tightened the eligibility requirements, but still lacked funding for such a large program, so Allred opted for a middle course, advocating pensions only for the needy elderly. Most of the money for his plan came from increased taxes on liquor. When Allred proposed new taxes on oil, gas, carbon black, and sulfur to cover other needed programs, the legislature balked. He had to call two special sessions of the legislature in 1936 to work out the details of the program. Even so, when Allred declined to run for another term in 1938 and accepted appointment as a federal judge, the state was $19 million in debt.

Hillbilly Politics

As the 1938 gubernatorial race got underway, a Fort Worth flour salesman, Wilbert Lee O'Daniel, entered the contest in an unconventional manner. He had been performing for several years on a radio program that featured country-and-Western music, and he told his audience that several listeners had suggested he run for governor. He feigned lack of interest in the idea, but asked members of the audience to write him if they thought he should run. After receiving more than 54,000 letters in one week, O'Daniel announced that he was a candidate for governor. In keeping with the homilies that he delivered on his program, he claimed that his motto would be the golden rule and his platform the Ten Commandments.

O'Daniel was not the hillbilly that he portrayed on his radio program. An Ohio native, he had moved to Fort Worth in 1925 to become general manager of a milling company. He discovered the potential of the relatively new medium of radio when he fired the "hillbilly" band, the Light Crust Doughboys—including the creator of "western swing," Bob Wills—that performed on a program his company sponsored. Thousands of fans wrote requesting that the show be put back on the air. O'Daniel did not like the band's music, but he recognized the opportunity. He rehired the Light Crust Doughboys, took over as master of ceremonies for the program, moved it to the strongest radio station in the area, WBAP in Fort Worth, and put it on the Texas Quality Network during the prime-time noon hour each day. After being fired from his general manager job, O'Daniel organized his own band, the Hillbilly Boys, and was soon selling "Hillbilly Flour" under his own label. His program began with a woman's voice asking, "Please, pass the biscuits, Pappy," and O'Daniel was soon known throughout the state as "Pappy."

O'Daniel's popular program consisted of hillbilly music, homely stories, advice on family life, and maudlin poems such as "The Boy Who Never Got Too Old to Comb His Mother's Hair." Although he was a bit aloof, even austere, in person, O'Daniel affected a folksy voice that worked on the radio. He composed and sang his own songs, such as "Beautiful Texas" and "Put Me in Your Pocket." By the time he ran for governor he may have been, according to some political observers, the best-known personality in Texas because of radio's popularity. Roy Bedichek, who traveled frequently in his job as head of the University Interscholastic League at the University of Texas, recalled seeing men all over the state "slapping their thighs with delight around filling station radios" as they listened to O'Daniel.

Once in the race, O'Daniel employed the same showmanship in his political campaign that he had in his flour business. He fitted out an old bus with a loudspeaker and, with his hillbilly band, traveled from town to town, drawing thousands of people at every stop. After entertaining the crowd with music, he would launch into his stump speech, proclaiming that he was for "less Johnson grass and politicians; more smokestacks and businessmen." Then he would ask for contributions to his campaign, and his daughter would walk through the crowd with collection plates that had been made in the form of barrels labeled "Flour—Not Pork." Some doubted that he was serious about the race. At one point he told a reporter, "I don't know whether or not I'll get elected, but boy! It sure is good for the flour business"—and few realized that it was all an act. Some of his most unpretentious comments and much of the campaign itself was the product of the fertile and expert mind of Dallas public relations executive Phil Fox, who was working with O'Daniel on behalf of conservative, anti–New Deal business interests.

The other candidates initially underestimated the attraction the voters had for "Pappy." When it became clear that he was a serious candidate, the opposition began to ridicule him as "the big town hillbilly candidate" and "the banjo man from Fort Worth." But he handled the attacks with aplomb. When a reporter asked how he would govern under his platform of the Ten Commandments, O'Daniel smiled and said, "Well, take the fourth commandment, Honor Thy Father and Thy Mother: Doesn't that mean old-age pensions just as plain as day?" The increasingly large crowds loved it. Former chair of the Railroad Commission, Ernest O. Thompson, who had been one of the favorites in the race, confessed that he "didn't even see O'Daniel. The first thing I knew he passed all of us and left me with a cloud of flour dust in my eyes."

Even an old pro like "Farmer Jim" Ferguson, who sat out this race, had to be impressed. O'Daniel conducted his campaign like an old-time religious revival, holding the rallies outside, "basking in God's sunlight." And he presented the issues in the same way as the camp meeting preacher: You were for him or against him, good for Texas or bad for Texas. Having never paid a poll tax or voted, O'Daniel called for abolition of the poll tax and capital punishment. Novelist George Sessions Perry of Rockdale aptly remarked that had O'Daniel "been even slightly less astute, had he made a slightly less careful analysis of his own talents and the emotional requirements of his constituents, he might very well have gone on the road with a medicine show." O'Daniel won without a runoff in one of the biggest upsets in state history, with his largest majorities coming from the WBAP listening area around Fort Worth.

The Conservative Backlash

Although O'Daniel appeared to some to be little more than a popular personality, his homilies cloaked his conservative agenda. He invoked President Roosevelt's name on the campaign trail, but in reality was more representative of the remnants of the Jeffersonian Democrats, a conservative group that had organized in an almost fatalistic attempt to defeat Roosevelt in 1936. The Jeffersonian Democrats adamantly opposed FDR's efforts to pack the Supreme Court and saw the attempted purge of anti-Roosevelt Democratic members of Congress in 1938 as un-American. As some measure of prosperity returned to the middle class, their message of limited government, lower taxes, and individual freedom gained adherents. Knowing that they had no chance as a third party, however, they worked against New Deal programs and candidates from within the Democratic Party. They undoubtedly played a role in the 1938 defeat of liberal congressman Maury Maverick of San Antonio and in the return to Congress of Martin Dies of Orange, initially a Roosevelt supporter but now chair of the Special Committee on Un-American Activities (renamed the House Committee on Un-American Activities in January 1945), an ardent anti–New Dealer. Men of such stripe were O'Daniel's friends, advisors, and supporters.

Because of the deficit that O'Daniel had inherited from the Allred administration, taxation became the dominant issue of his term. The state was still trying to catch up with its side of the funding under the Social Security Act, which had grown to $48–$60 million, but was so poor that members of the House had sat through the last legislative session with umbrellas when it rained because there was no money to repair the capitol roof. The governor and the legislature would have to work together to come up with that much new money.

O'Daniel had denounced a sales tax during the campaign but had not revealed where he would find the money to cover the deficit or the pensions that he had promised, and speculation began to spread that he would endorse an income tax. He waited until his inaugural, which attracted a crowd of approximately 60,000 to the University of Texas Memorial Stadium in January 1939, to unveil his plans for a "transactions tax" of 1.6 percent. It was a thinly disguised and regressive sales tax, of course, something that he had condemned during the campaign. He also scaled back on his primary campaign platform of universal old-age pensions for those over age sixty-five who did not have an income of at least $30 per month. Unable to get even these modest measures through the legislature, he identified those who disputed him in his folksy Sunday morning radio addresses from the porch of the governor's mansion, and the legislature soon was inundated with warnings from voters that the lawmakers should quit playing politics and support the governor. His tax plan had no chance of passing, but many of those who opposed him either did not run in the next election or were defeated.

Meanwhile, claiming lack of funds, he vetoed money for new buildings at state hospitals and cut more than 50 percent from the state Highway Department's budget. He slashed the Texas Rangers' budget to the point that they had to borrow bullets from Highway Patrol officers. The legislative session ended with no tax bill and an increase of some $10 million in the state's deficit. O'Daniel began appointing ultraconservative business people to the University of Texas Board of Regents with the intent of gaining control of the university without enduring the public drubbing that Ferguson had suffered.

World War II

War came to Europe in the fall of 1939 with a suddenness that few in Texas anticipated. There had been adequate warnings: Japan had invaded Manchuria in 1931 and China in 1937 and had gradually expanded its influence over the western Pacific. In the meantime, Germany, bristling under the onus of its World War I defeat and subsequent treaties, began its regeneration under Chancellor Adolf Hitler, while Benito Mussolini took power in Italy. Italy attacked Ethiopia in 1936, and the following year Germany successively occupied Austria, the Sudentenland (German-speaking Czechoslovakia), and Czechoslovakia itself. But it was the German invasion of Poland in 1939 that began the European phase of the war, and in April 1940, the German blitzkrieg overcame Denmark, Holland, and Belgium. France fell only a few weeks later. Then Hitler turned his bombers toward Britain.

Texans and National Politics

As President Roosevelt struggled with the delicate task of helping Britain while at the same time preparing a reluctant nation for war, he also had to decide whether he would seek a third term. O'Daniel faced a decision about his own political future in Texas. But, unlike Roosevelt, whose sense of duty called, O'Daniel's failure to accomplish even the more modest of his platform goals seemed to diminish his interest in reelection. Indeed, his poor performance inspired several challengers. The old veteran, "Pa" Ferguson, believed that the governor had made such a mess of things that "Ma," now almost sixty-five years old, would be a shoo-in to retake the mansion. He baited O'Daniel, calling him a "slickhaired banjo player who crooned his way into the governor's office" and "has been giving the people of Texas a song and dance ever since."

O'Daniel stuck to what he did best. He began his campaign on the radio, wondering aloud whether he should run for reelection. A few weeks later, he announced that "thousands of my friends" had beseeched him to run and that he would honor their request. Despite the fact that Europe was engulfed in war, he offered the same clichés as his platform, decried that state agencies were nothing more than "juicy play-pretties for professional politicians," and denounced the "powerful oligarchies" in Austin. In his few campaign appearances, he took little notice of the fact that the Nazis had occupied Paris and the Luftwaffe was bombing London, except to claim that he had sent President Roosevelt a telegram detailing the activities of fifth columnists in Texas, which, needless to say, he did not follow up on after the election. He won again without a runoff.

Vice President Garner momentarily diverted attention from the statehouse when he allowed his name to be put forward for the presidency in 1940 in an effort to keep Roosevelt from winning a third term. Though he had been crucial to the success of the New Deal, Garner now questioned the reforms, calling some of the New Deal program just "plain damn foolishness" in 1935. But the greatest rift had occurred when, in his second inaugural address in 1937, Roosevelt asked for expansion of the U.S. Supreme Court. The conservatives on the Court had declared both the National Recovery Act and the Agricultural Adjustment Act, as well as several other pieces of legislation, unconstitutional in a series of five-to-four decisions in 1935 and 1936. Roosevelt thought that adding a few friendly justices to the Court might solve the problem. Garner was one of many who fiercely opposed this proposal, and he became the silent leader of the Democratic opposition. Another Texan, Hatton Sumners, chair of the House Judiciary Committee, blocked the "court packing" plan in the House, and conservatives ultimately defeated it in the Senate. The difficulty passed when vacancies enabled Roosevelt to make several new appointments to the Court, but the split with Garner was irreparable. After the 1940 election, the seventy-one-year-old vice president retired from politics.

O'Daniel began 1941 with a renewed mandate, but he still had to face the need for a tax bill, and he again submitted his plan for a 1.6 percent transactions tax and a tax on natural resources and public utilities. The legislature virtually ignored him, and his bills died one by one in various committees. Eventually, the legislature put together its own plan, which became known as the Morris omnibus tax bill, and it passed both houses overwhelmingly. O'Daniel salvaged an antilabor bill but the session was an open rebuke of the governor, and the state seemed on the verge of another political crisis.

A solution of sorts appeared when U.S. senator Morris Sheppard, who had served the state in the Senate since 1913, died on April 9, 1941. O'Daniel saw an opportunity to take his antilabor campaign national, and many of his detractors saw an opportunity to get him out of the governor's mansion. The legislature even passed a resolution requesting that he appoint himself to the Senate. Instead, O'Daniel selected the ailing, eighty-seven-year-old son of Sam Houston, Andrew Jackson Houston, to replace Sheppard and announced it in his typically heavy-handed and ostentatious manner. He elbowed aside University of Texas folklorist and author J. Frank Dobie, the guest speaker at the San Jacinto Day ceremonies at the monument, to present Houston as the new senator, and led the crowd in singing "Beautiful Texas." It was only a ploy to reserve the position for himself in the upcoming election, of course, and Houston managed to attend only one committee meeting before he died.

O'Daniel then filed as a candidate in the winner-take-all 1941 special election to fill the seat, facing the young New Deal congressman from Johnson City, Lyndon Baines Johnson, who had the support of President Roosevelt; East Texas congressman Martin Dies; and Attorney General Gerald Mann. A total of twenty-nine candidates vied for the post. O'Daniel declared that his platform remained "one hundred percent approval of the Lord God Jehovah, widows, orphans, low taxes, the Ten Commandments, and the Golden Rule." If the United States had to get involved in the war, he mused, then perhaps Texas should have its own army and navy, and he emphasized his one legislative accomplishment, the passage of the antistrike law, which he said had driven labor organizers out of the state.

"Pa" Ferguson was able to play his last political trick in this election. Ferguson protégé Lieutenant Governor Coke Stevenson would advance to the governor's office should O'Daniel be elected to the Senate. Ferguson also had reasons to dislike O'Daniel, aside from "Ma's" 1940 defeat. O'Daniel was a staunch prohibitionist who had tried unsuccessfully to appoint three prohibitionists to the

Texas Liquor Control Board and complained when the Senate turned down these "good clean honest Christian dry citizens." With a few well-placed telephone calls to old friends in East Texas, "Pa" set in motion the process by which O'Daniel was elevated to the U.S. Senate and Coke Stevenson into the governor's office. Vote rigging, then standard procedure in Texas politics, was the tactic Ferguson and O'Daniel used. Because areas of the state favorable to Johnson had already reported their vote totals and because East Texas, a Ferguson stronghold, had not reported, it proved easy to alter the tally and secure an O'Daniel victory.

O'Daniel's departure for Washington did nothing to calm state politics, because he had to run again in the regular election in 1942 to hold onto his seat. He prepared for the campaign by introducing several antilabor, antistrike bills in the Senate, never gathering more than a handful of supportive votes. Yet he later claimed that he had enabled the United States to win World War II because his antilabor efforts had prevented strikes. In fact, Senator Connally, along with Virginia Democrat Howard Worth Smith in the House, authored the antistrike legislation, which added noting of substance to wartime labor policies.

O'Daniel's reelection in 1942 brought a period of relative political calm to the state, as Texans pitched into the war effort. For one thing, Coke R. Stevenson from Junction, the new governor, was a much quieter person, a man of few words. He smoked a pipe and had a habit of drawing on it several times before responding to a question, which led the capitol press corps to nickname him "Calculating Coke." Even then, his response was usually brief and uninformative. He was a seasoned official, having served as speaker of the House of Representatives before being elected lieutenant governor, and he managed to establish a cordial relationship with the capitol press corps by visiting with them frequently on an informal basis and inviting them to his ranch in the summers. Probably seeing himself as the guardian of the state's financial stability rather than as a politician, Stevenson espoused the simple life and conservative politics. He opposed enlargement of federal powers. Expansion of the state's economy during the war enabled him to balance the budget without excessive cuts to services, and he oversaw several improvements in the highway and educational systems. He faced no serious opposition and was easily reelected to the office in 1942 and 1944.

Texas in the War

Many Texans had continued to feel that a European war did not concern them, but on Sunday, December 7, 1941, a ham radio operator in South America picked up the news from Hawaii of the Japanese attack on the American naval base at Pearl Harbor and relayed it to amateur radio operators in Texas. The worst was soon confirmed: Nineteen ships had been sunk—most of the U.S. Pacific fleet—hundreds of men killed, and the harbor badly damaged. Before U.S. senator Tom Connally could get to the capitol the next morning to introduce the resolution declaring war against Japan, young Texans had already lined up in front of recruiting offices. Germany and Italy declared war on the United States three days later.

Ever since World War I, Texas had been a military training center, with the Third Army headquartered at Fort Sam Houston, and aviators stationed at Randolph, Brooks, and Kelly airfields, all in San Antonio. That infrastructure expanded during World War II. Fifteen major army camps in Texas trained more than 1.2 million troops between 1940 and 1945, and several prisoner-of-war camps were built in the state, ultimately housing almost 80,000 German, Italian, and Japanese prisoners of war by June 1944.

Approximately 750,000 Texans served in the armed forces, including 12,000 women, more than any other state. Two of the war's greatest military commanders were born in Texas—General Dwight D. Eisenhower at Denison and Fleet Admiral Chester W. Nimitz at Fredericksburg—and Audie Murphy of Farmersville became the war's most decorated hero before coming home to pursue a career in the movies. Prominent Texas women also enjoyed military careers. Oveta Culp Hobby served as the director of the Women's Army Corps. Initially, her job was to travel the country recruiting women to join the services. Upon receiving her appointment, Hobby told the press, "You have said the Army needs the Corps. That is enough for me." Women who served in the WACS performed support duties behind the lines and stateside, freeing men for combat service. One Texas woman who volunteered declared, "I'd get up in the morning and put my feelings on the bed and my hat on my head, and get on with it." Texas A&M University alone, which at the time was a male-only, military-oriented institution, provided some 14,000 officers during the war, more than both the U.S. Military Academy and the U.S. Naval Academy combined.

Wartime Economic Growth

The war finally brought an end to the depression. As the federal payroll stimulated local businesses, Texans sacrificed for "our boys overseas" and bought war bonds and planted "victory gardens," as they had during World War I. Rationing of sugar, coffee, meat, shoes, rubber, automobile parts, and gas became a way of life. Governor Stevenson accepted the rationing of everything except gasoline because, he said, Texas had plenty of it and with such vast distances to cover, it was as necessary as "the saddle, the rifle, the ax, and the Bible." Farmers now put all their land back in cultivation, got high prices for their crops, and helped feed the Allies.

With the assistance of the federal government, the largest petrochemical complex in the world developed along the gulf coast. Crucial to its growth was the construction of two pipelines from Texas to the Midwest and the East Coast. As early as 1940, Interior Secretary Ickes realized that German submarines might interfere with tanker ships along the coastline and urged the construction of the pipelines. It was not until the attack on Pearl Harbor, however, that he persuaded independent oilman J. R. Parten to head the Petroleum Administration for War and to undertake the construction of the pipelines. With financing from the RFC, construction was completed on the "Big Inch" (24 inches in diameter), to deliver Texas crude from East Texas to Illinois and then on to the East Coast, in August 1943; the "Little Inch" (20 inches in diameter), from the Houston-Beaumont area to New Jersey, was completed in 1944. After the war Texas Eastern Transmission Corporation, formed by George and Herman Brown and their partners, acquired the pipelines.

Other wartime industries were established all over the state: steel mills in Houston and Daingerfield; the largest tin smelter in the world at Texas City; aircraft factories at Garland, Grand Prairie, and Fort Worth; huge shipyards at Beaumont, Port Arthur, Houston, Galveston, and Corpus Christi. Building these plants was not easy. Members of the Texas delegation lobbied the executive branch hard to achieve these results. Rep. Wright Patman, a northeast Texas Democrat with populist leanings, argued such plants strengthened not only the state's economy but also the national economy and had international impact. The war reinvigorated the paper and wood-pulp industries in East Texas and supported synthetic rubber and munitions plants in other parts of the state, mitigating against Texas as a colonial economy responsible only for providing raw materials to the wealthier production centers in the northeast and Midwest.

The number of wage earners tripled, with opportunities now available in the workforce for minorities and women, including positions that had formerly been

Howard R. Hollem/Getty Images

Irma Lee McElroy, a former office worker, is shown painting the U.S. insignia on airplane wings at the Naval Air Base in Corpus Christi, Texas.

reserved for men. The popular song "Rosie the Riveter" heralded the accomplishments of women in new roles such as pipe fitter, lathe operator, and assembly-line worker. All told, manufacturing increased fourfold between 1939 and 1944, from $453 million to $1.9 billion. This newfound prosperity enabled Governor Stevenson to sweep away the $42 million debt that the state had accumulated and, at the same time, improve state highways, raise teaching salaries, and undertake a building program at the University of Texas. Still, one of his most important contributions was the adoption, early in his term, of the constitutional amendment (Article III, Section 49a) that put the state on a "pay-as-you-go" basis; it prohibits the legislature from spending more than the State Comptroller (tax collector) certifies will be on hand when the bills come due.

Minorities and the War

African Americans from all over the country trained in and staffed Texas camps, and they were expected to conform to the local customs regarding segregation. They lived separately from white troops, trained separately, and were not welcome in the white service clubs or movie theaters or had separate seating. Almost 258,000 African American Texans registered for the selective service, and about one-third of them were assigned to segregated units, usually commanded by white officers. As would be expected, there were racial incidents under such circumstances, and African American leaders protested the discrimination. The Fair Employment Practices Committee conducted investigations in some fifty cities, which in some cases heightened the existing tensions.

The urban areas were even more volatile because of the wartime growth. African Americans already made up one-third of the population in the Beaumont–Port Arthur area, but that number increased by 20 percent in the three years after 1940. On a hot summer night in 1943, the city erupted into racial violence as 2,000 white shipyard workers rioted in the African American section of Beaumont because it had been rumored (falsely) that an African American man had raped a white woman. Governor Coke Stevenson declared martial law. Three people were killed, more than seventy injured, and twenty black-owned homes and businesses were burned down before the local authorities, the Texas Rangers, and the National Guard restored order. Historian Luis Alvarez concluded the riots were "deeply layered with gender and sex." Such meanings explain why white Texans believed the rumors about rape. "These rumors constructed black male bodies as dangerous and oversexed. Black men were viewed not only as incapable of contributing to the war effort but also as subversive to U.S. nationalism for their alleged violence to white women," Alvarez contended, "who were most often caricatured as mothers of young children, wives of servicemen or defense workers, or defense workers themselves."

Although many minorities, both African Americans and Mexican Americans, fell between the cracks during the New Deal, the government programs and the war created an increased political awareness among them that enabled them to improve their situations. African American businesspeople and civil rights leaders such as Maceo Smith and Juanita Craft in Dallas and Hobart T. Taylor, Sr., Carter W. Wesley, and Lulu B. White in Houston took leadership roles in the local chapters of the NAACP. In the 1930s and 1940s the organization worked to eliminate segregation in the Democratic Party primary and to improve access to public education. The NAACP's challenge to the state's white primary law led to the 1944 Supreme Court decision, *Smith v. Allwright,* in which the Court held that the white primary was unconstitutional. Some white Texas politicians who previously had disdained their African American constituents found themselves campaigning for black votes in a matter of a few years. Meanwhile a few liberal white Texans challenged other discriminatory tactics. Jessie Daniel Ames, who had been active in the Texas suffrage movement, formed the Association of Southern Women for the Prevention of Lynching in 1930. By 1938 African American women in Texas were also fighting this battle.

Mexican Americans, meanwhile, had formed the League of United Latin American Citizens (LULAC) in an effort to eliminate racial prejudice and win equal rights. LULAC was largely a middle-class organization that opposed strikes, demonstrations, boycotts, and other acts that might be interpreted as disloyal. It encouraged Mexican Americans to vote and sent delegations to protest inequity and police brutality.

In El Paso, Mexican American women disputed their low wages, and in San Antonio 12,000 pecan shellers, mostly Mexican heritage women, walked off the job in 1938 in protest of low wages and awful working conditions. Labor leader Emma Tenayuca helped organize the strike. There were no indoor toilets, and the high concentration of pecan dust made tuberculosis a common disease for workers. Wages for shellers had been reduced from the already low 6 cents a pound to 5 cents a pound. Those who cracked the pecans had been paid 50 cents per a hundred pounds but saw their earnings fall to 40 cents a hundred pounds. Pecan shelling was one of the lowest paying industries in the nation with workers earning between $2 and $3 dollars a week. This strike was the largest in Texas to date. Local law enforcement officials behaved brutally toward the striking women.

In 1942, the United States and Mexico signed the Mexican Farm Labor Program Agreement, known as the Bracero program, to permit much-needed Mexican laborers to come into the United States to help alleviate the labor shortage. The agreement guaranteed the workers a minimum wage of 30 cents an hour and humane treatment. Because of the record of discrimination and mistreatment of Mexicans in Texas, however, the Mexican government refused to let Mexican laborers come into Texas under the program until 1947. For different reasons, Texas growers opposed the Bracero program during the war years, fearing that its requirements would be expanded to other low-wage markets. White Texas landowners preferred to hire Mexican migrants who crossed the border without government sanction. The program remained operative until 1964.

National Archives and Records Administration

Depiction of the crowded, poor working conditions for pecan shellers in San Antonio, Texas. Approximately 160 people worked in the factory shown. They sat on backless benches, earned five cents an hour (or less), and had access to only one functioning toilet.

President Roosevelt acted preemptively to maintain good relations with Mexico and the other Latin American countries by establishing the Office of Inter-American Affairs (OIAA). When Mexico banned laborers from coming into Texas under the 1942 Bracero program, which had been negotiated to ensure a supply of wartime field hands and other laborers, the OIAA brought the matter to Governor Stevenson's attention, and the following year he appointed a Good Neighbor Commission, funded by the OIAA. The commission worked to improve the treatment and living conditions of Mexicans in Texas, and became a state agency in 1945.

Conclusion

The labor shortage was only one indication of the major changes that had taken place in agriculture during the war. The diversification of crops continued, with increases across the board in the production of grain sorghums, cattle, sheep, goats, horses, turkeys, tomatoes, onions, spinach, pecans, and roses, in addition to cotton. The number of farms decreased during the war, but the average size of farms grew and total production increased by as much as 30 percent because of the increased use of machinery.

In 1945, Texas emerged from World War II fully industrialized and one of the most rapidly growing urban areas in the nation. Texas industry, propelled by war production, had greatly outstripped agriculture in economic importance. The state once again had a financial surplus, for which Governor Stevenson claimed credit, but which, in fact, was due more to the federal expenditures that poured into the state during and after the war. In addition to the federal payroll—perhaps one out of every ten members of the armed services trained in Texas—private industry expanded at an unprecedented rate. Fort Worth, Garland, and Grand Prairie boasted aircraft factories; Houston, Port Arthur, Orange, and Beaumont had new shipyards; and the huge petrochemical industry was firmly established on the coast. In addition, munitions plants, steel mills, and the Texas City tin smelter added to the state's industrial muscle. Needless to say, the older, established industries, such as oil and lumber, did equally well, and by 1945 Texas had replaced California as the leading petroleum producer in the nation.

Although Governor Stevenson was reelected in 1942 and 1944 virtually without opposition, the war years saw the beginning of a liberal-conservative rift in the Democratic Party that became even more pronounced after the war. The party remained united behind Vice President Garner as the U.S. presidential election approached in 1940, but when Roosevelt decided to run for a third term, Texas conservatives, who called themselves the Texas Regulars, split from the New Deal faction of the party. Two episodes, in particular, ignited their fury. The first was the supposed infiltration of the University of Texas by communists and other subversives (a specious charge), which led to the ultraconservative board of regents firing the president, Homer P. Rainey, an ordained Baptist minister, in November 1944. The second was the U.S. Supreme Court's *Smith v. Allwright* decision in April 1944, which brought an end to the all-white primaries. Within a few decades, this liberal-conservative split would evolve briefly into a two-party system.

Suggested Readings

Overviews of this period include Donald W. Whisenhunt, *The Depression in Texas: The Hoover Years* (1983); Lionel V. Patenaude, *Texas Politics and the New Deal* (1983); and James Smallwood, *The Great Recovery: The New Deal in Texas* (1983).

The Great Depression

For information on the Great Depression in Texas, see Robert C. Cotner et al., *Texas Cities and the Great Depression* (1973) and Kenneth B. Ragsdale, *Centennial '36: The Year America Discovered Texas* (1987). Robert S. Maxwell, *Texas Economic Growth, 1890 to World War II: From Frontier to Industrial Giant* (1981), is also helpful. For information on agriculture, see Donald E. Green, *Land of the Underground Rain: Irrigation on the Texas High Plains, 1910–1970* (1973). For information on the Dust Bowl, see Donald Worster, *Dust Bowl: The Southern Plains in the 1930s* (2004).

The New Deal

George Norris Green, *The Establishment in Texas Politics: The Primitive Years, 1938–1957* (reprint, 1984) is the best treatment of politics during this period. Robert Dallek, *Lone Star Rising: Lyndon Johnson and His Times, 1908–1960* (1991), and Randall Woods, *LBJ: Architect of American Ambition* (2006) are the best treatments of Lyndon B. Johnson. See also Jordan A. Schwarz, *The New Dealers: Power Politics in the Age of Roosevelt* (1994); Seth S. McKay, *W. Lee O'Daniel and Texas Politics* (1944); Steven Fenberg, *Unprecedented Power: Jesse Jones, Capitalism, and the Common Good* (2011); and biographical essays of Morris Sheppard, John Nance Garner, Jesse Jones, Tom Connally, Sam Rayburn, and Johnson in Kenneth E. Henderickson, Jr., and Michael L. Collins, eds., *Profiles in Power: Twentieth-Century Texans in Washington* (1993). For particular New Deal programs in Texas, see Philip Parisi, *The Texas Post Office Murals: Art for the People* (2004); James Wright Steely, *Parks for Texas: Enduring Landscapes of the New Deal* (1999); Keith J. Volanto, *Texas, Cotton, and the New Deal* (2004); and Cynthia A. Brandimarte, with Angela Reed, *Texas State Parks and the CCC* (2013); Ronald E. Goodwin, *Remembering the Days of Sorrow: The WPA and the Texas Slave Narratives* (2014). For information on oil in Texas in the 1930s see William R. Childs, *The Texas Railroad Commission: Understanding Regulation in America to the Mid-Twentieth Century* (2005).

Information on minorities and women may be found in Luis Alvarez, *The Power of the Zoot: Youth Culture and Resistance during World War II* (2009); Alwyn Barr, *Black Texans: A History of African Americans in Texas, 1528–1995* (1996); Julia Kirk Blackwelder, *Women of the Depression: Caste and Culture in San Antonio, 1929–1939* (1984); Darlene Clark Hine, *Black Victory: The Rise and Fall of the White Primary in Texas* (2003); Monica Perales, *Smeltertown: Making and Remembering a Southwest Border Community* (2010); Rebecca Sharpless, *Fertile Ground, Narrow Choices: Women on Texas Cotton Farms, 1900–1940* (1999); and Charles L. Zelden, *The Battle for the Black Ballot: Smith v. Allright and the Defeat of the Texas All-White Primary* (2004).

Texas in World War II

For details on Texans in the federal government during the war, see Nancy Beck Young, *Why We Fight: Congress and the Politics of World War II* (2013). More information on Texas in World War II is found in *The Handbook of Texas* and the *Southwestern Historical Quarterly*.

A "Confluence of Anxieties": Texas from 1946 to 1960

In 1949 a forty-one-year-old Texan named V. O. Key, Jr., who was then a professor at Johns Hopkins University in Baltimore, published the results of his seminal study of the political process in the South, *Southern Politics in State and Nation*. The South had long been recognized as the most depressed part of the nation, especially after President Franklin D. Roosevelt identified it as such in 1938. The question was how it would prevail over its problems to participate in the prosperity that the rest of the nation enjoyed. Many people assumed that the most difficult problem the South had to overcome was racism and segregation; Key agreed. The ruling oligarchy aggravated the situation by using race baiting for years to maintain the loyalty of poor whites. Key concluded that the lack of class conflict in the South prevented economic progress and electoral participation. In Texas, however, Key saw a glimmer of hope, suggesting that the beginnings of a class conflict had erupted there in the liberal-conservative split in the Democratic Party. He predicted that the one-party system, by which the ruling elite held power, would gradually succumb to the forces of urbanism, industrialism, and organized labor and would transform into a two-party system, with one liberal party and the other conservative. Because "politics generally comes down, over the long run, to a conflict between those who have and those who have less," he asserted, the two parties would argue about taxation and expenditure: who pays the taxes, and how the money is used. It was almost as if he had written a script for the postwar decades in Texas.

Chapter 13 A "Confluence of Anxieties": Texas from 1946 to 1960	
1946	World War II price controls are removed
1948	Lyndon Johnson elected to the U.S. Senate
1949	Gilmer-Aikin laws passed; fifty-first legislature adopts the state's first billion-dollar budget
1950	U.S. Supreme Court decides *Sweatt v. Painter* and Heman Sweatt admitted to University of Texas Law School; 59.8 percent of the state's population live in cities and towns; Korean War begins
1953	U.S. Congress enacts legislation confirming Texas ownership of its tidelands out to three leagues
1954	Texas Instruments produces first silicon transistor and first portable radio
1956	U.S. Congress approves national system of interstate highways
1957	Senator Lyndon B. Johnson is instrumental in the U.S. Congress's passage of the first civil rights act in more than eighty years; Soviet satellite Sputnik launches space race
1958	Texas pianist Van Cliburn wins the prestigious Tchaikovsky Piano Competition in Moscow

As World War II ended, Texan veterans came home to a changed state. Industrialization and a large population increase brought on by the war effort had transformed the economic, social, and political fabric of the state, and it would take some time before most people understood the ramifications. Opportunities in Texas, including the huge growth of the oil industry, attracted out-of-state veterans, such as the future president George Herbert Walker Bush, who came to Midland with his growing family after graduating from Yale in 1948. The "modified class politics" that Key had documented in Texas was not the product of a plantation oligarchy, as in other southern states, or of an "upthrust of the masses" that had forced the upper class to defend itself, but the result "of the personal insecurity of men suddenly made rich who are fearful lest they lost their wealth."

The extent of class politics quickly became apparent during the biennial gubernatorial races and subsequent sessions of the legislature as various constituencies fought over the commonly accepted solution: tax revenue—where to get it and how to use it. Race and gender, though, proved almost as important to understanding society and politics in the state in the two decades following World War II. Rapid urbanization and increased population forced the state to expand its educational institutions, social services, and bureaucracy, which, of course, required additional taxes. But increased taxation challenged the traditional agrarian-inspired approach to Texas government, and the only relatively new source of money in the state, the oil industry, had accumulated enough political and economic clout to ensure that it would not have to bear the brunt of these new initiatives.

As you read this chapter, consider the following questions:

1. Which groups benefitted from the political status quo in Texas? Which did not? Why were the conservatives effective in gaining control of state politics?
2. What were the key characteristics of modernization in Texas? Were the benefits of postwar modernization distributed evenly throughout the state? Why or why not?
3. Compare and contrast the Mexican American civil rights movement with the African American civil rights movement. What accounts for the successes and failures in each?

A Splintering One-Party System

The party harmony that had prevailed during World War II, which saw Coke Stevenson elected virtually unopposed as governor, dissolved after the war, as liberal and conservative factions renewed their battles. As the first postwar gubernatorial campaign began in 1946, the favorite seemed to be Homer P. Rainey, the former president of the University of Texas who was searching for vindication for his firing by the board of regents. Hosting a radio show in which he defended his official behavior, Rainey drew increasing support from liberals and newly enfranchised African Americans. He espoused, to one degree or another, academic freedom, civil rights, labor union rights, and taxes on natural resources; his opponents suspected him of, and accused him of, supporting integration— the kind of race-baiting that Key described—although he was on record against it. Rainey's proposed tax on natural resources was anathema to the oil industry, and, with the exception of a few liberal stalwarts such as independent oilman J. R. Parten of Madisonville, the industry unified behind the more moderate Beauford H. Jester, a member of the Railroad Commission, who positioned himself between conservatives and the liberal Rainey.

Rapid wartime industrialization had led to increased union membership in Texas. By 1946 approximately 350,000 Texans had joined unions, some 225,000 of them in unions affiliated with the American Federation of Labor (AFL), the largest labor group in the country. Another 60,000 belonged to unions associated with the Congress of Industrial Organizations (CIO), the second largest labor group, which had its state headquarters in Dallas and was making significant gains in East Texas. The largest numbers of union members were located in the heavily industrialized areas of Houston–Beaumont and Dallas–Fort Worth, although many unions were located near one specific industry, such as Daingerfield (steelworkers), Greenville (auto workers), and Tyler (oil field workers). At the same time, the state CIO became active in politics in 1944 and in 1946 supported Rainey for governor, which further tainted the former university president in the eyes of the conservative businesspeople. As election day neared, and the nation endured hundreds of strikes by union laborers trying to keep up with postwar inflation, including work stoppages at the General Tire and Rubber Plant in Waco and Consolidated Vultee Aircraft in Fort Worth, voters began to see Rainey in a new and, to them, more dangerous, light.

Modified Class and Gender Politics

Perhaps the most important component of the liberal coalition that worked on behalf of Rainey's campaign were activist women, several of whom had been leaders in the woman suffrage fight during the Progressive Era, notably Minnie Fisher Cunningham, and others who were younger. From the postwar years at least until the early 1970s, this loose coalition of women energized the various liberal factions within the state's Democratic Party. While they appreciated the need for compromise, they were, like the groups they joined, more firm in their ideological views than the national Democrats from Texas, namely Sam Rayburn and Lyndon Johnson, who benefited from their assault on the Texas Regulars.

The Regulars traced their origins to the Jeffersonian Democrats, a conservative group that formed in Texas in 1936 in opposition to Roosevelt's bid for reelection. Tensions continued in 1940. The 1944 presidential election intensified the warfare in Texas between the conservatives and the loyalists, the name taken by the more moderate and liberal faction of the Democratic Party in Texas that gave its loyalty to Roosevelt and the New Deal. That same year the Committee for Constitutional Government, the name a group of wealthy, conservative Texas oilmen took for themselves, organized and tried but failed to have the three most liberal members of the Texas delegation in the U.S. Congress defeated: Lyndon Johnson, Wright Patman, and Sam Rayburn. The presidential contest that year divided Texas Democrats. Conservatives controlled the party machinery in the state and arranged for a similarly minded delegation to go to the Democratic National Convention where they could vote against Roosevelt. A second state convention that fall undid the work of the conservatives earlier that year, naming a slate of loyalists as the Democratic electors. The conservatives then adopted the name the Texas Regulars, bolted the party, and assumed the posture of a third party.

In 1946 the Regulars fought hard against Rainey, whose female defenders in Texas formed a political organization called the Women's Committee for Educational Freedom (WCEF). It linked two generations of Texas women, revealed the challenges liberals faced in Texas, and contended political reform could not be achieved without female leadership. The WCEF drew on their status as mothers, their membership in women's clubs, and also on their religious faith. They believed that economic and political democracy were dependent on class and gender equality. Another former Texas suffragist compared Rainey's firing to affairs in Europe before World War II: "Hitler and Mussolini took over the great universities of Germany and Italy, established a gag rule and threw out all the professors who refused to approve their totalitarian doctrines."

One important weakness the WCEF faced resulted from the continuation of traditional gender roles in Texas and women's economic dependence on breadwinning husbands. This reality made it difficult to draw a large number of women into politics, especially when the Texas Regulars and the conservative establishment used tactics that equated nontraditional lifestyles with communism. Said one conservative critic of the WCEF: "It would seem that the Cunningham-Collier female gang had selected small segments of the various Red groups in the state and succeeded in getting together a fairly representative cross section of the lunatic fringe of Texas. The old she red foxes of the outfit may have known what they were doing, but it is doubtful about the youngsters." Still the WCEF undertook the necessary but unglamorous precinct organizational work to bring out voters on election day. They were much less successful getting Democratic men with a liberal outlook to listen to their suggestions for campaign strategy.

The Rainey campaign was the first in the state to profit from the emerging urban coalition of labor, minorities, women, and independent progressives that would ultimately challenge the state's Democratic establishment for control of the party itself, and it was here that Key had seen a flash of what he perceived as a budding "modified class politics." Key overlooked entirely the heightened role of women in politics, but the gendering of power in Texas made for a more complicated dynamic than the race and class struggles Key had identified. Although Rainey led in the polls right up to election day, Jester took a small lead in the first primary and concluded with a resounding victory in the runoff.

The postwar years also saw the emergence of an organization designed to inculcate high school girls with the importance of public service and the political process. In 1941, the Texas chapter of the American Legion Auxiliary formed the Bluebonnet Girls State program, a leadership camp analogous to Boys State, a program run by the American Legion since 1935. Attendees had to be seventeen years old and carry a B average in their high school coursework. Leaders put the Girls State program on hold for the duration of the war. It resumed in 1947 with Texas women knowledgeable about government in leadership positions. Frances Goff, a veteran of the Women's Army Corps and also an employee of the state legislature, was one of those women, and she ran the program from the early 1950s until her death in 1994. Whereas the WCEF sometimes encountered resistance in recruiting married women to politics, Girls State had the advantage of working with young, unmarried women. Attendees called themselves "citizens" and they assumed leadership roles in mock city governments and a mock state government. The nonpartisan program brought political leaders in to speak to the young women, and many women who later became important in state and national politics went through the program, including Governor Ann Richards, Carole Keeton Strayhorn, former Austin mayor and Texas Railroad commissioner, and Bea Ann Smith, former judge for the Court of Criminal Appeals. The impact of Girls State on Texas politics was slow to emerge given the ages of the participants and the average age at which people enter politics, but it is nonetheless significant that this organization emerged when it did, suggesting a postwar awareness of the importance of women to public policy in the state.

Industrial Workers and Labor Unions

Despite the fact that unions in Texas had not yet become a political force, their very presence concerned conservatives. Union membership increased in Texas by 225 percent in the 1940s, double the membership of any other southern state. Given that only 10 percent of the state's workers were union members in the late 1930s, though, this figure needs to be assessed with caution. Besides the state federations representing the AFL and the CIO, only the Oil Workers and the Communication Workers engaged very much in state politics. Too often the various union organizations spent more time squabbling among themselves than plotting strategy against conservative industrialists and their political allies in the state. Yet, the soaring growth of urban Texas and also of manufacturing employees, up by 130 percent, meant that labor had tremendous untapped power in the state.

This mattered in Texas because of the economic transformation in the state from a poor agrarian economy before the war to an industrial economy after the war. The tremendous industrial development Texas underwent in the war years—namely in oil refining and also in defense production—meant that there were more blue collar workers in the state potentially interested in union representation, something that would bring higher labor costs and lower profits. Moreover, many of these workers would likely join the CIO, a union known for its opposition to segregation and racial bias in the political economy. Labor

DeGolyer Library, Southern Methodist University, Dallas, Texas, Lawrence T. Jones III Photography Collection

Oil field worker, Gulf Oil Corporation, Waddell Gasoline Corporation, West Texas, 1956.

activists ignored the antagonism to unions and instead believed that workers would be ascendant in the postwar era. Sociologist C. Wright Mills predicted labor leaders would be the "new men of power."

The CIO strikes in the coal industry in 1943, led by John L. Lewis, did nothing to help postwar Texas labor organizers. An antiunion activist declared, "we read the Holy Bible [and] fail to find a provision that tribute must be first paid for this God-given right and duty [to work] to John L. Lewis." The 3,000 member strong Texas Manufacturing Association worked with major industrial firms in the state, including Brown and Root Construction Company, the Texas Power Saw Company, and Sheffield Steel, along with anti-Democratic political advocacy groups like the Christian American Association, which was formed in Houston and which funded much of the lobbying for Right-to-Work legislation. Oil industry types along with small business owners and some eastern industrialists funded Christian American, which developed Right-to-Work as a political slogan. A similar but smaller organization, Fight for Free Enterprise, was based out of San Antonio.

The Conservative Backlash

Jester opposed new taxes and labor unions, and he endorsed states' rights. When he ran for governor, Jester had urged enactment of several labor laws, such as voluntary mediation and arbitration in contract disputes and binding arbitration in public and quasi-public utility disputes. With conservative business support, however, the legislature went even further in 1947, passing laws requiring an "open shop," forbidding strikes by public employees, severely limiting picketing, and prohibiting picketing of utilities. Meanwhile, Jester's own proposals died for lack of support. Jester did not really agree with the antiunion laws, but he did not fight them, and an expanding, postwar economy enabled him to keep his promise of no new taxes. He swept into office a second time in 1948 without really having to campaign.

The postwar antiunion outlook in Texas was linked to the political schisms in the state's Democratic Party and concerns about maintaining Jim Crow. The Texas Regulars had long opposed Roosevelt and the New Deal, and for this faction the labor reforms won in 1935 presented significant problems for the wealthy Texas industrialists who bankrolled conservative politicians in the state. The far right wing in the state also opposed unions, and studying the process of winning Right-to-Work legislation reveals the fervor and diversity in the faction opposed to worker rights in Texas. Indeed, by the postwar years Right-to-Work had come to mean the right not to join a union, not the right to a job.

In 1947, there were few lawmakers in Austin sympathetic to labor, only 45 out of 149 in the House and 8 out of 30 in the Senate. Because of heavy lobbying by industry, the legislature passed and Governor Jester signed a stringent Right-to-Work bill into law. Other antilabor laws followed, including measures banning secondary boycotts, mass picketing, and public employee unionism. The antiunion legislation that the Texas Legislature passed in the 1940s served as a model for other states, mainly in the South, wishing to halt the advance of workers. Texas enacted its anti-union law before the Taft-Hartley Act was passed in the U.S. Congress, suggesting that postwar reform legislation would be conservative in ideology.

Organized Crime Texas-Style

By the late 1940s, several of the state's cities were plagued by organized crime. Gambling, bootlegging, and various kinds of rackets were prosperous endeavors for a number of notorious characters, including Lester "Benny" Binion of Dallas, who had become the local kingpin as the war ended. The Maceo brothers still ruled Galveston, where the local police commissioner bragged to an attorney that he was on the payroll of almost fifty brothels. A number of veterans, just home from making the world safe for democracy, felt that the gangsters threatened democracy at home and embarked on reform. In 1946 a crusading district attorney, Will Wilson, chased Binion out of Dallas to Las Vegas, where he became a fixture of the gambling establishment in that city. In 1949, Attorney General Marion Price Daniel, Sr. sent investigators into cities across the state to look into rumors of bookies and gambling and, on August 15, sent Texas Rangers on successful raids in Fort Worth, Odessa, and Beaumont. Advance warning permitted operators in Galveston, perhaps the most wide-open town in the state, to hide their equipment and escape prosecution, but in 1957 they fell victim to newly elected Attorney General Will Wilson, who closed them down.

The 1948 Elections

The 1948 elections sharply delineated the kind of liberal-conservative conflict that Key described, both on the national and state levels. The presidential race pitted President Harry S. Truman against New York's Republican governor Thomas E. Dewey, and the U.S. Senate race featured former governor Coke Stevenson and Rep. Lyndon B. Johnson. By comparison, the gubernatorial contest between Jester and seven other candidates was a mere sideshow, with Jester winning without a runoff.

Truman inherited all the anti–New Deal sentiment that had built up in Texas when he succeeded Roosevelt in 1945. Many of the conservatives who had called themselves the Texas Regulars, organized around Senator W. Lee O'Daniel and Rep. Martin Dies, and campaigned against Roosevelt now joined with the Dixiecrats, a short-lived political party that nominated Strom Thurmond of South Carolina to challenge Truman for the presidency. They opposed Truman on the basis of his continuation of New Deal policies, his foreign policy, and, specifically, his civil rights initiatives of 1947 and 1948. Truman carried Texas that fall by more than a million votes, his largest majority of any state, and upset Dewey. Governor Jester maintained control of the Democratic Party and helped Truman to his huge majority.

The senatorial primary was equally dramatic. Coke Stevenson represented the Texas establishment and was heavily favored over Lyndon Johnson, but the contest turned out to be one of the closest elections in the state's history. Stevenson had served as wartime governor for almost three terms (finishing O'Daniel's second term, then being elected twice on his own). Lyndon Johnson, his more liberal opponent, had gone into the campaign believing that he had been cheated out of victory in the 1941 special election against O'Daniel and determined not to let it happen again.

Johnson had continued to serve as a member of Congress from the Hill Country and had earned a reputation as a New Dealer. He was only forty years old in 1948 and tried to depict himself as a modern politician, relying heavily on radio commercials and crisscrossing the state in a helicopter named the "Johnson City Windmill." Johnson also worked twenty hours a day and ran a well-organized campaign, whereas Stevenson's campaign was poorly organized and haphazard. Johnson contrasted what he depicted as Stevenson's old-fashioned conservative, antigovernment views with his own stance as a responsible official who was attentive to his constituents. Campaign manager John Connally, a future Texas governor, had his advance team in each town ahead of Johnson to prepare for the brief visit. The helicopter brought out the crowds, enabling the candidate to talk to more voters, and during June and July Johnson visited 118 cities in seventeen days. He portrayed the sixty-year-old Stevenson as old, old-fashioned, and out of touch. He expected to win in the first primary, but finished more than 71,000 votes behind the better-known Stevenson. The third candidate in the race, Houston attorney George Peddy, got enough votes to force a runoff, saving Johnson from defeat.

Stevenson's runoff campaign was even more disorganized than the primary, and he soon made his biggest blunder of the election. A special session of Congress provided the occasion. The governor had announced that he would visit Washington, D.C. to talk with federal officials and foreign policy experts, undoubtedly an attempt to discount any advantage that Johnson might have in the runoff because of his experience and wide acquaintance in the nation's capitol. When Stevenson looked at possible office space in the Senate Office Building and met with real estate agents about purchasing a home, it appeared to many that he was taking the election for granted. But Stevenson's real difficulty occurred at a press conference.

Governor Stevenson tried to take advantage of Johnson's earlier efforts to protect his right flank. As a young congressman, Johnson had demonstrated his conservative credentials by supporting the Taft-Hartley Act, which reaffirmed workers' rights to join unions, bargain collectively, and strike, but prohibited closed shops, permitted states to pass "right-to-work" laws, and enabled the president to get a court-ordered injunction for an eighty-day "cooling off" period before unions could close down an entire industry. As a result, the Texas AFL had endorsed Stevenson, despite his antiunion record, and Stevenson had refused to take a position on Taft-Hartley during the primary. If he had opposed it he would have lost his conservative backers, and if he had favored it he would have lost the support of the AFL. So Johnson suggested that one of the reporters ask Stevenson to explain his position on the Taft-Hartley Act. At first Stevenson refused to answer, saying that his comments had already been published. When the reporter persisted, Stevenson replied, "All my notes and papers are back in Texas. I am facing these questions without any material." The syndicated columnist Drew Pearson, a friend of Johnson's, was unmerciful the next day, writing that Stevenson "evaded more issues and dodged more questions than any recent performer in a city noted for question dodging." The Johnson team spread thousands of copies of the column across the state as the runoff approached, and "Silent Coke's" refusal to take a stand became the theme of the Johnson runoff campaign.

An episode six years earlier provides insight into Stevenson's silence regarding matters of race. An African American man had been lynched in Texarkana, Texas on the specious charge of allegedly having raped a white woman. The white male vigilante group who murdered him also brutalized his body, dragging it through the streets before hanging him from a winch at a cotton gin. When asked by the press, Stevenson made no comment, but privately he is recorded as saying, "Well, you know these Negroes sometimes do those kinds of things that provoke whites to such action." Stevenson's views of Mexican Americans were no more enlightened, and he was also an isolationist in international affairs, known for his criticism of the Marshall Plan, the important postwar initiative for rebuilding Europe. Such views caused Texas liberal J. Frank Dobie to remark, "Coke Stevenson knows as much about foreign policy as a hog knows about Sunday."

Johnson won in a very close election, but Stevenson did not concede immediately. Rather than call for a statewide recount, which might have confirmed Johnson's victory, Stevenson felt that he could find evidence in the boss-ruled counties of South Texas that Johnson supporters had stuffed the ballot box and that he could have those votes disqualified. He went to Alice, Texas with longtime friend and ex–Texas Ranger Frank Hamer, who had tracked down Bonnie and Clyde, to investigate the matter of Box 13 in Jim Wells County, which had reported the additional 200 votes for Johnson a week after the election. They found their evidence: The last 200 names on the voting list were written in the same hand, but a different hand from the rest of the list, in a different color ink than the rest of the list, and in alphabetical order. Stevenson's attorneys even took depositions from several people whose names were on the list but who said that they had not voted.

Stevenson took his evidence directly to the state Democratic Election Committee, which upheld Johnson's victory by a vote of 29 to 28. Then, with fistfights punctuating the meeting and a delegate who suffered a heart attack in the hotel lobby assigning his proxy to a Johnson supporter before being taken to the hospital, the state convention confirmed the committee's decision. Stevenson challenged the election in U.S. District Court. He got a temporary restraining order from an anti–New Deal judge who blocked Johnson's name from being placed on the general election ballot. With Abe Fortas (whom Johnson later appointed to the Supreme Court) planning the strategy, the Johnson forces convinced Supreme Court Justice Hugo Black to set the order aside. The full Court later affirmed Black's ruling, and Johnson went on to win the general election. Stevenson, still unwilling to give up, contacted several Republican senators in an effort to have the Senate refuse to seat Johnson. But the Democrats won control of the Senate that fall, and Johnson had enough friends among them that no challenge would have been successful. Johnson realized that he entered the Senate with the reputation of a wheeler-dealer and a cloud of illegality hanging over his head, and he gave himself a nickname based on the event: In a radio speech, he jokingly referred to himself as "Landslide Lyndon" because of his eighty-seven-vote runoff victory, and it stuck.

Johnson's first committee assignments were Armed Services and Interstate and Foreign Commerce, which permitted him to push for more military bases in Texas, and to shape legislation that affected the oil and natural gas business. He soon had a hand in legislation that helped to build more houses around military bases, subsidized the tin smelting business in Texas City, loaned money to the Lone Star steel plant in northeast Texas, and sold surplus war equipment to the University of Texas for use in government-contracted research. Such results turned more than a few "recalcitrant and hardened Ag'inners" into "I told you so supporters," according to one business leader.

Modernizing Texas

The demographics of Texas had changed as a result of the war. Between 1930 and 1950, the state's population grew by almost 25 percent. Increasing numbers of immigrants from the North and the Midwest fueled the state's urbanization and then suburbanization. As racial and ethnic minorities—African Americans and Mexican Americans—began to exercise political power, old political allegiances faltered. The Democratic Party was splitting into liberal and conservative factions, but the conservative faction maintained control of the party apparatus. Much of this population growth was in the state's cities—Austin, Beaumont, Dallas, El Paso, Fort Worth, Galveston, Houston, and San Antonio—but the Valley and the oil-rich regions of West Texas also saw growth. Moreover, there was a concomitant decline in population in the rural East Texas, Central Texas, and Hill Country counties. In 1940, 45.4 percent of the population lived in cities; that figure increased to 59.8 percent by 1950, slightly higher than the percentage for the country as a whole (58.6 percent). The urbanization of the state paralleled the increased wealth in the state; in the postwar years Texas ceased being a state of impoverished rural farmers and became a state dominated by the middle class in urban and suburban settings.

In 1948, Governor Jester won reelection with ease, and he worked on social issues born in part as a result of the state's urbanization and industrialization.

For his second term, he unveiled an ambitious plan to deal with some of the state's increasingly serious problems. Unlike those who preceded and followed him, Jester was a moderate. Working with the legislature, he initiated an anti-lynching law and prison reforms and sought appropriations for the elderly and for the state's health services. They reformed the state's educational institutions, providing more money for higher education and establishing Lamar University in Beaumont. His support for a state antilynching law along with his call for a state constitutional amendment to eliminate the poll tax provides evidence of his moderate views on civil rights. He realized change was necessary, but he did not want that change coming from the federal government. In addition, Jester also spearheaded educational and economic reforms vital to the modernization of Texas.

Educational Reform

The most important reforms they made were in the area of public education. Lawmakers had failed to enact meaningful education reform two years earlier in the last legislative session. Under consideration had been a measure to provide a minimum level of pay for Texas teachers. Two lawmakers—Senator A. M. Aikin, Jr. and Rep. Claud Gilmer—were charged with overseeing a special committee to make recommendations for education reform in the next session. They recognized that public schools in Texas were underfunded and inadequate for a modernizing state. Opponents of reform charged that the Gilmer-Aikin proposals were akin to both communism and fascism. After much drama in the state House, the legislation was enacted into law. The Gilmer-Aikin laws brought about many changes: The laws consolidated 4,500 school districts into 2,900; instituted state equalization funding, based on attendance, which supplemented local taxes; required a minimum of 175 teaching days per year; and raised teacher salaries as well as educational requirements. Finally, the appointed nine-member State Board of Education and the elected state superintendent of public instruction became an elected twenty-one-member board with the power to appoint a commissioner of education, subject to confirmation by the Texas Senate, and a new agency, the State Department of Education (now the Texas Education Agency) was created to support the board and the commissioner.

An equally influential educational cocurricular development occurred in the postwar years, and that was the increasing importance given to high school football in Texas popular culture. Players have been lionized, especially when they went on to achieve glory on the college gridiron, but recent historians have noted the centrality of high school football coaches in making the sport achieve a larger-than-life position in state culture. Historian Ty Cashion argued that the school consolidation movement, economic modernization, the good roads movement, and the almost total authority coaches held over their players before the 1960s made it possible for high school football to become "one of the state's identifying social institutions."

Economic Reform

Texans also created the infrastructure necessary to support economic development during this period. The state legislature passed the Colson-Briscoe Act of 1949 (one of the sponsors, Dolph Briscoe, would later be elected governor), which included appropriations of $15 million a year from the Omnibus Tax Clearance Fund for construction of farm-to-market roads. The highway commission had authorized construction of 7,500 miles of rural roads funded equally by the state and federal government in 1945. This proved to be a popular program, and the legislature increased the appropriation in 1962 so that a minimum of $23 million would be spent each year. By March 1989 the Texas farm-to-market system included almost 42,000 miles of paved roads, the most extensive network of secondary roads in the world.

Although the fifty-first legislature passed the state's first billion-dollar budget in 1949, many of Jester's reforms needed additional funding, and he vetoed much of the second year of the biennial appropriation because the comptroller ruled that there was insufficient income. This decision would force the legislature to meet in special session the following year to fund state institutions for the second year of the biennium. The state still needed other sources of revenue because, in addition to increased expenses, the growing competition from Middle Eastern crude had cut into the state's oil revenues. The Gilmer-Aikin law, for example, was financed by a selective consumer tax. Jester had also convinced the legislature to propose a series of constitutional amendments to repeal the poll tax, prohibit discrimination on juries, establish civil-service protections, and require the legislature to meet annually. But before he could pursue these proposals, he died of a heart attack on July 11, shortly after the session ended. Lieutenant Governor Allan Shivers succeeded him, and that fall the voters rejected all of the proposed amendments.

In one isolated public policy arena, the state government began a process that shaped one key sector of the state's economy for the remainder of the century. During 1940s and early 1950s, a collaborative effort of Texas politicians, Houston philanthropists, and the state's university and medical community began to see results for a massive modernization of medical facilities, research, and training. In the early 1940s, trustees for the M. D. Anderson Foundation conceived of the construction of a major medical research and treatment facility in Houston, what is now the Texas Medical Center. Achieving success for the enterprise required tremendous political skill. The private medical community in the area was more than a little suspicious of the state-funded hospitals being constructed in the medical center area. Moreover, the addition of federal funds to the endeavor after the passage of the Hill-Burton Act by the U.S. Congress in 1946 added to the taint. That legislation provided federal funding for hospital construction in the states. Legislative efforts to secure state funding for construction in the Medical Center proved fruitful in 1949 and 1950, ensuring the success of the fledgling exercise.

Two of the first facilities to be planned were the University of Texas Hospital for Cancer Research (now the M. D. Anderson Center) and the Baylor University College of Medicine (now Baylor College of Medicine). These and six other medical facilities were built on 134 acres of city-owned land near the Hermann Hospital (now Memorial Hermann). Expansions to the complex have continued, and since 1960 over a dozen more major facilities have been constructed. By the turn of the century, the Texas Medical Center was the largest in the world, consuming almost 700 acres, multiple medical schools, colleges of nursing, university systems, and hospitals. Moreover it had earned an international reputation for excellence.

Challenging the Racial and Ethnic Status Quo

Questions about segregation and civil rights increasingly became an issue for lawmakers and statewide officials above and beyond other policy problems. The state's attorney general, Price Daniel, wanted to maintain the Jim Crow status quo, but Governor Jester realized that some form of civil rights reform would soon be required. His goal was making sure the state, and not the federal government controlled the process. Most white officials of the state government focused on the question of African American challenges to segregation, but in Texas the problem was more complicated with Mexican Americans also challenging discrimination in the court system. Because Mexican Americans achieved some early victories, these cases became models for African American attorney Thurgood Marshall working for the NAACP.

The Mexican American Civil Rights Movement

Mexican Americans defended their rights in several notable federal court cases, but, as historian Neil Foley has argued, a Mexican American tendency to construct a "Caucasian racial identity from the 1930s through the 1950s complicated, and in some ways compromised, what at first appeared to be a promising start to interracial cooperation." Racial identity, according to Foley, was not the extent of "whiteness," a concept that historians have evaluated in the past several decades. Indeed, being white made accessing tangible property rights, educational opportunities, and career advancement more obtainable. While native-born whites discriminated against immigrant groups by assigning them a "nonwhite" status, immigrants also claimed a white identity to secure equal treatment and opportunity.

Early Mexican American civil rights organizations—the League of United Latin American Citizens (LULAC) and the American G.I. Forum—were both founded in Texas. Their primary objective was to claim whiteness and U.S. citizenship. Official documents for the two organizations make no mention of the word Mexican, preferring instead to be called Latin American. Starting in the

1930s these and other organizations began challenging educational segregation against Mexican Americans. Their methods for doing so differed sharply from the NAACP strategy of emphasizing the unequal nature of the "separate but equal" doctrine as practiced in the South. Instead, Mexican Americans in the West contended that any segregation against them was wrong, arguing whites could not be segregated by other whites. As far back as 1930, the courts had readily ended educational segregation of Mexican Americans when a case could be made the discrimination was constructed for racial reasons.

Delgado v. Bastrop ISD (1948), prosecuted by LULAC and the American G.I. Forum of Texas, forced local school districts to cease de facto segregation whereby specific buildings on school campuses were designated for Mexican heritage children only. The argument, though, was not that segregation itself was wrong in a democracy of free people but that the use of a "language handicap" to segregate did not make pedagogical sense. Never, though, in their shared efforts to obliterate educational segregation did African American and Mexican American activists find a consistent common cause. The educator and activist George I. Sánchez made a statement that hints at why: "Let us keep in mind that the Mexican-American can easily become <u>the front-line defense</u> of the civil liberties of ethnic minorities. The racial, cultural, and historical involvements in his case embrace those of all . . . other minority groups. Yet, God bless the law, he is 'white'! So, the Mexican-American can be the wedge for broadening of civil liberties for others (who are not so fortunate as to be 'white' and 'Christian'!)."

Mexican Americans in other ways worked for equality. World War II veteran Dr. Hector García had organized the American G.I. Forum in 1948 to help Mexican American veterans get the benefits due them under the G.I. Bill of Rights of 1944, but quickly began to address other concerns. One such concern was the refusal of a Three Rivers funeral home director to permit the use of his chapel for the funeral of Félix Longoria, an American soldier who was killed in

Sign in Dimmit, Texas depicting the racializing of ethnic Mexicans and the imposition of segregation, 1949. Because there were very few Mexicans and Mexican Americans living in the town its target audience was migrant workers.

the Philippines during the last days of World War II but whose body had just been recovered. Longoria had won the Bronze Service Star, the Purple Heart, a Good Conduct Medal, and a Combat Infantryman's Badge for his service in the Philippines. The funeral home director explained his decision, saying "the whites would not like it." With García at her side, Beatrice Longoria, Felix's widow, spoke out publicly during the three-month period it took to get her husband a proper burial. Naturally a shy woman, she confronted her own personality as well as the gendered expectations for South Texas women when she demanded justice. Moreover, she challenged the white power structure, including Anglo dominance of the region's economy. The status quo had left Mexican Americans in positions of subservience. Historian Patrick Carroll has argued about the racial dynamics in the region, "Anglos eventually distinguished themselves as whites, as Texans, as Americans. They came to see Mexican Americans and Mexican nationals as one and the same: 'Mexicans,' brown, alien, and economically, socially, and politically retrogressive, to be segregated from 'Americans,' because they were 'un-American' and 'unfit' to become American."

García wrote to a number of Texas senators and members of Congress, but Senator Lyndon Johnson was the only one to respond. He said of the Longoria case: "I deeply regret to learn that the prejudice of some individuals extends even beyond this life. I have no authority over civilian funeral homes. Nor does the federal government. However, I have today made arrangements to have Felix Longoria buried with full military honors at Arlington National Cemetery, here at Washington, where the honored dead of our nation's War rest. . . . There will be no cost. . . . This injustice and prejudice is deplorable. I am happy to have a part in seeing that this Texas hero is laid to rest with the honor and dignity his service deserves." He arranged for Longoria to be buried in Arlington National Cemetery in 1949 with full military honors. While not the most egregious form of discrimination against Mexican Americans, this episode nonetheless galvanized the community and drew the attention of people as far away as Argentina.

The African American Civil Rights Movement

There were parallel developments in the African American struggle for civil rights, but unlike with Mexican Americans, few Anglo politicians were ready to advocate publicly on behalf of a black cause. Along with other southern governors, Jester opposed President Truman's civil rights program, but he advised University of Texas officials in the spring of 1949 that they would have to admit qualified African American students to medical school at Galveston unless the legislature created a separate medical school at the new Texas State University for Negroes (previously the Houston Colored Junior College then the Houston College for Negroes and now Texas Southern University) in Houston.

An African American applicant to the University of Texas law school, Heman Sweatt, had already filed suit against the university in 1946, claiming that he had been turned down for admission because of his race and challenging the segregation system itself. As that suit wound its way through the courts, two African Americans filed for application to the medical school in Galveston in 1949, and one of them was admitted that fall. The University of Texas, not unlike other institutions of higher education in Texas and the South, reflected racial views of the world that would not be tolerated in the early twenty-first century. This context is important to understanding just how difficult it was to prosecute and win the *Sweatt* case. T. S. Painter, who replaced Rainey as president of the university, wrote openly in his correspondence with conservative members of the board of regents his biased views about African Americans, including his support for segregation as the official policy of the university. In doing so, he relied on stereotypical arguments about biology that have been refuted as racist.

Civil rights litigants had been increasingly successful in the federal courts after World War II, and the Houston chapter of the NAACP, with the support of Thurgood Marshall, the well-known attorney and future Supreme Court justice, challenged segregation in Texas. Sweatt, a graduate of Wiley College in Marshall and a former medical student at the University of Michigan and now a postal employee and civil rights advocate in Houston, had become interested in law and applied to the University of Texas law school in 1946. Marshall successfully sued the university in the U.S. Supreme Court (*Sweatt v. Painter*), winning a major decision in 1950. Shivers led the segregationist forces, and the state attempted to resolve the dilemma by creating a law school for African Americans as part of the Texas State University for Negroes, but the Court held that the new school did not meet the "separate but equal" provision required by the 1896 *Plessey v. Ferguson* case and ruled that the university had to admit him. This decision, however, did not apply to undergraduate or primary and secondary education.

Heman M. Sweatt in line to register for courses at the University of Texas School of Law, 1950.

Four years after the *Sweatt* case, another important civil rights case from Texas was heard in the U.S. Supreme Court. *Hernández v. State of Texas* resulted when an all-white jury in Edna, Texas, found Pete Hernández guilty of murdering Joe Espinosa in 1950. Civil rights attorneys with the American G.I. Forum and the League of United Latin American Citizens appealed the verdict to the Supreme Court, arguing that Hernández's Fourteenth Amendment rights had been violated. They contended the amendment not only prohibited race-based discrimination but also class-based discrimination. Attorneys for *Hernández* and for the state agreed Hernández was white, but the Mexican American civil rights attorneys provided compelling evidence that class-based discrimination between Mexican Americans and Anglos had resulted in the exclusion of all persons with Spanish surnames from juries in that county for a quarter of a century. A unanimous Court ruled in favor of Hernández. Because Mexican American civil rights attorneys were using a very different strategy than African American civil rights attorneys, this case did not have much bearing on the status of blacks in Texas. It does suggest the very complicated nature of race and ethnicity in Texas, though.

The Conservatives Take Charge

Allan Shivers had begun his political career as a prolabor member of the legislature from Jefferson County. Like Jester, he graduated from the University of Texas, where he had been president of the student body. He earned the respect of his colleagues while in the legislature and emerged as a leader. In 1937 he married Marialice Shary, daughter of a wealthy Rio Grande valley land developer, John H. Shary, who was called the father of the Texas citrus industry. After service in the army during World War II, he returned to Texas in 1946 and was elected lieutenant governor (and reelected in 1948); he instituted changes that brought considerable power to the office, enabling him to become the first lieutenant governor to influence and shape the state's legislative agenda by controlling Senate committee appointments. Although he was considered a moderate, Shivers pursued a more conservative course on social and economic issues after election to statewide office.

Shivers was one of the ablest chief executives in the state's history. In preparation for a special session of the legislature, Shivers called a number of lobbyists and business leaders to the governor's mansion to convince them of the need for new taxes and then called a special session of the legislature for January 1950 to address the matter. In his speech before that session, he still exhibited some of his early liberal ideals. He also instituted administrative changes that, ironically, because he is generally known as one of the stronger chief executives, weakened the power of the governor but improved efficiency: He created the Legislative Council to research and draft bills and the Legislative Budget Board, with the lieutenant governor and speaker of the House as chair and vice chair, to prepare the annual budget. Previously, each agency had submitted a memorandum to the governor, who determined what to recommend to the legislature.

The reforms continued during the 1951 legislative session. Shivers asked the legislature for more money for roads, prisons, schools, and the mentally ill. He supported safety inspections for automobiles and liability insurance for motorists, with the intent that motorists must prove that they had sufficient resources to cover any accident that they might cause. The legislature also passed the first redistricting bill in thirty years, which began a long process of transferring power from the rural areas with diminishing population to the growing urban areas.

As Shivers expanded his political power, he began to express his conservative views more clearly. Early in 1951, he supported a measure that permitted candidates for public office to cross-file—that is, they could file in both the Democratic and Republican primaries. Such an approach to electoral politics gave conservative Democrats a decided edge, they benefitted from votes within the factionalized Democratic Party but also from votes of newcomers to Texas more comfortable with the nascent Republican Party, a voting tradition that many postwar migrants to Texas brought with them from the northeast and midwest. Liberals objected to some of the more conservative, antilabor legislation that Shivers had supported during the last session, and they finally broke with him when, because of the tidelands issue, he decided to support the Republican candidate, Dwight D. Eisenhower, in the 1952 presidential election.

Given Shivers's politicking for the Republicans, the factionalized Democratic Party did not heal its wounds in 1952. In what V. O. Key would have considered a prime example of the rising class conflict, Shivers won control of the executive committee of the state Democratic Party that year and purged the more liberal members. The liberals then formed a splinter group, the Democrats of Texas, and they coalesced around Ralph Yarborough. Frankie Randolph, a wealthy Houston woman, was one important component to the liberals' efforts as she funded the *Texas Observer,* a journal of political news told from a liberal perspective. Moreover, the liberals developed increased skepticism for moderate pragmatists like Johnson and Rayburn, who faced increased difficulty navigating the shoals of their home-state party from Washington, D.C. The consequence was an even more factionalized party with a greater level of mistrust between the liberals and the conservatives. Instead of settling matters, the fights in 1952 only expanded the intraparty animosity.

The Early Republicans

Shivers was not the only prominent Texan to support Eisenhower in 1952. One woman who epitomized postwar women's political activism was Oveta Culp Hobby, wife of the former governor Will Hobby, who had been the head of the Women's Interest Section in the army during the war and then became the first commander of the Women's Army Corps. Campaigning for Eisenhower in 1952 brought Hobby rewards in 1953 when the new president named her to his cabinet as the first secretary of health, education, and welfare. She held the post for two years, leaving Washington, D.C. following a controversy over the inadequate distribution of the newly developed polio vaccine. Hobby had the responsibility for approving all new "biologics," a category under which the vaccine fell, but she opposed government involvement in health care. The vaccine crisis prompted the federal government to take a greater role in regulating vaccine distribution. When Hobby returned to Houston in 1955, she resumed her position as president and editor of the *Houston Post* and, in 1956, became chair of the board of directors of the newly organized Bank of Texas. She was one of the most powerful people in Houston.

In retrospect, the 1952 election marked the beginning of an increasingly harsh rhetoric between liberal and conservative forces that signified deeper change in the state's politics—change that V. O. Key had predicted and that would continue until most of the conservatives had joined the Republican Party.

The Tidelands and the Oil Industry in Texas

Ownership of the tidelands, the submerged land from the point of low tide to three leagues (about ten and a half miles) out in the Gulf of Mexico, further split the Democratic Party and made Shivers a stronger states' rights advocate. After oil was discovered in the tidelands, federal officials claimed that the offshore lands belonged to the nation. California was the first state to press its claim to tidelands in 1945, but the Supreme Court decided against it. Congress even passed legislation guaranteeing California's ownership of the tidelands, but President Truman vetoed it, asserting national ownership. Texas pleaded that it was in a different situation than California, and Truman seemed to agree, saying during a presidential campaign stop in Austin in 1948 that "Texas is in a class by itself; it entered the Union by Treaty." In the meantime, Texans had miffed Truman by awarding leases in the tidelands without consulting him, and after the election (in which he handily carried Texas), he instructed his attorney general to file suit against the state, claiming that these lands too belonged to the nation. The Supreme Court ruled against Texas by a vote of 4 to 3 (with two abstentions). In 1952, Rayburn pushed another bill through Congress that would have given Texas possession of its tidelands, but Truman vetoed that one too. With Texas attorney general Price Daniel leading the fight, the tidelands became the foremost issue during the upcoming presidential election and one of the most serious conflicts between states and the federal government during the twentieth century.

The tidelands dispute split the state Democratic Party. Adlai Stevenson of Illinois, the Democratic presidential candidate, supported the Truman administration's position but native Texan Dwight D. Eisenhower, the Republican presidential candidate and revered commander of Allied forces in Europe during the war, supported the Texas claim. Maintaining control of the party machinery, Governor Shivers led the Democrats for Eisenhower campaign. Liberal Democrats, including the state's two most important national leaders, Sam Rayburn

> **"TIDELANDS" DRILLING**
>
> Out in the Gulf of Mexico, in an area owned by Texas public schools, the oil hunters drill their wells from small man-made islands of steel like this or from mammoth anchored barges.

Print depicting the process of offshore drilling that was at the root of the Tidelands controversy in the late 1940s and the early 1950s.

and Lyndon Johnson, remained loyal to Stevenson, but Texas voted Republican for only the second time in its history as a state. In the governor's race, Shivers defeated Ralph Yarborough, a liberal attorney and former judge, by more than 400,000 votes. In 1953 the Congress passed and Eisenhower signed a quitclaim bill that recognized that the tidelands extended three leagues into the Gulf of Mexico along the coast of Texas and the west coast of Florida. The General Land Office reported that by 1987 the Texas public school fund had received nearly $2 billion from leases, rentals, and royalties on this property.

Just as the tidelands issue had tremendous political impact in the state, it also held ramifications for the oil industry. A booming petrochemical industry saw Texas as a new frontier, and the tidelands were just a part of that. The war years were a significant turning point in the state's oil economy. The end of wartime price controls in 1946 sent oil prices higher than they had been in three decades. Pent up consumer demand throughout the country—for new automobiles, suburban homes, road trip vacations, and a host of consumer products—made fossil fuels and the states with abundant supplies of them central to the postwar boom. One of the most important growth regions in the state was the Permian Basin, and among the out-of-state transplants who moved there and into the state more generally to make money in the oil industry was future president George H. W. Bush, his wife Barbara Bush, and their oldest son and also future president George W. Bush, then just a toddler.

Several other notable industry developments occurred in the postwar years: industry consolidation, the growth of offshore production, and increased tensions between the independent producers and the major companies. With the onset of cheap, foreign oil being imported into the United States in the 1950s, domestic companies introduced production efficiencies and also expanded the petrochemical industry to insure their continued survival. In the late 1950s and running into the 1960s, a consolidation movement began and numerous independents folded. Moreover, exploration technologies improved making offshore production profitable; after the tidelands issue was settled in 1953, this aspect of the industry expanded rapidly.

Politics and oil connected in other ways in Texas. A very complicated tax benefit for oil companies became more controversial in the 1950s. The depletion allowance allowed oil companies regardless of size to take a tax write off for nonproductive wells that they drilled. The tax benefit was more beneficial to the independents, which often had a lower operating threshold and needed the tax deduction to stay in business. Perhaps two of the most important defenders of the depletion allowance in Washington, D.C., Johnson and Rayburn, nevertheless never earned the trust of the very independents they worked to protect. This consequence also helps explain the growing conservative tendency in Texas politics.

The Cold War and Class Politics

Shivers drifted toward conservatism not only on the tidelands issue but also on the wave of anticommunism in America that surged through the country at the beginning of the Cold War. Many date the Cold War from the famous 1945 Yalta Conference among President Roosevelt, British prime minister Winston Churchill, and Soviet premier Joseph Stalin—from the moment that Stalin asserted Russia's authority in Eastern Europe, dividing Europe along what Churchill dramatically called the "iron curtain" in a speech at Fulton, Missouri, the following year. By the end of 1949, the Soviet Union had detonated its first atomic bomb, ending the U.S. monopoly on atomic power, and the communists had driven the nationalists out of China; in June 1950, North Korean troops crossed the 38th parallel that separated the Communist north from the Western-oriented south, pushing the poorly prepared defenders before them. President Truman responded quickly, committing U.S. troops under the United Nations banner. But as the war dragged on, and the Chinese entered the conflict on the side of the North Koreans, Americans became increasingly frustrated. Shivers was among those who called Truman soft on communism and claimed that he was committed to a "no win" policy in Korea. Many Americans began to worry about the spread of communism, as the Soviet Union began to establish puppet regimes in Eastern Europe.

The "red scare" or McCarthyism of the 1950s was partly a result of the undocumented charges by Wisconsin senator Joseph McCarthy that Communist Party members had infiltrated the government, especially the State Department. But Martin Dies of Texas, who became the first chair of the Special Committee on Un-American Activities in 1938, practiced his own brand of anticommunism. Moreover, a Texas Senate committee, established in 1941 for the purpose of ferreting out communists, hunted for "reds" at the state level. Many political figures also mixed red-baiting with race-baiting. Key would have recognized it as a Cold War variation on a theme.

Dies's anticommunism was actually a thinly veiled attack on New Deal liberalism, especially the labor laws that protected union organizing and collective bargaining, and Dies himself was not uncomfortable with extremely conservative viewpoints. He also merged the politics of race and gender with his anticommunism, accepting arguments that "young white girls" were using sex "to play up to Negroes, by sleeping with them if necessary, in order to bring them into the movement." Dies's closest colleagues called him "der Fuehrer." After Dies left office, McCarthy said the Texas red-hunter was "a heroic voice crying in the wilderness" who had not deserved to be "damned and humiliated and driven from public life." Dies piloted many of the phrases more commonly associated with McCarthy during his World War II era tenure as chair of the Committee on Un-American Activities, including "I have here in my hand" and indicating possession of "reliable evidence" that nonetheless could not be disclosed. Democratic insiders in Congress did not realize the damage Dies could do, instead believing the committee was a relatively safe place to put him so that he would not make trouble for the war effort. This decision helped make possible the even more venal postwar red scare for Dies provided much of the language and the tactics of interchanging innuendo and fact, drawing names of suspected communists from letterheads and mailing lists, and requiring those charged to name other names. His East Texas district included a sizeable unionized, working class population, and according to one journalist who covered congressional politics, "The CIO fought Dies from hell to breakfast . . . and undoubtedly did him some considerable harm. Between the labor organization and the Texas demagogue there is a deep bond of mutual hate, disrespect, and disgust."

Yet many Texans supported Senator McCarthy, including Houston oilman Hugh Roy Cullen and Jesse H. Jones, publisher of the *Houston Chronicle*. Cullen even invited the Wisconsin senator to speak at the San Jacinto Day ceremonies in Houston in 1954. By the spring of 1951 chapters of the Minute Women of the U.S.A., whose goals were to fight communism in government and education and ensure that schools and colleges taught American heritage, had formed in Houston, Dallas, San Antonio, and Wichita Falls. Members came from the

Rep. Martin Dies receiving the "Heil Hitler" salute, 1938.

wealthy and the upper classes. Other issues that the Minute Women advocated included support for segregation, opposition to national health care, and support for the oil industry. The Houston chapter was the most active. Using a mixture of organizational tactics, including appointed leaders, no formal bylaws, and telephone trees to call meetings, the Minute Women practiced a newer form of grassroots political activism consistent with the tactics of other conservative organizations from the era. Among other things, the Minute Women forced the Houston school superintendent out of office. As historian Don E. Carleton has noted, "The Red Scare in Houston was the product of a complex mechanism of legitimation that gave a small fringe group of extremists credibility. Central to the local causes of Houston's Red Scare was the fact that the city was in a period of transition as a result of significant economic, demographic, and cultural changes stemming from World War II."

Largely on the strength of political activity among the Minute Women, Dies returned to the U.S. Congress in 1953, holding an at-large seat for the entire state. Dies's poor relations with the Democratic Party, however, left him without influence in the nation's capitol. Not even the House Committee on Un-American Activities welcomed Dies back to Washington. Leaders of the committee believed Dies had hindered the anticommunist movement. Instead, the Minute

Women worked with U.S. senator Price Daniel, who was happy to accommodate the movement. Dies's fate in his second political act suggests there was a
chasm between the electoral abilities of the Minute Women and other right-wing
groups and the potential for their candidates to succeed. Indeed, the group was
much more effective at tainting public individuals than it was in achieving policy
change from the inside of the political process.

The legislature required loyalty oaths of all public employees, but the crusade to get communists out of the public schools resulted in only one dismissal
out of more than 65,000 employees. In Dallas, Jerry Bywaters, director of the
city-supported Dallas Museum of Fine Art, came under attack from conservative
citizens who claimed that the museum exhibited paintings by communist artists.
Although some citizens may have been concerned about the Spanish artist Pablo
Picasso's communist sympathies, later research proved, ironically, that the accusations originated with a group of realist artists who probably felt threatened by
the modernist and abstract works that the museum was exhibiting rather than by
the artists' political sympathies.

Bywaters was not the only significant cultural figure from Texas who attracted
the attention of anticommunist activists. Texas-born folklorist John Henry Faulk
also became a victim of the postwar red hunt. He had researched African American sermons for his master's thesis, and he was a staunch defender of civil rights
throughout his life. A gifted storyteller, Faulk ultimately made his career on the
radio. His program, the *John Henry Faulk Show,* mixed politics with humor and
music, and he regularly incorporated western Texas folk themes. Working in radio in New York City in the 1950s, Faulk helped wrest control of the union for
entertainers away from an entity that aided McCarthy's investigations. His reward
was to be blacklisted. He brought suit, and in 1962 won the largest civil court libel
judgment recorded at that time in history—$3.5 million. The award was reduced
to $500,000 by an appeals court. Faulk's victory likely would not have been pos-
sible in the 1950s, showing just how powerful anticommunism was immediately
after World War II and how it subsided as a force in the next decade. The real
problem was that the "red scare" and the Cold War combined with social changes
such as urbanization and the expansion of civil rights to threaten the status quo,
causing many citizens to identify these needed changes as also un-American.

The Texas Response to the Civil Rights Movement

Another issue that split the state Democratic Party was integration. The decision that made racial separation illegal was *Brown v. Board of Education* in 1954,
which was far more sweeping in its effect than the *Sweatt* decision. In that decision, the Court brushed aside the "separate but equal" argument and held that
segregation of the public schools was unlawful because to separate children
"from others of similar age and qualifications solely because of their race gener-
ates a feeling of inferiority . . . that may affect their hearts and minds in a way
unlikely ever to be undone."

African Americans were still disenfranchised for reason of the poll tax even though the Supreme Court had overturned the white primary in 1944. The majority of white Texas voters opposed racial integration, and it became one of the central issues of the 1954 gubernatorial race, pitting Governor Shivers, seeking an unprecedented third term, against the garrulous and liberal Ralph W. Yarborough, an Austin attorney and former judge whom Shivers had defeated in 1952. The election confirmed several of Key's conclusions: that the poll tax and other repressive measures kept poor citizens from voting, that the coalition of organized labor and poor rural folk was developing, and that the liberal–conservative class conflict, represented by Yarborough and Shivers, was at hand. As the race grew closer, and after the Supreme Court had handed down the *Brown v. Board of Education* decision, Shivers charged not only that "Communist labor racketeers" supported Yarborough but that Yarborough also advocated full integration. Yarborough forced Shivers into a runoff, but Shivers won by fewer than 100,000 votes.

Integration continued to be an issue after the election. Conservative attorney general and fierce state's rights advocate John Ben Shepperd contended that the Supreme Court decisions did not apply to Texas. But the University of Texas and Texas Western College did admit their first African American undergraduate students in 1955. The San Antonio and El Paso school districts began integrating their schools in 1956. But when three African American students attempted that same year to enroll in the Mansfield school, near Fort Worth, members of the local community resisted federal court orders.

At the time of the incident, there were approximately 700 white students in the school and sixty African American students. The elementary school for black Mansfield students was substandard and the high school students were forced to ride city buses into nearby Fort Worth where they were dropped as many as twenty blocks from the school they were assigned to attend. After an NAACP suit, a federal court issued an order that the Mansfield schools desegregate, but the local mayor and police chief aided the white residents of the town in orchestrating a campaign of resistance. Mobs of hundreds of people gathered around the school in late August 1956 when the African American children were scheduled to integrate the campus.

Three African Americans were hung in effigy, but Governor Shivers called the incident a peaceful protest. By then a lame-duck governor, he sent Texas Rangers to preserve the status quo. Nor did President Eisenhower provide much help for his attention was on his reelection campaign that fall. The following year, the legislature passed segregation laws that enabled other districts to avoid desegregation. Not until 1965 and later when federal funding under the Elementary and Secondary Education Acts was made conditional upon compliance with other federal laws and Supreme Court rulings, that is, the 1964 Civil Rights Act and *Brown v. Board of Education,* did Texas school districts begin desegregating their campuses with "all deliberate speed."

Given these realities, it is no surprise that some members of the Texas delegation in the U.S. Congress signed the Southern Manifesto in 1956; what was odd was that few Texans added their names to this congressional document. Authored by rabid segregationist Rep. Howard Worth Smith of Virginia, the document stated openly white southern opposition to the *Brown* decision. Nineteen U.S. senators and eighty-two members of the House of Representatives signed it including the following Texans: Senator Price Daniel and Reps. John Dowdy, O. C. Fisher, Wright Patman, and Walter Rogers. Notably Lyndon Johnson did not sign the document; nor did the majority of the Texans in the U.S. House, including an odd assortment of liberals and conservatives: Jack Brooks, Omar Burleson, Martin Dies, Sam Rayburn, Albert Thomas, and Jim Wright. Nor did the lone Republican in the delegation, Bruce Alger, sign. Neither region within the state nor ideology explains who signed and who did not; instead the best explanation is that the Southern Manifesto was identified with Deep South segregationist mores, not the new identity Texas had been cultivating for itself in the twentieth century, one that could mask the racialized thinking that remained in the state.

Scandal and Political Upheaval Hurt Shivers

Shivers's historical reputation probably would have been better served if he had not run for a third term. The school crisis was an ugly affair, and he was beset with charges of corruption as insurance scandals eroded public confidence in his administration. Reporters exposed illegal operations in the Veterans' Land Board that resulted in the sentencing of General Land Office commissioner James Bascom Giles to six years in the penitentiary. Even worse were the insurance scandals. The state's regulation of the insurance industry was so lax that more insurance companies called Texas home than any other state. So many had failed that Yarborough made it an issue during the 1954 campaign. One of the largest debacles was U.S. Trust and Guaranty, which had grown quickly into a large company that controlled seventy-four other insurance companies in twenty-two states, but more troubling politically was the collapse of the Insurance Company of Texas. Its founder, Ben Jack Cage, was indicted for bribery and embezzlement and fled to Brazil, where he lived for the rest of his life.

These problems were not sufficient for Shivers to retire from Texas politics. Shivers again led Eisenhower's campaign in Texas in 1956, but the state Republican Party nominated only a few candidates for office. Realigning the state was a slow process with most conservatives still identifying as Democrats and voting for the conservative candidates in that party (cross-filing had been removed from the Texas Election Code in 1955). The liberal Yarborough made his third run for the governor's office, but lost to the more conservative Price Daniel, who had the support of Johnson and Rayburn and who resigned his U.S. Senate seat to become governor. Johnson, Rayburn, and Daniel formed a coalition with liberals to wrest control of the party machinery away from Shivers and the conservative establishment, and, in the major liberal victory of the decade, Yarborough won the open senatorial seat with only 38 percent of the vote in a winner-take-all special election over twenty-one other candidates.

Following his election to a third term, Shivers still faced the thorny problem of civil rights. Shivers appointed an Advisory Committee on Segregation in the Public Schools with the specific instructions that they prevent "forced integration." The committee presented a number of racist proposals to the legislature. In the debate, state senator Henry B. González of San Antonio, the lone Mexican American in the legislature, became a hero to liberals when he filibustered against the proposals. He had many supporters, but two of the bills eventually became law: (1) Local voters had to approve integration before state funds could be used for an integrated school, and (2) Any reason on a list of approved reasons could be legally used to prevent integration. Price Daniel, who succeeded Shivers as governor, signed the bills into law but made no effort to enforce them. Daniel had pledged to support local boards of trustees in their decisions, implying his support of segregation, but the new attorney general, Will Wilson, recognized that federal laws and Supreme Court decisions did apply to Texas, and segregation gradually came to an end in Texas over the next two decades.

Governor Price Daniel

The most important issues facing Texas as Price Daniel took the governor's office were taxation and expansion of state services such as water (the worst drought in the history of the state occurred from 1949 to 1956), schools, highways, care of the elderly, law enforcement, and prison reform. But the state's antiquated tax system creaked and groaned under the pressure, and little could be done without increased revenue. Daniel favored "sin" taxes (e.g., on tobacco and liquor) and business taxes, but, after two special sessions in 1961, and despite his public objections, the legislature presented him with a 2 percent general sales tax, which he permitted to become law without his signature. The regressive nature of the tax was somewhat tempered by the exemption of food, drugs, clothing, farm supplies, and some other items, but the subsequent need for additional funds has since caused some of those items to be added to the tax list. Daniel ran for an unprecedented fourth term in 1962 but was defeated because much of the electorate blamed him for the new sales tax.

Although Daniel would not be called a champion of civil rights, he seemed moderate in comparison to Shivers, and neither he nor Attorney General Wilson agreed with the positions taken earlier by Shivers and Shepperd. On the national scene, meanwhile, Johnson took a leading role in passing the 1957 Civil Rights Act, while Rayburn supported it behind the scenes so as not to offend voters in his home district. The act provided for a civil rights commission, a civil rights division within the Justice Department, and a compromised voter rights section. Practically, the law changed very little with regard to southern race relations. Still conservative southerners hated the law because its passage resulted only after the filibuster had been broken in the Senate, setting a precedent for the passage of more meaningful civil rights legislation. Liberals also hated the law because it changed nothing. One northern liberal critic said the legislation "was like soup made from the shadow of a crow which had starved to death" and blamed Johnson for allowing his southern senatorial friends to water the bill down prior to its passage. Johnson's support of the 1957 Civil Rights Act was based on his personal convictions as well as his belief that he needed a dramatic achievement to advance his national political aspirations.

Texas Society in the 1950s

Like people in the rest of the country, Texans in the 1950s experienced modernization in ways beyond macroeconomics. Most notable was the rise of the consumer culture, which was linked to the state's increased prosperity and urbanization. Increased consumption resulted in part from two otherwise distinct developments: construction of better roads and an expanding popular culture. Suburbanization proved the most important result of road construction, and Texans increasingly consumed the new popular culture through the medium of television. Large cities in the state opened television stations during these years, with the first in Fort Worth, WBAP, airing broadcasts in 1948. Two years later, there were six stations in Texas, three in Dallas and Fort Worth, two in San Antonio, and one in Houston.

Better Roads

The press of urbanization threatened to leave agricultural and rural areas of the state behind because Texas was, until the admission of Alaska in 1959, the largest state in the nation. Throughout the 1930s, rural Texans felt isolated from their neighbors and often had to drive for hours over unpaved roads to reach the nearest market community. The state tackled the problem in 1949 with the passage of the Colson-Briscoe Act for construction of farm-to-market roads. The real push came during the decade of the 1950s, however, when the federal government took the lead in the construction of superhighways as a part of national interstate highway construction.

A new road system was high on President Eisenhower's agenda when he took office. Ever since he had made a cross-country trip with an Army convoy in 1919, he had realized how badly the nation needed good roads. The trip from Washington, D.C. to San Francisco had taken sixty-two days, and the soldiers had encountered all kinds of difficulties caused by poor roads and extreme temperatures. Like most Americans, Eisenhower was impressed with the German *autobahns* and noted how much more rapidly American forces moved once they reached the good German roads. President Roosevelt and Congress had made several false starts on improving the roads during the 1930s, then postponed everything as the war effort consumed the country's attention and economic resources. Eisenhower began to work on the National System of

Interstate and Defense Highway Act as early as 1954, and Congress approved it in 1956. The goal was to link every major population center with a modern, high-speed expressway. The states had to finance the expensive roads, but the federal government reimbursed them for 90 percent of the cost. Texas was a major beneficiary of the system because of its size and geographical location. By 2007, the state had over 3,000 miles of interstate highways, more than any other state.

Better highways combined with war-related industrialization and the large number of military bases across the state greatly accelerated urbanization and also racial stratification. The construction of new highways not only divided some extant neighborhoods but also often separated in more obvious ways white, African American, and Mexican American neighborhoods. There were 28,357 miles of U.S. and state highways in the state by the early twenty-first century; increased construction of farm-to-market roads, the interstate highway system, and freeways such as North Central Expressway in Dallas (1954) accelerated the process during the next decades until, by 2007, Texas had approximately 300,000 miles of improved roads. This led to the proliferation of the suburbs, as mobility permitted workers to live outside the city centers. And that, in turn, led to the development of what one author has termed "edge cities"—suburban business districts, mini-cities, or service cities—smaller city cores outside the central business district of the larger cities, the Galleria areas in Houston and Dallas, for example, and Las Colinas in Irving. Today, these edge cities are marked by the presence of office towers and hotels and are usually located near interstate highway junctions.

Created by Squire Haskins Foto, Greer (Dewitt Carlock) Papers, di_05822, The Dolph Briscoe Center for American History, The University of Texas at Austin

From the ceremony opening Central Expressway in Dallas, Texas, August 19, 1949. The photograph depicting the new highway shows a view of Central from the north toward downtown Dallas in the south (at the top of the picture).

Arts and Culture

Postwar urbanization and economic expansion in Texas encouraged a cultural expansion. Music in Texas reflects the state's heterogeneous character. For years, German music could be heard in the beer halls and gardens of San Antonio, while just a few streets over, in La Plaza del Zacate or Haymarket Square, Tejanos played Mexican folk and popular music. Adopting the accordion from German musicians, Tejanos created the *conjunto* style, now popular through Texas and Mexico.

Meanwhile, the folk music of the South combined with the cowboy style of Texas to create what became known as "hillbilly" music, which later evolved into the upscale country-and-western tunes. The first national country-and-western star may have been the singer Jimmy Rogers, who moved to Kerrville in 1929. A few years later, Bob Wills borrowed from such great jazzmen as Benny Goodman to create "western swing" and became popular as part of the band on W. Lee O'Daniel's radio program. Maurice Woodward "Tex" Ritter carved a niche for himself and other singing cowboys in what became known as "western music" and smoothed the way for the stars of the B-grade western movies of the 1950s. One such star was Gene Autry (from Tioga), who parlayed his matinee stardom into a chain of radio stations and, ultimately, ownership of the California Angels major league baseball team and the establishment of the Autry Museum of Western Heritage in Los Angeles. Ernest Tubb took country music in another direction and pioneered what was widely known as "honky-tonk" music, whereas performers like George Jones retained his "country" style but moved more toward the popular genre. Meanwhile, Willie Nelson and a few others who had become disaffected with the growing mainstream of country music moved to Central Texas, where they developed the "Austin sound." Tejanos have contributed to country-and-western music, too, with singers like Trini López, Freddy Fender, Johnny Rodríguez, and Selena.

African Americans have also added much to the Texas arts mix. Ornette Coleman of Fort Worth has revolutionized the way the saxophone is used in what has been called "free jazz." Weldon Leo "Jack" Teagarden of Vernon became a famous jazz trombonist and orchestra leader and played with Benny Goodman, Louis Armstrong, and Paul Whiteman, among others. Perhaps the most famous African American Texan artist, however, is Alvin Ailey of Rogers, who debuted on Broadway in 1954 and stayed on in New York to study ballet and modern dance, founding the Alvin Ailey American Dance Theater in 1958. Drawing upon his "blood memories" of Central Texas, the blues, spirituals, and gospel music, he choreographed his masterpiece, *Revelations,* in 1960, and the company remains popular today with its unique blend of modern and African American expression.

Classical music also boomed in postwar Texas. Although the state had three major symphony orchestras during the 1950s (in Dallas, Houston, and San Antonio), it was pianist Van Cliburn's triumph at the prestigious

Tchaikovsky Piano Competition in Moscow in 1958 that really attracted the public's attention. Van Cliburn was born in Shreveport, Louisiana, but grew up in Kilgore. After winning international fame, in 1962 he helped establish the Van Cliburn International Piano Competition in Fort Worth. Meanwhile, smaller orchestras gained prominence and proficiency in Amarillo, Fort Worth, Austin, Wichita Falls, Corpus Christi, Beaumont, and Lubbock, and other cities. Opera companies performed throughout the state, but there were professional companies in San Antonio, Fort Worth, Houston, and Dallas.

Conclusion

The years between 1946 and 1960 saw tremendous growth in Texas, growth that proved some of V. O. Key's observations about Texas: "The Lone Star State is concerned about money and how to make it, about oil and sulfur and gas, about cattle and dust storms and irrigation, about cotton and banking and Mexicans. And Texans are coming to be concerned broadly about what government ought and ought not to do." The growth of the oil and gas industry (including the state's acquisition of the Tidelands), defense production, and medical research all had major impact on the economy, but not sufficient to offset the dramatic growth in population. The percentage of population growth in Texas outpaced that of the nation throughout the twentieth century. In 1962, the state passed the 10-million mark in population, but by 1950 most Texans lived in the cities. According to the census for that year in the decade, since 1940, the rural population in the state had declined by just over 400,000. The state's cultural institutions flourished after the war, with new museums, orchestras, and educational facilities being established, but, again, these improvements hardly kept pace with the needs that an increased population demanded.

Tensions regarding postwar growth were most acute in the nexus of politics and society. The one party politics in the state became all the more hostile as the liberal and conservative factions rallied around political leaders they supported. Using outdated and restrictive rules meant that urban Texans—many of the new migrants to the state—and minority Texans were disadvantaged in favor of rural residents. Women made inroads into politics, but female influence was most strong at the grassroots—among liberal and conservative women—and around the margins. The part-time legislature did nothing to modernize its functions, and too little regarding policy. The exceptions were school and road reform along with controversial right-to-work legislation that limited the rights of labor union members. Civil rights, for African Americans and for Mexican Americans, was the most important issue of the decade, and state officials did as much as they could to maintain the status quo. The result was an intensification of class and racial divides in the state, problems that remained in the 1960s.

Suggested Readings

A Splintering One-Party System

The best overview for these years is George Norris Green, *The Establishment in Texas Politics: The Primitive Years, 1938–1957* (1984).

For more on the politics of class and gender, see Judith N. McArthur and Harold L. Smith, *Minnie Fisher Cunningham: A Suffragist's Life in Politics* (2003); Ann Fears Crawford, *Frankie: Mrs. R. D. Randolph and Texas Liberal Politics* (2000); Nancy Beck Young and Lewis L. Gould, *Texas, Her Texas: The Life and Times of Frances Goff* (1997); Ruthe Winegarten, *Black Texas Women: A Sourcebook* (1996); Marc Dixon, "Limiting Labor: Business Political Mobilization and Union Setback in the States," *Journal of Policy History* 19 (2007): 313–344.

The best accounts of the 1948 senatorial election are found in the Johnson biographies: Robert Dallek, *Lone Star Rising: Lyndon Johnson and His Times, 1908–1960* (1991), and Randall Woods, *LBJ: Architect of American Ambition* (2006). See also Joe Phipps, *Summer Stock: Behind the Scenes with LBJ in '48* (1992).

Modernizing Texas

Information on the Gilmer-Aikin legislation is in Rae Files Still, *The Gilmer-Aikin Bills* (1950) and details about high school football are in Ty Cashion, *Pigskin Pulpit: A Social History of Texas High School Football Coaches* (2006).

For information on M.D. Anderson and the Texas Medical Center, see James Stuart Olson, *Making Cancer History: Disease and Discovery at the University of Texas M.D. Anderson Cancer Center* (2009).

Challenging the Racial and Ethnic Status Quo

Several scholars have written about the legal challenges to segregation. See Neil Foley, *Quest for Equality: The Failed Promise of Black-Brown Solidarity* (2010); Cynthia Orozco, *No Mexicans, Women, or Dogs Allowed: The Rise of the Mexican American Civil Rights Movement* (2009); Patrick James Carroll, *Felix Longoria's Wake: Bereavement, Racism, and the Rise of Mexican American Activism* (2003); Carl Allsup, *The American G.I. Forum: Origins and Evolution* (1982); and Guadalupe San Miguel, Jr., *Let All of Them Take Heed: Mexican Americans and the Campaign for Educational Equality in Texas, 1910–1981* (1987).

Conservatives Take Charge

One of the key books of the era is V. O. Key, Jr., *Southern Politics in State and Nation* (1949). Chandler Davidson, *Race and Class in Texas Politics* (1990) provides a thoughtful update and analysis of Key's theories. See also Paul Casdorf, *A History of the Republican Party in Texas, 1865–1965* (1965); Roger M. Olien, *From Token to Triumph: The Texas Republicans since 1920* (1982); and Don E. Carleton, *Red Scare: Right-Wing Hysteria, Fifties Fanaticism, and Their Legacy in Texas* (1985).

For more on Allan Shivers, see Sam Kinch, Jr. and Stuart Long's *Allan Shivers: The Pied Piper of Texas Politics* (1974); Ricky F. Dobbs, *Yellow Dogs and Republicans: Allan Shivers and Texas Two-Party Politics* (2005). For other postwar Texas politicians, see Dorsey B. Hardeman and Donald C. Bacon, *Rayburn: A Biography* (1987); Patrick Cox, *Ralph Yarborough: The People's Senator* (2001); Nancy Beck Young, *Wright Patman: Populism, Liberalism, and the American Dream* (2000).

For the oil industry, see William R. Childs, *The Texas Railroad Commission: Understanding Regulation in America to the Mid-twentieth Century* (2005); Don E. Carleton, *A Breed So Rare: The Life of J. R. Parten, Liberal Texas Oilman, 1896–1992* (1999); Roger M. Olien and Diana Davids Hinton, *Wildcatters: Texas Independent Oilmen* (2007); Tyler Priest, *The Offshore Imperative: Shell Oil's Search for Petroleum in Postwar America* (2007); and Joseph A. Pratt, Tyler Priest, and Christopher J. Castaneda, *Offshore Pioneers: Brown & Root and the History of Offshore Oil and Gas* (1997).

For agriculture, see Donald E. Green, *Land of the Underground Rain: Irrigation on the Texas High Plains, 1910–1970* (1973).

For the red scare, especially Martin Dies, see Nancy Beck Young, *Why We Fight: Congress and the Politics of World War II* (2013).

For information on African Americans, see Alwyn Barr, *Black Texans: A History of African Americans in Texas, 1528–1995* (1996); Robert D. Bullard, *Invisible Houston: The Black Experience in Boom and Bust* (1987); Merline Pitre, *In Struggle against Jim Crow: Lulu B. White and the NAACP, 1900–1957* (1999).

The Conundrum of Lyndon Johnson's Texas, 1960–1978

"Don't go for it unless it's already in your pocket," Lyndon Johnson had advised Texas state senator Barbara Jordan when she contemplated running for a seat in the U.S. Congress. Having the seat in her pocket must have been hard to imagine in her first two attempts to gain election to a Texas legislative seat in the early 1960s. Then, the African American attorney from Houston's fifth district had campaigned hard as part of a liberal Democratic coalition, only to see many of the white males in the coalition get elected while she did not. At the time, her family—loving and supportive but reflecting the traditional values of the era—had encouraged her to curtail her political activity and think about getting married.

The political picture for Jordan and other minority candidates had begun to change with the federal actions of the mid-1960s: The Voting Rights Act had struck down some of the barriers to voting African Americans had experienced, the "poll tax" that had kept many poor people and minorities from exercising their franchise had been abolished, and the Supreme Court had mandated redistricting efforts, giving urban areas with larger populations more representatives than rural areas and moving from at-large legislative seats to officeholders representing specific areas.

All of this meant that Jordan could run again in a new Houston eleventh district with a significant percentage of African American voters. In 1966, she won a state senate seat and by 1972 had proven herself a skilled team player, enjoyed the support of former president Johnson, and served as vice chair of the newest senate redistricting panel, allowing her to help control the shape her district would take. Running for the U.S. Congress seat from her district, she was opposed by another African American legislator, Curtis Graves. She had such solid support, however, both within the Texas political power structure and within her home district, that she became the "first black woman from a southern state to serve in Congress," the first African

435

American elected to Congress from Texas, and one of only two African American representatives elected from the South, which had not sent an African American to Congress since 1900. Chosen to speak before the Democratic National Convention in 1976, she would tell delegates, "[M]y presence here is one additional bit of evidence that the American Dream need not forever be deferred." Jordan's political success symbolized some of the changes that were taking place in Texas and the nation, but her victory did not necessarily mean that state politics as a whole would realign in similar fashion.

Chapter 14 The Conundrum of Lyndon Johnson's Texas, 1960–1978	
1960	John Tower becomes the first Republican U.S. senator from Texas since Reconstruction
1961	Legislature passes 2 percent general sales tax, and Governor Daniel permits it to become law without his signature
1963	President Kennedy assassinated in Dallas
1964	President Johnson's Great Society program, including the Civil Rights Act of 1964 and the Voting Rights Act of 1965, begins; the Twenty-fourth Amendment to the U.S. Constitution declares poll taxes illegal in federal elections; Southwest Airlines founded; Dr. Michael DeBakey of Methodist Hospital in Houston performs the first successful coronary artery bypass graft procedure
1965	The Astrodome, the world's first enclosed, domed, multipurpose sports stadium, opens in Houston
1965	First U.S. combat troops sent to Vietnam
1966	Rio Grande valley farm workers march on the state capitol
1967	Governor Connally leads in reorganizing higher education, including establishment of the University of Texas system
1968	Dr. Denton Cooley performs the first heart transplant in the United States at St. Luke's Hospital in Houston
1969	Neil Armstrong speaks first words from the lunar surface, "Houston, the Eagle has landed."
1971	Sharpstown scandal
1972	Equal Rights Amendment to the Texas constitution adopted
1972	Women and minorities gain greater visibility in Texas political elections
1974	State legislators reject new state constitution
1975	State legislators approve revised new constitution, but voters reject it

The 1960s and 1970s were transitional years in Texas society and politics. Midcentury establishment conservatives, operating under the banner of the factionalized Democratic Party, faced new challenges from moderates and liberals and from women and ethnic minorities, all of whom proved more insistent on gaining equal social and political rights. During the 1960s, two related themes dominated state affairs: social protest and political reform.

By 1972, economic and political power had shifted to the cities, raising the issues of urban poverty, crime, and pollution for Texas, problems that had long plagued urban centers in the eastern United States. No ideological unanimity prevailed regarding how best to solve these challenges. The rural political power structure was losing sway in Texas, but urban residents were not singularly aligned with the liberal wing of the state's Democratic Party. The new wealth created in Texas after the war years and the new migrants to the state resulted in a continuum of political and social views. Finally, at the same time Jordan and other liberal Democrats began changing the dynamics within their party, the Republicans gained a competitive foothold in the state.

As you read this chapter, consider the following questions:

1. Should the 1960s and 1970s be viewed as years of success or failure for the Texas Republican Party? Why?
2. Compare and contrast the African American civil rights movement, the feminist movement, and the Chicana/o movement in Texas in the 1960s and 1970s. Which faced the biggest obstacles? Why? Which was most successful in achieving its aims? Why?
3. What were the major political reforms of the 1960s and 1970s? Do they provide a larger legacy than the political scandals of the early 1970s? Why?

The Lyndon Johnson Era

Johnson had grown up in the Hill Country and graduated from Southwest Texas State Teachers College (now Texas State University) in San Marcos, where he earned his elementary teacher's certificate in 1928. He spent a year as principal and teacher at Cotulla, in South Texas, where the poverty of his students and their families deeply impressed him. His first important political job in 1935 was as director of the National Youth Administration in Texas, a position that he left in 1937 to run for Congress, and then for the Senate in 1948.

The 1960 Election

Johnson apparently had his eyes on the presidency all along and viewed the 1957 Civil Rights Act as necessary both for racial equality in the South and for his political career. But race relations deteriorated following Arkansas governor Orval Faubus's 1957 stand against the integration of Central High School in Little Rock.

Johnson avoided any involvement with the crisis. He was able to regain significant ground when the Soviets launched *Sputnik I,* the first artificial earth satellite, later that year, and he seized the moment to convene hearings on its impact and the American response. He received a large part of the credit when the Democrats gained twenty-eight seats in the Senate in the 1958 midterm elections.

Rather than immediately announce for the presidency in 1960, Johnson remained in Washington, presenting the image of a hardworking senator doing his job. Speaker of the House Sam Rayburn, also a Texan, and others portrayed him as a seasoned leader whose accomplishments and wisdom made him a far better choice than the young and inexperienced John F. Kennedy of Massachusetts, who was already campaigning hard around the country. Johnson felt that Kennedy's weaknesses would become apparent during the campaign and that a deadlocked convention would then turn to him as the only truly qualified candidate to lead the party. He had protected his Senate seat, however, by getting the Texas legislature to move the state's primary to May so that he could be a candidate for both the Senate and the presidency.

Johnson's strategy overlooked some very basic changes in the manner in which Americans elected presidents, namely the increased importance of the presidential primary and the decline of the convention system. Because Kennedy gained enough delegates in the states that held primaries, he avoided a deadlocked convention. Nominated on the first ballot at the Los Angeles convention, Kennedy was shrewd enough to realize that he needed Johnson's help to carry Texas and other crucial southern states. He offered Johnson the vice presidential slot, and, after adhering to the advice of Rayburn and other close advisors, Johnson accepted. The Republicans nominated Vice President Richard Nixon for

Rayburn (Sam) Papers, di_04781, The Dolph Briscoe Center for American History, The University of Texas at Austin

Senator Lyndon Johnson kissing Speaker Sam Rayburn on the head on the occasion of Rayburn's 74th birthday, January 8, 1956.

president and Henry Cabot Lodge III for vice president. The 1960 campaign featured the first televised debates between presidential candidates.

Everyone had predicted a close vote in Texas, and an incident in Dallas may have swung it toward the Kennedy–Johnson ticket. Campaigning with his wife, Lady Bird, in downtown Dallas, Johnson encountered some aggressive supporters of Dallas Republican congressman Bruce Alger, who cursed them, one of them hitting Lady Bird with a campaign sign, probably by accident. But the news media covered the event, and when the Alger camp showed little or no remorse, a number of voters probably expressed their disapproval at the ballot box. Another event that surely helped the Kennedy–Johnson ticket was Henry B. González's gubernatorial campaign of 1958. Although González had finished a poor second to incumbent Price Daniel, his political organization was still intact in 1960 and delivered a large percentage of the Hispanic vote to the Democrats; reversing the trend of the last two presidential elections, the Democrats carried Texas (by fewer than 50,000 votes out of the almost 2.3 million cast). Nationwide the margin was only 118,574 votes out of the more than 68 million cast. Kennedy was actually a minority president, garnering only 49.7 percent of the vote. Johnson had literally made it possible for him to become president.

The Rise of the Republicans and the 1961 Senatorial Election

Although their party had lost the presidency, Texas Republicans saw the 1960 election as something of a turning point. Republican ideas showed no significant decline in popularity in the state as Nixon and Lodge had captured more votes in Texas than any Republican candidate ever had. John Tower, an unknown assistant professor from Midwestern University (now Midwestern State University) in Wichita Falls, had polled more than 900,000 votes against Johnson for the Senate seat, a contest he lost. Moreover, the Republican Party was making a few inroads in selected pockets of the state, such as the Panhandle region of West Texas where an avowed member of the right wing John Birch Society was elected mayor of Amarillo in 1961.

The Kennedy–Johnson victory made a special senatorial election necessary. Governor Daniel appointed William A. "Dollar Bill" Blakley to fill the seat until the election could be held in 1961. Ironically, Blakley had served the interim appointment in 1957 when Daniel resigned his Senate seat to become governor of Texas. Blakley was a businessman with investments in airlines and banking, and his political views were very conservative.

Even when measured by Texas standards, the election was a wild affair. There were over seventy candidates with Tower as the lone Republican who vied for the seat. Given the growing might of the Republican Party in the state, this calculus did not bode well for the Democrats, a party that had been divided for the better part of the century and remained so in 1961. Tower had never really quit campaigning after his loss to Johnson in 1960, a contest in which he gained name recognition. The leading Democratic contenders were Henry B. González and

Maury Maverick Jr., both San Antonio liberals, and Rep. Jim Wright, a Fort Worth liberal with strong ties to organized labor. Given this three-way divide among the liberals and the excess of second and third tier candidates the Democrats had little hope of defeating Tower in the first round of voting in a winner-take-all contest that only required a runoff if no candidate secured a majority of the votes. The two top vote getters were Blakley and Tower. Liberals were so enraged that they boycotted the runoff election, saying they would "go fishing" and cede that contest to Tower. They wrongly believed that they could easily beat Tower in 1966 when he would have to stand for reelection. Tower ran an excellent campaign and defeated Blakley with 54 percent of the vote to became the first Texas and southern Republican senator since Reconstruction. He won reelection in 1966, 1972, and 1978.

John Connally and the Appeal to Minorities

As the Republicans became competitive in local and some statewide races, the Democrats engaged in divisive ideological and personal battles. In 1962, John B. Connally, Jr. challenged five other candidates, including the incumbent, Price Daniel, for the governorship. Connally had long been a friend of Johnson's and had served as manager for all of Johnson's major campaigns so he had the makings of a statewide network in place.

Many noticed a big difference between Connally's campaign and previous Democratic establishment efforts. Johnson's election to the vice presidency as well as the newly found potency of the liberal wing of the party, evidenced by Ralph Yarborough's election to the Senate in 1957, influenced Connally, a moderate, to openly court the votes of labor, African Americans, and Hispanics. After a close election, Connally took office saying that he wanted to be the "education governor" because he believed that education was the key to addressing the pressing social problems of race relations and poverty. Johnson's unexpected ascension to the presidency following Kennedy's assassination less than a year into Connally's term as governor changed the dynamics of Texas politics.

Dallas, 1963: The Kennedy Assassination

In hindsight, many have suggested that the incident in which Johnson and his wife were jostled—particularly when coupled with a later incident in which UN Ambassador Adlai Stevenson was heckled and hit with a placard—was illustrative of the sentiment in Dallas in the early 1960s. Dallas was home to retired general Edwin A. Walker, who had resigned from the army when he was reprimanded for distributing right-wing propaganda to his troops. General Walker had recently taken to flying the American flag upside down at his residence as a distress sign because of the federal government's integration policy. Others of similar sentiment, such as H. L. Hunt, the wealthy oilman who financed extremely conservative causes, lived in Dallas.

It was in that setting, on November 22, 1963, that President Kennedy was assassinated as he rode in a motorcade through downtown Dallas. He had come to Texas primarily in an attempt to heal the liberal–conservative rift in the state Democratic Party and to raise funds for his coming reelection campaign in 1964. Riding in the same car with the president, Governor Connally was seriously wounded, by the same sniper, Lee Harvey Oswald, shooting from the Texas Schoolbook Depository. Many blamed the city's conservatism for Kennedy's death, but the Warren Commission, established immediately after the assassination, concluded in 1964 that Oswald acted alone. In 1979, after reviewing the Warren Commission findings and gathering new information, the House Select Committee on Assassinations concluded that Kennedy "was probably killed as the result of a conspiracy," but was unable to identify any participants other than Oswald or the person or persons who planned the assassination. Despite passage of the President John F. Kennedy Assassination Records Collection Act in 1992, which unsealed all of the federal records pertaining to Kennedy's assassination, conspiracy theories continue to abound.

Kennedy's assassination changed the course of both national and state politics. Lyndon Johnson became president, and John Connally, who had narrowly defeated a political unknown in 1962, now became virtually unbeatable as governor. He won reelection in 1964 by a 3–1 margin and in 1966 with 72 percent of the vote. At the same time, Johnson's ascendance was a setback to state Republicans, and he momentarily stymied their surge in Texas and quieted the battle within the state Democratic Party. Johnson led the Democratic ticket in 1964 against Republican Barry Goldwater of Arizona, defeating him by more than 700,000 votes in Texas and almost 16 million nationally. The future Republican president George H. W. Bush failed in his bid to unseat Yarborough in the Senate race, and the Republicans lost both of their congressional seats and all but one of their legislative offices.

A Texan in the White House

Safely elected on his own, President Johnson embarked upon an ambitious program. He had already signed the Civil Rights Act of 1964, the most far-reaching civil rights act in the nation's history, which addressed voting rights, public accommodations, and discrimination both in education and on the job. During his campaign in 1964, Johnson had begun to talk about the Great Society program, which would include a "war on poverty." He viewed his electoral triumph in 1964 as a mandate to out Roosevelt Franklin D. Roosevelt, the New Deal president who was in office when he came to Congress and who was his political hero. Johnson spoke unashamedly about poverty and why it was a major problem for American society, the last American president to do so in such bold terms. In a campaign speech that year, Johnson had intoned, "Do something we can be proud of. Help the weak and the meek. Lift them up. Help them train and give them an education where they can make their own way instead of having to live off the bounty of our generosity."

Other social programs included health care for the elderly (Medicare) and the Neighborhood Youth Corps. Education reform was important to the former school teacher, and the Great Society included the Elementary and Secondary Education Acts, legislation that made compliance with federal law a prerequisite for gaining the new federal dollars. The result: accelerated efforts to end segregated education in the South, including Texas. Along with more than 200 other bills passed during Johnson's presidency, Congress enacted the Voting Rights Act of 1965. The other bills included the National Museum Act, the Public Broadcasting Act, and the national endowments for the arts and humanities. A political columnist wrote in 1965 that Johnson's Great Society "codif[ied] the New Deal vision of the good society."

At the same time, Lady Bird Johnson called attention to the environment with her well-received highway beautification program, which historian Lewis L. Gould described as "a new departure for a First Lady. The same is true for the work she did in beautifying Washington in its monumental areas and in its inner-city ghettos." LBJ pushed for congressional passage of other environmental and consumer protection laws: clean air, pesticide control, urban mass transit, wilderness areas, water pollution, truth in packaging, traffic and highway safety, and scenic rivers and trails. Nothing in the Great Society was sufficient to counterbalance the ill-effects of the growing war in Vietnam, which ultimately divided the country and eroded Johnson's political base to the point that he declined to run for reelection in 1968.

Political Reform in Texas

The Great Society had an immediate impact on Texas. Governor Connally had opposed the public accommodations section of the 1964 Civil Rights Act but endorsed the Head Start program, thinking that Johnson might have taken the idea from a language program for Mexican American children that he had begun in Texas. In other areas of the domestic legislative package, however, Connally feuded with Johnson, because, in Connally's view, they reduced the power of the state too much and he actually vetoed an eleven-county Neighborhood Youth Corps project drafted to take advantage of corresponding Great Society legislation.

With his new popularity and the political assistance of a new speaker of the House, his protégé Ben Barnes, Connally began to push his programs in higher education, increased tourism, and recruitment of out-of-state industry, and he proved himself to be one of the ablest and most powerful of the state's twentieth-century governors. Connally looked like most people thought a Texas governor should, tall in his elegant boots, with distinguished wavy gray hair frequently hidden under his white Stetson. He was articulate and, on occasion, rose to the level of oratory. *Dallas Morning News* political reporter Richard Morehead claimed that Connally was the only governor in the nation who could hold his own with California Republican governor Ronald Reagan at the annual governors conferences, where he frequently found himself defending Johnson's policies against Reagan's charges. Now he applied that power of persuasion and salesmanship to implementing his campaign promises. Early in his term, Connally had described his goal to State Department counselor and later Johnson aide Walt W. Rostow: He wanted to unify Texas, and in his opinion the best way to do that was to focus on higher education. There was plenty of room for improvement. Eighty-six percent of the graduates of the University of Texas at Austin who pursued graduate studies did so elsewhere; faculty salaries were forty-sixth in the nation; and New York produced five times more Ph.D.s annually than did Texas. Connally believed that education would be the engine that drove his other two goals.

Connally's record of achievement is impressive. He established a coordinating board for higher education and raised taxes so that he could increase faculty salaries, enlarge campuses, and create the University of Texas system in 1967. Under the leadership of his close friend, Frank C. Erwin, whom he appointed to the board of regents, appropriations for the flagship campus in Austin increased in little more than a decade from $40.4 to $349.7 million. The system's enrollment also increased rapidly, from 29,940 to 77,437 during the same period.

Connally's programs, plus a large infusion of federal grants from the Great Society program, also led to a major increase in medical research and the number of medical schools in the state. As World War II ended, the state had only three medical schools—the University of Texas Medical Branch at Galveston, Baylor College of Medicine in Houston, and Southwestern Medical College in Dallas—that graduated about 200 doctors per year, not enough to care for the state's growing population. With the availability of federal funding, however, Texas established four new schools during the 1960s and 1970s. Although it was a private institution, Baylor would begin to receive some state funds during the 1980s.

With increased federal financing for medical research as well as the Lyndon B. Johnson Space Center (originally known as the Manned Spacecraft Center), which the National Aeronautics and Space Administration (NASA) had located near Houston, doctors at several of the Texas medical schools produced significant medical breakthroughs. Perhaps the best known were Michael E. DeBakey of Methodist Hospital and Denton Cooley of St. Luke's Hospital in Houston, who were in the forefront of heart surgery and transplants since the 1960s. DeBakey performed the first successful coronary artery bypass graft procedure in 1964, and Cooley performed the first heart transplant in the United States in 1968. Both continued their research by working on mechanical hearts. In Dallas, meanwhile, Joseph L. Goldstein and Michael S. Brown of the University of Texas Health Science Center performed research in physiology and medicine that would be recognized with the Nobel Prize in 1985. Such initiatives proved important to the increased diversification of the Texas economy.

The Civil Rights Movement Intensifies

Coupled with these federal acts, African Americans and Hispanics continued to campaign for equal rights. Nonviolent protests that began in Greensboro, North Carolina, in 1960 spread to Texas. Students at two historically African American colleges, Wiley and Bishop, staged nonviolent demonstrations that year, and the following year students at Texas Southern, the University of Texas, North Texas State, and other colleges protested against segregated theaters and restaurants. Wiley and Bishop Colleges were both located in Marshall, Texas, a town of 25,000 located in deep East Texas. Though the African American population constituted 43 percent of the county's population there was no eagerness to get out in front of the civil rights movement. Things were different for the college students who had less to lose: they were not employed in the town and were not beholden to the white power structure in the same way that the majority of the working class African American population was. The local officials responded harshly to the protesters, turning fire hoses on them and resorting to other tactics common in the Deep South. A state-run investigation of the Wiley and Bishop College sit-ins contended that the movement was communist inspired, a specious finding but one that reflected the animosity of the local and the state government toward grass roots civil rights activists. This particular protest failed; local businesses made no concessions to the student protesters. The unfortunate result suggests the similarity of Marshall with other small Deep South towns where local officials used violence to foil civil rights protest efforts.

Important civil rights reformers hailed from Texas, namely James Farmer, who headed the Congress of Racial Equality (CORE). Farmer grew up in Marshall, where his father was a professor at Wiley. Farmer graduated from Wiley in 1938 after leading the school's debate team to a victory over the Harvard University team in 1935. He then studied divinity at Howard University and used his understanding of Gandhi and pacifism to guide his civil rights initiatives. His most important initiative with CORE was the Freedom Rides in 1961.

Fear of bad publicity and federal laws gradually brought segregation to an end in areas of Texas where the Deep South mores of Marshall did not prevail. In Houston, for example, local businesspeople quietly reached an agreement with a group of college students and community leaders that if they would not demonstrate, public facilities would be integrated. While cities throughout the nation dissolved into confrontations and riots, for the most part Texas cities remained calm.

A comparable story of protest occurred in the Hispanic regions of Texas. During the 1960 presidential campaign Viva Kennedy–Viva Johnson clubs brought more Hispanics into the political process. Meanwhile, in South Texas the Political Association of Spanish-Speaking Organizations (PASSO), assisted by Teamsters officials, helped organize Hispanic voters in Crystal City in 1963. The overwhelming majority of residents there were impoverished Mexican Americans working for Del Monte Foods, Incorporated, and many of the employees had joined the Teamsters. The new all-Hispanic city council held power for two years. This political transformation sent a message to the white minority population throughout South Texas that their rule would no longer go unchallenged. Hispanics in Carrizo Springs and Cotulla also won political power.

This newfound Hispanic activism resulted in one of Governor Connally's most embarrassing moments in the summer of 1966. In an effort to get the legislature to adopt a minimum wage of $1.25 per hour, organizers in South Texas decided to march the almost 500 miles from Rio Grande City to the capital to focus publicity on the effort.

Although he had planned to be out of the capitol building on Labor Day, when the marchers were scheduled to arrive, Connally told speaker of the House Ben Barnes, "I don't think it's right for them to just march up here and nobody be here." With Barnes and Attorney General Waggoner Carr in tow, he headed to New Braunfels, where he found the bedraggled little band. Shaking hands all around, Connally urged them to call off their march because "things can get out of hand in marches," a veiled reference to the riots, violence, and bloodshed that had occurred throughout the nation, and said that he would not receive them in Austin because he did not want to "lend the dignity" of his office to any such demonstration. When state labor leaders arrived at the scene, the mood turned more confrontational and developed into a standoff, and Connally, Barnes, and Carr departed in their executive limousine.

The marchers rallied and continued gathering supporters as they neared Austin and as word of Connally's rather highhanded attempt to stop them spread. Senator Yarborough met the marchers at the capitol on Labor Day along with a number of supporters, including labor leader Cesar Chavez of the United Farm Workers and Connally's brother, Golfrey, an economics professor at San Antonio College. The minimum wage law did not pass that year, but historian

Rep. Henry B. Gonzalez at a Labor Day Rally at the State Capitol, 1966.

Arnoldo de León considers this incident one of the formative events of the Chicano movement.

Just as important was the process by which the Chicana/o middle class in Texas cities like San Antonio demanded reforms to open up a closed political machine that benefitted an older style of crony politics. This demographic formed the Good Government League in the Alamo City to lobby for reform. African Americans, labor unions, white liberals, and Chicana/os made up this coalition, one that suggested the major factions in the Democratic Party for the remainder of the century. One of the beneficiaries of this process was Henry B. González, who was elected to the U.S. Congress from San Antonio in 1961. González has been criticized, though, for being too accommodating for the older Anglo power structure to the deficit of the Chicana/o working class and poor.

The New Left in Texas

The 1960s saw numerous groups challenging the political status quo on the state and the national level. In addition to the demands for equal political power by minorities, younger, college educated Americans questioned the ethics of liberalism and the U.S. government. This movement, known as the New Left, is typically associated with elite East Coast and West Coast universities such as Columbia University in New York City and the University of California at Berkeley as well as the University of Chicago. It also had deep roots in Texas, specifically at the University of Texas at Austin. White college students formed this movement because of their civil rights activism. The New Left advocated a grass roots style "participatory democracy" and by the late 1960s the movement ceased being a small cadre of intellectuals and swelled as college students across the country began protesting the Vietnam War. The New Left differed sharply from the left of the 1930s and 1940s in that it saw college campuses and not labor unions as the center of its recruiting and intellectual base. Its philosophy challenged the alienation and anxiety associated with industrialization and abundance in American society, arguing that its version of liberalism could save Americans from these problems.

Austin was the largest center of New Left activism in the South, and outside of California, New York, and Chicago, the most important in the country. Two national New Left leaders honed their skills while students at the University of Texas: Casey Hayden and Jeff Shero Nightbyrd. Historian Doug Rossinow explained that the Texas New Left followed a different trajectory from that found on the East and West Coasts: they had few ties with the old left, they were skeptical of the right wing anticommunists of the 1950s, they were sympathetic to the populist tradition of Texas, and they associated with dissident Christianity. The source of Christian liberalism at UT was the University YMCA-YWCA. Students who came to the New Left through this faith tradition believed in direct action, saw racism as the most important social problem the country faced, and remained committed to the existential search for authenticity. Police departments in major cities throughout the state reacted with violence toward the New Left protesters, and the Ku Klux Klan infiltrated department in Houston shot and killed one African American activist and shot two others.

As the decade wore on both universities and the Vietnam War became significant New Left targets. In 1967, the UT bureaucracy clamped down hard on New Left activists there following a protest rally against Vice President Hubert Humphrey's visit to Austin.

Regarding the war, the Texas New Left held control of the antiwar movement two years longer than was true on the coasts. There by 1965, antiwar activism had been taken over by those who did not share the anticapitalist, anti-imperialist views of the New Left. Nor did the shift in Texas result because of an abdication of New Left leadership but because of a rapid influx of new, less politically radical antiwar activists.

Texas Counterculture

By the 1970s, the New Left in Austin had morphed into a form of cultural liberalism that made the city unlike any other in the state. The celebration of individualism was central to this process. Austin's cultural liberalism included an attack

UT Texas Student Publications, di_05754, The Dolph Briscoe Center for American History, The University of Texas at Austin

Janis Joplin with Powell St. John and Kirk Lanier Wiggins, the Wednesday Night Folk Singers at the University of Texas at Austin, 1962, from the 1963 Cactus yearbook for the University of Texas.

on traditional sexual mores and a tolerance for alternative lifestyles. Moreover, one humorist wrote, "What can I tell you about Austin? This town, this community is so organic people will turn to compost before your very eyes." Austin became a breeding ground for counterculture capitalism in the form of the Austin-based Whole Foods supermarket chain, an antiunion operation that touted individualism as a reason for its low tolerance for unions.

Music also played a role in the individualistic Austin-bred counterculture. Port Arthur native Janis Joplin, perhaps one of the most important counterculture musicians of the 1960s, began her career playing at Threadgills Restaurant in Austin; she was then a student at the University of Texas. Joplin led a tortured life even as she earned a reputation as one of the best white blues singers ever. She died of a drug overdose in 1970. Finally, the Armadillo World Headquarters opened in Austin in 1970 to provide a venue for counterculture musicians. In addition to bringing important national acts like the Grateful Dead and Bruce Springsteen to Austin, the Armadillo also helped launch the careers of several musicians, including Stevie Ray Vaughan, Marcia Ball, and Joe Ely.

The Mainstream Arts and Popular Sports

Connally's establishment of the Texas Fine Arts Commission (now the Texas Commission on the Arts) in 1965, which also receives funds through the National Endowment for the Arts, called attention to the state's growing cultural facilities. Long famous for its philanthropists, Texas is fortunate that a number of them chose to establish museums. One of the first to do so was Jessie Marion Koogler McNay of San Antonio, who left her Mexican-Mediterranean style mansion and art collection as a private museum, which opened in 1954. The Amon Carter Museum, designed by New York architect Philip Johnson, followed in 1961. Five years later, the Museum of Fine Arts in Houston opened Bayou Bend, the mansion that architect John F. Staub had designed for Ima Hogg and her brothers, as a decorative arts center. Perhaps the best known of the Texas museums is the Kimbell Art Museum in Fort Worth, which opened in 1972 but one of the most eclectic, which opened to the public in 1978, is the Stark Museum of Art in Orange, containing H. J. Lutcher Stark's vast collections of Americana.

Museums also seemed to lead the way for modern architecture in the state. In 1950, John and Dominique de Menil hired architect Philip Johnson to design an International Style house for them in Houston. He went on to design the campus plan and several of the buildings for the University of St. Thomas in Houston in 1958, the same year that Ludwig Mies van der Rohe, one of the pioneers of the International Style, designed Cullinan Hall as an addition to the Museum of Fine Arts. At the same time, San Antonio architect O'Neil Ford was designing the campus of Trinity University with the revolutionary lift-slab construction technique that cut building costs considerably. Other distinguished architecture can be seen in the San Antonio Art Museum, which moved into the spectacularly renovated Lone Star Brewery in 1981; the new (1984) Dallas Museum of Art designed by Edward Larrabee Barnes; the Louis Kahn–designed Kimbell Art Museum in Fort Worth; and the new Museum of Fine Arts and the Menil Collection in Houston.

During the late twentieth century, perhaps the most recognizable building in the state after the Alamo was the Astrodome, the world's first fully air-conditioned, enclosed, domed, multipurpose sports stadium, which opened as the home of the Houston Astros baseball team in 1965. The team was created four years earlier as the Houston Colt .45s, gaining its new name with its new stadium. When it was determined that baseball players could not see fly balls against the bright glare of the plastic roof and crisscrossed girders during daylight, Judge Roy M. Hofheinz, head of the Houston Sports Association, ordered the roof painted. The lack of sunlight meant that natural grass could not grow in the stadium, so in a well-publicized event, Hofheinz obtained an artificial grass called Astroturf®. The Houston Oilers football team played there until moving to Nashville in 1997, and the domed stadium has hosted dozens of other sporting events as well as concerts, conventions, and religious meetings. Today the Astrodome is a relic, with both the Astros and the Houston Texans football team playing in other stadiums.

Houston was not the only sports city in Texas with an expanding national presence. Nor was it the first Texas city to earn for itself a professional football team. For one year in 1952, a team called the Texans played in Dallas. This team had previously played in the National Football League as the New York Yanks. It had little success and was sold and reconstituted as the Baltimore Colts. Later in 1959, Houston businessman Bud Adams worked with Dallas businessman Lamar Hunt to found the American Football League with teams placed in the two cities: the Oilers in Houston and the Texans (a different team) in Dallas. The Oilers were successful in the AFL, but the Texans did not fare well in Dallas where an NFL expansion team that Clint Murchison Jr. started in 1960, the Cowboys, seemed the more popular with fans. In 1963, the Texans relocated to Kansas City, becoming the Chiefs.

Texas sports teams have not only done well in their respective leagues but also have become another key factor in the gradual twentieth-century rebranding of the state as something apart from its rural, southern roots. The most successful, loved by some and hated by others, is the Cowboys, dubbed America's Team in 1978. The Cowboys have won five of the eight Super Bowls in which they played while the Oilers never advanced to a Super Bowl game. Other major league sports franchises in the state included the Texas Rangers baseball team, which moved to Arlington in 1972; three successful National Basketball Association teams, the San Antonio Spurs with five championships, the Houston Rockets with two, and the Dallas Mavericks with one; and one National Hockey League team, the Dallas Stars, which won the Stanley Cup championship once at the end of the century.

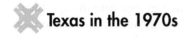

Texas in the 1970s

The Great Society ended almost as soon as it began in Texas and in the United States. This does not mean the Johnson era reforms failed but that Texans, like their counterparts elsewhere in the country, debated what place those reforms and the political ideology that begat them should have in the 1970s. Meanwhile, the civil rights legislation and the intervention of the federal government in state affairs forced changes in Texas government and society from above while the Chicano and women's movements transformed them from below.

A State Adrift

Both Johnson and Connally announced that they would not run again in 1968. Johnson was driven from office by the social unrest and urban riots accompanying the war in Vietnam. He returned to the Hill Country, where he wrote his memoirs and supervised construction of the Lyndon Baines Johnson Library and Museum on the campus of the University of Texas at Austin. The result was a state where politics were increasingly adrift without clear leaders or ideological preferences.

When Connally stepped down after three terms, Preston Smith of Lubbock, who had served the same length of time as lieutenant governor, was elected governor in 1968. Having grown up on a West Texas farm and worked his way through high school and college, Smith was a plainspoken, uncharismatic but sensitive person who suffered by comparison with Connally and was offended by suggestions that he lacked a vivid or humorous personality. His trademark polka-dot tie (Governor Price Daniel had advised him to wear something distinctive) seemed only to call attention to his bland personality. "He doesn't look very good," an editorial writer once said in comparing him to the former University of Texas All-American quarterback, Bobby Layne, also from Lubbock, "all he can do is beat you. "

Smith was an informal governor, who often answered his own telephone and placed calls himself, but Smith seemed to have an inherent mistrust of city dwellers, and the feeling was mutual. He immediately set the tone for his administration when he was called to Washington in the spring of 1969. There he learned the details of a federal plan designed to ease slum housing problems. He opposed the plan, he told reporters, because "some people just like to live in slums." Elected at the same time as Smith was Lieutenant Governor Ben Barnes, almost Smith's polar opposite and the apparent heir of the Johnson/Connally mantle. He had been the youngest person to serve as speaker of the Texas House when he was elected in 1965 at age twenty-six and polled more votes than any other Texas politician—more than 2 million—to win the lieutenant governor's office.

The third member of the leadership was House Speaker Gus Mutscher, who assumed the office with the opening of the legislative session in 1969.

A conservative from rural Washington County, Mutscher soon exercised surprising control over the House (even more than Barnes had exercised) by sticking to his motto, "never quit politicking and never underestimate your opponent." With Mutscher as Speaker and Barnes as lieutenant governor, Smith proposed a program that met with only limited success. He got a pay raise for schoolteachers, but his water plan, which proposed transferring water from East Texas or from outside the state to needy areas like West Texas, went down to defeat at the hands of East Texas legislators. He supported the establishment of two new medical schools, one in Houston and the other in Lubbock, and got funding for a minimum wage and for vocational education. In the face of a "housewives' revolt," he was embarrassed to have to back away from a Barnes/Mutscher proposal to add food to the list of items subject to a sales tax.

Federal Government Intervention

Federal interventions during the 1960s and early 1970s continued to alter the social and political fabric of Texas. First, U.S. Supreme Court decisions continued to have an impact: *Baker v. Carr* (1962) and *Reynolds v. Sims* (1964) brought about what became known as "one-man, one-vote," which meant that both houses of a state legislature had to be reapportioned regularly so that each representative and each senator would represent approximately the same number of citizens. Subsequent decisions affecting Texas held that a county could have more than one member of the Senate and more than seven members of the House. These were important legal victories for urban areas, for the first time permitting neighborhoods such as Houston's largely African American fifth ward to have its own representation.

Federal actions also continued to broaden the electorate. The Twenty-fourth Amendment to the U.S. Constitution in 1964 made it illegal to require a poll tax to vote in federal elections. The big change, however, came with the Voting Rights Act of 1965, which outlawed state and local restrictions on voters as being prejudiced against minorities and provided federal officials to monitor elections. Even after adoption of the Twenty-fourth Amendment, Texas had kept the poll tax for state elections, but it succumbed to the Voting Rights Act in 1966 when Judge Homer Thornberry, a Johnson protégé on the U.S. Court of Appeals of the Fifth Judicial Circuit, ruled it to be a violation of the Fourteenth Amendment. Subsequent to these reforms, Barbara Jordan from Houston's fifth ward became the first African American to be elected to the Texas Senate since Reconstruction, and Curtis Graves and J. E. Lockridge were elected to the House. In 1971, the Twenty-sixth Amendment to the U.S. Constitution gave eighteen-year-olds the right to vote.

These changes also opened up local elections and changed the face of governing bodies in Texas. The political complexion of the Senate changed overnight, for example, as moderates and liberals gained office. The impact of these changes also reached the local level, and organizations such as the Citizen's

Charter Association in Dallas and the Good Government League in San Antonio, which had dominated local politics for years, lost their control.

Gender Diversity in Texas Politics and Culture

The 1970s proved to be an important transitional decade between the old and new Texas. The entrance of women and minorities into the political arena reflected a new diversity in Texas politics, due in part, to the rise of the liberal coalition in the Democratic Party. This new political diversity also came from Republican inroads into, and eventual dominance of, state political power structures as other Texans reacted to the shift in the Democratic Party by choosing more conservative candidates.

Women—Mexican American, African American, and Anglo—began setting political agendas and winning local elections. In the late 1960s, Anita Martinez of Dallas had already become the first Mexican American woman to win a city council seat in Texas, and Wilhemina Delco had become the first African American, male or female, to be elected to the Austin school board. But the year 1972 proved to be a watershed for Texas women in politics. Other women saw Barbara Jordan campaigning for the U.S. Congress and Frances "Sissy" Farenthold for the governorship and began to see opportunities for themselves. Farenthold had directly challenged the power structure in her three years in the House. She recalled, "I went there knowing blacks weren't represented, knowing Mexican

Rep. Barbara Jordan delivering the keynote address at the 1976 Democratic National Convention.

Americans weren't represented. I found that Texans weren't even represented." She and Jordan cosponsored the Equal Legal Rights amendment to the Texas constitution.

Sefronia Thompson, a former junior- and senior-high-school teacher, remembered being galvanized by Jordan's and Farenthold's campaigns: "I just wanted to be part of this big harvest, so I ran. And I won." Thompson was one of a record half-dozen women elected to the Texas legislature, along with a young lawyer named Sarah Weddington, who was about to win a landmark Supreme Court case, *Roe v. Wade,* that legalized abortion in the United States. Among the other five were two African American women, Thompson and Eddie Bernice Johnson, and two Republican women, Betty Andujar and Kay Bailey.

Throughout the 1970s, women would continue to emerge in positions of local and regional political power. In 1973 Lucy Patterson became the first African American woman elected to the Dallas city council. In 1975 Lila Cockrell became the first female mayor of a major Texas city, in this case, San Antonio. The next year, Irma Rangel, a former teacher and lawyer from Kingsville, became the first Mexican American woman to take a seat in the Texas House of Representatives, and future governor Ann Richards became a Travis County commissioner.

After election, these women found themselves facing an entrenched power structure. "There was a great deal of questioning and suspicion and challenge we could see on the faces of those who had been there longer, because this was a new crop of people for a new era," Eddie Bernice Johnson recounted, "and we ushered in that era, and we made a lot of changes." Johnson worked on bills to eliminate credit discrimination against women and housing and home loan discrimination against minorities. She also labored to see that poor children got school breakfasts and pregnant teachers got benefits and job security.

The Feminist Movement in Texas

Not only were individual Texas women making a place for themselves within the state's political system but also they were fighting and winning important legal and social battles to make adjustments benefitting all Texas women. Some of the most dramatic changes during this time gave women many rights that they had been long denied. Indeed, there were multiple notable feminist accomplishments in Texas: early ratification of the federal Equal Rights Amendment, winning abortion rights, challenging images of female strength, and hosting a major international conference.

Norma L. McCorvey, more widely known to history as Jane Roe, challenged the restrictive Texas abortion laws that prevented access to this medical procedure except to preserve the life of the woman. Sarah Weddington, then a young attorney and graduate of the University of Texas School of Law, argued the case for Roe against Dallas County District Attorney, Henry Wade in the United States District Court for the Northern District of Texas. The three-judge panel overturned the Texas law, and Wade appealed to the U.S. Supreme Court.

On January 22, 1973, the Court in a 7–2 decision ruled that there could be no restrictions against abortion during the first trimester of pregnancy, that restrictions in the second and third trimesters could be drawn on the grounds of maternal health, and that laws to protect the fetus could only be applied for the third trimester and must contain provisions to permit abortion to protect the life of the mother. The Court argued that restrictive abortion laws violated a woman's right to privacy as articulated in the First, Fourth, Ninth, and Fourteenth Amendments. Reaction to the decision has been one factor in the late twentieth-century rise of cultural conservatism in Texas and in the nation.

Another controversial development from the early 1970s involved the Equal Rights Amendment. Dallas attorney Hermine D. Tobolowsky, president of the Texas Federation of Business and Professional Women, had been active in women's rights issues since the 1940s and had identified a number of laws that she considered discriminatory, such as the denial of women's right to control property they owned at marriage or had inherited. Tobolowsky testified before a state Senate committee hearing in support of a bill that would have changed a number of these laws. The bill failed, and her treatment before the committee caused her to resolve instead to support an equal rights amendment to the Texas constitution. She traveled around the state speaking to women and civic groups, rallying support for the amendment. It was introduced at each session of the legislature from 1959 until it was finally passed in 1972, after the introduction of the federal Equal Rights Amendment in Congress provided greater credibility for the effort. Tobolowsky became known as the mother of the Texas Equal Rights Amendment. Following federal passage of the national Equal Rights Amendment in 1972, the Texas state legislature was among the first in the country to ratify the ERA. Proponents of an ERA for the U.S. Constitution failed to convince the needed thirty-eight states to ratify it, though, falling three states short by the deadline in 1982.

Conflict also swirled around the 1977 International Women's Year National Conference in Houston, which was attended by 2,000 delegates who debated the social, legal, and economic inequities women endured, often because of government policy. Delegates faced a mixed reception by city officials. A Harris County Republican party official described the women as "a gaggle of outcasts, misfits, and rejects." The delegates were not all adherents of feminism, though, divided over increasingly contentious social issues such as abortion rights, gay rights, and the ratification of the ERA. National anti-ERA activist Phyllis Schlafly led the conservative group, which walked out of the proceedings rather than support the resolutions dealing with women's rights.

As the feminist movement gained strength nationally, many Texas women began to pay attention. The National Organization for Women (NOW) established chapters in Texas, and the Texas Women's Political Caucus encouraged women to get involved in the political process. New methods of birth control (such as the birth control pill) influenced many women to delay marriage and family while pursuing an education or a career. Again, actions of the federal government had an impact. Title VII of the 1964 Civil Rights Act (upheld by later court decisions) gave women control of their property and prohibited discrimination in the workplace. Title IX of the 1972 Education Amendments required universities receiving federal funds to allow women to participate in many activities that had been closed to them. In sports, for example, universities organized a number of teams for women athletes that had not existed before Title IX. A dramatic rendering of female athletic ability occurred in the famous battle of the sexes tennis match played in Houston's Astrodome between rising female star Billie Jean King and fading male star Bobby Riggs. King easily defeated Riggs, an outspoken male chauvinist, 6–4, 6–3, 6–3.

The Chicana/o Movement in Texas

Even as women focused on bringing gender issues into the public forum, members of ethnic minorities—male and female—continued to fight for their own distinctive identities as Texans and for inclusion in the political power structure. African Americans were building on the civil rights movement of the 1950s and the activism of the 1960s. So were Texas Hispanics, primarily Mexican Americans and Mexicans but also those with roots in other Central and South American countries.

In 1970, the census showed 2 million Mexican Americans in the state—about one in every five Texans. They were concentrated in the major cities, but also spread through the agricultural and cattle-raising towns of South and West Texas. Although many were laborers, an increasing number—some 40 percent—constituted a Mexican American middle class. Activism was growing among young urban Hispanics, particularly with the rise of the Mexican American Youth Organization (MAYO) after a 1967 activist meeting in El Paso and 1968 meetings in San Antonio and Laredo. MAYO leaders felt that institutional racism in the United States was so entrenched that only an alternate educational system delivered by Mexican Americans for Mexican Americans and through a separate political party could address their concerns. Their activism led to another political coup in Crystal City—and to a serious run by candidates of a Mexican American party for the offices of Texas governor and lieutenant governor.

The earlier Crystal City "electoral revolt" had come to naught by 1965, leaving many of the town's Mexican Americans wary when José Angel Gutiérrez returned to the town as a MAYO organizer in 1969. Gutiérrez, who had participated in the 1963 revolt as a college student, found that despite the wariness, many in the community were upset over the stipulation that candidates for the Crystal City High School homecoming queen and court must have a parent who had graduated from the school. In this era of limited schooling for most Mexican Americans, this requirement eliminated most Hispanic students. Now Gutiérrez, his wife Luz, activist Virginia Músquiz, and others organized a response that put pressure on the school board and mounted a student boycott that emptied the high school of almost 65 percent of its students.

By spring, a new political party was coalescing across South Texas—*La Raza Unida* (United Race or United People), which would come to be known as RUP (*Raza Unida* Party). In Crystal City, Gutiérrez and other RUP candidates captured school board and city council seats. Gutiérrez would explain, "We were Chicanos [a 1970s term for activist Mexican Americans] who were starved for any kind of meaningful participation in decision making, policy making and leadership positions."

Similar victories occurred in other South Texas towns, with RUP leaders pushing an agenda of Chicano power and pride, although the results were not as dramatic as in Crystal City, where Gutiérrez became school board chair. Here Anglo teachers uneasy with the new regime were replaced with RUP supporters; much of the curriculum centered on Mexican American experience; and militant stances became the norm—for example, the boycott of lettuce picked by exploited migrant workers.

La Raza Unida continued to challenge the traditional political power structure. Gutiérrez, who would go on to become judge for Zavala County, called for education and urban renewal that would take into account Mexican American claims, plans, and dreams for their city communities. Many of the activists advocated a brand of cultural nationalism that seemed as exclusive in its way as that of the Anglo-dominated institutional structures; these activists split off both from other Mexican American groups and from the RUP, with different ideologies and political plans. But they stimulated older organizations, such as the G.I. Forum and LULAC, to address issues of equality more boldly, and they demonstrated that Tejanos and Tejanas could and would participate in defining local and state government issues. Another organization, the Mexican American Legal Defense and Education Fund (MALDEF) led the way in creating court challenges to the imbalances in power.

The Sharpstown Scandal and Challenges to the Old Political Order

Another federal intervention in Texas helped bring down the curtain on an era, and make possible a gubernatorial election whereby a white male candidate representing the traditional Democratic Party values faced a feminist challenger in the Democratic primary and a candidate from *La Raza Unida* in the general election. In 1971 the Securities and Exchange Commission (SEC) charged several state officials and others with illegally profiting from a quick-turnover stock deal. According to the SEC, Houston businessman Frank Sharp wanted a banking bill passed that would provide state-backed depositor's insurance to exempt his bank, Sharpstown State Bank, from regulation by the Federal Deposit Insurance Corporation; he bribed several current and former state officials by loaning them money from his bank to purchase stock in one of his companies, the National Bankers Life Insurance Company, with the understanding that once the bill had passed, they could sell their stock at a handsome profit. Governor Smith included the bank bill in the agenda for the second special legislative session in 1971, and speaker of the House Gus Mutscher, Jr. and his allies pushed it through. Smith later vetoed the bill on the advice of the state's banking law experts, but not until he and several others had sold their stock at a profit. A Travis County grand jury indicted Mutscher, Representative Tommy Shannon, and Rush McGinty (an aide to Mutscher) for bribery and conspiracy, and in March 1972 they were convicted by an Abilene jury and given a sentence of five years' probation. The SEC alleged that Governor Smith, state Democratic chair and state banking board member Elmer Baum, and others had been bribed, but did not charge them.

The result was a political housecleaning and modest shift to the left in the state's politics. Conservative rancher Dolph Briscoe of Uvalde, who had run in 1968, won the Democratic gubernatorial nomination in the runoff. He appealed to voters with a "Mr. Clean" image, but he also seemed like a safe choice who would not demand too much change to the overall structure of state politics. His primary challenger had been Sissy Farenthold, a liberal in the party who ran second in the first primary. She attracted those voters disgusted both with corruption in state politics and with the male-dominated hierarchy. Her prominence in the contest surprised many because Lieutenant Governor Barnes had been expected to become governor of the state, given his earlier successes and his ties to Lyndon Johnson. Instead, this election ended Barnes's political career. He had also borrowed money from Sharp's bank. Though he was not named in the scandal, Barnes remained connected to it in the minds of most voters. The same fate awaited Governor Smith, who ran a poor fourth.

The Democratic primary also revealed the limits to which Texans as a whole would support liberalism and feminism. In this regard, Texas Democrats proved more conservative than the party nationally. At the Democratic National Convention that year, Farenthold finished second in the voting for the vice presidential slot on the Democratic presidential ticket. Forty percent of the

Supporters of gubernatorial candidate Frances "Sissy" Farenthold in Laredo, Texas with a sign reading, "Your vote can break the yoke on Texas: Vote Farenthold for Governor," 1972.

delegates were women—compared to a mere 13 percent only four years before. At the Republican convention as well, a previously unheard-of 30 percent of the delegates were women.

The general election in 1972 held more drama than had been typical in Texas history. Briscoe faced two opponents, Republican Henry C. Grover and RUP candidate Ramsey Muñiz, and their places on the ballot tell two important stories about Texas politics and society. Grover ran a vigorous campaign that suggested the likelihood Republicans could soon claim the governor's mansion. Moreover, Republicans picked up seats in the Texas House of Representatives. These accomplishments resulted as much because of national politics as what was happening in the state. The Democratic nominee for the presidency in 1972, liberal South Dakota senator George McGovern, had campaigned in favor of abortion rights, amnesty for Vietnam draft dodgers, and the legalization of drugs. Neither these positions nor his efforts to liberalize the rules of the Democratic Party, making it easier for women and people of color to have a voice in party affairs, pleased moderates and conservatives in the Texas Democratic Party.

Muñiz, Briscoe's other challenger, posed more a symbolic than real threat, but the enthusiasm that his supporters brought to the contest suggested the continued importance race and ethnicity would play in state affairs. RUP activists had debated whether the party was ready for statewide races in 1972. Even though key leaders advocated waiting out the 1972 races, the party nominated Muñiz, a twenty-nine-year-old attorney from Waco and MAYO member.

Muñiz, a former lineman on the Baylor University football team, traveled the state in a red 1962 Plymouth announcing that "the days of being led to the polls to vote straight ticket for these two other parties are over." He was personable and energetic, militant without being overbearing, and his campaign gained momentum when Dolph Briscoe beat Farenthold for the Democratic nomination, for Briscoe, to many, was an old-style Democrat unfriendly to minorities.

Muñiz's running mate for the lieutenant governor slot, Alma Canales, was only twenty-four years old, more radical, and less able or less inclined to court the middle class, whether Mexican American or Anglo. Her presence on the ticket signaled the depth of Tejana activism. In fact, in 1971 in Houston, Mexican American women had put together "the first national conference ever organized to deal specifically with Mexican-American women's concerns." Even the relatively conservative LULAC Women's Affairs Committee in this election year had a Texas convention at which they urged LULAC to work for women in important governmental positions.

With Muñiz officially a candidate, Gutiérrez became his campaign manager, and they persuaded an array of both militant and moderate Mexican Americans as well as liberal Anglos to consider voting for the third party. At the same time, they drew the ire of liberal Democrats unhappy with Briscoe but unwilling to desert the party. Lawyer Mark Smith warned ominously, "A vote for La Raza Unida . . . is nothing more than a vote for destruction of the liberal wing of the Democratic Party in Texas. It can only result in destroying any hope for a two-party state in which the Democratic Party is representative of the voice of the people and their aspirations for justice."

On election day, Muñiz's 6.28 percent of the vote may have looked negligible to some, but it was sufficient to worry the leaders of the Texas Democratic Party, for Muñiz almost became the spoiler in a race in which Briscoe could have expected the RUP votes. Indeed, Briscoe bested his Republican challenger, Henry C. Grover, by just under 100,000 votes, a much closer margin than had been typical in past gubernatorial races.

The voters elected moderate Houston newspaper executive William P. Hobby, Jr., son of Governor Will Hobby and former secretary of health, education, and welfare, Oveta Culp Hobby, as lieutenant governor over seven other Democratic candidates. The makeup of the legislature also changed significantly, with many newcomers winning election to both the House and the Senate. Virtually all of these newly elected officials were committed to reform of some kind, and Briscoe did not try to control the party machinery in the same way that his predecessors had.

The Sharpstown scandal proved a boon to Republicans. Coupled with it was former Governor John Connally's service as secretary of the treasury in Republican president Richard Nixon's administration and his support of Nixon against Democrat George McGovern in the 1972 presidential election. He even announced his formal switch to the Republican Party in May 1973, thinking that would enable him to run for and win the presidency in 1976.

 ## Governing a Changing State

Through this period, Texas government had to adapt to the needs and pressures of a burgeoning citizenry, to continued movement of Texans and out-of-state immigrants to key cities, to the changes in the state economy, and to increasingly complex relations with the federal government. And it had to do so with a constitution that was already dated when it was first adopted in 1876, with its emphasis on agrarian interests and a limited state government. Further, while redistricting in the 1970s had weakened conservative male influence on the legislature, the legislature continued to operate with traditional and limited responses to many pressing modern problems.

Government in the 1970s

In the early 1970s, reformers began pushing to rewrite the state constitution rather than continue the unwieldy system of multiple amendments. It took a constitutional convention amendment to start the process, which voters approved in 1972. Legislators were to meet for this purpose in January 1974. In the meantime, a commission appointed by state officials prepared a new constitution for their consideration. Proposed changes included convening the legislature every year rather than every other year and granting the governor more power.

When the legislature met as a convention, it rejected the document; the measure failed by three votes to gain the necessary two-thirds majority approval. Some had argued that the changes did not go far enough, others that they went too far. The governor at the time, Dolph Briscoe, had appeared indifferent to the initiative, and ultimately came out against it. The next legislature, in 1975, tried a different tack: Members put together eight amendments to the old constitution that resembled the one rejected the previous year. They won passage of the amendments in the legislature, but not among the voters. Texas would continue into the twenty-first century with the 1876 constitution and its elaborate set of amendments—ninety-one were approved in the decade of the 1980s alone, a total of more than 350 passed into law by the mid-1990s. It would also continue under this constitution with a chief executive with very limited powers and a legislature that shut down for long periods.

Governors of the 1970s provided uneven and generally uninspired leadership as they continued to grapple with where to get and how to use tax money, most of them focusing on educational initiatives and budget matters. Briscoe's predecessor, former legislator and lieutenant governor Preston Smith, demonstrated an impressive insider's knowledge of state government. His emphasis on school funding did yield a number of new colleges, professional schools, and branches of technological institutes, including some in his native West Texas, which had had few higher education options. But overall, as his comment on people "lik[ing] to live in slums" indicates, his administration largely maintained the status quo.

Briscoe focused primarily on his pledge of "no new taxes," in part by transferring much school funding from the state to local school districts. Funding for education, though, did not decline with $4 billion in new funding channeled to education at the public and the collegiate levels. The additional revenue for this and other needs came from the swollen state coffers from additional tax revenues, the product of a booming economy. Teachers and state workers both earned sizable raises during the Briscoe years. Funding for the Department of Mental Health and Mental Retardation increased.

His administration supported increased funding for highway construction and improvement and also the Texas Open Records Act and the Texas Open Meetings Act, passed in response to the Sharpstown scandal. New regulations were imposed on lobbyists. Lawmakers also were held to higher ethical standards as well as financial disclosure rules. The penal code was revised during the Briscoe administration, the first time in 100 years, and it included provision for the death penalty. The U.S. Supreme Court in 1972 had overturned the death penalty, calling it "arbitrary and capricious," and had said states could not reinstate it without more finely tuned laws.

Briscoe showed awareness of the new political landscape in his appointments. He named a significant number of women and minorities to offices within state government. His appointments included the first African Americans to serve on state boards and as district judge.

While he easily secured reelection in 1974, Briscoe lost his bid for a third term in 1978 when he was defeated in the Democratic primary (in 1972 Texas voters approved increasing gubernatorial terms from two to four years, effective with the 1974 election). These accomplishments need to be measured against the new demands placed on Texas government in the decade: the population was soaring and the need for increased state services paralleled this growth. Moreover, Briscoe's critics lambasted him for being dull and not terribly involved in running the state. Still, he achieved an enviable record, and he enjoyed a relatively united Democratic Party.

The governors of this era also contended with federal government involvement in Texas affairs. Federal courts enforced integration plans for public schools in the early 1970s. Federal agencies such as the U.S. Justice Department, the Occupational Safety and Health Administration, and the Environmental Protection Agency required compliance with federal regulations. The federal government at varying rates supplemented state coffers for public schools, cities, highways and transportation, and welfare costs, but Texas continued to rank low in federal grants awarded to states.

Economic Boom

During the 1970s, economic opportunity in Texas remained largely defined by the state's status as the chief oil-producing state in the nation. The 1974 Arab embargo on oil to the United States led to higher prices for Texas oil, and the oil and gas industry continued to fuel the Texas economy to the extent that the state gained a great degree of economic independence. This meant that the Texas economy was booming when the national economy struggled, both for the same reason, the Middle East and the politics of international oil supplies. Nationally, worries over the availability of foreign oil proliferated as high oil prices prevailed, taking another spike upward as a result of the Iranian revolution and reductions in Saudi Arabian oil production. By 1981, the industry generated more than one-fourth of the state's economic revenues and provided a bonanza of funds both for the state and for private enterprise. These funds gave the state legislature a surplus and stimulated prolific business growth and real estate speculation. Then, when the Middle Eastern Organization of Petroleum Exporting Countries dropped its prices, Texas oil revenues stopped climbing and soon began to drop, a problem that dominated the state's economy in the 1980s.

Growing cities, and the long distances between them, also fostered the development of commuting by air. Texas cities had long been served by Braniff Airways (founded in 1928) and Texas International Airways (founded in 1947 as Trans-Texas Airways). Meanwhile, Rollin King's small air-taxi service gave him the idea of establishing a commuter service between the state's three major cities: Houston, Dallas, and San Antonio. King joined with his attorney, Herb Kelleher, to create Southwest Airlines, which, by the turn of the century, had become one of the leading airlines in the nation. Just as important to the increasing modernization and economic significance of Texas on the national and the international stage was the opening of two major international airports in the state: Houston's Intercontinental Airport (now Bush Intercontinental Airport) in 1969 and Dallas Fort Worth International Airport in 1974.

Increasingly, consumer-driven industries became a vital component of the Texas economy. The suburban shopping mall was perhaps the quintessential midcentury development in the American consumer economy. Located near major freeways in middle-class suburban areas, the shopping mall displaced the downtown department stores such as Neiman Marcus, which became a symbol of new Texas wealth in the 1930s. Its brand had gained national panache, but to survive it had to remake itself as a high end mall anchor store. Small and independent store owners also suffered and had less chance of survival. Some of the earliest and most important malls in Texas include the Galleria in Houston (1970) and NorthPark in Dallas (1965). These malls catered to a more upscale demographic while others like Big Town in Mesquite (1959) and Sharpstown in the greater Houston area (1961) targeted the middle class suburbanites. As suburbia continued to sprawl outward from central city cores these malls were just as likely as not to go out of business in favor of newer, trendier malls located near the newer and more popular suburbs. This disposable mentality toward shopping had tremendous and negative environmental implications.

Tourism became another notable component of the Texas consumer culture, with options ranging from scenic explorations of the natural environment in places like Padre Island National Seashore and the Big Bend Mountains to artificial adventures in theme parks. While Texans did not invent the theme park, a concept that dates back to Coney Island in the late nineteenth century and Disneyland in the 1950s, they developed parks that both linked to the state's history, Six Flags over Texas (1961), at least nominally, and its vision of itself in the future, Astroworld (1968). In 1968, Hemisfair, an international exposition that highlighted southwestern cultures in a theme park setting, opened. While temporary, it commemorated the founding of San Antonio 250 years previously.

The Texas economy had historically been tied in one way or another to the land, either through farming or the extraction of natural resources from the earth. This became somewhat less true in the second half of the twentieth century, making it possible for an environmental movement to both gain adherents and also powerful critics. A fight in Congress over the fate of the Big Thicket illustrates this situation. Senator Ralph Yarborough was probably the most important congressional influence on the passage of legislation providing for federal protection for the Big Thicket. Yarborough and Senator John Tower both sponsored bills along with Houston liberal Robert Eckhardt to preserve the forested region. Yarborough condemned the publishing company, Time, Inc. and the Santa Fe Railroad Company for their logging practices in that region of Texas. A 1974 law placed almost 85,000 acres in the Big Thicket National Preserve.

Here protection for the environment trumped business exploitation of Texas's natural resources.

Other Texas business endeavors really had nothing to do with profits on a ledger sheet but can better be understood as an outgrowth of successful investing, profitable business models, and a passion for social betterment. By the middle of the twentieth century, philanthropies and charitable foundations had become a fairly standard device for wealthy Americans. Some on the political left were skeptical of such creations believing them to be a tax dodge for those families that established them and, more important, a usurpation of the government's responsibility for social welfare provision.

Several notable Texas foundations gained increased prominence in the 1960s and 1970s, and their impact on the state's economy is important. Philanthropic spending made up the gap in social and educational services in a state not known for its prioritization of such things. For example, Ima Hogg, the daughter of reformist governor James Stephen Hogg, had since the late 1920s been an advocate for better mental health services in Texas, and in 1964 she created the Ima Hogg Foundation with its purpose being provision for children's mental health care in Houston and Harris County. Earlier in 1940 she had used the proceeds of her brother's estate to create what became the Hogg Foundation for Mental Health at UT. Hogg was a typical Texas philanthropist in that her family money came from oil, the source of much of the early wealth in the state. Historians who have studied foundations argue that they proved to be an important factor in building community cohesion in the twentieth century. Moreover, Texas foundations typically operated without regard for race before the desegregation era. By the 1970s, there were over forty large private foundations created in Texas with the large majority engaged in charitable work.

Conclusion

Did Lyndon Johnson really have it in his pocket? Did the Democratic Party in Texas? Certainly Johnson revolutionized the political landscape in the nation and his home state, but did the domestic reforms of the Great Society, namely civil rights, beget a new political order that reflected these reforms? The Democratic Party in Texas by the end of the 1970s was more responsive to the views of minorities, women, and the poor, but it was also losing its position as the only political vehicle to power in the state.

Indeed, the political ferment of the 1960s and 1970s had made clear that Texans were not homogenous, in their political views or in their cultural and social values. It gave rise to a new or more widely shared appreciation for different cultural roots and ways of life. The Institute of Texas Cultures, first opened in 1968 as part of Hemisfair in San Antonio, began producing exhibits and information on Texans of various ethnic origins, its mission statement to encourage greater understanding the state's diversity. In 1973 San Antonio students and community members of Mexican heritage staged an original play, *El Alamo: Our Version of What Happened.* Visitors flocked to celebrations of traditional German holidays such as Oktoberfest and those adapted from their experiences in Texas, such as the Easter Fires pageant in Fredericksburg, which combines ancient custom with Texas frontier legend. Texans of African American descent reinvigorated the celebration of "Juneteenth," a holiday originally established to mark the public recognition of Texas slaves' freedom—the reading of the Emancipation Proclamation in Galveston with the arrival of federal troops after the Civil War. In 1979, the legislature voted to make the date, June 19, a state holiday.

The changes in public perceptions could be profound. After winning her seat in the U.S. Congress, Barbara Jordan had gone on to become a national figure: a formidable member of the House Judiciary Committee during the 1974 Watergate hearings, keynote speaker at the 1976 and 1992 Democratic National Conventions, professor at the Lyndon Baines Johnson School of Public Affairs in Austin, and ethics advisor to Governor Ann Richards. Jordan had traveled a long way from her modest beginnings in Houston's Fifth Ward and from the double challenge of growing up black and female in an era when African Americans did not share in the power structure and women were expected to focus on being wives and homemakers. After Jordan's death in 1996, Texas playwright Larry King's play *The Dead President's Club* included an appearance by God in the form of a strong, articulate black woman. No one could miss the resemblance to Jordan.

The conundrum, then, of the Johnson years in Texas is that a series of reforms that opened the political process to minorities and women also, and inadvertently, sped up the conversion of Texas to a two-party state, so much so that by the late 1970s the Republicans were on the verge of gaining more political power than they had held since Reconstruction. To be sure, there were other factors that contributed to the state's political realignment—its population increase and its economic boom—and the story of the conversion of Texas into a Republican state is one that unfolded in the last two decades of the twentieth century and the first decade of the twenty-first century.

Suggested Readings

The Lyndon Johnson Era

Among the more useful and readable biographies of Lyndon Johnson are Robert Dallek, *Flawed Giant: Lyndon Johnson and His Times, 1961–1973* (1998) and Randall Woods, *LBJ: Architect of American Ambition* (2006). For a short account of Johnson's background and presidency, see Bruce J. Schulman, *Lyndon B. Johnson and American Liberalism: A Brief History with Documents* (2006) and Gareth

Davies, *From Opportunity to Entitlement. The Transformation and Decline of Great Society Liberalism* (1996). See also Lewis L. Gould, *Lady Bird Johnson: Our Environmental First Lady* (1999). For the Kennedy assassination, see Steven M. Gillon, *The Kennedy Assassination—24 Hours After: Lyndon B. Johnson's Pivotal First Day as President* (2010) and Gerald Posner, *Case Closed: Lee Harvey Oswald and the Assassination of JFK* (1993).

James Reston, Jr.'s *The Lone Star: The Life of John Connally* (1989) provides an effective treatment of Johnson's protégé. For biographies of key members of the Texas delegation during these years see Patrick Cox, *Ralph Yarborough: The People's Senator* (2001); John R. Knaggs, *Two-Party Texas: The John Tower Era, 1961–1984* (1986); Nancy Beck Young, *Wright Patman: Populism, Liberalism, and the American Dream* (2000); Barbara Jordan and Shelby Hearon, *Barbara Jordan: A Self-Portrait* (1979); and Mary Beth Rogers, *Barbara Jordan, American Hero* (1998).

Treatments of race and politics during the 1960s are in Ignacio M. Garcia, *Viva Kennedy: Mexican Americans in Search of Camelot* (2000); Rodolfo Rosales, *The Illusion of Inclusion: The Political Story of San Antonio, Texas* (2000); David Montejano, *Anglos and Mexicans in the Making of Texas, 1836–1986* (1987); David Montejano, *Quixote's Soldiers: A Local History of the Chicano Movement, 1966–1981* (2010); David Montejano, *Sancho's Journal: Exploring the Political Edge with the Brown Berets* (2012); Brian Behnken, *Fighting Their Own Battles: Mexican Americans, African Americans, and the Struggle for Civil Rights* (2011); Marc Rodriguez, *The Tejano Diaspora: Mexican Americanism and Ethnic Politics in Texas and Wisconsin* (2011); Ignacio M. Garcia, *United We Win: The Rise and Fall of La Raza Unida Party* (1989); Arnoldo De Léon, *Mexican Americans in Texas: A Brief History* (1993); Carl Allsup, *The American G.I. Forum: Origins and Evolution* (1982); Alwyn Barr, *Black Texans: A History of African Americans in Texas, 1528–1995* (1996); Robert D. Bullard, *Invisible Houston: The Black Experience in Boom and Bust* (1987); Donald Seals Jr., "The Wiley-Bishop Student Movement: A Case Study in the 1960 Civil Rights Sit-Ins," *Southwestern Historical Quarterly* 106 (January 2003): 419–440; and Guadalupe San Miguel, Jr., *Let All of Them Take Heed: Mexican Americans and the Campaign for Educational Equality in Texas, 1910–1981* (1987).

The shifting political climate in Texas during these years is addressed in Chandler Davidson, *Race and Class in Texas Politics* (1990); Sherry L. Smith, ed., *The Future of the Southern Plains* (2005); Jeff Roche, ed., *The Political Culture of the New West* (2008); Sean P. Cunningham, *Cowboy Conservatism: Texas and the Rise of the Modern Right* (2010); Roger M. Olien, *From Token to Triumph: The Texas Republicans, since 1920* (1982).

For details on the New Left in Texas see Doug Rossinow, *The Politics of Authenticity: Liberalism, Christianity, and the New Left in America* (1998) and Sara Evans, *Personal Politics: The Roots of Women's Liberation in the Civil Rights Movement & the New Left* (1980).

Texas in the 1970s

For information on women, politics, and feminism in Texas see *Capitol Women,* by Nancy Baker Jones and Ruthe Winegarten (2000); *Texas Women Frontier to Future* (1998), by Ann Fears Crawford and Crystal Sasse Ragsdale; Ruthe Winegarten, *Black Texas Women: A Sourcebook* (1996); David J. Garrow, *Liberty and Sexuality: The Right to Privacy and the Making of* Roe v. Wade (1998); N. E. H. Hull and Peter Charles Hoffer, Roe v. Wade: *The Abortion Rights Controversy in American History* (2010); Rob Fink, "Hermine Tobolowsky, the Texas ELRA, and the Political Struggle for Women's Equal Rights," *Journal of the American West* 42 (Summer 2003): 52–57.

Governing a Changing State

For the politics of Texas in the 1970s see Brian McCall, *The Power of the Texas Governor: Connally to Bush* (2009).

Recognizing Old and New Realities

The matriculation of one undergraduate student is not usually noteworthy to historians. Michael Dell's arrival at the University of Texas in the fall of 1983 breaks with this pattern. This freshman, premed student made choices that previewed the new realities coming to the Lone Star State in the last decades of the twentieth century. He brought three computers with him and a lot of ideas about making and selling them. Dell's future, like the Texas economy, was about to take some interesting turns.

In his one year at the University of Texas, Dell registered his own company, PC's Limited, with the state of Texas, and incorporated the company under the name Dell Computer Corporation. On the proceeds of his direct sales of upgraded computers and components to Austin area residents, he rented office space in North Austin and hired an engineer to use the newly available chip sets (streamlined versions of the chips necessary to put together a PC) to create Dell's first computer. Dell developed a business model that allowed the company to avoid the costs of high levels of inventory by building the computers according to customer specifications.

By 2002, Dell Computer Corp. claimed 14 percent of the global market in computers and appeared poised to continue increasing its share. "If you want to be in the PC business, you have to compete against Dell," noted the chief executive officer (CEO) of another company, "and that is very, very difficult." Dell Computer Corp. became the largest employer in Austin and Michael Dell became the richest individual under the age of forty in the world. In 2014, it was listed at the top of information technology service providers for the health care industry, a ranking it first achieved in 2010.

Chapter 15 Recognizing Old and New Realities	
1978	William Clements, Jr. becomes the first Republican governor of Texas since Reconstruction
1979	Juneteenth is made an official state holiday
MID-1980s	The oil business in Texas goes from boom to bust; Michael Dell begins his successful personal computer business
1985	Joseph L. Goldstein and Michael S. Brown of the University of Texas Health Science Center in Dallas win Nobel Prize in medicine for their research on cholesterol
1988	George H. W. Bush is elected president of the United States
1989	Southwest Airline revenues top $1 billion
1992	United States, Canada, and Mexico enter into North American Free Trade Agreement (NAFTA)
1997	Senate Bill 1 creates a new state water-planning system
1998	After two decades of alternating Democratic and Republican administrations, Republicans consolidate control of state offices
2000	George W. Bush wins U.S. presidency; Hispanics are largest ethnic group in four major Texas cities
2001	Enron Corporation declares bankruptcy in Houston
2002	Rio Grande runs dry
2003	In *Lawrence v. Texas*, the U.S. Supreme Court overturns the state's sodomy laws; Horizontal drilling begins in the Barnett shale
2006	The U.S. Congress repeals the Wright Amendment
2008	Rick Perry becomes the longest serving governor in the state's history
2009	Annise Parker is elected mayor of Houston, the first openly lesbian to serve as mayor of a major American city
2011	A record is set for the highest amount lost in a drought, $7.62 billion

As Texans moved through the final decades of the twentieth century and into the twenty-first, their actions and attitudes as individuals and groups, along with broader economic and political trends, redefined Texas identity, moving away from one primarily celebrating white male ranching and oil culture. The state's population had grown even more diverse, but now that diversity was increasingly acknowledged and reflected in the political structures and culture of Texas. The state pursuit of economic opportunity remained a key characteristic, but this opportunity increasingly took new forms—or new variations on old forms. Independence and limited government still resonated with Texans, but now these values had to be balanced even more than before with the challenges of dynamic urban growth, rural decline, and federal–state relations. The scope and vitality of the land characterized Texans' vision of themselves and the state even as more of the population gravitated to urban and suburban zip codes. The remaining farmers and ranchers found the challenges of working and managing the land more and more daunting; and Texans, in general, faced the difficulty of preserving natural features and natural resources that they had previously taken for granted.

As you read this chapter, consider the following questions:

1. Define the characteristics and accomplishments of the late twentieth and early twenty-first century political realignments in the state. What factors distinguish these realignments from earlier ones in Texas history?
2. What social challenges did racial and ethnic minorities face in Texas during this time period? What did these groups achieve?
3. Should the Texas economy be viewed as a success story in the late twentieth and early twenty-first century? In both urban and rural Texas? Why?

Political Realignments

For more than a century, the traditional power structure in Texas had been strongly, consistently based in the Democratic Party. But with the changes of the 1960s and 1970s, liberals had gained power within the party and had drawn activist reformers and minority voters into it. Most of the women and minorities entering politics in the 1970s did so as Democrats. More conservative Texans—including many concerned with the rapid rate of societal and political change they saw the activists advocating—switched to the Republican Party, and in the 1980s it seemed as if a two-party culture was emerging in the state. Democrats typically performed better with minorities, women, and labor and Republicans with business and urban interests, and competitiveness existed between the two parties that had not been seen previously in the twentieth century. This realignment was already evident in 1972, when white middle-class voters uneasy with Lyndon Johnson's Great Society and affirmative action elected seventeen Republicans to the state House and three to the Senate.

Not until 1996 would Republicans gain control of the Texas Senate and 2002 the Texas House. By that time, though, Texas again took on the characteristics of a one-party state, but with some key differences when compared with the years of Democratic hegemony. While the Democrats in the twenty-first century no longer seemed capable of winning statewide office, the party did not fold. Nor was the Grand Old Party (GOP) ever as factionalized as the twentieth-century Democrats had been, though the emergence of the Tea Party in 2009 put stress on the GOP in Texas, and indeed priorities in the party have shifted over the past thirty years.

The state continued its rightward tilt in the 2014 midterm elections with the election of Republicans Greg Abbott and Dan Patrick as governor and lieutenant governor with Patrick openly appealing to the Tea Party constituency.

The Reemergence of the Republican Party in Texas

In the state elections of 1978, for the first time since Reconstruction, a Republican—Dallas oilman William P. Clements, Jr.—was elected governor of the state. Democrats faced stiff challenges in their bid to hold the governor's mansion: President Jimmy Carter was unpopular in the state; urban Texans gravitated toward the Republican Party; and Republican senator John Tower, popular in the state, was up for reelection. Moreover, Democrats were divided. Dolph Briscoe, the Democratic governor of the state since 1973, had lost his bid for reelection in the Democratic primary against challenger John Hill, the attorney general. Hill ran as an urban liberal discontent with Briscoe's passive leadership of the state, and their primary battle reignited the long-term divisions in the Democratic Party, making it easier for a Republican challenge in the general election. A self-made man who began his career as an oilfield roughneck, Clements defeated Hill, a gentlemanly trial lawyer with a long record of public service, by the narrowest of margins, just under 17,000 votes statewide in an election with over 2.3 million votes cast statewide. Issues that predominated then included growing government bureaucracy and concerns about education and energy. Later President George W. Bush said of Clements, "He broke the ice.... He showed Texas that a Republican could bring to the governor's office a philosophy that was acceptable to most Texans. He began the change at the state level for conservative Democrats to vote Republican for governor. That's a huge legacy."

Republican governor Clements focused on cost-cutting measures, as had Briscoe before him, in part by requiring state agencies to justify their existence and their work forces. He lobbied for cutting spending for prison construction and teacher salaries, even though both were necessary in a state noted for its high rates of incarceration and its large population of school students. During

Created by Guerrero Photographic Group. Hobby (Willam P., Sr.) Family Papers, di_04919, The Dolph Briscoe Center for American History, The University of Texas at Austin

Dolph and Jane Briscoe, Bill and Rita Clements, Bob and Jane Bullock, William P. Hobby, Jr., Ann Richards, and Preston and Ima Smith, 1991.

his first legislative session in 1979, he reduced state spending by $252 million by using the line item veto rather than through cooperation with the state legislature. Clements also undertook the work to build the Republican Party in Texas, especially rural Texas by appointing Republicans as judges and then encouraging them to run for election in their own right. He also campaigned for Ronald Reagan in 1980, calling President Carter a "God-damned liar." In 1981, Clements had better luck with the legislature, in part because he sought higher appropriations for education, including increasing spending for public education by 23 percent and teacher pay by 26 percent. His brusque personality left him immune to criticism but also won him the enmity of the state's Democrats, who were eager to run against him in 1982.

In the 1980s prison reform became a central issue, illustrating the tensions and complexities of federal–state relations. Texas had been convicting and incarcerating criminals at a rate far exceeding the national average, and although the state population had grown 19 percent between 1968 and 1978, the prison population had doubled. David Ruiz, an inmate who had been convicted of armed robbery, led other Texas inmates in filing suit against prison system director W. James Estelle in 1972, citing overcrowding and other substandard prison conditions. In 1980 federal judge William Wayne Justice agreed that the conditions constituted "cruel and unusual punishment" outlawed by the U.S. Constitution. The federal judge ordered the state of Texas to make major penal changes. Officials scrambled to comply, in part by establishing new prison facilities. But the prison population continued to swell disproportionately to the general population.

During these years, the American South as a whole shifted heavily from Democratic to Republican, the majority voting in national elections for Ronald Reagan for president, then for his former vice president and former Texas congressman George H. W. Bush, who was elected president in 1988, but this political realignment did not necessarily mean the reduction of political opportunity for women and minorities. Instead, GOP success became something of a foil for many minority and women candidates in the state who effectively ran against the restrictive positions Republicans took on policy questions regarding issues like civil rights and women's health care.

By the 1980s, Texas had become a two-party state with more opportunities for women and minorities. In 1981, Democrat Henry Cisneros was elected mayor of San Antonio; not since the administration of Juan Seguín 140 years earlier had a Hispanic headed the city government. That same year, President Ronald Reagan appointed El Paso–born and Arizona-raised Sandra Day O'Connor to be the first woman on the U.S. Supreme Court. In 1982, Democrat Ann Richards won election as Texas state treasurer; not since the second election of Ma Ferguson in 1932 had a woman achieved election to statewide office.

In the gubernatorial election of 1982, attorney general and Democrat Mark White defeated Clements. White put much emphasis on education. Students continued to swell the state's college population, particularly at its two flagship public universities, the University of Texas and Texas A&M University, as well as at other state schools funded and regulated by a legislatively approved co-ordinating board. White led in the legislature's passing of House Bill 72, or the Educational Reform Act, a weighty and far-reaching education law that reconfigured the state board of education. The bill instituted a "no pass, no play" requirement for students in public schools—barring students who had failed a class from participating in extracurricular activities in the next grading period—and tried to balance the state funding allocated to poor and wealthy districts. Many saw the "no pass, no play" law as aimed at student athletes and feared it would undermine high school sports programs in a state where high school foot-ball has often been a focal point for whole communities. After a legal challenge in which a Texas court upheld the rule, the U.S. Supreme Court refused to consider the issue. The law stood, although it was modified in the mid-1990s, shortening the suspension period and allowing the suspended student to practice or rehearse with the extracurricular group.

Although the "no pass, no play" rule was controversial, most problematic was the attempt to balance the funding allocated to Texas K-12 school districts. Because most of the money for schools came from property taxes in the areas served by the schools, wealthier communities received more money per student than poorer communities. In the late 1980s, the Alamo Heights independent school district had more than fourteen times the property value per student of the Edgewood independent school district, also in Béxar County. Unsatisfied with White's attempts at reform, the Edgewood independent school district pur-sued a lawsuit asserting that the state's reliance on local property taxes made its educational system imbalanced and unconstitutional. The lawsuit would domi-nate Texas politics until the 1990s.

Clements returned and defeated White in 1986, as White struggled with the education issues and as the state experienced an economic downturn brought on by falling oil prices. In Texas, Clements could enjoy a "veto-proof" second term, as the 1986 elections had given Republicans more than one-third of the House votes.

Other results in 1986 show the two party tenor of voting in the state. That year, Democrat Judith Zaffirini of Laredo joined the Texas state senate as its first Mexican American woman. A former volunteer lobbyist for the mentally ill and mentally retarded, Zaffirini set out to effect what she termed a "momma agenda," advocating legislation that reflected her concerns as a mother, such as requir-ing immunizations for Texas children. Her agenda ran counter to the ideological trends in the state. Yet she proved effective in the upper chamber. She playfully reminded a fellow legislator, "[Y]ou study legislation from the perspective of Bubba. I study legislation from the perspective of Momma."

In his second term, Clements faced the loss of one-fourth of the state's rev-enue as a result of the mid-1980s oil crash, and he struggled to keep the state government functioning, reluctantly abandoning his own "no new taxes" stance and dealing with a new state court ruling that indicated the need for more taxes to maintain the public schools. Under his administration, the legislature continued to work to equalize school expenditures per student across the state, as poorer districts still had less than half of what the richer districts had to spend per student. In 1989, as a result of the Edgewood lawsuit, the Texas Supreme Court instructed the legislature to put into place an equitable system before school started in the fall of 1990.

A Texas Republican in the White House

Just as important as the political developments in Austin in the late 1980s were those in Washington, D.C. Vice President George H. W. Bush ran for and won election to the presidency in 1988, and his four-year term in the White House reflected the political transformations taking place in Texas. Bush proved to be a transitional figure in Republican politics. He had been an early participant in the efforts to realign Texas, and his concerns were in sync with the business community preferences for fewer federal regulations. Bush was less comfortable with the cultural conservatism that was building in the state and the nation: opposition to abortion rights, gay rights, and feminism and support for evangelical Christian conservatism. To gain the presidential nomination in 1988, he had to bridge the gap in his party between cultural conservatives and economic conservatives while also suggesting he would take a hard line against the Democratic-controlled Congress in Washington. He did so by promising he would not raise taxes even though he knew modest tax increases would likely be necessary to address the nation's spiraling deficit. Bush's "no new taxes" pledge suggested his allegiance to economic conservatism and made criticism of him on social issues more difficult.

The shifting priorities of Republican conservatives, from antistatist, antitax and spend, anti–New Deal views to a more diverse mélange of economic conservatism mixed with social conservatism occurred gradually. Elements of social conservatism existed throughout twentieth-century Texas and manifested in debates about prohibition and the Ku Klux Klan from the 1910s and the 1920s. Later antilabor views from the 1930s, 1940s, and 1950s offered a different precursor to modern conservatism. Finally, opposition to civil rights reforms in the 1950s and 1960s provided another foundation for the construction of modern conservative values. Still, scholars have debated the degree to which social conservatism (antiabortion, antifeminism, anti-immigration, opposition to civil rights, antigay rights, etc.) should be viewed simply as a backlash to the liberalism of Lyndon Johnson's Great Society from the 1960s. The prominence, though, of social and evangelical conservatism in Texas, as in the rest of the country, dates to the 1970s and 1980s.

Two developments, one in foreign affairs and one in the domestic economy, marked Bush's presidency. In the 1990 budget deficit reduction negotiations, Bush agreed to a congressional plan to attack the deficit with a mixture of spending cuts and tax increases, a move that caused conservatives in the Republican

Courtesy George H. W. Bush Presidential Library

Vice President George H. W. Bush and President Ronald Reagan, 1981.

Party to criticize the president for lacking loyalty to the party's agenda and compromising too easily with Democrats.

Foreign affairs changed the conversation in Washington. In August 1990, Iraq invaded Kuwait and threatened U.S. access to Middle Eastern oil supplies, and Bush worked through the United Nations to have sanctions imposed before going to war. When Iraq refused to adhere to the sanctions and leave Kuwait, Bush led an international alliance that pushed Iraq out of Kuwait in January and February 1991. The successful conclusion of that conflict at the end of February boosted his popularity immensely with the American people, but not enough to offset the criticisms he endured regarding the recession of the early 1990s. Unemployment nationwide was almost 8 percent in the summer of 1992, allowing Arkansas governor Bill Clinton to run an effective campaign about the slumping economy and defeat Bush in his bid for reelection to the presidency that fall.

Governor Ann Richards and Liberal Democrats

As Texas conservatives migrated to join the Republican Party, liberals became a more powerful force within the Texas Democratic Party. In the 1990 election, Ann Richards, a liberal Democrat, won the governor's seat. She had already earned a national reputation for herself when she derided then presidential candidate George H. W. Bush at the 1988 Democratic National Convention, saying, "Poor George, he can't help it. He was born with a silver foot in his mouth." This and other similar statements earned her the enmity of conservative Texans who liked Bush and supported his presidency. Her 1990 election showed both the potential of women, minorities, labor, and the poor working together but also the importance of personality. Her GOP opponent, oilman and rancher Clayton Williams, made unwise and inappropriate jokes about rape, suggesting that it was inevitable and that women should "relax and enjoy it." Williams made other mistakes: he admitted not knowing the content of a proposed constitutional amendment on the ballot that year, he acknowledged he had not paid income taxes in 1986, and he refused to shake Richards's hand during a televised debate. Richards outpolled Williams, and became the first woman to be elected governor of Texas solely based on her own career accomplishments (as opposed to Ma Fergusen).

Also in 1990, Republican Kay Bailey, now Kay Bailey Hutchison, won election as state treasurer, earning recognition as the first Republican woman to secure a statewide elective position, and Democrat Dan Morales became the first Hispanic attorney general. Two years later, Morris Overstreet became the first African American to gain statewide office with his election as a judge on the Texas Court of Criminal Appeals.

Despite these gains—and Richards's appointments of women, Hispanics, and African Americans to various boards and commissions—the percentages of women and minority officeholders remained low. For example, in the early 1990s, city councils in Texas, on average, had one Hispanic for every twenty members, even though the Hispanic population statewide was one in five. In 1997, the Texas House and Senate had thirty-three women members, but this constituted less than 20 percent of the total membership.

In response to federal court orders regarding public school funding and prison overcrowding, the Richards administration focused on educational and prison reforms. Richards also contended with an antiquated tax structure and a $5 billion budget shortfall. She took a firmer hand with the directors of the state agencies, and she usually got her way. New ethics standards were created during her term and environmental protections were strengthened. Insurance reforms included the requirement that drivers carry automobile insurance. To raise additional funds for education, Richards supported legislation creating a state lottery over the protests of conservative religious groups. Legislation to outlaw stalking was enacted. Moreover, Richards succeeded in her efforts to get General Motors to keep open its plant in Arlington, Texas. She also convinced Southwestern Bell Corporation to relocate its headquarters to San Antonio from Missouri.

Among her efforts at prison reform included the implementation of what she called "the largest drug-and-alcohol treatment system in the world" as a component of the Texas Department of Criminal Justice. As a recovering alcoholic, she realized that addiction played a role in the commission of crime, making treatment as important as punishment to prevent recidivism. She also oversaw the

Texas State Library and Archives Commission, Austin, Texas

Gov. Ann Richards purchases the first scratch-off lottery ticket in Texas at Polk's Feed Store in Oak Hill, Texas, May 29, 1992.

construction of new prisons, the imposition of mandatory sentencing guidelines, and the reduction of parole approval rates. Her prison construction program resulted in the doubling of the state's capacity to incarcerate inmates.

After the courts rejected a series of legislative initiatives, Governor Richards worked with the legislature in 1993 to devise an acceptable plan that got public education out from under the federal court order. According to this plan dubbed "Robin Hood," each school in the wealthy districts would aid redistribution in one of five ways: by combining its tax base with that of a poorer district, giving the state money "to help pay for students in poorer districts," "contracting to educate students in other districts," simply consolidating with another district or other districts, or "transferring some of its commercial taxable property to another district's tax roles." By the end of the twentieth century, the law had led to much dissatisfaction. The limited but important state funding for schools declined and districts judged "wealthy" fought to hang onto their resources, many of them in the midst of major spurts in enrollment. In 2001, a number of these school districts sued to get "Robin Hood" overturned, but a district judge affirmed its legality.

Economic Growth, Urbanization, and Changing Political Identities

The governors of the 1990s enjoyed an improving economy in a state that was changing rapidly. In the oil boom of the 1970s and early 1980s, Texas had attracted 2.5 million immigrants, making it the third most populated state. As we will see later in the chapter, the oil bust of the 1980s sparked economic diversification. Now, in the 1990s, as more people were drawn to business opportunities or high-tech jobs and the warm climate, Texas shot to second place, behind California. Large numbers of urban professionals from other states flocked to Texas where they helped solidify the growing base of the Republican Party.

By 2002, despite some slowdown in growth and employment, three of the fastest-growing counties in the nation were located in Texas, as people immigrated to Texas from other states and from Mexico. Not only was the minority population becoming the majority in many cities, but key cities and outlying areas were experiencing staggering population growth. In El Paso and other urban areas outside the five magnet cities, rapid growth was the rule, but not prosperity. City governments faced infrastructure problems, including clogged highways, urban sprawl, crowded new schools, and a general drain on city services. Even in the magnet cities— primarily Dallas, Houston, and Austin—unemployment sometimes jumped dramatically, as more hopefuls poured in and the economy shifted.

In the midst of such urban challenges, there remained among much of the populace a resistance to local, state, and federal government regulation. At its most pronounced, this resistance was manifested in the separation of the Branch Davidians under David Koresh until their final fatal encounter with federal agents at the Branch Davidian compound outside Waco in 1993, and in the 1990s activities of a group in West Texas calling itself the "Republic of Texas" and asserting that Texas remains independent of the United States. On a milder level, Texans repeatedly rejected the idea of a state income tax, including a brief attempt by officials to introduce one in the late 1980s. Residents of Houston in the 1980s also resisted attempts to institute standard zoning measures that would regulate the city's growth; in doing so, they maintained Houston's record as "the largest unzoned city in the United States." Smaller communities wrangled over the rules and regulations that would come with incorporation, particularly those involving land use.

The Era of George W. Bush

The economic and demographic transformations of the 1990s facilitated the consolidation of Republican power in the state. George W. Bush, son of the former president, won the governorship in 1994. That Ann Richards was his opponent did not hurt. Bush loyalists in the state had never really forgiven her for her disparaging comments about George H. W. Bush. George W. Bush also benefitted from a focused campaign with promises to improve education, juvenile justice, and welfare services. During his governorship, he implemented a program of testing in the public schools while also reducing by 50 percent the number of Texans receiving welfare. Moreover, he signed two large tax cuts into law.

Bush prided himself on his cross-partisan political style, identifying himself as a "compassionate conservative" as he readied himself for a White House campaign in 2000; and, during his gubernatorial years, the Republican Party gained the control of all but the state house. Bush won reelection in 1998 with 69 percent of the vote, making Republican inroads even in heavily Hispanic counties identified with the liberal Democrats. In 1998, Republicans also won the offices of lieutenant governor, attorney general, comptroller, land commissioner, and agriculture commissioner. Republicans were a majority in the Texas state senate and close to a majority in the House. Among these numbers were women and minorities; for example, Susan Combs served as the first female agriculture commissioner, and Michael Williams, an African American, became a railroad commissioner.

Texas also became a lightning rod for national and international debate in its use of the death penalty. The death penalty had been reinstated by the state legislature during the Briscoe administration, reflecting a national trend in which most Americans polled favored it. In response to the state's conservative "tough on crime" attitudes, Texas became far more rigorous than other states in employing capital punishment. By 2002, Texas's thirty-three executions for the year made up almost half of the U.S. total for the year. In 2013, Texas executed its five hundredth person since 1976 when the U.S. Supreme Court reinstated death penalty. Texas leads the nation in the use of capital punishment.

The growing power of the Texas Republican Party in the 1990s reflected in the national events, including a "Republican revolution" in 1994 during the Clinton administration. The Republican Party vowed to regain the control it had lost when incumbent George H. W. Bush lost the presidency to Clinton in 1992, and it did so in large part by propelling Texas governor George W. Bush into the White House in the election of 2000. Governor Bush ran against Democrat Al Gore, Clinton's vice president, for the presidency. Vote-count problems, particularly in Florida, delayed election results, but a Supreme Court ruling on the returns confirmed totals that led to Bush's victory in the electoral college.

At the state level, although the economy was strong during the 1990s, many problems remained. For example, in 1998, Texas ranked first among the states in people without health insurance, second in the number of people in state prisons, and third in the number of people living below the poverty level. There also remained a violent strain of racism, as evidenced that year by the dragging death of African American James Byrd, Jr., by three white men in East Texas. The men were captured and tried, and hate-crime legislation was developed to address such crimes of racism and prejudice.

George W. Bush's presidency proved to be controversial even though many Americans liked the affable Texan for his demeanor as an average person. He used his identity as a Texan to craft his political image. He regularly vacationed at his Crawford, Texas ranch where he took the press to observe him cutting underbrush. He promised he would be a different kind of conservative, that he would rid Washington of scandal and corruption, and that he would work collaboratively with Democrats in Congress. He cited his record in Austin as evidence that he could cooperate effectively across the aisle.

The first eight months of Bush's tenure in the White House included challenges to the constitutionality of his presidency, an economic recession, and corporate corruption scandals including the Texas energy company Enron. His early domestic policy accomplishments included the faith-based and community initiative, severe limits on stem cell research, a massive $1.35 trillion tax cut, and the No Child Left Behind education reforms, which brought the Texas testing model to Washington, D.C.

The al Qaeda attacks on the World Trade Center in New York City and the Pentagon on September 11, 2001, re-centered his presidency with a new focus on terrorism, including wars in Afghanistan and Iraq to root out the "axis of evil." Mixed results in these wars along with domestic problems—namely Hurricane Katrina's devastation of New Orleans and the beginning of the Great Recession in 2007—led to a resurgent Democratic Party. Bush returned to Dallas after his administration ended, and he did not assume a public role in national affairs.

Social Conservatism and Republican Dominance

With Bush vacating the governorship for the presidency, the post passed to Lieutenant Governor Rick Perry, who identified transportation and higher education as his priorities. During Bush's presidency, Perry was elected governor in his own right in 2002 and 2006, and again in 2010 after Bush left office, making him the longest serving governor in the state's history. He appealed to both fiscal and social conservatives advocating pro-business measures and speaking openly of his Christian faith. His tenure was known for drastic cuts to education and other public services during the recession that began in 2008, choices that satisfied his donors and his evangelical conservative base that opposed government intervention.

He fought hard against what he termed federal intrusion into the state, contemplating the possibility of secession in 2009, a position he later rejected. He was among the first politicians to identify with the Tea Party. Perry bragged of his ability to bring new jobs to Texas, crediting the low tax, low regulation environment in the state. He did break ranks with conservatives on immigration issues, calling for a more moderate policy than was favored by GOP conservatives. This position along with several verbal gaffes rendered his 2012 presidential bid unsuccessful.

As Texas moved into the twenty-first century, government officials grappled with urban and suburban growth and rural decline, lack of a state income tax, and Texas's low ranking in a number of health-and-welfare areas, including welfare payments, mental health care, and immunizations. They also faced the knowledge that Texas ranked first among the states in releases of toxic chemicals into the air and was developing serious problems in meeting the water needs of communities, farms, ranches, and industries. Although conservation efforts were underway, much of the Texas landscape had been polluted, depleted, and scarred.

In 2014, Texans elected Republican Greg Abbott as governor of Texas. Abbott is the first Texas governor with a disability. He became a paraplegic at age 26. An economic and social conservative, Abbott assumed his new office in January 2015. Earlier as attorney general he sued the federal government over thirty times on issues ranging from health care to the environment and gun rights. He won a case before the U.S. Supreme Court protecting the placement of the Ten Commandments on the Texas State Capitol grounds. He once described his job as the state's top lawyer, "I go into the office, I sue Barack Obama and I go home."

Social and Cultural Diversity

As the state urbanized and modernized economically during the 1990s and first decades of the twenty-first centuries, social and ethnic groups created a place for themselves within Texas society, revealing the heightened diversity within the state.

Hispanic Texas

The Hispanic population of Texas, primarily Mexican and Mexican American, continued to grow, with census figures doubling between 1970 and 1990. Since 2000, the Hispanic population, which remains the fastest growing segment of Texas society, has increased by 10 percent. This growth played a critical role in making Texas a majority-minority state, a metric accomplished in 2004, placing the state in the same category as California, Hawaii, and New Mexico. In 2012, whites accounted for 44.5 percent of the state's population, Hispanics 38.2 percent, African Americans 12.3 percent, and Asians 4.2 percent.

Holidays such as Cinco de Mayo and Mexican Independence Day were more widely celebrated. In many parts of the state, Hispanic families staged elaborate *quinceañeras* (fifteenth-birthday parties) for their daughters, complete with formal dresses and tuxedos for the honoree and attendants, with dances and dinners. In this era, Tejano music became more widespread and prevalent. The biggest Tejana sensation in this period was a young woman from South Texas, Selena Quintanilla Perez, who became the "queen of Tejano music." Known only as Selena, she achieved national prominence in the early 1990s, before her untimely death in 1995.

The new acknowledgment of cultural and ethnic diversity did not come without some friction. Prominent Hispanic author Sandra Cisneros sparked controversy by painting her house a vivid shade of purple in the King William district of San Antonio, a historic area in which homeowners agreed to restrictive codes to maintain nineteenth-century appearances. When some neighbors and other city residents complained, Cisneros argued before the San Antonio Historic Review Board that the color was historically accurate for the population of Mexican heritage. The new exterior paint stayed.

Larger issues emerged based on ethnic identity, such as historic claims to land ownership, with Hispanics descended from pre-Revolution Spanish and Mexican families fighting in court for title to lands taken over years before by Anglos. Prominent in this regard was the Balli family, which included hundreds of descendants of a Spanish priest who had received an eighteenth-century grant to what is now Padre Island. The Ballis had arrived in Spanish Texas in 1749 and had amassed over a million acres of ranchland by 1800. By 1938, however, the family was struggling economically, and eleven family members sold their portions of the island to a New York lawyer named Gilbert Kerlin.

Family members contended in subsequent lawsuits that Kerlin had cheated them out of agreed-upon mineral rights and had failed to return a portion of the island to them in a 1942 settlement of competing claims. Generations of the Balli family vowed to carry on the fight as Kerlin's wealth, in part from oil and gas royalties from Padre Island, soared. In late 2000, a Brownsville jury sided with them, granting almost 300 family members a judgment of $2.7 million.

Cultural Diversity

Texas's cultural diversity was apparent to the most casual observer, much of it of a strong ethnic character and much of it simply reflecting a range of cultural expression. New immigrants to Texas, most of them urban and many of them from Asian and African nations, added to the mix of perspectives and experiences. They joined long-term residents in both challenging and celebrating the stereotypes of Texans as oil-rich ranchers, as "urban cowboys" and rural ones, as "outlaws" in keeping with the country music scene of the 1970s, when Willie Nelson, Waylon Jennings, and others brought a fresh Texas-based perspective to the genre. Texans could navigate the steps of the cotton-eye Joe in country dance halls and attend local opera productions in Houston, Dallas, Fort Worth, San Antonio, Austin, and Beaumont. They could visit exhibits of art produced in the state and also study the paintings of the old masters at the Kimbell Art Museum in Fort Worth; they could camp out at the Kerrville Folk Festival and attend the symphony orchestra productions in Texas's major cities.

Dilworth (Coke H) Photographic Archive, di_08103, The Dolph Briscoe Center for American History, The University of Texas at Austin

Audience members at Willie Nelson's Fourth of July Picnic, 1976.

Native American Land Claims

Another issue was the rights of the three remaining Native American tribes in Texas. The Alabama-Coushattas of East Texas, a small group with long ties of loyalty and friendship to the state, had been recognized by the state as a tribe in the nineteenth century. The Kickapoos, who in the nineteenth century had sought refuge from land and cultural pressures by moving through Texas to Mexico, had established enough of a presence on the Rio Grande border that in 1983 they were granted recognition from the U.S. government and land in Texas near El Indio. The Tiguas of Ysleta had been considered virtually extinct and had received no state or federal recognition, and therefore had no official tribal identity or claim to government benefits. The Tiguas's quest for federal recognition and the introduction of gambling operations by the three tribes reminded other Texans of the continued presence of Native American groups and of the challenges posed by the new awareness of diversity.

Earlier in the 1960s, El Paso city officials had contacted the Bureau of Indian Affairs to report that the Tiguas, descendants of Pueblo Indians who had settled near El Paso after the 1680 Pueblo revolt against the Spanish, were living in the expanding city on land tribal members had occupied for centuries and were unable to pay their property taxes.

The Tiguas had never been under the jurisdiction of the Bureau of Indian Affairs, but the federal government rather grudgingly acknowledged the Tiguas as a tribe, leading the way to tax exemption. It insisted, however, that the state rather than the federal government act as their trustee. State funds proved inadequate and uneven, and the Tiguas continued a marginal existence, relying in large part on the development and management of a restaurant and tourist center.

Then, in 1984, state attorney general Jim Mattox ruled that it was against the state constitution for Native American tribes to have rights not granted to other Texans. This meant that the Tiguas would lose both the limited state funds and their tax exemption. Tribal members responded by petitioning for federal trust status, along with the Alabama-Coushatta tribe, which was seeking a restoration of this status.

In August 1987, the Tiguas—1,124 individuals—won federal trust status, thereby protecting their land claims and securing federal funds and services. Some tribes nationally were turning to gaming operations to improve employment rates and living conditions the federal government had not effectively addressed. As part of the trust agreement, however, the Tiguas acknowledged that gambling would not occur where it was not already legal in the state. The state government did not want to open the door to Native American gaming, and the Tiguas were expected not to maneuver around this stipulation by claiming federal reservation rights.

But when the state entered the lottery business in 1992, the Tiguas argued that gambling was now permitted across Texas, and they opened a bingo hall, then a high-stakes gambling casino. By 1999, the casino was pulling in almost $60 million a year in profits and had become a major economic force in the El Paso area, employing 800 people, less than half of whom were tribal members.

In 1999, Texas attorney general John Cornyn filed suit against the Tiguas, arguing that they had violated the 1987 trust status provision against gambling where gambling was not permitted in the state. In September 2001 he won against the Tiguas in district court, and in early 2002, having lost an appeal, they closed the casino. The ruling also affected the Alabama-Coushattas, who only briefly opened a casino in 2002, but despite the judgment, the state was unable to stop a Kickapoo gaming operation at Eagle Pass on the Mexican border.

In the 2000 census, Native Americans added up to 0.5 percent of all Texans; the African American population continued to hover at about 12 percent of the state total; and the Hispanic population was growing rapidly, at 32 percent constituting almost one-third of the census total. Although a little over half of the population was categorized as "white," by 2000, in El Paso and San Antonio as well as Houston and Dallas, Hispanics were the largest ethnic group, outnumbering African Americans and Anglos. The effect of such shifts was dramatically demonstrated in the Democratic primary runoff for the governorship in 2001, when for the first time the two contenders, Dan Morales and Tony Sanchez, publicly debated in both English and Spanish.

The LGBT Movement

By the late twentieth century, cultural diversity did not just involve ethnicity but also sexuality. As was true in other major cities throughout the country, the largest cities in Texas, especially Houston, Dallas, and Austin, saw the emergence of active gay rights organizations as early as the 1960s and 1970s. While Austin was regarded as a liberal oasis within Texas in the 1960s, the city housed only a few gay bars. Houston, however, was "the homosexual playground of the South" for its numerous bars and organizations. Dallas also had an active gay culture. In Houston, the Gay Political Caucus became an important organization in city politics with its endorsement of candidates for mayor and city council often determining the outcome of races. Gay and lesbian activists also cooperated to address issues of great importance to their community, including the AIDS crisis and discriminatory legislation.

Gay and lesbian Texans, however, were routinely subjected to police brutality and arrests for violating the state's sodomy laws, codes that had been revised numerous times. Such laws appeared in numerous states, but Texas had long been fixated on the topic. One particular couple from Snyder, Texas, had been arrested and convicted three times, causing them to receive a life sentence as habitual criminals. In Houston in 2002, police arrested John Lawrence and Tyron Garner for engaging in consensual sexual relations in the confines of Lawrence's apartment. The police had entered the apartment after being told that weapons had been used in the home. The report was false. Lawrence and Garner challenged the arrest and the case went to the Supreme Court. In a *Lawrence v. Texas,* which was decided in 2003, a 6–3 Court overturned the sodomy laws in Texas and the rest of the nation.

Perhaps the most important development, one that revealed a wider public acceptance of gays and lesbians, came in Houston city politics. In 2009, Houston voters elected the first openly gay mayor, Annise Parker, of a major U.S. city. She won reelection in 2011 and was a candidate for a third term in 2013. Attitudes in the state as a whole were very different, though. In 2005, Texas voters adopted a state constitutional amendment banning gay marriage.

Developing Economic Opportunity

As new faces and agendas appeared on the Texas political scene, the economic landscape of the state was changing as well. Wealth in the state remained with the oil industry but that sector redefined itself with a more diverse focus on multiple aspects of energy production. It also expanded to include technology, tourism, aerospace, and international trade. Not all Texans benefited equally from the state's economic boom.

The Energy Industry

In the mid-1980s, the economy built on oil teetered and crashed. Rigs closed down; large numbers of oil workers lost jobs. Even more ominous for the state as a whole, the state government lost revenues from oil and property taxes from oil producers and was forced to cut back services. At the same time, the spiraling real estate market that had been tied to oil prosperity took a nosedive; people were suddenly stuck with mortgages that far exceeded the new value of their property, and new office space now sat empty.

Then, to make things worse, the savings and loan industry in Texas blew apart. Federal deregulation during the Reagan administration meant savings and loan institutions had been operating with little restraint and foresight. These institutions offered generous interest rates to depositors, generous loans to the real-estate speculators and energy developers, and—in many cases—generous payouts to their top personnel. As an economic recession took hold, the savings and loans failed at a rate not seen since the Great Depression of the 1930s, and out-of-state investors claimed them, again undercutting an independent Texas economic base. The whole banking industry in Texas was affected, the ten largest banking operations passing out of the control of state corporations by 1990.

By 1993, money generated by the oil and gas industry had dropped to 7 percent of total state revenues, and one-third of the jobs in the petroleum industry from the early 1980s had vanished. This trend continued as oil prices remained low— at $10 a barrel in 1999, less than a third of what the prices had been in the early 1980s. The same year, 6,658 wells were drilled, less than a quarter of the number drilled in the peak year of 1984.

Although oil prices started rising in 2000, even the most optimistic observers no longer saw the petroleum industry as a viable foundation for the Texas economy. The lesson of the mid-1980s was to diversify, and Texans had done so, reviving the economy with a variety of enterprises by the mid-1990s. Still during the first decade of the twenty-first century new technology aided oil and gas exploration in the state. This was most evident in the Barnett Shale formation near Fort Worth and the Eagle Ford Shale formation in South Texas. With horizontal drilling capabilities and also the use of hydraulic fracturing, these deposits have generated tremendous revenues. The former is estimated to contain approximately 44 trillion cubic feet of natural gas that will be produced by 2030 when the field is expected to expire. The Barnett Shale is the largest onshore natural gas field in the United States, and the Eagle Ford Shale contributed $60 billion to the South Texas economy, including the creation of over 116,000 jobs. The technologies developed in this field have been applied in other shale formations around the world. The new drilling methods, in addition to being a tremendous boost to the Texas economy, have also generated significant controversy about the environment, including water and air quality issues and potential negative health consequences for humans in the area.

Research and development into wind power became another critical component of the Texas energy industry in the early twenty-first century. The Lone Star State became the nation's largest producer of wind energy, and this renewable energy source contributed as much as 38 percent of the electricity generated in Texas for the state's power grid, the Electric Reliability Council of Texas (ERCOT), in 2014. Development of solar power in the state, though, lagged far behind the industry in California, the nation's leader in that category.

Texas as a Technology Hub

Perhaps the most prominent success stories were in the field of electronics and computer technology. Texas businessman H. Ross Perot had already become a billionaire in the 1960s with his Electronic Data Systems (EDS) in Dallas, which supplied software and services for the fledgling computer industry. Dallas-based Texas Instruments, which had introduced the first portable handheld calculator in 1971, struggled in the 1970s and early 1980s. But it rebounded, continuing to provide electronics and electronic research for the military and for commercial use, extending its research and development into computer graphics and related areas. Microelectronics and Computer Technology Corporation (MCC), begun by people in computer and semiconductor manufacturing in Austin in 1982, became one of the biggest research and development consortia for the U.S. electronics industry; it drew together government and university researchers, high-tech companies, and users of their technologies. By 1983, as we saw in the chapter opening, Michael Dell had established what would become an IT giant for decades to come.

Another significant research and development venture got underway in Texas in the early 1990s. The U.S. Department of Energy had selected the state as the location for a superconducting super collider, a huge particle accelerator that would serve as a research tool for particle physicists studying the dynamics of matter by accelerating the subatomic particles in an extended tunnel. With congressional funding, more than 2,000 employees were brought together at a site outside Waxahachie, where a laboratory and tunnel were under construction. As the cost of the project climbed, however, a nervous Congress withdrew funding, halting progress on the project in 1993, and the project facilities have remained vacant ever since.

The Enron Scandal

Other innovative, entrepreneurial growth appeared as solid but proved chimerical. In 1986, Enron Corporation, an energy-trading firm that had grown out of a small gas-pipeline operation, moved its headquarters to Houston and in an age of energy deregulation proceeded to become the largest energy-trading company in the world; by 2000 Enron reported over $100 billion in annual revenues and mounted what was touted as "the most successful Internet effort of any firm in any business." The company built a handsome forty-story headquarters, with a million-dollar hand-etched glass relief map of the world suspended in the atrium. It subsidized the arts in Houston and the Astros new baseball stadium (now Minute Maid Park), putting its distinctive "E" logo on the facility, and even sponsored a venture capital initiative to aid and nurture minority businesses in Houston's Fifth Ward.

In late fall 2001, after corporate leaders cashed out their stock options, it became clear that Enron's reported revenues had little basis in fact. Not only did thousands of Enron employees and individual investors lose their substantial investments in the company, but Texas's teacher retirement system and employee retirement system together lost almost $60 million in stocks and bonds. In the litigious aftermath of Enron's fall, Houston itself felt the pinch as not only 4,000 jobs but vital community funding disappeared. Enron became a symbol of corrupt corporate practices, not only in Texas, but nationally.

Diverse and Robust Industries

Stable economic activity characterized a wide range of enterprises. The timbering industry employed almost 100,000 people in 1999. Tourism drew more than 1 million international visitors in 1999; the overall tourist rate was second only to California's, and the Sea World Amusement Park in San Antonio rivaled— but did not surpass—the Alamo as the top tourist attraction. The construction industry was robust, and exports in 2001 made up more than 13 percent of all U.S. exports. Most of these exports fell into four categories: electronics, industrial machines and computers, chemicals and petrochemicals, and transportation equipment. Also significant were retail trade, health services, and some manufacturing. Nor did the Texas economy suffer as badly as the rest of the country during the recession that began in 2008. Houston proved to be the most important job generating city in the nation, recovering 230.5 percent of the jobs it lost during the recession by March of 2013. Second was Dallas at 164.2 percent. These results were attributed to the lessons Texas learned from the economic downturn of the early 1980s: avoid overbuilding the real estate market and avoid firing too many workers in key economic sectors like the energy industry.

The aerospace industry continued to develop. In the 1990s, NASA partnered with other agencies, private firms, and Texas universities to develop new methods of exploring outer space. The airline industry in Texas continued to grow as well. American Airlines, which had relocated its headquarters from the New York area to the Dallas–Fort Worth area, had set up the first of a series of hubs at Dallas–Fort Worth airport in 1981. Meanwhile, entrepreneur Herb Kelleher's discount carrier, Southwest Airlines, had, by 1989, amassed annual revenues of $1 billion. It would go on to become the "most consistently profitable airline" in the United States.

Its profitability was linked with the carrier's expansion outside the Texas market. In 1979, Southwest made its first flight to a city outside of Texas, going from Houston to New Orleans. Interstate travel from Dallas Love Field, the airline's home airport, proved more difficult, though, with the passage of the Wright Amendment in the U.S. Congress in December 1979. That legislation, authored by Rep. Jim Wright, a Fort Worth Democrat, aimed to protect the recently opened DFW Airport from competition, and it limited flights out of Love Field to airports in Texas and only in the four states bordering Texas: Louisiana, Arkansas, Oklahoma, and New Mexico. In the early 1980s, service out of cities other than Dallas opened to West Coast destinations including Los Angeles and San Francisco. Expanded service to the Midwest, the South, and the Northeast followed in the 1980s and 1990s. Congress passed legislation to repeal the Wright Amendment in 2006. Because its business model involves a point-to-point system and not a hub system, Southwest has been able to amass thirty-nine consecutive years of profitability as of 2012.

Other Texans with a vision made their fortunes in a wide variety of ways. West Texas native Mary Kay Ash started a modest beauty business in Dallas in the 1960s with a formula for face cream and parlayed it into an industry bringing in $2 billion annually. Her business model afforded women an opportunity to earn an income by becoming sales consultants; Mary Kay products were sold through at-home parties, not in department or drug stores.

Urbanization and the Income Divide

As some Texans parlayed their visions into corporate enterprises, others found employment in the major cities. According to the 2010 census, Texas had the second highest number of urban residents in the nation, lagging behind California, but it also had the highest number of rural residents. This meant that fourteen states and the District of Columbia had a higher percentage of urban residents. By 2010, 84.7 percent of Texans lived in urban areas, and eight out of every ten new jobs were located in only five "magnet" cities: Dallas, Fort Worth, Austin, San Antonio, and Houston. In these cities, the median household income ranged between $40,000 and $49,000, whereas in the rest of Texas it was $50,920 a year, compared with a national average of $52,762. A very different story, though, must be told for the wealthy suburbs fringing the state's major metropolitan areas. For example, the median household income for Sugarland outside of Houston was over $97,000 while Flower Mound outside of Dallas was over $123,000.

Metrics from 2009 for per capita income, meanwhile, give a sense of the poverty problems in Texas. The state's average per capita income was $38,609 and the nation's was $39,635. The five poorest counties in Texas—Hidalgo, Maverick, Zapata, Zavila, and Starr—are all located in the Rio Grande Valley and have per capita incomes ranging from $16,433 to $20,509.

Organized labor had been in a decline since the 1970s, as workers increasingly entered fields without strong unionizing traditions—fields such as retail trade and government—and as employment shrank in jobs associated with unions, such as oil and manufacturing. From the early 1970s to the early 1990s, the percentage of the unionized labor force dropped by more than half, from 47 to 21 percent. Other factors were involved as well, including a political climate less receptive to unionizing, corporate practices such as contracting with outside firms and individuals, and development of the computer and other industries in which management proved resistant and workers unresponsive to labor organizing.

NAFTA

One controversial economic measure in this era was a national free trade agreement that promised to impact Texas more than it would other states. In 1992, President George H. W. Bush joined Canadian and Mexican leaders in signing the North American Free Trade Agreement (NAFTA). This agreement promised a gradual reduction of trade barriers throughout North America, making it easier and more economical for the three nations to move their goods across the borders. It greatly altered U.S.–Mexican trade, and most of that trade centered in or moved through Texas.

Critics feared that the increased Mexican truck traffic would strain the state's highways and that there would be environmental costs, especially along the border where Mexico's *maquiladoras* (industrial plants) multiplied under the new agreement. These *maquiladoras* were notorious polluters with poor working conditions and very low wages.

But the pact did significantly increase commerce between Texas and Mexico, infusing money and thousands of jobs into the state's economy. One study by the Texas Public Policy Foundation showed that trade with both Mexico and Canada had increased Texas exports to these countries by $16 billion between 1993 and 1999. Further, 70 percent of all American exports to Mexico moved through Texas. These trends continued into the twenty-first century with 86 percent of all U.S. rail traffic into Mexico going through Texas and 67 percent of all truck

October 7, 1992 signing ceremony for NAFTA. President Carlos Salinas of Mexico, President George H. W. Bush, Prime Minister Brian Mulroney of Canada, standing left to right; Mexican Secretary of Commerce and Industrial Development Jaime Serra Puche, U.S. Trade Representative Carla Hills, and Canadian Minister of International Trade Michael Wilson, seated left to right.

traffic going through Texas. Indeed, three of the top five ports of entry on the U.S.–Mexico border are located in Texas (Laredo, Hidalgo, and El Paso). In 2012, approximately $195 billion in goods was traded between Texas and Mexico, or almost 35 percent of the total U.S.–Mexico trade for the same year. Between 2004 and 2012, trade between Texas and Mexico increased by almost 109 percent.

Ranching and Farming in Texas

The three components of an earlier state economy—farming, ranching, and oil—seemed far removed from the lives of most Texans. Large operations and small remained, however. The fabled King Ranch, invigorated by oil and gas royalties totaling more than $1 billion between 1945 and 1994, had become a corporation with its own exploratory oil and gas division and international cattle operation. Most Texas ranches were far more modest in scope, even economically marginal, but the flush oil years of the 1970s and early 1980s had stimulated the ranching business in some areas of the state. A study of Washington County, a portion of Stephen F. Austin's old colonies, showed oilmen and other wealthy investors buying up ranches after World War II and making improvements to the land and to the breeding of the cattle. This "rural gentrification" became more pronounced in the 1970s, as wealthy Houston residents continued to buy Washington County farms and ranches and raise cattle, often consulting with local agricultural extension agents. There was a certain extravagance and simple hobbyist mentality to much of the activity in the late 1970s and early 1980s, as the "mink and manure set" gave lavish parties to show off their pricey purebred cattle. The phenomenon was fueled primarily by their ability to sink large amounts of money into ranching. But many of them did preserve and improve the ranch lands and participate in the modernization of ranching practices.

By the 1990s, only about 1 percent of Texas workers earned their livings directly from the soil, and the number of people in the ranching industry had dwindled as well. Nevertheless, Texas continues to claim an important role nationally in farming and ranching. In 1999, even though the number of Texas farms had dropped by more than 40 percent since 1940, the 227,000 remaining constituted the largest number of farms in any American state, as did the land they covered—131 million acres. They also were valued at more than 18 times their 1950 prices. Texas continued to lead all states in cotton production in most annual tallies, producing one-fourth of all cotton grown in the United States and exporting large amounts to Mexico, Japan, and South Korea. In the meantime, ranchers were contributing almost 65 percent of the agricultural revenues in Texas, with almost all of the 254 counties ranking cattle first among their agricultural revenues. The state was also unmatched in the United States not only in beef cattle but also in cattle "on feed," wool, mohair, goats, sheep, and lambs.

These achievements required great diligence and modern approaches. Many people were surprised to learn that more cattle were being raised in East Texas and more cotton grown in West Texas, the latter thanks to extensive irrigation. But heat and drought, frigid and changeable winters, rains at the wrong time, the heavy expenses of maintaining a farm or a ranch—all conspired to keep farmers and ranchers sweating out their profit margins. Those ranchers who could do so depended on oil production on their ranch land to help finance their livestock and other agricultural losses.

With a continued increase in mechanization and improved equipment, many of the old jobs of farm and ranch workers were completed more efficiently. State-of-the-art working pens on cattle ranches, for example, made herd management much easier. Such technology made possible working a herd of 300 cows and 300 calves in half a day, a job that would have taken a full day or more earlier in the century.

The small segment of the population still intimately tied to the land, however, also faced the vagaries of the weather in ways the majority of Texans could no longer fully appreciate. In the extended drought of 1994–96, farmers lost their crops and ranchers sold off their cattle, but the cattle market then became saturated and prices fell. In the meantime, the feed on which ranchers depended in dry times for their remaining herds grew more expensive. A frigid winter in 1996–97 compounded problems for many, and when it was followed by more drought conditions in 1998, 1999, and 2000, farmers and ranchers faced billions of dollars of agricultural losses, including an estimated $515 million in 2000 alone. Some gave up on staple crops; even though cotton remained big business in Texas in 2002, farmers could not sell it for even half of what it cost many of them to grow it. Drought conditions returned in 2005, and continued to plague the state for the next six years. In 2011 the losses from the drought totaled $5.2 billion, a record high. That same year was the driest in the state's history with just 11.18 inches of rain.

In the Rio Grande Valley, continuing drought combined with the Mexican government's failure to deliver on a shared water treaty turned the Rio Grande into a trickle and left farmers' fields high and dry. Third-generation farmers converted citrus groves to goat pastures and cotton, vegetable, and sugarcane fields into grain sorghum fields, the latter a good dry-weather crop but one that produces little profit. Almost half of the valley's irrigated cropland had become dry farmland in only six years. Bud Wentz, a long-term farmer outside Brownsville, told a reporter, he no longer cared about preserving his farm for the next generation. He expressed an eagerness to walk away if only he could sell for a fair price.

Most held on, however, and the overall productivity remained impressive, with agriculture generating $20 billion of business in the state in 2010. The Texas economy itself performed well that year, given a boost by improved export markets and by a new upturn in oil and gas activity. Unemployment rates were lower than they had been in more than twenty years. Texans continued to look for ways to innovate and diversify in a new world in which "knowledge work" and service work predominated, the former based on the use, manipulation, interpretation, and transmission of information. The economic growth of the cities, however, generated new problems, including how the cities could absorb the new immigrants and continue to provide jobs. Further, the social and economic disparities between the vital cities and the rest of the state became more pronounced, leading Pampa representative Warren Chisum to note that rural Texas faced a significant crisis. In the meantime, Texas government officials sought to address the shifting contours of Texans' lives and work.

Tending the Land

In the last few decades of the twentieth century, the federal and state governments passed legislation reflecting a new awareness of the need to preserve and protect the land and its resources. In this, they were aided or spurred by national environmental organizations such as the Sierra Club and Audubon Society and also by local Texas grassroots organizations concerned about vanishing species, an altered landscape, and air, ground, and water pollution. In particular, water pollution, shortages, and anticipated shortages began to come to the fore as a major issue for twenty-first-century Texas.

The Environment

The environment in Texas had been transformed since the first Europeans traversed the land. Indeed, the Texas environment was much altered and diminished from the days when the Spanish explored its grasslands and flowing rivers. Texas in the 1700s had over 12 million acres of Blackland Prairie, over 16 million acres of bottomland hardwood forests, and over 12 million acres of coastal wetlands. For example, most of the Big Thicket, a biological treasure trove in East Texas, which had gained federal protection as the first national biological preserve in 1974, was home to "relict" plants, located nowhere else and nurtured by the unique combination of soil and humidity. In the late 1990s, the preserve provided sustenance for hundreds of bird and plant species, as well as fifty kinds of reptiles and sixty mammal species. By the late 1990s, the prairies, forests, and wetlands had been reduced by more than half, endangering a range of plants and animals—from ocelots to brown pelicans, from red-cockaded woodpeckers to Kemp's ridley sea turtles.

Texas had boasted the largest expanses of prairies in the United States, with as many as 300 native plant species and with great stands of Indian grass, switchgrass, big bluestem, and little bluestem predominating. Yet even on the remaining prairie acreage, plowing had destroyed the native grasses.

The picture was far from uniformly grim. Environmental organizations were seeking to preserve and expand the pockets of native grasses, rich in nutrients and part of a healthy ecosystem. The East Texas forests had benefited from efforts by the U.S. Forest Service and the Civilian Conservation Corps of the 1930s, as well as improved timbering practices by companies in the late twentieth century, so significant reforestation occurred in some of the areas already stripped or "farmed out."

In addition, farmers, ranchers, and even suburbanites had worked with biologists, game wardens, and other state and federal officials on stewardship of their land and its resources. The federal Endangered Species Act of 1973 with its rules for habitat protection had not always been popular in the state, as landowners struggled with requirements that sometimes seemed harsh and unreasonable. Many landowners were deeply committed to caring for their property but felt constrained by government regulations made at a distance. Yet good land-use and wildlife management practices, whether imposed by law or sought out and adopted, had yielded thriving wild turkey and deer populations and made Texas the premier bird-watching area in the world.

The government and citizens' groups tried to stop or reduce industry pollution in Texas as aging smokestacks continued to belch out sulfur dioxide and nitrogen oxide compounds. For example, in late 2001, the Central Texas environmental group Neighbors for Neighbors spurred the state to investigate Alcoa, Inc.'s Rockdale plant by charging that it was releasing unsafe amounts of these chemicals into the air, then in 2002 joined a lawsuit to force the plant to spend hundreds of millions of dollars to clean up emissions. More recently, by

2014, air pollution from oil and gas production in the Eagle Ford Shale had become a major challenge for south Texans. A toxic, yellow-brown haze is common in the 400 mile wide, 50 mile long swath of territory. Among the chemicals released into the atmosphere include hydrogen sulfide, the carcinogen benzene, sulfur dioxide, carbon monoxide, and carbon disulfide poisons that cause nausea, nosebleeds, headaches, body rashes, respiratory problems, neurological damage, and cancer in area residents. State officials have shown a greater interest in protecting the industry from regulation than in protecting people from health problems.

Even relatively benign development, such as light, "clean" industry, or housing, put a strain on those cities and counties that were burgeoning; officials and neighbors of the new development struggled with everything from traffic problems and school overcrowding to loss of natural habitat for animals and plants. But increasingly, the greatest strain became how to ensure enough clean water.

Water Challenges

Water quality and availability in the late twentieth century became a chief concern for Texans, from the wetlands of the coast to the *playas* (shallow rainwater pools of the High Plains far to the northwest), from the state's many southward flowing rivers to its aquifers, the ancient, shallow underground seas fed by rainwater. The legislature, prodded by Lieutenant Governor Bob Bullock, slowly awoke to the issue, in 1997 passing Senate Bill 1, which split the state into sixteen water-planning areas. In each area, a regional water-planning group would project water needs and strategies for the next fifty years; all of these plans were consolidated in 2002 and updated every five years.

The coastal wetlands, in particular, had suffered from the industrial development of the twentieth century. The Texas gulf coast shared with the Louisiana coast a distinction as "the petrochemical center of the nation," the Texas portion claiming almost 60 percent of American petrochemical capacity. Galveston Bay, the seventh largest estuary in the United States, remained a busy port and the site of extensive petroleum refining and chemical production. Although the Texas Solid Waste Disposal Act of 1969 helped protect Galveston and other gulf bays from direct discharge of industrial waste, this estuary, also the location of a vital fisheries industry, continued to absorb pollution from the Houston Ship Channel, which connects it to the city of Houston. The channel, still narrow and shallow despite mid-twentieth-century attempts to improve it, continued to be the site of oil spills and other freighter, barge, and tanker accidents and collisions, many of the damaged ships carrying poisonous cargo.

Far away on Texas's High Plains, the *playas* hosted more than a hundred species of migrant waterfowl, such as lesser Canada geese and mallards, and were home to sandhill cranes and other bird species. Almost half of the *playa* region was in Texas; beginning in the 1980s, the United States, Mexico, and Canada shared an agreement to protect these sites.

Major concern centered on Texas rivers. By 2002, some had appeared on lists of the most endangered U.S. rivers, among them the Clear Creek, the Trinity, the San Jacinto, the Concho, and the Guadalupe and its tributaries. In the last case, the environmental group American Rivers charged, the state was allowing too much of the Guadalupe's water to be used by urban areas, industries, and farmers, thereby adding to the ravages of drought and not only affecting water quality and flow but also doing damage to the coastal estuaries that normally received that flow. In 1993 the Rio Grande, a vital water source for Mexico, New Mexico, and Texas and tied with the St. Lawrence for the fourth longest river in the nation, was named one of the top ten endangered rivers in the United States and compared with a sewer for its high level of filth and contamination. In its more than 40,000 square miles of drainage in Texas, it provided irrigation for the cotton, pecan, and vegetable crops of West Texas and the citrus fruits, cotton, and vegetables of the lower Rio Grande valley in South Texas. But dams, drought, and too many people relying on what water existed took their toll. In addition, the proliferation of *maquiladoras* along the river border meant more human crowding, with inadequate sanitary conditions, and more industrial water and air pollution, with associated hazardous waste disposal issues. In 2013, the San Saba river was listed as the third most endangered river in the United States. Its troubles resulted because area farmers were pumping too much water from the river for irrigation purposes, so reported American Rivers.

These water woes were exacerbated by the treaty struggle between the United States and Mexico that had Rio Grande valley farmers worried and incensed. A 1944 agreement ensured the United States would receive from Mexico one third of the water from six tributaries to the Rio Grande, amounting to at least 114 billion gallons. Conversely, the United States was to grant to Mexico water from the Colorado River on an annual basis defined as at least 1.5 million acre-feet of water. An acre-foot was the amount of water required to inundate an acre to the depth of a foot. By 1950, the United States was fulfilling its part of the agreement. But over the years between 1944 and 2002, Mexico built up a huge water debt while increasing irrigated acreage and claiming deferments based on drought conditions. In 2013, the debt stood at 471,000 acre-feet.

In the meantime, the Rio Grande shrank dramatically in just twenty years (1982–2002), its flow at El Paso reduced from 33.39 cubic meters per second to 11.79 cubic meters. In the spring of 2002, the river simply ran dry before reaching its gulf outlet near Brownsville.

Aquifers presented an equally troubling picture. Texas was blessed with an abundance of these underground water sources—nine major ones (including the Edwards Aquifer) and twenty smaller ones spreading under four-fifths of the state. The problems with their depletion were illustrated when businessman Ron Pucek tapped the Edwards Aquifer, which spread through a maze of channels, fractures and limestone formations underlying nine central Texas counties. In 1991, Pucek spent $1 million drilling "the world's largest water well" into the aquifer to create the 85-acre Living Waters Artesian Springs Catfish Farm, confident that he could do this under the "right of capture" on which Texas water law is based: the idea that a landowner can draw as much water as he can pump from underneath his land.

In the same year, a scientific study showed that the Edwards Aquifer was being rapidly depleted and warned what would happen if a drought of the severity of the 1950s struck central Texas again. San Antonio alone made heavy demands upon the aquifer for its municipal water supply. Although the right of capture had made some sense in an earlier era when untapped ground water could not be accurately mapped or measured, most states had adopted more cautious approaches to groundwater supplies. Though he ceased operations after just one year in business, finally, in 2000, after almost a decade of legal wrangling, Pucek sold the catfish farm and most of his water rights for $9 million to the trustees of the San Antonio water system. Legally, he had retained the right of capture, and he walked away a financial winner by selling the water rights.

As Texas entered the new century, the tapping of groundwater, primarily for farmer's irrigation and use by cities but also for ranching, mining, and manufacturing, was still depleting the aquifers faster than they could refill through the natural slow percolation of rainwater. The largest aquifer, the Ogallala Aquifer underpinning the Texas High Plains, had been pierced by more than 50,000 irrigation wells. Some scientists have estimated that the natural refilling of the Ogallala would take 6,000 years. In 2013, other scientists estimated the aquifer risked going dry by 2070 were significant conservation measures not implemented.

Water projections were grim in many areas of the state. In Williamson County, one of the three Texas counties among the ten fastest-growing in the United States, it was estimated that by 2050, the county would face a massive shortfall of potable water. Planners were considering a variety of costly options, including piping water from the Carrizo-Wilcox Aquifer. But this would require landowners in nearby counties to grant pumping rights, a risky proposition for the grantees. Though the state has a Water Plan, one that relies on a mixture of conservation and new reservoir construction, it does not have the funding identified to pay for the necessary measures. The stakes remained high in 2014. Architects of the plan acknowledged that the state "does not and will not have enough water to meet the needs of its people, its businesses, and its agricultural enterprises." Should a drought as bad as the one in the 1950s hit the state, then Texans would lose money, approximately $116 billion, over a million jobs, and would face a population decline of approximately 1.4 million people.

Conclusion

In the last two decades of the twentieth century, recognition of old realities and new shaped a Texas for the twenty-first century. The historical experience of all who called Texas home took on greater meaning, diversity was acknowledged, and members of groups formerly excluded from political power began to share in that power. New ways of making money developed to reshape the Texas economy, but the old economic staples of oil, ranching, and farming remained integral to the economy through ups and downs and to Texans' sense of identity. An old independent spirit wary of government had to be balanced with challenges born of rapid, shifting population growth and the intricacies of state–federal relations. The land and its resources no longer seemed endless and therefore needed renewed care and communal effort.

All of these changes brought to the fore issues of Texas identity, and Texas myth: the stories about Texas identity that Texans—and non-Texans—have created or absorbed as part of their understanding of the world. Of course, these stories had been shaped through the region's history in a number of ways, from "Texians" embracing images of their land as a cradle of liberty in the Revolutionary era to the conscious adoption of western images by framers of the Texas Centennial. Stereotypes ranged from stalwart pioneers, Texas Rangers, ranchers, and cowboys to larger-than-life businessmen engaged in boom-and-bust enterprise. Key elements included an emphasis on rugged individuality and a rather testy and exploitative frontier mentality.

But myths evolve. By the twenty-first century, some of the old myths have been exposed as skewed in favor of the group getting to tell the story; for example, many Anglos over the course of the nineteenth and twentieth centuries accepted and transmitted negative characterizations of Mexicans and Tejanos. Some myths can be seen to lack the basis in truth they may have had in an earlier era—for example, the images of Texas as having limitless land and resources. Some can be affirmed and adapted: If Texas is distinctive as a place, then its environment is worth protecting and preserving.

Many of the changes described in this chapter, then, are attempts to rewrite the myth, to address old ways of thinking that turned out to be wrong, no longer viable, or true in a different, more complex sense. In the process, Texas has retained a distinctive dynamic.

The Texas entering the twenty-first century, then, was poised to further sharpen and enhance its identity as a distinctive land of opportunity and diversity. It remained immense with possibilities for new economic, social, and political visions, new forms of innovation, new community configurations. Possessed of a rich, checkered, and complex history, it remained a place to, in the words of republic president Anson Jones, "commence the world anew."

Suggested Readings

Information on this era comes largely from the *Texas Almanac* (2001 and 2012-2013), the 2010 U.S. Census, and from newspaper articles listed in the bibliography; much of the history of Texas in the late twentieth and early twenty-first centuries remains to be written. For discussions of Texas myth, see "Texas Values/Texas Future," in the Philosophical Society of Texas *Proceedings of the Annual Meeting at Austin, Dec. 3–5, 1999,* and Robert F. O'Connor, ed., *Texas Myths* (1986).

Political Realignments

For information on the governors of this period, see Brian McCall, *The Power of the Texas Governor: Connally to Bush* (2009); Carolyn Barta, *Bill Clements: Texian to His Toenails* (1996); Jan Reid, *Let the People In: The Life and Times of Ann Richards* (2012). The best books on George H. W. Bush include Herbert S. Parmet, *George Bush: The Life of a Lone Star Yankee* (1997); John Robert Greene, *The Presidency of George Bush* (2000); Michael Schaller, *Right Turn: American Life in the Reagan-Bush Era, 1980–1992* (2006); Kevin Phillips, *American Dynasty: Aristocracy, Fortune, and the Politics of Deceit in the House of Bush* (2004). For background on George W. Bush see Julian E. Zelizer, ed., *The Presidency of George W. Bush: A First Historical Assessment* (2010); George C. Edwards III and Desmond S. King, *The Polarized Presidency of George W. Bush* (2007); David R. Farber, *The Rise and Fall of Modern American Conservatism* (2010).

The *New Handbook of Texas* includes useful information on this period on such topics as education and the prison system. For a recent history of prisons in Texas see Robert Perkinson, *Texas Tough: The Rise of America's Prison Empire* (2010).

Useful works that deal with Texas women in politics during this era include *Capitol Women,* by Nancy Baker Jones and Ruthe Winegarten (2000); *Texas Women Frontier to Future* (1998), by Ann Fears Crawford and Crystal Sasse Ragsdale; and *Claytie and the Lady: Ann Richards, Gender, and Politics in Texas* (1994), by Sue Tollison-Rinehart and Jeanie R. Stanley.

Social and Cultural Diversity

For changing concepts of Texas identity, see Leigh Clemons, *Branding Texas: Performing Culture in the Lone Star State* (2008). For one account of Mexican family land claims, see Abel Rubio's *Stolen Heritage: A Mexican-American's Rediscovery of His Family's Lost Land Grant* (1998). Information on the Tiguas appears in Jeffrey M. Schulze's "The Rediscovery of the Tiguas: Federal Recognition and Indianness in the Twentieth Century" in *Southwestern Historical Quarterly* (2001). For details on gays and lesbians in Texas, see James T. Sears, *Rebels, Rubyfruit, and Rhinestones: Queering Space in the Stonewall South* (2001). Dale Carpenter, *Flagrant Conduct: The Story of Lawrence v. Texas: How a Bedroom Arrest Decriminalized Gay Americans* (2012).

Developing Economic Opportunity

In addition to the *Texas Almanac* and newspapers, the *New Handbook of Texas* contains numerous helpful entries on public and private enterprises in Texas— see, for example, "AMR Corporation" and "Southwest Airlines." Michael Dell's story can be found in his *Direct from Dell: Strategies that Revolutionized an Industry* (1999).

Newspaper articles chronicle the challenges of farming, but ranching continues to draw loving book-length appraisals; see, for example, Lawrence Clayton's

Contemporary Ranches of Texas (2001) and Kathleen Jo Ryan's *Deep in the Heart of Texas: Texas Ranchers in Their Own Words* (1999), from which some of the quotes in this section were drawn. Also useful is Mark Friedberger's "'Mink and Manure': Rural Gentrification and Cattle Raising in Southeast Texas, 1945–1992" in *Southwestern Historical Quarterly* (1999).

Tending the Land

A good general source is Richard C. Bartlett's *Saving the Best of Texas* (1995). Information on Ron Pucek's catfish farm and other environmental matters can be found on the Internet at the Edwards Aquifer home page, *www.edwardsaquifer .net*. Consult the *New Handbook of Texas* for a variety of related articles—see, for example, "Environmental Health."

Texas Chief Executives

Governors of Spanish Texas

Domingo Terán de los Ríos	1691–92
Gregorio de Salinas Varona	1692–97
Francisco Cuerbo y Valdez	1698–1702
Mathías de Aguirre	1703–05
Martín de Alarcón	1705–08
Simón Padilla y Córdova	1708–12
Pedro Fermín de Echevérs y Subisa	1712–14
Juan Valdez	1714–16
Martín de Alarcón	1716–19
Joseph de Azlor, Marqués de Aguayo	1719–22
Fernando Pérez de Almazán	1722–27
Melchor de Media Villa y Azcona	1727–30
Juan Antonio Bustillos y Ceballos	1730–34
Manuel de Sandoval	1734–36
Carlos Benites Franquis de Lugo	1736–37
Prudencio de Orobio y Basterra	1737–41
Tomás Felipe Wintuisen	1741–43
Justo Boneo y Morales	1743–44
Francisco García Larios	1744–48
Pedro del Barrio Junco y Espriella	1748–51
Jacinto de Barrios y Jáuregui	1751–59
Angel Martos y Navarrete	1759–66
Hugo Oconor	1767–70
Barón de Ripperdá	1770–78

Domingo Cabello	1778–86
Bernardo Bonavía	1786 (appointed, but did not serve)
Rafael Martínez Pacheco	1786–90
Manuel Muñoz	1790–99
José Irigoyen	1798–1800 (appointed, but did not serve)
Juan Bautista de Elguézabal	1799–1805
Antonio Cordero y Bustamante	1805–08
Manuel María de Salcedo	1808–13
Juan Bautista Casas	Jan.–Mar., 1811 (insurgent governor)
José Bernardo Gutiérrez de Lara	Apr.–Aug., 1813 (insurgent governor)
José Alvarez de Toledo	Aug. 1813 (insurgent governor)
Cristóbal Domínguez	1813–14
Ignacio Pérez	1816–17
Manuel Pardo	May–Oct., 1817
Antonio Martínez	1817–22 (continued to serve after Mexican independence)

Governors of Provincial Texas

José Félix Trespalacios	1822–23
Luciano García	1823

Governors of Coahuila y Texas

Rafael Gonzales	1824–26
José Ignacio de Arizpe	1826
Victor Blanco	1826–27
José Ignacio de Arizpe	1827
José María Viesca y Montes	1827–31
José María Letona	1831–32 (died in office)
Rafael Eca y Músquiz	1832–33
Juan Martín de Veramendi	1833 (died in office)
Francisco Vidaurri y Villaseñor	1833–34
Juan José Elguézabal	1834–35
José María Cantú	1835
Marciel Borrego	1835
Agustín Viesca	1835
Miguel Falcón	1835
Bartolomé de Cárdenas	1835
Rafael Eca y Músquiz	1835

Provisional Governor of Texas during Texas Revolution

Henry Smith	Nov. 1835–Mar. 1836

Presidents of the Republic of Texas, 1836–1846

David G. Burnet	Mar.–Oct., 1836 (interim)
Sam Houston	Oct. 1836–Dec. 1838
Mirabeau B. Lamar	Dec. 1838–Dec. 1841
Sam Houston	Dec. 1841–Dec. 1844
Anson Jones	Dec. 1844–Feb. 1846

Governors of the State of Texas

J. Pinckney Henderson	Feb. 1846–Dec. 1847
George T. Wood	Dec. 1847–Dec. 1849
Peter Hansborough Bell	Dec. 1849–Nov. 1853
J. W. Henderson	Nov. 1853–Dec. 1853
Elisha M. Pease	Dec. 1853–Dec. 1857
Hardin R. Runnels	Dec. 1857–Dec. 1859
Sam Houston	Dec. 21, 1859–Mar. 1861 (removed from office by Secession Convention)
Edward Clark	Mar. 1861–Nov. 1861 (appointed to office by Secession Convention)
Francis R. Lubbock	Nov. 1861–Nov. 1863
Pendleton Murrah	Nov. 1863–June 1865
Andrew J. Hamilton	June 1865–Aug. 1866 (appointed by President Andrew Johnson)
James W. Throckmorton	Aug. 1866–Aug. 1867 (removed from office by Gen. Philip H. Sheridan during Reconstruction)
Elisha M. Pease	Aug. 1867–Sept. 1869 (appointed by Gen. Philip H. Sheridan but resigned in protest of radical Reconstruction policies)
Edmund J. Davis	Jan. 1870–Jan. 1874
Richard Coke	Jan. 1874–Dec. 1876
Richard B. Hubbard	Dec. 1876–Jan. 1879
Oran M. Roberts	Jan. 1879–Jan. 1883
John Ireland	Jan. 1883–Jan. 1887
Lawrence Sullivan Ross	Jan. 1887–Jan. 1891
James Stephen Hogg	Jan. 1891–Jan. 1895
Charles A. Culberson	Jan. 1895–Jan. 1899

Joseph D. Sayers	Jan. 1899–Jan. 1903
S. W. T. Lanham	Jan. 1903–Jan. 1907
Thomas Mitchell Campbell	Jan. 1907–Jan. 1911
Oscar Branch Colquitt	Jan. 1911–Jan. 1915
James E. Ferguson	Jan. 1915–Aug. 1917
William Pettus Hobby	Aug. 1917–Jan. 1921
Pat Morris Neff	Jan. 1921–Jan. 1925
Miriam A. Ferguson	Jan. 1925–Jan. 1927
Dan Moody	Jan. 1927–Jan. 1931
Ross S. Sterling	Jan. 1931–Jan. 1933
Miriam A. Ferguson	Jan. 1933–Jan. 1935
James V. Allred	Jan. 1935–Jan. 1939
W. Lee O'Daniel	Jan. 1939–Aug. 1941
Coke R. Stevenson	Aug. 1941–Jan. 1947
Beauford H. Jester	Jan. 1947–July 1949
Allan Shivers	July 1949–Jan. 1957
Price Daniel	Jan. 1957–Jan. 1963
John Connally	Jan. 1963–Jan. 1969
Preston Smith	Jan. 1969–Jan. 1973
Dolph Briscoe	Jan. 1973–Jan. 1979
William P. Clements	Jan. 1979–Jan. 1983
Mark White	Jan. 1983–Jan. 1987
William P. Clements	Jan. 1987–Jan. 1991
Ann W. Richards	Jan. 1991–Jan. 1995
George W. Bush	Jan. 1995–Dec. 2000
James Richard Perry	Dec. 2000–Jan. 2015
Greg Abbott	Jan. 2015–present

Sources: Vito Alessio Robles, Coahuila y Texas desde la consumación de la Independencia hasta el Tratado de Paz de Guadalupe Hidalgo, 2 vols. (1945, reprint, Mexico: Editorial Porrua, 1979); Arturo Berrueto González, comp., *Diccionario biográfico de Coahuila* (Saltillo: Gobierno del Estado, 1999); H. P. N. Gammel, comp., *The Laws of Texas, 1822–1897*, vol. 1 (Austin: Gammel Book Co., 1898); "About Texas," Texas State Library website, http://www.tsl.state.tx.us/ref/abouttx/prerepub.html; *Handbook of Texas Online*, http://www.tshaonline.org/

Comparative Population Statistics

Year	Province of Texas[1]	New Spain[1]
1731–39	1,499	
1740–49	3,203	
1750–59	3,683	
1760–69	3,436	
1770–74	3,076	
1780–89	2,919	
1790		4,636,074
1790–99	3,316	
1803		5,764,731
1805–09	4,329	
1810		6,122,354
1815–19	3,778	
1820		6,204,000

	Department of Texas[1]	Mexico[2]
1834–35	23,621	6,854,193

	Republic of Texas[3]	
1845	125,000	7,263,246

	State of Texas[4]	United States[4]
1850	212,592	23,191,876
1860	604,215	31,443,321
1870	818,579	38,558,371
1880	1,591,749	50,189,209
1890	2,235,527	62,979,766
1900	3,048,710	76,212,168
1910	3,896,542	92,228,496
1920	4,663,228	106,021,537
1930	5,824,715	123,202,624
1940	6,414,824	132,164,569
1950	7,711,194	151,325,798
1960	9,579,677	179,323,175
1970	11,196,730	203,211,926
1980	14,229,191	226,545,805
1990	16,986,335	248,765,170
2000	20,851,820	281,421,906
2010	25,145,561	308,745,538

Sources: [1]Colonial-period estimates exclude independent Indian groups, which Meacham estimates to have declined in population from 35,600 in the seventeenth century to 20,100 early in the nineteenth century. Movement of Indians in and out of missions, the opening and closing of new mission fields, and the transfer of troops all kept the colonial-period population in flux. Estimates based on the work of Tina Laurel Meacham, "The Population of Spanish and Mexican Texas, 1716–1836" (Ph.D. diss., The University of Texas at Austin, 2000).

[2]"Population: 1821–1910," *Encyclopedia of Mexico: History, Society & Culture* (Chicago: Fitzroy Dearborn, 1997).

[3]"Census and Census Records," *Handbook of Texas Online*, http://www.tshaonline.org/handbook/online /articles/ulc01

[4]http://www.tsl.state.tx.us/ref/abouttx/census.html

Glossary of Spanish Terms

acequia: irrigation ditch

adelantado: governor with broad powers; usually reserved for the leader of a royally chartered expedition

agregado: additional or secondary settler

alcalde mayor: district magistrate; lieutenant governor

alcalde ordinario: municipal magistrate

alguacil mayor: constable, sheriff, jailer

ayuntamiento: municipal government

bracero: from *brazo,* arm; one who works with his hands; term applied to field laborers, particularly those who came to the United States during and after World War II

capitulación: royal charter

casas reales: town hall

castas: general term for mixed-bloods

compadrazgo: ritual kinship, godparenthood

corregidor: district magistrate

criado: reared or raised; a servant who is part of the household

criollo: American-born Spaniard

dictamen: official opinion

diezmero: a tithe collector

empresario: colonization agent; one who contracts with the government to introduce families into Texas

encomienda: grant of Indian tributaries to a Spaniard as a reward for services in an entrada

entrada: conquest, colonization, or settlement expedition

escribano: public scribe, notary

gachupín: derogatory term for European Spaniards, particularly popular at the end of the colonial period

genízaro: New Mexican term for a detribalized Indian incorporated into Spanish society

gente de razón: people of reason; term applied to all members of colonial society excepting Indians *grito:* yell, scream, cry; a political declaration

hacendado: the owner of a hacienda

hacienda: large landed estate producing both livestock and crops for market

hidalgo: literally, "son of something"; lowest rung of Spanish nobility

intendencia: late colonial administrative unit based on French model intended to replace the old Hapsburg colonial structure

intendente: administrative head of an intendencia

junta: committee, governing directorate

justicia mayor: district magistrate

labor: tilling or plowing; an agricultural field; a Mexican-era unit of land measure of approximately 177.1 acres

mayordomo: overseer

mesteña or mesteño: unbranded stock

mestizaje: term applied to the process of race mixing among the European, African, and Indian populations of Spanish America

mestizo: offspring of a Spaniard and an Indian

patrón: master

peninsular: European-born Spaniard

peón: lowest category of permanent *hacienda* employee

porción: portion or allotment; long lot along the Rio Grande originally surveyed in 1767

primeros pobladores: first or original settlers

procurador: municipal attorney

pueblo: village, settlement, people; in New Mexico and Arizona, term applied to the various town-dwelling Indian tribes

quinto real: royal fifth; Spanish Crown's portion of treasure taken in an expedition or precious metals mined

rancho: term for a mixed-use, small-to-medium rural property that in Texas referred to a large livestock estate

reducción: gathering of nonsedentary Indians into a mission community

regidor: alderman, town councilman

regimiento: town council

república de españoles: one of two major divisions of Spanish colonial society composed of all non-Indians covered by a separate code of law

república de indios: one of two major divisions of Spanish colonial society composed of all Indians under Spanish rule covered by a separate code of law

requerimiento: summons, demand; formal statement of Spanish right to dominion in the New World, required to be read to Indians before war could be made on them

sistema de castas: ordering of Spanish American society according to racial-ethnic characteristics

sitio: place; a unit of land equivalent to approximately 4,500 acres of grazing land

subdelegado: district magistrate under the intendencia system

Tejano: a Texan of Mexican heritage

vaquero: cowboy

vecino: citizen

visitador: inspector general

Bibliography

Abbott, E. C., and Helena Huntington Smith. *We Pointed Them North: Recollections of a Cowpuncher.* Norman: University of Oklahoma Press, 1955.

Alessio Robles, Vito. *Coahuila y Tejas en la época colonial.* Mexico City: Editorial Cultura, 1938.

———. *Coahuila y Texas desde la consumación de la Independencia hasta el Tratado de Paz de Guadalupe Hidalgo.* 2 vols. 1945. Reprint, Mexico City: Editorial Porrúa, 1979.

Allen, Ruth A. *East Texas Lumber Workers.* Austin: University of Texas Press, 1961.

———. *The Great Southwest Strike.* Austin: The University of Texas Bulletin No. 4214, 1942.

Allsup, Carl. *The American G.I. Forum: Origins and Evolution.* Austin: University of Texas Press, 1982.

Almaráz, Félix D., Jr. *Governor Antonio Martínez and Mexican Independence in Texas: An Orderly Transition.* 1975. Reprint, San Antonio: Bexar County Historical Commission, 1979.

———. "The Legacy of Columbus: Spanish Mission Policy in Texas." *Journal of Texas Catholic History and Culture* 3 (1992): 17–36.

———. "San Antonio's Old Franciscan Missions: Material Decline and Secular Avarice in the Transition from Hispanic to Mexican Control." *Americas* 44 (July 1987): 1–22.

———. *Tragic Cavalier: Governor Manuel Salcedo of Texas, 1808–1813.* Austin: University of Texas Press, 1971.

Alonzo, Armando. *Tejano Legacy: Rancheros and Settlers in South Texas, 1734–1900.* Albuquerque: University of New Mexico Press, 1998.

Alvarez, Luis. *The Power of the Zoot: Youth Culture and Resistance during World War II.* Berkeley: University of California Press, 2009.

Ambrose, Stephen E. *Eisenhower: Soldier and President.* Rev. ed. New York: Simon & Schuster, 1990.

Anders, Evan. *Boss Rule in South Texas: The Progressive Era.* Austin: University of Texas Press, 1982.

Anderson, Gary Clayton. *The Conquest of Texas: Ethnic Cleansing in the Promised Land, 1820–1875.* Norman: University of Oklahoma Press, 2005.

———. *The Indian Southwest, 1580–1830: Ethnogenesis and Reinvention.* Norman: University of Oklahoma Press, 1999.

Anderson, H. Allen. "The Delaware and Shawnee Indians and the Republic of Texas, 1820–1845." *Southwestern Historical Quarterly* 94 (October 1990): 231–260.

Anna, Timothy E. *Forging Mexico, 1821–1835.* Lincoln: University of Nebraska Press, 1998.

Arnn, John Wesley III. *Land of the Tejas: Native American Identity and Interaction in Texas, A.D. 1300–1700.* Austin: University of Texas Press, 2012.

Aten, Lawrence E. *Indians of the Upper Texas Coast.* New York: Academic Press, 1983.

Bacarisse, Charles A. "Baron de Bastrop." *Southwestern Historical Quarterly* 58 (January 1955): 319–330.

———. "The Union of Coahuila and Texas." *Southwestern Historical Quarterly* 61 (January 1958): 341–349.

508

Bagur, Jacques D. *A History of Navigation on Cypress Bayou and the Lakes*. Denton: University of North Texas Press, 2001.

Bainbridge, John. *Super-Americans*. Garden City, NY: Doubleday, 1961.

Banks, Jimmy. *Money, Marbles, and Chalk*. Austin: Texas Publishing Co., 1971.

Barksdale, E. C. *The Meat Packers Come to Texas*. Austin: Bureau of Business Research, 1959.

Barnes, Donna A. *Farmers in Rebellion: The Rise and Fall of the Southern Farmers Alliance and People's Party in Texas*. Austin: University of Texas Press, 1984.

Barr, Alwyn. *Black Texans: A History of African-Americans in Texas, 1528–1995*. Norman: University of Oklahoma Press, 1996.

———. *Reconstruction to Reform: Texas Politics, 1876–1906*. Austin: University of Texas Press, 1971.

———. *Texans in Revolt: The Battle for San Antonio, 1835*. Austin: University of Texas Press, 1990.

Barr, Alwyn, and Robert A. Calvert, eds. *Black Leaders: Texans for Their Times*. Austin: Texas State Historical Association, 1981.

Barr, Juliana. *Peace Came in the Form of a Woman: Indians and Spaniards in the Texas Borderlands*. Chapel Hill: University of North Carolina Press, 2007.

Barta, Carolyn. *Bill Clements: Texian to His Toenails*. Austin: Eakin Press, 1996.

Bartlett, Richard C. *Saving the Best of Texas*. Austin: University of Texas Press, 1995.

Bartley, Earnest R. *The Texas Tidelands Controversy: A Legal and Historical Analysis*. Austin: University of Texas Press, 1953.

Behnken, Brian. *Fighting Their Own Battles: Mexican Americans, African Americans, and the Struggle for Civil Rights*. Chapel Hill: University of North Carolina Press, 2011.

Benavides, Adán, Jr., comp. and ed. *The Béxar Archives (1717–1836): A Name Guide*. Austin: University of Texas Press, 1989.

Benson, Nettie L. "Bishop Marín de Porras and Texas." *Southwestern Historical Quarterly* 51 (July 1947): 16–40.

———. "A Governor's Report on Texas in 1809." *Southwestern Historical Quarterly* 71 (April 1968): 603–615.

———. "Texas Failure to Send a Deputy to the Spanish Cortes, 1810–1812." *Southwestern Historical Quarterly* 64 (July 1960): 14–35.

———. "Texas as Viewed from Mexico, 1820–1834." *Southwestern Historical Quarterly* 90 (January 1987): 219–291.

Berrueto González, Arturo. *Diccionario biográfico de Coahuila*. Saltillo: Gobierno del Estado de Coahuila, 1999.

Bethell, Leslie, ed. *The Independence of Latin America*. Cambridge, UK: Cambridge University Press, 1987.

Biles, Roger. *The South and the New Deal*. Lexington: University of Kentucky Press, 1991.

Bishop, Bill. "Major Urban Areas See Most of Texas' Growth: As Cities' Amenities Attract Talented Workers—Companies, Jobs Follow." *Austin American Statesman* 3 March 2002—A1.

Bixel, Patricia Bellis, and Elizabeth Hayes Turner. *Galveston and the 1900 Storm*. Austin: University of Texas Press, 2000.

Blackwelder, Julia Kirk. *Women of the Depression: Caste and Culture in San Antonio, 1929–1939*. College Station: Texas A&M University Press, 1984.

Blaufarb, Rafe. *Bonapartists in the Borderlands: French Exiles and Refugees on the Gulf Coast, 1815–1835*. Tuscaloosa: University of Alabama Press, 2005.

Blodgett, Jan. *Land of Bright Promise: Advertising and the Texas Panhandle and South Plains, 1870–1917*. Austin: University of Texas Press, 1988.

Bolton, Herbert E. *Coronado: Knight of Pueblos and Plains.* 1949. Reprint, Albuquerque: University of New Mexico Press, 1964.

———. *The Hasinais: Southern Caddoans as Seen by the Earliest Europeans.* 1987. Reprint, Norman: University of Oklahoma Press, 2002.

———. *Texas in the Middle Eighteenth Century: Studies in Spanish Colonial Administration.* 1915. Reprint, Austin: University of Texas Press, 1970.

———, ed. and trans. *Athanase de Mézières and the Louisiana-Texas Frontier, 1768–1780.* 2 vols. Cleveland: Arthur H. Clark, 1914.

Boswell, Evault. *Texas Boys in Gray.* Plano: Republic of Texas Press, 2000.

Brading, David A. *Miners and Merchants in Bourbon Mexico, 1763–1810.* Cambridge, UK: Cambridge University Press, 1971.

Bradley, Ed. "Fighting for Texas: Filibuster James Long, the Adams-Onís Treaty, and the Monroe Administration." *Southwestern Historical Quarterly* 102 (January 1999): 323–342.

Brandimarte, Cynthia A. with Angela Reed. *Texas State Parks and the CCC.* College Station: Texas A&M University Press, 2013.

Bricker, Richard W. *Wooden Ships from Texas: A World War I Saga.* College Station: Texas A&M University Press, 1998.

Brister, Louis E., ed. *John Charles Beales's Rio Grande Colony: Letters by Eduard Ludecus, a German Colonist, to Friends in Germany in 1833–1834, Recounting His Journey, Trials, and Observations in Early Texas.* Denton: Texas State Historical Association, 2008.

Britten, Thomas A. *The Lipan Apaches: People of Wind and Lightning.* Albuquerque: University of New Mexico Press, 2009.

Brown, Norman D. "Garnering Votes for 'Cactus Jack': John Nance Garner, Franklin D. Roosevelt, and the 1932 Democratic Nomination for President." *Southwestern Historical Quarterly* 104 (October 2000): 148–188.

———. *Hood, Bonnet, and Little Brown Jug: Texas Politics, 1921–1928.* College Station: Texas A&M University Press, 1984.

Bruseth, James E., and Nancy A. Kenmotsu. "From Naguatex to the River Daycao: The Route of the Hernando de Soto Expedition Through Texas." *North American Archaeologist* 14 (1993): 199–225.

Bryant, Keith L., Jr. *Arthur Stillwell: Promoter with a Hunch.* Nashville: Vanderbilt University Press, 1971.

———. *History of the Atchison, Topeka and Santa Fe Railway.* New York: Macmillan, 1974.

Buckley, Eleanor C. "The Aguayo Expedition into Texas and Louisiana, 1719–1722." *Quarterly of the Texas State Historical Association* 15 (July 1911): 1–65.

Buenger, Walter L. *Secession and the Union in Texas.* Austin: University of Texas Press, 1984.

———. *The Path to a Modern South: Northeast Texas Between Reconstruction and the Great Depression.* Austin: University of Texas Press, 2001.

Buenger, Walter L., and Arnoldo De León, eds. *Beyond Texas Through Time: Breaking Away from Past Interpretations.* College Station: Texas A&M University Press, 2011.

Buenger, Walter L., and Robert A. Calvert, eds. *Texas Through Time: Evolving Interpretations.* College Station: Texas A&M University Press, 1991.

Bullard, Robert D. *Invisible Houston: The Black Experience in Boom and Bust.* College Station: Texas A&M University Press, 1987.

Burton, H. Sophie, and F. Todd Smith. *Colonial Natchitoches: A Creole Community on the Louisiana-Texas Frontier.* College Station: Texas A&M University Press, 2008.

Calvert, Robert A., and Arnoldo De León. *The History of Texas.* 3rd ed. Wheeling, IL: Harlan Davidson, Inc., 2002.

Campbell, Randolph B. *An Empire for Slavery: The Peculiar Institution in Texas, 1821–1865.* Baton Rouge: Louisiana State University Press, 1989.

———. *Grass Roots Reconstruction in Texas, 1865–1880.* Baton Rouge: Louisiana State University Press, 1997.

———. *Sam Houston and the American Southwest.* New York: HarperCollins, 1993.

Cantrell, Gregg. *Kenneth and John B. Rayner and the Limits of Southern Dissent.* Urbana: University of Illinois Press, 1993.

———. "Racial Violence and Reconstruction Politics in Texas, 1867–1868." *Southwestern Historical Quarterly* 93 (January 1990): 333–356.

———. *Stephen F. Austin: Empresario of Texas.* New Haven: Yale University Press, 1999.

Carleton, Don E. *A Breed So Rare: The Life of J. R. Parten, Liberal Texas Oilman, 1896–1992.* Austin: Texas State Historical Association, 1999.

———. *Red Scare: Right-Wing Hysteria, Fifties Fanaticism, and Their Legacy in Texas.* Austin: Texas Monthly Press, 1985.

Carlson, Paul H. *The Plains Indians.* College Station: Texas A&M University Press, 1998.

———. *Texas Woollybacks: The Texas Sheep and Goat Industry.* College Station: Texas A&M University Press, 1982.

Carmody, Kevin. "Guadalupe Is in Jeopardy, Group Warns: Water Rights Issue Puts River System on Conservationists' List." *Austin American Statesman* 2 April 2002—B1.

Caro, Robert A. *The Years of Lyndon Johnson: Master of the Senate.* New York: Alfred A. Knopf, 2002.

———. *The Years of Lyndon Johnson: Means of Ascent.* New York: Alfred A. Knopf, 1990.

———. *The Years of Lyndon Johnson: The Path to Power.* New York: Alfred A. Knopf, 1982.

Carpenter, Dale. *Flagrant Conduct: The Story of Lawrence v. Texas: How a Bedroom Arrest Decriminalized Gay Americans.* New York: W. W. Norton, 2012.

Carraro, Francine. *Jerry Bywaters, A Life in Art.* Austin: University of Texas Press, 1994.

Carrigan, William D. *The Making of a Lynching Culture: Violence and Vigilantism in Central Texas, 1836–1916.* Urbana: University of Illinois Press, 2006.

Carroll, John M., ed. *The Black Military Experience in the American West.* New York: Liverwright, 1971.

Carroll, Mark M. *Homesteads Ungovernable: Families, Sex, Race, and the Law in Frontier Texas, 1826–1860.* Austin: University of Texas Press, 2001.

Carroll, Patrick James. *Felix Longoria's Wake: Bereavement, Racism, and the Rise of Mexican American Activism.* Austin: University of Texas Press, 2003.

Carter, Cecile Elkins. *Caddo Indians: Where We Come From.* Norman: University of Oklahoma Press, 1995.

Carter, William B. *Indian Alliances and the Spanish in the Southwest, 750–1750.* Norman: University of Oklahoma Press, 2009.

Casdorf, Paul. *A History of the Republican Party in Texas, 1865–1965.* Austin: Pemberton Press, 1965.

Cashion, Ty. *Pigskin Pulpit: A Social History of Texas High School Football Coaches.* Austin: Texas State Historical Association Press, 2006.

Cashion, Ty, and Jesús F. de la Teja, eds. *The Human Tradition in Texas.* Wilmington, DE: SR Books, 2001.

Castañeda, Carlos E. *Our Catholic Heritage in Texas.* 7 vols. Austin: Von Boeckmann-Jones, 1936–1958.

Chabot, Frederick C., ed. *Texas in 1811: The Las Casas and Sambrano Revolutions.* San Antonio: Yanaguana Society, 1941.

Champagne, Anthony. *Congressman Sam Rayburn.* New Brunswick, NJ: Rutgers University Press, 1984.

Chapa, Juan Bautista. *Texas & Northeastern Mexico, 1630–1690*. Ed. William C. Foster. Austin: University of Texas Press, 1997.

Chávez, Thomas E. *Spain and the Independence of the United States: An Intrinsic Gift*. Albuquerque: University of New Mexico Press, 2002.

Childs, William R. *The Texas Railroad Commission: Understanding Regulation in America to the Mid-Twentieth Century*. College Station: Texas A&M University Press, 2005.

Chipman, Donald E. "In Search of Cabeza de Vaca's Route Across Texas: An Historiographical Survey." *Southwestern Historical Quarterly* 91 (October 1987): 127–148.

———. *Spanish Texas, 1519–1821*. Rev. ed. Austin: University of Texas Press, 2010.

Chipman, Donald E., and Harriett Denise Joseph. *Notable Men and Women of Spanish Texas*. Austin: University of Texas Press, 1999.

Christian, Garna L. *Black Soldiers in Jim Crow Texas, 1899–1917*. College Station: Texas A&M University Press, 1995.

Clark, L. D., ed. *Civil War Recollections of James Lemuel Clark and the Great Hanging at Gainesville, Texas in October 1862*. Plano: Republic of Texas Press, 1997.

Clayton, Lawrence. *Contemporary Ranches of Texas*. Austin: University of Texas Press, 2001.

Clemons, Leigh. *Branding Texas: Performing Culture in the Lone Star State*. Austin: University of Texas Press, 2008.

Coerver, Don M., and Linda B. Hall. *Texas and the Mexican Revolution: A Study in State and National Border Policy, 1910–1920*. San Antonio: Trinity University Press, 1984.

Conkin, Paul. *Big Daddy from the Pedernales: Lyndon Baines Johnson*. Boston: Twain, 1986.

Cook, John R. *The Border and the Buffalo: An Untold Story of the Southwest Plains*. 1907. Reprint, Austin: State House Press, 1989.

Copelin, Laylan. "As Enron Sank, State Pension Funds Invested, Lost." *Austin American Statesman* 26 December 2001—A1.

Cordell, Linda. *Archaeology of the Southwest*. 2nd ed. San Diego: Academic Press, 1997.

Cotner, Robert C. *James Stephen Hogg*. Austin: University of Texas Press, 1951.

Cotner, Robert C., et al. *Texas Cities and the Great Depression*. Austin: Texas Memorial Museum, 1973.

Cox, Patrick. *Ralph Yarborough: The People's Senator*. Austin: University of Texas Press, 2001.

Crawford, Ann Fears. *Frankie: Mrs. R. D. Randolph and Texas Liberal Politics*. Austin: Eakin Press, 2000.

Crawford, Ann Fears, and Crystal Sasse Ragsdale. *Texas Women Frontier to Future*. Austin: State House Press, 1998.

Crawford, Ann Fears, and Jack Keever. *John B. Connally: Portrait in Power*. Austin: Jenkins Co., 1973.

Crimm, Ana Carolina Castillo. *De León: A Tejano Family History*. Austin: University of Texas Press, 2003.

Crouch, Barry. *The Freedman's Bureau and Black Texans*. Austin: University of Texas Press, 1992.

Cruz, Gilbert R. *Let There Be Towns: Spanish Municipal Origins in the American Southwest, 1610–1810*. College Station: Texas A&M University Press, 1988.

Cummins, Light T. "Church Courts, Marriage Breakdown, and Separation in Spanish Louisiana, West Florida, and Texas." *Journal of Texas Catholic History and Culture* 4 (1993): 97–114.

Cunningham, Sean P. *Cowboy Conservatism: Texas and the Rise of the Modern Right*. Lexington: University Press of Kentucky, 2010.

Cutrer, Emily F. *The Art of the Woman: The Life and Work of Elisabet Ney*. Lincoln: University of Nebraska Press, 1988.

Dabbs, J. Autrey. "The Texas Missions in 1789." In *New Foundations: Preliminary Studies of the Texas Catholic Historical Society III*. Ed. Jesús F. de la Teja, 119–40. Austin: Texas Catholic Historical Society, 2000.

Dallek, Robert. *Flawed Giant: Lyndon Johnson and His Times, 1961–1973*. New York: Oxford University Press, 1998.

———. *Lone Star Rising: Lyndon Johnson and His Times, 1908–1960*. New York: Oxford University Press, 1991.

Dary, David. *Cowboy Culture: A Saga of Five Centuries*. Lawrence: University Press of Kansas, 1989.

Davidson, Chandler. *Race and Class in Texas Politics*. Princeton: Princeton University Press, 1990.

Davies, Gareth. *From Opportunity to Entitlement: The Transformation and Decline of Great Society Liberalism*. Lawrence: University Press of Kansas, 1996.

Davis, Graham. *Land: Irish Pioneers in Mexican and Revolutionary Texas*. College Station: Texas A&M University Press, 2002.

Davis, William C. *The Pirates Laffite: The Treacherous World of the Corsairs of the Gulf*. Orlando, FL: Harcourt, Inc., 2005.

———. *Three Roads to the Alamo: The Lives and Fortunes of David Crockett, James Bowie, and William Barret Travis*. New York: HarperCollins, 1998.

Dawson, Sr., John C. *High Plains Yesterdays: From XIT Days Through Drouth*[sic] *and Depression*. Austin: Eakin Press, 1985.

De León, Arnoldo. *Mexican Americans in Texas: A Brief History*. 2nd ed. Wheeling, IL: Harlan Davidson, Inc., 1999.

———. *They Called Them Greasers: Anglo Attitudes Toward Mexicans in Texas, 1821–1900*. Austin: University of Texas Press, 1983.

———, ed. *War along the Border: The Mexican Revolution and Tejano Communities*. College Station: Texas A&M University Press, 2012.

De Zavala, Adina. *History and Legends of the Alamo and Other Missions in and Around San Antonio*. 1917. Reprint, Houston: Arte Publico Press, 1996.

Deaton, Charles. *The Year They Threw the Rascals Out*. Austin: Shoal Creek Publishers, 1973.

Dell, Michael. *Direct from Dell: Strategies That Revolutionized an Industry*. New York: HarperBusiness, 1999.

Din, Gilbert C. "Spain's Immigration Policy in Louisiana and the American Penetration, 1792–1803." *Southwestern Historical Quarterly* 76 (January 1973): 255–276.

Dixon, Marc. "Limiting Labor: Business Political Mobilization and Union Setback in the States." *Journal of Policy History* 19 (2007): 313–344.

Dixon, Olive K. *Life of "Billy" Dixon*. Reprint, Austin: State House Press, 1987.

Dobbs, Ricky F. *Yellow Dogs and Republicans: Allan Shivers and Texas Two-Party Politics*. College Station: Texas A&M University Press, 2005.

Doughty, Robin W. *At Home in Texas: Early Views of the Land*. College Station: Texas A&M University Press, 1987.

———. *Wildlife and Man in Texas: Environmental Change and Conservation*. College Station: Texas A&M University Press, 1983.

Downs, Fane. "Governor Antonio Martínez and the Defense of Texas from Foreign Invasion, 1817–1822." *Texas Military History* 7 (Spring 1968): 27–43.

———. "'Tryels and Trubbles': Women in Early Nineteenth Century Texas." *Southwestern Historical Quarterly* 90 (April 1987): 35–56.

Dugas, Vera Lee. "Texas Industry, 1860–1880." *Southwestern Historical Quarterly* 59 (October 1955): 151–183.

Dugger, Ronnie. *Our Invaded Universities: Form, Reform and New Starts: A Nonfiction Play for Five Stages*. New York: W. W. Norton, 1974.

———. *The Politician: The Life and Times of Lyndon B. Johnson*. New York: W. W. Norton, 1982.

———. *Three Men in Texas: Bedicheck, Webb, and Dobie.* Austin: University of Texas Press, 1967.

Dunn, William E. "Apache Relations in Texas, 1718–1750." *Quarterly of the Texas State Historical Association* 14 (January 1911): 198–274.

Eckhardt, Gregg A. "Ron Pucek's Living Waters Catfish Farm." *The Edwards Aquifer Home Page* 28 June 2002. <http://www.edwardsaquifer.net/pucek.html>.

Edwards, George C., III, and Desmond S. King. *The Polarized Presidency of George W. Bush.* New York: Oxford University Press, 2007.

Elliot, J. H. *Imperial Spain, 1469–1716.* 2nd ed. New York: Penguin, 2002.

Enstam, Elizabeth York. *Women and the Creation of Urban Life: Dallas, Texas, 1843–1920.* College Station: Texas A&M University Press, 1998.

Evans, Sara. *Personal Politics: The Roots of Women's Liberation in the Civil Rights Movement & the New Left.* New York: Vintage Books, 1980.

Everett, Dianna. *The Texas Cherokees: A People Between Two Fires, 1819–1840.* Norman: University of Oklahoma Press, 1990.

Exley, Jo Ella Powell. *Texas Tears and Texas Sunshine: Voices of Frontier Women.* College Station: Texas A&M University Press, 1985.

Fagan, Brian M. *The Great Journey: The Peopling of Ancient America.* Rev. ed. Gainesville: University Press of Florida, 2003.

Farber, David R. *The Rise and Fall of Modern American Conservatism.* Princeton, NJ: Princeton University Press, 2010.

Faulk, Odie B. *The Last Years of Spanish Texas, 1778–1821.* The Hague: Mouton, 1964.

———. "The Penetration of Foreigners and Foreign Ideas into Spanish East Texas, 1793–1810." *East Texas Historical Journal* 2 (October 1964): 87–98.

———. "Ranching in Spanish Texas." *Hispanic American Historical Review* 45 (May 1965): 257–266.

Faulk, Odie B., and Laura E. Faulk. *Defenders of the Interior Provinces: Presidial Soldiers on the Northern Frontier of New Spain.* Albuquerque: Albuquerque Museum, 1988.

Fenberg, Steven. *Unprecedented Power: Jesse Jones, Capitalism, and the Common Good.* College Station: Texas A&M University Press, 2011.

Fink, Rob. "Hermine Tobolowsky, the Texas ELRA, and the Political Struggle for Women's Equal Rights." *Journal of the American West* 42 (Summer 2003): 52–57.

Flannery, Tim. *The Eternal Frontier: An Ecological History of North America and Its People.* New York: Atlantic Monthly Press, 2001.

Flint, Richard. *No Settlement, No Conquest: A History of the Coronado Expedition.* Albuquerque: University of New Mexico Press, 2008.

Flint, Richard, and Shirley Cushing Flint, eds. *The Coronado Expedition to Tierra Nueva: The 1540–1542 Route Across the Southwest.* Niwot: University Press of Colorado, 1997.

Flores, Dan L. *Jefferson and Southwestern Exploration: The Freeman and Custis Accounts of the Red River Expedition of 1806.* Norman: University of Oklahoma Press, 1984.

Foik, Paul J. "Captain Don Domingo Ramón's Diary of His Expedition into Texas in 1716." In *Wilderness Mission: Preliminary Studies of the Texas Catholic Historical Society II.* Austin: Texas Catholic Historical Society, 1999.

Foley, Neil. *Quest for Equality: The Failed Promise of Black-Brown Solidarity.* Cambridge: Harvard University Press, 2010.

———. *The White Scourge: Mexicans, Blacks, and Poor Whites in Texas Cotton Culture.* Berkeley: University of California Press, 1997.

Forman, Maury, and Robert A. Calvert. *Cartooning Texas: One Hundred Years of Cartoon Art in the Lone Star State.* College Station: Texas A&M University Press, 1993.

Forrestal, Peter J., trans. "The Solís Diary of 1767." In *Preparing the Way: Preliminary Studies of the Texas Catholic Historical Society I.* Austin: Texas Catholic Historical Society, 1997.

Foster, William C. *Historic Native Peoples of Texas.* Austin: University of Texas Press, 2008.

———. *Spanish Expeditions into Texas, 1689–1768.* Austin: University of Texas Press, 1995.

Fowler, Will. *Santa Anna of Mexico.* Lincoln: University of Nebraska Press, 2007.

Frantz, Joe B. *Texas: A Bicentennial History.* New York: W. W. Norton, 1976.

Frantz, Joe B., and Julian Ernest Choate. *The American Cowboy: The Myth and the Reality.* Norman: University of Oklahoma Press, 1955.

Frazier, Donald S. *Blood & Treasure: Confederate Empire in the Southwest.* College Station: Texas A&M University Press, 1995.

Freehling, William W. *The Road to Disunion: Secessionists at Bay, 1776–1854.* New York: Oxford University Press, 1990.

Friedberger, Mark. " 'Mink and Manure': Rural Gentrification and Cattle Raising in Southeast Texas, 1945–1992." *Southwestern Historical Quarterly* 102 (January 1999): 269–293.

"The Future Is Texas." Reprinted from *The Economist. Austin American Statesman* (5 January 2003): H1+.

Galbraith, John Kenneth. *The Great Crash, 1929.* Boston: Houghton Mifflin, 1955.

García, Ignacio M. *United We Win: The Rise and Fall of La Raza Unida Party.* Tucson: University of Arizona Press, 1989.

———. *Viva Kennedy: Mexican Americans in Search of Camelot.* College Station: Texas A&M University Press, 2000.

García, Mario T. *Desert Immigrants: The Mexicans of El Paso, 1880–1920.* New Haven: Yale University Press, 1981.

Gard, Wayne. *The Chisholm Trail.* Norman: University of Oklahoma Press, 1954.

———. *Frontier Justice.* Norman: University of Oklahoma Press, 1949.

Gardien, Kent. "Take Pity on Our Glory: Men of Champ d'Asile." *Southwestern Historical Quarterly* 87 (January 1984): 241–268.

Garrett, Julia K. *Green Flag Over Texas: A Story of the Last Years of Spain in Texas.* New York: Cordova Press, 1939.

Garrow, David J. *Liberty and Sexuality: The Right to Privacy and the Making of* Roe v. Wade. New York: Macmillan Publishing Co., 1998.

Gee, Robert W. "Dry Fields Threaten Way of Life for Valley Farmers." *Austin American Statesman* 17 March 2002—A1.

Gerhard, Peter. *The Northern Frontier of New Spain.* Princeton: Princeton University Press, 1982.

Gillon, Steven M. *The Kennedy Assassination—24 Hours After: Lyndon B. Johnson's Pivotal First Day as President.* New York: Basic Books, 2010.

Goodwin, Ronald E. *Remembering the Days of Sorrow: The WPA and the Texas Slave Narratives.* Buffalo Gap: State House Press, 2014.

Goodwyn, Lawrence. *Democratic Promise: The Populist Movement in America.* New York: Oxford University Press, 1976.

Gould, Lewis L. *Lady Bird Johnson: Our Environmental First Lady.* Lawrence: University Press of Kansas, 1999.

———. *Progressives and Prohibitionists: Texas Democrats in the Wilson Era.* Austin: Texas State Historical Association, 1992.

Graham, Joe S. *El Rancho in South Texas: Continuity and Change from 1750.* Denton: University of North Texas Press, 1994.

Green, Donald E. *Land of the Underground Rain: Irrigation on the Texas High Plains, 1910–1970.* Austin: University of Texas Press, 1973.

Green, George Norris. *The Establishment in Texas Politics: The Primitive Years, 1938–1957.* 1979. Reprint, Norman: University of Oklahoma Press, 1984.

Green, James R. *Grass-Roots Socialism: Radical Movements in the Southwest, 1895–1943.* Baton Rouge: Louisiana State University Press, 1978.

———. "Tenant Farmer Discontent and Socialist Protest in Texas, 1901–1917." *Southwestern Historical Quarterly* 81 (October 1977): 133–154.

Green, Stanley C. *The Mexican Republic: The First Decade, 1823–1832.* Pittsburgh: University of Pittsburgh Press, 1987.

Greene, John Robert. *The Presidency of George Bush.* Lawrence: University Press of Kansas, 2000.

Groneman, Bill. *Eyewitness to the Alamo.* Plano: Republic of Texas Press, 1996.

Habig, Marion A. *The Alamo Chain of Missions: A History of San Antonio's Five Old Missions.* Chicago: Franciscan Herald Press, 1969.

Hackett, Charles W. "The Neutral Ground Between Louisiana and Texas, 1806–1821." *Louisiana Historical Quarterly* 28 (October 1945): 1001–1128.

———, ed. and trans. *Pichardo's Treatise on the Limits of Louisiana and Texas.* 4 vols. Austin: University of Texas Press, 1931–1946.

Haggard, J. Villasana. "The Counter-Revolution of Béxar, 1811." *Southwestern Historical Quarterly* 43 (October 1939): 222–235.

Haley, J. Evetts. *Charles Goodnight, Cowman and Plainsman.* Norman: University of Oklahoma Press, 1949.

———. *George W. Littlefield, Texan.* Norman: University of Oklahoma Press, 1943.

Hämäläinen, Pekka. *The Comanche Empire.* New Haven: Yale University Press, 2008.

Hardeman, Dorsey B., and Donald C. Bacon. *Rayburn: A Biography.* Austin: Texas Monthly Press, 1987.

Hardin, Stephen L. *Texian Iliad: A Military History of the Texas Revolution.* Austin: University of Texas Press, 1994.

———. *Texian Macabre: The Melancholy Tale of a Hanging in Early Houston.* Abilene: State House Press, 2007.

Harmon, Dave. "The Fight for a Historic Birthright: Padre Island Ruling Gives Hope to Latino Families." *Austin American Statesman* 10 January 2000—A1.

Hatcher, Mattie Austin. "The Expedition of Don Domingo Terán de los Ríos into Texas." In *Wilderness Mission: Preliminary Studies of the Texas Catholic Historical Society II.* Austin: Texas Catholic Historical Society, 1999.

———. *The Opening of Texas to Foreign Settlement, 1801–1821.* 1927. Reprint, Philadelphia: Porcupine Press, 1976.

Haynes, Sam W. "Anglophobia and the Annexation of Texas: The Quest for National Security." In *Manifest Destiny and Empire: American Antebellum Expansionism,* eds. Sam W. Haynes and Christopher Morris. College Station: Texas A&M University Press, 1997.

———. *Soldiers of Misfortune: The Somervell and Mier Expeditions.* Austin: University of Texas Press, 1990.

Haynes, Sam W., and Cary D. Wintz, eds. *Major Problems in Texas History: Documents and Essays.* Boston: Houghton Mifflin, 2002.

Henderson, Richard B. *Maury Maverick, A Political Biography.* Austin: University of Texas Press, 1970.

Henderson, Timothy J. *The Mexican Wars for Independence.* New York: Hill and Wang, 2009.

Hendrickson, Jr., Kenneth B. *The Chief Executives of Texas: From Stephen F. Austin to John B. Connally, Jr.* College Station: Texas A&M University Press, 1995.

Hendrickson, Jr., Kenneth E., and Michael L. Collins, eds. *Profiles in Power: Twentieth-Century Texans in Washington.* Arlington Heights, IL: Harlan Davidson, Inc., 1993.

Henson, Margaret Swett. *Juan Davis Bradburn: A Reappraisal of the Mexican Commander of Anahuac.* Reprint, College Station: Texas A&M University Press, 2011.

———. *Lorenzo de Zavala: The Pragmatic Idealist.* Fort Worth. Texas Christian University Press, 1996.

———. *Samuel May Williams, Early Texas Entrepreneur.* College Station: Texas A&M University Press, 1976.

Henson, Margaret Swett, and Deolece Parmalee. *The Cartwrights of San Augustine: Three Generations of Agricultural Entrepreneurs in Nineteenth-Century Texas.* Austin: Texas State Historical Association, 1993.

Hester, Thomas R. *Digging into South Texas Prehistory: A Guide for Amateur Archaeologists.* San Antonio: Corona Publishing, 1980.

Hickerson, Nancy P. "How Cabeza de Vaca Lived with, Worked Among, and Finally Left the Indians of Texas." *Journal of Anthropological Research* 54 (Summer 1998): 199–218.

———. *The Jumanos: Hunters and Traders of the South Plains.* Austin: University of Texas Press, 1994.

Hight, Bruce. "Tiguas Roll Snake Eyes in Court Fight; El Paso Tribe Must Close Casino after Nine Years but Can Continue Appeal." *Austin American Statesman* 12 February 2002—A1.

Hill, Patricia Everidge. *Dallas: The Making of a Modern City.* Austin: University of Texas Press, 1996.

Himmel, Kelly F. *The Conquest of the Karankawas and the Tonkawas, 1821–1859.* College Station: Texas A&M University Press, 1999.

Hine, Darlene Clark. *Black Victory: The Rise and Fall of the White Primary in Texas.* Columbia: University of Missouri Press, 2003.

Hinojosa, Gilberto M. *A Borderlands Town in Transition: Laredo, 1755–1870.* College Station: Texas A&M University Press, 1983.

Hodge, Frederick W., and Theodore H. Lewis, eds. *Spanish Explorers in the Southern United States, 1528–1543.* 1907. Reprint, Austin: Texas State Historical Association, 1990.

Hogan, William Ransom. *The Texas Republic: A Social and Economic History.* 1946. Reprint, Austin: University of Texas Press, 1969.

Holden, William C. *Alkali Trails, or, Social and Economic Movements of the Texas Frontier, 1846–1900.* Dallas: Southwest Press, 1930.

Holmes, Jack D. L. "Showdown on the Sabine: General James Wilkinson vs. Lieutenant-Colonel Simon de Herrera." *Louisiana Studies* 3 (1964): 46–76.

Hudson, Linda S. *Mistress of Manifest Destiny: A Biography of Jane McManus Storm Cazneau, 1807–1878.* Austin: Texas State Historical Association, 2001.

Hull, N. E. H., and Peter Charles Hoffer. Roe v. Wade: *The Abortion Rights Controversy in American History.* Lawrence: University Press of Kansas, 2010.

Humphrey, David C. *Austin, an Illustrated History.* Northridge, CA: Windsor Publications, 1985.

Hyman, Harold. *Oleander Odyssey: The Kempners of Galveston, Ca. 1850–1987.* College Station: Texas A&M University Press, 1990.

Ibarra, Ana Carolina, ed. *La independencia en el septentrión de la Nueva España: Provincias Internas e intendencias norteñas.* Mexico: Universidad Nacional Autónoma de México, 2010.

Iber, Jorge. "Bidal Aguero and *El Editor* Newspaper: The Varied Roles of a Spanish Surnamed Entrepreneur in a Lubbock, Texas Barrio, 1977–1999." *West Texas Historical Association Yearbook* 75 (1999): 54–61.

Jackson, Jack. *Indian Agent: Peter Ellis Bean in Mexican Texas.* College Station: Texas A&M University Press, 2005.

———. *Los Mesteños: Spanish Ranching in Texas, 1721–1821.* College Station: Texas A&M University Press, 1986.

Jackson, Jack, ed., and John Wheat, trans. *Almonte's Texas: Juan N. Almonte's 1834 Inspection, Secret Report and Role in the 1836 Campaign.* Austin: Texas State Historical Association, 2003.

———. *Texas by Terán: The Diary Kept by General Manuel de Mier y Terán on His 1828 Inspection of Texas.* Austin: University of Texas Press, 2000.

Jackson, Jack, ed., and William C. Foster, annot. *Imaginary Kingdom: Texas as Seen by the Rivera and Rubí Military Expeditions, 1727 and 1767.* Austin: Texas State Historical Association, 1995.

Jackson, Ron. *Alamo Legacy: Alamo Descendants Remember the Alamo.* Austin: Eakin Press, 1997.

Jacobs, Louis. *Lone Star Dinosaurs.* College Station: Texas A&M University Press, 1995.

Jasinski, Laurie. *Hill Country Backroads: Showing the Way in Comal County.* Fort Worth: Texas Christian University Press, 2001.

John, Elizabeth A. H. *Storms Brewed in Other Men's Worlds: The Confrontation of Indians, Spanish, and French in the Southwest, 1540–1795.* College Station: Texas A&M University Press, 1975.

John, Elizabeth A. H., ed., and John Wheat, trans. "Inside the Comanchería, 1785: The Diary of Pedro Vial and Francisco Xavier Chaves." *Southwestern Historical Quarterly* 98 (July 1994): 27–56.

Johnson, Benjamin Heber. *Revolution in Texas: How a Forgotten Rebellion and Its Bloody Suppression Turned Mexicans into Americans.* New Haven: Yale University Press, 2005.

Jones, Billy Mac. *Health Seekers in the Southwest, 1817–1900.* Norman: University of Oklahoma Press, 1967.

———. *The Search for Maturity.* Austin: Steck-Vaughn Co., 1965.

Jones, Nancy Baker, and Ruthe Winegarten. *Capitol Women.* Austin: University of Texas Press, 2000.

Jones, Oakah L., Jr. *Los Paisanos: Spanish Settlers on the Northern Frontier of New Spain.* Norman: University of Oklahoma Press, 1979.

Jordan, Barbara, and Shelby Hearon. *Barbara Jordan: A Self Portrait.* Garden City, NY: Doubleday, 1979.

Jordan, Terry G. "A Century and a Half of Ethnic Change in Texas, 1836–1986." *Southwestern Historical Quarterly* 89 (April 1986): 385–422.

———. *German Seed in Texas Soil: Immigrant Farmers in Nineteenth-Century Texas.* Austin: University of Texas Press, 1966.

———. *North American Cattle-Ranching Frontiers: Origins, Diffusion, and Differentiation.* Albuquerque: University of New Mexico Press, 1993.

———. *Texas: A Geography.* Boulder, CO: Westview Press, 1984.

———. *Trails to Texas: Southern Roots of Western Cattle Ranching.* Lincoln: University of Nebraska Press, 1981.

Kearns, Doris. *Lyndon Baines Johnson and the American Dream.* New York: Harper & Row, 1976.

Kenner, Charles L. *The Comanchero Frontier: A History of New Mexican-Plains Indian Relations.* Norman: University of Oklahoma Press, 1969.

Kessell, John L. *Spain in the Southwest: A Narrative History of Colonial New Mexico, Arizona, Texas, and California.* Norman: University of Oklahoma Press, 2002.

Key, Jr., V. O. *Southern Politics in State and Nation.* New York: Alfred A. Knopf, 1949.

Kinch, Jr., Sam, and Ben Procter. *Texas Under a Cloud.* Austin: Jenkins Publishing Co., 1972.

Kinch, Jr., Sam, and Stuart Long. *Allan Shivers: The Pied Piper of Texas Politics.* Austin: Shoal Creek Publishers, 1974.

King, Larry L. *Confessions of a White Racist.* New York: Viking Press, 1971.

Kinnaird, Lawrence, ed. *The Frontiers of New Spain. Nicolás de Lafora's Description, 1766–1768.* Berkeley, CA: Quivira Society, 1958.

Knaggs, John R. *Two Party Texas: The John Tower Era, 1961–1984.* Austin: Eakin Press, 1986.

Knaut, Andrew L. *The Pueblo Revolt of 1680: Conquest and Resistance in Seventeenth-Century New Mexico.* Norman: University of Oklahoma Press, 1995.

La Vere, David. "Between Kinship and Capitalism: French and Spanish Rivalry in the Colonial Louisiana-Texas Indian Trade." *Journal of Southern History* 64 (May 1998): 197–218.

———. *The Caddo Chiefdoms: Caddo Economics and Politics, 700–1835.* Lincoln: University of Nebraska Press, 1998.

———. *The Texas Indians.* College Station: Texas A&M University Press, 2004.

La Vere, David, and Katia Campbell, eds. and trans. "An Expedition to the Kichai: The Journal of François Grappe, September 24, 1783." *Southwestern Historical Quarterly* 98 (July 1994): 59–78.

Lack, Paul D., ed. *The Diary of William Fairfax Gray from Virginia to Texas, 1835–1837.* Dallas: De Golyer Library and William P. Clements Center for Southwest Studies, Southern Methodist University, 1997.

———. *The Texas Revolutionary Experience, A Political and Social History 1835–1836.* College Station: Texas A&M University Press, 1992.

Larson, Erik. *Isaac's Storm: A Man, a Time, and the Deadliest Hurricane in History.* New York: Vintage Books, 2000.

Lemée, Patricia R. "Tios and Tantes: Familial and Political Relationships of Natchitoches and the Spanish Colonial Frontier." *Southwestern Historical Quarterly* 101 (January 1998): 341–358.

Leutenegger, Benedict, ed., and Marion A. Habig. "Report on the San Antonio Missions in 1792." *Southwestern Historical Quarterly* 77 (April 1974): 487–498.

Liebmann, Matthew. *Revolt: An Archaeological History of Pueblo Resistance and Revitalization in 17th Century New Mexico.* Tucson: University of Arizona Press, 2012.

Lindell, Chuck. "Texans Take Mexico Water Fight to D.C.; Growers Want U.S. to Push Mexico on Releasing Water to Rio Grande." *Austin American Statesman* 25 April 2002—B1.

Linklater, Andro. *An Artist in Treason: The Extraordinary Double Life of General James Wilkinson.* New York: Walker Publishing, 2009.

Linsley, Judith Walker, Ellen Walker Rienstra, and Jo Ann Stiles. *Giant Under the Hill: A History of the Spindletop Oil Discovery at Beaumont, Texas, in 1901.* Austin: Texas State Historical Association, 2002.

Little, Carol Morris. *A Comprehensive Guide to Outdoor Sculpture in Texas.* Austin: University of Texas Press, 1996.

Malone, Ann Patton. *Women on the Texas Frontier.* El Paso: Texas Western Press, 1985.

Marks, Paula Mitchell. *Hands to the Spindle: Texas Women and Home Textile Production, 1822–1880.* College Station: Texas A&M University Press, 1998.

———. *Turn Your Eyes Toward Texas: Pioneers Sam and Mary Maverick.* College Station: Texas A&M University Press, 1989.

Martin, Robert L. *The City Moves West: Economic and Industrial Growth in Central West Texas.* Austin: University of Texas Press, 1969.

Martin, Roscoe. *The People's Party in Texas: A Study in Third-Party Politics.* 1933. Reprint, Austin: University of Texas Press, 1970.

Matovina, Timothy. *The Alamo Remembered: Tejano Accounts and Perspectives.* Austin: University of Texas Press, 1995.

———. *Tejano Religion and Ethnicity in San Antonio, 1821–1860.* Austin: University of Texas Press, 1995.

Maxwell, Robert S. *Sawdust Empire: The Texas Lumber Industry, 1830–1940.* College Station: Texas A&M University Press, 1983.

———. *Texas Economic Growth, 1890 to World War II: From Frontier to Industrial Giant.* Boston: American Press, 1981.

McArthur, Judith N. *Creating the New Woman: The Rise of Southern Women's Progressive Culture in Texas, 1893–1918.* Urbana, IL: University of Illinois Press, 1998.

McArthur, Judith N., and Harold L. Smith. *Minnie Fisher Cunningham: A Suffragist's Life in Politics.* New York: Oxford University Press, 2003.

McCall, Brian. *The Power of the Texas Governor: Connally to Bush.* Austin: University of Texas Press, 2009.

McCarty, Kieran. "Before They Crossed the Great River: Cultural Background of the Spanish Franciscans in Texas." *Journal of Texas Catholic History and Culture* 3 (1992): 37–44.

McCaslin, Richard B. *Tainted Breeze: The Great Hanging at Gainesville, Texas, 1862.* Baton Rouge: Louisiana State University Press, 1994.

———. "Wheat Growers in the Cotton Confederacy: The Suppression of Dissent in Collin County, Texas, During the Civil War." *Southwestern Historical Quarterly* 96 (April 1993): 527–539.

McComb, David G. *Galveston, A History.* Austin: University of Texas Press, 1986.

———. *Houston: A History.* Austin: University of Texas Press, 1986.

———. *Texas: A Modern History.* Austin: University of Texas Press, 1989.

McConal, Patrick M. *Over the Wall: The Men Behind the 1934 Death House Escape.* Austin: Eakin Press, 2000.

McDonald, David. *José Antonio Navarro: In Search of the American Dream in Nineteenth-Century Texas.* Denton: Texas State Historical Association, 2010.

McKay, Seth S. *Texas and the Fair Deal.* San Antonio: Naylor Press, 1954.

———. *Texas Politics, 1906–1944.* Lubbock: Texas Tech University Press, 1952.

———. *W. Lee O'Daniel and Texas Politics.* Lubbock: Texas Tech University Press, 1944.

McKay, Seth S., and Odie B. Faulk. *Texas After Spindletop.* Austin: Steck-Vaughn Co., 1965.

McMath, Robert C., Jr. *American Populism: A Social History, 1877–1898.* New York: Hill and Wang, 1993.

———. *Populist Vanguard: A History of the Southern Farmer's Alliance.* Chapel Hill: University of North Carolina Press, 1975.

Meinig, D. W. *Imperial Texas: An Interpretive Essay in Cultural Geography.* Austin: University of Texas Press, 1969.

Meyer, Michael C. *Water in the Hispanic Southwest: A Social and Legal History, 1550–1850.* Tucson: University of Arizona Press, 1984.

Meyer, Michael C., William L. Sherman, and Susan M. Deeds. *The Course of Mexican History.* 6th ed. New York: Oxford University Press, 1999.

Miller, Thomas L. *The Public Lands of Texas, 1519–1970.* Norman: University of Oklahoma Press, 1972.

Moneyhon, Carl. "Edmund J. Davis in the Coke-Davis Election Dispute of 1874: A Reassessment of Character." *Southwestern Historical Quarterly* 100 (October 1996): 131–151.

Montejano, David. *Anglos and Mexicans in the Making of Texas, 1836–1986.* Austin: University of Texas Press, 1987.

———. *Quixote's Soldiers: A Local History of the Chicano Movement, 1966–1981.* Austin: University of Texas Press, 2010.

———. *Sancho's Journal: Exploring the Political Edge with the Brown Berets.* Austin: University of Texas Press, 2012.

Moorhead, Max L. *New Mexico's Royal Road: Trade and Travel on the Chihuahua Trail.* Norman: University of Oklahoma Press, 1958.

————. *The Presidio: Bastion of the Spanish Borderlands.* Norman: University of Oklahoma Press, 1975.

Morehead, Richard. *Fifty Years in Texas Politics.* Burnett: Eakin Press, 1982.

Morgenthaler, Jefferson. *La Junta de los Rios: The Life, Death and Resurrection of an Ancient Desert Community in the Big Bend Region of Texas.* Boerne, TX: Mockingbird Books, 2007.

Morfi, Juan Agustín. *History of Texas, 1673–1779.* Trans. and ed. Carlos E. Castañeda. 2 vols. Albuquerque: Quivira Society, 1935.

Morris, John Miller. *El Llano Estacado: Exploration and Imagination on the High Plains of Texas and New Mexico, 1536–1860.* Austin: Texas State Historical Association, 1997.

Murph, Dan. *Texas Giant: The Life of Price Daniel.* Austin: Eakin Press, 2002.

Myers, Sandra L. *The Ranch in Spanish Texas.* El Paso: Texas Western Press, 1969.

Nackman, Mark E. *A Nation Within a Nation: The Rise of Texas Nationalism.* Port Washington, NY: Kennikat Press, 1975.

Navarro, José Antonio. *Defending Mexican Valor in Texas: José Antonio Navarro's Historical Writings, 1853–1857.* Ed. David R. Navarro and Timothy M. Matovina. Austin: State House Press, 1995.

Navarro García, Luis. *Don José de Gálvez y la Comandancia General de las Provincias Internas del Norte de Nueva España.* Seville: Escuela de Estudios Hispano-Americanos de Sevilla, 1964.

Neu, Charles E. "In Search of Colonel Edward M. House: The Texas Years, 1858–1912." *Southwestern Historical Quarterly* 93 (July 1989): 25–44.

Neugebauer, Janet M., ed. *Plains Farmer: The Diary of William G. DeLoach, 1914–1964.* College Station: Texas A&M University Press, 1991.

Newcomb, W. W., Jr. *The Indians of Texas: From Prehistoric to Modern Times.* Austin: University of Texas Press, 1961.

————. *The Rock Art of Texas Indians.* Paintings by Forrest Kirkland. Austin: University of Texas Press, 1967.

Newkumet, Vynola Beaver, and Howard L. Meredith. *Hasinai: A Traditional History of the Caddo Confederacy.* College Station: Texas A&M University Press, 1988.

Nunley, Parker. *A Field Guide to Archeological Sites in Texas.* Austin: Texas Monthly Press, 1989.

Oates, Stephen B., ed. *Rip Ford's Texas.* Austin: University of Texas Press, 1963.

O'Connor, Kathryn Stoner. *Presidio La Bahia del Espiritu Santo de Zuniga, 1721–1846.* Austin: Von Boeckmann-Jones, 1966.

Olien, Diana Davids, and Roger M. Olien. *Oil in Texas: The Gusher Age, 1895–1945.* Austin: University of Texas Press, 2002.

Olien, Roger M. *From Token to Triumph: The Texas Republicans Since 1920.* Dallas: Southern Methodist University Press, 1982.

Olien, Roger M., and Diana Davids Hinton. *Wildcatters: Texas Independent Oilmen.* College Station: Texas A&M University Press, 2007.

Oliphant, Dave. *Texas Jazz.* Austin: University of Texas Press, 1996.

Olivera, Ruth R., and Liliane Crété. *Life in Mexico Under Santa Anna, 1822–1855.* Norman: University of Oklahoma Press, 1991.

Olmsted, Frederick Law. *A Journey Through Texas, Or, A Saddle-Trip on the Southwestern Frontier.* 1857. Reprint, Austin: University of Texas Press, 1978.

Olson, Donald W., et al. "Piñon Pines and the Route of Cabeza de Vaca." *Southwestern Historical Quarterly* 101 (October 1997): 174–186.

Olson, James Stuart. *Making Cancer History: Disease and Discovery at the University of Texas M.D. Anderson Cancer Center.* Baltimore: Johns Hopkins University Press, 2009.

Ornish, Natalie. *Ehrenberg: Goliad Survivor, Old West Explorer.* Dallas: Texas Heritage Press, 1997.

Orozco, Cynthia. *No Mexicans, Women, or Dogs Allowed: The Rise of the Mexican American Civil Rights Movement.* Austin: University of Texas Press, 2009.

Osante, Patricia. *Orígenes del Nuevo Santander (1748–1772).* Mexico: Universidad Nacional Autónoma de México, Instituto de Investigaciones Históricas, 1997.

Owens, William A. *A Season of Weathering.* New York: Scribner, 1973.

Parisi, Philip. *The Texas Post Office Murals: Art for the People.* College Station: Texas A&M University Press, 2004.

Parmet, Herbert S. *George Bush: The Life of a Lone Star Yankee.* New York: Scibner, 1997.

Pate, J'Nell L. *Livestock Legacy: The Fort Worth Stockyards, 1887–1987.* College Station: Texas A&M University Press, 1988.

Patenaude, Lionel V. *Texas Politics and the New Deal.* New York: Garland Publishing, 1983.

Paulissen, May Nelson, and Carl McQueary. *Miriam: The Southern Belle Who Became the First Woman Governor of Texas.* Austin: Eakin Press, 1995.

Perales, Monica. *Smeltertown: Making and Remembering a Southwest Border Community.* Chapel Hill: University of North Carolina Press, 2010.

Pérez de Villagrá, Gaspar. *Historia de la Nueva México, 1610.* Albuquerque: University of New Mexico Press, 1992.

Perkinson, Robert. *Texas Tough: The Rise of America's Prison Empire.* New York: Metropolitan Books, 2010.

Perttula, Timothy K. *"The Caddo Nation": Archaeological and Ethnohistoric Perspectives.* Austin: University of Texas Press, 1992.

———, ed. *The Prehistory of Texas.* Rev. ed. College Station: Texas A&M University Press, 2013.

Phillips, Kevin. *American Dynasty: Aristocracy, Fortune, and the Politics of Deceit in the House of Bush.* New York: Viking, 2004.

Phillips, William D., Jr., and Carla Rahn Phillips. *A Concise History of Spain.* Cambridge: Cambridge University Press, 2010.

Phipps, Joe. *Summer Stock: Behind the Scenes with LBJ in '48.* Fort Worth: Texas Christian University Press, 1992.

Pickering, David, and Judy Falls. *Brush Men and Vigilantes: Civil War Dissent in Texas.* College Station: Texas A&M University Press, 2000.

Pitre, Merline. *In Struggle Against Jim Crow: Lulu B. White and the NAACP, 1900–1957.* College Station: Texas A&M University Press, 1999.

———. *Through Many Dangers, Toils and Snares: The Black Leadership of Texas, 1868–1900.* Austin: Eakin Press, 1985.

Platt, Harold L. *City Building in the New South: The Growth of Public Services in Houston, Texas, 1830–1915.* Philadelphia: Temple University Press, 1983.

Posner, Gerald. *Case Closed: Lee Harvey Oswald and the Assassination of JFK.* New York: Random House, 1993.

Powers, John, and Deborah Powers. *Texas Painters, Sculptors and Graphic Artists: A Biographical Dictionary of Artists in Texas before 1942.* Austin: Woodmont Books, 2000.

Poyo, Gerald E., ed. *Tejano Journey, 1770–1850.* Austin: University of Texas Press, 1996.

Poyo, Gerald E., and Gilberto M. Hinojosa, eds. *Tejano Origins in Eighteenth-Century San Antonio.* Austin: University of Texas Press, 1991.

Pratt, Joseph A. Tyler Priest, and Christopher J. Castaneda. *Offshore Pioneers: Brown & Root and the History of Offshore Oil and Gas.* Houston: Gulf Publishing Co., 1997.

Priest, Tyler. *The Offshore Imperative: Shell Oil's Search for Petroleum in Postwar America.* College Station: Texas A&M University Press, 2007.

Priestley, Herbert I. *José de Gálvez, Visitor General of New Spain, 1765–1771*. 1916. Reprint, Philadelphia: Porcupine Press, 1980.

Prindle, David F. *Petroleum Politics and the Texas Railroad Commission*. Austin: University of Texas Press, 1981.

Procter, Ben H. *Just One Riot: Episodes of Texas Rangers in the Twentieth Century*. Austin: Eakin Press, 1991.

———. *Not Without Honor: The Life of John H. Reagan*. Austin: University of Texas Press, 1962.

Pruitt, Bernadette. *The Other Great Migration: The Movement of Rural African Americans to Houston, 1900–1941*. College Station: Texas A&M University Press, 2013.

Pupo-Walker, Enrique, ed., and Frances M. López-Morillas, trans. *Castaways: The Narrative of Alvar Núñez Cabeza de Vaca*. Berkeley: University of California Press, 1993.

Ragsdale, Crystal Sasse. *The Golden Free Land: The Reminiscences and Letters of Women on an American Frontier*. Austin: Landmark Press, 1976.

Ragsdale, Kenneth B. *Centennial '36: The Year America Discovered Texas*. College Station: Texas A&M University Press, 1987.

Ramos, Raúl A. *Beyond the Alamo: Forging Mexican Ethnicity in San Antonio, 1821–1861*. Chapel Hill: University of North Carolina Press, 2008.

Ramsay, Jack C., Jr. *Jean Laffite, Prince of Pirates*. Austin: Eakin Press, 1996.

Ratcliffe, Sam D. "'Escenas de Martirio': Notes on *The Destruction of Mission San Sabá*." *Southwestern Historical Quarterly* 94 (April 1991): 507–534.

———. *Painting Texas History to 1900*. Austin: University of Texas Press, 1992.

Reed, S. G. *A History of the Texas Railroads*. Houston: St. Clair Pub. Co., 1941.

Reichstein, Andreas. *Rise of the Lone Star: The Making of Texas*. College Station: Texas A&M University Press, 1989.

———, ed. "The Austin-Leaming Correspondence, 1828–1836." *Southwestern Historical Quarterly* 88 (January 1985): 247–282.

Reid, Jan. *Let the People In: The Life and Times of Ann Richards*. Austin: University of Texas Press, 2012.

Reindorp, Reginald C. "The Founding of Missions at La Junta de los Ríos." In *Preparing the Way: Preliminary Studies of the Texas Catholic Historical Society III*. Austin: Texas Catholic Historical Society, 2000.

Reséndez, Andrés. *Changing National Identities at the Frontier: Texas and New Mexico, 1800–1850*. Cambridge: Cambridge University Press, 2005.

———. *A Land So Strange: The Epic Journey of Cabeza de Vaca*. New York: Basic Books, 2007.

Reston, James, Jr. *The Lone Star: The Life of John Connally*. New York: Harper & Row, 1989.

Reston, Maeve. "Growth Drains Williamson Water Supplies." *Austin American Statesman* 18 August 2000—B10.

Rhinehart, Marilyn D. *A Way of Work and a Way of Life: Coal Mining in Thurber, Texas, 1888–1926*. College Station: Texas A&M University Press, 1992.

Rice, Lawrence D. *The Negro in Texas, 1874–1900*. Baton Rouge: Louisiana State University Press, 1971.

Richards, David. *Once Upon a Time in Texas: A Liberal in the Lone Star State*. Austin: University of Texas Press, 2002.

Richardson, Rupert N. *Colonel Edward M. House: The Texas Years, 1858–1912*. Abilene: Hardin-Simmons University Publications in History, 1964.

Richardson, Rupert N., Adrian Anderson, and Ernest Wallace. *Texas: The Lone Star State*. 8th ed. Englewood Cliffs, NJ: Prentice-Hall, 2001.

Richmond, Douglas W., and Sam W. Haynes, eds. *The Mexican Revolution: Conflict and Consolidation, 1910–1940*. College Station: Texas A&M University Press, 2013.

Ricklis, Robert A. *The Karankawa Indians of Texas: An Ecological Study of Cultural Traditions and Change.* Austin: University of Texas Press, 1996.

Rister, Carl Coke. *Comanche Bondage.* 1955. Reprint, Lincoln: University of Nebraska Press, 1989.

Rivaya Martínez, Joaquín. "Diplomacia interétnica en la frontera norte de Nueva España. Un análisis de los tratados hispano-comanches de 1785 y 1786 y sus consecuencias desde una perspectiva etnohistórica." *Nuevo Mundo Mundos Nuevos*, Debates, 2011. <http://nuevo-mundo.revues.org/62228>.

Roberts, Randy, and James S. Olson. *A Line in the Sand: The Alamo in Blood and Memory.* New York: The Free Press, 2001.

Robertson, Robert J. *Her Majesty's Texans: Two English Immigrants in Reconstruction Texas.* College Station: Texas A&M University Press, 1998.

Roche, Jeff, ed. *The Political Culture of the New West.* Lawrence: University Press of Kansas, 2008.

Rodnitzky, Jerry L., and Shirley R. Rodnitzky. *Jazz Age Boomtown.* College Station: Texas A&M University Press, 1997.

Rodriguez, Marc. *The Tejano Diaspora: Mexican Americanism and Ethnic Politics in Texas and Wisconsin.* Chapel Hill: University of North Carolina Press, 2011.

Roell, Craig H. *Matamoros and the Texas Revolution.* Denton: Texas State Historical Association, 2013.

———. *Remember Goliad! A History of La Bahía.* Austin: Texas State Historical Association, 1994.

Rogers, Mary Beth. *Barbara Jordan, American Hero.* New York: Bantam Books, 1998.

Rosales, Rodolfo. *The Illusion of Inclusion: The Political Story of San Antonio, Texas.* Austin: University of Texas Press, 2000.

Rosenbaum, Robert J. *Mexicano Resistance in the Southwest: The Sacred Right of Self Preservation.* Austin: University of Texas Press, 1981.

Rossinow, Doug. *The Politics of Authenticity: Liberalism, Christianity, and the New Left in America.* New York: Columbia University Press, 1998.

Rubio, Abel. *Stolen Heritage: A Mexican-American's Rediscovery of His Family's Lost Land Grant.* 1986. Reprint, Austin: Eakin Press, 1998.

Rundell, Walter, Jr. *Early Texas Oil: Photographic History, 1866–1936.* College Station: Texas A&M University Press, 1977.

Ryan, Kathleen Jo. *Deep in the Heart of Texas: Texas Ranchers in Their Own Words.* Berkeley, Calif.: Ten Speed Press, 1999.

Salinas, Martín. *Indians of the Rio Grande Delta: Their Role in the History of Southern Texas and Northeastern Mexico.* Austin: University of Texas Press, 1990.

Sanders, Leonard. *How Fort Worth Became the Texas most City.* Fort Worth: Amon Carter Museum, 1973.

San Miguel, Guadalupe, Jr. *Let All of Them Take Heed: Mexican Americans and the Campaign for Educational Equality in Texas, 1910–1981.* Austin: University of Texas Press, 1987.

Santos, Richard G. *Aguayo Expedition into Texas, 1721: An Annotated Translation of the Five Versions of the Diary Kept by Br. Juan Antonio de la Peña.* Austin: Jenkins Publishing, 1981.

———. *Santa Anna's Campaign Against Texas, 1835–1836: Featuring the Field Commands Issued to Major General Vicente Filisola.* Waco: Texian Press, 1968.

Schaller, Michael. *Right Turn: American Life in the Reagan-Bush Era, 1980–1992.* New York: Oxford University Press, 2006.

Schmelzer, Janet L. *Where the West Begins: Fort Worth and Tarrant County.* Northridge, CA: Windsor Publications, 1985.

Schulman, Bruce J. *From Cotton Belt to Sunbelt: Federal Policy, Economic Development, and the Transformation of the South, 1938–1980.* New York: Oxford University Press, 1991.

Schulze, Jeffrey M. "The Rediscovery of the Tiguas: Federal Recognition and Indianness in the Twentieth Century." *Southwestern Historical Quarterly* 105 (July 2001): 15–39.

Schulman, Bruce J. *Lyndon B. Johnson and American Liberalism: A Brief History with Documents.* Boston: Bedford/St. Martin's, 2006.

Schwartz, Jeremy. "Wimberley Seeks to Restore Harmony After Bitter Campaign." *Austin American Statesman* 12 May 2002—B1.

Schwartz, Ted. *Forgotten Battlefield of the First Texas Revolution: The Battle of the Medina, August 18, 1813.* Ed. Robert H. Thonhoff. Austin: Eakin Press, 1985.

Schwarz, Jordan A. *The New Dealers: Power Politics in the Age of Roosevelt.* New York: Vintage Books, 1994.

Seals, Donald, Jr. "The Wiley-Bishop Student Movement: A Case Study in the 1960 Civil Rights Sit-Ins." *Southwestern Historical Quarterly* 106 (January 2003): 419–440.

Sears, James T. *Rebels, Rubyfruit, and Rhinestones: Queering Space in the Stonewall South.* New Brunswick: Rutgers University Press, 2001.

Serwer, Andy, and Julia Boorstin. "Dell Does Domination." *Fortune* (Asia) 145, 2 (21 January 2002): 43.

Sharpless, Rebecca. *Fertile Ground, Narrow Choices: Women on Texas Cotton Farms, 1900–1940.* Chapel Hill: University of North Carolina Press, 1999.

Shockley, John S. *Chicano Revolt in a Texas Town.* Notre Dame: University of Notre Dame Press, 1974.

Sibley, MarilynMcAdams. *Lone Stars and State Gazettes: Texas Newspapers Before the Civil War.* College Station: Texas A&M University Press, 1983.

———. *The Port of Houston.* Austin: University of Texas Press, 1968.

———. *Travelers in Texas, 1761–1860.* Austin: University of Texas Press, 1967.

Silverthorne, Elizabeth. *Ashbel Smith of Texas: Pioneer, Patriot, Statesman, 1805–1886.* College Station: Texas A&M University Press, 1982.

———. *Plantation Life in Texas.* College Station: Texas A&M Press, 1986.

Simmons, Marc. *The Last Conquistador: Juan de Oñate and the Settling of the Far Southwest.* Norman: University of Oklahoma Press, 1991.

Skaggs, Jimmy M. *The Cattle-Trailing Industry: Between Supply and Demand, 1866–1890.* Lawrence: University Press of Kansas, 1973.

Smallwood, James. *The Great Recovery: The New Deal in Texas.* Boston: American Press, 1983.

Smith, F. Todd. *The Caddo Indians: Tribes at the Convergence of Empires, 1542–1854.* College Station: Texas A&M University Press, 1995.

———. *From Dominance to Disappearance: The Indians of Texas and the Near Southwest, 1786–1859.* Lincoln: University of Nebraska Press, 2005.

———. *The Wichita Indians: Traders of Texas and the Southern Plains, 1540–1845.* College Station: Texas A&M University Press, 2000.

Smith, Sherry L. ed. *The Future of the Southern Plains.* Norman: University of Oklahoma Press, 2005.

Smithwick, Noah. *The Evolution of a State, or Recollections of Old Texas Days.* 1900. Reprint, Austin: University of Texas Press, 1983.

Soukup, James R., et al. *Party and Factional Division in Texas.* Austin: University of Texas Press, 1964.

Spearing, Darwin. *Roadside Geology of Texas.* Rev. ed. Missoula, MT: Mountain Press, 1991.

Spellman, Paul N. *Forgotten Texas Leader: Hugh McLeod and the Texan Santa Fe Expedition.* College Station: Texas A&M University Press, 1999.

———. *Spindletop Boom Days.* College Station: Texas A&M University Press, 2001.

Spratt, John S. *The Road to Spindletop: Economic Change in Texas, 1875–1901.* Dallas: Southern Methodist University Press, 1955.

———. *Thurber, Texas: The Life and Death of a Company Coal Town.* Austin: University of Texas Press, 1986.

Stagg, J. C. *Borderlines in Borderlands: James Madison and the Spanish-American Frontier, 1776–1821.* New Haven: Yale University Press, 2009.

Steely, James Wright. *Parks for Texas: Enduring Landscapes of the New Deal.* Austin: University of Texas Press, 1999.

Stewart, Kenneth L., and Arnoldo De León. *Not Room Enough: Mexicans, Anglos, and Socioeconomic Change in Texas, 1850–1900.* Albuquerque: University of New Mexico Press, 1993.

———. *Tejanos and the Numbers Game: A Socio-Historical Interpretation from the Federal Censuses, 1850–1900.* Albuquerque: University of New Mexico Press, 1993.

Still, Rae Files. *The Gilmer-Aikin Bills.* Austin, TX: Steck Co., 1950.

Struve, Walter. *Germans and Texans: Commerce, Migration, and Culture in the Days of the Lone Star Republic.* Austin: University of Texas Press, 1996.

Sweet, David. "The Ibero-American Frontier Mission in Native American History." In *The New Latin American Mission History,* eds. Erick Langer and Robert H. Jackson. Lincoln: University of Nebraska Press, 1995.

Taylor, Alex. "Little Divides Manor Hopefuls: Schools Candidates Unified in Opposition to Wealth-Sharing Laws." *Austin American Statesman* 26 April 2002—B7.

Taylor, Virginia H., trans. and ed. *The Letters of Antonio Martínez, Last Governor of Texas, 1817–1822.* Austin: Texas State Library, 1957.

Teja, Jesús F. de la. "The Colonization and Independence of Texas: A Tejano Perspective." In *Myths, Misdeeds, and Misunderstandings: The Roots of Conflict in U.S.-Mexican Relations,* eds. Jaime E. Rodríguez O. and Kathryn Vincent. Wilmington, DE: Scholarly Resources, 1997.

———. " 'A Fine Country with Broad Plains—the Most Beautiful in New Spain': Colonial Views of Land and Nature." In *On the Border: An Environmental History of San Antonio,* ed. Char Miller. Pittsburgh: University of Pittsburgh Press, 2001.

———. " 'Only Fit for Raising Stock': Spanish and Mexican Land and Water Rights in the Tamaulipan Cession." In *Fluid Arguments: Five Centuries of Western Water Conflict,* ed. Char Miller. Tucson: University of Arizona Press, 2001.

———. *San Antonio de Béxar: A Community on New Spain's Northern Frontier.* Albuquerque: University of New Mexico Press, 1995.

———. "Spanish Colonial Texas." In *New Views of Borderlands History,* ed. Robert H. Jackson. Albuquerque: University of New Mexico Press, 1998.

Teja, Jesús F. de la, ed. *A Revolution Remembered: The Memoirs and Selected Correspondence of Juan N. Seguín.* 2nd ed. Austin: Texas State Historical Association, 2002.

Teja, Jesús F. de la, and John Wheat. "Béxar: Profile of a Tejano Community, 1820–1832." *Southwestern Historical Quarterly* 89 (July 1983): 7–34.

"Texas Values/Texas Future." *Proceedings of the Annual Meeting at Austin, December 3–5, 1999.* Austin: The Philosophical Society of Texas, 2002.

Thomas, Alfred B. *Teodoro de Croix and the Northern Frontier of New Spain, 1776–1783.* Norman: University of Oklahoma Press, 1941.

Thompson, Jerry D. *A Wild and Vivid Land: An Illustrated History of the South Texas Border.* Austin: Texas State Historical Association, 1997.

———. *Cortina: Defending the Mexican Name in Texas.* College Station: Texas A&M University Press, 2007.

———. *Mexican Texans in the Union Army.* El Paso: Texas Western Press, 1986.

———. *Vaqueros in Blue and Gray.* Austin: Presidial, 1976.

———, ed. *Civil War in the Southwest: Recollections of the Sibley Brigade.* College Station: Texas A&M University Press, 2001.

Thompson, Jerry D., and Lawrence T. Jones. *Civil War and Revolution on the Rio Grande Frontier: A Narrative and Photographic History.* Austin: Texas State Historical Association, 2004.

Thonhoff, Robert H. *El Fuerte del Cíbolo: Sentinel of the Béxar-La Bahía Ranches.* Austin: Eakin Press, 1992.

Tijerina, Andrés. *Tejano Empire: Life on the South Texas Ranchos.* College Station: Texas A&M Press, 1998.

———. *Tejanos and Texas Under the Mexican Flag, 1821–1836.* College Station: Texas A&M University Press, 1994.

Timmons, W. H. *El Paso: A Borderlands History.* El Paso: Texas Western Press, 1990.

———. "The El Paso Area in the Mexican Period, 1821–1848." *Southwestern Historical Quarterly* 84 (July 1980): 1–28.

Tjarks, Alicia V. "Comparative Demographic Analysis of Texas, 1777–1793." *Southwestern Historical Quarterly* 77 (January 1974): 291–338.

Tolleson-Rinehart, Sue, and Jeanie R. Stanley. *Claytie and the Lady: Ann Richards, Gender, and Politics in Texas.* Austin: University of Texas Press, 1994.

Tous, Gabriel, trans. "The Espinosa-Olivares-Aguirre Expedition of 1709." In *Preparing the Way: Preliminary Studies of the Texas Catholic Historical Society I.* Austin: Texas Catholic Historical Society, 1997.

———. "Ramón Expedition: Espinosa's Diary of 1716." In *Preparing the Way: Preliminary Studies of the Texas Catholic Historical Society I.* Austin: Texas Catholic Historical Society, 1997.

Turner, Elizabeth Hayes. *Women, Culture and Community: Religion and Reform in Galveston, 1880–1920.* New York: Oxford University Press, 1997.

Turner, Ellen Sue, and Thomas R. Hester. *A Field Guide to Stone Artifacts of Texas Indians.* Austin: Texas Monthly Press, 1985.

Tyler, Ron. "Art in Texas: The First Hundred Years," In *Deep in the Art of Texas: A Century of Paintings and Drawings,* ed. Michael W. Duty. Fort Worth: TCU Press, 2014: 46–58.

———. "The Arts in Early Texas: A Cultural Crossroads." In *American Material Culture and the Texas Experience: Itinerant and Immigrant Artists and Artisans in 19th Century Texas,* David B. Warren Symposium, vol. 4, Bayou Bend Collection and Gardens. Houston: The Museum of Fine Arts, 2014.

———. *The Big Bend: A History of the Last Texas Frontier.* College Station: Texas A&M University Press, 2007. 4th printing.

———. "Cotton on the Border, 1861–1865." *Southwestern Historical Quarterly,* LXXIII (April 1970): 456–477.

———. *The Cowboy.* New York: Ridge Press and Morrow, 1975

———. "Fugitive Slaves in Mexico." *The Journal of Negro History,* LVII (January 1972): 1–12.

———. *Santiago Vidaurri and the Southern Confederacy.* Austin: Texas State Historical Association, 1973.

———. *Views of Texas: The Watercolors of Sarah Ann Hardinge, 1852–1856.* Fort Worth: Amon Carter Museum, 1988.

Tyler, Ron, ed. *Wanderings in the Southwest in 1855,* by J. D. B. Stillman. Spokane, WA: The Arthur H. Clark Company, 1990.

Tyler, Ron, and Lawrence R. Murphy, eds. *The Slave Narratives of Texas.* Austin: Encino Press, 1974; State House Press, 1997.

Utley, Robert M. *Lone Star Lawmen: The Second Century of the Texas Rangers.* New York: Oxford University Press, 2007.

―――. *Lone Star Justice: The First Century of the Texas Rangers*. New York: Oxford University Press, 2002.

Valerio-Jiménez, Omar S. *River of Hope: Forging Identity and Nation in the Rio Grande Borderlands*. Durham, NC: Duke University Press, 2013.

Vázquez, Josefina Zoraida. "The Colonization and Loss of Texas: A Mexican Perspective." In *Myths, Misdeeds, and Misunderstandings: The Roots of Conflict in U.S.-Mexican Relations*, eds. Jaime E. Rodríguez O. and Kathryn Vincent. Wilmington, DE: Scholarly Resources, 1997.

Vega, Garcilaso de la. *The Florida of the Inca*. Trans. and eds. John Grier Varner and Jeannette Johnson Varner. Austin: University of Texas Press, 1980.

Vigness, David M. *Spanish Texas, 1519–1810*. Boston: American Press, 1983.

Vincent, V. A. "The Frontier Soldier: Life in the *Provincias Internas* and the Royal Regulations of 1772, 1766–1787." *Military History of the Southwest* 22 (Spring 1992): 1–14.

Volanto, Keith J. *Texas, Cotton, and the New Deal*. College Station: Texas A&M University Press, 2004.

Wade, Maria F. *The Native Americans of the Texas Edwards Plateau, 1582–1799*. Austin: University of Texas Press, 2003.

Walker, Donald. "Governor Preston E. Smith." *West Texas Historical Association Yearbook* 75 (1999): 6–17.

Wallace, Ernest, and E. Adamson Hoebel. *The Comanches: Lords of the South Plains*. Norman: University of Oklahoma Press, 1952.

Wallace, Ernest, David M. Vigness, and George B. Ward. *Documents of Texas History*. 1963. Reprint, Austin: State House Press, 1994.

Walsh, Patrick J. "Living on the Edge of the Neutral Zone: Varieties of Identity in Nacogdoches, Texas, 1773–1810." *East Texas Historical Journal* 37 (1999): 3–24.

Warren, Harris G. *The Sword Was Their Passport: A History of American Filibustering in the Mexican Revolution*. Baton Rouge: Louisiana State University Press, 1943.

Weaver, John D. *Brownsville Raid*. 1973. Reprint, College Station: Texas A&M University Press, 1992.

Weber, David J. *The Mexican Frontier, 1821–1846: The American Southwest Under Mexico*. Albuquerque: University of New Mexico Press, 1982.

―――. *The Spanish Frontier in North America*. New Haven: Yale University Press, 1992.

Weddle, Robert S. *The French Thorn: Rival Explorers in the Spanish Sea, 1682–1762*. College Station: Texas A&M University Press, 1991.

―――. *San Juan Bautista: Gateway to Spanish Texas*. Austin: University of Texas Press, 1968.

―――. *The San Saba Mission: Spanish Pivot in Texas*. Austin: University of Texas Press, 1964.

―――. *Spanish Sea: The Gulf of Mexico in North American Discovery, 1500–1685*. College Station: Texas A&M University Press, 1985.

―――. *Wilderness Manhunt: The Spanish Search for La Salle*. Austin: University of Texas Press, 1973.

―――. *The Wreck of the Belle, the Ruin of La Salle*. College Station: Texas A&M University Press, 2001.

Weems, John Edward. *Dream of Empire: A Human History of the Republic of Texas, 1836–1846*. New York: Simon & Schuster, 1976.

Whisenhunt, Donald W. *The Depression in Texas: The Hoover Years*. New York: Garland Publishing Co., 1983.

―――, ed. *Texas: A Sesquicentennial Celebration*. Austin: Eakin Press, 1984.

Wilkison, Kyle G. *Yeomen, Sharecroppers and Socialists: Plain Folk Protest in Texas, 1870–1914*. College Station: Texas A&M University Press, 2008.

Willoughby, Larry. *Texas, Our Texas*. Austin: Holt, Rinehart and Winston, 1993.

Wilson, Carol O'Keefe. *In the Governor's Shadow: The True Story of Ma and Pa Ferguson.* Denton: University of North Texas Press, 2014.

Wilson, Maurine T., and Jack Jackson. *Philip Nolan and Texas: Expeditions to the Unknown Land.* Waco: Texian Press, 1987.

Winders, Richard Bruce. *Crisis in the Southwest: The United States, Mexico, and the Struggle Over Texas.* Wilmington, Del.: SR Books, 2002.

Winegarten, Ruthe. *Black Texas Women: A Sourcebook.* Austin: University of Texas Press, 1996.

———. *Texas Women: A Pictorial History, from Indians to Astronauts.* Austin: University of Texas Press, 1986.

Winegarten, Ruthe, and Sharon Kahn. *Brave Black Women: From Slavery to the Space Shuttle.* Austin: University of Texas Press, 1997.

Worster, Donald. *Dust Bowl: The Southern Plains in the 1930s.* New York: Oxford University Press, 2004.

Woods, Randall. *LBJ: Architect of American Ambition.* New York: Free Press, 2006.

Wooster, Ralph A. *Lone Star Generals in Gray.* Austin: Eakin Press, 2000.

———. *Texas and Texans in the Civil War.* Austin: Eakin Press, 1996.

Wooster, Ralph A., and Robert A. Calvert. *Texas Vistas: Selections from the Southwestern Historical Quarterly.* Austin: Texas State Historical Association, 1980.

Wooster, Robert. *Soldiers, Suttlers, and Settlers: Garrison Life on the Texas Frontier.* College Station: Texas A&M University Press, 1987.

Young, Nancy Beck. *Why We Fight: Congress and the Politics of World War II.* Lawrence: University Press of Kansas, 2013.

———. *Wright Patman: Populism, Liberalism, and the American Dream.* Dallas, TX: Southern Methodist University Press, 2000.

Young, Nancy Beck, and Lewis L. Gould. *Texas, Her Texas: The Life and Times of Frances Goff.* Austin: Texas State Historical Association Press, 1997.

Zamora, Emilio. *World of the Mexican Worker in Texas.* College Station: Texas A&M University Press, 1993.

Zelden, Charles L. *The Battle for the Black Ballot:* Smith v. Allwright *and the Defeat of the Texas All-White Primary.* Lawrence: University Press of Kansas, 2004.

Zelizer, Julian E., ed. *The Presidency of George W. Bush: A First Historical Assessment.* Princeton: Princeton University Press, 2010.

Index

530